NATHAN SCHACHNER

Alexander Hamilton

New York • THOMAS YOSELOFF • London

TO BARBARA AND LUDWIG

CONTENTS

CHAPTER		PAGE
I.	West Indies Background	1
II.	Young Man of Business	16
III.	New World to Conquer	27
IV.	From Pen to Sword	35
V.	Hamilton Goes to War	45
VI.	Call Colonel Hamilton!	56
VII.	From Sword to Pen	77
VIII.	Love and Treason	102
IX.	Hamilton Quits the War	120
X.	Final Victory	133
XI.	No Taxation with Representation	144
XII.	Hamilton in Congress	153
XIII.	Conservative Lawyer	168
XIV.	Preliminary Maneuvers	184
XV.	Birth of a Constitution	195
XVI.	The Fight for Ratification	207
XVII.	Mr. Secretary of the Treasury	228
XVIII.	The Great Reports	242
XIX.	The Great Reports, *continued*	265
XX.	Years of Strife	282
XXI.	Rum and Politics	304
XXII.	More Rum and More Politics	325

v

Contents

CHAPTER		PAGE
XXIII.	Private Statesman	341
XXIV.	Public Emergency and Private Scandal	360
XXV.	The War Clouds Gather	374
XXVI.	Twilight of the Federalists	389
XXVII.	Achilles Retires to His Tents	403
XXVIII.	Death and Transfiguration	419
	Notes	435
	Bibliography	473
	Index	483

Alexander Hamilton

CHAPTER I

West Indies Background

I. A QUESTION OF BIRTH

THAT ALEXANDER HAMILTON was illegitimately born was well known in his own day, and accepted without great ado by the generality of his friends and political followers. It is true that a political hack was to denounce him in public print as "the son of a camp-girl," [1] and John Adams, filled with a sense of unredressed wrongs, sneered at him in private as "the bastard brat of a Scotch pedlar," [2] but such ungenerous animadversions on the accident of his birth were remarkably few, considering the passionate personal and political enmities that Hamilton aroused in the course of a tempestuous career.

It is certain that the bar sinister was no obstacle to the satisfaction of Hamilton's most vaulting ambitions. In the West Indies, where the facts of his birth were common property, devoted friends and relatives raised a fund to provide him with the best educational opportunities available in the British colonies. On the mainland, the taint of "bastard" did not prevent him from storming the highest positions in army and state or, what is even more significant, from marrying into one of the proudest families of the infant nation.

Not until his contemporaries had vanished with him from the scene did the legend of Hamilton's respectable paternity begin to flourish. This legend was initiated by his biographer-son, John C. Hamilton, and sedulously fostered by later descendants. [3] So successful were their pious labors that for almost a century the fiction of legitimacy was generally accepted as true by historians, who attributed the unflattering references of Adams, Jefferson and others to the libels of party warfare.

The twentieth century had already commenced when Gertrude Atherton, the novelist, painstakingly unearthed the true facts of Hamilton's birth so far as they could be determined at that late date. [4] These facts are lamentably few—the long passage of time, the loss or destruc-

[1] Notes for this and subsequent chapters will be found at the end of the text, beginning on page 435.

I

tion of records and the uncooperative attitude of the Hamilton family combined to prevent much chance of fuller knowledge.

With this regained knowledge, however, another thesis arose to trouble the clear waters of Hamiltonian biography: to wit, that Hamilton's career, his bold assertiveness, his will to power, his genius, were in effect the products of a pathological compensation for the irregularity of his birth. This thesis owes its origin to the current trend toward psychoanalytical interpretations of historical figures. Whatever may be the value of psychoanalysis in the hands of competent practitioners with patients under immediate observation and control, it is obviously a dangerous instrument in the hands of lay biographers for probing the minds and motives of men long dead and of whom we have at best incomplete sources of information.

That Hamilton's earliest urge toward fame and fortune, his manifest impatience with every obstacle to the rapid expansion of his career, his consuming appetite for the quick glory to be had on the field of battle, were bottomed in part on the knowledge that there was no cushion of family respectability and inheritable estate for him to fall back upon, it would be idle to deny. Yet to offer the condition of Hamilton's birth as the sole motivating force or complete explanation of the man is to simplify unwarrantably a complex personality and a complex era.

It was an age of great men. The times were propitious, and the yeasty ferment of revolution thrust the ablest rapidly to the top. Some of his contemporaries were almost as precocious in talent and ability. The will to power in others was quite as strong. Ambition soared as high in many. A surprising number drove as purposefully toward a clearly defined goal. The competition was keen, but not stifling. There was room for all. If Hamilton went further than most and exercised a profounder influence on the destinies of a nation still in the process of parturition, it was chiefly because he combined to a pre-eminent degree those qualities which others possessed singly or only in part.

2. MARITAL LAPSES

The island of Nevis, where Alexander Hamilton was born, was and still is a part of the British West Indies. It rises out of the tropic seas in the shape of a majestic cone, lifting its central peak to an elevation of over three thousand feet. Though its total area is not more than fifty square miles, its luxuriant, semi-volcanic soil and lapping warmth, its romantic situation and abundant slave labor made it a particularly inviting haven for adventurers and refugees from the Old World. Here were plantations that yielded the generous cane, from which sugar, molasses and rum flowed profitably and in great measure. Here were strange, delicious fruits, exotic plants and lordly houses white-gleaming in the sunshine, all to be possessed and enjoyed with a minimum of cash or effort—at least, so ran the tales returned to the world of Europe.

John Faucette, a French Huguenot, listened eagerly to the tales. It was essential that he find a place of refuge immediately. For France, his native country, had decided to revoke its long toleration of the Huguenot creed and it meant death for any Huguenot to remain, unless he agreed to abjure his former faith. Some yielded and vowed belief in the prevailing Catholicism, but by far the greater number preferred exile and the hazards of new fortunes. They emigrated to the neighboring Protestant countries of the Netherlands and England, and many turned their backs forever on the Old World to seek new lives and religious freedom in the vast expanses of the New.

Among the latter was John Faucette. He landed on Nevis in the year 1685. Penniless, yet possessed of that native shrewdness and stern determination which characterized the Huguenot emigrants, he refused to succumb to the langorous drift of a tropical island. He adopted the more English spelling of Fawcett and studied medicine with one of the local practitioners.

After a short apprenticeship he set up for himself. So successful did he become in the course of a few years that he was able to purchase an ample estate at Gingerland, a town house in the island capital, Charlestown, and still have a sufficient surplus to invest substantially in a number of London trading ventures.

On achieving this satisfactory status in life, Dr. Fawcett decided it was time for him to marry. Since he was now a man of considerable means he found no difficulty in persuading a girl twenty years his junior to fall in love with him. Of his young wife nothing is known except that her first name was Mary. Neither tradition nor documents cast any light on her surname or family connections. Not even the date of the marriage is known, except that it must have been prior to 1714.[5]

For twenty six years or more Dr. Fawcett and his wife lived together on his estate at Gingerland, in what was known throughout the island as the "Great House." Two daughters were born to them; and these grew up and were married in turn. The elder, named Mary after her mother, wedded Peter Lytton, a moderately comfortable planter on the neighboring Danish island of St. Croix. The younger, whose name seemingly was Ann, followed her sister to St. Croix and married Thomas Mitchell, also a planter. The Leeward Islands were a homogeneous group, geographically, economically and socially, though split up politically among several European nations, and English colonists shifted indifferently from one island to another in search of land, trade and fortune.

The Great House was empty of children now. Dr. Fawcett was getting along in years, and the fortune he had accumulated was ample for his needs. Accordingly he retired from active practice and thought to enjoy a well-earned leisure.

But his wife was to assert later that his retirement was directly responsible for her ensuing misfortunes. He was an old man and unused to leisure. Gout, the scourge of the eighteenth-century wealthy, tormented his limbs and confined him to a chair. He became irritable and explosive of temper. He resented his wife's comparative youth, good looks and love of dancing and parties. He grew increasingly jealous of the gallant attentions paid her by the neighboring planters. He not only discouraged their visits to his own home, but forbade Mary's attendance at the occasional balls of the countryside or excursions to Charlestown, the center of island society. In effect she was a prisoner in the lonely Great House.

As though these troubles were not enough, bad news came from England. Dr. Fawcett had been persuaded by his London agents to invest his funds in some highly speculative enterprises. The speculations crashed, and with them went the greater part of the old man's fortune.

In the midst of these personal and financial difficulties Mary unexpectedly presented her husband with another daughter. The child was born in 1736 and was christened Rachel.

This proved to be the final straw for the gouty and embittered old doctor. He had neither anticipated the possibility of another child at his advanced age nor desired it. In the face of this new calamity he lost all control over speech and action. The Great House resounded with his violent upbraidings. His jealous vigilance over his wife redoubled, and probably his constant recriminations included some plain-spoken doubts as to the paternity of little Rachel.

Mary Fawcett packed her personal belongings, bundled up her baby and quit Gingerland and her husband forever. She took refuge with friends on the island who advised a legal separation to safeguard her rights. Dr. Fawcett refused his consent to a peaceful settlement, whereupon Mary addressed a petition for her separate maintenance and support to "His Excellency, William Matthews, Esq., Chancellor and Ordinary in Chief for the Leeward Caribbee Islands." Faced with the prospect of legal proceedings Dr. Fawcett grudgingly yielded. He signed an agreement settling upon Mary an annuity of fifty-three pounds, four shillings annually for life, and relinquishing all claims to her separate property. In return Mary renounced her dower rights in his estate.[6]

On the satisfactory termination of these legal proceedings Mary Fawcett went with little Rachel to the neighboring island of St. Christopher, or St. Kitts, as it was more familiarly known, where she owned a small estate. Here she lived modestly within the limits of her annual allowance until Dr. Fawcett's death, which occurred a few years after the separation. Under the terms of the agreement Mary had no rights in her husband's property, but Rachel, as his daughter, was entitled to an equal share with her older sisters. The estate consisted chiefly of land and buildings; the remainder of his assets had long since been dissipated. She received as her share in the division the vacant town house in Charlestown. But the little girl naturally continued to live with her mother on St. Kitts.

Rachel Fawcett grew rapidly and with all the lushness of tropical adolescence. She was given a grounding in those accomplishments which were deemed essential to a woman of family. She mastered English, French and Latin; she learned to play the piano, to sing, dance, embroider and paint pretty water-colors. Aside from these conventional aids, she showed herself to be intelligent, high-spirited and impetuous. Her wilful beauty and marked appeal soon attracted the attention of all the eligible males on the islands.

The chief suitor for the hand of the sixteen-year-old girl was a wealthy Danish-Jewish planter of nearby St. Croix, where both her married sisters lived. His name was John Michael Levine; though it has been spelled by later commentators—in conformity with the fashion set by Alexander Hamilton—Lavine. He himself spelled it indifferently Levine, Lawein and Lavion.

Levine was much older than Rachel, but her mother, embittered by the genteel poverty into which they had sunk and dazzled by the elderly suitor's wealth and position, without doubt pressed the connection upon the young girl.

They were married in style—probably in 1752—and sailed for an extended honeymoon to Copenhagen, the former home of the groom. Mary Fawcett went along with them, but returned to St. Kitts before the newly wedded couple had exhausted the delights of the Danish metropolis. Finally Levine and his bride also returned and settled down to normal marital life on St. Croix. Shortly afterward Rachel gave birth to a son, Peter.

But the marriage was foredoomed to failure. Middle age and sixteen do not mix. Mary Fawcett had permitted the allurements of wealth and position to blind her to the parallel with her own unfortunate marriage. Levine was sedate and elderly; Rachel was hot-blooded and young. Therein are sufficient elements for an explosion. What actually occurred is not clear. It has been maintained by John C. Hamilton, Rachel's grandson, and by succeeding biographers, that Levine treated his girl-bride with the utmost brutality and that she was forced to leave him on that account. But this assertion must be taken with a certain sceptical reserve. For the filial biographer, in his anxiety to gloss over the situation, further insisted that Rachel thereafter obtained a divorce from Levine, married James Hamilton in respectable fashion, and that his father, Alexander Hamilton, was the lawful fruit of this second venture into matrimony.[7] All of which is untrue.

Whatever the reasons for her decision, Rachel did desert her husband, leaving four-year-old Peter in his paternal custody, and in 1756 went to the Barbados, still another of the close-clustered West Indies Islands. Her adventures there are wrapped in impenetrable fog. But the divorce papers which Levine later filed against his errant wife declared with brutal plainness that she had "absented herself and went whoring in the Barbados."[8]

In any event young Rachel soon quit the Barbados and went to live with her mother on St. Kitts. The ladies of the islands now had additional matter for gossip. First the mother, Mary Fawcett, had separated from her husband. Now the daughter, Rachel Levine, deserted the man she had wed. The male members of the compact island society did not prove as censorious as their wives. They had stoutly taken Mary's part when she fled to St. Kitts. They rallied to Rachel's side with equal vigor.

Peter Lytton and Thomas Mitchell, across the water on St. Croix, naturally supported their young sister-in-law. So did the Stevens family, probably related on her mother's side. But the most vehement defense of the runaway beauty came from a group of men wholly outside the family circle. These included Archibald Hamm, a wealthy

planter; Dr. Hugh Knox, a Presbyterian minister of Irish birth who
had studied for his calling at Princeton and whose nature was incurably
romantic; and Will Hamilton, a Scotch medico.

Dr. Hamilton, the indigent son of a noble Scottish house, had come
many years before to seek his fortune in the West Indies. Between
the practice of medicine and the prudent management of a plantation
he finally achieved a competence; and the report of his success, with
the customary exaggerations, traveled back to his far-flung kinsmen
in Scotland.

Stirred by the tale, the family now shipped another impoverished
cadet to the islands to seek a similar fortune. This was James Hamilton,
a handsome, easy-going, rather shiftless youngster for whom there
seemed no prospects on the barren, run-down domains at home. He
was the fourth son of Alexander Hamilton and his wife Elizabeth.
Alexander Hamilton was known as the Laird of the Grange, which
was located in the Parish of Stevenson, County of Ayrshire. The Hamiltons could trace their ancestry back to a great ducal house that had
scattered branches throughout the British Isles. Elizabeth was the
daughter of Sir Robert Pollock, whose lineage was equally well
attested.[9]

Young James Hamilton arrived in the West Indies either in 1755 or
1756. Just as uncertain is the place of his landing; or when or where
he first met Rachel. If he came in 1755 it is possible he may have met
Rachel while she was still living with Levine on St. Croix. In that case
the advent of the good-looking young Scot might have had something
to do with her decision to quit her husband. It is much more likely,
though, that he was introduced to her by his kinsman, Dr. Will Hamilton, after she had come to St. Kitts to live with her mother. Rachel
was twenty now, in the prime of her beauty, and particularly impres-
sionable to a young man of similar years, tastes and romantic
inclinations.

The inevitable happened. They fell in love. But a serious obstacle
blocked the normal progress of events. Rachel was legally still the
wife of John Michael Levine. Had she proper grounds, and wealth
and influence enough, she might have been able to obtain a divorce
under the liberal Danish law of St. Croix. But later developments indicate that she had no grounds, and it was Levine who had wealth and
influence.

On St. Kitts, which was a British colony, the obstacles to a divorce
were almost insurmountable. The British laws were extremely rigor-

ous: only an Act of Parliament could dissolve the bonds of matrimony. To obtain such an Act required a petition to England, a vast deal of money and powerful connections to push the bill. Even if Rachel and James Hamilton desired a legalization of their love they had neither money enough nor sufficiently powerful friends in England to command it.

They decided therefore to live together without benefit of law or clergy. It was not a difficult decision to make. Customs and morals in the West Indies were free and easy at the time. Many other couples were in the same predicament. The difficulties in the way of divorce were well known. So that no scandal or ostracism seems to have attached to the imprudent pair as a result of their openly avowed relation.

Now that James Hamilton had committed himself to the moral, if not legal, obligations of matrimony it was necessary for him to seek a means of livelihood. With Will Hamilton's assistance he became a partner in a trading venture on St. Kitts. To cut down expenses until the venture showed a profit, the young couple moved over to Nevis and occupied the town house which Rachel had inherited from her father. A strait two miles wide separated Nevis and St. Kitts, and each morning James ferried over to St. Kitts and each evening returned to Nevis.

Not long after this new arrangement was made Mary Fawcett died. She had little cash to leave her youngest daughter, who had followed so closely in her footsteps. But she left what she could, and in addition had executed a deed of trust before her death: "I, Mary Fawcett, widow of the Island of St. Christopher, desiring to provide for the future of my three dear slaves, Rebecca, Flora and Esther, transfer them to my friend, Archibald Hamm, or to his heirs; they to remain in my possession during my lifetime, to pass thereafter to my beloved daughter, Rachel Lavion." [10]

For a while James and Rachel struggled to make a go of their irregular relationship. But James was not cut out to be a merchant. He soon quarreled with his partners, separated from the firm, and tried to establish a business on his own account. He used for this purpose the small sum of money that had been left to Rachel on her mother's death. The new venture failed almost at once.

In the midst of this latest defeat, with both present and future hopelessly dark, Alexander Hamilton was born. Over the exact date of his birth much controversy has raged, nor has the matter been properly settled even to this day. For the records of Nevis are barren on the subject.

The only extant evidence consists of two items. One is the fact that Hamilton, in later life, celebrated his birthday on the eleventh of January. The other is the solitary documentary allusion to the *year* of his birth, contained in a letter by Hamilton to his Scottish relatives, written when he was famous and close to the end of his life. Even here the reference is vague. He states merely that "at about sixteen" he came to the continental colonies to seek an education and his fortune, and that at nineteen he entered the American Army as captain of artillery.[11]

The date of his commission, however, is known with certainty. It was March 14, 1776; which would place the year of Hamilton's birth, if his own chronology is to be believed, in 1757. And as such it has been generally accepted, though not without opposition.

For there is in existence a legal document, dated 1766, and executed on the island of St. Croix, to which Alexander Hamilton's name is affixed as a witness.[12] But if Hamilton was born on January 11, 1757, as alleged, it would mean that at the age of nine he was deemed competent to witness a formal document.

This, however, is not as insurmountable a hurdle as has been usually supposed. While he was certainly considerably below the age of legal competence as a witness, the same lack of competence would equally apply if Hamilton had in fact been thirteen or fourteen at the time. And no one has ever ventured to maintain that Hamilton was four or five years older than he claimed. It must also be considered that the West Indian planters were rather lax in the signing and witnessing of papers. What more logical than to believe that the signer of the deed, requiring a witness in a hurry, and finding none present except young Hamilton, requested his attestation without bothering his head about the age of the providential witness?

It has also been claimed that if he were in truth born in the year 1757 this would make him an infant prodigy in the most complete sense of the term. For did he not, at the age of fourteen, manage with the greatest skill and maturity of judgment during an extended absence of his master the trading business to which he had been apprenticed several years before?

Yet young lads ripened fast under the particular conditions that existed in the American colonies at the time, and Hamilton had the added incentive of knowing that his future depended almost entirely on his own unaided efforts. It is not intended to detract from the amazing precocity of these efforts, but merely to point out that such precocity cannot be taken as proof positive that Hamilton was lying about his age.

The question of Hamilton's paternity has equally perturbed investigators. Yet their surmises as to the father—if James Hamilton be omitted from consideration—are wholly conjectural, without probative value or the slightest shred of evidence to support them.

Such, for example, is the attribution to George Washington because he happened to be in the Barbados at the time when Rachel was there and later displayed a warm affection for Hamilton. Such is the attempt to pin the fact upon Stevens, the planter, because it had been noted that Hamilton and Ned Stevens, the planter's son, strongly resembled each other. For this assertion Timothy Pickering, then collecting materials for a biography of Hamilton, is responsible. But his manuscript notes indicate that the man to whom he went for information on this vital point—a brother-in-law of young Stevens—proffered no such explanation for the resemblance, "altho' it seemed apparent that he thought them near of kin." [13]

It has even been seriously suggested that John Michael Levine himself might have been the father. But Levine obviously had no such belief. In fact, he won a law suit involving the disposition of Rachel's property on the ground that young Alexander was not his son.

An examination of the available evidence, therefore, discloses no valid reason for doubting that Alexander Hamilton was born on January 11, 1757, or that James Hamilton was his father.

3. A FURTHER ABANDONMENT

His own business ventures having failed disastrously, James Hamilton was compelled to accept aid from Rachel's family. Peter Lytton, her brother-in-law, offered him the management of his plantation on St. Croix. Though the aggrieved husband, Levine, dwelt on that island and Rachel, by her return, came within Danish jurisdiction again, the offer was accepted. The couple quit the house on Nevis for St. Croix and, with their infant son, received a hearty welcome from the Lyttons and the Mitchells. In 1762 a second son was born to them and was christened James, after his father.

But the welcome soon wore thin. James Hamilton's management of another's estate proved as ineffectual as the conduct of his own. There was a quarrel. Perhaps Rachel, by this time fully aware of the short-comings of her lover, sided with her relatives. In a huff, as so often before, James quit his job. More words followed. In a greater huff, and about three years after his settlement in St. Croix, James Hamilton took boat and deserted Rachel and their two small boys. The romance was over. The unwed mother who had quit her husband was now in turn abandoned by her lover.

The further career of James Hamilton is dim, pierced only by momentary flashes in the letters of his famous son. From St. Croix he went to the island of St. Vincent, a British possession; but the fatal defects of his character prevented him from ever rising above poverty and obscurity.

That Alexander Hamilton in later life was anxious, nay eager, to avow himself the son of James Hamilton, is understandable. It connected him with the eminently respectable Hamiltons of Scotland, and gave him a solid footing in the very insecure matter of his birth. After he came to the mainland, he tried hard to keep in touch with his father, in spite of any natural resentment he may have felt over the desertion of his mother and himself. He also continued to maintain an interest in his younger brother.

Curiously enough, neither aging parent nor younger brother reciprocated his interest, at least not until Alexander had made his way in the world. Once the elder brother had achieved success, however, James Hamilton, the younger, suddenly broke his silence. From the island of St. Thomas he wrote in 1785 for assistance and to inform Alexander that he had drawn a sight draft on him for fifty pounds. He also hinted strongly that his brother do something for him in New York.

Hamilton was then married and busily engaged in getting a foothold for himself in the law. Nevertheless he wrote back promptly:

The situation you describe yourself to be in gives me much pain, and nothing will make me happier than, as far as may be in my power, to contribute to your relief. I will cheerfully pay your draft upon me for fifty pounds sterling whenever it shall appear. I wish it was in my power to desire you to enlarge the sum; but, though my future prospects are of the most flattering kind, my present engagements would render it inconvenient to me to advance a larger sum.[14]

He was not very anxious, however, to have a poverty-stricken brother whom he hadn't seen since early childhood appear suddenly on the scene. He had made for himself a definite niche in New York society, and the apparition of an awkward colonial, down at the heels and involved in who knew what matrimonial entanglements, did not fit in with his plans. He therefore sidestepped the hint with a vague promise that within a year or two he might be able to settle the younger James on a farm. Nothing further materialized and Alexander was never to see him again, though he continued to send him regular remittances of money.

The case of the elder James was on an entirely different footing. Black sheep though he had been, he was still the undoubted scion of an ancient Scottish family, and *his* presence could assist Alexander in achieving that proper background which he so ardently needed.

He had in fact written to his father in 1780 to inform him of his impending marriage with Elizabeth Schuyler. Yet even that arresting bit of news had not aroused any paternal sentiments in the man who had abandoned his family; and there had been no reply.[15]

Now, however, that the younger James had broken the ice of long silence, Hamilton sought information concerning his recalcitrant parent.

But what has become of our dear father? [he inquired of his brother.] It is an age since I have heard from him, or of him though I have written him several letters. Perhaps, alas! he is no more, and I shall not have the pleasing opportunity of contributing to render the close of his life more happy than the progress of it. My heart bleeds at the recollection of his misfortunes and embarrassments. Sometimes I flatter myself his brothers have extended their support to him, and that now he is enjoying tranquillity and ease; at other times I fear he is suffering in indigence. I entreat you, if you can, to relieve me from my doubts, and let me know how or where he is, if alive; if dead, how and where he died. Should he be alive inform him of my inquiries, beg him to write to me, and tell him how ready I shall be to devote myself and all I have to his accommodation and happiness.

Just when it was that the elder Hamilton first decided to begin a correspondence with his son is not clear from the evidence. But, from the tone of the only letter of his that now seems extant, there had been some communication by 1793, when he wrote from St. Vincent:

DEAR ALEXANDER:
I wrote you a letter, inclosed in one to Mr. Donald, of Virginia, since which I have had no further accounts from you. My bad state of health has prevented my going to sea at this time—being afflicted with a complication of disorders.

The war which has lately broken out between France and England makes it very dangerous going to sea at this time. However, we daily expect news of a peace, and when that takes place, provided it is not too late in the season, I will embark in the first vessel that sails for Philadelphia. . . .

I beg you will drop me a few lines, letting me know how you and your family keep your health, as I am uneasy at not having heard from you for some time past. I beg my respectful compliments to Mrs. Hamilton and your children, and wishing you health and happiness, I remain, with esteem, dear Alexander,

Your very affectionate
FATHER [16]

But the old man was never to come to the United States, in spite of his son's pleadings. He preferred to remain in the West Indies, among his cronies, and accept at long range the funds that Alexander contributed for his support until the time of his death.

These were considerable, though Alexander, for all his fame and brilliant career, was never to become a wealthy man. From 1796 to 1799 alone he honored drafts for his father and younger brother amounting to several thousand dollars.[17]

The old man died on June 3, 1799 and was buried in St. George's Cathedral, in the town of Kingston, on St. Vincent Island.[18] He had never stirred from his island sanctuary since he deserted his family many years before.

His Scottish relatives had long considered him the black sheep of the family. And the irregularity of his connection with Rachel Levine, coupled with the scandal of his subsequent abandonment, certainly strengthened their desire to have nothing to do with him or his two young sons. Nor is there any evidence that they ever assisted him in any way during the poverty of his old age.

But when Alexander, his son, rose to power and influence in the subsequent years, it dawned on them that here was a blood connection whom it would be well to cultivate. There were other cadets of the noble, if impoverished, family in Scotland who might be able to find fortune in the new country under the guiding auspices of this new-found relative. Whereupon one of the Scottish Hamiltons wrote with great cordiality in 1797 to place under his protection a younger son who was even then on his way to New York.

Alexander Hamilton was pathetically flattered by the letter. He seized the opportunity to establish once and for all the essential respectability of his birth and lineage. He hastened to reply:

The mark it affords of your kind attention, and the particular account it gives me of so many relations in Scotland are extremely gratifying to

me. You, no doubt, have understood that my father's affairs at a very
early day went to wreck, so as to have rendered his situation during the
greatest part of his life far from eligible. This state of things occasioned
a separation between him and me, when I was very young, and threw me
upon the bounty of my mother's relatives, some of whom were then wealthy,
though by vicissitudes to which human affairs are so liable, they have
been since much reduced and broken up. Myself, at about sixteen, came
to this country.

Not a word of complaint against his father; not a hint of reproach
for the Scottish Hamiltons who had not inquired these many years
as to their fate. He proceeded to give a short biography of himself, his
marriage into the Schuyler family and his subsequent fortunes. He was
obviously trying to impress these far-off Hamiltons.

"Though I have been too much in public life to be wealthy, my
situation is extremely comfortable, and leaves me nothing to wish for
but a continuance of health." Concerning his father: "I have strongly
pressed the old gentleman to come and reside with me, which would
afford him every enjoyment of which his advanced age is capable; but
he has declined it on the ground that the advice of his physicians leads
him to fear that the change of climate would be fatal to him."

He would be happy, he went on, to receive his correspondent's son
in New York, and concluded that "it is my intention to embrace the
opening which your letter affords me to extend my intercourse with
my relations in your country." [19]

A few years later he was again host to one of the younger members
of the Hamilton family and obtained for him a berth in the American
Navy.

4. THE DIVORCE AND DEATH OF RACHEL LEVINE

With Rachel Levine, however, fate took a more decided stand. She
was afforded no opportunity of availing herself of her son's later good
fortune or of spinning out a lengthy term of years in the peaceful web
of her native islands.

The first great blow descended in 1759, three years after she had
fled from her husband. She had been living openly with James Hamilton all this time, a son had been born as the fruit of this new connection, yet John Michael Levine had bided his time. Now he moved
swiftly. He commenced proceedings for divorce in the Ember Court
in Christianstadt, on the island of St. Croix, which had jurisdiction
over the marriage and the offense. He charged adultery and desertion.

The court was tactful. Though seemingly the case was uncontested, and the adultery was notorious, it made no reference to this particular charge in the final decree. Instead, it granted Levine his divorce on the ground that Rachel "had absented herself" and gave him permission to remarry; no similar permission, however, was given the defendant.[20] Levine was free, but Rachel was not.

Yet Levine was not content. Nine years later, immediately following Rachel's death, he raked up the old scandal with another public court proceeding. Rachel had left to Alexander and James, her sons by James Hamilton, the three female slaves bequeathed to her by her mother, Mary Fawcett. Levine claimed them in behalf of her "only lawfully begotten heir Peter Lawein" and won his suit.[21]

The second great blow was James Hamilton's desertion in 1763. This was the ultimate disaster—she was worse than widow, though both husband and lover were still alive. Two small children were left in her disconsolate care: Alexander, aged six, and James, an infant in arms.

Her relatives sought to soften this final blow. The Lyttons took her in and exerted themselves in her behalf. The Mitchells were kind and understanding. Sympathetic friends gathered around. But the passionate spirit of Rachel was broken. She could not survive long this last stroke of misfortune.

For a few years more she lingered and declined. Happiness had turned its face away. There was nothing left. On the 26th day of February, 1768, Rachel Levine died. She was only thirty-two at the time. They buried her in the family cemetery at Tuite's plantation on the island of St. Croix.[22] Left behind were the two children to make their way as best they could in a hostile world. Alexander was now eleven, and James was six.

CHAPTER II

Young Man of Business

I. ABORTIVE LEGACIES

OF ALEXANDER HAMILTON's early youth little is known. It was quite probably the typical life of a youngster on a West Indian plantation at the time. There would be much outdoor activity and little formal education; colored in Hamilton's case, however, by the omnipresent facts of a vanished father, an unhappy mother, and their utter dependence on the charity and kindness of relatives.

That the path was made as easy as possible for him is evidenced by the gratitude he later displayed toward Mrs. Ann Mitchell, his aunt. For his account book shows the following item under the date, July 11, 1796: "Donation to my Cozen Mrs. Mitchell; draft upon me $100." [1] That he called her "cozen" has unduly confused commentators as to the relationship between them. It was a term often used for any relative not in the direct line of descent.

And much later, in the last moments of his life, while arranging his affairs on the eve of his duel with Aaron Burr, Hamilton found time and thought for this same Mrs. Mitchell who had come, old and broken in health, to live with him in America. "Cherish her tenderly!" he admonished his wife. [2]

After the duel's tragic ending she continued to live with Mrs. Hamilton for some weeks in the grief-haunted Grange; then she went on to Burlington where she was stricken blind. Ultimately a collection was made in her behalf by Hamilton's friends, who paid her passage back to her native West Indies. [3]

Young Alexander's closest boyhood friend was Edward Stevens. Edward and his brother, Thomas, were cousins on his mother's side, and the resemblance between Alexander and Edward was striking. The two lads played together and confided to each other their hopes and ambitions. Young Ned wanted to become a doctor; Alexander would be content with nothing less than a great captain in war.

When the need for a formal education became apparent the three boys were sent off to Christianstadt, the capital of St. Croix, to be tutored by Dr. Hugh Knox, the Presbyterian divine who had so staunchly defended both Rachel Levine and Mary Fawcett.

The change was most welcome to young Alexander. Life in the town was more bustling and exigent than on the plantation; and Dr. Knox proved an enthusiastic teacher and invaluable friend. The boy's keen mind and quick intelligence rejoiced in the intellectual fare that was spread before him. He learned French well—a necessity in the West Indies, where French trade was important—and he was inducted into the rudiments of Latin and mathematics. It is said that he even achieved a smattering of Hebrew by voluntary attendance at the school of a Jewish schoolmistress.[4]

But this formal education came abruptly to an end when his mother died. At the age of eleven he found himself without father, without mother, and dependent wholly on the bounty of his maternal relations and his own efforts.

The Lyttons and the Mitchells, however, had lost their once substantial fortunes and were themselves in dire need. There was no one else to whom he could turn for aid. Even the small legacy of slaves that Rachel had bequeathed to him was taken away by the judgment of the court in the suit that John Michael Levine immediately commenced in behalf of his own son, Peter.

Hamilton and his older half-brother, Peter, must certainly have met, for the narrow limits of Christianstadt precluded complete avoidance. But it is just as certain that they passed by each other without speech and with resentful looks. Peter later emigrated to South Carolina and prospered mightily. He had small satisfaction from his prosperity, however, for in 1782, when he was only about twenty-eight, he took ill and died.

When the news of Peter's death came to Hamilton, he had been married a little over a year and was struggling with the problem of personal finances and a war not yet ended. He wrote to his wife about it. "Engrossed by our own immediate concerns, I omitted telling you of a disagreeable piece of intelligence I have received from a gentleman of Georgia. He tells me of the death of my brother Levine. You know the circumstances that abate my distress, yet my heart acknowledges the rights of a brother. He dies rich, but has disposed of the bulk of his fortune to strangers. I am told he has left me a legacy. I did not inquire how much."[5]

In spite of this fine appearance of nonchalance, Hamilton immediately added a postscript to a letter on military operations he was then writing to General Nathanael Greene, who was in command of the southern theater of war.

"I take the liberty to enclose you a letter to Mr. Kane Executor to the estate of Mr. Lavine a half Brother of mine who died some time since in South Carolina, Cape Roberts. If you should not be acquainted with him, [name erased from manuscript] can inform you, who he is. I shall be much obliged to you to have my letter carefully forwarded." [6]

Whether Hamilton ever received anything from Peter Levine's estate is not known. No record of its disposition seems to be available.

In 1786 he learned of another legacy.

On the recommendation of Mr. Nicholas Cruger of this city [he wrote to a firm in St. Croix], I take the liberty to commit to your care a small matter in which I am interested. I am informed that Mr. John Hallwood, a relation of mine, who died some time since in St. Croix, has, by his will, left me one-fourth part of his estate. The amount, I imagine, is not very considerable, but, whatever it may be, I shall be glad to have it collected and remitted. Mr. Hallwood's estate, I believe, consisted entirely in his share in his grandfather's estate, Mr. James Lytton, whose affairs have been a long time in a dealing court, but one would hope are now ready for a final settlement. Dr. Hugh Knox can give you further information on the subject.[7]

But this second attempt was evidently as unfortunate as the first. For he heard later from Dr. Knox: "I am sorry to inform you that no justice seems to be done in the dealing of Mr. Litton, and that as things are situated and perplexed, I fear little will come out of it for any of the heirs." [8]

2. DREAMS IN A COUNTING HOUSE

Now that young Hamilton was an orphan in every practical sense of the word, and his relations no longer able to support him, it became urgently necessary to make some provision for his future.

An opening was found for him as apprentice clerk and general fac- totum in the trading house of Nicholas Cruger, one of the wealthiest merchants of St. Croix. His white-painted, rambling establishment was located in Christianstadt, not far from the big stone store that Mr. Mitchell had occupied on the corner of Strand and King Streets in the days of his prosperity.

The boy entered on his new duties in the autumn of 1769, at the age of twelve. He did not look twelve—his slight frame, small bones and smaller stature gave him the appearance of a child, while his constitution was "rather delicate and frail." [9] But he made up for these shortcomings by a keen intellect, a passion for reading and self-improvement, and a boundless ambition that consumed his slight body with internal fires.

He did not like the counting house in which he had been placed. He despised the humdrum drone of business, the exact measurements of pounds and bushels and quarts. As he pushed a newly sharpened quill over the documents on his slanting desk, his small feet barely gripping the upper rungs of the high stool on which he was perched, his vision burst the confining walls of the room to soar outward toward grander, more splendid things—such as, the heroic fields of war!

To make matters worse, his cousin and playmate, Ned Stevens, had sailed off for New York and the glowing prospects of King's College. Barely had young Hamilton been installed before a desk when his discontent burst forth in a torrent of words to his distant friend.

"To confess my weakness, Ned, my ambition is prevalent," he wrote with passion, "so that I contemn the grovelling condition of a clerk or the like, to which my fortune, etc., condemns me, and would willingly risk my life, though not my character, to exalt my station. I am confident, Ned, that my youth excludes me from any hopes of immediate preferment; nor do I desire it; but I mean to prepare the way for futurity. . . . I shall conclude saying, I wish there was a war." [10]

These are youthful daydreams and divine discontents that are not unusual in boys of his age. What makes the letter outstanding is the fact that these naïve dreams were to be realized to the full in the years to come.

In spite of young Alexander's contempt for "the grovelling condition of a clerk" he nevertheless thrust himself into his work with that ardor of impetuous spirit and complete concentration for which he was later to become famous. Already the traits that were to be perpetually at war within the man were clearly visible in the boy. Two radically different principles tugged impatiently at each other and sought to tear apart the slight, spare frame that contained them both. On the one hand Hamilton was clear-headed, practical, compact, a master of detail and scornful of windy generalities and utopian visions. On the other he was a wild romantic, bumping his head on innumerable occasions against the clouds, filled with Renaissance conceptions of chivalric honor, yearning for vague new worlds to conquer. It was a strange dualism whose uneasy yoke explains much that might otherwise remain inexplicable in Hamilton. If one believes in the inheritance of racial characteristics, one might attribute the combination to Scotch practicality and French effervescence. Yet his father was indubitably ineffectual and the Highlanders were notoriously romantic, while the Huguenots of his mother's side were just as notoriously hard-headed.

The youthful clerk labored with such diligence that within a few short months his employer advanced him to the position of bookkeeper and sent him over to Frederikstadt on the other side of the island to take charge of a branch store.

He had been there only a little while when opportunity knocked loudly. Nicholas Cruger was taken seriously ill and was forced to sail for New York to receive competent medical treatment. Someone had to be left in complete control of the thriving business on St. Croix. To everyone's astonishment he decided on his boy clerk and bookkeeper, Alexander Hamilton.

Cruger sailed on October 15, 1771. Hamilton, not yet fifteen, found himself faced with the heavy responsibilities of a large and far-flung trading establishment.

Nicholas Cruger dealt in everything. The trade of the island to a considerable extent was in his hands. There was buying and selling with the planters; there were complicated negotiations with ship captains and the loading of cargoes; there was endless correspondence with foreign merchants. A vast number of commodities passed through his warehouse—flour, grain, apples, lumber, mules, sugar, rum, clothing, butter, codfish, alewives, candles, cheeses, tea.

All this was now plumped into the lap of the boy. He rose to the occasion. Perhaps the visions of war and glory faded; perhaps they were only thrust temporarily into the tidy corners of his mind. In any event they did not interfere with the full and exact necessities of his position.

It was a splendid discipline. It swept out some of the cobwebs of impracticality from his brain; it forced him into a definite groove of arduous endeavor; it gave him a firm foundation of facts and figures and a precise familiarity with the processes of commerce and trade; above all else, it nurtured independent judgments and a habit of responsible and immediate decisions.

Throughout Cruger's long sojourn on the mainland, young Hamilton reported to the merchant at regular intervals. Only a few of these illuminating letters have ever been published. He made duplicates of his reports in a round, fair hand and placed them in the firm's letter books.

Less than two weeks after Cruger had quit St. Croix, the first business communication from his youthful substitute was on its way after him by fast ship. He had promptly answered all the mail recently arrived, he wrote Cruger. In particular there was a letter from Cruger's brother, John Harris Cruger, who lived on the mainland and shared in a trading venture with Nicholas and a third brother, Tileman. Hamilton thought John Harris was wrong in his division of the profits and told Nicholas as much: "He says that he will remit Mr. Tileman Cruger for his 1/3 part of the Sloops first Cargo ... & should depend upon your Honour for the other two—being £400. in advance for you, exclusive of your part of her Cargo out. I therefore just inclose a little state[ment] of matters between you that you might be able more clearly to convince him of his Mistake." [11]

The boy worked so hard those first few weeks, and the initial responsibilities were so grave, that his delicate health broke down. Yet he refused to take to bed or to yield even temporarily the duties with which he had been intrusted. "I am so unwell—" he wrote Cruger on November 4th, "that it is with difficulty I make out to write these few lines." Nevertheless, in spite of illness, "I have sold about 30 bbls. flour more & Collected [a] little more money from different people." [12]

By the following week he had recovered and was again plunged deep into a swirl of business.

He sent copies of all letters received and his replies to the ailing merchant. He discoursed on the state of the market and the price of butter. He was particularly indignant about the quality of the flour.

Your Philadelphia flour is realy very bad—being of a most swarthy complexion—& withal very untractable; the Bakers complain that they cannot by any means get it to rise. Wherefore & in consideration of the quantity of flour at Market and the little demand for it I have some thought not to refuse 8 p[ence] from any good person that will give it—taking 40 or 50 Barrels. Upon opening several barrels I have observ'd a kind of Worm very common in flour about the surface—which is an indication of Age—it could not have been very new when twas skipd. [13]

A few days later he was sending to Tileman Cruger, also a partner in several trading ventures, a complete set of instructions that display a remarkably full and detailed grasp of the business of shipping and trading. [14] Not many mature and long-established merchants could have done nearly as well.

On the same day he wrote out precise orders for Captain Newton, who was handling a cargo for the firm. He was to proceed immediately "to Curracoa" and deliver his cargo. From there he was to go "to the Main, for a load of Mules—& I must beg if you do—you'll be very choice in Quality of your Mules.... Remember you are to make three trips this Season & unless you are very diligent you will be too late—as our Crops will be early in. Take care to avoid the Guarda Costas [where pirates lurked]. I place an intire reliance upon the prudence of your Conduct." [15]

But difficulties arose concerning these very mules. Captain Newton had barely cleared upon his voyage before a ship belonging to a rival firm put into St. Croix with seventy mules on board for sale to the planters. Yet the youthful business man was not alarmed. "A large Sloop with 70 Mules from the Main arrived here two days ago—" he informed Cruger, "the terms of Sale Cash down—which gives me high hopes that he will be obliged to go further—Cash of all kinds being very scarce here.... The Captain talks largely of Dangers & difficultys upon the Coast—but no doubt exaggerates a good deal by way of Stimulation." [16]

And so the letters go on, at intervals of two to four days, giving the absent merchant a complete picture of his business and of his clerk's activities.

At the beginning of the new year he heard from Cruger that his health was now restored, but that he would stay on in America to transact some important business. He was well satisfied with the conduct of his affairs on St. Croix.

Hamilton replied promptly: "Nothing cou'd be more pleasing to me than to hear of the reestablishment of your Health, and I sincerely wish you a permanent possession of that invaluable blessing." Meanwhile, "the 101 barrels superfine Flour from Philladelphia are just landed, about 40 of which I have already sold at 11½ ... but as tis probable there will be much less imported than I expected—I intend to insist on 12 for the rest." He closed by sending his employer "many thanks for the Apples you were so kind as to send me." [17]

Captain Newton returned with his cargo of mules from the mainland; but the sea voyage had been too much for the poor brutes. "Two days ago Capt. Newton delivered me ... 41 Mules," Hamilton told Tileman Cruger mournfully, "in such order that I have been oblig'd to send all of them to pasture—and of which I expect at least a third will die." [18]

This was a blow; and another followed on its very heels. He wrote to Henry Cruger, the fourth of a family of merchants.

Capt. Gibbs was ready to sail seven days after his arrival, but was detained two days longer by strong Contrary winds which made it impossible to get out of the Harbour.

Believe me Sir Nothing was neglected on my part to give him the utmost Dispatch, & considering that his Cargo was stowed very Hicheldy-picheldy—the proceeding part of it rather uttermost, I think he was dispatched as soon as could be expected....

The delay, however, was the least of the trouble.

You'll be a little surprised [he continued], when I tell you Capt. Gibbs was obligd to leave his freight money behind, the reason is this—Mr. B[urling] could by no means raise his part—tis true he might have been compeld by Law but that would have been altogether imprudent—for to have enforced payment...would have been attended with a detention of at least 10 or 12 days & the other freights were very trifling; so that the whole now rests with me, and God knows when I shall be able to receive Mr. B[urling's] part who is long winded enough.[19]

Meanwhile Cruger's new sloop, grandiosely named the *Thunderbolt*, had arrived in port with another cargo of mules and news of pirates, and privateers that were as bad as pirates, infesting the high seas. The boy's military ardor flamed. In letter after letter he insisted that the *Thunderbolt* be at once equipped with cannon to withstand attack, "as she went intirely defenceless to the Main—notwithstanding several Vessells had been obligd to put back to get out of the way of the Launches with which the Coast swarms."[20]

Nicholas Cruger returned to St. Croix in March, 1772, his health good and his American business transacted.[21] He found his establishment in flourishing condition, and the fifteen-year-old boy become a man during his absence.

Alexander Hamilton had met his first test and emerged triumphant.

3. THE HURRICANE LETTER

So well pleased was the merchant that in August of the same year he sent his chief assistant on a tour of the neighboring islands to buy and sell for him and to report on business conditions generally. Hamilton came back to St. Croix from this trip just in time to witness and experience one of those terrific hurricanes that sweep the West Indies with deplorable frequency. Christianstadt was almost wrecked, and the island flattened under a howling, tearing twister of wind and rain.

When calm came again to the shattered island, and the inhabitants emerged to count their dead and estimate their losses, young Hamilton seized his quill and commenced to write. He had been reading voraciously in his spare time—especially in Pope and Plutarch—and he burned to emulate their flair for the heroic. The hurricane seemed a worthy subject for such an exhibition of his talents.

The storm had struck St. Croix on the night of August 31st; his composition was dated September 6th. With that pardonable trembling known to all youthful authors he sent the child of his brain to *The Royal Danish-American Gazette*, the chief English newspaper of the Danish Islands. It was accepted and on Saturday, October 3, 1772, it appeared in the full panoply of print.

The sensations it aroused in the breast of its only begetter are understandable; the pride and delight with which it was received by the circle of friends and relatives are forgivable; but the general acclaim it attracted from the substantial, hard-headed business men of the islands, and even from officialdom itself, can only arouse puzzled conjecture.

It has indeed been the fashion among Hamilton's biographers to follow suit and to praise the youthful effusion in extravagant terms. Inasmuch as the actual performance was not available until the turn of this century, when Mrs. Atherton unearthed it, earlier writers simply followed tradition and judged the composition by its after-effects. Most later biographers, it is to be suspected, never read it.

As a matter of fact, the so-called "Hurricane" letter is a performance characterized in every word and line by the pomposities of youth, no better, if no worse, than a hundred thousand similar outpourings of word-intoxicated young men. It is stilted to a painful degree; it is replete with mouth-filling religiosities, no doubt imitated from the pulpit flights of Dr. Hugh Knox, his teacher and advisor. It has none of the terse style of Hamilton's business letters or the clear logic of his maturer years.

I take up my pen [he began], just to give you an imperfect account of the most dreadful hurricane that memory or any records whatever can trace, which happened here on the 31st ultimo at night....

Good God! what horror and destruction—it's impossible for me to describe—or you to form any idea of it. It seemed as if a total dissolution of nature was taking place. The roaring of the sea and wind—fiery meteors flying about in the air—the prodigious glare of almost perpetual lightning—the crash of the falling houses—and the ear-piercing shrieks of the distressed, were sufficient to strike astonishment into Angels....

This, the description of the actual hurricane, was however no more than mere introduction. The letter proceeds almost at once to the meat of the matter: a series of apostrophes, of which the following is but a single example.

Where now, Oh! vile worm [he demands rhetorically of the race of man], is all thy boasted fortitude and resolution? what is become of thy arrogance and self-sufficiency?—why dost thou tremble and stand aghast? how humble—how helpless—how contemptible you now appear. And for why? the jarring of the elements—the discord of clouds? Oh, impotent presumptuous fool! how darest thou offend that omnipotence, whose nod alone were sufficient to quell the destruction that hovers over thee, or crush thee to atoms? . . . He who gave the winds to blow and the lightnings to rage—even him I have always loved and served—his commandments have I obeyed—and his perfections have I adored.—He will snatch me from ruin—he will exalt me to the fellowship of Angels and Seraphs, and to the fulness of never ending joys.[22]

Yet this composition, strained and wholly derivative as it seems today, marked the turning point in Hamilton's life.

It became an immediate sensation. Governor Walsterstorff himself inquired after the author of this masterpiece. The Reverend Hugh Knox was beside himself with delight. The Lyttons and the Mitchells beamed. A conference was called. Obviously such talent must be encouraged.

There were no institutions of learning worthy of the name in the islands. The wealthier planters sent their children to England to finish their education. But the merchants preferred the mainland where their New York and Philadelphia correspondents could watch over and guide the young men during the long process of learning.[23] In fact, Dr. Witherspoon, fourth president of what is now Princeton University, had recently circularized the islands with an "Address to the inhabitants of Jamaica and West India Islands on behalf of the College of New Jersey," in which he discoursed on the advantages of his college for the education of West Indian youth.[24]

The matter was arranged with lightning speed. Dr. Knox took charge of the proceedings, urging that his young protegé go to Princeton, of which he himself was a graduate.[25] The aunts agreed to the proposition and pooled their limited resources. Dr. Knox added what he could, and no doubt a general collection was made among others who had been impressed with the letter.

Still dazed at the sudden turn of events, Hamilton found himself within a week on board ship, headed for Boston, and in his pocket letters of introduction to New York merchants and certain prominent personages with whom Dr. Knox was acquainted.

The passage proved not without terrors. Midway to port the ship caught fire, and both crew and passengers worked frantically to extinguish the blaze. This was accomplished only after much difficulty, and the blackened hulk limped safely into Boston Harbor in the latter part of October, 1772.[26]

The boy, now almost sixteen, did not spend much time in that troubled town. He had probably shipped for Boston because no boat was due to leave for New York for a considerable time. He took the first stagecoach out of Boston and lumbered over rutted roads, already stiff with autumnal frosts, toward New York—and a glittering future.

CHAPTER III

New World to Conquer

I. HAMILTON GOES TO COLLEGE

NEW YORK CITY, in 1772, was not the metropolis it is today. It was not even the largest town in the colonies. Philadelphia and Boston surpassed the city on the Hudson in population, volume of trade, and the amenities of civilized life. It barely covered the lower tip of Manhattan Island, its streets were dirty and crooked, its water supply came from a few precarious wells, and epidemics caused by accumulated filth and lack of all sanitary measures were startlingly regular occurrences.

Yet to the lad of fifteen, accustomed only to the limited islands and provincial towns of the West Indies, New York must have proved a dazzling vision. Here at last spread before him the illimitable opportunities of which he had dreamed even as he checked with meticulous care barrels of flour and hogsheads of molasses, or entered in his ledgers pounds and pence and farthings.

But he was sensible enough to realize that this gleaming new world could not be conquered by mere yearning. Tools were required to open the deceptively inviting gates, and these tools were knowledge and discipline.

Young Hamilton had brought with him as the most precious part of his baggage certain letters of introduction. The most practical of these related to finances. Nicholas Cruger, his erstwhile employer, recommended him to the firm of Kartwright & Company, substantial New York merchants with whom he had a running account. Besides placing the boy under their protection, Cruger arranged with them to sell at various intervals shipments of produce from the West Indies and credit the proceeds to Hamilton's account.[1]

The connection with Kartwright & Company proved to be particularly fortunate. One of the members of the firm was Hugh Mulligan. His brother, Hercules Mulligan, took an immediate liking to the youth who had been brought under their wing and devoted himself unremittingly to his interests.

This Irishman with the classical name ran a fashionable tailor shop for the upper-class Tory elements in the city. When the British later occupied New York, it was impossible for his snobbish customers to believe that their polite, dapper tailor held anything but the most correct Tory sentiments. But Hercules was in fact a fiery patriot and known to Washington as such. So well did he conceal his feelings that he was able to continue at his trade and gather valuable information which he sent secretly through the lines to the American encampment.

His sub rosa activities were hidden even from the patriots, who sullenly avoided this seeming Tory toady. In fact, when peace was declared and Washington, immediately following his triumphant entry into New York, breakfasted openly with his faithful spy, the incident became "the wonder of the Tories and the perfect horror of the Whigs," neither of whom understood why the aristocratic general thus honored the man of pins and needles.[2]

Dr. Knox had likewise furnished the boy with letters to former Princeton classmates and influential friends. These included Drs. Rogers and Mason, gentlemen of the cloth; Elias Boudinot, who was to play a leading role in the politics of the Revolution; and William Livingston, of the powerful Livingston clan, and then governor of New Jersey.

All of these gentry took a profound interest in the young West Indian's welfare and proceeded to exert themselves in his behalf. On their united advice it was determined to place the lad in the grammar school of Frances Barber at Elizabethtown, New Jersey.

Hamilton spent a year under the tutelage of the kindly and scholarly schoolmaster, preparing himself at breakneck speed for entry into college. Curiously enough, another resident of Elizabethtown during that same year of 1773 was Aaron Burr, recently graduated from Princeton, who was devoting himself to leisured reading and less leisured dalliance with the young ladies of the town.[3] Though Elizabethtown was not a large place, and there was barely a year's difference in age between the two young men, it is hardly probable that they encountered each other. The lordly college graduate would have little occasion to notice the humble grammar-school student.

During this year Hamilton cemented his relations with Boudinot and Governor Livingston. To the obligations imposed on them by Dr. Knox were soon added the personal charm and attractiveness of the eager youth. He was made welcome in their houses and he spent all his leisure hours equally between them. He applied himself with fierce energy to his lessons; yet he found time to compose youthful verses, including an elegy on the death of Boudinot's baby. He even wrote the prologue and epilogue to a play that was otherwise never completed.[4]

By the end of the year he had advanced so far in his studies that he considered himself ready for college.

He applied to Princeton, the alma mater of his beloved tutor, Dr. Knox. Hercules Mulligan accompanied the youthful aspirant to his interview with Dr. Witherspoon, its dour, if learned, president. The Scotch divine examined Hamilton as to his qualifications and found them satisfactory enough. Entrance requirements were meager in those days—a little Latin, some acquaintance with morals and religion, and the ability to read and write.

But the eager youngster was in a hurry to get over with his formal education as soon as possible so as to come to grips with the real business of life. Accordingly, he insisted on immediate entry to an advanced class and demanded a promise that he could proceed as rapidly as the progress of his studies justified, without regard to the college rules regulating promotions.

The startled doctor gravely agreed to submit these demands to the trustees for consideration. Within a fortnight Hamilton received their reply—the trustees regretted that such exemptions were contrary to the usages of the college, and therefore his application must be denied.[5]

Nothing daunted by the rebuff, Hamilton applied next to King's College in New York—later known as Columbia. King's—then under the presidency of Dr. Myles Cooper, English by birth and fiercely loyal to his mother country—was not as fastidious in its requirements as Princeton. It agreed to accept the lad on his own terms.

King's College was then a small institution, bounded by what are now Church, Greenwich, Barclay and Murray Streets. It did not rank with Harvard or Yale; even Princeton, recently established, exceeded it in prestige. The faculty consisted of three instructors. Dr. Cooper, the president, taught Latin, Greek, English, mathematics and philosophy. Dr. Samuel Clossey confined himself to natural philosophy and anatomy. Dr. Peter Middleton specialized in chemistry.

Hamilton threw himself into these new studies with the same burning impatience that had characterized his short grammar-school career. Life beckoned, and the turmoil that was already gripping the colonies added to his anxiety to be finished with cloistered studies. Of all his courses he paid most attention to anatomy. A good number of his mother's friends had been doctors. His maternal grandfather had been a doctor. Ned Stevens, his boyhood friend, who had preceded him to New York, was also a student at King's College, and taking up anatomy in preparation for a medical career. It is probable that Hamilton had some idea at this time of studying medicine. If he had, the swift tide of events soon banished the thought.

It was not all grind, however. Besides Ned Stevens, he made the acquaintance of a congenial group of fellow-students. These included two brothers, Samuel and Henry Nicoll, Nicholas Fish and Robert Troup. Troup became a lifelong friend whose friendship grew to idolatry with the passage of the years.

The young students organized a club for mutual improvement in composition, debating and public speaking. Hamilton, the youngest, in a short space of time became their acknowledged leader, outshining all the rest in debate and oratory.[6]

There was no lack of topics to debate. Events in the colonies were moving rapidly toward the final dénouement. The period of comparative calm that followed the exciting events of the sixties was suddenly broken by the passage of the tax on tea and the ensuing explosion of the Boston Tea Party. At once the colonies were in an uproar.

New sensations followed thick and fast. The New York Sons of Liberty joined their Boston brethren in resistance; they compelled the tea ship to quit New York harbor without unloading. Expresses thundered over the roads; committees of correspondence went into action.

The seething excitement in the city had its echoes within the cloistered walls of King's College. The club debated the issues, and its earnest young members declaimed in set phrases against the tyranny of George the Third. The faculty of King's College might be thoroughly British in sentiment; not so the students.

That Hamilton took the part of the colonies in these debates may be taken for granted, though Troup, reminiscing as an old man, claimed that his friend had been monarchical and pro-British until a visit to Boston, soon after the Tea Party, converted him to the cause of resistance.[7] But there is no evidence of such a journey outside of Troup's confused recollections. It is not plausible that Hamilton deserted his studies at King's College in the middle of his first year in order to make the long and tedious trip to Boston and back.

Nor is it necessary to seek long for an explanation of his sympathy with resistance and later rebellion. The merchants and planters of the West Indies were watching the struggles of the continental colonies against the regulatory acts and repressive trade policies of the mother country with equal sympathy. The British system of mercantilism coerced *their* trade just as much into narrowly defined channels. They were just as resentful of the restrictions, and Hamilton had heard their grumblings and discussions as a boy in St. Kitts and Nevis.

In fact, these two islands had greeted the Stamp Act with an outburst of indignation equal to that of the mainland. Bands of rioters, calling themselves the "Sons of Freedom," forced their way into the warehouses where the obnoxious stamps were stored and destroyed them.[8]

Furthermore, Dr. Hugh Knox, Hamilton's special mentor and adviser, enthusiastically opposed what he termed British oppression. All through the war to come he followed the fortunes of his protegé and the American Army with an ardor equalling that of the combatants themselves. As for Ned Stevens, who quit New York and went to the University of Edinburgh to study medicine before the Revolution finally broke out, *his* vicarious participation in the emotions of the day outpaced those of the patriots in the field. When the news of Burgoyne's surrender reached Scotland he cried out his delight. Hanging, it seems, would have been too good for "Gentleman Johnny."

"Why," he demanded of Hamilton, "did you grant *the Puffer, the Boaster, the Savage* (for such his Proclamation proves him to be) such favorable terms?"[9]

2. HAMILTON MAKES A SPEECH

After the Boston Tea Party, Hamilton decided that the walls of his debating club too sharply limited his activities. His hand itched for the pen, if not yet for the sword. He remembered how his first great opportunity in life had stemmed from a composition published in a West Indian newspaper. Who knew what vista might open up for him on this vaster stage?

Between lectures on anatomy and Greek, during hours stolen from study, he composed a "Defence of the Destruction of the Tea" and mailed it off to *Holt's Journal,* one of the polemic sheets of the day. Probably to his surprise, and no doubt to his delight and satisfaction, the piece was accepted and published.[10]

Encouraged by this initial success Hamilton wrote a whole series of articles and *Holt's Journal* duly published them as they came in. The articles made an impression upon the leaders of resistance, who did not know the age of this new literary addition to their ranks. John Jay wrote to his friend, McDougall: "I hope Mr. Hamilton continues busy: I have not received Holt's paper these three months, and therefore cannot judge of the progress he makes." [11]

The summer of 1774 brought freedom from formal lectures for a space of months, but no freedom from political turmoil and pamphleteering. The port of Boston had been closed by an enraged British government, troops filled the city, and the alarm of these allegedly tyrannous acts spread flaming over the other colonies. New York called a mass meeting to decide on plans of joint action with the other colonies.

On the sixth of July the people gathered in the "Fields," where City Hall Park is now located. Alexander McDougall presided on the hastily erected platform. Seated with him were the bolder spirits of revolt. The Sons of Liberty came out in force. The rough sailors from the waterfront, the mechanics and draymen, the apprentices and their merchant employers, packed the Fields in a solid mass. Loyalists and conservatives prudently kept to their houses. The debating club of King's College squirmed through the excited people until they stood close to the platform.

The speeches were fiery, the speakers impassioned. McDougall offered a set of resolutions urging non-importation of all English goods. The resolutions passed by acclamation. But the meeting refused to end. The crowd clamored for more. Hamilton and his group were swept with the common enthusiasm. Someone of the club yelled to Hamilton: "Give 'em a speech, Alexander. You're good at it." The others took up the cry. Before he knew quite what had happened eager hands had thrust him upon the speakers' platform.

Hamilton gazed out over the sea of faces. Something like stage-fright assailed him. He had never spoken to an audience larger than the debating club. He faltered a moment; then confidence returned. His voice grew strong and vigorous. He painted a picture of the long oppressive action of the mother country, insisted upon the sacred duty of resistance to such tyranny, and ended with a peroration in which revolt became a mighty tidal wave sweeping from the shores of the New World back upon the doomed headlands of England the wrecks of her power and the shattered remnants of her glory.

The huge assemblage swayed to the ringing oratory. "Who is he?"

they asked each other. "A collegian!" ran the reply. Then all voices joined in a roar of approval as the boy of seventeen, flushed and conscious of his powers, descended from the platform.[12] His maiden try at public speech had been as successful as his first effort with the pen.

Hamilton, however, kept a level head. In spite of rising agitation, in spite of pamphleteering and oratory, he held diligently to his studies. When the fall term opened at King's College, we find a significant item in the private ledger of Dr. Robert Harpur: "Sept. 20, 1774—Mr. Alexr. Hamilton at £3..4 p Quar[ter], Dr. entered with me this day to study Mathem[atic]s."[13]

That Dr. Harpur labored satisfactorily to instil that abstruse science in the mind of his pupil is evidenced by a further entry in the same manuscript ledger nine years later: "1783. By Cash recd. from him, now Col. Hamilton as a present at the close of the War—5 Guin[ea]s. = £9, 6 s. 8 d."[14]

And there is on deposit with the Library of Congress a slender volume of Hamilton's school exercises during this troubled period, in which, neatly copied, are excerpts from the *Iliad* in the original Greek, together with extended notes from ancient history and geography.[15]

That Hamilton did not permit even the advent of war to interfere with his studies is evidenced by his pay book while in command of a company of artillery. Side by side with notations of the sums paid out to the members of his company are comments and excerpts of books read in the interim of drills and war's alarums. Among others he read Cicero, Demosthenes, Plutarch, Bacon's *Essays*, Rousseau's *Emile*, Hobbes' *Dialogues*, Robinson's *Charles V*, Millot's *History of France*, Smith's *History of New York*, and Ralt's *Dictionary of Trade and Commerce*.[16]

The list is solid in history, morals and travels; but the notes relate chiefly to economics, trade and government—interesting evidence that even at this early age Hamilton's feet were placed upon the path he was to follow undeviatingly through life. Especially illuminating is this question he propounded to himself as early as 1776: "Quere. Would it not be advisable to let all taxes, even those imposed by the States, be collected by persons of Congressional appointment; and would it not be advisable to pay the collectors so much per cent. on the sums collected?"[17] In these few words is implicit the germ of Hamilton's later nationalism and advocacy of a strong central government.

A study of his excerpts and quotations from the books he read show conclusively that Hamilton had already formed the basis of his mature philosophy and course of action. From the *First Philippic* of Demosthenes he carefully copied the following:

"As a general marches at the head of his troops, so ought with politicians, if I dare use the expression, to march at the head of affairs; insomuch that they ought not to wait the *event*, to know what measures to take; but the measures which they have taken, ought to produce the *event*."

Here, in admirably succinct form, is the essence of the future Hamiltonian system and the heart of his quarrel with Jeffersonian laissez-faire in government.

CHAPTER IV

From Pen to Sword

I. THE PAMPHLETEER

AT ABOUT THE time Hamilton began the study of mathematics under Dr. Harpur, the First Continental Congress assembled in Philadelphia. The colonies had finally determined to seek ways and means together to defend their threatened liberties. Yet, while all were agreed upon the necessity of defense, the means to be employed was another matter. A violent controversy arose. The radicals were all for extreme measures; the conservatives and moderates shrank from anything that might permanently endanger the relations between the mother country and the colonies. After a struggle that almost wrecked the congress the radicals won control. They forced through resolutions calling for a boycott of all English goods. Thereby, they argued, England must soon be brought to her senses. Her most sensitive nerve was her pocketbook; hit her there, and she must yield.

To enforce the boycott, committees of inspection were organized throughout the colonies. They were authorized to use such measures as were necessary. Everyone knew what that meant.

The conservatives among the colonists were frightened at these vigilante tactics; those of Tory sympathies aghast. Dr. Samuel Seabury, an eminent divine who later became Bishop of Connecticut, decided on a counterblast. He addressed a tract to the farmers and tillers of America, designed to bring them back to their proper allegiance to the crown. He called it "Free Thoughts on the Proceedings of the Continental Congress" and signed it anonymously, "A Westchester Farmer." Almost immediately he followed it with another blast, entitled "Congress canvassed by a Westchester Farmer."

These were skilful performances, written in a hearty and popular style, as became a pretended yeoman of the soil. Contrary to the general trend of the pamphlets of the era they contained very little billingsgate. Instead they appealed to the plain common sense of the landed farmers, plausibly arguing that they had been beneficently

35

treated by the British crown and parliament, and that they had little to gain and much to lose from the radical turmoil of the period.

The pamphlets created a considerable stir among those conservative patriots who were already drawing back from what they considered the excesses of the Sons of Liberty and resented the approval stamped upon their methods by the congress.

The radicals became alarmed. It was necessary to counteract the effects of Seabury's pseudo-pastoral arguments. But who could write a proper reply?

While the regular radical pamphleteers were being canvassed for this purpose there appeared from the press of James Rivington in New York on December 15, 1774, a lengthy, paper-backed affair bearing the formidable title, "A Full Vindication of the Measures of Congress from the calumnies of their enemies, in answer to a letter under the signature of a Westchester Farmer." No name was signed to the pamphlet.

At the time no one but Hamilton's immediate circle of friends knew that he was the author. What had prompted him to spring to the defense of congress and the patriot cause is unknown. Certainly none of the regular radicals had urged the task upon him. He was still not yet eighteen, he was a student at college, and the articles he had written for *Holt's Journal* were limited in circulation and not important enough to have justified his choice for the responsibility of replying to Seabury.

It is doubtful, however, if he required any outside urgings. He had already tasted the sweets of authorship. Arguments flowed readily from his tongue, but his pen was even more nimble. He enjoyed the shock of controversy; next to the trial by sword he loved more than anything else the ordeal by argument. He was a natural-born pamphleteer. In a few years he was to become incomparable in an age of noted adversaries. Only Tom Paine may be said to have surpassed him. Their methods, indeed, were wholly different. Paine dealt with emotions, and struck off immortal phrases white-hot from the passion that consumed him. Hamilton coined no immortal phrases, but he employed with deadly effect relentless logic, masterful legalisms, and downright strokes of the bludgeon.

"A Full Vindication" was not only Hamilton's first important contribution to the cause of the colonies, it displayed as well much of the technique he was to use in later years. Though shot through with immaturities and phrases which should have betrayed the youth of its author to the observant, it was nevertheless a surprising performance. It skilfully marshaled the arguments that were current property, and added to them many that were peculiarly Hamilton's own. It tickled the ears of the groundlings; yet appealed in measured accents to the economic interests of the rich and respectable. It frankly incited to racial and religious prejudices while at the same time invoking with impassioned fervor the democratic doctrine of the rights of man. It moved by swift transitions from homely plain speaking to the most glittering generalities. In short, it was a catch-all, a net in which to gather all classes and conditions of society for a single defense against British aggression. Its philosophy was not deep-rooted, its economic and political theses ill-considered, but it served its purpose to quicken the multitude and act as a brake on Seabury's influence.[1]

One passage, however, adumbrated the future "Report on Manufactures." The timid feared the effects of a boycott on America itself. How could she exist? they asked. Quite well, Hamilton retorted. We have food and clothing in plenty; as for those articles we now import from abroad, why not manufacture them ourselves? "If, by the necessity of the thing, manufactures should once be established, and take root among us, they will pave the way still more to the future grandeur and glory of America."[2]

The Reverend Samuel Seabury considered the anonymous pamphlet important enough to deserve a refutation. He countered with "A View of the Controversy." He was sufficiently perturbed to descend to the scurrility he had avoided in his initial pamphlets. For, he declared, his opponent had employed "artifice, sophistry, misrepresentation and abuse," weapons which he wielded "like an old experienced practitioner."

With amazing speed Hamilton issued a counterblast. Barely a month after the appearance of Seabury's reply, "The Farmer Refuted" was in print and hawked about in village and town. From the standpoint of sheer bulk alone it is an impressive performance, running to more than one hundred and twenty pages of text in Lodge's edition of the *Works*.[3]

He retorted scurrility to scurrility, but very sensibly added more effective arguments. He examined the basis of the relations between Great Britain and America. To prove his point that the colonies owed allegiance to the crown alone, and not to parliament, so that parliament had no legal right to tax the Americans, he delved into the history of the several colonies. In each case, he pointed out with much detail, the charter had come directly from the king, and there was a compact between king and colony in which there was no mention of obedience to a British parliament.

But when he came to the case of New York, his whole thesis floundered. For New York had no charter; it was a province conquered and wrested from the Dutch.

Whereupon Hamilton cast aside the ingenious line of legal argument he had been pursuing and rose to the winds of declamation, all in capitals. Now he thundered: "THE SACRED RIGHTS OF MANKIND ARE NOT TO BE RUMMAGED FOR AMONG OLD PARCHMENTS OR MUSTY RECORDS. THEY ARE WRITTEN, AS WITH A SUNBEAM, IN THE WHOLE VOLUME OF HUMAN NATURE, BY THE HAND OF THE DIVINITY ITSELF, AND CAN NEVER BE ERASED OR OBSCURED BY MORTAL POWER." [4]

It is in purple passages like these that the reader is brought back abruptly to a realization of the author's extreme youth. The later Hamilton would never have been guilty of such obvious substitutes for logical argument.

He was on much more substantial ground when he hammered at the tremendous importance of the American trade to the economy of Great Britain. With a remarkable grasp of his facts he dissected the economic life of the mother country to show how precariously fine-drawn it was and how easily it could be upset. Hence non-intercourse must prove the most effective weapon of coercion and force Britain speedily to restore the ravished liberties of the colonies.

His conclusion was surprisingly mild: "I earnestly lament the unnatural quarrel between the parent state and the colonies, and most ardently wish for a speedy reconciliation—a perpetual and *mutually* beneficial union." But, he hastened to add, "the best way to secure a permanent and happy union between Great Britain and the colonies, is to permit the latter to be as free as they desire." [5] Words of wisdom, whose full force England has only recently come to understand.

The two pamphlets made a deep impression on the colonial leaders. Speculation ran rife as to the author. It was obvious, they agreed with Seabury, that "an old experienced practitioner" had written them. John Jay, perhaps? But John Jay denied it. Who, then?

When it was finally disclosed that the pamphleteer was a mere collegian, and a fledgling youth, the astonishment was profound. Dr. Myles Cooper, staunch old Tory, refused to believe that his student was responsible. "He had no doubt the answers were from Jay's pen," he told Troup, "and he ridiculed the idea of their having been written by such a stripling as Hamilton." But, reported Troup, "I well knew the contrary, as Hamilton wrote the answers when he and I occupied the same room in college, and I read them before they were sent to the press." [6]

Later on, according to tradition, Dr. Cooper became finally convinced that his pupil wielded a trenchant pen and offered him a substantial sum to employ his talents on the side of the British Ministry. Hamilton turned the offer down.[7]

Flushed with the acclaim that had greeted his efforts Hamilton sought other topics on which to try his rapid pen. One was not long in coming.

One June 22, 1774, parliament enacted what is known as the Quebec Act, granting full religious liberty to the French Catholics of Canada and restoring to them the legal and political institutions under which they had been governed prior to the English conquest. Today historians are agreed that this particular act is a shining example of statesmanlike qualities and liberal legislation. But the American colonists felt far otherwise.

In the south that section of the Act which annexed to Quebec all the territory north of the Ohio River was the focal point of attack. The Virginia planters had speculated considerably in the ill-defined lands across the Ohio and they resented bitterly the loss of all their prospects. In the north, however, it was the clause granting freedom of worship to the Catholics of Quebec that evoked the storm. The Protestant ministers thundered from the pulpits; the ancient cry of "Popery" brought horrid visions to their auditors.

Hamilton joined that hue and cry. Here was a further issue with which to widen the gap between England and America. On June 15, 1775, he published his "Remarks on the Quebec Bill." [8] The "Remarks" made no pretense to logic or reasoned discussion of the facts; they were a frank appeal to racial and religious prejudice. This odious Act, he cried, "develops the dark designs of the ministry more fully than any thing they have done." What were these dark designs? Nothing else than "the subjugation of the colonies, and afterward that of Great Britain itself."

The youthful propagandist found it easy to prove this horrendous thesis for the benefit of trembling Protestant ears. For the Popish re-

ligion was the "great engine" of arbitrary power. A grateful priest-
hood, in return for the solid establishment of its superstitious reign
and the compulsory extraction of tithes from an unwilling people,
would support the contemplated despotism of king and ministry. The
Protestants, abandoned to the tender mercies of a triumphant Popery,
must yield on every side. Even the lands of the Ohio, especially dear
to southern speculators, must soon be flooded with "innumerable hosts"
of Popish aliens who, in a short space of time, would surround on every
side the devoted Protestants of the colonies. This, in effect, was the
sinister design concealed in the provisions of the Quebec Act.

That sentiments such as these, though agreeable enough to the majority of the colonists to whom they were addressed, did infinite harm
to the cause of revolution, did not occur to Hamilton or to his audience. More than anything else, the agitation over the Quebec Act and
the vituperation poured over the Catholic sensibilities of the Canadians
were to hold them loyal to the cause of England in the forthcoming
struggle.

2. THE SWORDSMAN

But Hamilton did not rely solely on his talents with the pen to
further the conflict that was now inevitable. Here was the war of
which he had dreamed as he sat on his stool in Cruger's establishment.
Here was the opportunity for that military glory which exalted the
soul and brought the young and hitherto obscure to the heights of
popular applause. Grimly the young student determined not to be
found wanting.

Everywhere was hasty drilling and martial preparation. Muskets
were removed from their pegs and carefully cleaned; powder and ball
were stored against the day. King's College did not lag behind. Edward
Fleming, a former adjutant in the British army, formed a company of
college students and other youngsters of New York, and taught them
the "manual exercise." Hamilton and his friend Troup joined immediately. Every morning, before classes, they met in the churchyard of
St. George's Chapel for drill. With the naïve enthusiasm of youth they
accoutered themselves in gaudy uniforms, emblazoned grandiose inscriptions on their attire and adopted a high-flown name.

The "Corsicans," they called themselves. They wore short green
coats and small round hats cocked rakishly on one side. Round the
crowns flaunted the stirring sentiment, "Liberty or Death." Flaming
red hearts of tin rode their jackets, inscribed "God and our Right." [9]

While the collegians applied themselves to the manual of arms, the Revolution began. Lexington and Concord touched off the powder keg. Ethan Allen marched on Ticonderoga, and the Second Continental Congress assembled in Philadelphia.

In New York City rioting broke out. The impassioned patriots moved against the hated Tories. The chief Tory was Dr. Myles Cooper, president of King's College and Hamilton's mentor in education. That irascible old man minced no words in denouncing what he termed the excesses of a vile rabble. On the night of May 10, 1775, the rabble went into action. Carrying along with them buckets of bubbling tar and feathers hastily stripped from beds and pillows, they poured in a shouting swarm through the narrow, ill-paved streets, headed for the stately domicile of the Tory.

Hamilton, roused from his slumber, heard the uproar and saw the tossing torches that illumined the rioters on their way. Hastily dressing and calling on Troup, his roommate, to accompany him, he rushed into the street.

"What's up?" he demanded breathlessly.

"We're going to give that damned Tory, Cooper, a taste of tar and feathers," they shouted back.

"Quick!" Hamilton whispered to Troup. "We've got to head them off. If they harm Dr. Cooper, it will be a disgrace the cause will never live down. Follow me!"

They sped by a short cut to the house of the unsuspecting doctor, and leaped upon the steps of the porch just as the mob surged up. The building was dark; the educator was fast asleep.

"Stop, men!" Hamilton shouted with outstretched hand. The rioters paused momentarily at the apparition of the two collegians. Hamilton was known to them as an active patriot—had he not already exhorted them in the Fields? Had he not written flaming pamphlets in their behalf? Was he not even then drilling in readiness to fight the British?

Hamilton seized the moment of their indecision. "Bethink yourselves," he cried, "on the impropriety of your conduct; on the disgrace you are bringing on the cause of liberty, of which you profess to be the champions."

Just then Dr. Cooper, clad only in shirt and nightcap, peered out of his bedroom window. He saw the night filled with angry men and Hamilton gesticulating to them from the porch steps. "Ha!" he thought to himself in alarm, "that rebellious young rascal is rousing the rabble to do me hurt!"

Thrusting his head out, he cried in great excitement: "Don't listen to him, gentlemen. He is crazy, crazy!" Then, thrusting a cloak over himself, he rushed to the rear of the house to make his escape. The mob howled with laughter, and in the confusion Hamilton ran after him, swift with explanations. Calming the agitated doctor, he hustled him into the darkness just in time. Already the hotter spirits among the mob had battered their way into the house.

Piloted by Hamilton, Dr. Cooper fled to the banks of the Hudson and made his way down toward the harbor. A Mr. Stuyvesant gave him refuge, and on the evening of the following day he went stealthily in a small boat to the protection of the British man-of-war, *Kingfisher*. Eventually he embarked for England, where he embalmed his terrifying experiences in enthusiastic verse.[10]

A few months later, on the 23rd of August, occurred another in the mounting series of explosive incidents in which Hamilton was directly involved. Several British warships, including the *Asia*, lay at anchor in the bay, and a rumor spread that the ships intended to land an armed force to seize twenty-one pieces of cannon that were stationed at the Battery. Accordingly, the newly created Provincial Congress of New York met in hasty session and resolved to remove the endangered pieces to a place of safety.

That evening a militia company of artillery under the command of Captain John Lamb, accompanied by an outpouring of citizens, descended upon the Battery to drag the cannon away. Hamilton, Troup and Mulligan, with their "Corsican" comrades, seized their muskets and joined the hurrying patriots. An armed barge of the *Asia*, surprising the swarm of men at the task, fired on them. Lamb's company promptly returned the fire, and so did a battalion under Colonel Lasher that had come up in support. The *Asia*, lying at anchor, swung into action with a broadside.

The drums of the city beat to arms, the populace caught up weapons and rushed to the waterfront. While the regular companies fired, reloaded and fired again at the dim-seen boats in the harbor, the citizenry tugged and heaved at the cannon. Hamilton and Mulligan helped with one of the great guns. Hamilton "exhibited the greatest unconcern," though solid shot and musket balls whined all about him. After they had managed to haul the cannon away, Hamilton discovered he had left his musket behind. He went back to retrieve it, in spite of the continued bombardment. Three men on shore had been wounded, and one of the crew of the *Asia's* barge killed in the fighting. But the guns had been snatched from British hands.[11]

In spite of all these exciting events, his drilling and writing, Hamilton somehow found time to continue his studies. King's College in effect closed down with Dr. Cooper's melodramatic escape; yet the student continued to read diligently in history, finance and political economy. Also, in view of the times, he applied himself to military studies, especially in those relating to artillery. His pay book and other documents testify to the extent and range of his reading.

For matters were proceeding rapidly toward direct war in New York, as was already the case in Massachusetts. Governor Tryon, last of the royal governors, quit the rebellious province in great haste, threatening to return with a British army at his back. The new Provincial Congress of patriots attempted to take over authority and restore order, but the rioting got wholly out of hand.

One of the worst of the affrays was an irruption into the city by a body of Connecticut horsemen under Captain Sears for the express purpose of wreaking vengeance on James Rivington, one of the most influential printers in the colony. He was accused of Tory leanings, though he had also published pamphlets on the patriot side: among them Hamilton's "A Full Vindication." The raiders clattered into town, gutted his printing plant, and carried off the type.

The affair aroused considerable indignation, even among the New York patriots. They resented this violent meddling with local concerns by an outside group. Hamilton was one of the first to voice his protest. He wrote a strong letter to John Jay, with whom he had become acquainted as a result of his writings. Jay was then in Philadelphia as a delegate from New York to the Second Continental Congress.

Though I am fully sensible how dangerous and pernicious Rivington's press has been [he wrote] and how detestable the character of the man is in every respect, yet I cannot help disapproving and condemning this step.... In times of such commotion as the present, while the passions of men are worked up to an uncommon pitch there is great danger of fatal extremes. The same state of the passions which fits the multitude, who have not a sufficient stock of reason and knowledge to guide them, for opposition to tyranny and oppression, very naturally leads them to a contempt and disregard of all authority.... In such tempestuous times, it requires the greatest skill in the political pilots to keep men steady and within proper bounds, on which account I am always more or less alarmed at every thing which is done of mere will and pleasure, without any proper authority.[12]

As in the case of Dr. Cooper, Hamilton showed himself a vigorous proponent of a strong governmental hand, law and order, and a respect for property rights. Just as vigorous was his openly expressed contempt for the multitude and the necessity for wise leaders to keep them within bounds.

Later, after a formal remonstrance from the New York Congress to the governor of Connecticut, the kidnapped type was returned intact to its owner.

In spite of the riots against them, however, the Tories increased their activities. Within a month, Hamilton was again writing to Jay; but this time it was to warn him against Tory intrigues. "I have much reason to suspect," he advised, "that the tories have it in contemplation to steal a march upon us, if they can, in respect of a new Assembly. I believe the governor [Tryon] will shortly dissolve the old and issue writs for a new one." The scheme was to gain control of the new Assembly while patriot eyes were focussed on more stirring events and use it to throw the people "into divisions and ferments." To prevent this artful intrigue from becoming successful, Hamilton told Jay, he had already "thrown out a hand bill or two to give the necessary alarm, and shall second them by others." [13]

These handbills have vanished. They represent his last attempt to influence public opinion with the pen for a long time to come. Hamilton was now to turn decisively to the sword.

CHAPTER V

Hamilton Goes to War

I. ARTILLERY CAPTAIN

On January 6, 1776, the New York Provincial Congress resolved that a company of artillery be raised for the defense of the colony. This was the opportunity for which Hamilton had been waiting and preparing himself with studies in gunnery and pyrotechnics. He promptly applied for the command of this company which existed as yet only on paper, and induced Colonel McDougall, whom he had met in the course of his manifold activities, to endorse his application.

The congress, however, hesitated to grant such a post to a nineteen-year-old boy whose single experience with cannon consisted in dragging one away from the Battery. But Hamilton had influential friends who bestirred themselves in his behalf. The congress yielded to the pressure and decided, in order to preserve the proprieties, to examine the youth in the theory of artillery and ballistics. McDougall was one of the examiners. Hamilton had grounded himself thoroughly and impressed the committee with his grasp of fundamentals.

Whereupon the Provincial Congress hesitated no longer. On March 14, 1776, it "Ordered: That the said Alexander Hamilton be, and he is hereby appointed Captain of the Provincial Company of the Artillery of this Colony." [1]

But Hamilton's difficulties had only commenced. According to the cheerful custom of the time he was a captain without a company. The cannon, of course, were taken from the public store; but the congress could furnish no gunners to man them. The duty of raising men devolved on Hamilton personally. And since the congress, an extra-legal body, had no funds, it was also incumbent on the new-fledged officer to furnish and equip his troops out of his own pocket. Furthermore, there was the problem of bounties. Hardly a patriot could be induced to enlist unless a substantial cash sum offered in advance smoothed the path.

The young captain did not hesitate. The last remittance from his sore-pressed relatives in St. Croix had just arrived, with a gloomy note to the effect that no more would be forthcoming. Hamilton took the money and went out to raise his company. So persuasive were his appeals and so effective the distribution of his funds that within a few days he had lined up thirty men, all in uniform and properly outfitted for war. He purchased each piece of equipment himself and was careful to get only the best. By the time he was through not a penny remained to him of his remittance, but he had the satisfaction of knowing that no other local company presented as smart or lavish appearance as his.[2]

Having a company was not enough. It was necessary to lick these raw, untrained recruits into soldiers. Hamilton applied himself to this task with single-minded devotion. He paraded his men daily to the Fields and drilled them until they were ready to drop. Whereas the other companies of militia drilling on the Fields came irregularly, straggled and loafed in the ranks, obeyed orders or not as the whim seized them, Hamilton enforced strict and rigorous discipline. War, he knew, was a grim business at best, and he hammered unremittingly at his men until they were letter-perfect in the handling of their guns. Officers of the line came to watch the little company snapping through evolutions at the terse commands of the young captain and nodded approval at such a refreshing novelty among the militia. His fame began to spread.

Meanwhile William Alexander, who called himself Lord Stirling, had been placed in command of the Continental forces in New York. This was on March 6, 1776. Through the good offices of Elias Boudinot, who had befriended the boy on his arrival in America, he offered Hamilton a position on his staff. Boudinot hastened to New York from Newark with the good news. Hamilton received it coldly. He was expecting his commission shortly in the militia and, while the staff appointment was flattering, he preferred a command in a fighting force, no matter how humble, to the dignity and emolument of an aide. He told Boudinot as much. Disappointed, Elias Boudinot returned to Newark and had his brother, Elisha, convey the refusal to Stirling. Elisha was tactful. It wouldn't do to tell the noble lord that their protegé had turned down his offer for a still tentative militia captaincy. Accordingly he wrote: "Mr. Hamilton had already accepted the command of Artillery, and was therefore deprived of the pleasure of attending your Lordship's person as Brigade Major."[3]

On April 2nd the New York Committee of Safety ordered Captain Hamilton's company, now swollen to sixty-eight men, to the task of guarding the records of the colony.[4] This was inglorious work enough, if necessary, and it may well be imagined that the fiery, newly appointed captain chafed at the assignment.

Nevertheless he continued to drill his troops during the day—and to study at night. He worked his men hard; yet he was quick to advance their interests on every possible occasion. He demanded promotions for those privates in the ranks who in his opinion deserved them.[5] He insisted on an advance in pay for his troops equal in amount to that received by the regular artillery, even though his own pay would not be affected.[6]

All requests were promptly granted. The New York Congress had learned to respect the judgment of its appointee. On the very day it received the demand for an increase, it passed a resolution to raise the pay, ordered frocks for his men, and decreed that "the said Captain *Hamilton* receive ten Shillings for every man he has or shall inlist, not exceeding one hundred men." [7]

Yet it seems there was discontent in the company. The young captain was a hard taskmaster and his ideas of discipline ruthless. The manuscript orderly book of Colonel Webb, to whose regiment Hamilton's Company was attached, discloses several significant items. On April 20, 1776, four men in Hamilton's command—including two sergeants and a corporal—were tried for mutiny. Two were found guilty as charged—a sergeant and the corporal. The sergeant was reduced to the ranks and fined a month's pay; the corporal went also into the ranks and was sentenced to imprisonment for a fortnight. The other two were convicted of a lesser offense—disobedience of orders—and got off with a reprimand.[8]

Still the trouble did not cease. Two weeks later a man who tried to desert was sentenced to six days' imprisonment on bread and water, and a week after another deserter was given "39 Lashes on his Bare Back." [9]

In spite of penalties and floggings, the men continued to desert. It became so bad that the Provincial Congress finally gave Hamilton permission to take a search squad and board all the ships then at anchor in the harbor in quest of the fleeing soldiers.[10]

The situation, however, should not be held against Hamilton. The militia companies were notoriously averse to discipline and the rigors of military life, and Hamilton was a strict disciplinarian. They preferred to fight when they would and relax when they wished. All through the war Washington was to be plagued by the equally unaccountable bursts of valor and of sudden flight on the part of state militias.

2. HAMILTON MEETS BURR

Nevertheless Hamilton managed to keep his company up to its complement and to a proper state of fitness. In June he was relieved of his humdrum duties of guarding paper records and ordered to Bowling Green at the tip of Manhattan where his cannon commanded the harbor.

On July 12th the long expected British fleet, led by the *Phoenix* and the *Rose*, sailed up the narrows and into the harbor to invest New York. Tense with excitement, Captain Hamilton ordered his men to their guns. The days of drilling were past; the time for action had arrived. Solid shot went screaming and whistling over the water. But the company proved unlucky in its first engagement. The warships of the British received no hurt from the cannonade, while one of the cannon burst as it was being fired and killed two of its own crew.[11]

General Howe, commanding an army of 34,000 men and accompanied by a huge armada, effected a landing on Staten Island, wholly unperturbed by the scattered firing from the city. His orders called on him to crush the rebellion once and for all, and it seemed quite probable that he would do so forthwith. Washington had hastened down from Boston to New York to meet this formidable threat, but his force was small, badly equipped and poorly disciplined. New York was indefensible; yet Washington, with an eye for the political situation and the wavering attitude of some of the colonies, resolved to attempt its defense.

His first act was to insist that the local militia be incorporated into the ranks of the regular Continental Army, so that they might be subject to his orders. The Continental Congress, sitting in Philadelphia, obliged with the necessary Enabling Act. The New York Congress, which had authority over the militia, followed suit with a series of resolutions. As a result, Hamilton found himself on August 9th an officer in the Continental Army, and his artillery company attached to General Scott's brigade.[12] He must have viewed the transfer with considerable satisfaction. The discipline among the Continental troops, poor as it was, was much more rigorous than in the militia, and the penalties for mutiny and desertion proportionately severe.

The situation that confronted Washington offered almost insuperable difficulties. To prevent Howe from seizing Brooklyn Heights across the river and from that commanding elevation throw cannon shot at will into New York, Washington was compelled to divide his already numerically inferior forces. One part he held in Manhattan to defend the city; the other he ordered over to the Heights. Scott's brigade and Putnam's division were among the latter.

Hamilton had barely taken his men and guns across the river when he realized that the position was wholly untenable. Another fiery young warrior, landing with General Putnam, whose aide he was, came to an identical conclusion. The name of the young man whose opinion coincided thus independently with Hamilton's was Aaron Burr.

With both young officers to think was to act. Burr reported his findings in caustic language to General Putnam. Hamilton scribbled off a note to Washington himself. He was sufficiently prudent, however, not to sign his name. He had carefully inspected the terrain, he wrote, and was convinced that any attempted defense under the guns of the fleet, with Howe certain to land farther down in a flanking movement, would prove suicidal. It would be better, he advised, to retreat at once back across the river before the British attacked and to consolidate the little army on more advantageous ground on upper Manhattan.

He handed the anonymous letter to his faithful friend, Hercules Mulligan, who in turn gave it to Colonel Webb who commanded the regiment.[18] Whether Webb transmitted the advice to Washington, and whether Washington, if he received it, had a chance to read the note before battle was joined is not known.

The ensuing events justified to the full the forebodings of Hamilton and Burr. On August 27th Howe attacked. His tactics were brilliant. He landed on undefended ground, turned the American left at Jamaica and thrust it crumpled and broken back upon the main body on Brooklyn Heights. Had Howe pressed his advantage with decision, he might have cut the whole army on Long Island to pieces while Washington watched helplessly from Manhattan, and perhaps have ended the war then and there. But Howe was strangely content with his initial victory and went into camp instead. Time and again he was to save the cause of the American Revolution by a similar curious dilatoriness at crucial moments.

Nevertheless the situation was desperate. In front, commanding the water, lay the British fleet. Behind sat Howe's victorious legions. And even he must, when morning came, attack the hemmed-in regiments. With a heavy heart Washington ordered the troops to attempt the dangerous crossing to Manhattan under cover of night. Fortunately it commenced to rain and a strong wind blew up, easing the vigilance of the blockading fleet.

It was a slow, terrible retreat in darkness and storm across the East River. The small boats were frequently swamped and the shivering men drenched to the skin. Hamilton managed to ferry his guns safely over and took up a position at Bunker's Hill, a small fort located at what is now the intersection of Grand and Mulberry Streets.

Here confusion reigned. Orders came one moment and were countermanded the next. Washington still hoped to hold New York, though the British fleet commanded all the waters around the island and a landing by Howe at the northern end of Manhattan would cut off half his troops. But again Howe delayed. When he finally did move into action, it was to throw a force across to Kip's Bay, much lower down the island. Even so the disheartened Continentals fled for safety. They swept in a great, disordered mass up the island, each man for himself, heedless of ranks or officer's exhortations, not to pause until Washington met them with oaths and the flat of his sword at Harlem Heights, far beyond the range of battle.

The British horse galloped along the fleeing flanks, cutting them down and exulting at the easy victory. Scott's brigade clung in indecision to the tiny fort at Bunker's Hill while the tide of panic-stricken Continentals and the pursuing British swept past and beyond them. Silliman's brigade, under the temporary command of General Knox, equally bewildered, flung panting into the fort. Here seemed a measure of protection; Hamilton's guns looked comforting to officers and men. They did not realize that each moment's delay increased their peril; that already the victorious British had cut them off from the main body on Harlem Heights.

In this situation a slight youth of twenty, bearing the insignia of a major of the staff, came galloping into the fort. It was Aaron Burr, attached to General Putnam, but himself cut off from his division. His eye flashed around the crowded, huddled men. Why, he demanded, hadn't they already retreated? General Knox, his obese frame shaking with his recent exertions, replied that retreat was impossible. There was nothing left but to defend the fort, and he intended to do so to the last man. "I know the roads," retorted Burr. "I can lead you to safety." But Knox clung to the fort with the obstinacy of a distracted man. He refused to go.

In a passion Burr swung from the panting general and addressed himself directly to the troops who had clustered around, listening in silence to the dispute. "Do you wish to remain here and end up in a dungeon or hung like dogs," he shouted, "or will you follow me who can bring you to safety? Better that half of you die bravely fighting than all of you be sacrificed like cowards."

Among those who heard his ringing speech was Alexander Hamilton. It was probably the first time these two, whose lives thereafter became so tragically intertwined, had met in person.

Both men were young—Burr was barely a year older than Hamilton—and both were aflame with a similar thirst for power and glory. Even in appearance there were striking similarities. Both were short of stature, erect, compact, and filled with an indescribable élan. Both were capable of great friendships and equally great hatreds. Both were irresistible to women and delighted in turn in their numerous conquests. Both were brilliant far beyond their years and possessed of intellects as tight and compact as their bodies. Both were extremely solicitous of their dignity, as is usual with men of slight physique. Burr was five foot six; Hamilton topped him by an inch. Burr had soft, brown hair and piercing black eyes; Hamilton was of a fair, ruddy complexion and wore his hair brushed back from his forehead in a carefully powdered club. There was an almost feminine hue to his cheeks. Both were easy and vivacious in manner, and handsome. In conversation Hamilton's face was mobile and his smile attractive; in repose it assumed a severe and thoughtful expression.[14]

Such were the two young men who now met under such striking circumstances. It may well be that here, at this first meeting, was laid the foundation for Hamilton's later intense dislike for the man who in so many particulars resembled himself. Certainly it must have chafed the captain of artillery, himself avid for dramatic glory, to stand by and see this other youth, hardly older than himself, steal the show away.

For Burr's impassioned speech, insubordinate as it was, proved brilliantly successful. The troops disregarded their own officers and clamored that he lead them. Burr put himself in command, while Knox puffed and glowered, yet followed unwillingly. The young major knew the terrain intimately. He took them along unfrequented back roads and led them safely into the main lines at Harlem Heights. Only once had they caught sight of an enemy patrol and beat it off easily. In the haste and necessary disorder of the retreat, however, Hamilton lost all of his baggage and one of his beloved cannon. This, too, must have rankled.[15]

When, finally, in his own good time, Howe decided to attack the American position at Harlem Heights, Washington had managed to rally his beaten men and complete his line of breastworks. The British were thrown back and the wearied troops were enabled to quit their untenable position and retreat in good order to a stronger position among the low hills near White Plains.

It does not appear that Hamilton was involved in the limited skirmish at Harlem Heights, where his role at best was purely defensive. But at White Plains, for the first time, he was given the chance to prove his courage and steadiness under heavy enemy fire.

3. TRIAL BY BATTLE

Washington took up his position on two hills. His right rested on a patch of elevated ground; his left on Chatterton's Hill, with McDougall in command. The small stream known as the Bronx River meandered along the base of the hills, affording additional protection against a frontal attack.

The British followed the Americans at a leisurely pace to White Plains and, with equal deliberation, made preparations for an assault. Howe had under him a mixed force of British regulars and Hessians, well-disciplined and battle-hardened. The Americans were in the main newly incorporated militia with a leavening of Continentals, whose experience thus far was chiefly in retreat.

It was obvious that when the assault came, Chatterton's Hill would be the prime target. Hamilton's artillery was therefore ordered to take up a position on its flanks so as to command the approaches over the stream. Fortunately recent rains had swollen the little river to an unwadable torrent.

The Hessians, under Colonel Rahle, commenced the attack. They moved slowly across the farther plain while a company of engineers flung a wooden bridge over the stream. A rise of ground sheltered them from Hamilton's guns. The young captain swiftly trundled his two field pieces from his prepared position to a rock ledge that overlooked the newly constructed bridge. The sweating men swung them around and depressed the muzzles just as the Hessians, bayonets fixed, charged across and plunged up the slope.

The guns blazed. The cannoneers reloaded and fired again. Several of the workmen, still engaged in strengthening the bridge supports, were killed outright. Gaps appeared in the Hessian ranks. They wavered and fell back in disorder across the bridge. Meanwhile British regulars, under Leslie, forded the stream some distance below and now came sweeping up the hill on the farther slope in an effort to silence and spike his guns. Hamilton promptly swung his pieces around to meet the new attack, while Smallwood's infantry, higher up on the hill, poured down a galling fire into the oncoming ranks. The combined hail of musketry and cannon shot was too much for Leslie's men. They were compelled to give ground.

But Rahle's Hessians took advantage of the diversion to reform and recross the bridge. As they advanced they met the retreating regulars. Lesile rallied his men, the two columns joined and charged up the hill again. This second wave proved too much for Smallwood's militia. They broke and fled. Hamilton's battery was now without support and in grave danger of capture. McDougall sent him a message to withdraw at once. With the utmost difficulty he managed to save his pieces just as the triumphant enemy swarmed over and around. Putnam, coming up too late with reinforcements, was nevertheless able to cover McDougall's retreat without further losses. But the British had captured the hill.[16]

That night Washington slipped his troops away and retired to North Castle where Howe, with his accustomed politeness, left him alone. But the capture of Fort Washington, the American strong point on the Hudson, threatened to cut off the Americans once more. Washington abandoned North Castle, ferried his men across the river and began his long, disheartening retreat through New Jersey.

It was a gloomy period—and the fires of the Revolution flickered and threatened to quench entirely. The Americans had been defeated in every major engagement, the men were deserting in droves, and much of their equipment and supplies had fallen into the hands of the British. Three thousand troops—all that were left—marched weariedly on; with Lord Cornwallis, commanding eight thousand well-fed, well-equipped men, in hot pursuit.

Cornwallis caught up with the retreating army at the Raritan River.

The Americans were already across and the bridge had been destroyed, but the river was fordable. To check the British advance Washington detached a rear-guard, including Hamilton's battery. Grimly he set up his two field pieces on the farther bank. Time and again the British tried to cross and were thrown back by a steady fire. When, finally, they broke through and Hamilton whipped his guns around in retreat, the delaying action had served its purpose. Washington's ragged and footsore soldiers had already reached a temporary shelter at Princeton.

It was here that Hamilton first attracted Washington's personal attention. The commander-in-chief, observing the coolness and skill with which the young artillery captain was handling his guns, sent one of his aides to inquire the name of the gallant officer and to invite him to his headquarters at the first halt of the exhausted forces. Hamilton had won his spurs.[17]

The Americans made a sorry spectacle as they straggled into Princeton. But Hamilton's long months of hard driving now showed their effect. *His* company drew all eyes by the disciplined appearance of its ranks and the brisk, soldierly stride of its men. Hamilton himself, reported a spectator admiringly, "a youth, a mere stripling, small, slender, almost delicate in frame," marched on foot "beside a piece of artillery, with a cocked hat pulled down over his eyes, apparently lost in thought, with his hand resting on a cannon, and every now and then patting it, as if it were a favorite horse or a pet plaything." [18] Perhaps his thoughts were back in St. Croix, when he was a boy seated on a high stool and wishing there were a war.

It was December now and bitter both in the elements and in men's hearts. Christmas approached, but the Americans had nothing about which to make merry. They were hungry, discouraged, shivering. Cornwallis lay encamped at New Brunswick, snug in winter quarters, waiting cheerfully for spring when he would rouse himself and crush this little band of rebels. Down at Trenton, across the ice-strewn Delaware, the Hessians were in camp and preparing to celebrate the advent of the Prince of Peace with true Teutonic jollification.

The sudden brilliant stroke by which Washington descended on the drunken Hessians and revived the failing fortunes of the Revolution is too well known to require extended description. During the assault Hamilton's artillery was in the reserve. But he reached the crossroads in time to unlimber his guns and shell Von Lossberg's regiment as it emerged, disordered and sleepy, from Church Alley.

At the battle of Princeton he took a more active part. Some of the British had sought refuge in Nassau Hall, the main structure of the college. Hamilton brought his cannon to bear upon the building and demanded their surrender. The British refused. Whereupon he gave the order to fire. The very first shot crashed through the chapel for a direct hit upon the painted features of His Majesty, King George the Second, whose portrait graced the wall. The second shot fell among the hidden troops. Under cover of the shelling the militia swarmed cheering to the attack. Within minutes the disheartened British surrendered.[19]

But the constant fighting and long marches had taken dreadful toll of Hamilton's little company. By the time the remnants of Washington's army encamped in winter quarters on the heights at Morristown, they had been reduced to a bare twenty-five men, hardly enough to serve the two field pieces that were more precious even than human lives.

In that dreary camp Washington rested and refused to be lured out by the blandishments of the enemy. Hamilton and his corporal's guard rested with him.

CHAPTER VI

Call Colonel Hamilton!

I. OFFICIAL AIDE

THE ENCAMPMENT AT Morristown lasted through the winter, and in the enforced idleness of close quarters Washington was able to estimate and appraise more closely the talents and character of his officers. General Greene had already recommended young Hamilton to his attention; he himself had witnessed the stand on the banks of the Raritan. But gallantry in action was a rather general commodity among the young officers of his army. What Washington was looking for just then were talents of a different kind. All communications, all orders, all correspondence with a thousand clamoring individuals and official bodies, had to be written out laboriously in long hand and then copied with equal labor into the letter books. Washington was not a ready letter writer; his ideas did not flow with ease and fluency onto paper. And there was a war to be fought.

He had aides for the task, to be sure. But most of them, sprightly enough young men, were readier with the sword than with the pen. The turnover among them was heavy, and the documents to be drafted increased steadily in volume and importance. Despairingly he wrote to Joseph Reed, an absent aide: "At present my time is so much taken up at my desk, that I am obliged to neglect many other essential parts of my duty: it is absolutely necessary, therefore, for me to have persons that can think for me, as well as execute orders." [1]

These specifications fitted Hamilton exactly. He had written voluminous pamphlets and the words came easily. His ideas were logical and clear. He wrote rapidly and in a precise, vigorous hand. He knew military tactics and was an excellent disciplinarian. He was a student and had displayed an unwonted grasp of the political situation. What more could a harassed commander desire?

Whereupon Washington called the young captain into his quarters one day and offered him a position on his official staff as aide-de-camp—with the rank of lieutenant-colonel.

It was a dazzling offer and Hamilton should have jumped at the chance. At one bound he leaped from captain to lieutenant-colonel, from the obscurity and toil of the artillery to the prominence and intimate contacts of the commander's family. Yet, strangely enough, Hamilton hesitated.

Once before he had refused a staff appointment. War was still the essentially romantic affair of his early dreams, in spite of Long Island, Bunker's Hill, White Plains and New Jersey. In the line there were opportunities for the bright fame he craved—the glorious shock of battle, the keen smell of powder. As a member of the staff, no matter how high-sounding his title, he would be merely an ink-stained scrivener.

But an invitation from the commander-in-chief was not lightly to be refused. In effect it was a command. After much hemming and hawing and with a reluctant heart he finally accepted. On March 1, 1777, Alexander Hamilton, aged twenty, was duly commissioned a lieutenant-colonel and inducted into Washington's official family.

Dr. Hugh Knox, in distant St. Croix, rejoiced mightily in Hamilton's impending appointment to the staff of the "Great and Good General Washington." The clergyman, whose advancing age in no wise dimmed his enthusiasms, took an unmeasured pride in the young man whose career, now unfolding under such splendid auspices, was in large part due to his kindly offices. On the slender basis of the Hurricane Letter he had surmised the literary abilities implicit in his ward. Now he had visions of a newer and greater effort. "*Mark this*," he underscored: "You must be the Annalist and Biographer, as well as Aide-de-Camp, of General Washington—and the Historiographer of the American War! I take the liberty to insist on this...few men will be as well qualified to write the history of the present glorious struggle." [2] Even if he desired to follow the worthy old doctor's suggestion, however, Hamilton soon found himself too engrossed in daily duties and political problems to do anything about it.

It seems that Hamilton had fallen seriously ill immediately on entering winter quarters at Morristown—probably as a result of the arduous campaigning of the preceding months—but by the time he was appointed to the staff he had fully recovered. For Dr. Knox congratulated him on his recovery "from a long and dangerous illness," and on April 8th the Convention Committee of the New York Provincial Congress belatedly assured him that they were most happy to hear of his return to health. "The smallness of our numbers will not permit the loss of one useful citizen," they wrote flatteringly. "It is, therefore, a determined point, that, sick or well, you are by no means to die." [3]

All through his life Hamilton's slender frame was to find it difficult to support the furious energy and ceaseless activity of his mind. He was never a completely well man for any extended period of time.

Hamilton's first duty after his appointment was to apprise the New York Convention of the change in his status and to suggest that his depleted company be formally transferred to the Continental forces. The convention approved of the suggestion and authorized its Committee of Correspondence—Gouverneur Morris, Robert R. Livingston and William Allison—to invite the fledgling aide to send them reports on the activities of the army, and whatever observations he wished to make on the general state of affairs.

Hamilton replied promptly that "with cheerfulness I embrace the proposal of corresponding with your convention through you, and shall from time to time ... communicate such transactions as shall happen, such pieces of intelligence as shall be received, and such comments upon them as shall appear necessary to convey a true idea of what is going on in the military line." [4]

It has been generally assumed that this flattering mark of attention to a stripling of twenty from the eminent men who composed the convention is proof positive of the prominence which Hamilton had already achieved. Nothing could be further from the truth.

The colonies at this time, and for a long time to come, were suspicious of all operations over which they did not exercise complete local control. By subsidizing some one close to the center of events to send them detailed reports, they thought to keep a vigilant scrutiny on the situation. One of Washington's aides, naturally, would be the best possible source for such information. Nor was Hamilton the first to be so employed by the distrustful convention.

Almost a year before they had engaged Tench Tilghman for the purpose. A little later they used Robert H. Harrison. Both of these young men were on Washington's staff. The letter which William Duer, of the Convention Committee, addressed to young Tilghman to that effect seems to have been overlooked in this connection. On September 22, 1776, he wrote:

The Convention of this State have appointed a committee of Correspondence for the Purpose of obtaining Intelligence from the army, of which Committee your acquaintance Mr. R. R. Livingstone, and myself are members. They have empowered this Committee to employ a Gentleman near Head Quarters for communicating Intelligence to whom they have engaged to make an adequate compensation—Mr. Livingstone and myself are anxious you should undertake this task; in consequence of which I am requested to know your sentiments on this head—The Sum Ideal of your office will be to write a daily Letter which our Express will wait on you for.[5]

Tilghman accepted and performed the duty from September 22nd to October 21st. Then Harrison took over. By March, 1777, however, both young aides grew weary of the ceaseless task, and Hamilton was then requested to fill the place.

But as the reports came in from their new correspondent, the convention soon realized that here was a young man who would decidedly bear watching. They were composed with such clarity and force, they displayed such a thorough grasp of military tactics and knowledge of the course of the war, their comments on campaigns and general events were so just and perspicacious that a good history of the Revolution—such as Dr. Knox had begged for—might be assembled from these hasty communiques, for which an impatient express was always waiting.

The daily correspondence brought Hamilton to the personal attention and intimate confidence of such important personages as Gouverneur Morris, Robert R. Livingston, William Duer and Philip Schuyler, representing the wealth and aristocracy of New York. Already these men were laying their lines for the future. There were forces engaged in the Revolution that they viewed with considerable dislike and alarm—radical, egalitarian, propertyless. They had no intention of yielding their power or property to the tender mercies of small, debt-ridden farmers and artisan Sons of Liberty who thought themselves as good as their employers. It was necessary to work with them to throw off the common yoke of England; once peace was established, however, they must be put firmly in their proper place.

In the coming struggle which they envisaged, the leaders realized they must have assistance. They examined Hamilton's comments and ideas and murmured approval. Here was a young man—without family or money, it was true—but vigorous and ambitious, possessed of uncommon common sense and sound ideas, firm in his devotion to law and order and the rights of property, and as much distrustful of the rabble as they were. Already men like John Jay, Boudinot and William Livingston of New Jersey were his friends and ready to vouch for him. It would be well to attach such a rising young man to their own interests.

That Hamilton, for his own part, thought something along similar lines when he entered into the correspondence is quite likely. He needed the Schuylers, Livingstons and Morrises as much as they needed him. Through them he could achieve his entrée into the inner circles of that small, influential society to which he felt himself fitted by nature and inclination.

In almost his first report Hamilton wisely dissociated his private opinions from Washington's, and this caution met with the committee's approval. Morris replied that "your favor gave great pleasure, as well to the committee as to several members of the House, who are much pleased with your judicious caution, to distinguish between what you sport as your private opinions, and the weighty sentiments of the General." [6]

When Washington, exasperated by the growing boldness of the Tories, especially in New Jersey, determined on stern measures to suppress them, Hamilton dutifully sent his old friend, Governor Livingston, a list of those who had been imprisoned under military law. "A spirit of disaffection shows itself with so much boldness and violence in different parts of this State," he wrote, "that it is the ardent wish of His Excellency, no delay, which can be avoided, might be used in making examples of some of the most atrocious offenders." [7]

To the New York Committee, however, he stated his own views on the subject of the Tories. "Lenity and forbearance have been tried too long to no purpose..." he acknowledged. "But," he was quick to add, "in dispensing punishment, the utmost care and caution ought to be used. The power of doing it, or even of bringing the guilty to trial, should be placed in hands that know well how to use it. I believe it would be a prudent rule to meddle with none but those whose crimes are supported by very sufficient evidence, and are of a pretty deep dye." He also laid down a general rule for dealing with offenders. Either pardon them entirely, or inflict capital and severe punishments. "Inflicting trifling punishments," he properly observed, "only embitters the minds of those on whom they fall, and increases their disposition to do mischief without taking away the power of doing it." [8] This pregnant observation, delivered by a young man in the eighteenth century, might well be pondered by those in the twentieth who are faced with a remarkably similar situation.

Thus, within a month after commencing what was supposed to be merely a series of reports on military matters, Hamilton was giving advice to the august convention of his state on political and internal affairs. The convention did not resent the advice; it asked for more.

In fact, Morris submitted a draft of the proposed New York Constitution for his consideration. At first Hamilton hesitated to commit himself. "While I view it in the main as a wise and excellent system," he wrote back, "I freely confess it appears to me to have some faults which I could wish did not exist." Yet he did not wish to name or discuss these faults at length, since to do so would be both useless and presumptuous on his part.[9]

When Morris, however, opened the door with his own criticisms of the defects of the Constitution, Hamilton availed himself of the opportunity to be equally candid. Nor did he hesitate to disagree with the views of Morris when necessary. For one thing he did not like the proposed division of the legislature into two bodies. "Your Senate," he declared, "from the very name, and from the mere circumstance of its being a separate member of the Legislature, will be liable to degenerate into a body purely aristocratical." This was democratic thought; on the other hand, Hamilton opposed the principle of a general election for governor. "To determine the qualifications proper for the chief executive magistrate," he asserted, "requires the deliberate wisdom of a select assembly, and cannot be safely lodged with the people at large."[10]

More and more the great men of the convention came to lean upon the advice and opinions of the stripling of twenty. When New York murmured over Washington's Fabian tactics in the conduct of the war he hastened to defend his chief. "The liberties of America are an infinite stake," he lectured Livingston. "We should not play a desperate game for it, or put it upon the issue of a single cast of the die. The loss of one general engagement may effectually ruin us." Delay, he told the impatient people at home, is the only policy, even at the cost of continued enemy depredations. Each day we wait brings aid from Europe that much closer. Each day we wait our army grows stronger, and the enemy dwindles away.[11] If Hamilton was perhaps unduly optimistic, such encouragement was essential to keep in line the local Solons who controlled the sinews of war. Without doubt Hamilton's reports were a considerable factor in preventing New York from joining the swelling pack that yelped for Washington's blood.

2. MILITARY AMANUENSIS

The duty of reporting to the New Yorkers, however, was extra-official and could not be permitted to interfere with the performance of his proper duties. These were specific, and the real reason for his appointment to the staff.

On that staff Hamilton found himself in the company of a number of very congenial young men, all quite young, all filled with martial ardor and a superabundance of high animal spirits, and all with a marked preference for the sword over the laborious pens they unwillingly wielded. The youths welcomed their new comrade with open arms—both for his personal qualities and because he was going to assume the job they most detested. They were good fellows—Robert H. Harrison of Maryland, who fixed upon Hamilton the soubriquet of the "Little Lion," Tench Tilghman, who had tired so quickly of correspondence with New York, Richard K. Meade and, at a later date, John Laurens and James McHenry. The easy camaraderie of camp and field developed into close friendships. They quickly tell under the spell of their new companion—and Hamilton was to find no more devoted partisans and followers than this little group of laughing, carefree aides who made up Washington's family.

Washington was equally pleased with his new aide. Within a day or two after Hamilton took over the post of private secretary, the harassed commander breathed a sigh of relief. His troubles were over. To a clear head and logical mind Hamilton added a talent for phrasing, a bold but thoroughly controlled imagination, a rapid, fluent pen and a masculine and legible hand. Washington's specifications for the ideal aide who could *think* for him as well as execute orders had been happily filled.

It is difficult, if not impossible, to determine which of the countless communications, orders, dispatches that exist in Hamilton's handwriting represent the general's personal dictation appropriately clothed by his aide, or are in fact Hamilton's own compositions and ideas.

Yet the difficulty has not prevented an acrimonious controversy from raging between the supporters of Washington and the proponents of Hamilton. Robert Troup started the ball rolling with the flat assertion that "the pen for our army was held by Hamilton; and for dignity of manner, pith of matter, and elegance of style, General Washington's letters are unrivalled in military annals." [12] This evoked loud cries of anguish from the Washingtonians, who resented the insinuation that it was *Hamilton* who was responsible for these laudable qualities.

A careful comparison of Washington's correspondence during the period of Hamilton's incumbency with the periods before and after does unquestionably disclose a divergence in manner and style, with the palm for fluent phrasing and easy expression going to Hamilton's secretarial pen. But it is equally unquestionable that there is no such divergence in the matter expressed or the ideas involved. Without doubt Washington outlined in general form what he desired to say, and Hamilton clothed the skeleton in appropriate language. The same controversy is to arise again when we come to a consideration of the great Farewell Address many years later.

Happily such considerations did not trouble Washington at the time. He came more and more to rely upon the good sense and sobriety of judgment of his heaven-sent aide. Each night, when the day's dispatches were brought to his tent, his first command invariably was: *"Call Colonel Hamilton!"* [13] Then, under the guttering light of the candles, the gigantic general and his slight-statured aide would bend over the documents, discuss their contents and the general nature of the replies where replies were necessary. Hamilton would jot down notes as they went along. Then, with a bow, he would pick up the papers, depart for his own tent, light his candles and labor far into the night. His gray quill pen moved rapidly over the paper, each stroke precise and bold as he wrote on and on. Only rarely did he have to pause for thought, or to erase and amend. Formal or official documents he signed with Washington's name; others, relating to the business of the camp, he signed with his own name. It was unnecessary to add the words, "Aide-de-camp." Officers and men both knew he was speaking for the commander.

In spite of these manifold duties there were relaxations to be found at Morristown. Patriotic ladies, married and single, journeyed rather frequently to the wintry encampment and received a hearty welcome. The bored officers dined and flirted with their pretty guests, and Hamilton, who had already achieved something of a reputation as a ladies' man, did nothing to lose that reputation. A male visitor to the camp reported that it was there "for the first time, I had the pleasure of knowing Colonel Hamilton. He presided at the General's table, where we dined; and in a large company in which there were several ladies, among whom I recollect one or two of the Miss Livingstons and a Miss Brown, he acquitted himself with an ease, propriety and vivacity, which gave me the most favorable impression of his talents and accomplishments." [14]

3. DREARY DAYS

The war dragged wearily through the spring and early summer of 1777. The outlook was doubly dark for the Americans. General Burgoyne, thrusting to separate New England from the rest of the country, was already on the march. General Howe set sail from New York to seize Philadelphia. He hoped by this maneuver to compel Washington to abandon his entrenched position in the Jersey hills in an attempt to save the threatened city. Once out in the open, Howe felt he would have no difficulty in smashing this army whose mere existence was a constant threat to his line of communications.

But Washington refused to be lured down into the open plains. His strategy is clearly revealed in a letter Hamilton wrote to Dr. Knox: "It may be asked, If, to avoid a general engagement, we give up objects of the first importance [such as Philadelphia], what is to hinder the enemy from carrying every important point, and ruining us? My answer is, that our hopes are not placed in any particular city or spot of ground, but in preserving a good army, furnished with proper necessaries, to take advantage of favorable opportunities, and waste and defeat the enemy by piecemeal." [15]

Unfortunately Washington was not permitted to adhere long to this wise decision. The clamor of the Philadelphians, and above all, the outcries of the Continental Congress, then in session within the beleaguered city, forced Washington into the very action he dreaded. With much misgivings he moved his army down to intercept Howe as he came up from the Head of Elk, in Maryland, where his flotilla had landed on August 25th. The two armies clashed at the Brandywine, twenty-five miles southwest of Philadelphia. After a bitter battle the Americans gave ground and fell back.

What part Hamilton took in this battle is not known, but as the defeated troops retreated to the hills and the British pressed on toward Philadelphia, he was ordered on just such an adventure as was most congenial to his military soul.

The Americans were falling back in such haste that there had been no time to salvage certain stores of supplies cached on the Philadelphia road for the use of the army. To prevent their falling into enemy hands Washington ordered Hamilton and Captain Henry Lee to take a small party of horse and destroy the mills in which they were contained. It was a dangerous mission, since the British for once were moving fast and might well reach the designated mills before they did.

But Hamilton was delighted. On the morning of September 18th he gathered his troop and galloped across the misty countryside. Henry Lee, as second in command, rode with him. The ground sloped gently upward as they spurred foam-splashed horses to their destination; then dropped sharply in a long hill to a little stream where the mills lay visible in the morning light. A bridge spanned the mill-race. Just beyond gleamed the waters of the Schuylkill.

At the brow of the hill the troop reined in. No enemy was in sight, but Hamilton, for all his daring, prudently posted two of his men on the high ground as vedettes. With the remainder he galloped down to the mills. Once again prudence overcame impatience. He divided the little band into two sections. One, under Lee, was ordered to seize a flat-bottomed boat he saw moored on the banks of the Schuylkill. The other, under his own command, lit torches and ran to fire the buildings with their contents.

His foresight was immediately justified. He was inside one of the mills, thrusting his torch to the inflammable flour, when he heard shots ring out. He ran into the open, calling on his men to follow. Down the hill at breakneck speed tore the two vedettes. Behind them in hot pursuit galloped a large body of British horse. The vedettes thundered across the bridge and toward the Schuylkill, shouting the unnecessary news as they flew by. Lee and two of his men, who had meanwhile returned to the mills, were still by their horses. They swung into their saddles and made for the river. Together with the vedettes they pushed their horses into the stream and swam safely across to the other side.

Hamilton, with his contingent of four, had no time to get to their horses. They ran down to the river bank, clambered into the boat and sheered off bare seconds before the British were upon them. The river was in flood, and the little craft tossed downstream like a cockleshell. Lee, on the farther shore, turned in his saddle. He saw the boat struggle vainly in the violent current, the disappointed British lined on the bank and pouring furious volleys after it, with only a single shot or two fired in return. Then a turn of the road cut off further sight.

Lee galloped on, saddened at the obvious fate of his comrades. As soon as he reached a safe place of refuge he dispatched the woeful tidings to Washington. The general had opened the tragic missive and was in the very act of reading it when Hamilton, disheveled and dripping, burst into his tent to report a similar fate for Lee. After tremendous exertions and under continuous fire he had finally managed to land the boat on the opposite shore. Of the five on board, however, one was dead and another badly wounded.[16]

Hamilton had seen enough to convince him that Philadelphia was doomed. That same day he sent an express post-haste to John Hancock, president of the Continental Congress. "If Congress have not left Philadelphia they ought to do it immediately without fail...," he warned. "I just now passed the Valley Forge—in doing which a party of the enemy came down and fired upon us in the boat, by which means I lost my horse—one man was killed, and another wounded. The boats were abandoned, and will fall into their hands. I did all I could to prevent this, but to no purpose." [17]

This abrupt message created consternation in the city. The valiant members of congress tarried not on the order of their going. They fled that same night, each for himself, snatching up what baggage they could. They did not pause until they reached Lancaster, where they judged it safe to reconvene and become once more a dignified legislature.

John Adams, who was not a coward, recorded in his diary the panic of the moment.

SEPT. 19, 1777—At three, this morning, was awakened by Mr. Lovel, and told that the members of Congress were gone, some of them, a little after midnight; that there was a letter from Mr. Hamilton, aide-de-camp to the General, informing that the enemy were in possession of the ford and the boats, and had it in their power to be in Philadelphia before morning, and that, if Congress was not removed, they had not a moment to lose. Mr. Marchant and myself arose, sent for our horses, and, after collecting our things, rode off after the others.[18]

Congress need not have been in such a hurry, for the British did not march into Philadelphia until September 26th. Hamilton himself was in town on the 22nd collecting a supply of clothing and blankets for the army before the enemy should arrive and commandeer them.[19]

Working at top speed, he sent the military stores on ships to places of safekeeping up the Delaware and salvaged what he could for the needs of the ragged, ill-fed army. So successful were his efforts that the British found little public property to seize when they finally arrived, bands blaring and the Philadelphia Loyalists cheering.[20]

His work done, the young lieutenant-colonel returned to Pott's Grove, where Washington had set up temporary quarters. But congress, from the distant safety of Lancaster, continued to flay the general for his alleged inaction. Stung by their complaints, Washington essayed a surprise attack upon the main body of Howe's forces at Germantown just before the dawn of October 4th.

The plan of battle was tactically correct, but it called for split-second timing, perfect discipline and a liaison system of a high order of efficiency. Four columns, starting from widely separated points, were to converge upon the sleeping enemy and attack in a single simultaneous smash. But Washington's troops were comparatively untrained, the system of intercommunication haphazard and, adding to the difficulties, a heavy fog rolled over the terrain, obliterating all landmarks.

Even so the assault might have succeeded had not the column commanded by General Knox stumbled upon a stone house north of Germantown, where several hundred British were barricaded. Knox drew up his troops and called a council of war. Hamilton, who had been attached to the column, with Pickering and other junior officers urged that a small force be left to contain the beleaguered enemy, while the main body outflanked the house and proceeded to the appointed destination.[21]

But Knox vowed that he would leave no enemy in his rear and ordered a frontal attack upon the stronghold. For hours the column of three thousand Americans hurled themselves in vain against the stone walls, while the day rode high and the other columns found an enemy fully aroused by the distant thunder of guns and a wide gap in their own line of battle. By the time Knox finally overcame the resistance of the little band of British and recommenced his march toward the main attack, Howe had ample opportunity to bring up his reserves, the American Army had been routed and was falling back in great disorder. It was the second time Hamilton had been a witness to Knox's gross blundering. But this time there was no Aaron Burr, as at Bunker's Hill, to retrieve the situation by effective insubordination.

4. MISSION TO THE NORTH

The campaign around Philadelphia had ended badly. But in another sector, an event took place that electrified the disheartened colonies, stiffened their resistance and brought France to an open espousal of their cause. Burgoyne, marching down from Canada, had been surrounded by an American army under General Gates and compelled to capitulate at Saratoga.

Gates, a vain man and already sufficiently convinced of his own talents, allowed the victory to go to his head. He believed, with many others in congress and out, that Washington was grossly overrated and that he, Gates, was a much better general. In this belief he was bolstered by the testimony of sycophants and of those who had schemes of their own in mind. With a studied disdain, therefore, he sent off an express direct to congress, announcing the victory; but he sent none to Washington, the commander-in-chief.

The news of Burgoyne's surrender reached Washington through indirect channels. Others knew of it long before he did. It was an open insult, yet Washington was compelled to swallow it and hold his temper. It was no time for quarrels. There was more at stake than personal vanity. With the capture of Burgoyne it would be possible for Gates to release several divisions for desperately needed service near Philadelphia. Once such reinforcements joined him, Washington might well be able to recapture the city from Howe.

But Washington realized that a mere dispatch to the general in the north ordering the transfer of the necessary divisions would not be in itself sufficient. Gates already considered himself the savior of the country. An influential group in congress was working secretly and in haste to depose Washington and replace him by Gates, Conway or Charles Lee. It was most probable that Gates would refuse to obey his order.

Under these circumstances the choice of a proper messenger to Gates was of the utmost importance. He must combine boldness with tact, determination with prudence. Without hesitation Washington picked his youthful aide-de-camp, Alexander Hamilton, for the delicate mission.

Hamilton started northward on October 30, 1777. He carried no written instructions or dispatches to Gates, only a simple letter of introduction and a congratulatory message, in the course of which Washington managed to insinuate a gentle reproof:

I cannot but regret [he wrote mildly] that a matter of such magnitude, and so interesting to our general operations, should have reached me by report only, or through the channel of letters, not bearing that authenticity, which the importance of it required, and which it would have received by a line under your signature, stating the simple fact.

With these few words he dismissed the insult and came to the meat of the mission.

Our affairs having happily terminated at the northward, I have by the advice of my general officers sent Colonel Hamilton, one of my aids, to lay before you a full state of our situation, and that of the enemy in this quarter. He is well informed upon the subject, and will deliver my sentiments upon the plan of operations, that is become necessary to be pursued.... From Colonel Hamilton you will have a clear and comprehensive view of things, and I persuade myself you will do all in your power to facilitate the objects I have in contemplation.[22]

Compelled to take a devious route to avoid British and partisan bands, Hamilton nevertheless rode so hard that he was at Fishkill on the Hudson, over a hundred and fifty miles away, by the morning of November 2nd. There he found General Israel Putnam, from whom Washington also desired troops for the campaign against Howe. The youthful aide delivered his message, made a tour of inspection of the encampment and took it upon himself to make various changes in the orders on the basis of his observations. Then, after hurrying off a long report to Washington of what he had done, the indefatigable young soldier swung back into his saddle, and spurred on to Albany that same night.[23]

He reached Albany at noon on November 4th. Tired as he was, dusty, unshaven, and without sleep, he hurried at once to the quarters of the victorious general. He found the great man swimming in a sea of adulation, surrounded by flatterers and convinced of his own tremendous abilities.

Yet Gates listened politely enough while Hamilton delivered his instructions. In brief, Gates was to detach three brigades from his troops and send them down to Philadelphia. With this substantial augmentation and with an addition from Putnam, Washington felt certain he would be able to recapture that vital city.

But the conqueror of Burgoyne lolled pudgily in his chair while the young aide spoke rapidly and eagerly. Giving up three brigades, he reflected, meant divesting himself of the larger part of his army. A general without an army is a man without any importance. Did Washington hope in sly fashion to rob him of his importance and push him into the background after a victory such as Washington had never achieved? He wouldn't let him, by God! He didn't have to take orders from Washington any more. Hadn't his adherents in congress, with an eye to just such an eventuality, pushed through a bill giving him, Gates, what was practically an independent command?

Nevertheless he temporized. The situation in New England was still dangerous, he told Hamilton. He was willing to send some troops; but certainly not three brigades. The impetuous aide kept his temper and tried to argue the point, but Gates refused to be budged from his position. The best that Hamilton could gain was the promise of *one* brigade.

He retired from headquarters discomfited and at a loss just how to proceed. He knew only too plainly that Washington was in desperate need of much larger reinforcements; yet he dared not insist. Suppose Gates became angry and refused to send any?

He unfolded the delicate situation in a letter to his chief. "General Gates has won the entire confidence of the Eastern States; if disposed to do it, by addressing himself to the prejudices of the people he would find no difficulty to render a measure odious which it might be said, with plausibility enough to be believed, was calculated to expose them to unnecessary danger."

This was not all. To complicate matters there was congress to be considered. That body was already sufficiently jealous of the commander's power and would welcome an opportunity to lessen or even subvert it altogether. With this in mind Hamilton added a significant note: "General Gates has influence and interest elsewhere; he might use it if he pleased to discredit the measure there also. . . . These considerations, and others I shall be more explicit in when I have the pleasure of seeing you, determined me not to insist upon sending either of the other brigades remaining here." [24]

Dispatching the letter Hamilton with a heavy heart went to inspect Patterson's brigade, which Gates had so grudgingly promised. What he saw made him white with anger. He hurried back to his room and penned a blistering note to Gates; he dared not trust his hasty temper to another personal encounter with the general. But in the note he cast diplomacy to the winds. In sharp peremptory accents he laid down the law to the mighty Gates.

By inquiry I have learned that General Patterson's brigade, which is the one you propose to send, is by far the weakest of the three now here, and does not consist of more than about six hundred rank and file fit for duty. Under these circumstances, I cannot consider it either as compatible with the good of the service or my instructions from His Excellency, General Washington, to consent that that brigade be selected from the three to go to him; but I am under the necessity of desiring, by virtue of my orders from him, that one of the others be substituted instead of this,—either General Nixon's or General Glover's—and that you will be pleased to give immediate orders for its embarkation.[25]

The veteran general read the communication with astonishment and some perturbation. This plain-spoken aide had forced him into a position where he must yield or come to an open conflict immediately. He was not yet prepared for the latter. Giving time for tempers to cool, he arranged another meeting. Hamilton came pale but determined. He found the general in an unusually placating mood. Gates had backed down so far that he granted more than the aide had demanded in his letter. He would, he averred, send not only Patterson's brigade but Glover's brigade as well.[26] Hamilton had boldly bearded the lion and come off victorious.

His mission to Albany semi-successfully completed, Hamilton took horse again back to Fishkill and Windsor to find out whether the orders he had left with Putnam on his way up had been put into effect. These were for two brigades—Poor's and Larned's—to march. To his astonishment and disgust he found the two brigades still in quarters without a sign of movement.

By this time Hamilton had come to the end of his patience. First it had been Gates; now it was Putnam who was sabotaging Washington's plans. He sought out the old general and told him hotly what he thought of him. Before the bewildered veteran could recover himself Hamilton had dashed out, mounted horse and was galloping away to George Clinton, governor of New York. That gentleman, himself brusque, downright and given to plain talk, nodded approvingly at Hamilton's complaints. He had had plenty of opportunity to observe Putnam's set ways and stubborn refusals.

On Clinton's advice Hamilton sat down to write to Putnam. His pen fairly burned the paper. "I cannot forbear confessing that I am astonished and alarmed beyond measure to find that all his Excellency's views have been frustrated, and that no single step of those I mentioned to you has been taken to afford him the aid he absolutely stands in need of, and by delaying which the cause of America is put to the utmost hazard." The young man who had already tilted successfully with the hero of Saratoga minced no words with the old man of Connecticut. "How the non-compliance can be answered to General Washington you can best determine," he wrote pointedly. "I now, sir, in the most explicit terms, by his Excellency's authority, give it as a positive order from him, that all the Continental troops under your command may be immediately marched to King's Ferry, there to cross the river and hasten to reinforce the army under him." [27]

So furious was he that he sent another letter off to Washington advising him to remove Putnam from the command of the post, and put Clinton in his place. "The blunders and caprices of the former," he declared bluntly, "are endless."

But if Hamilton was furious, Putnam became almost apoplectic when he received what he called "Hamilton's most unjust and ungenerous reflections." Trembling with wrath he dispatched a copy of them to Washington and demanded redress for the insult.[29] Washington, however, backed up his aide to the hilt. He replied coldly to Putnam's irate complaints that "the urgency of Colonel Hamilton's letter was owing to his knowledge of our wants in this quarter. . . . I cannot but say there has been more delay in the march of the troops, than I think necessary; and I could wish that in the future my orders may be immediately complied with, without arguing upon the propriety of them. If any accident ensues from obeying them, the fault will lie upon me and not upon you." [30]

The stinging rebuke wilted Putnam, and thereafter he placed no further obstacles in the way. But Hamilton had not waited for his acquiescence. Going over Putnam's head, he sent for Colonel Bailey, in command of Larned's brigade, and ordered him to proceed at once to the south. Bailey protested that the brigade would refuse to stir until its arrears of pay had been paid in full. The resourceful young aide thereupon appealed to Clinton, who borrowed some five to six thousand dollars for the purpose. With back pay jingling in its pockets, the brigade commenced its southern trek.[31]

It has been the fashion of historians to excoriate Putnam for gross disobedience. Yet there were palliating circumstances. It is true that Putnam had visions of duplicating the triumph of General Gates. He thought to move down against New York and drive the British out of the city. Naturally, if Washington took away his best brigades, he must forego these dreams.

There is another side to the story, however. When Hamilton first came to him, Putnam had honestly, if reluctantly, attempted to comply with his instructions. He had actually ordered General Poor's brigade to march on the following day to reinforce Washington. But the men were mutinous. They had received no pay for almost eight months; half the men were on the sick list, and the other half grumbled and swore they would not budge until their grievances had been adjusted. Major Hughes, of Gates' staff, was with Putnam when Hamilton arrived, and in a hitherto unpublished letter to his superior, portrays the situation.

When Putnam issued the marching orders, he writes, both officers and men mutinied. The officers "determined to resign, rather than march without Money and Clothes. The men desert in numbers." A loyal captain ran a soldier through when he refused obedience, and was promptly shot dead by the soldier's comrades. Furthermore, "the Brigade have complained of being diseased with the Itch. Genl. Putnam has order'd them in the Hospital to be cured, and I believe they will march in 3 or 4 days. Genl. Poor is very sick at Poughkeepsie. Such is the *poor* State of Poor's Brigade." [32]

We have already seen that Larned's brigade likewise refused to march until Clinton raised sufficient money to pay their arrears. With illness, back pay and outright mutiny to face, it is no wonder that Putnam found it difficult to comply with Hamilton's demands.

Hamilton himself acknowledge these difficulties, but he attributed them—aside from the itch and kindred troubles—to Putnam's negligence. "I am sorry to say," he informed Washington, "the disposition for marching, in the officers and men in general, does not keep pace with my wishes or the exigency of the occasion." [33]

He wrote these lines propped up in bed. The strain of pushing through his instructions against negligence, evasion and downright treachery proved too much for his slender frame. On the 10th of November he came down with "a fever and violent rheumatic pains throughout my body."

Yet illness could not stop him in the pursuit of his duty. From his bed he continued to scourge Putnam's conduct and fume about the reprehensible delays. Still weak and ill, he hurried across the river for still another denunciatory interview with Putnam and then rushed down to Peekskill to make certain that the recalcitrant troops were actually on the march. At Peekskill, however, his outraged frame collapsed entirely. Once more he went to bed, this time with a high fever. [34]

His condition became critical. Governor Clinton heard of his illness and in alarm ordered his private physician, Dr. John Jones, to hasten to Peekskill to attend him. Unfortunately the doctor was himself sick, and another physician, less well known, had to be called. [35]

For thirteen days Hamilton's life was despaired of. The doctor gave up hope. Then, on the fourteenth day, the fever broke. One of Clinton's aides, who had been in constant attendance, reported the period of crisis to the anxious governor.

On the 25th in the evening he seem'd to all appearances to be drawing nigh his last, being seized with a coldness in the extremities, & remained so for the space of two hours, then surviv'd. He remained calm & the fever not so high on the 26th. On the 27th in the morning the Coldness came on again, and encreased (he was then cold as high as his knees,) in so much the Doct'r Thought he could not survive; he remained in this situation for near 4 hours, after which the fever abated very much, and from that time he has been getting better. The Doct'r now pronounces him out of danger.[36]

During his illness a letter came from Washington that must have done much to assist his recovery. Unaware that his aide was in the shadow of death, the commander wrote in the most cordial tone that "I approve entirely of all the steps you have taken; and have only to wish, that the exertions of those you have had to deal with, had kept pace with your zeal and good intentions." [37]

It was early in December when Hamilton, still weak and shaken, rejoined the staff at Whitemarsh and found the army ready to move into winter quarters at Valley Forge. But he had the satisfaction of knowing that his mission had proved remarkably successful. Four brigades from the northern forces had moved down, no matter how unwillingly, to join Washington. Yet the delays, for all his efforts, had proved decisive. The storms of winter forced Washington into camp without having executed his contemplated campaign.

5. CONWAY'S CABAL

The forces opposed to Washington had not been idle. For some time there had been a definite movement on foot, though clothed in secrecy and subterranean intrigue, to supersede him as commander-in-chief. The conspiracy, known to history as "Conway's Cabal," had influential support both in the army and in congress. The army malcontents numbered among them such generals as Gates, Conway and Mifflin, with a large group of lesser officers. In congress the cabal commanded a working majority. The first step was to create—by Congressional enactment—a new title of Presidency of the War-office. This office was to be given to General Gates, hero of Saratoga, and its sole purpose was to hedge in and restrict Washington's power.

The next step in the scheme was to bring Washington into contempt with the country at large. The conspirators dared not do so by direct, frontal attack on a commander whom the people still trusted. Instead they sniped continuously at his loyal officers and aides—and Hamilton was not the least against whom they directed their sneers and abuse. Commenting on this period Lafayette later remarked that "the people attach themselves to prosperous generals, and the commander-in-chief had been unsuccessful. His own character inspired respect and affection; but Greene, Hamilton, Knox, his best friends, were sadly defamed. The Tories fomented these dissensions." [38]

Whether the Tories were actually involved is a moot question. There is no question, however, that a considerable number of indubitable patriots were involved—even some who sincerely believed that Washington had outlived his usefulness and who were afraid of his continued lease of power.

It is certain that the conspiracy had gained considerable headway and might eventually have proved successful, had not the whole business been betrayed to Washington by two concurring accidents. One was the delivery into his hands of a damning letter from Conway to Gates. The other was the drunken indiscretion of the ineffable James Wilkinson, then on Gates' staff, and later to become in succession commander-in-chief of the American Army, Spanish spy and the betrayer of Aaron Burr.

Wilkinson tells of both accidents in his extremely unreliable and apologetic *Memoirs*. Conway had written an incautious letter to Gates in which the nature and purposes of the conspiracy had been plainly revealed. Wilkinson, as Gates' aide, had seen the letter and probably discussed it with his chief. But Wilkinson was congenitally incapable of keeping any secrets but his own. He addressed himself to several bottles of liquor in the tavern company of Major McWilliams. In the course of the evening and the due diminishment of the liquor he became expansive and boastful. Among other things he bragged of the coming downfall of Washington and quoted the fatal letter of Conway in support of his thesis. The shocked major hurried to report the conversation to Washington, who immediately sent off a dignified inquiry to Gates, omitting, however, to disclose the source of his information.

Gates was thrown into great agitation. How, in Heaven's name, had he been betrayed? He rushed to the strongbox where he kept the letter and found it still there. Then he remembered Hamilton's recent visit to his quarters and light presumably dawned on him. Vehemently he cried out to Wilkinson: "I have had a spy in my camp.... Colonel Hamilton has been sent up to me by General Washington; and, would you believe it, he purloined the copy of a letter out of that closet." Yes, the more he thought of it the more he was certain what had happened. "The family being called out by business, he [Hamilton] was left alone an hour in this room, during which time, he took Conway's letter out of that closet, and copied it, and the copy has been furnished to Washington." [39]

Wilkinson pretended great surprise over this affront to all the decencies—Gates still did not know he had been responsible for the disclosure—yet he offered to defend Hamilton against a charge of actual spying. On Gates' staff with him at the time was Colonel Robert Troup, the student friend of Hamilton, and Wilkinson didn't like him. Perhaps, he suggested insidiously to Gates, it was Troup who had inadvertently communicated the contents of the letter to his old friend, Hamilton.

When Gates finally discovered that it was Wilkinson alone who had betrayed him, he wrote a furious note to the offender: "I am astonished if you really gave Major McWilliams such information how you could *intimate* to me, that it was *possible* Colonel Troup *had conversed* with Colonel Hamilton upon the subject of General Conway's letter." [40]

Whereupon, says the unblushing Wilkinson, he promptly challenged Gates to a duel, and Gates backed down. But the latter, attempting to exculpate himself with Washington, directly accused Wilkinson of trying to fix suspicion on Hamilton and Troup in order to free himself from blame. "I did not listen to this insinuation against your aide-de-camp and mine," Gates declared virtuously. "I considered it even as ungenerous." In fact, so he assured Washington, the whole affair was a plot on the part of Wilkinson, who had forged the incriminating letter in order to discredit both Conway and Gates. [41]

It suited Washington to let it go at that. The conspiracy collapsed with its premature unfolding, the principal authors scuttled for cover, Hamilton's honor was cleared and Wilkinson, under pressure, resigned from the army. Wilkinson's eclipse, however, was only temporary. The next summer congress appointed him clothier-general to the army that had repudiated him, and this snug position enabled him to amass a tidy sum for future adventures in chicanery and double-dealing.

CHAPTER VII

From Sword to Pen

---

1. PRISONER EXCHANGE

THE TRAGIC STORY of Valley Forge is familiar to every school child: the long, bitter winter, the suffering of the soldiers and the bloody imprints on the iron-hard snow. In vain Washington begged congress for the barest necessities for his naked, starving men. Congress was too busy playing politics to heed.

Hamilton's wrath and contempt poured forth in a blazing letter to Clinton. "The great men who composed our first council; are they dead, have they deserted the cause, or what has become of them?" he cried. Certainly the men who compose the present congress, with a few exceptions, are a lesser breed. "Economy" is the watchword, even if it leads to famine, nakedness and mutiny among the soldiers; favoritism in promotions is the pastime. Let a foreigner come before them, no matter how rascally, and he is promptly given rank over competent Americans who have fought since the beginning.

No! he answered himself. The great men are not dead, nor have they deserted the cause. They have seen fit to quit congress for the battlefield or the civil offices of their respective states. "The only remedy then," thought Hamilton, "is to take them out of these employments and return them to the place where their presence is infinitely more important. . . . It is time that men of weight and understanding should take the alarm, and excite each other to a proper remedy." [1]

Hamilton had placed his finger squarely on one of the crying evils of the time. The spirit of a common nationalism was still woefully weak; men of ability preferred to run their own state governments than enter a congress whose authority was limited and depended entirely on the good will of the individual states. Even as late as 1787 it was almost impossible to attract competent leaders for positions in the federal body. Time and again some of the largest states had no

77

representation at all in Congress, and sessions were adjourned for lack of a quorum.

At this time Governor Clinton agreed with Hamilton, though later he was to become the strongest supporter of localism and States' Rights. He wrote back with a reckless disregard for the English language. "I wish the Defects of a certain great Body [Congress] were lass apparent. Even their Want of Wisdom but too Evident in most of their Measures woud in that Case be less Injurious.... Coud our Soldiery subsist on Resolves, they woud never want Food or Cloathing." [2]

Hamilton returned to the attack. Clinton, as governor of New York, was powerful; perhaps he might be goaded into action. This time he concentrated on the wanton conduct of congress in refusing to honor Washington's engagements with Howe for an exchange of prisoners. Such a course, he insisted, was not only against all good faith and humanity, but "will injure drafting and recruiting, discourage the militia, and increase the discontents of the army. The prospects of hopeless captivity cannot but be very disagreeable to men constantly exposed to the chance of it." [3]

This problem of prisoners was sufficiently knotty without the intervention of congress. Within ten days an American commission was to meet with British delegates in an attempt to unsnarl the tangle. As the American representatives Washington appointed three colonels— Hamilton, Harrison and Boudinot. [4]

The commissioners had to contend not only with the British but with congress, which had appointed a committee of its own to reform and watch the army, much as the French were later to send political commissioners to keep an eye on suspect generals, and the Russians to attach commissars to each military unit. This congressional committee was vehemently opposed to the idea of a general exchange of prisoners. Such an exchange, they thought, would work to the disadvantage of the Americans. Most of those who languished in British prison hulks were untrained militiamen, and there were plenty more of them to be had. The captive British, however, were well-trained regulars whose replacement must prove a matter of considerable difficulty. From a coldly military point of view the logic was impeccable. The fallacy lay, as Hamilton had pointed out, in treating men as unthinking machines to be moved about at the pleasure of a higher will.

Congress itself realized that the open adoption of such a realistic policy would provoke a storm of anger in the army and among the relatives and friends of those in British hands. Its committee therefore proposed a most jesuitical scheme to Hamilton and his fellow-commissioners. Let the cartel you intend to offer the British be a mere pretence, they said. Maneuver so that the negotiations break down, but do it so skilfully that the blame for the break will fall on the British. We can then explain to our army and our people that we have done our best, and everything will remain as it is.

This stultifying scheme was rejected by the commissioners with the contempt and indignation it deserved, and the congressional Machiavellians retired in high dudgeon to report to their parent body. In hot anger congress passed a resolution assailing Washington for having appointed commissioners "to settle the Cartel, whom he knew held principles adversary to the true interests of America."

The three commissioners promptly offered to resign, but, reports Boudinot, Washington sternly "ordered us to the Duty, and told us to make the best treaty in our power, and he would ratify it, and take the risk upon himself." [5]

Later on, when Boudinot himself went to congress as a delegate, he was told by fellow-members that "Congress was so ashamed of the measure that was run upon them by the Committee from the Army, that in two or three days after, they had expunged the whole from their minutes." [6]

Under such inauspicious circumstances the Americans finally met the British at Perth Amboy on December 11, 1778. In the meantime Colonel Grayson had joined the original trio, and a certain very delicate and important part of the negotiations was entrusted to his capable hands. Boudinot narrates that the negotiators "agreed to Dine together—we were very sociable—We had previously obtained the Characters of our opponents and were convinced that they depended much on out drinking us, we knew Coll Grayson was a match for any of them, and therefor left all that part of the business with him—They soon found themselves foiled." [7]

In spite of this preliminary victory the negotiations were finally broken off because the British had no plenary powers to settle the matter. The real bone of contention was the principle on which exchanges were to be made. The Americans insisted that officers be exchanged for officers, and privates for privates. The British, who had more officers than they needed, preferred to regain their more valuable privates first and let the unfortunate officers stew in enemy jails.

Hamilton and Harrison drafted a formal protest against the British position. "We join with you in lamenting that the purpose of our meeting have been frustrated, and we assure you, that it is to us matter of equal concern and surprise to find, that there should be a difference in our respective constructions of the Resolve, to which you refer." The protest, bearing the stamp of Hamilton's logical style, carefully reviewed the history of the negotiations and placed the onus for the rupture squarely on the British.[8]

The commissioners themselves parted on the most cordial personal terms. Colonel O'Hara, on whom the British had depended to drink the Americans under the table, shook hands and said chuckling: "Now if I am ever taken prisoner, I shall call on Colonel Hamilton, Colonel Harrison and Colonel Boudinot, and I expect you'll immediately come to my aid and take care of me."

The jest turned into good earnest. O'Hara was second in command at Yorktown when the British surrendered. When his turn came to deliver up his sword he called out for Hamilton. Hamilton came up. "Now, sir," cried O'Hara, "perform your promise, though when you made it, I little thought that I should ever have an opportunity of requiring your performance of it." Hamilton, fresh from the storming of a redoubt, smiled, bowed, and took charge of his erstwhile boon companion.[9]

2. THE STRANGE CASE OF GENERAL LEE

With the coming of spring in 1778 the tide of war began slowly to shift. The rigors and sufferings of the winter were over, the period of inaction at Valley Forge had been put to the useful purpose of drill under the severe eyes of Baron Steuben, and Sir Henry Clinton replaced Howe at Philadelphia. Clinton decided his forces were too widely dispersed and determined to abandon Philadelphia for a concentration based on New York.

Since he had not enough ships to transport his troops by sea, he left the city by land on June 18th. Washington promptly quit Valley Forge and started in pursuit. Lafayette was given command of a mobile advance guard to establish contact with the retreating British. Hamilton was detailed to spur ahead and obtain intelligence as to the enemy's position.

He rode into Cranberry on the night of June 25th to find everything in confusion and Lafayette fuming. He had thrown out detachments to locate the British, and the detachments had vanished together with the elusive foe. The young French nobleman, not much older than Hamilton himself, greeted the aide with joy. Would he be good enough to seek out the missing parties, establish some measure of co-operation between them and bring back word as to the whereabouts of the British?

It was late at night and Hamilton had already ridden long and hard. Nevertheless he mounted his horse again and galloped on to Hightstown and Allentown, where the advance scouts were supposed to be operating. To his dismay he found only the wildest disorder. Not a single precaution had been taken by the scattered detachments; each was operating blindly on its own; not a solitary patrol was anywhere near the enemy or could be heard from before morning. Hamilton issued sharp orders to the bewildered commanders to send out new parties at once, since it was vital to determine the exact dispositions of the enemy forces. But by this time dawn was already streaking the skies and the British were on the march again. A splendid chance to cut them off during the night had been missed. Nevertheless Hamilton dashed off a note to Washington that he was still in favor of a swift, smashing blow at the retreating foe.[10]

After reporting to Lafayette he hastened back to rejoin Washington. The commander was ready to follow his advice for immediate action, but a strange and complicated situation had meanwhile arisen. Major-General Charles Lee was the senior general under Washington. To him Washington had first offered the command of the advance guard, and he had declined it in favor of Lafayette. Now that battle seemed imminent, he demanded the honor. When Washington patiently agreed, Lee wavered and decided again not to take it.

On June 28th Lafayette caught up with Clinton's army at Monmouth and engaged it in battle. The thunder of the guns could be heard plainly by the main body of Americans, some miles to the rear. Lee changed his mind again. To Washington's exasperation and Hamilton's intense disgust, he reasserted his claim to the post of honor. It was no time for argument, so Washington ordered him to the front with five thousand men; and once there, to assume command of the attack.[11]

Meanwhile Hamilton spurred ahead to reconnoiter beyond Monmouth Court-house. Lafayette's troops were locked in desperate battle with the full British army, and the smoke of thousands of guns lay in a heavy pall on the rolling fields. Suddenly Lee's reinforcements poured helter-skelter out of a wood. To Hamilton's trained eye their formation was bad; they came out raggedly and their flanks were unsupported.

He galloped over to meet them, and attained a little rise of ground which gave him a view of the British. Out of the wavering smoke he saw a troop of cavalry deploying swiftly to the left, where they could fall with crushing force upon Lee's exposed and unprotected flank. Clapping spurs to his horse he raced on to Lee and warned him of what he had seen. It would be wise, he suggested, to detach a battalion to counteract the maneuver and catch the British in turn on their own left flank. Lee approved of the idea and authorized Hamilton to give orders to that effect to the column on the right. Hamilton did so, then hastened back to report to Washington.[12]

Washington was already hurrying up to the front, accompanied only by his staff. Hamilton joined the troop of officers and retraced his path at a breakneck pace. When they reached the field where he had left Lee it was to come upon a scene of utter disaster. Lee was retreating in wild disorder, his troops flying pell-mell for the safety of the woods, and the entire battle seemed lost. Yet not a single enemy was in sight to account for the debacle.

What happened then is clouded with the fumes of controversy. The accepted version for a long time had it that Washington flew into a towering rage and, flaying the luckless Lee with a burst of magnificent swearing, ordered him off the field in disgrace. Hand in hand with this version went another. According to this, Hamilton leaped from his horse, drew his sword and melodramatically exclaimed: "We are betrayed, your excellency, and the army are betrayed, and the moment has arrived when every true friend of America and her cause must be ready to die in their defence."

But Washington glanced at him coldly and observed: "Colonel Hamilton, you will take your horse." Then he turned away to the task at hand.[13]

Both stories must go into the scrap heap of discarded legends. There is no doubt that Washington was angered, and he may well have used expressions that were vigorous and forthright. But he did not order Lee off the field. In fact, he commanded him to rally his men, while he galloped on to the front where Lafayette's forces, deserted and disheartened, were giving way before the entire British army.

The tale of Hamilton's melodramatic stand must likewise be corrected in certain vital details. Lee himself, within a few days of the event, gave his own version at court-martial proceedings, and Hamilton, who also took the stand, did not deny its accuracy. According to him Hamilton was left with Lee after Washington had pushed on to Lafayette. "Flourishing his sword, [Hamilton] immediately exclaimed, that's right, my dear General, and I will stay, and we will all die here on this spot." Lee, as he told the story, professed to be much surprised at this outburst, "but observing him much flustered and in a sort of frenzy of valour, I calmly requested him to observe me well and to tell me if I did not appear tranquil and master of my faculties; his answer was, that he must own that I was entirely possessed of myself; well, then (said I), you must allow me to be a proper judge of what I ought to do." Which testimony Lee's aide, Captain Mercer, confirmed in full, and Colonel Harrison, Hamilton's friend and fellow-aide, in part.[14]

Thus rebuffed, Hamilton dashed after Washington who, with the utmost coolness, was taking vigorous measures to reform the panicky troops and check the British advance.

Washington dispatched him to Colonel Livingston with orders to proceed at once to the support of some exposed artillery. From there he galloped over to a shattered remnant of Varnum's brigade that its commander, Colonel Olney, was vainly trying to bring to a stand. Hamilton's appearance stiffened the fleeing men and the two officers succeeded in forming them behind a fence just as the British swept up to capitalize on the expected rout. To their surprise they were met with a withering fire. Hamilton flung himself into the action. As he led the troops in a countercharge a musketball wounded his horse. The animal stumbled and threw him headlong. Fortunately the British gave way and he was rescued. But he was badly bruised and the pain of his hurts, coupled with the excessive heat and the fatigue of his former ceaseless exertions, compelled him to retire from the field.[15]

Washington's personal assumption of command finally converted an impending disaster into a modified victory. By nightfall the British had withdrawn and left the Americans on the battle-field. But their army was intact and safely on its way to New York. A splendid opportunity to smash it completely had been muffed through Lee's curious behavior.

The battle of Monmouth made Hamilton into something of a hero. His praises were universally sung—except by Lee. James McHenry, most recent member of Washington's official family, wrote an account to Boudinot:

I am happy to have it in my power to mention the merit of your friend Hammy. He was incessant in his endeavours during the whole day —in reconnoitering the enemy, and in rallying and charging. But whether he or Col. Laurens deserves most of our commendation, is somewhat doubtful—both had their horses shot under them, and both exhibited singular proofs of bravery. They seemed to court death under our doubtful circumstances, and tryumphed over it as the face of war changed in our favor.[16]

Hamilton also wrote to Boudinot. He was modest about his own exploits, and lavish in his praise of Washington. "America owes a great deal to General Washington for this day's work. A general rout, dismay and disgrace would have attended the whole army in any other hands but his." When he came to speak of Lee, however, his wrath knew no bounds. "This man," he blazed, "is either a driveler in the business of soldiership or something worse.... Whatever a court Martial may decide, I shall continue to believe and say—his conduct was monstrous and unpardonable." [17]

To which Boudinot, with McHenry's praise already before him, responded that "I had concluded your Laurels had produced a forgetfulness of your old friend, but am now rejoicing in my disappointment." As for the battle, both Hamilton and the country were to be congratulated "on the kind Interposition of Heaven in our favour on the 28 Ultimo." [18]

Neither Hamilton nor his army comrades were willing to be content with the "Interposition of Heaven." They felt that Lee's failure to support Lafayette and his retreat from a non-existent enemy smacked strongly of betrayal. Washington placed Lee under arrest and convened a court-martial to try him. Hamilton was called to give testimony. He stated the facts as he knew them, with an account of his own movements during the battle. Notwithstanding his obvious animus in private speech, he tried to be impartial and careful in his testimony relating to Lee. In one or two instances, however, he couldn't resist the temptation to slip in a few cutting remarks. He said that Lee "seemed to be under a hurry of mind," and that, while his men retreated, he had found Lee "sitting on his horse, doing nothing that I saw." [19]

These comments hurt the sensitive general, and when he took the stand in his own defense, he admitted with a tinge of sarcasm that "it has hurt me the more, as it comes from a man of esteem'd sense, and whose valour I myself was a witness of, although it is not that sort of valour, unless by practice and philosophy he can correct, will ever be of any great use to the community."

In proof of this depreciatory judgment he proceeded to tell the story of his encounter with Hamilton on the field of battle, very much, doubtless, to the discomfiture of that young officer.

The court brought in a verdict of guilty on several of the charges and suspended Lee from his command for one year. There were further repercussions. Baron Steuben wrote Lee roundly denouncing his conduct, a copy of which letter Hamilton read "with pleasure," he told Steuben. "It was conceived in terms which the offense merited, and if he had any feeling, must have been felt by him. Considering the pointedness and severity of your expressions, his answer was certainly a very modest one, and proved that he had not a violent appetite for so close a tête-a-tête as you seem disposed to insist upon. This evasion, if known to the world, would do him very little honor." [20]

Nor was the fiery young colonel content with mere approbation of the attempts of others to provoke a challenge from Lee, who had made disparaging remarks about Washington both during and after the court-martial proceedings. He wished to challenge the offender himself, but a brother-aide, John Laurens, forestalled him, and Hamilton was forced to act instead as Laurens' second. The duel took place on December 24, 1778, in a little glade in a nearby wood. Pistols were the weapons. On the first exchange Lee received a slight wound. He demanded a second fire, but the two seconds intervened and halted the duel. [21]

This encounter did not end the affair as far as Hamilton was concerned. Lee's supporters—and they were many—felt that Hamilton's testimony had been chiefly responsible for the conviction of their idol. A certain Major John S. Eustace wrote to Lee a full year after the trial that he had recently proclaimed in the presence of many officers that he *"thought Colonel Hamilton was perjured,"* and the matter might *"be decided as he chose."* [22] Very likely Hamilton never heard of the provocative remarks, for nothing came of it.

Several months later, however, the persistent Eustace again reported to Lee:

I met Hambleton [sic] the other day in company with the favourite Green [General Nathanael Greene] the *Drunkard* Stirling, and their several classes of attendants—He advanced towards me, on my entering the room with presented hand—I took no notice of his polite intention, but sat down, without bowing to him or any of the clan...he then asked me if I was come from Camp—I say'd, *shortly, no,* without the usual application of SIR, rose from my chair—left *the room* and him *standing before the chair.* I cou'd not treat him much more rudely—I've repeated my *suspicions* of his *veracity on the tryall* so often that I expect the son of a bitch will challenge me when he comes.[23]

Since the episode ends abruptly on this note, it is highly probable that Eustace colored the story considerably in the telling.

3. ATTACK ON SAMUEL CHASE

Lee's court-martial was still in session when news came of tremendous import to the final outcome of the war. The French, their doubts as to the staying power of the Americans settled by the pleasing spectacle of Saratoga, decided to render open aid to the embattled nation. On the 8th of July, 1778, thirteen ships of the line sailed majestically into the Delaware under the command of Admiral D'Estaing. He had hoped to arrive in time to intercept Howe's inferior fleet of transports at Philadelphia, but an unnecessarily long trip across the Atlantic permitted Howe to gain the shelter of the guns in New York harbor. D'Estaing, annoyed at finding his victim fled, followed in pursuit and demonstrated in force outside Sandy Hook, daring the British to come out and fight.

Meanwhile Washington, whose prey in the form of General Clinton had also reached safety in New York, marched his army across New Jersey to Haverstraw, on the banks of the Hudson, where he encamped. With D'Estaing blockading by sea and himself standing astride all land and river lines, he hoped to squeeze the British out of their principal base by means of a great pincer movement. To effectuate his plan required proper coordination between the French fleet and the American army.

As usual when he had a particular important mission on hand, he sent Hamilton. "I am sending you Colonel Hamilton," he wrote D'Estaing, "in whom I place entire confidence. He will be able to make you perfectly acquainted with my sentiments, and to satisfy any inquiries you may think proper to propose; and I would wish you to consider the information he delivers as coming from myself." [24]

But D'Estaing, though outnumbering the British fleet in ships and guns, finally decided against the risk of a decisive battle, and Hamilton arrived barely in time for a single meeting, after which the French admiral weighed anchor and proceeded to Rhode Island where General Sullivan was operating with ten thousand men. Yet that solitary interview with Hamilton made such a permanent impression on D'Estaing that, months later, in forwarding a highly confidential communication to Washington he added a postscript: "I entreat you not to confide the secret to any person, except Colonel Hamilton. His talents and his personal qualities have secured to him for ever my esteem, my confidence, and my friendship." [25]

More than any other officer in the American ranks, Hamilton attracted the warm friendship of the numerous foreigners in the service. They appreciated his high spirits, martial bearing, Gallic polish and vivacity. He also spoke French, the universal language of Europe, with fluency, and this was a godsend in an army where only a bare handful—who did not include Washington—knew any tongue but English. These friendships were to survive the days of battle and become permanent possessions—Lafayette, D'Estaing, Baron Steuben, Du Portail, Fleury and many others.

Hamilton fell ill in Newark after seeing the French fleet sail away with Washington's hopes for the recovery of New York crumbling in its wake, and it was several days before he was able to return to Haverstraw with the sad news of D'Estaing's departure.

His health continued poor all that summer. James McHenry, who had given up a budding medical practice to join Washington's staff, harkened to his symptoms and put on his most learned frown. "In order to get rid of your present accumulations," he prescribed, "you will be pleased to take the pills agreeable to the directions; and to prevent future accumulations observe the following table of diet. This will have a tendency also to correct your wit," he added slyly. His dietary provisions, however, were sound. Tea sweetened with brown sugar for breakfast, "beef or mutton, either boiled or roasted" for dinner, washed down with plenty of water and very little wine. Vegetables were all right, but "you must not eat as many vegetables as you please—a load of vegetables is as hurtful as a load of any other food." [26]

The long inactivity of camp spurred Hamilton to take up his pen again. There was ample need for his polemic prowess in the state of the nation. Congress had touched bottom in incompetence and total indifference to the needs of the army. Its own president, Henry Laurens, father of Hamilton's comrade-in-arms, John Laurens, openly accused it of "venality, peculation and fraud." And now a particularly atrocious example of such "venality, peculation and fraud" brought Hamilton into public print.

Samuel Chase, delegate to congress from Maryland, learned as a result of his official position that congress had secretly determined to purchase in the open market vast quantities of grain for the use of the French fleet. Acting on this advance knowledge Chase sent out agents to buy up all available supplies. When the congressional emissaries came to buy, they found that their fellow-member had cornered the market. "Business is business!" thought Chase, as he compelled his poverty-stricken country to pay through the nose.

The congressional speculator had hidden his identity behind a screen of agents, but the true principal in the infamous "corner" was revealed to Hamilton by two reliable informants. Hamilton never disclosed their names, but it is probable they were his fellow-aides, Laurens and McHenry. The former's father had already unleashed a blast against congressional thievery, and McHenry came from Chase's home state, besides taking a prominent part in the later dénouement.

Hamilton sat down and tossed off at white heat a series of fiery denunciations which *Holt's Journal*, the publisher of his first American pamphlets, printed under the pseudonym of Publius.

The first letter was a scathing castigation of "that tribe who, taking advantage of the times, have carried the spirit of monopoly and extortion to an excess which scarcely admits of a parallel." Any member of congress who turns "the knowledge or secrets to which his office gave him access to the purposes of private profit... ought to feel the utmost rigor of public resentment, and be detested as a traitor of the worst and most dangerous kind." [27]

The following week he got down to cases. His "Open Letter to the Honorable ———, Esq." mentioned no names, but by this time everyone knew to whom he referred. "Had you not struck out a new line of prostitution for yourself," he thundered, "you might still have remained unnoticed and contemptible—your name scarcely known beyond the little circle of your electors and clients." [28]

A few weeks later he ended the series with a final crushing blow. Savagely sarcastic, he painted the picture of what an honest congressman was like; then he held up Chase for public inspection. Hamilton belabored the contrast, employing every printable phrase in his arsenal of denunciations. "I advise you," he said ironically, "by a timely and voluntary retreat to avoid the ignominy of a formal dismission. Your career has held out as long as you could have hoped." In fact, you are "admirably fitted in many respects for the meridian of St. James, you might there make the worthy representative of a venal borough, but you ought not to be suffered to continue to sully the majesty of the people in an American Congress." [29]

The letters created an immense sensation, and desperate attempts were made by Chase and his friends to discover their author. But *Holt's Journal* held the secret of Publius well. Chase, politically powerful in Maryland, denied the charges to his home state. His opponents, however, aided by Hamilton's friend, McHenry, and flaunting the Publius letters unweariedly, kept the issue alive until the Maryland legislature, controlled though it was by Chase's followers, was finally compelled in 1781 to bring the matter to a formal hearing. But the hearing and the ensuing trial was in the nature of a whitewash. He was acquitted of the accusation on a strictly partisan division.

With this vindication in hand a friend of Chase, Major Giles, determined to exact retribution from the author of the pamphlets. But the author was still discreetly garbed in anonymity. It was suspected, however, that McHenry knew his name. Giles therefore called on him to reveal the true identity of Publius. McHenry refused and hastened to notify Hamilton of the demand.[30]

Hamilton was troubled in spirit. This sudden revival of an ancient matter had come at a most inopportune time. For he was by now married and only a month before a son had been born. Obviously Giles' demand was the prelude to a challenge. McHenry wanted to know what to do. For the first time in his life Hamilton was at a loss for words. The hitherto unpublished draft of his reply to McHenry's query is unwontedly crossed and recrossed with emendations.

Nothing [he wrote finally] gives me greater pleasure on all occasions than to see suspected and injured innocence vindicated, nor would any person more chearfully retract an ill-founded accusation on conviction of its error, than myself. You know the motives and the grounds of my charges against Mr. C[has]e, at a period fertile in practices as pernicious, as base ——— You know that I *can have no* personal enmity to him, and that considerations of public good alone dictated my attack upon his conduct and character.

Yet his information had come from two most respectable and reliable witnesses; and he could not consider the vindication by the Maryland Assembly as conclusive or binding. "I have too often seen public assemblies," he pointed out, "acquit guilt from prepossessions

[of] party spirit, want of formality or certainty (though there has been the greatest probability) in the evidence."

Nor would he avow himself to Giles as Publius. "As to the discovery of my name demanded with such preposterous vehemence, by a volunteer in the dispute, I conceive myself under no obligation to make it; especially to a person uninterested in the matter." [31]

Chase never did discover who his relentless assailant really was. It is an ironical footnote to history that Chase later became a Federalist high in the councils of the party and a political bedfellow to Hamilton. Nor did Hamilton then do anything to prevent his appointment by a Federalist President to the Supreme Court of the United States, from which high office Jefferson tried later to tumble him by a famous, though ineffectual, impeachment.

4. NEGROES, TOMCATS AND MILITARY PARSONS

If Hamilton's pen was active, his sword rusted in its scabbard. The war in the north had resolved itself into a period of dreary waiting at West Point while holding Sir Henry Clinton safely bottled up in New York. Some fertile mind, bored with inaction, sought to relieve the tedium by concocting a most romantic plot. Why not, he suggested, kidnap the somnolent Sir Henry right out of his own house in New York? It should prove a comparatively simple matter, since the house was located at the tip of the island and only a few yards away from the Hudson River. A few light whaleboats with muffled oars could steal down the river at night, land stealthily, pounce upon the unsuspecting Britisher and bring him back in triumph to the American lines.

Washington thought the plan feasible and went so far as to appoint Colonel Humphreys the leader of the kidnap party, when Hamilton raised an objection.

"There could be little doubt of its success," he admitted, "but, sir, have you examined the consequences of it?"

The general stared at his aide. "In what respect?"

"Why," replied Hamilton, "it has occurred to me that we shall rather lose than gain, by removing Sir Henry Clinton from the command of the British army, because we perfectly understand his character. By taking him off we only make way for some other, perhaps an abler officer, whose character and dispositions we have to learn."

Washington was so struck by the justice of these observations that he immediately countermanded his orders, and Sir Henry's sleep remained uninterrupted.[32]

With the coming of the new year John Laurens, who had become Hamilton's closest comrade on the staff, grew restless. While he was stagnating at West Point his own home state, South Carolina, reverberated with the thunder of war. He didn't intend to rot in camp, he announced to Hamilton one day; he would go south and participate in a real war.

Hamilton was excited. He would have loved to accompany his friend, but he had no such convenient excuse as Laurens and he was certain Washington would not hear of it. The two aides discussed the coming trip daily when one of them had a brilliant idea. Fresh troops were badly needed by the hard-pressed American forces in the south. But where could they come from? The levies of the southern states were exhausted. The Negro slaves, of course! Here was a vast, untapped source of manpower. The more the pair thought of the idea the more enthusiastic they became. Laurens would go down to South Carolina, raise battalions of slaves and hurl them upon the British.

His friend sat down at once and wrote a letter to John Jay, then president of Congress, which Laurens was to use to further the great scheme. The letter throws a flood of light upon Hamilton's cynical conception of the art of soldiery.

Dated March 14, 1779, it read:

I have not the least doubt that the negroes will make very excellent soldiers, with proper management. It is a maxim with some great military judges, that, with sensible officers, soldiers can hardly be too stupid....I mention this because I have frequently heard it objected to the scheme of embodying negroes, that they are too stupid to make soldiers. This is so far from appearing to me a valid objection, that I think their want of cultivation (for their natural faculties are as good as ours), joined to that habit of subordination which they acquire from a life of servitude, will enable them sooner to become soldiers than our white inhabitants. Let officers be men of sense and sentiment; and the nearer the soldiers approach to machines, perhaps the better.[33]

Armed with this epistle Laurens departed, while Hamilton settled down a little more resentfully to his clerical work in camp. But Laurens soon discovered it was not as simple as they had thought to raise regiments of "machines." Doubtless the slaveowners of his native state turned hostile ears to his proposals. They had no intention of exposing valuable slaves to the hazards of war, nor did they view with the proper enthusiasm the idea of placing arms in the hands of their blacks. In a little while young Laurens gave up the whole scheme and instead joined the active campaigning of his fellow whites.

The next officer to become disgusted with northern inaction and to heed the call of southern adventure was James Monroe. Monroe was thin, slight, studious and hardly the proper subject for such roving flights of fancy, but spring was in the air and his pulses stirred. Hamilton furnished him a humorous note of introduction to Laurens.

"Monroe is just setting out from Head Quarters and proposes to go in quest of adventures to the Southward. He seems to be as much of a knight errant as your worship; but as he is an honest fellow, I shall be glad he may find some employment, that will enable him to get knocked in the head in an honorable way.... You know him to be a man of honor a sensible man and a soldier." [34]

In later years Hamilton was to revise most drastically this present estimate of James Monroe, Virginian.

With his friend gone and the rumors of war mere distant echoes, Hamilton sought, and found, other diversions to beguile the passing days. The settled camp swarmed with ladies—wives, daughters, sisters and mere curiosity seekers. They overran the place and the bored young officers were only too happy to arrange balls and dances, whisper sweet nothings in the shadows of the barracks and promenade in the moonlight along the majestic river. Young Hamilton soon outdistanced all the rest in these activities, and his reputation as a gallant spread far beyond the confines of the camp.

A Tory newspaper managed to weave Hamilton's notoriety and the proposed new American flag into a single withering sneer. "Mrs. Washington," it reported, "has a mottled tom-cat (which she calls, in a complimentary way, 'Hamilton') with thirteen yellow rings around its tail, and that his flaunting it suggested to the Congress the adoption of the same number of stripes for the rebel flag." [35]

The same sheet pursued its attentions to Hamilton further. It accused him of writing a history of the war. "It is said little Hamilton, the poet and composer to the Lord Protector Mr. Washington, is engaged upon a literary work which is intended to give posterity a true estimate of the present rebellion and its supporters." [36] Why such a task should evoke the malicious chuckles of the Tories is hard to say; nor do we know what truth there was in the accusation. No such history, or even a proposed sketch of it, is to be found among Hamilton's papers; yet he may well have started writing one and then thrown it aside in favor of more immediate occupations. Dr. Hugh Knox on several occasions had strongly urged the composition of a history upon him.

If he had no time for serious writing, perhaps it was because he was too busily engaged in writing letters of introduction for all and sundry. A constant stream of the most motley applicants came to plague him with all manner of requests, since he was known to have the ear of the general and considerable influence. Hamilton good-naturedly turned no one down and obliged with a letter for the favor-seeker. In his present mood of youthful gayety and nocturnal pursuits he managed to infuse each letter with a touch of humorous bawdry and flippant cynicism; nevertheless he always ended on a note of compassionate understanding. There is the introduction to Governor Clinton which he penned for an importunate old woman. He starts flippantly enough:

The bearer of this is an old woman, and of course the most troublesome animal in the world. She wants to go into New York. It was in vain we told her no inhabitant could be permitted by us to go within the enemy's lines without permission from the civil power. Old and decriped [sic] as she is, she made the tour of the family, and tried her blandishments upon each.... As she showed a disposition to remain with us till she carried her point with true female perseverance—as we are rather straitened in our quarters, and not one of the gentlemen of the family would agree to share his bed with her, and as you must at all events have the favor of a visit from her, I at last promised her a letter to you—the direct and sole end of which is to get rid of her.

Then the flippancy vanishes, and he adds a final sentence: "She seems to be in distress, and to have a claim upon our compassion." [37]

The same phenomenon appears in a letter introducing an elderly chaplain to Anthony Wayne. The bawdry is eliminated in the published version of this letter, here rendered intact from the manuscript:

Dr. W. Mendy is one of those characters that for its honesty simplicity and helplessness interests my humanity. He is exceedingly anxious to be in the service and I believe has been forced out of it not altogether by fair play. He is just what I should like for a military parson except that he does not whore or drink. He will fight and he will not insist upon your going to heaven whether you will or not.... Pray take care of the good old man. [88]

5. WHISPERING CAMPAIGN AND FRENCH LEAVE

During the summer of 1779 Hamilton became the target of a series of malicious accusations which aimed to get at Washington through the more vulnerable person of his confidential aide. For the various conspiracies against the commander had not been abandoned with the collapse of the Conway Cabal; they merely went underground to await a more favorable moment for resumption of activities. That moment seemed to have arrived. The plotters had had ample time to work out a scheme. It was not enough, they realized, to gain adherents in Congress and among discontented army officers. It was necessary to ruin Washington once and for all with the common people—those stupid, average folk who clung unthinkingly to their trust in him through defeat and dragging warfare.

Accordingly, whispers were set in motion. Washington was plotting secretly to make himself military dictator. Congress was to be done away with—jailed; perhaps murdered. All civil authority would end. How was this known? Through Hamilton, of course. While carousing in a Philadelphia tavern (the conspirators remembered Wilkinson's earlier indiscretion), hadn't that hot-headed aide called roundly on the people to rise, join General Washington, and turn an impotent congress neck and crop out of doors?

The whisper spread like wildfire. People began to nod their heads and add other damning details as they sent the scandal merrily on its way. Finally it reached Washington and Hamilton.

In a cold fury Hamilton set about the task of running down the author of the calumny and challenging him to prove his words with pistols. He wrote short, sharp notes to two men who had been heard repeating the tale—William Dana and Colonel John Brooks of Massachusetts.

Dana admitted his guilt in spreading the report, but offered in defense that he had had it from Brooks, who, in turn, had received it from the Reverend Dr. William Gordon. But, added Dana hastily, since Hamilton denied making the incriminating remarks, he would believe him.[39]

With the name of Dr. Gordon before him, Hamilton now wrote to that gentleman of the cloth to demand from whom *he* had received the tale. Hamilton knew the clergyman well. The Reverend Doctor had been born in England and noticeably leaned to the Tory side. He was then engaged in writing a long-winded History of the American Revolution that betrayed on every page a clamorous partisanship and a reckless disregard for truth.

What happened next is described in detail and in an attempt at jest by Hamilton to his friend, John Laurens, in South Carolina.

You well remember the old Jesuit [he alluded to Gordon]. He made us a visit at Fredericksburg, and is writing the history of America. The proverb is verified,—"There never was any mischief, but had a priest or a woman at the bottom." I doubt not subornation and every species of villainy will be made use of to cover the villainy of the attack. I have written to Gordon and what do you think is his answer?—he will give up his author if I will pledge my honor "neither to give nor accept a challenge, to cause it to be given or accepted, nor to engage in any encounter that may produce a duel." Pleasant terms enough. I am first to be calumniated, and then, if my calumniator takes it into his head, I am to bear a cudgelling from him with Christian patience and forbearance....I have ridiculed the proposal, and insisted on the author, on the principle of unconditional submission. What the Doctor's impudence will answer, I know not.[40]

Gordon evaded the issue, and finally Hamilton accused him of being the real author of the slander—as indeed he was—ending: "I only lament that respect to myself obliges me to confine the expression of my contempt to words." [41]

Thereupon the worthy clergyman, emboldened by this obvious allusion to the sanctity of his calling, took his accusation direct to Washington. The general replied curtly that he had turned his complaint over to Hamilton; if Gordon had any charges to make "cognizable by a military tribunal, you have only to signify your wish and the time you will be able to procure your witnesses, and I shall proceed in it accordingly." [42]

But Gordon had no stomach for official proceedings—it seems that Hamilton threatened to thrash him publicly—and the matter was dropped. Yet the purpose of the author and of those who instigated him had been served. It was one of many similar strands employed to weave a net of calumny and poisonous lies about the patient form of the commander-in-chief.

Meanwhile the war was getting nowhere. Ever since the French joined in, the people of America had felt that there was no further necessity for exertions on their own behalf. The French will take care of everything! was the universal thought. The lethargy infected congress. To every request for army supplies it interposed indifference and a tangle of red tape. As a result the troops were in a bad way. The quaintly Englished complaint of Colonel Fleury to Hamilton is most illuminating: "The officers of the two A Battalions of L'Infantery, which I actually command, have applied to me for ceasing to run over those craggy mountains barefooted, and beg that I would write to head quarters to have an order from his Excellency to get one pair of shoes for each; the shoes they hint to are at New Windsor, and their intention is to pay for." Since his excellency, however, had only that day seen these same unfortunate officers respectably shod, let Fleury's good friend, Hamilton, explain the reason to the general. "N. B. As his Excellency could form a very advantageous idea of our being lucky in shoes by the appearance of the officers who dined to-day at head quarters, and were not quite without, I beg you would observe to him, if necessary, that each company had furnished a shoe for their dressing." [43]

It was Washington's idea to make a final gigantic effort to recapture New York with the cooperation of the French fleet. "If your excellency will engage to cooperate with your whole naval and land force against the enemy's fleet and army at New York . . .," he wrote D'Estaing, "I will bring twenty-five thousand effective men into the field." The estimate was optimistic, to say the least. He was sending Hamilton and Du Portail as liaison officers.[44]

But the two emissaries never found D'Estaing. That too-cautious admiral had suffered a wound in assaulting Savannah. The failure of the attack sent him hurrying over to the French West Indies instead of sailing toward the north, as he had promised. There he paraded for a while, awaiting a blow from the British fleet that never materialized. The blow that finally fell came in the shape of a tropical storm that scattered his fleet in all directions. Disgusted, a part of the mighty armada on which such high hopes had been pinned returned to France. Nothing had been accomplished, and the British still controlled the seas.

Hamilton and Du Portail knew nothing of these developments. Obedient to Washington's orders, they hastened to Lewiston to watch for his coming; then they rushed to Great Egg Harbor on the rumor of his arrival. But the sails of the ships of the line never broke the clean edge of the horizon. Disappointed, they went to Philadelphia and there for the first time heard of the inglorious saga of the disappearing French.

Nevertheless life must go on. In the same letter that conveyed the disastrous information to Hamilton were some personal details. "Your Cloths are not yet finished," his correspondent confessed. "The Taylor has disappointed me but promises to have them done in a day or two, when they shall be sent to you." [45] After all, the lieutenant-colonel was only twenty-two, his wardrobe needed replenishing, and the ladies of Philadelphia and at headquarters (where Martha Washington chaperoned a bevy) were extremely critical.

6. HOW TO FINANCE A WAR

By the time Hamilton returned to his duties, the army had gone into winter quarters again at Morristown. There, in the ensuing lull, he began to cast into shape certain ideas that had been slowly fermenting in his mind as a result of prolonged reading and intimate association with the desperate financial straits of the country.

The business of raising money to fight a war had proved a task far beyond the capabilities of the gentry who made up the Continental Congress. It must be confessed, indeed, that the limitations under which they labored were well nigh insuperable. They had been given no power to levy taxes—all they could do was *request* the several states to furnish funds when needed. They had to create a national treasury where none had ever existed before. National credit was a highly speculative novelty. In desperation congress resorted to a series of loans and—what amounted to the same thing—issued paper money.

But paper money, without hard specie to back it up, follows an inevitable course, and the currency printed by the Continental Congress was no exception to the rule. It slid with accelerating rapidity. A paper dollar at the end of 1779 was worth exactly two cents in real coin. As a result prices rose to astronomical figures; the printing presses ground out more paper; prices soared higher; again more paper in interminable spiral. "It's not worth a Continental!" is still in use today as an expression of utter worthlessness. Indeed, had not the French made substantial loans to their struggling ally, the Revolution must soon have collapsed of its own weight.

Hamilton knew of these pressing problems as much as any man. A large part of his correspondence consisted of letters to congress begging for supplies, for money with which to pay the soldiers. With his own eyes he saw the currency plunge to lower and lower depths and read the mournful replies of the congressional financiers that were confessions of hopeless defeat. Yet money was the necessary sinew of war, and sound finances were of more importance than a victory in the field. Moved by these considerations he composed a long and carefully thought-out letter analyzing the entire situation and offering suggestions for its improvement. He placed the bulky epistle in the mails, addressed to General John Sullivan, a member of congress from New

Hampshire, who was particularly interested in the financial crisis. Then he sat back and waited for results.

With unusual modesty Hamilton did not sign his own name. "If a personal conference with him should be thought material," he wrote at the end, Sullivan might communicate with him by a letter "directed to James Montague, Esquire, lodged in the Post Office at Morristown." [46]

This letter is an astonishing performance. Here, for the first time, Hamilton displays his mature powers. There are no flights of exuberant fancy, no glittering generalities such as had disfigured his earlier pamphlets. His facts are correct and impressively marshaled, his reasoning cogent, his logic sober. Here, in rare combination, emerges the close student of the theory of government and the practical man of affairs. For Hamilton, in this letter to Sullivan, was not writing for popular consumption and for a reading public he at heart despised; he was discussing a matter of weight and importance with a single individual who was himself a leader and man of influence. Hamilton was always at his happiest in these private letters.

The pressing issue before the country, he pointed out, was the deplorable state of the currency. To fight a war required money, and a money revenue was usually derived from taxation. But congress had no power to tax; only to make requisitions upon sovereign states which had it in their own discretion to comply or not. And even if congress had such a power, the amounts that could be raised would be insufficient. Didn't the wealthiest nations of Europe, with the fullest recourse to taxes, always float foreign loans in time of war? Why then shouldn't the United States adopt the same method?

"Taxes are limited," he declared pertinently, "not only by the quantity of wealth in a state, but by the temper, habits, and genius of the people; all of which, in this country, conspired to render them moderate; and as to loans, men will not be prevailed upon to lend money to the public when there is a scarcity, and they can find a more profitable way of employing it otherwise, as was our case." Hamilton had no illusions about the self-sacrificial patriotism of the average moneyed man.

Since income from taxes was not sufficient, and native men of wealth were too intent on high profits, the only remedy was to borrow abroad where the interest rate would prove attractive. There was another argument in favor of foreign loans. The sums realized could be converted on the spot into merchandise and brought to this country for government sale at a profit, which profit in turn would tend to support the currency.

From foreign loans he turned his attention next to the problem of the farmers. Since they were largely self-sufficient they purchased little outside goods on which taxes were levied and therefore contributed hardly at all to the support of the government. Yet they insisted on, and obtained, high prices for their products, which led to inflation and further diminution of the currency. To compel them to pay their proper quota and at the same time keep food prices down Hamilton advocated a tax on farmers in kind—a government levy of a percentage of the annual crops.

But even these two remedies, he realized, could not alone restore the currency to a sound level. "The only plan that can preserve the currency," he admitted, "is one that will make it the *immediate* interest of the moneyed men to co-operate with government in its support."

Thus early Hamilton enunciated the principle that was to form the chief bastion of his philosophy of government, and to which he returned again and again in later papers and actions. A government could only be strong, its finances stable—and these propositions, to Hamilton, were synonymous—if the men of wealth were given a financial stake in its durability. The small artisans and the propertyless might be taxed against their will (note his later procedure in the so-called Whisky Rebellion); the farmers' crops might be seized for the national use; but "the moneyed men" must be wheedled and given good inducements.

To obtain such cooperation Hamilton proposed that a national bank be chartered for a test period of ten years, though he did not "suppose it will ever be discontinued." Part of its stock was to be paid for by a foreign loan of two million pounds; part by a domestic subscription of two hundred millions in Continental currency, repayment of which at the end of the charter period was to be guaranteed by the government in Spanish dollars in the ratio of twenty to one. Since a Spanish dollar was worth on November 17, 1779 (about the time of his proposal), thirty-eight and one-half Continental dollars, Hamilton's scheme meant a tidy profit to "the moneyed men" of almost one hundred per cent on their original investment.

From this bank congress would be permitted to borrow two millions annually at four per cent; private loans would pay six. The bank stock would be negotiable and would circulate as additional currency. Half the stock and half the profits were to go to the government;

the other half to the private subscribers. The actual management of the bank was to be placed in a private board of trustees, chosen by the private owners, though it would be subject to inspection by a governmental board.

He concluded his proposal with an expression of complete confidence in its feasibility, because, he said frankly, it "stands on the firm footing of public and private faith;... it links the interest of the State in an intimate connection with those of the rich individuals belonging to it;... it turns the wealth and influence of both into a commercial channel, for mutual benefit, which must afford advantages not to be estimated."

This was the first time, so far as is known, that a bank with governmental assistance and, in part, for governmental purposes was proposed in America. The idea was not original; Hamilton readily admitted he was modeling his institution on the existing Bank of England. Though he was presently engaged in a war against the mother country, he never made a secret of his admiration for the foundations and ordered stability of English government. Throughout life he trumpeted its superiority over that of all other nations, and he constantly rendered it the tribute of imitation wherever such imitation was possible in the American scene.

The letter to Sullivan showed that at the age of twenty-three Hamilton's ideas were fully grown. Later years may have ripened them; rarely did they change or evolve. His basic philosophy in 1789 and in 1800 was remarkably consistent with the fundamentals of 1779. The bank he finally put into effect when he became Secretary of the Treasury bore a marked family resemblance to the outline he sent General Sullivan. Not once did he swerve from his firm conviction that the interests of the rich must be linked to the interests of the state if it is to survive and wax powerful. The young man of twenty-three was as realistic, or as cynical, if you wish, as the older man who later helped rule the nation.

It is quite probable that Sullivan replied to "James Montague, Esquire," and that several interviews resulted. Sullivan was impressed, yet in the present state of things he could do nothing. Certainly the proposed bank was impossible of fruition. The states were sufficiently jealous of any attempt at centralization not to set up a tremendous outcry at such a national instrument which would deprive them of all financial control, and the obvious advantages to "the moneyed men" would not go well with the propertyless radicals who thought they were fighting a social as well as a political revolution.

The one proposal of all those incorporated in Hamilton's letter that congress did consider and adopt was the one that called for requisitions in kind from the farmers. But the yield proved inconsiderable. The farmers resisted it fiercely and hid their crops when the tax collectors came to requisition. They may well have inquired why no similar requisitions were being levied on the goods of the merchants and traders.

CHAPTER VIII

Love and Treason

I. ENGAGEMENT TO ELIZA

THE WINTER QUARTERS of the American army at Morristown during the waning months of 1779 and the beginning of 1780 were a far cry from the tragic suffering of the previous winter at Valley Forge. Food was fairly abundant, the quarters were comfortable, and visitors streamed in endlessly. Martha Washington came up from Virginia to give a touch of domesticity to her general's battle-scarred existence; the married officers brought their wives and daughters to comfort them during the dull winter months. Gay young ladies fluttered about the camp, much to the delight of the spruce young aides who interspersed plodding hours of duty with soulful gazing into bright eyes, witty badinage and tender gallantries, formal dinners and more agreeable balls.

Hamilton threw himself into the round of entertainments with gusto. He appreciated a neatly turned ankle and a roguish smile as much as any man. Rising from the desk where he had just completed a lengthy financial dissertation, bristling with figures and fortified with learned quotations, he would shift with easy grace to the brightly brittle repartee and airy nonsense that only the young are privileged to enjoy.

Yet, as Christmas came, his heart and his imagination were still untouched by the beauty or wit of any of the belles who cast eyes in his direction. Such at least is the inference to be drawn from the high-flown and high-spirited letter he sent to his good friend, John Laurens, down in South Carolina. While "we are upon the subject of wife," he wrote playfully,

I empower and command you to get me one in Carolina. Such a wife as I want will, I know, be difficult to be found, but if you succeed, it will be the stronger proof of your zeal and dexterity. Take her description—she must be young, handsome (I lay most stress upon a good shape), sensible (a little learning will do), well bred (but she must have an aversion to the word *ton*), chaste, and tender (I am an enthusiast in my notions of fidelity and fondness), of some good nature, a great deal of generosity (she must neither love money nor scolding, for I dislike equally a termagant and an economist). In politics I am indifferent what side she may be of. I think I have arguments that will easily convert her to mine. As to religion a moderate stock will satisfy me. She must believe in God and hate a saint.

But as to fortune, the larger stock of that the better. You know my temper and circumstances and will therefore pay special attention in the treaty.

However, after this minute schedule of qualifications, he wound up suddenly: "Do I want a wife? No. I have plagues enough without desiring to add to the number that greatest of all." [1]

The letter begins and ends as a jest. But there is no doubt that Hamilton was perfectly serious when he listed what he most desired in a wife. Fortune, especially, was an exceedingly desirable commodity for an impecunious young man, whose sole income consisted of the doubtful salary of an aide and who had no family or ancestral inheritance upon which to fall back.

But even as he was dashing off this itemized statement of attributes and particularized charms, he had already met the girl he was to marry. By and large she filled his requirements, except that she might not have been as handsome as the specifications, and her piety was deeper than his theory demanded. But she was able to add some highly important items to his list. There was no more powerful family, viewed politically, socially or financially, to be found in the state of New York.

There were four great families in New York at the time—the Van Rensselaers, the Van Cortlandts, the Livingstons and the Schuylers. Of these not the least were the Schuylers. Philip Schuyler represented the fourth generation of Dutch patroons whose holdings were princely along the Mohawk River and in the region surrounding Albany. He dwelt on his immense estates like a feudal baron, his word law and his will supreme. From his fertile valleys came flax and from his endless forests prime lumber. He built his own ships and floated them down the Hudson to trade with England and the West Indies.

With the coming of the Revolution he cast in his lot unhesitatingly with the colonies and rose rapidly to a major-general's post. He commanded the northern forces in the Canadian campaign, but his haughty, unbending air and aristocratic pretensions made him sufficient enemies to bring about his downfall. When he lost Ticonderoga to the British they were quick to accuse him of incompetence and even disloyalty;

and caused him to be superseded by General Gates. The affair went as far as a court-martial, from which he emerged vindicated, though embittered.

The old patroon families intermarried a great deal, and Philip Schuyler duly took as his wife Catherine, the daughter of John Van Rensselaer of Claverack. Of their large brood of daughters the most brilliant, Angelica, eloped in 1779 with an unknown Englishman who had suddenly appeared in the colonies under the name of John Carter. At first Schuyler was furious. "Carter and my eldest daughter ran off and were married on the twenty-third of July," he lamented to William Duer. "Unacquainted with his family connections and situation in life the matter was exceedingly disagreeable and I signified it to them." [2]

But the mystery was shortly cleared up to everyone's satisfaction. The pretended John Carter was in fact John Barker Church, of good English stock, who had been forced to quit England as a result of a duel. Married to the charming and witty Angelica, and with Schuyler's belated blessing upon him, he became commissary to Admiral Rochambeau and General Wadsworth, accumulated a large fortune as a result, and was later able to return to England, accompanied by his wife, to live in the most lavish style. Both husband and wife were to play important roles in Hamilton's later career.

The second daughter of Philip and Catherine Schuyler was Elizabeth, born on August 9, 1757, and therefore some seven months younger than Hamilton. She was not as much of a belle as her older sister, nor did she have the vivacity, the exquisite charm, the wit or brilliance of Angelica. Nevertheless she possessed solid and estimable qualities of her own that, four years before, had been sufficient to attract the admiring attention of such a gay young blade as Tench Tilghman.

Writing in his journal, under the date of August 22, 1775, he described his first introduction to "Miss Betsy Schuyler, the Generals 2d daughter." The same night he commented: "I was prepossessed in favr of this young Lady the moment I saw her. A Brunette with the most good natured lively dark eyes that I ever saw, which threw a beam of good temper and benevolence over her whole Countenance. Mr. Livingston informed me that I was not mistaken in my Conjecture for that she was the finest tempered Girl in the World." [3]

Hamilton first made her acquaintance in November, 1777, during the few days of his mission to Gates, when he spent a day at the

Schuyler home in Albany. At that time his thoughts were busy with more serious business than the "beam of good temper" displayed on a young girl's countenance.

Now, however, in the idleness and relaxation of Morristown, he was able to devote more of his attention to this paragon of good temper with the lively dark eyes. For Schuyler, out of the army and a member of that congress which had once demoted and disgraced him, had leased a house close to the army camp where he installed his family while he attended sessions in Philadelphia.

For a while Betsy was only one of a numerous bevy of young ladies to Hamilton, all equally charming and all equally flattered by the gallantries of the dashing young aide.

With the turn of the year, however, Hamilton became a more frequent visitor in the Schuyler establishment. General Schuyler, coming in from Philadelphia whenever possible, welcomed him cordially. He knew the young man from the days when Schuyler was a member of the New York Congress and had read Hamilton's reports as its army correspondent.

The older man and the younger were soon on the most intimate terms. Both were interested in the same things—a strong, forceful government, the maintenance of Washington's command against the machinations of the politicians—and a common dislike for the laxity of the times. They talked at length over these and kindred topics and warmed to each other in the glow of general agreement. By virtue of his wealth and connections, Schuyler was an important political figure in state and national politics, and an alliance with him through the close ties of marriage must be of inestimable benefit to an ambitious young man.

It is impossible to say whether considerations such as these came consciously into Hamilton's mind when he directed his gaze and his addresses to the good-natured Betsy. Subconsciously, however, they must have had their influence. There is no doubt that he sincerely loved Elizabeth Schuyler, though perhaps her solid qualities appealed to his good sense more than they stormed his emotions. There is certainly no doubt that Betsy fell utterly in love with the glamorous young aide and was to remain loyal and faithful to him even beyond his tragic death.

The path of love in this particular instance ran smoothly enough. The proud old aristocratic father not only raised no objections to the match, but extended to it his warmest paternal blessing. His experience with the headstrong Angelica had obviously chastened him. After their marriage the following year he hastened to congratulate his new son-in-law: "You can not my Dear Sir be more happy at the connection you have made with my family than I am. Until a Child has made a judicious choice the heart of a parent is continually in anxiety, but this anxiety vanished in the moment I discovered where you and she had placed your affections." [4]

Betsy had in fact made an excellent choice, as Schuyler realized. By this time Hamilton was well and favorably known throughout the army and among men of substance and influence. His talents were universally acknowledged and it was freely predicted that he would travel far. His manners were polished, his bearing dignified and his ideas sound. The only rub lay in his family connections. It was known he had come from the West Indies while still a boy; very little more of his antecedents were known at the time. That General Schuyler must have asked him point-blank before giving his final consent may be taken for granted. That Hamilton avowed that his mother had been first married to Levine, and later divorced, is evident from the letter he wrote his wife a year or two later. [5]

It is also certain that he gave his father's name, his circumstances and stressed the solidity of the Scottish Hamiltons. But that he told the entire truth, namely, that James Hamilton and Rachel Levine never legally married, and that therefore his own birth was illegitimate, is extremely unlikely. No doubt he slid over that delicate point as quickly as possible. For Schuyler was a rigid and unbending man, with the pride of heritage behind him, and he would never have consented to such a marriage for his daughter. The unsettled condition of the times also prevented him from making such inquiries in the West Indies as must have occurred to any prudent father.

Later on, when the rumors about Hamilton became common property, it was not only too late to do anything about it, but Schuyler had completely yielded to his son-in-law's spell and become his most ardent admirer and follower. Nothing mattered then except Hamilton's vivid personal charm and political genius.

Early in his courtship Hamilton wrote in flowerly style to Eliza's sister, Angelica Church, who was then in New Rochelle with her husband. (Elizabeth was called by her intimates indifferently Eliza, Betsy or Betty.) "I venture to tell you in confidence," declared the young suitor gallantly, "that by some odd contrivance or other your sister has found out the secret of interesting me in everything that concerns her; and though I have not the happiness of a personal acquaintance with you, I have had the good fortune to see several very pretty pictures of your person and mind which have inspired me with a more than common partiality for both." [6]

That this was not mere empty gallantry toward the sister of his beloved is borne out by later events. When Hamilton and Angelica finally met, they were instantly attracted to each other, and it is quite probable that had Angelica been still unattached and at home before Hamilton finally placed his affections, she would have cast her younger sister entirely in the shade. But she was now safely married, and Hamilton was engaged to Eliza, whose domesticity, gentleness and good nature satisfied needs in him other than those which Angelica might have plumbed.

For the benefit of the absent Angelica he went on to paint a flattering portrait of Eliza which has more of the earmarks of conventional extravagance than of sincere emotion. Eliza, he proclaimed with a flourish, was turning the heads of the entire army. "It is essential to the safety of the state, and to the tranquillity of the army—that one of two things take place, either that she be immediately removed from our neighborhood, or that some other nymph qualified to maintain an equal sway come into it. . . . I solicit your aid." Meaning, of course, that he was most curious to meet Angelica.

Early in March, 1780, Hamilton went to Amboy on another of the interminable missions looking toward an exchange of prisoners. He found to his disgust that the proceedings, as once before, depended more on the quantity of wine drunk than on the merits of the case. Eliza, Angelica and Peggy, the three Schuyler sisters, he wrote Eliza, were "the daily toasts at our table, and for this *honor* you are chiefly indebted to the British gentlemen; though, as I am always thinking of you, this naturally brings Peggy to my mind, who is generally my toast."

But this left-handed compliment is soon displaced by irritation over his companions.

I have learned a secret by coming down here. Our interview is attended with a good deal of sociability and good humor, but I begin, notwithstanding, to be tired of our British friends. They do their best to be agreeable and are particularly civil to me, but, after all, they are a compound of grimace and jargon and, out of a certain fashionable routine, are as dull and empty as any gentleman need to be. One of their principal excellencies consist in swallowing a large quantity of wine every day, and in this I am so unfortunate that I shall make no sort of figure with them.[7]

The short absence from Eliza spurred Hamilton's ardor. When he returned from his bibulous encounter with the British he proposed formally to his beloved, was accepted, and sought an interview with General Schuyler. The old general expressed his joy at the event, but shook his head when the ardent swain asked for an immediate wedding. Mrs. Schuyler had in the meantime returned to Albany, and he wished to write for her approval first.

On April 8th he reported to Hamilton that "yesterday I had the pleasure to receive a line from Mrs. Schuyler in answer to mine on the subject of the one you delivered me at Morris town. She consents to comply with your and her daughters wishes." But this related only to the engagement. As for Hamilton's insistence on an immediate marriage, "you will see the Impropriety of taking the dernier pas when you are. Mrs. Schuyler did not see her Eldest daughter married. That also gave me pain, and we wish not to Experience it a second time." [8]

Hamilton bowed to the reasonable request of the parents, and the wedding was postponed until it was possible for it to be performed in fitting style at the ancestral mansion of the Schuylers in Albany.

By July he had sufficiently recovered from his disappointment to order certain finery through his good friend, Colonel Laurens, then in Philadelphia. Laurens agreed to execute the commission "about your feather—the whole will be committed to the care of Colonel Gui-mat—I will mount a beaver and plumage in the same stile, as soon as I have a prospect of joining the Corps." [9]

Hamilton's soldier friends reacted variously to the public announcement of his engagement. Tench Tilghman's letter to his brother, William, when he heard the news, poses some curious problems. "Alas poor Polly! Hamilton is a gone man, and I am too old for his substitute—She [Polly] had better look out for herself and not put her trust in Man. She need not be jealous of the little Saint [a reference to Elizabeth Schuyler's piety]—She is gone to Pennsylvania and has no other impressions than those of regard for a very pretty good tempered Girl, the daughter of one of my most valuable acquaintances." [10]

We have no other information about the girl, Polly, with whom, it would seem, Hamilton was seriously entangled right up to the announcement of his engagement. It would also appear that Hamilton's courtship of Eliza had been so discreetly conducted that Polly, a comparative stranger to the Schuylers, though well known to the Tilghmans, left Morristown without the slightest knowledge that she had been displaced in his affections.

Colonel Fleury, on the other hand, congratulated his friend, Hamilton, with a Gallic frankness that requires no explanation. His letter has never before been published. "Mrs. Carter [Angelica Church] told me you was soor [sure] to be married to her sister, Miss Betty Schuyler, & congratulate you heartily on that conquest; for many Reasons: the first that you will get all that familly's interest, & that a man of your abilities wants a Little influence to do good to his country. The second that you will be in a very easy situation, & happiness is not to be found without a large Estate." [11]

Now that the engagement was officially declared, Hamilton attempted to remake the submissive and adoring Eliza. She was not an intellectual, as was her sister, Angelica. The latter had had the advantages of attending a fashionable ladies' seminary in New Rochelle while Eliza remained home to learn the arts of domesticity under the supervision of her mother. But the imperious young man had no doubt he could mold the willing clay to his heart's desire.

I entreat you, my charmer, not to neglect the charges I gave you, particularly that of taking care of yourself and that of employing all your leisure in reading. Nature has been very kind to you, do not neglect to cultivate her gifts and to enable yourself to make the distinguished figure in all respects to which you are entitled to aspire. You excel most of your sex in all the amiable qualities, endeavor to excel them equally in the splendid ones. You can do it if you please, and I shall take pride in it.— It will be a fund too to diversify our enjoyment and amusements and fill all our moments to advantage.[12]

Like many another lover, however, Hamilton soon discovered it was easier to exhort than to accomplish. After a little while he dropped his schoolmaster attitude and with it Eliza's self-improvement schemes quietly vanished. She was never to shine in salons with any brilliance. Her talents were of the domestic order, and her particular contribution to Hamilton's life was to furnish him with a haven of humble and undeviating devotion—even in those too many moments when she had the best reason to believe he had been unfaithful to her. Hamilton may have sought diversion elsewhere, but invariably he returned, secure in the knowledge of her tender ministrations and forgiveness.

2. A PLAN OF GOVERNMENT

Very early in his career Hamilton had made the acquaintance of James Duane of New York. Duane was just one of those leaders to whom Hamilton unerringly gravitated. He was a man of considerable property, influential, and conservative in his social and economic views even while in revolt against English rule. At the present moment he represented New York in the Continental Congress.

In turn Duane had been impressed by the remarkable talents of young Hamilton. In common with the Livingstons, John Jay, Schuyler and an ever-growing group of solid, substantial men he listened to the youthful aide's ideas and opinions with marked respect, and consulted him on the knotty problems that confronted the infant government. Right now, late in the summer of 1780, these problems seemed almost unsolvable. Congress was passing through one of the worst of its innumerable crises. The state of the country was shocking; the Continental currency was practically worthless; the army was disintegrating for lack of supplies and pay; the states ignored the feeble requests of the so-called national government for funds and were busy with wildcat schemes of their own. To most thinking men the Revolution was fast approaching an end.

Duane came up from Philadelphia to the camp at Morristown to discuss the desperate situation with Washington and his generals. He met Hamilton and talked with him. What did Hamilton think of the times? Hamilton thought they were bad—very bad, but in striking contrast with most of the others with whom Duane talked, he proposed definite remedies. Apply these, he asserted with confident conviction, and the country can yet be saved. Duane was struck with his ideas. Put them in writing, he suggested, and forward them to me in Philadelphia. Hamilton sat down and wrote his reflections in the form of a letter addressed to Duane.[13]

This letter, composed amid the distractions of camp and in time snatched from his regular duties, is an astounding performance. Buttressed with historical analogies, informed with statesmanship of the highest order, it set forth a plan for the reorganization of the national government that was sensible, practical and necessary if the government was to continue to exist. The pamphleteer has vanished; the statesman has emerged.

Almost the first sentence goes straight to the heart of the problem. "The fundamental defect is a want of power in Congress." But this want of power was largely due to the timidity of Congress itself. He brushed aside impatiently the arguments of those who said that congress had no authority to act because the Articles of Confederation granted it no definite powers. It might recommend, they said, but not command. Nonsense! Hamilton retorted, a bold congress would have assumed the necessary powers. "The public good required that they should have considered themselves as vested with full power *to preserve the republic from harm.*"

Nevertheless it was true that congress was not all to blame. "The Confederation itself is defective, and requires to be altered. It is neither fit for war nor peace." As long as each state has complete sovereignty in internal affairs, there can be no proper union. What makes for a strong and vigorous nation? A central power with independent control of its funds. "Without certain revenues, a government can have no power. That power which holds the purse-strings absolutely, must rule." This bit of realism Hamilton had learned from his reading and from the present example.

But under the confederation the states held the purse strings. This was intolerable. Let perpetual sources of revenue be placed at the sole disposal of congress. Hamilton suggested for this purpose a poll tax, a general tax on land and imposts on commerce.

With the problem of finances disposed of, he turned now to an attack upon the congress he had just defended. If it had assumed too little control over money, it had arrogated to itself too much power in another direction. It had viewed with suspicion all attempts to set up an independent executive. "Congress," he declared, "have kept the power too much in their own hands, and have meddled too much with details of every sort. Congress is, properly, a deliberative corps, and it forgets itself when it attempts to play the executive."

Hamilton proposed his remedies; they were clear-cut, forthright, definite. Let congress immediately invest itself with those powers which he maintained were inherent in its original appointment. If the delegates were too timid to adopt such an outright course, then call a convention of all the states with full authority to form a general confederation. This confederation should grant to congress complete and unhampered sovereignty over war and peace, foreign affairs, trade, finance, coinage, banks and treaties. Only those matters should be left to the states which relate "to the rights of property and life among individuals."

This congress was to appoint at once a series of executives, who in turn would be solely responsible for the administration of a department. Audaciously Hamilton told congress just whom to appoint: Schuyler, his prospective father-in-law, for President of War, Mc-Dougall for the Marine, and Robert Morris for Finance.

Let the war be fought with a regular army enlisted for the duration, he advised, not with a worthless state militia. If such an army cannot be raised by voluntary enlistment, introduce conscription, according to the Swedish plan. Then supply this army from funds raised by congress. Where would the money come from? Borrow from France, raise taxes, and above all, create a bank.

The bank was Hamilton's favorite scheme. He had advocated it strongly to Sullivan; now he insisted on it to Duane. He repeated all the old arguments and added some new ones. Paper credit was of no value unless it was founded "on a joint basis of public and private credit." Public credit alone was not enough. John Law had tried that scheme in France and the results had been disastrous. Similar attempts in America had proved just as devastating. For the new emissions of paper were depreciating just as rapidly as the old. Why? Because— and here Hamilton hammered home his fundamental thesis—"the moneyed men have not an immediate interest to uphold its credit. They may even, in many ways, find it their interest to undermine it."

Hamilton wasted no time in deploring this lack of patriotism and public spirit on the part of his "moneyed men." It was a fact of nature, to be accepted as such. To establish a permanent paper credit, you must set up a bank in which the people of wealth would be granted a preponderating share and control and "the whole or a part of the profits." Everyone would then be happy: the wealthy would gain large profits, the government would have a ready source of loans, paper money would circulate at par and trade would thrive. Not for a moment did it occur to Hamilton that in time of war wealth might just as properly be conscripted as men.

In conclusion Hamilton enunciated a psychologic law. "Men are governed by opinion," he said; "this opinion is as much influenced by appearances as by realities. If a government appears to be confident of its own powers, it is the surest way to inspire the same confidence in others."

The practical statesmanship and vision of the future course of the government of the United States displayed in this letter are amazing in so young a man. At a time when the centrifugal tendencies of the respective states were most in evidence, he called boldly for a centralized, unified national government. At a time when congress had shown itself weak, incompetent and corrupt, he demanded more power for it. With cold clarity he punctured the fallacy of unlimited paper money, unbacked by anything but government fiat. With unblushing frankness he dismissed idealism as a means of governing, and made wealth the sole support of government for mutual profit. "The sacred rights of mankind" and "the parity of privileges" to which all men are entitled by nature, so eloquently upheld in "The Farmer Refuted," are quietly laid aside, never to be resuscitated.

As a conservative and man of wealth, James Duane could readily perceive the advantages of Hamilton's plan. Yet as a practical politician he also realized it would not go well with a set of congressmen who were primarily local, rather than national, statesmen, and whose suspicions would certainly take alarm at such a candid disclosure of the venality of wealth. Hence it is not likely that he showed the plan *in toto* to more than a select group of like-minded men, who by training and moneyed instinct would agree to such a bank. Actually, only one of Hamilton's proposals bore immediate fruit—a plan for the creation of executive departments which Duane himself sponsored. The remainder had to wait for the future.

3. BENEDICT ARNOLD, TRAITOR

While Duane was digesting this amazing document and cautiously showing it to his friends, the theater of war had shifted to the south. Matters were going badly. The French fleets had been immobilized by strong British squadrons, and South Carolina was almost completely in enemy hands. General Gates, hero of Saratoga, was dispatched south to stem the tide. At Camden he met Cornwallis and the results were disastrous for Gates. It was one of the great defeats of the war. His militia fled at the first onslaught, and Gates, according to all accounts, outdistanced his men. A thousand were killed or wounded; another thousand were taken prisoner; the brave De Kalb died in a vain attempt to rally the panic-stricken troops. But Gates was safe at Hillsborough, one hundred and eighty miles away!

It was Hamilton's chance to strike back at the self-satisfied general who had once treated him so shabbily. He told Betsy Schuyler with malicious sarcasm that Gates "seems to know very little what has become of his army. He showed that age and the long labors and fatigues of a military life had not in the least impaired his activity, for in three days and a half he reached Hillsborough, one hundred and eighty miles from the scene of the action, leaving all his troops to take care of themselves, and get out of the scrape as well as they could." [14]

Though he also told Betsy that "this misfortune affects me less than others . . . because I think our safety depends on a total change of system, and this change of system will only be produced by misfortune," the news of the defeat toppled over an accumulated load of despair. Everything was wrong—the state of the army, the justifiable discontents of officers and men, the carping complaints against Washington and against himself as the chief of his aides. It required only a well-meant attempt by his friend, Laurens, to palliate and soothe to touch off a violent explosion.

'Tis in vain you attempt to appease [he retorted bitterly]; you are almost detested as an accomplice with the administration. I am losing character, my friend, because I am not overcomplaisant to the spirit of clamour—so that I am in a fair way to be out with every body. With one set I am considered as a friend to military pretensions however exorbitant, with another as a man who, secured by my situation from sharing the distress of the army, am inclined to treat it lightly. The truth is I am an unlucky honest man, that speak my sentiments to all and with emphasis.

The load was too much for him. In the blackness of that moment he cried out with terrible disillusionment: "I hate Congress—I hate the army—I hate the world—I hate myself. The whole is a mass of fools and knaves." [15]

The mood did not last. Hamilton was too young and too tough-minded to view the world, and especially himself, through such jaundiced spectacles for any length of time. In fact, when Benedict Arnold put a full period to the series of misfortunes that had bedeviled the American cause, Hamilton not only took the treason in his stride but found time for a display of generous and chivalric sentiments.

Benedict Arnold had long considered himself unjustly treated by congress. Time and again his brilliant gifts had been overlooked and less able officers promoted over his head. But such had also been the lot of other competent commanders in the army, yet none turned traitor to his country. Arnold, however, brooding on his wrongs and embarrassed in his personal fortunes by his own reckless expenditures and the extravagances of his pretty wife, the former Peggy Shippen, entered into secret negotiations with Sir Henry Clinton. On the promise of a large sum of money and a command in the British army he agreed to surrender West Point, key fortress to the Hudson River Valley and vital to communication lines between New England and the other states.

In pursuance of this plan he sought and obtained from Washington the command of the post at West Point. Once securely installed, he notified Clinton who sent his handsome young aide, Major John André, to arrange the final details of the surrender. André came under a pretended flag of truce and with a safe-conduct signed by Arnold himself. At West Point the traitorous officer furnished André with instructions for a sudden raid by British troops from New York and promised to offer only a token resistance before yielding the great fortress.

With Arnold's instruction secreted inside his boot André quit West Point and started down the river, expecting to be picked up by the British sloop, *Vulture*, which had anchored unostentatiously below, out of range of the guns of the fort.

But here fate took a hand. Directly opposite the point where the *Vulture* anchored, an American gun was in position. It was only a four-pounder pop-gun and the ship was out of range, but the officer in charge enthusiastically opened fire. The balls fell harmlessly into the river considerably short of their mark, but the *Vulture* took alarm, weighed anchor and moved farther down the stream. So that André, coming to the rendezvous, found the ship gone. In some perturbation he returned to West Point, from where he ferried across to the eastern bank, took horse and sought to make his way by land down to the British lines. Near Tarrytown a party of irregulars disregarded his flag of truce and safe-conduct, searched him and found the incriminating dispatches.

Colonel Jameson, to whom they brought André, was sorely puzzled. The documents were obviously treasonable, but the Englishman carried a signed pass from Arnold. Somewhat befuddled, he decided finally to forward the captured plans to Washington and return André himself to Arnold under guard, with a letter of explanation. Fortunately Major Tallmage expostulated in time to cause a patrol to be sent out to recall André, but the letter continued on its way to Arnold.

Meanwhile General Washington, who had been at Newport in a vain attempt to persuade Rochambeau to join him in a combined attack on New York, was journeying back by easy stages toward West Point. Evening fell as the general and his staff reached a point about fifteen miles from the fort. It had been his intention to press on that same day to West Point, but the Chevalier Luzerne politely invited him to spend the night at his lodgings and await the morning before continuing his journey. Washington accepted and sent Hamilton and

McHenry ahead with his baggage to notify Arnold that he would breakfast with him in the morning.

Arnold had established himself in comfortable quarters on the east bank of the Hudson, across the river from the main fortifications. When the two aides rode in at dawn to present their compliments Arnold, who did not know that André was already under arrest, rejoiced mightily at this most unexpected stroke of good fortune. Not only would he deliver West Point to the British, but the commander-in-chief of the American forces and his entire staff as well.

Hamilton and McHenry, unwitting participants in a tense, unfolding drama that might have changed the entire course of the Revolution and their country's future, took their ease after their long night ride. They ate and drank while waiting for the arrival of the entourage and chatted amiably with Arnold and his wife. They knew and respected Arnold as a brave and brilliant officer; they knew and admired pretty Peggy Shippen who had been a leading Philadelphia belle.

The sun was already high and still Washington did not arrive. With Lafayette and Knox he had turned aside to examine a newly completed redoubt instead of proceeding directly to Arnold's quarters. Arnold was on tenterhooks and Hamilton and McHenry were puzzled, but the four of them continued their light, amusing gossip.

Then a messenger strode into the room and handed Arnold a letter. It was the letter from Jameson that had been unaccountably forgotten when Tallmage forced André's recall. Arnold ripped open the enclosure, to read the horrifying news that "John Anderson"—André's name on the safe-conduct—was captured. Turning deathly pale, he hurriedly excused himself and went to his own room. In a frenzy of haste he snatched up all incriminating papers, thrust them into his saddlebags, then sent an orderly to get his wife out on some excuse and to notify Hamilton and McHenry that he had been called suddenly across the river to West Point, but would return shortly.

When Peggy burst breathlessly into his room, filled with premonitions, he told her swiftly that the jig was up. With a moan she sank down in a faint. Leaving her so, and without an attempt to revive her, Arnold went quietly out the back way, mounted horse and fled unperceived down the river bank to where the *Vulture* lay at its new anchorage. There he jumped into a boat, was rowed out to the ship and to safety.

In the meanwhile Washington and his escort had completed their inspection and rode into Arnold's quarters. The two aides were alone;

Arnold, they explained, had gone to West Point and Peggy Arnold had excused herself and left them to their own devices. Without any suspicion of what had taken place the travelers ordered breakfast, ate, and crossed over to West Point, while Hamilton remained behind. But Arnold was not at West Point, nor had he been there at all. For the first time Washington's mind "misgave" him, and he hastily recrossed the river. There was Hamilton, with a face of repressed tragedy.

During Washington's absence, the packet of André's dispatches had come from Jameson. Hamilton opened them, and found the whole tale of incredible treason displayed. He had barely finished when Washington was back, himself uneasy and disturbed. The young aide beckoned him aside and in low tones told him the news. Washington was stunned. Arnold, whom he regarded as one of his best officers, turned traitor! Recovering swiftly, he ordered Hamilton and McHenry to ride at top speed to Verplanck's Point, some eight miles down the river, where there was an American post from which Arnold might be intercepted if he had not already reached the *Vulture*. But when the two aides galloped into the Point, they found that the *Vulture* was under sail and moving down the tide. The bird had flown.[16]

Hamilton scribbled a note to Washington, advising him of Arnold's escape and that he was taking steps on his own responsibility to meet the emergency.

You will see by the enclosed that we are too late. Arnold went by water to the *Vulture*. I shall write to General Greene, advising him, without making a bustle, to be in readiness to march, and even to detach a brigade this way; for, though I do not believe the project will go on, yet it is possible Arnold has made such dispositions with the garrison as may tempt the enemy, in its present weakness, to make the stroke this night, and it seems prudent to be providing against it. I shall endeavor to find Meigs, and request him to march to the garrison, and shall make some arrangements here. I hope your Excellency will approve these steps, as there may be no time to be lost. The *Vulture* is gone down to New York.[17]

Luckily, Clinton had decided that the chance was gone and did not move. But Washington must have felt comforted that he had in Hamilton an aide who could act promptly and with decision in an emergency, without waiting for orders or an authorization.

When he had done all he could to safeguard West Point from sudden attack, Hamilton hastened back to Arnold's quarters. Everything was in a turmoil. Peggy Arnold had been revived from her faint and had gone into a prolonged fit of hysterics. Hamilton was deeply touched. Here was beauty in distress, lovely woman deserted by a traitor husband and crying out her anguish at the mocking fates. Of her innocence he had not the slightest doubt.

That night he wrote of her in sympathetic accents to Eliza as

an amiable woman, frantic with distress for the loss of a husband she tenderly loved; a traitor to his country and to his fame... it was the most affecting scene I ever was witness to. She, for a considerable time, entirely lost herself. The General went up to see her, and she upbraided him with being in a plot to murder her child. One moment she raved, another she melted into tears.... We have every reason to believe that she was entirely unacquainted with the plan.[18]

He might have saved his sympathy. Both Hamilton and Washington, as well as the vast majority of patriotic Americans, were completely taken in by Peggy Arnold's histrionics. Only Aaron Burr, who never allowed emotion to interfere with logic, was not deceived.[19] For this he was to be assailed as an assassin of noble womanhood by later historians. But recent discoveries among the papers of Sir Henry Clinton have proved conclusively that she was involved in Arnold's schemes from the very beginning.[20]

Arnold had escaped, but André remained in American hands. In spite of almost universal pressure to save him, Washington was firm in his determination to hang the young English major as a spy. Today the wisdom of that decision is questioned; at the time it aroused equal doubts. Hamilton misliked it completely and did not hesitate to tell his granite-spirited superior so. The gallantry of the Englishman, the spirit with which he pleaded his cause, the injustice of executing André while the chief culprit was free, made a deep impression on Hamilton. Though he reluctantly admitted that ruthless policy might demand an execution, his indignation grew white hot when Washington turned down André's last request for a soldier's death at the hands of a firing squad rather than a felon's fate by the rope.

On the day the unfortunate man was hanged Hamilton wrote two letters. One was to his future wife.

Poor André suffers to-day. Every thing that is amiable in virtue, in fortitude, in delicate sentiment, and accomplished manners, pleads for him; but hard-hearted policy calls for a sacrifice. He must die— ...I urged a compliance with André's request to be shot; and I do not think it would have had an ill effect; but some people are only sensible to motives of policy, and sometimes, from a narrow disposition, mistake it. [This was a direct slap at Washington.] When André's tale comes to be told, and present resentment is over, the refusing him the privilege of choosing the manner of his death will be branded with too much obstinacy. It was proposed to me to suggest to him [André] the idea of an exchange for Arnold; but I knew I should have forfeited his esteem by doing it, and therefore declined it....I confess to you, I had the weakness to value the esteem of a dying man, because I reverenced his merit.[21]

The other letter was to his old comrade-in-arms, John Laurens. It is a masterpiece of reporting. It sketched the progress of Arnold's treason from its initial phases to its inglorious end; it gave a full account of André's capture and the execution Hamilton had just been most unwillingly compelled to witness. It is a deeply felt and moving narrative, and achieves the qualities of great prose in the description of the condemned man's last moments and affecting death.[22]

But from this time on Hamilton was no longer to survey his commander-in-chief with the eyes of unquestioning loyalty; a certain coldness faintly tinged their relations, almost imperceptible at first, but to grow secretly in strength until the final explosion.

CHAPTER IX

Hamilton Quits the War

I. DISCONTENT

As THE YEAR 1780 drew to a close Hamilton became more and more impatient with his present situation. He had hesitated in the very beginning at joining Washington's staff. He disliked his secretarial duties heartily, and the years had intensified the dislike. His spirit chafed at this dull routine of correspondence and yearned for posts where glory and power were to be had. Nor did it add to his content that the titled foreigners in the army considered the office of amanuensis, even to the commander-in-chief, somewhat beneath the proper dignity of a gentleman.

As far back as July Hamilton gave vent to these sentiments in a hitherto unpublished letter. James McHenry, his comrade on the staff, was equally discontented with his duties and desired a change. Hamilton obliged him with a note to Congressman Duane, requesting Duane to use his influence to obtain for young McHenry an appointment in the line. "He [McHenry] wishes to quit a station which among foreigners is not viewed in a very reputable light—and to get into one more military." [1] As Hamilton penned these lines he must have smiled sardonically. He was seeking for a friend what he was too proud to ask openly for himself.

By October another element was added to Hamilton's general discontent—a personal resentment against Washington himself. Doubtless this resentment had been growing slowly through the years. It was impossible for two such strong characters to be in constant contact without friction. But Washington, as the superior, and appreciating the worth of his aide's services, could afford to overlook small irritants. Hamilton, the subordinate, chafing at the bit and unwontedly sensitive about his dignity, could not. Each fancied discourtesy was brooded on and magnified. Each imagined slight became a rankling sore. And, in October, the tragic business of Major André brought resentment to a head. Yet even prior to that episode Hamilton had made several

Alexander Hamilton *(Engraved from the painting by Chappel.)*

Alexander Hamilton as an officer of the Continental Army *(From the painting by Charles Willson Peale. Courtesy The Bettmann Archive.)*

Alexander Hamilton *(From the painting by Trumbull.)*

Alexander Hamilton *(Engraved from the miniature by Robertson.*
Courtesy Culver Service.)

Elizabeth Schuyler Hamilton (*Engraved from the painting by Earl.*)

Elizabeth Schuyler Hamilton in old age (*From the painting by Inman.*)

Aaron Burr *(From the painting by Vanderlyn. Courtesy The New-York Historical Society.)*

Thomas Jefferson *(Engraved from the painting by Stuart.)*

John Adams *(Engraved from the painting by Chappel.)*

Alexander Hamilton's home, "The Grange," as it was in 1895
(The J. Clarence Davies Collection. Courtesy Museum of the City of New York.)

discreet attempts to cut loose from what he considered a humiliating subordination.

Hamilton would have much preferred a transfer to a line regiment, such as he had requested for McHenry, but he knew that Washington would never give his assent. A second alternative was a position in the diplomatic service, to which Washington's consent was not necessary. Hamilton looked about him and found something to his liking—the post of Secretary to the Embassy to France. He commenced pulling wires.

So well did he conceal his activities that his future father-in-law wrote him from congress as a piece of fresh news that "you have been mentioned in private conversation to go as Secretary to the Embassy at the Court of Versailles; there is but one obstacle which prevents me from making up my mind on the subject; that you will know when I have the pleasure of seeing you. In the meantime revolve the matter in yours." [2]

It was precisely that "one obstacle" which had decided Hamilton against taking Schuyler into his confidence or utilizing his undoubted influence. For, if he gained the post, the marriage with Eliza must be postponed indefinitely or hurried so that she might go with him. Either course was objectionable to Eliza's father.

The immediate object of the mission was to obtain a loan from France, and Hamilton had time and again urged the loan upon congress as one of the most important steps in stabilizing American finances. He would have been eminently suited for the mission. He had studied the subject matter thoroughly and well, he knew exactly the arguments that would appeal to the French mind, and his connections, through his French comrades-in-arms, were admirable. Yet when congress finally decided on the post, they chose John Laurens instead.

It was a curious business. On December 9th both Hamilton and Laurens were placed in nomination, with other. On December 11th a vote was taken, and Hamilton "on the first ballot had as many votes as Colonel Laurens." [3] On succeeding ballots, however, votes shifted from the minor candidates to Laurens, while Hamilton received no additional strength. Finally his supporters gave up the struggle and Laurens was elected unanimously. [4]

Laurens had not known he was being considered for the mission. He felt that the vote in his favor was rather a vote for his father, who had been president of congress, and certainly he did not wish to oppose himself to Hamilton, his best friend. On receiving the news he promptly declined the post and suggested Hamilton in his place as much better qualified.[5]

Congress paid no attention to his suggestion. On December 17th they nominated James Lovell, who also declined in favor of Hamilton.[6] But congress remained adamant. After some more inconclusive balloting, they tendered the mission again to Laurens. He now felt compelled to accept, writing, however, to Washington that he still considered Hamilton the better choice.

Your Excellency will not be a little surprised to learn, that Congress have determined to send me to France, for the special purpose of representing the present state of our affairs and soliciting the necessary succours. I was in great hopes, that Congress would have availed themselves of the abilities of Colonel Hamilton for these important objects, and that I should have been suffered to persevere in a line of duty, to which I feel myself more adequate. But, unfortunately for America, Colonel Hamilton was not sufficiently known to Congress to unite their suffrages in his favor.[7]

What the true reasons of congress were for refusing Hamilton can not be gleaned from the dry husks of the *Secret Journals*, but one suspects that Schuyler had an active role in the matter, for by this time Hamilton was in the very midst of wedding ceremony and honeymoon.

Even before he knew the final result, Hamilton was already seeking other modes of escape. In the preceding fall he had expressed his views to Washington with the greatest candor. He desired above all glory in battle; his ambition was to raise himself "above mediocrity." This matter of "mediocrity" was a perpetual goad to Hamilton, and now more than ever, when he wished to appear before the powerful Schuyler clan as an equal and not a mere appendage son-in-law. He proposed to Washington that he be given a battalion command in Lafayette's expedition against the British on Staten Island. Washington refused.

On November 22nd he tried again. Though he saw Washington every day, he made his request in writing. "Some time last fall, when I spoke to your Excellency about going to the southward, I explained to you candidly my feelings with respect to military reputation, and how much it was my object to act a conspicuous part in some enterprise that might perhaps raise my character as a soldier above mediocrity. You were so good as to say you would be glad to furnish me with an occasion." Yet when that occasion arose at Staten Island, he had been turned down. Now there was another occasion. An attack was contemplated on Bayard's Hill, to the south. Give him the command of a corps of two hundred men, begged Hamilton, and he would engage to storm and capture the hill.[8]

Washington turned down this request also.

Filled with secret rage, Hamilton tried still another path. Colonel Scammel, the incumbent adjutant, had just been promoted to the rank of brigadier-general, and the post of adjutant-general fell vacant. Hamilton set to work at once.

Among his warmest friends in the army were young Lafayette, then at the height of his popularity, and General Nathanael Greene, whose gallantry and hard-riding strategy were changing the face of the war in the south.

Lafayette respected the young aide's abilities, admired his talents and loved him with all the ardor that a romantic Frenchman can bring to the service. A few months later he was to write to his wife in Paris that "amongst his [Washington's] aides-de-camp there is one man I like very much, and of whom I have often spoken to you; this is Colonel Hamilton." [9]

Greene had also been on the friendliest terms with Hamilton, though he was much the older man. Long after the war, when Greene died, it was Hamilton who delivered his funeral oration.

These two powerful and influential men now tried to obtain the vacant post for Hamilton.

Lafayette wrote to Washington:

If...you were to cast your eye on a man, who, I think, would suit better than any other in the world, Hamilton is, I confess, the officer whom I should like to see in that station.... His knowledge of your opinions and intentions on military arrangements, his love of discipline, the superiority he would have over all the others, principally when both armies shall operate together, and his uncommon abilities, are calculated to render him perfectly agreeable to you.... On every public or private account, my dear general, I would advise you to take him.[10]

Greene followed suit with an equally strong letter of recommendation.[11]

Washington read these communications with astonishment and some perturbation. Hamilton had been seeing him every day, consulting him on every imaginable army matter, handling his correspondence; yet this was his first intimation that his aide desired the post of adjutant. Coming as they did close on the heels of Hamilton's coldly formal letter, it was obvious that there no longer existed a spirit of warmth or trust between commander and secretary.

Much troubled, he replied to Greene: "Without knowing that Colo. Hamilton ever had an Eye to the office of Adj.-General, I did... recommend Genl. Hand for reasons which may occur to you." These reasons were chiefly that the adjutant-general was "the Second officer in that line. It would have been disagreeable therefore, to the present Sub-Inspectors, some of whom are full Colonels, to have a Lt.-Colonel put over them." [12]

To Lafayette he wrote along the same lines, adding that in any event it was too late, since he had already sent along his recommendation to congress. Lafayette, in his anxiety to help his friend, promptly offered to send an express to intercept the fatal letter, but Washington gently pointed out the utter impropriety of such a course.

Hamilton was now in Albany, closeted with the Schuylers and preparing for the long-delayed wedding with Betsy. The Schuylers were determined to do the thing properly with full pomp and circumstance. Everything was bustle and confusion, Betsy was radiant, while General Schuyler and his wife forgot the disappointment of Angelica's furtive elopement in the joy of the present occasion. But the bridegroom wandered preoccupied, dissatisfied with his material position, occupied with plans and stratagems for advancing himself, wondering how each scheme was progressing.

Into this atmosphere of marital expectation Lafayette's report of complete failure dropped like a thunderbolt. He apologized for "interrupting your Amorous occupations" in Albany, but "I have been Angry with you for not permitting my speaking immediately to the General on your Affair—this Curs'd way of a letter you have insisted upon has been the cause of my miscarrying, as the General had innocently put it out of his own power to oblige you." [13]

2. MARRIAGE

On the 14th of December, 1780, Alexander Hamilton and Elizabeth Schuyler were married in the First Reformed Church of Albany.[14] Immediately following the ceremony there was a great reception in the stately Schuyler mansion.

It was a gala occasion. The Schuyler family and all its powerful connections appeared en masse; on behalf of the groom came no family, but his fellow-officers made a satisfactory military show. Young James

McHenry bubbled over with enthusiasm. Filled with the divine afflatus and with more substantial wine, he wrote out a lengthy *Epithalamium* celebrating the marriage of his "dear Ham." [15] The wedding song was not particularly good, but "dear Ham" was properly flattered. "I thank thee Dear Mac for your poetry and your confidence," he wrote in acknowledgement. "The piece is a good one—your best.... You know I have often told you, you wrote prose well, but had no genius for poetry. I retract." [16]

Hamilton had finally achieved security. Allied to the Schuylers he no longer need worry about his own lack of social status or the irregularity of his birth. His friends were legion, and numbered among them were men of wealth, influence and position. He had a reputation for talent, energy and even genius. He was Washington's trusted and indispensable secretary. Most young men of not quite twenty-four would have been well content and would have slipped into a comfortable, pleasant groove.

But not Hamilton. His ambition goaded with relentless scourge. He believed his abilities required a larger arena than Washington's staff. Yet on all sides he had met with failure. The battle-field had been blocked; the office of adjutant-general had proved a mirage; and news now came that the special mission to France had been placed in the reluctant hands of John Laurens. Undismayed, his fertile brain began to revolve new possibilities. But first he must return to camp.

On December 19th he wrote to Washington: "Mrs. Hamilton presents her respectful compliments to Mrs. Washington and yourself. After the holidays we shall be at headquarters." [17]

The first of the year found him back in harness again. Betsy established herself cosily in the circle of official wives, flushed and proud of her new status. Martha Washington knew her well and welcomed her with cordial kindness. But her husband's mind was already fixed on far horizons, of which marriage covered only an inconspicuous sector.

After much debate congress had finally adopted a part of Hamilton's long-advocated plan for reforming the finances of the Revolution. It was decided to replace the inefficient and inept Committee on Finances by a single, responsible financier. The question was—who would be financier?

General Sullivan, member of congress, remembered well how he had been impressed with a series of remarkable proposals he had received from a certain "James Montague, Esq.," who turned out to be Hamilton. James Duane, another member of congress, was reminded of the brilliant essay on government and finance *he* had received. Isaac Sears, of New York, an influential politician, was still busily engaged in reading to his equally influential friends a letter dated October 12, 1780, which this same Hamilton had sent him. In short, crisp sentences it gave the gist of those more voluminous essays. "We must have a Government with more power. We must have a tax in kind. We must have a foreign loan. We must have a Bank, on the true principles of a Bank. We must have an Administration distinct from Congress, and in the hands of single men under their orders. We must, above all things, have an army for the war, and an establishment that will interest the officers in the service." [18]

Sullivan was the first to act. On January 29th he wrote Washington: "I wish your Excellency would be so obliding (when you have Leisure to favor me with another Letter) as to give me Yr. opinion with respect to Colo. Hamilton as a Financier." [19]

Washington was startled. He knew his aide was a remarkable and many-sided young man, but he had never dreamed he was a "Financier." He was also perplexed. Here was another in an endless bombardment of letters animated with a single purpose—to deprive him of the services of his secretary. If he was also annoyed, his generous reply showed no traces of it. "How far Colo. Hamilton, of whom you ask my opinion as a financier, has turned his thoughts to that particular study, I am unable to ansr., because I never entered upon a discussion of this point with him. But this I can venture to advance, from a thorough knowledge of him, that there are few men to be found, of his age, who have a more general knowledge than he possesses; and none, whose soul is more firmly engaged in the cause, or who exceed him in probity and sterling virtue." [20]

With this recommendation in hand, Sullivan put out some quiet feelers among his fellow-congressmen. The results were discouraging, and he so reported to Washington: "I am happy to find your Excellency entertains the Same Sentiments of the virtues and abilities of Colo. Hamilton, as I have Ever Done myself. After I wrote your Excellency I found The Eyes of Congress Turned on Robert Morris, of this City as Financier. I did not therefore nominate Colo. Hamilton as I foresaw that it would be but a vain attempt. I shall this Day nominate him as Secretary of Foreign Affairs in which I think I shall meet the approbation of most of the States." [21]

In this belief he was equally mistaken. The post of Foreign Affairs was likewise given to another. Not enough congressmen were interested in this young man whose political fortunes certain of the New York and New England delegates were so anxious to advance.

3. BREAK WITH WASHINGTON

But by the time this letter reached Washington, Colonel Hamilton was no longer his aide. The long-deferred explosion had taken place. Believing—though without justification—that Washington had blocked his advancement at every step—Hamilton waited only for an opportunity to tender his resignation. On February 16th the opportunity arose—or rather, Hamilton created one.

He was hurrying downstairs in headquarters with an order for immediate delivery to the commissary department. Halfway down, he met Washington coming up.

The general paused. "I would like to speak to you, Colonel Hamilton," he said.

Hamilton nodded. "I will wait upon you immediately, sir." Then he continued down. On the lower floor he found Tench Tilghman and turned the order over to him with instructions for its delivery. His task finished, he started back to attend on Washington. In the hall he ran into Lafayette, who stopped him. They spoke together for a minute or two on a matter of business; then Hamilton excused himself rather abruptly and hastened up the stairs.

Washington was waiting for him on the top landing. His hand was clenched on the balustrade and his face was dark as a thunder-cloud. "Colonel Hamilton," he exploded angrily, "you have kept me waiting at the head of the stairs these ten minutes. I must tell you, sir, you treat me with disrespect."

"I am not conscious of it, sir," Hamilton flared back, "but since you have thought it necessary to tell me so, we part."

Washington stared at him. "Very well, sir," he said coldly, "if it be your choice."

They separated at once, and general and aide departed each for his own room in a passion.

But Washington's anger cooled almost immediately. He called for Tench Tilghman and sent him within the hour bearing the olive branch to his touchy aide. The general had great confidence in his abilities, integrity and usefulness, Tilghman told his friend. Would he not come to see Washington and in a candid conversation heal the difference between them that could not have happened except in a moment of passion?

Hamilton stood his ground, very dignified and severe. With the greatest formality he ticked off the points of his reply.

Tell his Excellency, 1st—that I have taken my resolution in a manner not to be revoked. 2nd—that, as a conversation could serve no other purpose than to produce explanations which must be mutually disagreeable— though I certainly would not refuse an interview if he desired it—yet I should be happy if he would permit me to decline it. 3rd—that, though determined to leave the family, the same principles which have kept me so long in it would continue to direct my conduct towards him when out of it. 4th—that, however, I do not wish to distress him, or the public business, by quitting him before he can derive other assistance by the return of some of the gentlemen who are absent. 5th—that, in the mean time, it depends on him to let our behavior to each other be the same as if nothing had happened.

Whereupon he bowed his astonished friend out of the room. A little later Tilghman returned. Washington had consented to waive any explanatory conversation, and thanked him for his offer to continue temporarily as aide.[22]

What immediately strikes the detached observer is the triviality of the incident that brought about the breach. General Washington, commander-in-chief of all the American forces, harassed beyond the endurance of ordinary men by the gigantic problems with which he had to cope, had flashed briefly into anger at what he believed to be the nonchalant dilatoriness of his aide. The language he used was mild, so mild that a modern "brass hat" would have considered it breathtakingly polite. Certainly he had not expected his imperious young secretary to seize upon the occasion as an irrevocable break.

The anger passed quickly on his side. On Hamilton's it hardened. Yet Washington, with the true humility of a great man, offered the way to a reconciliation. Hamilton refused his offer and thereby inflicted further humiliation upon his chief. Many of Hamilton's biographers view the unfortunate affair merely as the rash, impulsive act of a supersensitive young man whose pride pushed him into a situation from which he could not recede.

Actually, however, Hamilton's explosion was the result of months of cool deliberation. The particular incident that fired the train did not matter. Any pretext would have served his purpose. Hamilton was determined to cut loose from what had become, for him, an intolerable situation. He had tried other means; they had failed. Nothing now remained but to force a clean-cut separation.

It is unfortunate that he did not simply resign, without a quarrel. But he knew how much Washington relied on his pen and ability, and he feared long arguments and pleas to remain. Furthermore, he no longer felt the old affection and loyalty for his chief. There were certain flaws in the great man that irritated him. There had been the André affair. There was Hamilton's own aversion to a subordinate position.

Under these circumstances the following paragraphs from his letter to General Schuyler, written immediately after the event, may be taken as his considered judgment on Washington during this period.

I always disliked the office of an aid-de-camp, as having in it a kind of personal dependence.... Infected, however, with the enthusiasm of the times, an idea of the General's character which experience taught me to be unfounded overcame my scruples, and induced me to *accept his invitation* to enter into his family. It was not long before I discovered he was neither remarkable for delicacy nor good temper, which revived my former aversion to the station in which I was acting, and it has been increasing ever since. It has been often with great difficulty that I have prevailed upon myself not to renounce it; but while, from motives of public utility, I was doing violence to my feelings, I was always determined, if there should ever happen a breach between us, never to consent to an accommodation. I was persuaded that when once that nice barrier, which marked the boundaries of what we owed to each other, should be thrown down, it might be propped again, but could never be restored. I resolved, whenever it should happen, not to be in the wrong. I was convinced the concessions the General might make would be dictated by his interest, and that his self-love would never forgive me for what it would regard as a humiliation.

I believe you know the place I hold in the General's confidence and counsels, which will make it the more extraordinary to you to learn that for three years past I have felt no friendship for him and have professed none. The truth is, our dispositions are the opposites of each other, and the pride of my temper would not suffer me to profess what I did not feel. Indeed, when advances of this kind have been made to me on his part, they were received in a manner that showed at least that I had no desire to court them, and that I desired to stand rather upon a footing of military confidence than of private attachment.

You are too good a judge of human nature not to be sensible how this conduct in me must have operated on a man to whom all the world is offering incense. With this key you will easily unlock the present mystery.

At the end of the war I may say many things to you concerning which I shall impose upon myself till then an inviolable silence.

The picture of the war-worn general, lonely for all his eminence, making overtures to his youthful aide for friendship and understanding, and being rebuffed under the guise of a strictly correct military behavior, has in it elements of almost insupportable pathos.

Yet Hamilton tried to be fair. He acknowledged Washington's good qualities, and realized that he alone could bring the nation to victory. For that reason he would continue to support him outwardly. "The General," he went on, "is a very honest man. His competitors have slender abilities, and less integrity. His popularity has often been essential to the safety of America, and is still of great importance to it. These considerations have influenced my past conduct respecting him, and will influence my future. I think it necessary he should be supported." [23]

In this concluding paragraph may be found the key to what has puzzled certain commentators—Hamilton's later close connection with this man whom he professed not to love.

To James McHenry, Hamilton was much briefer and more unbuttoned.

The Great man and I have come to an open rupture. Proposals of accommodation have been made on his part, but rejected. I pledge my honor to you that he will find me inflexible. He shall for once at least repent his ill-humour.... I wait till more help arrives, at present there is beside my self only Tilghman, who is just recovering from a fit of illness.... Except to a very few friends our differences will be a secret, therefore be silent.

I shall continue to support a popularity that has been essential—is still useful.

Adieu, my friend. May the time come when characters may be known in their true light.[24]

He also wrote to Lafayette and Greene, but in more cautious vein, for fear that the letters might be intercepted and read. To Greene he closed: "This, my dear General, is not an affair of calculation, but of feeling. You may divine the rest, and I am sure you will keep your divinations to yourself." [25]

Washington wrote to no one, nor mentioned the breach to a single person.

Schuyler replied almost at once to his son-in-law. The old general was troubled. He was torn between loyalty to Washington and an unbounded faith in, and admiration for, Hamilton. He was, he wrote, very sorry to hear of Hamilton's resignation; not, he added quickly, "that I discover any impropriety in your conduct in the affair in question, for of that, I persuade myself, you are incapable; but as it may be attended with consequences prejudicial to my country, which I love." He felt, and others felt, that no one could take Hamilton's place in the delicate and important task of aiding and counseling Washington. "Your quitting your station must, therefore, be productive of very material injuries to the public; and this consideration, exclusive of others, impels me to wish that the unhappy breach should be closed, and a mutual confidence restored." [26]

Lafayette also interposed his good offices, but neither Schuyler nor Lafayette nor anyone else could change Hamilton's stubborn determination. He continued to perform his duties with meticulous care until April 30th, when the return of the absent aides made it possible for him to tender his formal resignation.

Now that the matter was thus brought to public notice, Lafayette impulsively informed Washington that he had known about it all along, since Hamilton had confided the secret to him immediately after the occurrence.[27]

Washington received this gratuitous information with a resurgence of his old anger. He had kept silence about the break, as had been agreed upon. Yet now it was evident that Hamilton had not been as regardful of the niceties. "The event, which you seem to speak of with regret," he replied stiffly, "my friendship for you would most assuredly have induced me to impart to you in the moment it happened, had it not been for the request of H——, who desired that no mention might be made of it. Why this injunction on me, while he was communicating it himself, is a little extraordinary. But I complied, and religiously fulfilled it." [28]

Now that Hamilton had resigned as aide, he expected it would be an easy matter for him to obtain that command of an infantry regiment for which his heart had yearned these past three years. Unfortunately, the rules of the service required that such an application must be made direct to Washington. Galling as the request must have been to his pride, Hamilton wrote a formal letter to the general, three days before his resignation became effective, in which he recited his previous service and qualifications and asked for an appointment at least to a command in the light corps.[29]

The application placed Washington in a most embarrassing position. The regular officers of the line were already resentful at being pushed aside to make room for what they considered staff interlopers, whose previous experience consisted chiefly of a certain facility with the pen. In three recent cases, in fact, such superseding appointments had given rise not merely to loud complaints, but almost to mutiny. On the other hand, if Washington refused Hamilton's request, he would lay himself open to the charge that he was revenging himself for earlier humiliations.

With something of a sigh Washington sat down to answer Hamilton as tactfully as possible. He explained the nature of his embarrassment and the reason why he could not grant the application. Such an appointment would, "I am certain, involve me in a difficulty of a very disagreeable and delicate nature, and might perhaps lead to consequences more serious than it is easy to imagine." He ended on a pleading note: "My principal concern arises from an apprehension, that you will impute my refusal of your request to other motives than those I have expressed." [30]

His apprehensions were not ill-founded. Hamilton retorted with a cold insistence that his case was "peculiar and dissimilar to all the former" that Washington had cited. As far as *he* was concerned, he could see no "insuperable obstacles to a compliance." [31]

But Washington remained adamant, and Hamilton found himself out of the army and out of the war.

CHAPTER X

Final Victory

1. THE BANK AGAIN

RESIGNATION FROM SERVICE did not signalize for Hamilton even a temporary period of slippered relaxation or matrimonial dalliance. His restless brain and active mind permitted no intervals of quiet thought. On the very day he resigned as aide, he sealed and placed in the mail an essay addressed to Robert Morris, setting forth a comprehensive plan for placing the shaky finances of the country on a sound and durable basis. It was the third such plan he had composed within the space of a year and a half.

Robert Morris had just been appointed Financier. It was the post for which Hamilton felt himself supremely fitted; all his studies and meditative energies were devoted to considerations of finance and government. Yet he harbored no resentment toward the successful rival. Morris was experienced; he commanded the respect and confidence of the moneyed classes, and Hamilton himself had long before advised his appointment. More than anyone else, Hamilton understood the colossal difficulties that confronted the new Financier in solving the financial problems of the confederation.

These problems were manifold in character. The costs of the war were enormous; there was very little hard coin in circulation; the paper money of congress had depreciated over forty to one; but the chief trouble was that the Articles of Confederation had failed to give congress the power to levy taxes.

As before, the national government was dependent on the iniquitous requisition system for its support and for the support of the war. The states, jealous of each other, reluctant to burden their own citizens, complaining always that their particular allotments were unfair and onerous, failed invariably to supply anything like the sums requisitioned. Had it not been for loans and outright gifts from France, the war would have bogged down long ago; but France was becoming chary of further drains, and it was essential to secure more money, and at once.

How to raise such funds was the burden of Hamilton's lengthy essay. Essentially it was the same scheme he had urged on Sullivan and Duane and on everyone else he could induce to listen. In effect it was the draft of a charter for a bank. In it he embodied the fruits of past experience—crystallized by the Bank of England—with certain modifications of his own conforming to American conditions.[1]

The first step, he advised Morris, was to estimate the country's capacity for revenue. Hamilton himself thought this did not amount to more than $6,000,000 annually. Since the cost of government and the war ran to $10,000,000, there was an annual deficit of $4,000,000, "which deficiency must of course be supplied by credit, foreign or domestic, or both."

There was little chance of borrowing this sum abroad. France, Spain and Holland, the logical lending countries, had troubles of their own. Nor was it easy to borrow from domestic sources, since there was "the want of confidence of a sufficient number of men with sufficient moneyed capitals to lend the sums required, and the want of confidence in those who are able to lend to make them willing to part with their money."

Hamilton was not the man to decry such a situation, or to moralize over it. The timidity of capital was a part of the natural order of things. Therefore it was necessary to tempt it out of its hiding places by the attractive prospect of profits plus safety. Only a national bank could do this. By incorporating it under public and private auspices, it would

erect a mass of credit that will supply the defect of moneyed capital, and answer all the purposes of cash; a plan which will offer adventurers immediate advantages, analagous to those they receive by employing their money in trade, and eventually greater advantages; a plan which will give them the greatest security the nature of the case will admit for what they lend; and which will not only advance their own interest and secure the independence of their country, but, in its progress, have the most beneficial influence upon its future commerce, and be a source of national wealth and strength.

Here in a nutshell is the essence of his philosophy of government: to combine in happy union the private, selfish interests of the men of money with the solid interests of the national government. Hamilton was first and last a political realist and viewed with scornful suspicion any appeal to sentiment or idealism. His own ideas had solidified at the early age of nineteen; they were the same now at twenty-four; they were not to change essentially in the succeeding years.

The bank he proposed was in most respects similar to the ones he had suggested to Sullivan and Duane, only developed in far greater detail and expanded to conform to present needs. Of its capital stock of £3,000,000 no more than half might be subscribed by the United States government and foreign citizens, for "it is of primary importance that the money men among ourselves should be deeply interested in the plan."

The bank would have the power to issue "sight notes" that bore interest at four per cent so that it would be profitable to use them in place of specie. These notes would be legal tender for taxes and customs, but *not* for private debts. The bank would be obligated to lend £1,200,000 to congress at eight per cent, the loan to be amortized over twenty years from governmental revenues. For the duration of its charter—thirty years—no other bank, public or private, might be chartered. Its management was to be placed in a directorate of twelve—eight chosen by the private stockholders, and four by congress.

To most men, the idea that the infant government should burden itself with debts that must eventually be repaid held terrors that could only be overcome by a stern necessity. But Hamilton deliberately welcomed the imposition of such a burden and hailed a national debt as a positive good in itself. "A national debt," he asserted, "if it is not excessive, will be to us a national blessing. It will be a powerful cement of our Union. It will also create a necessity for keeping up taxation to a degree, which, without being oppressive, will be a spur to industry." No other plank in his program was to arouse as much vehement opposition from the *non*-moneyed people as this one.

Having disposed of the financial troubles of the country, Hamilton devoted the remainder of his letter to his second insistent theme—the lack of a strong, central government with sovereignty independent of and superior to the several states. The Articles of Confederation were worse than useless and, unless immediately revised, must inevitably lead to disastrous dissolution. He had a plan for that, too. "It has ever been my opinion," he told Morris, "that congress ought to have complete sovereignty in all but the mere municipal law of each State; and I wish to see a convention of all the States, with full power to alter and amend, finally and irrevocably, the present futile and senseless Confederation." With these terse words he fired the opening gun in the campaign that was finally to end in the Constitutional Convention of 1787 and the adoption of the Constitution.

Morris studied the plan submitted by his youthful adviser. In many points it coincided with his own ideas. Just how much of it he could safely advocate to congress and the country at the present moment was another matter. Nevertheless he wrote back with becoming modesty and flattery. "My office is new, and I am young in the execution of it. Communications from men of genius and abilities will always be acceptable; and yours will always command the attention of Robert Morris." [2]

Some few days after he received Hamilton's letter, Morris submitted to congress a plan of his own calling for a bank. His bank, however, was drawn to a considerably more modest scale, calling for the subscription of a mere 400 shares of $400 each. On the very day he replied to Hamilton congress set its seal of approval on his scheme, and the Bank of North America was duly incorporated and ready for business by the last day of the year. [3]

But the subscriptions proved disappointingly few. The terms of the charter held no such attractive provisions for private investors as those embodied in Hamilton's scheme. Only $70,000 was subscribed to it out of an authorized $160,000, and congress was compelled to deposit with the bank $200,000 it had received as a loan from France to set its machinery in motion. The bank doubtless helped somewhat in financing the Revolution, but only in a small way, and it fell into popular disfavor soon after the end of the war. In 1787 the Bank of North America was compelled to drop its national status and obtain a new charter as a local bank in Pennsylvania.

The times were not yet ripe for either part of Hamilton's twofold plan.

2. THE PATHS OF GLORY

On the day he posted his proposals to Morris, Hamilton packed his gear and quit the headquarters at New Windsor. What was he to do now? Every avenue of activity seemed closed against him. Yet his father-in-law, General Schuyler, was even then working in his behalf. He felt sincerely that Hamilton should go into congress, where his undoubted abilities must prove a valuable asset to that moribund body. On May 30th he wrote from Albany that he was down with the quinsy, "but I propose to attend the [New York] Legislature the latter end of next week, when I shall have the pleasure of seeing you at Fishkill [where the Legislature met] on the Sunday following. I believe you may prepare yourself to go to Philadelphia, as there is little doubt but you will be appointed." [4]

But Hamilton was not yet ready to enter politics. The incurable dichotomy of his nature asserted itself with overwhelming force. The letter to Morris proclaimed the realist, the practical man of affairs; his next step as loudly trumpeted the romantic. Above all else he desired military glory. It was the breath of his nostrils, his strange and particular passion all the days of his life. Before the war ended he must lead at least one charge against a foe and, wreathed in smoke and thunder, redeem the years of bloodless pen and ink.

Politely, but firmly, he turned down Schuyler's well-meant offer, though the rumor of his impending election as delegate to congress had already traveled to the ears of his friend, John Laurens.

I am indebted to you, my dear Hamilton [wrote Laurens], for two letters; the first from Albany, as masterly a piece of cynicism as ever was penned; the other from Philadelphia, dated the second March: in both you mention a design of retiring, which makes me exceedingly unhappy. I would not wish to have you, for a moment, withdrawn from the public service: at the same time, my friendship for you, and the knowledge of your value to the United States, makes me most ardently desire, that you should fill only the first offices of the Republic.... I must confess to you, that, at the present stage of the war, I should prefer your going into Congress, and from thence becoming a minister plenipotentiary for peace, to your remaining in the army, where the dull system of seniority, and the *tableau*, would prevent you from having the important commands to which you are entitled; but at any rate I will not have you renounce your rank in the army, unless you entered the career above mentioned. Your private affairs cannot require such immediate and close attention. You speak like a *paterfamilias* surrounded with a numerous progeny.[5]

This was flattering, but a letter he received about the same time from Lafayette, down in Richmond, was far more to his taste. "Come here, my dear friend," urged the Frenchman, "and command our artillery in Virginia. I want your advice and your exertions." [6]

But the one man who could place him in a military command—Washington—remained obstinately silent, and Hamilton perforce remained in Albany, hugging his useless commission to his bosom and seeking solace for his disappointments in the company of his wife.

Meanwhile the war took a sudden turn. Sir Henry Clinton had depleted his northern forces to support Cornwallis in the south. Washington seized upon the opportunity to propose again to the French his pet scheme for a joint assault by land and sea on New York. Rochambeau favored a similar combined blow in the south, but he finally gave his reluctant consent to Washington's pleadings. It eventually turned out that Rochambeau was right and Washington wrong.

Hamilton, however, was not interested in grand strategy. All he wanted was a chance for a battle in which he held a command, no matter where the battle took place. Hearing of the proposed assault he hastened from Albany to Dobb's Ferry to meet Washington. He arrived on July 4th and found himself cooling his heels while the general busied himself with more important matters. It was too much for his proud, impatient spirit. In an outburst of spleen he practically threw his commission in Washington's face. He was through with the army.

Washington read the curtly cold letter that accompanied the discarded commission and, instead of exploding into anger, he sent Tench Tilghman to Hamilton on another mission of appeasement. As it was later described to Betsy by her husband, Washington "pressed me to retain my commission, with an assurance that he would endeavor, by all means, to give me a command, nearly such as I could have desired in the present circumstances of the army. Though I know you would be happy to hear had I rejected this proposal, it is a pleasure my reputation would not permit me to afford you. I consented to retain my commission, and accepted the command." [7]

Poor Betsy, it seems, had no stomach for her husband's military ardors. Her peaceful honeymoon had been all too short.

On July 31, 1781, Hamilton finally achieved his heart's desire: a battalion, composed of the light companies of the 1st and 2nd New York regiments with two newly raised companies, was formally placed under the command of Lieutenant-Colonel Hamilton and ordered to join the advanced corps of Colonel Scammell. What added to his satisfaction was the fact that his subordinate in command was Major Nicholas Fish, one-time comrade in the debating society at King's College. [8]

While Washington was marshaling his forces for the grand assault on New York, news came from the southern theater of war to prove Rochambeau had been better advised than Washington. For Cornwallis was laying waste to Virginia in utter contempt of Lafayette's small opposing force, while Clinton had received substantial reinforcements from England, making a frontal assault on New York almost impossible of success. Without consulting Washington, Rochambeau ordered Comte de Grasse to the Chesapeake instead of north, as previously arranged.

Washington hastily revised his own plans. With a last reluctant look at New York, the center and focus of his strategy, he determined to march swiftly upon Virginia and Cornwallis. The plan was cloaked in utmost secrecy—neither Clinton in New York nor Cornwallis in Virginia was to know until too late of this major shift of American forces—but Hamilton could not resist notifying Betsy in Albany.

A part of the army, my dear girl, is going to Virginia, and I must, of necessity, be separated at a much greater distance from my beloved wife. I cannot announce the fatal necessity, without feeling every thing that a fond husband can feel. I am unhappy; I am unhappy beyond expression. I am unhappy, because I am to be so remote from you; because I am to hear from you less frequently than I am accustomed to do. I am miserable, because I know you will be so; I am wretched at the idea of flying so far from you, without a single hour's interview, to tell you all my pains and all my love. But I cannot ask permission to visit you. It might be thought improper to leave my corps at such a time and upon such an occasion. I must go without seeing you—I must go without embracing you;—alas! I must go.[9]

The style is stilted and literary; Hamilton was dissembling his eagerness to be off under the stock expressions of a despairing husband whose despair is not too extreme.

The expeditionary force moved by forced marches down to the Head of Elk in Maryland, where they were to take ship across the bay to Yorktown. Hamilton utilized the brief halt to dispatch another note to the young wife who prayed daily for his safe return. "Every day confirms me in the intention of renouncing public life and devoting myself wholly to you. Let others waste their time and their tranquillity in a vain pursuit of power and glory; be it my object to be happy in a quiet retreat with my better angel." [10] Such renunciatory sentiments were strictly for home consumption.

With the landing of the Americans astride the peninsula of which Yorktown formed the tip, Cornwallis found himself in an awkward situation. For this his superior, Clinton, was at fault. Alarmed by Washington's proposed attack on New York and unaware of the reinforcements already on the way from England, Clinton had hurriedly called on Cornwallis to send him every man he could possibly spare and assume a defensive position with the remainder at Yorktown, where the fleet could protect him with its guns and men. Reluctantly and against his own judgment, Cornwallis obeyed and moved into the trap. For a trap it turned out to be. Comte de Grasse defeated the British fleet in a five-day-long battle, and the battered remnants fled toward New York, leaving Cornwallis to his fate. The naval victory permitted a French convoy of troops to enter the Chesapeake safely and join the Americans.

Cornwallis was now wholly hemmed in. Holding a narrow strip of peninsula he had the triumphant French fleet on his sea side, and a combined Franco-American army barring all land approaches. On October 14th the allied forces prepared to storm the defenses of the numerically inferior British. Rochambeau commanded the French. The Americans were in two detachments—one under General Lincoln and the other under Lafayette. Hamilton, with two battalions of light infantry, joined Lafayette. The two friends met joyfully, as they had long eagerly anticipated, on the field of battle.

Hamilton literally quivered with excitement. Here at last was the coveted chance to win the glory he craved. He had quarreled with Washington; he had hazarded his fortune and his future for this single opportunity. Once Cornwallis was beaten—and no one doubted the result—the war would be practically over. Another such opportunity would never again present itself.

The British had constructed two advance redoubts from which a destructive crossfire could be poured on any frontal attack. It was therefore necessary to destroy these redoubts before the main assault began. A French force under Baron de Viomenil was given the task of storming the redoubt on the left; the one on the right was assigned by Lafayette to Colonel Barber.

When Hamilton heard of these dispositions, all seemed lost. The supreme chance had slipped once more through his eager fingers. Pale with fury, he rushed to Lafayette. The command on the right was his, he protested, and not Barber's. Was he not the officer of the day?

Lafayette regretted the situation, but the responsibility was not his. The order had come from Washington and he, Lafayette, was unable to change it. To the over-excited young officer this must have seemed proof positive that Washington was exacting a belated revenge for the humiliation he had suffered at the hands of his former aide.

Grim with determination, Hamilton dashed off a letter of appeal to Washington, claiming the command for his own. With a rare magnanimity, the harried general issued the necessary order superseding Barber with Hamilton. Wild with joy, Hamilton flourished the precious order at Major Fish, his subordinate: "We have it! We have it!" he shouted.[11] What Barber thought of the business is not known.

The attack took place at six that evening. On the left Viomenil's French swept forward. On the right Hamilton's contingent, with Gimat and Fish, crouched in readiness. Night strained slowly over the field, punctuated by flashes of gunfire as the French stormed ahead. To the left of Hamilton, Colonel Laurens, Hamilton's old comrade, led a detachment of eighty men with orders to sweep around the enemy's flank.

The men waited impatiently behind their palisade; and no one more impatiently than Hamilton. The French were already engaged in hand-to-hand conflict when he finally gave the signal. Too short to climb over the palisade, Hamilton ordered a soldier to kneel and present his back. Jumping nimbly on the man's shoulders, he swung himself upon the parapet.[12] Three men, taller than he, climbed to his side. Brandishing his sword and shouting for the others to follow, he leaped down into the ditch. The battalions swarmed after him.

The orders were to use the bayonet only and to make certain of obedience the muskets carried no ball. As they scurried across the intervening ground, enemy sentinels raised the alarm and a ragged storm of bullets greeted them. But it was now quite dark and the fire was wild and undirected. They reached the counterscarp without firing a single answering gun. Hamilton was running well in advance of his men, yet without hesitation he leaped into the moat and was lost to sight. For a moment it was thought he had been hit. But as his men rushed after him he reappeared, formed them in battle line and pressed on with bayonets fixed.

Meanwhile Laurens was attacking simultaneously on the flank. Taken from both front and rear, the British officer, Major Campbell, who had only sixty men to defend the redoubt, hoisted a white flag. Not a gun had been fired by the Americans; of their number nine were dead and thirty-two wounded. Gimat and Barber had been hit; Hamilton came through without a scratch.[13]

As Campbell surrendered, a New Hampshire captain lunged at him with his bayonet, shouting he would revenge upon him the death of Colonel Scammell. Scammell had been slain by the British a few days before under atrocious circumstances. The indignant Americans considered it murder and had threatened to kill any British officer who fell into their hands. But Hamilton threw himself between the enraged captain and his intended victim and sternly ordered the former back. He would have no reprisals, and not a man was injured after resistance ended.[14]

In later days, the story gained color. The Reverend William Gordon, in his embellished history of the war, alleged that Lafayette had demanded the right to retaliate British brutalities upon them, and Washington had given his consent. Whereupon Lafayette ordered Hamilton to put every man in the redoubt to the sword, but Hamilton had nobly refused to obey.[15] Why Gordon should have thus played up an exploit of the man who had once threatened publicly to thrash him is difficult to understand, unless it be that it afforded him an opportunity to malign a greater hate—Washington.

This added tale was to bob up again and again until, as late as August 10, 1802, Hamilton was compelled to publish a denial in the New York *Evening Post*.

The exploit of the redoubts created quite a stir—Viomenil's French had captured the other at a much greater cost in killed and wounded. Hamilton wrote a dramatic report for Lafayette. In it he praised everyone else's gallantry and modestly omitted his own.[16]

Lafayette forwarded the report to Washington with an enthusiastic comment. "I beg leave to refer your excellency to the report I have received from Colonel Hamilton, whose well known talents and gallantry were on this occasion most conspicuous and serviceable. Our obligation to him, to Colonel Gimat, to Colonel Laurens, and to each and all the officers and men, are above all expression." [17]

The capture of the redoubts broke the resistance of the British. On October 16th Cornwallis tried a half-hearted sortie but was easily driven back. Difficulties, however, arose in a new and unexpected quarter. Comte de Grasse had suddenly decided to withdraw his troops within forty-eight hours. Washington remonstrated that he had too few men of his own to assault a fortified position and he would be compelled to raise the siege on the very brink of victory. De Grasse refused to change his mind.

In despair Washington resorted to stratagem. Hamilton and some other officers sauntered over to the British lines under a flag of truce. During a casual conversation—the amicable sortie was supposedly a private venture—they mentioned that an assault in force was in the making; that everyone was so "exasperated at the Conduct of the British to the Southward, that they could not answer for the Consequences, as they did not think they could be restrained by authority

and Discipline." No doubt Hamilton told his story about Major Campbell and the difficulty with which he had been saved.

However, they added deftly, they knew Washington's "humane
Temper," and if the British would surrender now, before the attack
commenced, he would certainly grant them favorable terms and hold
them harmless.[18]

The stratagem worked. A few hours later, Cornwallis proposed an
armistice. On the 18th, commissioners met. On the 19th, Cornwallis
surrendered.

CHAPTER XI

No Taxation with Representation

I. HAMILTON DECIDES ON LAW

WITH THE CAPTURE of Cornwallis the war came virtually to an end. Hamilton had achieved his dearest wish. He had led a successful assault and tasted the sweets of glory. There was no further need to remain in the army. It was time now to remember that he was a married man with a child already on the way, and that, as far as immediate prospects were concerned, he was penniless.

It was true that the Schuylers were amply provided with worldly goods, and the old general would have been only too happy to aid his son-in-law in every possible way. But Hamilton was too proud and independent of spirit to accept financial assistance, except in the most temporary fashion. He grimly intended to provide for his own, and time was pressing.

Some time in November, 1781, Hamilton bade his fellow officers farewell and set out on the long journey to Albany. There he found Eliza big with child and radiant with joy at his safe return. The Schuylers welcomed him affectionately and insisted that the young couple remain in the ample Schuyler mansion until more definite prospects unfolded. Two months later, on January 22, 1782, Eliza gave birth to a son, whom they named Philip in honor of his maternal grandfather. He was the first of a numerous progeny—eight, all told, remained alive.

With the advent of a son the problem of making a living became urgent. But Hamilton knew exactly what he wanted to do. The most honorable, as well as the most lucrative, of the professions open to talent in the colonies had been the law. It became even more attractive in the youthful nation. A substantial number of the older lawyers—especially those with solid practices—had leaned toward the Tory side. They had guessed wrong. Now they paid the penalty for their inability to read the times aright. The enraged patriots of New York enacted a law which required all lawyers to take a stringent oath of loyalty to the revolutionary cause. The test oath automatically disbarred not only the avowed Tories, but even those of lukewarm faith. The ensuing vacuum afforded a splendid opportunity for lawyers of the right persuasion. Also, the Schuyler interests were far-flung and their legal complexities many. Hamilton therefore decided to study law.

In his private reading he had already grounded himself in Blackstone and the treatises of Grotius and Puffendorf. A knowledge of Blackstone alone was sufficient for most purposes in the eighteenth-century state of the law. What he required now was not so much additional theory as a practical acquaintance with the rules of evidence and the daily routine of a working office.

It was March, however, before he was able to buckle down to real work. There had been many interruptions between his return from Yorktown in November and the spring of 1782. For one thing, Philip had been born. For another, he had been compelled to journey to Philadelphia to straighten out his military status in order to retain his commission on a semi-active list.[1] And, in spite of Hamilton's protests, his father-in-law still persisted in his efforts to get him into congress as a delegate from New York.[2]

As he explained to Colonel Meade, his former comrade-in-arms, he was determined to refuse the siren call of public affairs. Private life and the company of his wife and infant son had become more glamorous than fame and glory. At least, so it seemed to him at the moment. "You cannot imagine how entirely domestic I am growing," he wrote. "I lose all taste for the pursuits of ambition. I sigh for nothing but the company of my wife and my baby. The ties of duty alone, or imagined duty, keep me from renouncing public life altogether. It is, however, probable I may not any longer be engaged in it."[3]

On his return from Philadelphia Hamilton moved his family into separate quarters. His legal studies had been intermittent; now he determined to compress the remainder into the shortest possible period of time. Keen young men were quitting the army in droves, though the war was not yet actually over, and hurrying to obtain footholds in the law. Soon there would arise a new hierarchy of lawyers, and it was a case of first come, first served.

Among those already engaged in practice was Robert Troup, Hamilton's old college friend. Troup agreed to make his home temporarily with the fledgling student and assist him in his studies. He moved into Hamilton's house in April, and for three months the two friends devoted every spare moment to the study of the law. Lights burned in Hamilton's room until the early hours of the morning. He was throwing himself into the business with that concentrated energy which he brought to bear on everything he did. As he conned texts and decisions, he jotted down the salient points and later worked them up into an outline in order to fix them more firmly in his memory. This outline was so beautifully logical and schematic that later students borrowed it and made copies for their own use. Eventually it became so popular that subsequent manuals of practice utilized Hamilton's manuscript as a fundamental base. [4]

So diligently did he apply himself that he passed the oral examinations for admission to the bar with flying colors. At the July term of the State Supreme Court he was duly admitted to practice as an attorney-at-law; in October he was granted the additional license of counsellor. Armed thus at every point, Hamilton was ready to begin his professional career.

2. TAX RECEIVER

Yet he was unable to commence immediately with the business of making money, as he had planned. His friends, and those interested in the struggles of the infant nation, now interfered. They considered his talents too valuable to be wasted in private life.

On May 2nd, Robert Morris had already called on him for assistance. New York's quota of the Continental taxes had been set at $375,598. But Morris knew, and everyone else knew, that congress would be lucky to obtain even a substantial fraction of this sum. If any man could approximate the required amount, thought Morris, that man was Hamilton. He therefore offered him the thankless job of Receiver of Continental Taxes for New York. [5]

Hamilton promptly turned it down. He was then immersed in his legal studies, the position was politically unimportant, and the pay was trifling compared with the labor required. [6] But Morris was insistent. Hamilton could handle the job easily as a part-time affair, he explained, and he had misunderstood the terms of compensation. Actually, the fees, based on a percentage of the collections, would amount to about $940 annually. The young lawyer pondered, sought advice and after considerable hesitation agreed to accept the position. [7]

He soon found, however, that collecting money was only part of his duties. He was expected also to exert pressure on a recalcitrant state legislature.

I must request you [wrote Morris in the letter accompanying his commission] to exert your talents in forwarding with your Legislature, the views of Congress. Your former situation in the army, the present situation of that very army, your connections in the State, your perfect knowledge of men and measures, and the abilities which heaven has blessed you with, will give you a fine opportunity to forward the public service, by convincing the Legislature of the necessity of copious supplies, and by convincing all who have claims on the justice of Congress, that those claims exist only by that hard necessity which arise from the negligence of the States.[8]

Morris used fulsome words of compliment, but they were sincerely meant. He had chosen Hamilton as the best man available for the task, because of his ability and because of his supposed influence—*via* Schuyler and others—on the legislature. Nevertheless it was an impossible business, and the outcome proved conclusively to Hamilton how feeble and ineffectual was the confederacy.

The mechanism for collection of the quotas was exceedingly obscure. Congress fixed the amounts, but the manner in which they were to be raised lay wholly in the discretion of the various state legislatures. When and if the latter levied taxes for the purpose of congressional use, local state collectors attempted the gathering. These officials were by and large lukewarm in their efforts, and the citizens on whom the taxes were levied interposed every obstacle that ingenuity could suggest. The receipts, scanty enough to begin with, suffered further shrinkage through ill-defined deductions at the hands of the collectors before they were ultimately, and most reluctantly, turned over to the Continental Receiver.

In New York this unsatisfactory situation was still more complicated by the fact that George Clinton was governor. Stubborn, provincial in character and agrarian in outlook, he represented the small yeoman farmer and the artisan rather than the great proprietor and the seaboard merchant. He was deeply suspicious of any attempt to subtract one jot or tittle of the sovereign powers of the states in favor of a central, consolidated government. One of the first of the so-called democrats, he fought the steady drive toward centralization tooth and nail and did as much as any man to delay its final consummation. Hamilton and he had worked together amicably enough during the war, but now the lines of cleavage were beginning to show plainly. Within a short period the two were to become bitter personal and political enemies.

The state legislature, on the other hand, under the skilful direction of Schuyler and other like-minded men, was more amenable. The year before it had passed Hamilton's pet measure, granting to congress the import duties at the port of New York, to be levied and collected "under such penalties and regulations, and by such officers, as Congress should from time to time make, order and appoint." But this grant was contingent on similar grants by all the other states (which were never made) and had been passed over Clinton's bitter opposition. He saw clearly enough that such control over finances would soon render congress independent of the states.[9] In fact, he plainly notified congress that "they entertain very slender Hopes of their Ability in the present exhausted Condition of the State to comply with any of the requisitions of Congress." [10]

It was under such adverse conditions that Hamilton went to work. He started energetically. On the morning of July 14th he sailed down the river to Poughkeepsie, where the legislature was in session. "I will endeavor by every step in my power to second your views," he informed Morris, "though, I am sorry to add, without any sanguine expectations." [11]

Two days later he landed, forwarded his credentials to Governor Clinton and requested that a conference be arranged for him with a committee representing both houses.[12]

Clinton made the appointment. Hamilton appeared before the joint committee and presented his views as to the necessity of a solid financial system. The committee agreed with him that the present system was most unsatisfactory, yet they refused to consent to his proposed remedy, viz.: that congress be given the power to levy and collect import duties within the state without waiting for a similar grant by the other states. They were so far impressed with Hamilton's arguments, however, that they immediately laid before the legislature and caused to be passed certain significant bills. One of these was an appropriation of £18,000 to Morris's order. But, Hamilton reported to the Financier, "I cannot hope that it will produce in the treasury above half the sum, such are the vices of our present mode of collection." The second measure was far more important. "Both Houses have unanimously passed a set of resolutions, to be transmitted to Congress and the several States, proposing a convention of the States, to enlarge the powers of Congress and vest them with funds. I think this a very eligible step, though I doubt of the concurrence of the other States; but I am certain without it they will never be brought to co-operate in any reasonable or effectual plan." [13] He did not tell Morris that these resolutions had been written by himself.

This was the first call for a convention to alter the Articles of Confederation. It was the beginning of a movement that culminated in the Constitutional Convention of 1787. And Hamilton had been the prime instigator of the call. The way it was handled displayed a particularly clever bit of political maneuvering. Schuyler was political boss of the senate, while certain of his coterie were in the assembly, though heavily in the minority. The majority of the combined houses, and the governor of the state, were firmly opposed to any further centralization of authority in a national government. Yet they permitted this resolution to pass without a dissenting vote. Why? Because Hamilton argued persuasively that such a call did not bind New York to any particular course of action; that the proposed powers to congress were left unspecified; and that, in any event, there was small likelihood that any other state would follow suit. It was, in other words, from Clinton's point of view, a gesture that showed New York's good will and harmed no one. In such fashion did he permit the wool to be pulled over his eyes. It is true that for the moment nothing definite followed, but the resolution proved an entering wedge which Hamilton and his cohorts were to use diligently and with good effect in the near future.

Hamilton was not yet through in his persuasive course. On the very same day an obedient legislature, under the spell of his oratory, passed two other measures. He wrote Morris concerning one of these. "The Legislature have also appointed, at my instance, a committee to devise, in its recess, a more effectual system of taxation, and to communicate with me on this subject." [14] He made no mention of the other measure. It might have affected Morris unpleasantly. The legislature had voted to send Hamilton as a delegate to the Continental Congress.

3. COLLECTIONS ARE POOR

For the benefit of the committee Hamilton devised a hitherto unpublished "Plan of Taxation." He brushed aside the prevailing mode of assessments as inefficient and inequitable. In its place he proposed a series of flat taxes—on land, dwellings, salt, tobacco, carriages, taverns, household servants, lawyers and the privilege of remaining a bachelor. In addition he advised import duties on sundry specified articles. These new sources of revenue, he estimated, would yield more than £100,000 per annum, and would be allocated as follows: the revenue from land would support the state government, the tax on lawyers, the judiciary, while the house tax would go to congress "when the other states shall provide *similar* funds." The salt, tavern and tobacco taxes were "to form together with the Interest on the late emission a fund for a *loan office*." [15]

The scheme, however, was much too comprehensive for adoption. The people of the state, accustomed to former haphazard and easy-going methods of taxation, would undoubtedly have rebelled at such rigorous burdens. Though privately agreeing with Hamilton on a good many of his measures, the committee dared not propose them to the legislature and adjourned "without doing anything decisive." [16]

Meanwhile Hamilton was attempting to collect nebulous funds from elusive state officials for the benefit of congress. The county treasurers, who were generally charged with the collection of taxes, knew nothing of accounting methods, were exceedingly vague as to what part of their revenues belonged to the national government and resented Hamilton as an alien intruder on their cherished prerogatives.

To cap everything, the economic situation in New York was desperate. Hamilton himself admitted it to Morris. Five of its fourteen counties, including its chief source of income, New York City, were still in enemy hands. Two more had revolted and gone Tory, two were ravaged and desolate and four others were partially overrun. Refugees swarmed from the areas of conflict, yet the constant drain of able-bodied men into the army had brought about a serious labor shortage. The state was exhausted, there was a universal scarcity of hard money, and foreign trade was practically non-existent. So that there was some excuse for the difficulty in tax collections.

Yet there is no question that the county treasurers failed wholly in their duty. In vain Hamilton exhorted them in the name of the public emergency, the public faith and the reputation of the state. "While the other States are all doing something," he lashed them in a circular letter, "as a citizen of this, I shall feel a sensible mortification in being obliged to continue publishing to the others, that this State pays nothing in support of the war, as I have been under the necessity of doing the last two months." [17]

This, of course, was purposeful exaggeration. It was true that New York was far down the list of contributors, but there were some states who had in fact paid nothing whatever into the Continental treasury during 1782.

The whole sad story may be read in a manuscript report rendered by the receivers for that year. Congress had assessed $8,000,000 on the several states. Only $422,161.63 had been collected, and of this paltry sum $302,734.84 had actually found its way into the treasury coffers. The states showing the best records were Pennsylvania, Massachusetts, New Jersey, Rhode Island and Connecticut—and *they* delivered approximately *ten per cent* of their quotas! Then the percentages slide rapidly down the scale until New York is reached. Her assessment was $365,000; Hamilton collected $6,250 or less than two per cent!

Yet Virginia, with a quota of over a million, paid not a cent! Neither did New Hampshire, Delaware or North Carolina, while Georgia and South Carolina considered themselves absolved from all contributions because they had furnished certain unspecified supplies to the southern army.[18]

There can be no better commentary on the state of the country's finances than this bald factual record!

It is small wonder then that Hamilton resigned from his ineffectual office in disgust and entered congress, where at least he could agitate more publicly for the sweeping changes in government he had in mind.

When, in August, 1781, he finally notified Morris of his resignation, effective on October 30th, the Financier was sorry to hear it. He hoped, however, that Hamilton would be able to remedy matters in this new field. Mournfully he wrote: "Your description of the mode of collecting taxes, contains an epitome of the follies which prevail from one end of the continent to the other. . . . God grant you success in your views to amend it." [19]

Before he quit, Hamilton felt under an obligation to seek out and recommend a successor. He might have failed as receiver, he thought, because the ruling faction of Governor Clinton had deliberately interposed obstacles in his way. They had resented his appointment and spread rumors that he had accepted the position because he was greedy for the perquisites of office. Very well, then, he thought grimly, let *them* wax fat on the perquisites if only they manage to collect the money.

With these considerations in mind he approached Abraham Yates, Jr., who was Clinton's lieutenant and influential in his party. The tenor of their conversation was reported by Yates in a weirdly composed and hitherto unpublished letter.

About a month or better ago In Conversation with Coll. Hamilton, occasioned as he said that the People Blamed him supposing that he had got this office upon his own Sollicitation: I told him I Never Blamed him that the world was open to him Indeed I thought [it] hard that he should Possess an office by way of Sine Cure with Immediate pay Torn as it [were] from the Loan Office while I had served as Loan Officer Near three years and had R[eceive]d Nothing.

Hamilton managed to convince the disgruntled politician that these rumors were wholly false.

In this Conversation [Yates admitted handsomely] and from letters he showed me it appeared that so far from being the Solicitor that he had Reluctantly taken the office upon him he then told me he Intended to resign the office and would have no pay for what he had Done—Explained to me the views of the Financier that it was Necessary the Receiver of Taxes should be able to Look Continentally, should have Continental Eyes should not be under governmental Regulation &c That the Loan Officer was in some Measure a Provincial officer was under [state] governmental Influence and Regulations &c.

With the path thus cleared, Hamilton proceeded to sound Yates on his views if he were appointed. "He then asked me whether if the Financier appointed me Receiver of Taxes I would promise on Every Occasion to promote the views of the Financier tho It should be against my opinion & should Even I conceive it to be against the Interest of the State. I got a little out of Temper I told him I was an Honest Man and Acted agreable to the Dictates of my Conscience." [20]

His moral indignation cost him the job, for Benjamin Tillotson, evidently more amenable than he, was later appointed to the office.

CHAPTER XII

Hamilton in Congress

1. "THE CONTINENTALIST"

HAMILTON HAD RESIGNED from one public office only to take up duties in another public field. In the Continental Congress, weak and shifting though it was, he had a chance to put his ideas into action. Step by step he had pushed forward his plan for the reorganization of the national government, for the concentration of power into its hands. His procedure had been carefully considered and moved in logical sequence. First came preparatory discussions with those men of influence and conservative wealth who felt as he did; then he wrote a series of solidly constructed letters which passed from hand to hand; these were followed by an overwhelming concentration of argument in the public prints; and finally, he had induced a state legislature (New York), after lulling the opposition into negligence, to issue a call for a convention of all the states. Now his field of activity must shift to the wider stage of congress in order to obtain a general audience of the other states.

The argument in the public prints had been going on for some time. As far back as July 12, 1781, immediately following his resignation from Washington's staff, he had opened fire with a pamphlet which he called "The Continentalist." Anonymously initialed A.B., it was the first of a series of six that appeared at regular intervals; the last appeared on July 4, 1782, just before he was elected to the congress they so vigorously defended.

The six essays brought into the open the private campaign Hamilton had theretofore conducted. They hammered a single theme and a single argument: the theme was implicit in the name—Continental nationalism; the argument was—*More power to Congress!* [1]

The fatal defect in the Articles of Confederation, he insisted over and over again in recurring leitmotiv, was "a want of power in Congress." It was this lack which was responsible for all the ills that afflicted the unhappy country and dragged the war out interminably. There were

those who were jealous of increasing the central power and professed
to see despotism in the offing. Yet they failed to see that, "as too much
power leads to despotism, too little leads to anarchy, and both, eventually, to the ruin of the people." It was ridiculous to believe, however,
that the federal system of the United States could ever lend itself to
despotism. The danger was all on the other side—"that the members
will be an overmatch for the common head."

People were wont to blame congress for all their troubles. "That
body," he acknowledged, "is no doubt chargeable with mistakes, but
perhaps its greatest has been too much readiness to make concessions of
the powers implied in its original trust."

Since congress was perhaps justifiably fearful of assuming these implied powers, grant them openly. He laid down a minimum program:
the right to regulate trade and impose import duties, to appoint its own
officers, to levy a land and poll tax and to become the custodian of
the western territories.

He examined in detail the question of the regulation of trade by
congress. He had read and digested Adam Smith, but he followed a
cautious middle course between the old mercantilism and the heady new
doctrine. "To preserve the balance of trade in favor of a nation ought
to be the leading aim of its policy." New openings of trade, beyond the
resources of private capital, "may require no small assistance, as well
from the revenue, as from the authority of the state." Yet, he added
quickly, he was utterly opposed to any governmental interference with
prices, or to any restrictions on private enterprise. With this doctrine
Hamilton laid the foundations for that happy combination of benevolent assistance to business and laissez-faire as to the administration of
that business which was later to become the fundamental tenet of the
Republican party.

In the sixth and final article he sought to prove for the benefit of
the landed interests and "the laboring poor" that they too ought to
advocate federal control of external commerce. Otherwise, he argued,
each state, fearful of imposing import duties lest commerce be diverted
to other, and freer, ports, would be compelled to rely on heavy land
taxes for revenue. This in turn would raise the prices of food and other
necessities, and the poor would suffer both from the higher cost of
living and unemployment because of foreign competition.

He was trying to placate the small farmer and the laborer who felt
that any system of federal regulation must necessarily be in the interests
of the trading and mercantile classes. But he never was very good at

such a task. His usual logic deserted him, and his argument limped. Inconsistencies crept in. In almost the same breath he maintained that "the laboring poor" would be thrown out of work and that labor would in fact command too high a price, "to reduce which, and not to increase it, ought to be a capital object of our policy." Such a significant admission was not calculated to gain any adherents among the laborers, no matter how welcome it might be to the merchant and manufacturer.

His peroration, however, was at once a stirring vision and a warning.

There is something noble and magnificent in the perspective of a great Federal Republic, closely linked in the pursuit of a common interest, tranquil and prosperous at home; respectable abroad; but there is something proportionably diminutive and contemptible in the prospect of a number of petty states, with the appearance only of union, jarring, jealous, and perverse, without any determined direction, fluctuating and unhappy at home, weak and insignificant by their dissensions in the eyes of other nations.

2. FIRST BATTLES IN CONGRESS

Now that Hamilton was in public life again, with the zeal of the proselyte he tried to induce his friends to adopt the same course. Of these the most valued was John Laurens; and Hamilton wrote him on August 15, 1782:

Peace made, my Dear Friend, a new scene opens—The object then will be to make our independence a blessing—To do this we must secure our *union* on solid foundations; an herculean task and to effect which mountains of prejudice must be levelled! It requires all the virtue and all the abilities of the Country. Quit your sword my friend, put on the *toga*, come to Congress. We know each other's sentiments, our views are the same; we have fought side by side to make America free, let us hand in hand struggle to make her happy.[2]

Alas, Hamilton was never to have Laurens' aid in the task at hand! Even while this moving appeal was on its way to him, that gallant young soldier died in an obscure skirmish far to the south.

The death of John Laurens was a great blow to Hamilton. The youthful southerner had been as close to him as a brother. They had shared camp and bivouac together; they had laughed and discussed; they had fought the same battles and plodded through the same rain and snow. Youth and high spirits had made them comrades; never again was Hamilton to achieve such close-knit intimacy with any man.

While Laurens, had he remained alive, would have hailed Hamilton's determination to enter congress with delight—for he had urged just

such a course on him months before—another of that group who had
made up the "family" viewed the matter with a jaundiced eye. This
was James McHenry, now retired from the army and practicing medicine in Baltimore.

From that vantage point he wrote cynically to Hamilton: "I see that
the good things of this world are all to be purchased with money and
that the man who has money may be whatever he pleases." Drop politics, he advised, and practice your law instead. "A few years practice
at the bar would make you independent, and do you more substantial
good than all the fugitive honors of Congress. . . . The moment you
cease to be a candidate for public places, the people will lament your
loss and wait with impatience till they can persuade a man of your
abilities to serve them. In the mean time, you will be doing justice to
your family." [3]

Hamilton paid no attention to this worldly and realistic advice. He
wound up his affairs as receiver, received his license as counsellor, and
wrote to Lafayette, who had gone to France soon after the victory at
Yorktown:

I have been employed for the last ten months in rocking the cradle and
studying the art of *fleecing* my neighbors. I am now a grave counsellor-
at-law, and shall soon be a grave member of Congress. The Legislature,
at their last session, took it into their heads to name me, pretty unanimously, one of their delegates.

I am going to throw a few months more in public life, and then retire
a simple citizen and good *paterfamilias*. I set out for Philadelphia in a few
days. You see the disposition I am in. You are condemned to run the
race of ambition all your life. I am already tired of the career, and dare
to leave it. [4]

Whatever his intentions at the moment, Hamilton, no less than Lafayette, found it almost impossible ever to drop quietly out of the race.

On November 25, 1782, Hamilton attended his first session of the
Continental Congress in Philadelphia, just four months after he had
been elected.

He found that futile body in a state of morbidity. Day after day the
straggling members adjourned because they had no quorum. Some of
the states had not even a single delegate present. Business stagnated,
and the few conscientious members thought longingly of their distant
homes.

New York was as much an offender as the others. On July 22nd her legislature had chosen five delegates—Hamilton, James Duane, William Floyd, Ezra L'Hommedieu and John Morin Scott. Duane, L'Hommedieu and another delegate named Phelps were hold-overs from the previous session. But the trio were waiting only for the arrival of Hamilton and Floyd so that they could go home. As for Scott, he took his election lightly, and had no intention of assuming his post.

The reasons for such lackadaisical conduct on the part of the delegates were simple. Few men relished the idea of posturing in a vacuum, of debating endlessly and passing resolutions that more often than not were ignored by the states. Practical politicians preferred to sit in their own state legislatures, where authority was a substance, not a shadowy phantom. In addition, living expenses in crowded Philadelphia were high, and often the states forgot to pay the meager salaries accredited to the delegates.

Duane and Phelps were among these forgotten men. Not a penny in pay had been received by either of them since they had taken their seats. New York's finances were not in good shape and Governor Clinton availed himself of the excuse to starve out her representatives. The less power these friends of Schuyler had the better he liked it. In the case of Phelps, a poor man personally, he succeeded.

Duane wrote Clinton a letter of protest in his behalf. Poor Phelps, he said, was

terribly distressed; without Cloaths fit for the season: without money or Credit to pay for his board: and leaning on the scanty support which the exhausted purses of your Delegates can afford. What is to be done for him? I hope your Excellency may be able to remit the supply for which I took the Liberty to write; otherwise I must hasten home. It is my wish to wait for Relief as I suppose Col. Hamilton and Col. Floyd will be here pretty early in the ensuing month—but propriety must yield to necessity.[5]

When Hamilton and Floyd finally did arrive, they found that the three resident delegates had carried Duane's threat into execution. Failing to receive remittances from Governor Clinton they had already decamped, leaving New York wholly unrepresented in congress. And Scott had not come at all.

Yet Hamilton was undismayed. He had entered congress for definite purposes, and he proposed to carry them through against all obstacles. On the day following his arrival, he rose to make his maiden speech. The point at issue was minor, but Hamilton was testing his ground. The speech was favorably received, and he was forthwith given a committee assignment.[6]

For ten days he marked time, studying his fellow members and waiting for an opening to unlimber his guns. On December 6th his opportunity came. The little state of Rhode Island furnished the ammunition.

The confederation was bankrupt. The interest on the domestic debt was in default; there was no money for the army and the war. The requisitions of congress upon the states were either evaded or quietly ignored. Finally, after a long and bitter struggle, state after state reluctantly agreed to allocate a portion of its import duties to congress. Even New York, swayed by Hamilton's eloquence and Schuyler's influence, had entered its assent over Clinton's opposition. But to make the assignment of funds effective a unanimous vote of all the states was required. And Rhode Island, smallest and most individualistic of them all, defiantly refused to yield. On November 30th its legislature met and flatly rejected the proposition.

Hamilton rose on the floor of congress and moved two resolutions. The first called on the states to fill their allotted quotas under the old requisition system. The second proposed that a congressional deputation be sent to Rhode Island to persuade her to grant the import duties. Both resolutions passed.[7]

Rhode Island, in its rejection, had issued an argumentative blast. Hamilton was made chairman of a committee to answer her objections. James Madison of Virginia and Fitzsimmons of Pennsylvania were associated with him. Hamilton wrote the reply at top speed: the manuscript is in his handwriting, with a few corrections and emendations by the other members. The report is a cogent and powerful document.[8]

He took up Rhode Island's objections in detail. To the first, that the proposed duty would bear hardest on a commercial state like Rhode Island, he countered with the utmost frankness "that every duty on imports is incorporated with the price of the commodity, and ultimately paid by the consumer, with a profit on the duty itself as compensation to the merchant for the advance of his money." Hamilton was perfectly correct, of course, though later tariff advocates have invariably soft-pedaled this particular argument. In fact, Hamilton himself, when writing "The Continentalist" for general public consumption, had argued exactly to the contrary. He then had insisted that the merchant, in order to meet competition, "must... content himself with smaller profits and lose the value of the duty, or at least part of it." [9]

To the second objection that there would be introduced into the state "officers unknown and unaccountable to them," he retorted that the congress had already introduced "unknown" post-office officials without any great harm.

To the third objection that if congress had the power to collect moneys without being accountable to the states for its expenditure, it would become independent of them altogether, Hamilton readily admitted the principle, though pointing out that the time *was* limited and coextensive with the debts contracted during the war.

Hamilton's Memorial, in conjunction with other more devious forces, finally persuaded the stubborn legislature of Rhode Island to acquiesce in the imposition of the tax. A great victory had seemingly been won. But the victory turned to ashes with a surprising *volte-face* by Hamilton's own state—New York.

On March 15, 1783, New York, instigated by Governor Clinton, repealed the grant of its imposts made in 1781, thereby throwing the whole system once more into the discard.

Why this reversal? The reasons are not hard to find. When the grant was originally made, it was considered a mere gesture—the war was still on, trade non-existent, and the port of New York was in British hands. Now, however, the war was practically over, and New York City, through whose harbor flowed the goods that fed the entire state, and most of Connecticut, New Jersey and Vermont as well, would soon be recovered. Why, argued the proponents of States' Rights, should this immensely profitable revenue be permitted to slip out of our hands? The duties, paid chiefly by consumers of other states, should go to swell New York's coffers and thereby lessen the tax burdens of the natives. The argument was devastatingly successful, even among Schuyler's followers, and Clinton won his point. National considerations yielded to strictly local aggrandizement.

Hamilton was temporarily defeated, but he had gained nation-wide attention by his spectacular fight. The eyes of the merchants, the hard-money men, the creditors and the nationalists turned to him as their spokesman and champion. Schuyler, in Philadelphia to observe the struggle, felt he had made no mistake in his son-in-law. Pridefully he wrote to Eliza, who had remained in Albany with little Philip:

Participate afresh in the satisfaction I experience from the connection you have made with my beloved Hamilton. He affords me satisfaction too exquisite for expression. I daily experience the pleasure of hearing enconiums on his virtues and abilities from those who are capable of distinguishing between real and pretended merit. He is considered, as he certainly is, the ornament of his country, and capable of rendering it the most essential services, if his advice and suggestions are attended to. In short, every true patriot rejoices that he is one of the great council of these States.[10]

3. CHAMPION OF NATIONALISM

In the meantime, financial worries obtruded themselves on the young congressman. His scanty funds were exhausted, and the state had failed, as usual, to remit the small allowance it granted its delegates. On December 18th Hamilton was compelled to send an urgent letter to Clinton.

"I shall very shortly be out of cash, and shall be much obliged to you to forward me the State allowance. It will answer as well in Mr. Morris' notes as specie, provided the notes have not more than a fortnight or so to run. It will be better if they are due. A disappointment in this will greatly embarrass me." [11] Clinton obliged with a remittance on December 29th and Hamilton was enabled to carry on.

On the floor of congress he became immediately one of its most active figures. Motions and resolutions poured from him in an endless stream, directed chiefly toward two definite goals—themselves inextricably intertwined—finances and centralized power. He was placed on innumerable committees—in many instances as chairman—and his facile pen was constantly employed in drafting reports, memorials and bills. Madison, already noted for scholarly and philosophic thought, worked with him. At this period Madison was almost as strong a proponent of a vigorous national government as Hamilton.

For years congress had solemnly voted its requisitions on the respective states, and received in return anywhere from five to ten per cent of the amounts demanded. As a result every state was burdened with a staggering mythical debt for the unpaid balances. Ever the realist, Hamilton moved on December 20th to reduce the requisitions. He contended "that the exorbitancy of the demands produced a despair of fulfilling them which benumbed the efforts for that purpose." But the members preferred to continue to vote sums which they knew could never be collected, and "the motion meeting with little patronage was withdrawn." [12]

As Hamilton sat through the daily sessions of congress, he realized more and more the utter futility of the proceedings. They were a shadow body shadow-boxing with realities. While they orated and passed resolutions, the ultimate power resided in thirteen jealous and particularistic state legislatures. He unbosomed himself to Clinton.

"Every day proves more and more the insufficiency of the Confed-

eration. The proselytes to this opinion are increasing fast, and many of
the most sensible men acknowledge the wisdom of the measure recommended by your Legislature at their last sitting." [13] This measure was
the call for a convention of the states pushed through by Schuyler and
Hamilton. Clinton, reading the letter, must have found it slightly
ironical.

Yet Hamilton refused to be discouraged. Congress *must* be made
strong and substantial in spite of itself. On January 27, 1783, James
Wilson of Pennsylvania introduced a resolution calling for the establishment of general funds to be collected solely by congress. Instantly
Hamilton was on his feet to speak in favor of the resolution. He distinguished sharply between the permanent revenue, universal and uniform throughout the United States, with congressional-appointed collectors in charge, advocated by Wilson's bill, and the present system
of separate funds drawn at the will of each state from whatever sources
it wished and through its own collectors. The first, he argued, was
simple, direct, invariable and required only a few officials. The second
was complicated, uncertain and peculiarly vicious in that the state
collectors, popularly elected, were more interested in maintaining their
vote-catching popularity than in collecting the revenues. [14]

The speech was forceful, but left most of the members unimpressed.
They did not share Hamilton's aversion to popular elections, and they
still feared a national government financially independent of their native
states.

On the following day Hamilton replied to their objections. The bone
of contention seemed to be congressional as against state-appointed
revenue collectors. He attacked again and with vehemence the inef-
ficiency of the state officers. Then, heated with debate, he let slip
a remark that revealed the true reason for his insistence on federal
collectors. "It was expedient," he declared, "to introduce the influence
of officers deriving their emoluments from, and consequently interested
in supporting the power of Congress."

Madison, who agreed with him, noted however that

this remark was imprudent & injurious to the cause w[hi]ch it was meant
to serve. This influence was the very source of the jealousy which rendered the States averse to a revenue under collection as well as appropriation of Congress. All the members of Congress who concurred, in any
degree with the States in this jealousy smiled at the disclosure. Mr. B[land]
& still more Mr. L[ee], who were of this number took notice in private
conversation, that Mr. Hamilton had let out the secret. [15]

As indeed he had. Hamilton had not the true politician's knack of concealing his inner motives. On the few occasions when he condescended to placate opposition he despised, he displayed a singular ineptitude. This was the reason he was always to remain a leader of leaders instead of a leader of the rank and file of his party and his country.

Sensing the storm which Hamilton's frank avowal had raised against the resolution, Madison offered a compromise amendment, omitting for the present the objectionable phrase that the funds "were to be collected under the authority of Congress." [16]

The opposition was not to be placated. They raised further objections. Why, they demanded, should foreign and domestic creditors be paid equally in specie? Foreign creditors, yes; but the domestic debts arose chiefly from the loan of money to congress in depreciated currency or from the sale of goods to the army at exorbitant prices. It was neither necessary nor just to recoup them in full.

Hamilton rose in protest against this new assault. He denounced any plan "that made but partial provision for the public debts." The attempt was thoroughly dishonorable, and he warned the opposition that the domestic creditors, resentful of discrimination, would flock to the state legislatures and exert their influence in favor of a general fund for congress.[17] He did not say that he himself was to be foremost in mobilizing the embattled creditors in a compact pressure group.

The emasculated bill, its teeth drawn by Madison's amendment and other changes, finally came up for a vote on February 12th. The appointment of the collectors—the most controversial issue—was "left to the States, they to be amenable to & under the controul of, Cong[res]s." In this form the measure passed, only New York and Pennsylvania dissenting. Hamilton grimly voted *nay*.[18]

Neither he nor Wilson was finished with the fight. On February 18th Hamilton proposed, and Wilson seconded, that "whereas Congress was desirous that the motives & views of their measures s[houl]d be known to their constituents in all cases where the public safety w[oul]d admit, that when the subject of finances was under debate the doors of Cong[res]s s[houl]d be open."

The motion was obviously political and recognized as such by his fellow members. On no other occasion, either in the Continental Congress or in the Federal Convention, did Hamilton evince such a tender solicitude for public sessions. In this instance he expected that the numerous creditors residing in Philadelphia would flock into the chamber and frighten the recalcitrant legislators into compliance. But congress, reported Madison, "adjourned it being the usual hour & the motion being generally disrelished." [19] When it finally came up for a vote, it suffered overwhelming defeat, only Pennsylvania voting *aye*. Even Hamilton's colleague, Floyd, voted against and thereby lost New York's ballot in a tie.

Though defeated in this maneuver, Hamilton returned stubbornly to the attack on the main issue, seeking to reinstate the emasculated provisions of Wilson's original measure. These were two—that congress should have the right to import duties for the life of the public debt, instead of the twenty-five year limit actually passed, and that congress should appoint the collectors. But for all his relentless hammering, and Wilson's able assistance, both motions were definitely lost on March 11th.[20]

It was April 18th when the final report on the funds was passed by a debate-weary congress. Every state voted for it, except bitter-end Rhode Island and New York divided. Hamilton, too, was a bitter-ender. As Madison acidly explained to Jefferson, "the latter vote was lost by the rigid adherence of Mr. Hamilton to a plan which he supposed more perfect."[21]

4. MUTINY

Other problems pressed upon the attention of congress and the country. American commissioners were in Paris negotiating a peace treaty, and news traveled slowly back to an impatient nation. The army was in ferment. It was still under arms, idle, its pay many months in arrears, while civilian legislators bickered and quarreled over sources of revenue as it starved. In a little while the discontent took on the proportions of a mutiny.

By February 13th Hamilton was already aware of the critical state of affairs. He wrote to Washington about it.

It appears to be a prevailing opinion in the army that the disposition to recompence their services will cease with the necessity for them, and that if they once lay down their arms, they will part with the means of securing their rights. It is to be lamented that appearances afford too much ground for their distrust.

Sympathetic though he was with the needs of the army, he seized the opportunity to employ them as a means of forcing through the measures he advocated in congress. He continued:

The claims of the army urged with moderation, but with firmness may operate on those weak minds which are governed by their apprehensions more than their judgments, so as to produce a concurrence in the measures which the exigences of affairs demand.... So far a useful turn may be given to them. But the difficulty will be to keep a *complaining* and *suffering* army within the bounds of moderation.

This Your Excellency's influence must effect. In order to [do] it it will be advisable not to discountenance their endeavours to procure redress, but rather by the intervention of confidential and prudent persons, to take direction of them.

He advised Washington, however, to remain aloof and hold the confidence of both army and the country, so as to "enable you in case of extremity to guide the torrent, and bring order perhaps even *good* out of confusion."

In a postscript he added: "General Knox has the confidence of the army and is a man of sense. I think he may be safely made use of." [22]

Washington was sorely troubled by the receipt of this letter. He had not known the government was in such financial distress. As for the army, he wrote back that "I shall pursue the same steady line of conduct, which has governed me hitherto.... The just claims of the army ought, and it is to be hoped will have their weight with every sensible legislature in the United States, if Congress point to their demands." [23]

This was on March 4th. Eight days later the situation had changed considerably for the worse. Hamilton's private views on the use to be made of the army discontent had somehow leaked out, and those with axes to grind promptly seized upon them and spread them abroad.

Washington was now thoroughly alarmed. An anonymous emissary (later discovered to be Major John Armstrong, an aide of General Gates) suddenly appeared in camp. At once wild rumors began to circulate: for example, "that it was universally expected the army would not disband until they had obtained justice; that the public creditors looked up to them for redress of their own grievances; would afford them every aid, and even join them in the field, if necessary; that some members of Congress wished the measure might take effect, in order to compel the public, particularly the delinquent States, to do justice...." There was even vague talk of a *coup d'état* to establish a monarchy and offer Washington the crown.

Washington was certain there was "something very mysterious in this business," and begged Hamilton to urge upon the delegates of the reluctant states to do something for the army speedily and without delay. "If any disastrous consequences should follow, by reason of their delinquency," he ended solemnly, ". . . they must be answerable to God and their Country for the ineffable horrors which may be occasioned thereby." [24]

Hamilton was not unduly perturbed. He calmly admitted that

I have myself urged in Congress the propriety of uniting the influence of the public creditors, and the army as part of them, to prevail upon the States to enter into their views. I have expressed the same sentiments out-of-doors. Several other members of Congress have done the same. The meaning, however, of all this was simply that Congress should adopt such a plan as would embrace the relief of all public creditors, including the army, in order that the personal influence of some, the connections of others, and a sense of justice to the army, as well as the apprehension of ill consequences, might form a mass of influence in each State in favor of the measures of Congress.[25]

But Hamilton and those who thought like him had evoked forces they could not control. It was a dangerous business arousing the passions of starving, desperate men with arms in their hands and hardened by years of bloodshed. Anonymous pamphlets appeared magically in the Newburgh encampment announcing a great meeting of army officers for forceful action instead of meek petition. A great throng of angry men assembled. But Washington acted with decision. Before any agitators could start to work he appeared before the crowd with a moving plea for patience and trust in the good faith of congress and their country. At first they listened in sullen silence; then his words took effect and they promised grudgingly not to act in haste.

Back in Philadelphia congress was stirred to feverish action by the news of the semi-revolt. It hastily adopted a resolution introduced by Hamilton praising Washington and the army alike for their restraint, and voted to grant the officers five years' full pay in the form of interest-bearing securities.

But the storm had been only temporarily allayed. Washington warned Hamilton that the army had a well-founded suspicion that congress intended using them "as mere puppets to establish continental funds, and that rather than not succeed in this measure, or weaken their ground, they would make a sacrifice of the army and all its interests." [26]

It has since been charged, on the one hand, that Hamilton was using the army as a threat to frighten the states into granting plenary powers to congress and funds for the benefit of the public creditors; and on the other hand, that he intended the army to overthrow congress and set up a military monarchy with Washington as its head.

The first charge is partly true. He openly avowed as much. But he also wanted justice to be done for the army itself. The soldiers were also creditors of the country, and the records disclose how he fought and voted in their behalf.

The second charge has no support in the evidence. Disgusted as he was with the timidity and provincialism of the delegates he nevertheless was the chief instigator and exponent of the slogan: "More power to Congress!" Yet the assertion that Hamilton intended Washington and himself to be the men on horseback spread widely and found easy belief. The rumor came to Washington's ears and he hinted about it to Hamilton, who replied: "I do not wonder at the suspicions that have been infused; nor should I be surprised to hear, that I have been pointed out as one of the persons concerned in playing the game described." [27]

The army disorders, temporarily allayed, soon blazed up again. Several detachments, encamped near Philadelphia and at Lancaster, refused to be discharged from the army without immediate payment of their claims. On June 15th they petitioned congress to that effect. The petition was disregarded. Three days later the disaffected battalions joined hands and threatened to enter Philadelphia to enforce their demands. The city fell into a panic. The most alarming rumors spread. Shops and homes would be looted, banks robbed and congress slaughtered in its seat.

Hamilton reacted promptly. A military demonstration in force was no part of his schemes, though he ought to have foreseen it as a probable result. The very thought of an untrammeled and riotous soldiery interfering with the orderly processes of government was abhorrent to him.

He rose in congress with a resolution denouncing the menacing attitude of the troops and calling for effectual measures "for suppressing the present revolt and maintaining the dignity and authority of the United States." [28] The frightened delegates passed it in a hurry and gave Hamilton the doubtful honor of taking the necessary measures in conjunction with the Pennsylvania officials to suppress the mutiny.

Even as Congress sat in the State House and voted on the resolution, three hundred men led by seven sergeants surrounded the building, rifles loaded and bayonets sinister in the sun. They gave congress twenty minutes, they shouted, to meet their demands; otherwise they'd enter and clear them out.

The members did not wait out the twenty minutes. They adjourned immediately and scattered out of the beleaguered building to a running accompaniment of jeers and catcalls. Hamilton, smarting at the indignity, gathered his committee and went hastily to see John Dickinson, president of the state of Pennsylvania, and demanded that he call out the state militia. Dickinson, however, and his assembly, were not altogether sorry to see congress taken down a peg. Besides, the mutineers had seized the arsenals and were in an ugly mood. Dickinson therefore temporized and evaded. He would, he claimed, first have to find out if the militia would be *disposed* to take up arms against regular soldiers. Fuming, Hamilton demanded that he set down his position in writing. Dickinson refused.

Whereupon congress packed up and decamped to Princeton, out of reach of the rioters. Once there, Hamilton moved that Major-General Howe be ordered with loyal troops to Philadelphia to disarm and arrest the mutineers and hold them for trial.[29] He also reported on the result of his negotiations with the Pennsylvania Executive Council. In scathing language he denounced their attitude, charging that they refused to act "till some outrage should have been committed by the troops." And they meant by *outrage*, he added bitterly, not merely a repetition of insults to congress, but actual physical violence to its members.[30]

The mutiny was finally settled without the shedding of blood. The mutineers retired before the report of marching loyal troops. Congress shipped funds for their pay to Lancaster and agreed to a full pardon.

But Hamilton remained furious at the evasive tactics of the Pennsylvania council; he had been all for immediate force to counter force. There was something to be said for Pennsylvania's course: it was most doubtful if its militia would have fought the regulars, and in any event a pitched battle would have set the whole army ablaze. Hamilton, however, and many with him, considered that the dignity of the United States had been hopelessly compromised.

Such a storm was raised that the Pennsylvania Council felt compelled to issue a statement justifying itself. Hamilton countered with a public letter to Dickinson defending congress and attacking Pennsylvania.[31] The city of Philadelphia was disgruntled that it had lost the presence and lucrative business of congress. It set rumors in motion insinuating that Hamilton had been influenced by ulterior motives in removing congress to another state.[32] But we have Madison's word for it that Hamilton had opposed the ignominy of flight and had yielded only to the expostulations of other and more timid members.[33]

CHAPTER XIII

Conservative Lawyer

I. LAST BATTLES IN CONGRESS

THE LONG EXHAUSTING war had finally ended. Victory perched on the tattered banners of the colonists. Faced with an armed coalition of Europe and America, England reluctantly yielded in the first defeat she had suffered in many decades. But with her accustomed cleverness she sought to drive a wedge between the newly independent United States and her allies. To that end she intimated to the American commissioners at Paris, headed by Benjamin Franklin, that France was deliberately delaying peace until her own interests could be taken care of, and that better terms might be arranged for the Americans in separate, secret negotiations.

Though such separate action violated the arrangements between France and the United States as well as the express instructions of congress, the commissioners readily assented to the British proposal and in secret sessions wrote a treaty which in truth was exceedingly favorable to the Americans. Consciences were salved by a proviso that the treaty was not to become effective until a general peace had been signed, but included in its terms was a special, secret clause relating to the disposition of the Floridas that ran expressly counter to the interests of our ally, Spain.

When the news of the secret treaty reached congress, a lively debate sprang up. There were those who were furious with the commissioners for their breach of faith. Others defended them as vehemently. Hamilton rose to placate the angry passions. He urged coolness and moderation on both sides. From the beginning he had opposed the congressional resolution directing the commissioners to seek French advice before negotiating with the British; but, he said, since the resolution *had* been passed, Franklin and his associates must be denounced for signing the preliminary peace articles without at least having first disclosed them to France. Still more strongly did he denounce the secret special clause. Yet such denunciation must not be made public, otherwise both internal and external dissensions could not be avoided; in fact, he proposed that the commissioners be publicly commended, but that the separate clause be immediately communicated to the allies.[1] In the main this moderate advice was adopted.

New problems arose fast and thick. Peace, for some time to come, proved almost as tumultuous a proceeding as war. A nation had to be organized. An army had to be demobilized and a peacetime military establishment properly prepared. Hamilton was called upon to draft a plan for the latter.

Hamilton's report, when finally submitted, was a carefully elaborated scheme providing for a Continental standing army of six regiments, paid out of federal funds, and augmented by a universal militia of "all free male inhabitants in each State, from twenty years to fifty, except such as the laws of each State shall think it proper to exempt." Hamilton would have much preferred a larger federally-controlled army, but he was well aware, as he told Washington, that "our prejudices will make us wish to keep up as few troops as possible."[2]

Within the militia itself he set up a curious division, reminiscent of the ancient Greek practice: those "who are willing to be at the expense of equipping themselves" could join the cavalry and be classed as dragoons; those who could not afford the expense or were not willing, would plod along as lowly infantry. He also advocated the establishment of foundries, arms and powder factories, but disapproved of military academies at this particular time for the training of professional officers.[3] The plan was read, commended and then filed without action with a host of other abortive reports.

Meanwhile trouble was brewing in connection with one of the crucial clauses of the treaty of peace. The treaty specifically set forth that no legal obstacles be placed in the way of the collection of debts owed by American to British merchants from before the war, and that further confiscations of Loyalist property by the states be prohibited. In addition, congress was to recommend to the states that any British or Loyalist holdings, already confiscated, be restored to their former owners.

It was easier to write such clauses into a treaty than to enforce them. A British agent in New York reported to his superiors that while the Americans generally acknowledged that the peace terms "were much more liberal than they had any right to expect, at the same time they rediculed [sic] that Article which says that Congress should recommend to the different Assemblys the restoration of ye property of the

Loyalists, well knowing that no attention woud be paid to it by the
Assembly's; and Col. Hamilton, a member of Congress, acknowledged
to me that he was of the same opinion." [4]

Though Hamilton knew the temper of his countrymen on the subject, he nevertheless determined to press the fight for the enforcement
of these clauses. It was a matter of national good faith and honor with
him; besides, he foresaw that the Loyalist class—conservative, propertied
and solidly substantial in the main—would prove the heartiest and most
effective supporters for his national program.

On May 30, 1783, he introduced a resolution "that the several states
be required, and they are hereby required to remove all obstructions
which may interpose in the way of the entire and faithful execution
of the 4th and 6th articles" of the peace treaty; and further, that the
states consider liberally the fifth recommendatory article relating to
restitution.

Richard Peters of Pennsylvania was immediately on his feet to move
for a commitment of the resolution, which in effect would defeat it
without a record vote. Hamilton heatedly demanded that the delegates
place themselves on record on Peters' motion. They did so with a will;
only Hamilton's vote was in the negative, and he saw his resolution go
into the limbo of discarded things. [5]

So hot was the sentiment against either debt collections or restoration
of confiscated properties that Virginia peremptorily instructed its
delegates in congress "neither to agree to any restitution of property
confiscated by the State, nor submit that the laws made by any independent State of this union be subjected to the adjudication of any
power or powers on earth."

Congress mildly reproved this fiery defiance with a statement that
"the commissioners of these states cannot retract without a violation of
the national faith." [6] With such a verbal obeisance to the letter of the
treaty, congress gingerly dropped the whole matter. The questions at
stake were to remain a plague spot in British-American relations for
many years to come, and were only settled, in half-hearted fashion, by
the Jay Treaty of 1794.

Defeated all along the line, Hamilton somewhat despairingly returned
to his main thesis—that a new and closer-knit confederation be formed
between the states.

On June 30th he formally introduced a resolution which, after re-
citing the shortcomings of the Articles of Confederation, called upon
the states to appoint delegates to a convention "with full powers to

revise the Confederation, and to adopt and propose such alterations as to them shall appear necessary; to be finally approved or rejected by the States respectively." [7]

Congress was lukewarm, if not wholly hostile. The resolution was referred to a committee, where it rested quietly. When, on September 2nd, it was momentarily brought into the light of day, a motion to postpone further action indefinitely passed overwhelmingly, and the resolution retired to its slumbers again.

Hamilton had been in congress for some six months now. He had gone there with certain definite objects in view, and he had fought vigorously and persistently to put them into effect. Now, as he took stock of his accomplishments, the net results were disappointingly slim. His major resolutions had gone down in defeat; the states continued triumphant, sovereign entities, and congress remained in a slough of quaking futilities, without power, without respect. It was time for him to depart: he had a wife and child to support and a livelihood to gain.

He notified Governor Clinton of his intention on May 14th. "I wish two other gentlemen of the delegation may appear as soon as possible, for it would be very injurious for me to remain much longer here. Having no future views in public life, I owe it to myself without delay to enter upon the care of my private concerns in earnest." [8]

So low had congress sunk in the public estimation that no one wanted the doubtful honor. New York had elected five delegates; only Floyd and Hamilton thought enough to attend, and Floyd retired early from the scene, leaving Hamilton solitary and alone.

No one having showed up to relieve him, Hamilton reiterated his request on June 1st. He wanted to go home, and quickly. [9] Much as Clinton disliked a national congress and suspected even its subservience, he felt it was necessary for New York to be represented, if only to keep a check on its actions. He wrote sharply to the three officially elected delegates who were still at home. "It is the business of the Delegates to make such Arrangements among themselves as to prevent the State being unrepresented, as I can have no agency therein but barely that of informing You of what ought not to have taken place." [10]

Duane was finally shamed into making his appearance at Princeton on July 16th. As soon as he came, Hamilton left for Albany. He was through with congress. At the time he left congress was merely the shadow of a shadow. Only six of the thirteen states had any delegates

present at all, and hardly one of even these states was fully represented.[11]

His fellow-members viewed Hamilton's going with regret. He had
made a deep impression during his term of office. Both those who
agreed with him and those who did not acknowledged that he was to
be reckoned with in the future of the nation. McHenry, who had not
long before advised Hamilton to flee politics as he would the plague,
had himself yielded to the contagion and was now in congress as a delegate from Maryland. He hastened to pass on to his friend the good
things he heard. "The homilies you delivered in Congress are still recollected with pleasure," he informed Hamilton. "The impressions they
made are in favor of your integrity; and no one but believes you a
man of honor and republican principles. Were you ten years older
and twenty thousand pounds richer, there is no doubt but that you
might obtain the suffrages of Congress for the highest office in their
gift." [12]

2. TORY DEFENDER

Hamilton had impatiently counted the days until he could be back
again in Albany with his "beloved Eliza" and his infant son. But now
that he was there he found himself once more marking time. Even before his return he had realized that the sleepy little Dutch town was not
the proper place in which to build up a successful law practice. New
York City, thriving metropolis and center of trade and commerce,
beckoned to the lawyer.

But it was necessary to wait for British evacuation before he could
enter the promised land. That event was skilfully delayed on various
pretexts by the British commander, Sir Guy Carleton, and it was not
until November 25th that the Americans were able to march triumphantly into the long-occupied city.

Close on the heels of the army and the government came a horde of
eager lawyers, avid for the lucrative business and fat fees of the
metropolis. Hamilton was among the briefless barristers; so were Aaron
Burr, Robert Troup, John Jay, Rufus King, Egbert Benson and others,
soon to make a brilliant company surpassing in learning and political
influence any similar group in the entire nation. The Tory lawyers,
disfranchised, disbarred and fearing physical vengeance from an embittered people, sadly departed with their protectors and left the field
clear for the newcomers.

Hamilton opened his law office at 57 Wall Street and employed as his managing attorney a young lawyer named Balthazar de Heart. Almost at once he forged to the head of his profession. His practice was equally lucrative and successful. The far-flung Schuyler interests served him well, and the substantial merchants of the community flocked to him. But in the beginning his chief income came from claims arising out of war damages and the confiscations of Loyalist property.

The problem of the Loyalists who had elected to remain after the British withdrawal and face the wrath of their victorious countrymen was to agitate New York State for years to come. More than any other, New York had held a considerable Tory element during the Revolution. In certain sections, notably in Long Island, the Tories had actually been in the majority. They had exulted openly in the British occupation and had lived, for the most part, easy, comfortable lives while their patriot neighbors had suffered and starved.

It was natural, therefore, that the resentment of those who had been driven from their homes and occupations should have risen to fever pitch. Governor Clinton declared with many an oath that he would "rather roast in hell to all eternity than be dependent upon .Great Britain or show mercy to a damned Tory." [13] Following suit, the state legislature proposed to deal with all Loyalists in the most ruthless fashion. Whenever and wherever they could be found, they were arrested, imprisoned, fined, banished, and their goods declared confiscated.

In 1779 a Confiscation Act had been passed by acclamation, declaring "the forfeiture and sale of the estates of persons who had adhered to the enemy."

With the coming of peace, the implacable hatred intensified rather than decreased. Governor Clinton personally led the pack. Confiscations were on a wholesale scale, and thousands of Loyalists flocked to Nova Scotia and New Brunswick, forsaking their country and their homes rather than submit to the persecutions of the victors.

Hamilton viewed these proceedings with considerable indignation and alarm. Even in wartime he had advocated moderate and sensible measures respecting the Tories. It was his contention that they should be punished only if and when they gave active aid and comfort to the British. Now that the war was over, he believed strongly that the best interests of the nation demanded conciliation and oblivion for past sins.

Hamilton was an outsider, still without deep roots in his adopted land. As such he was capable of an objectivity hardly possible to those whose homes had been burned or occupied by the enemy. Furthermore, he recognized in the Loyalist group a type of society in which he felt most at ease. He had joined the rebellion initially because that way pointed fame and opportunity and because the merchants of Nevis and St. Kitts among whom he had passed his boyhood had been out-spokenly critical of British measures. Yet it must not be thought that Hamilton at any period was a radical or a revolutionary by nature. All his instincts were on the side of property, respectability and con-servatism. He advocated a strong national government because he was convinced that only under such a centralized power could property rights be adequately safeguarded, and the excesses of the mob held in check. He never concealed his contempt for that "mob," including in the term the mass of propertyless people. The famous outburst of later days represented a settled conviction. "The people, Sir; the people is a great *beast!*"

The loyal followers of King George for the most part were the gentry, the wealthier merchants, the substantial lawyers and ministers, the doctors and the leaders of the provincial society. The mass of the revolutionaries, on the other hand, were chiefly the debt-ridden small farmers and artisans, radical in thought and action. To them the revolu-tion was not merely a political shift, but a social and economic upheaval as well.

The more conservative patriots, who had fought only for a break with England, were deeply concerned at the rising tide of radicalism. They were men of property themselves and wished for no such do-mestic upheaval. Yet they recognized the fact—and Hamilton, Schuy-ler, Duane, John Jay and Washington were among them—that they were approaching a critical period. Either "men of good will"—such as themselves—must rule, or the "mob" would gain control and render insecure those sacred property rights which Hamilton believed to be the very life-blood of society.

At this particular moment the "mob'" in New York had both a majority and control. Dangerous rumblings were heard from some of the other states. It was necessary, therefore, to mobilize immediately all the forces in opposition. Hamilton realistically recognized the essential kinship and community of interests between the outlawed Tories and the conservative patriots. If the radicals were to be checked, it was necessary to call on the Tories for aid. And to render their aid effective their wealth and influence must be left undisturbed.

Hamilton had first protested to Clinton in June against further con-fiscations, putting his argument on the legal ground that such for-

feitures directly contravened the treaty. On August 5th he went down
to New York City to attend to some legal business for Schuyler. The
city was still in British hands, but Hamilton was able to mingle freely
with the frightened Loyalists. He wrote back that "some late indict-
ments in our State have given great alarm here. Many who have all
along talked of staying now talk of going. We have already lost too
large a number of valuable citizens." [14]

A week later he found that the picture had worsened. "The spirit
of emigration has greatly increased of late," he reported. "Some violent
papers sent into the City have determined many to depart, who hitherto have intended to remain. Many merchants of second class, characters of no political consequence, each of whom may carry away
eight or ten thousand guineas have I am told lately applied for shipping
to convey them away. Our State will feel for twenty years at least,
the effects of the popular phrenzy." [15]

The treaty rights of the Tories were being disregarded by a venge-
ful legislature, the recommendations of congress contemptuously thrust
aside. The argument ran that the British themselves had violated the
treaty, inasmuch as they had not yielded the frontier posts as agreed
and had carried away with them slaves and other property of Americans. The British retorted that the Americans had been the first vio-
lators and pointed especially to the continued persecution of the
Loyalists.

On March 17, 1783, New York aimed its heaviest blow against the
pariah Tories. It passed a law that any citizen whose property, while
inside the British lines, had been occupied by any person other than its
lawful owner, might sue such occupant for damages. Even a British
order permitting the occupancy could not relieve the trespasser from
liability.[16]

It was this so-called Trespass Act that gave Hamilton his first great
opportunity as a lawyer and as an opponent of the Tory-baiting mania.
Elizabeth Rutgers, a widow, with her son, Robert, owned a brewery
and dwelling house on the north side of Maiden Lane in New York
City. When the British occupied the town in September, 1776, the
patriotic Mrs. Rutgers and her son fled with the retreating American
Army.

The British took possession of the brewery and used it for public
purposes and under military control until June 10, 1778. On that date
the commissary-general granted a license to the premises to two British merchants, Benjamin Waddington and Evelyn Pierrepont, at an

annual rental of £100. They entered into possession on September 28, 1778, and remained as tenants under the British license until March 17, 1783.

Mrs. Rutgers recovered her property when New York was finally surrendered. As far as the record shows, the brewery suffered no substantial damage during its period of occupancy. Yet she brought suit at once under the provisions of the Trespass Act against Waddington, who had rashly elected to remain behind after the British left. Pierrepont, it seems, had been prudent enough to flee the town. She claimed the rental value of the brewery and the dwelling house for the full period of four and a half years.

The case was the first of its kind and attracted widespread attention. If the plaintiff won her suit, there would be a flood of similar actions, with total damages running into millions of pounds.

The patriot bar flocked to the widow's assistance. An imposing and formidable array of counsel appeared in her behalf, including Robert Troup, John Lawrence and William Wilcox, with Egbert Benson intervening as the attorney-general of the state.

The matter at issue seemed simple. The facts were undisputed and the statute clear and definite. In addition, popular opinion was overwhelmingly in favor of Mrs. Rutgers and passionately aroused. She was a widow who had suffered because of her adherence to the revolutionary cause, and that added to the public tumult. It would prove rather dangerous business to advocate the cause of the unfortunate Waddington. Yet Hamilton promptly undertook the defense, in association with Brockholst Livingston and Morgan Lewis. He threw all the powers of his intellect and his political sagacity into the task. He considered the suit more than a mere legal issue; he intended to transform the courtroom into a forum from which he would denounce once and for all the whole business of Tory-baiting and treaty violation.

On August 7, 1784, the case came on for a hearing before the Mayor's Court of New York City. Sitting on the bench were James Duane, then mayor of the city and Hamilton's staunch friend and political ally, and Richard Varick, the recorder. Interest was intense; passions super-heated. Everyone was certain that Hamilton had assumed a hopeless defense; that there could be only one outcome.

Hamilton studied the complaint carefully and interposed a demurrer—in effect, a plea which assumes the truth of the allegations of the complaint and denies that they are sufficient in law for a judgment.

The demurrer was founded on two legal pleas. The first alleged that the property of the plaintiff had been abandoned by her and seized by the British general for the use of his army "as by the laws customs and usages of nations in time of war he lawfully might do," and that he had later licensed the property to "British Merchants under the protection of the said army."

The second plea alleged that after the passage of the Trespass Act, a treaty of peace had been signed and ratified with Great Britain whereby all claims for damage arising out of the war were mutually renounced between the nations and their respective subjects and citizens. Since Waddington was a British subject and Mrs. Rutgers an American, the complaint must be dismissed.[17]

Briefs were submitted by both parties, and the demurrer was argued before a packed and hostile courtroom. Hamilton hammered away at his two salient points—that the rules of warfare justified Waddington, and that the treaty specifically overruled the Trespass Act. In support of his first position he cited the law of nations, the English authorities, and Vatel, Grotius, Molloy, Domat and Barbeyrac, the great international lawyers. On the second—and vital—point, he took the bold position that a treaty constituted the supreme law of the land, overriding all conflicting local laws, and that congress had full power to enter into a compact which would bind by its terms all the states. Facing the judges squarely, he warned them in impressive tones that the disposition of the case would "remain a record of the spirit of our courts and will be handed down to posterity." [18]

Benson, for the plaintiff, rose in rebuttal. New York, he argued, was a sovereign state, not to be bound by congressional treaty or an inchoate law of nations. The statute was specific and must control.

On August 27th Duane read the decision of the court on Hamilton's demurrer. The little courtroom was again jammed to the bursting point. Partisan passions had been aroused in the interim to explosive proportions. It would prove an exceedingly dangerous business to dismiss the complaint. Duane sympathized wholly with Hamilton's point of view, yet he dared not decree complete victory. His decision was therefore a compromise.

On the major point of Hamilton's argument he expressed himself as in agreement. A congressional treaty, he declared, was the supreme law of the land, and "we are clearly of opinion, that no state in this union can alter or abridge, in a single point, the fœderal articles or the treaty." But in the instant case, he went on rapidly, he must find against the defendant, Waddington. The court had discovered a technical loophole—since "the rights of the British general ... could only be communicated by his *immediate* authority; the agency of the Commissary General in disposing of those rights, was an act of usurpation." Therefore Waddington was in effect illegally domiciled, and the case must be remanded to a jury for an assessment of damages.[19] A jury was later impaneled and brought in a verdict on September 2nd for the plaintiff in the sum of £791 13s. 4p.[20]

Curiously enough, most historians have failed to note this final disposition of the matter and have written down the case of Rutgers *vs.* Waddington as a complete victory for Hamilton and his client.

Duane thought that he had done very well. He had placated the adherents of the poor widow, yet at the same time he had laid down a fundamental doctrine which ought to cement the union and save the vast majority of the Tories from further harassment.

But the upholders of state sovereignty and the populace detected the maneuver at once. There was an explosion of wrath. Huge mass meetings denounced both Duane and Hamilton. The newspapers screamed violently. The state legislature passed a vote of censure against Duane and his court, and called on the Council of Appointment to be more careful in the future what manner of person it appointed to office.[21]

Successive legislatures wholly disregarded Duane's *obiter dictum*, insisting that the Trespass Act should continue to be enforced. It was not until 1788, when the Federalists won control in New York, that the then legislature finally repealed all statutes that were inconsistent with the treaty.

The controversy spilled over into pamphlets, broadsides and the newspapers. This shift in forum enabled Hamilton to display his talents on a wider stage and more effectively than in the confines of a courtroom. Under the pseudonym of Phocion he addressed two pamphleteering letters "To the Considerate Citizens of New York, on the Politics of the Time, in Consequence of the Peace." [22]

In the first letter he pleaded for justice and moderation in the treatment of the Tories. He raised his voice in protest against the artifices of politicians who attempted to inflame the passions of the people and to inculcate a spirit of revenge, cruelty and bloody persecution. Turning to the broader legal ground, he argued that the laws against the Tories were a violation of the treaty with Great Britain, and that congress had the right to bind the states by its action. New York had accepted the benefits accruing from the treaty; it must therefore accept the liabilities. Otherwise England would be justified in voiding the entire treaty and hold permanently the line of forts and trading posts within the boundaries of New York which she had agreed to yield.

The pamphlet aroused a tremendous flurry of excitement among the Clintonians. They rushed replies into print. The best of these was signed Mentor and was written by Isaac Ledyard, personally and politically close to Governor Clinton. He denied the validity of Hamilton's arguments and upheld the irresponsible sovereignty of New York. He ended with an excoriating attack upon Hamilton for his aspersions on the personal motives of his political opponents.[23]

Hamilton's second Phocion letter was an answer to Mentor. It was an attempt at conciliation. While reiterating his former position on the general principle, he apologized for the injudicious warmth of the first pamphlet, alleging that his anger had been directed only against a small group who were seeking their own advantage in the current agitation. By implication he omitted Mentor and Governor Clinton from this group.

The storm did not abate. The conservatives backed Hamilton, but the vast number of small farmers, mechanics, artisans and little merchants were determined to crush the Tories. To them Hamilton was the head and front of the agitation in their favor. So great was the resentment against him that certain hotheads proposed to challenge him successively in a series of duels until a well-aimed bullet finally removed this Tory champion from their path. But Ledyard heard of the mad scheme and denounced its perpetrators so effectively that the plan was dropped.[24]

Hamilton was later advised of the plot and took the occasion to thank Ledyard for his intervention. He exercised his personal charm with such success that Ledyard forsook the ranks of the Clintonians and enrolled himself as a follower of Hamilton.

Though Hamilton had gained the bitter ill-will of the masses, even to the point of personal threats, there were compensations. The Tories were properly grateful, and they had both legal business in abundance and money enough to pay substantial fees. He soon found himself overwhelmed with cases. He had no time even to reply to important letters, he wrote Gouverneur Morris, since "a legislative folly has afforded so plentiful a harvest to us lawyers that we have scarcely a moment to spare from the substantial business of reaping." [25]

3. FORENSIC SUCCESS

The "business of reaping" proved especially lucrative in Hamilton's instance. The case of Rutgers *vs.* Waddington had made him famous. His name and talents were on everyone's tongue—either for good or for ill. In a single bound he rose to the top of the New York bar—a position he was to maintain throughout his career. Only Aaron Burr could compete with him for that honor. At this early period they were friendly enough rivals. They fought each other amicably or appeared on the same side of an argument as associated counsel. Burr devoted himself exclusively to the practice of law and did not bother as yet with politics. The ominous cloud of future discord still lay invisible on the distant horizon.

Besides this flood of Tory business, Hamilton took full legal charge of the vast Schuyler interests. His old college teacher, Dr. Peter Middleton, employed him as counsel in some litigation over a will. He examined titles, submitted briefs on land patents, drafted wills and mortgages and tried cases that ranged from a petty cattle trespass to the defense of a murder indictment. His fees were usually modest, and whenever possible he preferred a compromise to extended court action so as to save his clients heavy legal expense.[26]

James Kent, himself an outstanding lawyer and judge, spoke of Hamilton's "clear, elegant, and fluent style, and commanding manner. He never made any argument in court without displaying his habits of thinking, and resorting at once to some well-founded principle of law, and drawing his deductions logically from his premises. Law was always treated by him as a science founded on established principles. His manners were gentle, affable and kind. He appeared to be frank, liberal, and courteous in all his professional intercourse." [27]

The merchants and large landowners of New York came to rely on Hamilton as a sound, conservative lawyer who believed in "established principles" and who possessed considerable political influence as well. Therefore, when the project of a bank was agitated, it was to Hamilton that its proponents came for advice.

The country at large had still not come around to his views on the necessity of such an institution for the concentration of capital and the extension of credit. The agrarians were suspicious of banks and bankers as instruments designed to crush them into helpless dependence on the machinations of a money economy. The nation's first bank—the Bank of North America—had been founded in Philadelphia through the efforts of Robert Morris and Hamilton. There had been some talk of a second bank in that thriving town, but the scheme fell through. Neither New York nor Boston had a bank.

John Barker Church, who had married Angelica Schuyler, Eliza's younger sister, was definitely interested in a proposition to establish a bank in New York. He was essentially a money man, and everything he touched had turned to gold coin. After his elopement with Angelica under an assumed name, he had managed to obtain the Commissary for the French Fleet and made himself a tidy fortune. With this sum he returned to England while the war was still on. The business of the duel had been cleared up, and he resumed his former name and station. His brilliant, witty and socially-minded wife went with him. English projects proved just as successful as the provisioning of the French fleet. With a splendid indifference to the war that still raged, or from what source he made his money, Church sent his surplus funds to America to be invested for him by Hamilton. Now that the war was over, his thoughts turned more and more to America as a field of operations and a home. And the prospect of a bank tempted his business instincts.

He asked Hamilton to buy secretly for him 250 shares in the proposed new bank of Pennsylvania, but the scheme collapsed. The idea of a New York bank, under his control, also engaged his interest. From Paris he wrote to Hamilton about the idea and his plans for the future. "We are taken [sic] measures to vest our Property in America by exporting from here and England a large quantity of ready money Articles and I hope we shall be at New York June or July." [28]

Such a bank as he—and Hamilton—envisaged, would be one based on "established principles." In other words, a bank that would do business chiefly with merchants and substantial business men, with a capital made up wholly of money, bonds and commercial paper. But Robert R. Livingston, chancellor of the state and a large landowner to boot, had just petitioned the legislature to grant a charter for a land bank based on wholly different principles.

A land bank would accept mortgages on land as collateral for subscriptions to its stock and would deal largely with loans based on the security of acres and farms instead of bills of lading and commercial notes. Its clientele would therefore be drawn chiefly from the agrarian, debtor class.

The merchants rose promptly in arms against such a perversion of first principles. Their vested rights in the monopoly of all financial transactions would be threatened by such a radical move. Hamilton rose in arms with them. The reasons he gave his brother-in-law, Church, for his opposition were extremely candid.

In the first place it would interfere with Church's own project. In the second place, it would interfere with "the commercial interests of the State." Therefore he started "an opposition to this scheme and took occasion to point out its absurdity and inconvenience to some of the most intelligent merchants, who presently saw the matter in a proper light and began to take measures to defeat the plan."

These measures included a petition to the legislature against granting a charter to the land bank and a movement to organize a money bank instead. Hamilton was asked to subscribe to the latter. "I was a little embarrassed how to act," he told Church, "but upon the whole I concluded it best to fall in with them, and endeavor to put the business upon such a footing as might enable you with advantage to combine your interests with theirs." [29]

Unluckily for Church, who wanted a controlling interest in any new bank, Hamilton hesitated so long that the initial subscribers had already incorporated in the charter a provision giving a maximum of seven votes to any individual stockholder, no matter how large his holdings. Once Hamilton had decided to purchase shares for his brother-in-law, however, he managed to persuade the subscribers to amend the constitution to grant an additional vote for each block of five shares owned above ten.

With this clearly understood, Hamilton engaged himself in the scheme, drafted the constitution and application for a charter, piloted them safely through the legislature and became one of the directors of the newly organized Bank of New York. On the other hand, he used his influence to such good effect that the proposed land bank was denied a similar charter.

Associated with Church in his original scheme for a bank of his own was Jeremiah Wadsworth, Connecticut merchant and politician, then also in London. When Church heard of Hamilton's activities in his behalf, he wrote back approvingly: "The establishment of the New York Bank has determined Wadsworth and myself to give up all Thought of carrying our banking Plan into execution, but I should be glad to be interested in the Shares of that Bank if they are not disposed of." [30]

Hamilton not only managed to reserve for them large blocks of stock, but he later made room for them in the board of directors as well. Even after he resigned from active participation because of the pressure of other affairs he continued to be strongly interested in this creation of his and worked diligently to establish the bank as a pillar of conservatism and a prop of the commercial and industrial interests in New York against all opposition during the ensuing turbulent years.

The years 1784 and 1785 slipped by rather quietly. Hamilton busied himself with consolidating his position in the law and in the substantial bosom of society. He cast only passing glances at the political field, devoting his attention to the business of making a living and rearing a family.

A second child was born on September 25, 1784—a girl whom they named Angelica in honor of Eliza's sister. Six more followed at fairly regular intervals—Alexander, James Alexander, John Church, William Stephen, Eliza, and finally, on June 2, 1802, Philip, named after Philip, their first-born, who had died tragically in a duel a little while before.

Hamilton also interested himself in the manumission of slaves, which appears to have been a pet scheme of a good many prominent New Yorkers. A society was formed to work for this laudable object, with John Jay as its first president. Hamilton was made chairman of a committee to devise ways and means, and he proposed a resolution that the members of the society begin by freeing their own slaves. Such direct action found no favor with the humanitarian members and the resolution was quashed. Hamilton himself, though it has been asserted to the contrary, continued to own slaves all through his life.[31] However, he remained a member of the society until his death and was annually re-elected as one of its counsellors.

His relations with his father-in-law, Philip Schuyler, grew even warmer with the passage of the years. Eliza herself was happy and adored her brilliant husband. Schuyler beamed benignly on the pretty picture of marital happiness. He never missed an opportunity to voice his approval of his favorite son-in-law. He wished, he told Eliza, that her brother and his son would copy "the virtues and good humours" of "your amiable husband." [32]

But this idyllic interlude was necessarily brief. The state and nation were in flux; events were plunging headlong toward a showdown battle between contending forces. Hamilton snuffed the battle from afar, like a veteran war horse. In a short time he was to spring into action and abandon the practice of law for the more strenuous and sterner conflict of politics.

CHAPTER XIV

Preliminary Maneuvers

I. HAMILTON PLANS HIS STRATEGY

BY THE BEGINNING of the year 1786 conditions in the country at large had become generally chaotic. Foreign trade was at a standstill, agriculture was in the throes of a depression, the farmers owed staggering debts to the city merchants and bankers, starving ex-soldiers were compelled to sell their Continental scrip—issued to them at face value in payment of their services—at a ratio of fifteen to one to speculators, interest on public loans was not only heavily in arrears but there seemed no prospect of ever meeting it, and hard money was almost wholly out of circulation.

To meet the admittedly distressful situation and yielding to the clamor of multitudes of debtors for relief, thirteen sovereign states tried thirteen different methods of alleviating matters. These generally took the form of printing paper money as fast as the presses could run it off and declaring these unsupported issues legal tender. In addition, "stay" laws were enacted, declaring a moratorium on the collection of debts. Faced with these desperate remedies on the part of the debtor class, the merchant and banker creditors declared they would fall into ruin and fled their debtors, armed with worthless paper payments, as they would the plague.

The national government dropped to an even lower level of powerlessness and general disregard than ever before. Rufus King reported succinctly: "There is no money in the federal Treasury—the civil list is in arrear—the troops in service mutinous for pay—the loans abroad exhausted—the foreign ministers destitute of Funds to draw on for their Daily Support—and the payments maid [*sic*] by the four Eastern & three Southern States for 15 months past not equal to 4 thousand Dollars." [1]

Congress continued to be the forgotten body. No one paid any attention to it, not even the delegates accredited to it. Nathan Dane, an unusually conscientious congressman hailing from Massachusetts, wrote back home in utter disgust: "There were only seven States assembled till the first inst.—since we have had eight—Dr. Johnson [of Connecticut] proposes to go home next week, which will probably reduce us to seven...we have done little or no business since you left us—and formed no interesting determination—this inattention, this negligence, stupidity in some of the States, in administring our government, will ruin us, if suffered to continue." [2]

In New York Governor Clinton and his party were determined that the national government, of which congress was the visible, if somewhat pallid, symbol, should continue in its present state of impotence. The Clintonites represented chiefly the debt-ridden rural and frontier districts who saw in a stronger central government a hegemony of the mercantile classes to whom they were indebted, heavy taxes, strict enforcement of the payment of debts, abolition of the easy paper money that rid them somewhat of the load, and an effective ban on the confiscations of Tory property.

The same reasons that impelled the Clintonites to resist centralization turned the merchants of the seaboard and the great landowners of the interior in the opposite direction. They had control of the state senate—voting for which depended on a heavy property qualification—but as long as the more popularly elected assembly followed Clinton, they were powerless.

In desperation they put their heads together and consulted: Schuyler, Hamilton, Duane, the Van Rensselaers, the Livingstons and others of similar views. Hamilton mapped out the strategy for the embattled conferees. He had in mind a double-pronged attack. The first was a direct assault, for which a weapon had been fortuitously placed in his hand by the recent action of the Virginia legislature at the instance of his friend, James Madison. It declared that the separate governments of the thirteen states had brought about a muddled and chaotic condition in the trade and commerce of the United States which had become intolerable, and invited the states to send commissioners to a convention at Annapolis in order to examine the situation and consider the possibility of a uniform system of commercial regulation which, if ratified by their respective states, would enable congress effectually to provide for the same.

Hamilton saw at once the enormous hidden potentialities of such a comparatively mild assemblage. Of its avowed purpose he had no great expectations or faith, but the convention might, in skilful hands, become the opening wedge for a more thoroughgoing and fundamental change in the federal structure.

The second prong of his scheme was in the nature of a flanking movement toward the same final aim. If congress would be granted the right to the import duties of the states, independently and under its own control, such regular, definite income would immediately give the national government a firm foundation and a solid basis of sovereignty. He had worked tirelessly both in New York and in congress for such a consummation—long before, New York had resolved for such a grant and then had suddenly withdrawn the offer. Now he was determined to force the fight again and bring it to an issue.

But to gain both ends it was necessary to obtain control of the New York legislature. The senate was safe enough under Schuyler's wing; the assembly, fortress of the Clintonians, had to be stormed. It was not an easy task; the broader base of its suffrage gave too much expression to the popular will. A determined coalition of all forces, however, the combined influence of the great families in the rural districts, the concerted assault of the merchants in the city, might effect a breach. Already Robert Livingston had significantly pointed the way to success in an upstate county. His report to Hamilton deserves quotation in full.

I feal happy in finding your Sentiments so justly accord with mine, and my Sons. As we observed for some time past the pernitious intentions of those you mention, & in order to prevent, & counter act, as much as in us laid, their politics,... we did endeavour the last year for an alteration in the representation, but without the desired Success, while we stood almost alone, as if no one saw the danger, but ourselves, nor did this falure discourage us, but reather hightend our diligence in this last Election, by Compleating the necessary Junction previous to the day of Election we have so often desired & endeavoured for; by uniting the interests of the Rensselaer, Schuyler, & our family, with other Gent[le]m[en] of property in the County in one Interest; by which means we carryed this last Election to a man as you must have heard from your friends, and I trust we shall always have the like success provided we stick close to each other.[3]

This rather breathless, weirdly spelled report gave Hamilton his clue. Let the merchants, bankers and similar "Gentlemen of property" in the city of New York likewise combine and elect a powerful delegation to the assembly. He chose his slate with care—Robert Troup, William Duer and Colonel Malcolm—all loyal and devoted followers of his.

The combination proved effective, and the trio went triumphantly to the assembly, while Hamilton remained in New York to busy himself with law practice and master strategy.

On March 14, 1786, Governor Clinton rather doubtfully communicated to the legislature the resolutions from Virginia. The trio immediately proposed the appointment of commissioners from New York to attend. The assembly hesitatingly yielded, with express reservations that the convention be limited to commercial objects and that the commissioners take no final action but report back to it.

It was a limited enough victory, but the trio redoubled their efforts and managed, with Schuyler's assistance in the senate, to name all six of the commissioners. The six were Robert C. Livingston, Leonard Gansevoort, Chancellor Robert R. Livingston, James Duane, Egbert Benson and the redoubtable Hamilton himself.[4]

On the other business on their agenda—the granting by New York of the impost to congress—they met with decisive defeat. In spite of a monster petition from the people of the city of New York, personally drafted by Hamilton and disseminated for signatures by his adherents,[5] in spite of the valiant efforts of his group in the legislature, all that the stubborn Clintonians would consent to was an emasculated bill which yielded the impost only on condition that it be handled by state collectors and provided that the depreciated state paper money be acceptable in payment thereof.[6] Since these conditions effectually ruined the grant, congress turned it down and requested Clinton to call a special session of the legislature to reconsider its action. Clinton refused, pleading his inability to comply on the ground that this was not "an extraordinary occasion" as demanded by the state constitution.[7]

But before this last point had come to an issue, Hamilton had determined to stand himself for election to the next session of the assembly. His cohorts already in the assembly were well-meaning and brave, but they had neither the oratorical powers nor the quickness of maneuver to meet and defeat the stubborn, but wily old governor in this central bastion of his influence. Hamilton alone, as his friends pointed out, possessed the necessary qualifications.

Schuyler wrote to Stephen Van Rensselaer, upstate, of the decision and the prospects of election. "Colo Hamilton will serve if elected. the Quakers, Merchants and some of the Mechanics are for him, but part of the latter averse; I am inclined however to think he will be returned." [8]

Hamilton *was* returned, but only after a bitter struggle.[9] Only those

"Mechanics" voted for him who were subject to the pressure of merchant employers; the rest distrusted both his policies and his insufficiently concealed opinion that they ought to leave voting and government to their betters.

2. THE ANNAPOLIS CONVENTION

Early in September Hamilton journeyed down to Annapolis in Maryland to take part in the convention. When he started out he knew that the gathering would end in failure. For, of the six delegates chosen by New York to represent it, Egbert Benson was the only other to accompany him. The rest gave various excuses—business, illness, general disinclination.

On reaching Annapolis he found his misgivings further confirmed. Only five states attended—New York, New Jersey, Pennsylvania, Delaware and, of course, Virginia—with a total of twelve delegates. The reasons for the sparse attendance at the convention have been generally misstated. It was not that the several states could not even get together to discuss such matters of mutual interest as trade and commercial relations. The proponents of states' sovereignty were rightly suspicious of the motives of those who had initiated the call, and decided to sabotage the proceedings from the beginning. In their private letters to each other they said so quite frankly, and named the names of the men who had other purposes in mind than a mere conference on trade. Among these names were Hamilton and Duane of New York, Robert Morris of Pennsylvania and Madison of Virginia.

Stephen Higginson of Massachusetts was one of the percipient men. He declined to attend the convention, though his state had chosen him as a delegate. He told John Adams that "the ostensible object of that convention is the regulation of Commerce; but when I consider the men who are deputed from New-York, Pennsylvania and Virginia, and the source from whence the proposition was made, I am strongly inclined to think political Objects are intended to be combined with commercial, if they do not principally engross their Attention." [10]

James Monroe was another. Strangely enough, he tried to warn Madison about the conspiracy (though Madison was in fact one of the leaders involved). "I consider the convention at Annapolis as a most important æra in our affairs—the eastern men be assur'd mean it as leading further than the object originally comprehended. If they do not obtain that things shall be arranged to suit them in every respect, their intrigues will extend to the objects I have suggested above." [11]

But Madison had already been discouraged at the opposition aroused, and was willing now to obtain at least the ostensible purpose of the meeting.[12]

Hamilton, on the other hand, was not so easily discouraged. He had not really anticipated any results from this particular convention, but it could be used as a stepping stone to higher things. When the few delegates met in dreary conclave and decided it would be a waste of time to discuss the matters for which they had assembled, Hamilton seized the opportunity to make his suggestion. Why not report back to their respective states that it was inadvisable to proceed under such unfavorable auspices, and request a new call to be issued for *all* the states to meet in another convention?

The delegates agreed to the suggestion and appointed John Dickinson of Pennsylvania chairman of a committee to draft the report. Though Hamilton had not been placed on the committee (perhaps the majority of the delegates mistrusted the extremity of his views) he promptly offered his services, and Dickinson gladly yielded him the arduous task.

Hamilton's first draft was in fact vigorous and forthright, setting out plainly the serious condition of the states and demanding a convention with broad powers to organize immediately a more efficient central government.

Governor Edmund Randolph of Virginia protested vehemently against the far-reaching tone of the report and declared he would not sign such a document. Madison took Hamilton aside to advise him: "You had better yield to this man, for otherwise all Virginia will be against you." [13]

Reluctantly Hamilton yielded. Without the aid of Virginia, on which he had counted heavily, his whole scheme must collapse. He rewrote his report, toning it down and using purposely vague phrases to assuage the recalcitrant governor. Randolph, mollified, signed the report; so did the other delegates. On September 14th, with the document in their pockets, they disbanded and went home.

The report he had ultimately drawn was a disappointment to Hamilton. He had hoped for more. But at least it was something definite on which to act. After a brief preamble setting forth the reasons why the delegates felt unable to proceed under the existing circumstances, it urged "that speedy measures may be taken to effect a general meeting of the States in a future convention for the same [*i.e.*, to discuss "a uniform system in their commercial intercourse"], *and such other pur-*

poses as the situation of public affairs may be found to require [italics mine]."

He proposed that the meeting be held at Philadelphia for "the second Monday in May next, to take into consideration the situation of the United States, to devise such further provisions as shall appear to them necessary to render the Constitution of the Federal Government *adequate to the exigencies of the Union.*" [14]

It was all very vague, but hidden in the italicized phrases were the weapons by which he intended to forge a new government and a new nation.

3. A PLACE IN THE ASSEMBLY

Returned to New York, Hamilton waited impatiently for the convening of the new legislature of which he had been elected a member. While he was marking time several events occurred that encouraged him mightily. One was the prompt favorable reaction of the Virginia Assembly to his report. His mollification of Randolph had not been without result. On October 16, 1786, Virginia voted to send delegates to the proposed convention in Philadelphia.

A second was the outbreak of a serious uprising in Massachusetts, known to history as Shays' Rebellion. The farmers in the western part of the state, rendered desperate by the eastern political control which discriminated against them in the apportionment of taxes and through subservient courts mercilessly distrained their cattle, foreclosed their farms and sent them to debtors' jails in default of payment on debts and taxes, rose under the leadership of Daniel Shays, a veteran of the Revolution, to rid themselves of their insupportable troubles. In great armed bands they moved across the western counties, compelling the courts to close, burning the records, forcibly preventing sales of foreclosed property and finally marching toward Boston to enforce their demands upon the merchant-controlled legislature. In great alarm the eastern merchants roused themselves, the militia turned out and overcame the advancing army. Once defeated, the embattled farmers scattered and a merciless man hunt ensued, rendered more cruel by the fright under which the seaboard merchants and wealthy classes had labored.

The revolt had been crushed, but the fear of another continued to trouble the dreams of the propertied people, and all over the country they turned their thoughts, as never before, to the idea of a strong national government with a strong, efficient standing army that could deal promptly and effectively with any such future menace to their well-being.

The New York state legislature opened its tenth session in an atmosphere of anticipation and excitement. As Hamilton took his seat in the assembly on January 12, 1787, he gathered his cohorts about him for the impending struggle. In the senate, he knew, Schuyler still held control, but the assembly was another matter. Here the followers of Clinton were in the majority, and it was his task to break into its ranks and sever enough votes to swing the tide in favor of the proposed grant of the impost to congress.

On the very next day the issue was joined. Governor Clinton, in his opening message, laid the request of congress for that all-important grant before the legislature without any comment. As was the custom, a committee was appointed to draft a reply, and Hamilton managed to get a place on it. If he hoped to be able to swing the other two members to his way of thinking, however, he was disappointed in the next move by his opponents, which resolved the assembly into a committee of the whole to consider the message.[13]

Almost at once a Clintonian was on his feet with a proposal to insert in the reply a clause expressing "approbation of your Excellency's conduct in not convening the Legislature at an earlier period." This was a direct slap at congress and at the Hamiltonian contingent who had demanded such a special session during the previous autumn. The proposal was passed by a large majority.[14]

Defeated at the outset, Hamilton regrouped his forces and maneuvered for a favorable position. In the interim, while feeling his ground for the larger fight, he introduced several other bills. One proposed to permit divorces on the ground of adultery. Theretofore only a legislative enactment could dissolve the bonds of matrimony. The assembly passed the measure by a non-partisan vote and the senate concurred. The Council of Revision objected to that section of it which forbade remarriage to the guilty party, arguing that though "it might not, perhaps, be an improper punishment, to confine offenders of this class, to a state of perpetual celibacy and mortification within the walls of a cloyster, ... to suffer them to remain in society, without a possibility of remarrying, is, in a degree, to compel them by law, to live in the open violation of the rules of chastity and decency." [15] Nevertheless the legislature repassed the bill over the veto, and Hamilton's enactment on divorce still remains substantially the law of New York.

He also displayed an active interest in educational matters, introducing a bill to strengthen the charter and privileges of King's College and permitting it to change its name to a less odious one, and to erect a University of the State of New York with supervisory powers over all institutions of higher learning within the state and administered by a board of twenty-one regents.[16] Here again he was successful. King's promptly became Columbia College; and Hamilton was appointed one of the regents of the new university, a position he was to hold for a considerable period.[17]

On February 15th Hamilton decided that it was time to force the major issue. A bill was brought in to grant congress the duties received on specific items of importation. It passed easily. But this was merely a preliminary step. The Clintonians had no objection to such a grant in itself; the battle was over the question of *who* was to appoint the collectors and *who* was to control them.

Hamilton took the next step and proposed, first, that congress both appoint and control the collectors; second, if this was not acceptable, that congress at least have the control, even if the state have the appointment.[18]

In a deathly silence Hamilton rose to make his speech in favor of the bills. A large audience packed the chamber to follow his remarks. It was composed chiefly of the "respectable" classes, assembled to support their idol and make their pressure felt by recalcitrant legislators. Under the benign influence of the gallery Hamilton exerted his utmost eloquence. He repeated all the old arguments he had ever made and added some new ones. New York and Pennsylvania, he pointed out, were the only states making any real contributions to the national treasury, and Pennsylvania was about to quit. Connecticut and New Jersey had already formally refused to make any further payments. Did New York then want to shoulder the whole national burden itself or, likewise refusing, see the whole fabric of the nation that had cost so much blood and tears to raise, perish because of its selfishness? Other states had been willing to make an unrestricted grant, but only if *all* the states likewise assented. Everything then depended on New York's action. It could make or break the struggling nation. His opponents asserted they had already passed the impost, but without congressional control of collectors what was that worth? Hadn't he, Hamilton, been a receiver of taxes under the present dispensation and seen how futile such a system was? Congress had rightly refused the gesture. It was all or nothing.[19]

The gallery of the "respectable" followed his argument with loud approval and black, indignant looks at those on the floor known to be opposed. But the Clintonians sat through the speech in stony silence and held their silence when Hamilton finally resumed his seat. No one from their ranks rose to refute him; no one of them attempted to answer his charges. In the same deadly silence the measures came up for vote, while the audience bent forward breathlessly to listen to the result.

When the vote was finally announced, showing that the resolutions had been decisively defeated, the audience broke into cries of disapproval. They filed out muttering angrily and declaiming against the absent governor who had pulled the strings to which the legislators danced obediently. In truth, Clinton had seemingly won a great victory.

But Hamilton and Schuyler saw certain signs of uneasiness among the members of Clinton's majority that determined them to seek advantage in an even more important field out of the ashes of this tactical defeat. The Clintonians had listened in silence and voted by order, but Hamilton's speech and the indignation of the gallery had made an impression. Some of them were ashamed of what they had done, and, reported Schuyler, "wished an opportunity to make some atonement." The pair quickly gave them that opportunity.[20]

They introduced bills simultaneously in the senate and the assembly to instruct the New York delegates in congress to recommend to the states a convention "for the purpose of revising the Articles of Confederation." The friends of Clinton fought the measure tooth and nail, but many of his more lukewarm followers had been seen privately by the bill's proponents and cleverly made to commit themselves in its favor. Their votes, now called for publicly, were sufficient to pass the measure.[21]

The delegates in congress wasted no time. New York and Massachusetts submitted similar motions, and congress quickly adopted the Massachusetts resolution as the more specific one.[22] The convention call was rushed back to the states, and Hamilton and Schuyler speedily moved for adoption. Their opponents were caught off balance by these lightning tactics, and those who had been tricked into committing themselves on the recommendation found now "it was too late to retract, and they acquiesced with chagrin in a resolution for the appointment of delegates to the convention."

The governor's men in turn resorted to a parliamentary trick. They demanded that the delegates be appointed by both houses jointly. With a senate almost evenly divided, and an assembly heavily Anti-Federal, this meant that the delegates would necessarily be all Anti-Federal. Schuyler saw through the trick and had it rejected by the senate. In turn, however, similar tactics by Hamilton in the assembly to gain a Federal representation were defeated in that body. With a stalemate in sight, the opposing factions were forced into a compromise. The names of three delegates were agreed on — two Anti-Federal, Robert Yates and John Lansing, and one Federal, Alexander Hamilton.

From this Pyrrhic victory Hamilton could take what comfort he chose. New York had finally committed herself at least to representation and attendance at the convention in Philadelphia; but New York also, voting under the unit rule, would invariably cast its ballot against the plans which Hamilton had in mind to bring up in the convention.[24]

There was one bit of unfinished business, though, that Hamilton wished to complete before he departed from the assembly for the larger arena of Philadelphia. Congress had become increasingly embarrassed in its relations with England over the obstinacy of New York in refusing to repeal those laws which contravened the terms of the peace treaty, and especially those which disfranchised the Tories. On April 13th the president of congress sent a personal letter to Clinton requesting such repeal, and Clinton submitted the letter to the legislature on the 14th.

Aside from considerations of what Hamilton believed to be justice, fair dealing and legality, he was deeply interested in the event. The lines of cleavage in the impending struggle for a stronger union were deepening and widening. At present the Federals were in the minority. But the Tories, if enfranchised, could be counted on to support solidly a national government with power enough to protect them against local prejudice and hatred, and as men of property they would naturally be on the side of a conservative union as against the more radical local legislatures.

Hamilton's last speech in the assembly was a moving plea for repeal.[25] But the Anti-Federal majority listened and took no action. It was only in the following year, after a Federalist victory, that the obnoxious measures were finally taken off the books.

With this last defeat, Hamilton packed his clothes and went to Philadelphia.

CHAPTER XV

Birth of a Constitution

---

1. SETTING THE STAGE

THE FIFTY-FIVE MEN who finally gathered in Philadelphia on the second Monday in May, 1787, had been given the vaguest of mandates by congress and the legislatures of their respective states. In effect they were merely a recommendatory body, an advisory commission, without plenary powers of any kind. Their duties, as defined in the several resolutions, were to consider alterations, amendments and revisions in the existing Articles of Confederation and to report their suggestions thereon to congress and the states from which they derived their authority. Nothing else.

Even such a limited role had aroused considerable opposition, and it was only deft maneuvering and skilled political action that had made the convention possible at all. Certainly the vast majority of the country did not dream of any *radical* change in the Articles or in the ties that bound the states so loosely to each other. Had there been any suspicion in the minds of most of the local legislators who voted to send representatives just what would eventually emerge from this convention, it may be said confidently that a good number of the states would not have gone at all, and there would have been no convention. Even so, Yates and Lansing of New York were present primarily to see to it that the convention did not stray from its purported purposes, and to cast New York's ballot firmly and unequivocally against any major change in the Articles.

The fifty-five men represented some of the finest political minds of the nation. Virginia sent a notable delegation—Washington, Madison, Edmund Randolph, George Mason, George Wythe; Pennsylvania was equally well represented by Franklin, Robert Morris, Gouverneur Morris, James Wilson; South Carolina sent the two Pinckneys and John Rutledge; Connecticut Roger Sherman and William S. Johnson; from little Delaware came John Dickinson; and from New York Alexander Hamilton.

It must be remembered, however, that these men did not represent the whole nation, nor even all of the best minds therein. Jefferson, Samuel Adams, John Hancock, Patrick Henry, Tom Paine and others who had been prime movers in the Revolution were not present. Nor were the people whose views they championed—the small farmer, the artisan, the debtor—at the convention. Aside from Luther Martin of Maryland and the lackadaisical Yates and Lansing of New York, they had few to present their problems or consider their difficulties. By and large, the convention delegates spoke for the conservative, propertied classes of the country. Whatever cleavages disclosed themselves at the convention were primarily sectional in character or between the interests of the commercial and the landed gentry groups.

Hamilton arrived early in Philadelphia. Here was the convention of which he had dreamed these many years. Here was the first real opportunity to forge a strong and sovereign nation from its quarreling, discordant elements. He had no illusions about the tremendous difficulties of the task. The call had been merely to tinker with the present Articles of Confederation. He knew that no tinkering, no patching, could solve the problem. There must be a clean sweep, and a fundamental change. He knew further that his own state was opposed to him—that his two colleagues would invariably, under the unit rule, cast New York's vote against any real change.

Nevertheless he set to work. He saw Madison constantly, whose ideas on federalism, if not as advanced as his own, were nevertheless sympathetic. He conferred with Washington, who everyone agreed was the proper presiding officer for the convention. He sought out young Rufus King of Massachusetts, whose state was as pivotal as New York and torn with domestic strife. His charm and personal fascination, as well as his arguments, shifted King from the opposition to a whole-hearted conviction of the necessity of a stronger union. "I revolutionized his mind," Hamilton boasted to a friend.[1]

On May 25, 1787, the convention opened in the Pennsylvania State House, later renamed Independence Hall. As expected, Washington was made chairman, and Hamilton was given a place on the committee to draft the rules of procedure.[2] Then the assemblage settled down to work.

Almost at once, by tacit consent, the delegates quietly proceeded to scrap the Articles of Confederation as a basis of organization for the nation and to propose in its place wholly different and novel plans of union. Virginia was the first to come forward with a reasoned plan of government. On May 29th Edmund Randolph introduced the Virginia plan. In effect it provided for a bicameral legislature and a national executive to be appointed by that body. Vested in the legislature were the right to veto any state law contravening the federal Articles and the power to employ force against a recalcitrant state. The executive, in conjunction with a national judiciary, would have a similar power of veto over both state and federal enactments, but such veto might be overridden. Since the plan proposed a representation in the legislature proportional to contributions or to population, the Virginia proposal was considered as favoring the larger states.

Promptly the small states came forward in the person of William Paterson of New Jersey with a counterplan which, as they supposed, protected their rights against the overshadowing domination of the large and populous communities. The plan attempted to hold on to as much as possible of the Articles of Confederation, with a *single* national legislature in which representation was by states, each with an equal vote. The powers of the congress, however, were to be increased by grants of imposts and other revenues, by the regulation of foreign and interstate commerce, and by the significant right to enforce its laws over the objections of the states.

Thus the issue was joined almost at the outset. But neither plan met with Hamilton's approval. Neither, for him, established that strong, centralized government which would make of the United States an irresistible unity instead of a mere aggregate of semi-independent states. On June 4th, in conjunction with Wilson of Pennsylvania, he proposed an amendment to the two plans, but with an especial eye to Virginia, which would empower the executive with a complete and absolute negative on all laws, both state and federal. To the objections raised that such a veto savored too much of the King of England, he remarked that that was no objection, since in England the King had not exercised his veto once since the Revolution. Whatever many of the delegates may have thought privately of the proposal, they felt it would damn all chance of future ratification, and voted overwhelmingly against the amendment. Only the votes of the proponents, and Hamilton's recent convert, Rufus King, were recorded in its favor.[4]

With this initial defeat Hamilton practically withdrew from all active participation in the proceedings of the convention. Except for a few minor resolutions and one great speech setting forth his views, he washed his hands of the entire matter and played little or no part in the long debates, in the give and take whereby that Constitution was forged which still governs the destinies of the United States. Why this strange withdrawal after years of spade work from the very task it had been his life's ambition to initiate? The answers so far given are eminently unsatisfactory. Perhaps the most plausible explanation may be found in the springs of Hamilton's character. He was essentially incapable of compromise. With him, as with Ibsen's Brand, it was *all or nothing*. He was perfectly willing to place himself at the head of a small band of devoted followers and lead a forlorn cause against the enemy; but here was no enemy, and he had no gallant little last-ditch band—if we except the new convert, Rufus King. The delegates to the convention were in the main solid, conservative men of the type in which Hamilton usually delighted; yet they saw what he failed to see—that their tenure was precarious and the country at large highly suspicious of their secret proceedings. If their work was to take root they must proceed with great caution, yielding ground in one instance in order to gain in another, balancing power against power, placating the small states, soothing the sections and taking care not to stir up too vehement hostilities.

Hamilton was both disheartened and disgusted with these tactics. He had hoped for a truly *national* government to emerge from these deliberations; one which had little or no room for the states except as purely local subdivisions with limited authority; one which patterned itself after the model of Great Britain. Yet such a system, he realized after only a few days in Philadelphia, had no chance of acceptance. Even the Virginia Plan, weak and middling as it was from his point of view, was meeting with strong opposition. As for the New Jersey Plan, why, the country might just as well continue under the present Articles.

2. HAMILTON PROPOSES

Yet it was not in Hamilton's nature to retire from the field of battle supinely and without at least one mighty effort. He determined to set forth to the assembled delegates his own ideas on the subject and the type of constitution that he considered necessary.

On June 18th he arose in the convention with a sheaf of papers in his hands. The delegates settled back in their chairs curiously. He was known to most of the eastern delegates and to many of the southern as a young man of considerable ability and strong convictions. But they also knew that his own state was against him.

For five hours he spoke to a deathly silent convention, referring occasionally to the notes he held in slim, long fingers. He employed no artifices of blazing oratory, though occasionally he embroidered the severe logic of his argument with sudden flights of fancy. His voice rarely raised above conversational pitch, and he paused at intervals as if searching for the very roots and foundations of the matter under discussion. He stood stiffly and not easily, and his manner was tinctured with a certain degree of vanity which, to one observer at least, was "highly disagreeable." [5]

He had been hitherto silent, he began, because of "his delicate situation with respect to his own State, to whose sentiments, as expressed by his colleagues, he could by no means accede." But the serious nature of the crisis had overcome his scruples. He was opposed to both plans before the convention because they left to the states much of their former sovereignty. "I have well considered the subject," he declared, "and am convinced that no amendment of the Confederation can answer the purpose of a good government, so long as the state sovereignties do, in any shape, exist." What good were the states? They gathered to themselves the loyalties that should belong to the nation; they constantly pursued internal interests adverse to the interest of the whole; they were not necessary for commerce, revenue, or agriculture; they added vast and useless expenses to the cost of government. In short, if they were reduced to mere local corporations or even altogether extinguished, the nation would be far the better for it.

What, then, did he propose? A plan of government as closely approximating the English model as circumstances and the temper of the people would permit. He didn't mind telling the convention that he personally almost despaired of a republican form of government over so vast an area, though he was "sensible, at the same time, that it would be unwise to propose one of any other form. In my private opinion," he continued confidentially, "I have no scruple in declaring . . . that the British government is the best in the world; and that I doubt much whether anything short of it will do in America."

While the assembled delegates digested this startling avowal, and perhaps wondered why then they had taken the trouble to break away from such an ideal form of government, Hamilton ruffled the sheets in his hand. He had before him, he said, a plan of his own in the form of a constitution. He was well aware that it went "beyond the ideas of most members" and he did not mean to offer it formally to the convention as a proposition, but "only to give a more correct view of my ideas, and to suggest the amendments which I should propose to the plan of Mr. Randolph."

Whereupon he read his draft constitution, commenting on each section as he went along. He called for a bicameral legislature, of which the assembly was to be elected by universal suffrage for a term of three years. To overbalance this concession to democracy, however, he proposed that the senate be elected for life, not directly by the people, but by electors chosen by them for the purpose, and that the senators be required to own substantial landed estates. Here, in other words, were the American counterparts of the British Parliament.

For the executive—he avoided the outlaw word *king*—who was to be chosen for life, during good behavior, he proposed an amazing pyramided hierarchy of voting carefully designed to keep the power of selection as far from the hands of the people as possible. Only those of means were permitted to vote for a group of "first electors." These in turn, if no absolute majority for a governor issued from their balloting, nominated "second electors" to complete the job.

The national executive was to have an absolute veto over all laws, both of the state and of the national legislatures. In addition, to make sure that no state would sneak through a law contrary to the wishes of the national government, the governors of the states were to be appointed by it, and these governors in turn had an absolute veto over legislation in their states.

Hamilton readily admitted that his scheme was not in essence republican, and certainly not democratic. He expounded his philosophy in very significant phrases.

All communities [he asserted] divide themselves into the few and the many. The first are the rich and well born, the other the mass of the people. The voice of the people has been said to be the voice of God; and, however generally this maxim has been quoted and believed, it is not true in fact. The people are turbulent and changing; they seldom judge or determine right. Give, therefore, to the first class a distinct, permanent share in the government. They will check the unsteadiness of the second; and, as they cannot receive any advantage by a change, they therefore will ever maintain good government.[6]

When Hamilton sat down, the leaves of his "Constitution" still rustling in his hands, the total silence of his auditors continued. No one rose to agree with him or to confute him; no one offered those additional remarks that were normal in the confidential give and take of the convention. After a little while, some one broke the silence with a remark on a wholly different topic, and the convention came to life again. It was as though Hamilton had not spoken at all nor held them in their chairs for five long hours.

What Hamilton's thoughts were at this silent treatment of his master effort are not known. He had taken care to forestall the sting of defeat by remarking that his plan was merely a statement of his own position and not intended as a formal proposition to be placed before the convention; nevertheless it is impossible to believe that he had not expected some reaction, some debate. Only Madison, privately taking those notes which constitute the chief source of our knowledge of the convention proceedings, came up to him and asked for a copy of the "Constitution" for entry into his minutes.

It is true that in private and outside the Convention Hall a good number of the more conservative delegates hastened to congratulate the daring young man; but, as Johnson of Connecticut remarked satirically a few days later "The Gentleman from New York is praised by every gentleman, but supported by no gentleman." [7]

There were evidently some vehement objections as well, for the next day Hamilton felt compelled to declare that "he had not been understood yesterday." He had not really intended "a total extinguishment of state governments" as some had gathered; they could continue as local and police subdivisions; but the authority of the national government must be indefinite and unlimited, without any hindrance from the states. [8]

Two days later he disclosed the true reason for his otherwise surprising insistence that the representatives be elected by universal suffrage, rather than by the state legislatures. The latter course "would increase that State influence which could not be too watchfully guarded against." [9] He did not worry too much about the radical possibilities of such a universally elected body; in the Senate and in the Executive he expected to see strong counterweights to any uneasy motions from the lower House.

For a few brief days after his abortive speech he continued his presence and rapidly diminishing participation in the debates of the convention. On June 26th he readily acknowledged that he did not "think favorably of republican government, but addressed his remarks to those who did think favorably of it, in order to prevail on them to tone their Government as high as possible." [10]

There were many obstacles to any such "toning" as Hamilton might suggest, however. As Gouverneur Morris pertinently remarked at a later date in the proceedings, "it was extremely doubtful whether the Constitution they were framing could ever be passed at all by the people of America; that to give it its best chance, however, they should make it as palatable as possible, and put nothing into it not very essential, which might raise up enemies." [11]

Thereafter Hamilton for the most part held his peace, except for a single flash of wit two days later. The convention had been dragging on for dreary days and the delegates seemed further from agreement than ever, when the patriarchal Franklin suggested that perhaps it might be a good idea to open the sessions hereafter with a prayer "imploring the assistance of Heaven" in their tedious deliberations. Hamilton made a little humorous speech in opposition. Coming at this late date, he remarked, such a resolution might "lead the public to believe that the embarrassments and dissentions within the convention, had suggested this measure." Furthermore, he was certain they were competent to transact the business which had been entrusted to their care without "the necessity of calling in foreign aid!" Accordingly, the convention decided to do without the services of a chaplain.[12]

3. HAMILTON RETIRES

The following day Hamilton quit the convention. He felt that there was no useful purpose to be gained by remaining. His ideas, and the ideas of the other delegates, were poles apart; and his attempts to "high-tone" the gathering had proved fruitless. Nor was his vote of any avail. Yates and Lansing, voting together, cast the unit vote of New York invariably against his futile ballot. Such complete ineffectuality galled his pride; besides, he hoped to accomplish more by outside pressure from influential men than within the convention itself. In the field of private conversation and private urging he was unrivaled; in public debate he was not nearly as good.

Disgruntled though he was, he did not remain inactive. On his journey back to New York through New Jersey and immediately upon reaching the city, he saw key men. He thought he was testing public sentiment in these talks; actually, he was sampling only the views of a small though powerful group who thought along his own lines. These men, as he wrote to Washington, agreed "that there has been an astonishing revolution for the better in the minds of the people." While the delegates still immured in the convention feared to go too far toward "a strong, well-mounted government" in the belief that the people would not stand for it, and while he admitted that the people were not yet ripe for his own plan, yet he was certain that this same people would adopt "one equally energetic, if the Convention should think proper to propose it." He expected to remain in New York ten or twelve days. Then, "if I have reason to believe that my attendance at Philadelphia will not be mere waste of time, I shall, after that period, rejoin the Convention." [13]

It has been the fashion to believe that Hamilton stood alone in the convention in his views. That is not so. It was merely the extremity of his position that brought him no public signs of approval; that, and the sobering knowledge that anything they fashioned required ratification in the state legislatures. Washington agreed with him at least in principle. Replying to his letter Washington avowed: "I *almost* despair of seeing a favorable issue to the proceedings of the Convention, and do, therefore, repent having any agency in the business. The men who oppose a strong and energetic government are in my opinion narrow-minded politicians, or are under the influence of local views." Tactfully, yet unmistakably, he rebuked Hamilton for his desertion. "I am sorry you went away; I wish you were back. The crisis is equally important and alarming, and no opposition under such circumstances should discourage exertions, till the signature is fixed." [14]

But others beside Hamilton thought longingly of quitting what seemed a mere barren proceeding. Rufus King felt sorry he not left Philadelphia "with our very able and sagacious Friend Hamilton." [15] Hamilton's own colleagues, Yates and Lansing, did in fact quit on July 5th, never to return, for an entirely different reason. As they explained to Governor Clinton, they had been appointed to revise the Articles of Confederation, *not* to draw up a wholly new constitution. Since the tenor of the proceedings at Philadelphia proved to them that the latter was the definite purpose of the delegates, they had determined to withdraw from further participation.[16] Obviously, since both extreme factions were dissatisfied, the convention was making progress. In the meantime, however, New York was not represented.

Though Hamilton himself had abandoned the convention, he was furious when he heard that Yates and Lansing had done the same thing. On July 21st he attacked Governor Clinton in the public press as the author of their withdrawal and accused him of working openly for the disruption of the proceedings in Philadelphia. Though his name was not signed to the article, the Clintonians countered with a fierce assault on Hamilton as the "anonymous scribbler" and raked up the hoary insinuation that he had "palmed" himself upon Washington in the days of the war and that Washington had finally dismissed him from his service. This charge, as always, touched Hamilton in his tenderest spot. He never was able to develop the thick political skin that sheds accusations of this nature without the dignity of notice. He called on Washington for an immediate statement of the true facts, and that harassed gentleman, then resting in Mount Vernon from his convention labors, hastened to comply, adding, however, that "it is with unfeigned concern I perceive that a political dispute has arisen between Gov. Clinton and yourself. For both of you I have the highest esteem and regard." [17] Washington was well aware that Hamilton's forthright assaults on Clinton were pushing that stubborn man completely into the ranks of the irreconcilables.

For a short space Hamilton plunged into his private law practice which he had necessarily neglected during his sojourn in Philadelphia, but his original disgust slowly turned to a restlessness at being thus away from the center of things. Yet he would not return alone. Without the other two delegates from New York his position in the convention was anomalous, not to say ridiculous. Alone, his ballot had no official standing, and even if the two Clintonians continued to cast New York's vote in opposition to everything he stood for, he felt that their mere presence in the convention might finally induce them to support the final verdict, no matter how dissatisfied they might be with the result.

Accordingly he swallowed his pride and wrote to his colleagues, informing them "that if either of them would come down I would accompany him to Philadelphia. So much," he added sarcastically in a note to King, telling him of what he had done, "for the sake of propriety and public opinion." In any event, though, he was determined to be present at the wind-up of the convention.[18]

Neither Yates nor Lansing responded to the invitation of their political enemy. As the brother of one wrote to the brother of the other, "I find but little Inclination in either of them to repair again to Philadelphia, and from their General Observations I believe they will not go.... Mr. Hamilton will consequently be disappointed and chagrined." [19]

In spite of the rebuff, Hamilton's anxiety increased. Again he asked King when he thought the convention would finish its work, as he wanted to be present before the end "for certain reasons" which he failed to enumerate. He had also heard whispers "that some late changes in your scheme have taken place which give it a higher tone. Is this the case?" [20]

In fact there had been changes during Hamilton's absence, if not wholly in the direction of a "higher tone." The large states were adamant against the New Jersey Plan; the small states equally opposed the Virginia Plan. Just as deadlock appeared certain, the practical men in both ranks got together and evolved a compromise known as the Connecticut Plan, whereby the small states gained equality in the Senate, if not in the House. With this chief obstacle out of the way, the path for further compromises on other controversial questions was made easier. Slowly but surely the document known as the Constitution was being hammered into shape.

4. THE FINISHED DOCUMENT

Hamilton did not wait for an answer from King, but suddenly appeared in Philadelphia on September 2nd and resumed his abandoned seat in Convention Hall. He found the weary delegates in the very last stages of their monumental work. They were putting the finishing touches on the document. Hamilton, again on the ground, could not refrain from entering into the final debates. "He had been restrained from entering into the discussions by his dislike of the Scheme of Government in General," he is reported as saying, "but as he meant to support the plan to be recommended, as better than nothing; he wished in this place to offer a few remarks."

The remarks were of a surprisingly liberal tone. He opposed the plan to let the Senate choose the President in case there were no clear electoral majority; he demanded a broad base for the lower House and an easier method of amending the Constitution; and he turned sharply on those malcontents "who say they will vote against the report because they cannot get all parts of it to please them." With the accents of sincerity he declared for himself that "*he* will take any system which promises to save America from the dangers with which she is threatened." [21]

On September 17th the finished document was presented to the convention for signature. Hamilton arose and made a moving speech. He urged *every* delegate present to sign the Constitution, no matter how he might have voted against particular provisions. It was essential to show a united front for the benefit of the people back home. "A few characters of consequence," he said with the utmost earnestness, "by opposing or even refusing to sign the Constitution, might do infinite mischief by kindling the latent sparks which lurk under an enthusiasm in favor of the Convention which may soon subside. No man's ideas were more remote from the plan than his own were known to be; but is it possible to deliberate between anarchy and Convulsion on one side, and the chance of good to be expected from the plan on the other?" [22]

With a bold, steady hand he wrote his name, singular and alone, under the heading of "New York." Lansing and Yates were home, preparing the ground for a tremendous struggle against this document they had no part in making; within the hall other delegates, unmoved by Hamilton's plea, refused to sign. They were Mason and Randolph of Virginia, and Gerry of Massachusetts.

Then the convention adjourned, and the delegates hastened home to justify their work to the sharply critical people of their respective states.

CHAPTER XVI

The Fight for Ratification

1. THE FEDERALIST PAPERS

THE CONSTITUTION, as it had been welded together in the controversial fires of the convention, was certainly not the instrument of government that Hamilton had hoped for. It held on to the states as the fundamental units of the nation; it severely limited the powers of the central government; and Hamilton could hardly envisage a great and powerful country arising on such insecure and tottering foundations. Privately, and for the balance of his life, he considered it a "frail and worthless fabric," and doubted audibly that it could last for any considerable length of time without falling to pieces.

But he also realized that it was superior to the present Articles of Confederation, and he was statesman enough to rise above his private prejudices and come publicly to its defense with the same degree of ardor and skill as though it were in truth the ideal document he pretended.

That the proposed Constitution would require a great deal of defending was obvious to Hamilton even while he was in the convention, and the full force of the opposition became immediately plain to him on his return to New York. If the Constitution did not meet with his approval because it did not go far enough, there were too many others to whom it had gone entirely too far. As the homecoming delegates brought back to their states the instrument of their adoption a clamor arose on every side. The chief support came from the wealthy merchants and their followers on the narrow fringe of eastern seaboard towns. In the hinterlands, among the small farmers and even the larger landed proprietors, the debtors and the frontiersmen, and also the more radical artisans of the cities, the opposition was intense. So intense, in fact, that it seemed hardly likely that it could ever be ratified by the requisite number of states. Knowing that the chances of success in the state legislatures were indeed slim, the convention had called for ratifying conventions, popularly elected, to decide on its handiwork, and added the revolutionary proviso that the consent of nine of the thirteen states would be sufficient to start off the new nation as a going concern.

In New York the prospect was especially dark. Barely had Hamilton returned when Clinton fired the first gun in opposition with a series of blasts in the New York *Journal* which he signed Cato. Hamilton promptly accepted the challenge with a series of articles in the *Daily Advertiser* signed Caesar, and the two Romans fought all over again the ancient battle of the loose Republic and the centralized State.

Neither series is particularly good, and the controversy soon degenerated to name-calling and *ad hominem* arguments. Hamilton particularly lost his temper, calling Clinton a "designing croaker," and what is worse, rashly betraying his contempt for the very populace in whose hands lay the final decision on the Constitution he advocated. "For my part, I am not much attached to the *majesty of the multitude*," he declared scornfully, "and therefore waive all pretensions (founded on such conduct), to their countenance. I consider them in general as very ill qualified to judge for themselves what government will best suit their peculiar situations; nor is this to be wondered at. The science of government is not easily understood." Only educated men like himself were competent to judge.[1]

Fortunately, Hamilton soon realized, or some of the more moderate men in his own party brought it forcibly to his attention, that this particular tack was not calculated to win votes or influence people, and the Caesar letters came to an abrupt halt.

Yet Hamilton could not stand idly by and watch the Constitution fail in New York for lack of effort. Clinton showed no immediate disposition to call the legislature into session in order to devise the machinery for the election of a ratifying convention. Each day of delay the tide of opposing opinion rose higher and higher. To combat the trend it was necessary to act decisively and at once. Caesar had failed; perhaps another and less offensive Roman might prove palatable to the New York electorate.

The facts as to the genesis of the Federalist Papers are unknown. It is plausible, however, to assume that the idea was Hamilton's. The initial number of the Papers was written by him; all of them appeared first in the New York press and were addressed "To the People of the State of New York."

But if the idea was originally his, as the scheme unfolded in his thoughts it became obvious that the task was far too vast for any one man to accomplish, even for such a facile writer as himself. His law practice claimed the major part of his attention—he had a wife and children to support; hence it was necessary to call on others for assistance. He consulted with John Jay, and Jay agreed to take over a certain part of the papers in contemplation. But Jay was a slow, methodical writer and a trifle tedious in tone. Whom else, then, could he call to his aid? Hamilton had an inspiration. James Madison had been one of the chief architects of the Constitution. Madison agreed in the fundamentals with Hamilton's view of a strong union. Madison was a scholarly writer, with a mind well-stocked with precedents and logical arguments. Madison had been present at each stage of the unfolding of the Constitution. But Madison was in Virginia, preparing for a desperate fight over ratification. Virginia was equally crucial with New York in the impending struggle, and the forces in opposition equally as strong. Yet when the matter was broached to him, he agreed to participate substantially in the scheme, and the triumvirate set themselves immediately to work.

Haste and speedy publication were essential. Pennsylvania, New Jersey and Delaware had already made provision for their conventions; other states were preparing to follow suit. If the Federalist Papers were to influence the decisions of the delegates, they must appear rapidly and in swift, consecutive order.

The problem that Hamilton, Jay and Madison had set themselves was far removed from the personal and polemic tone of Caesar. In its simplest form it called for a series of papers defending the proposed Constitution and urging its adoption by the several states, with the New York electorate particularly in view. But as the plan unfolded in the minds of the associates it became something larger and more truly philosophical. From an analysis of the various clauses and sections of the Constitution there should emerge a coherent essay on the purposes and nature of government, on political philosophy in the concrete as adapted to the American scene. That such a plan of composition was plainly visible to the trio in the beginning is most unlikely; yet as the work proceeded, and paper after paper was tossed into the hungry maw of the printer, the skeletal architecture of the whole grew more and more evident. Had *The Federalist* been written at leisure and brooded over for years before the first word was put on paper, it could not have been more unified, more architectonic in its structure. What makes the performance more remarkable is the fact that one of the contributors was remote from the other two and in imperfect communication with them.

Hamilton wrote the first paper of the series and signed it Publius. Thereafter all of the papers were similarly signed, no matter who was the author. It appeared on October 27th in the *Independent Journal;* and immediately the readers of that newspaper were aware that here was no ordinary polemic. From the very first paragraph the muddied controversy of abuse and violent imputation was shifted to a higher and more Olympian level of calm and ordered exposition.

It has been frequently remarked that it seems to have been reserved to the people of this country, by their conduct and example, to decide the important question, whether societies of men are really capable or not of establishing good government from reflection and choice, or whether they are forever destined to depend for their political constitutions on accident and force. If there be any truth in the remark, the crisis at which we are arrived may with propriety be regarded as the era in which that decision is to be made; and a wrong election of the part we shall act may, in this view, deserve to be considered as the general misfortune of mankind.[2]

While it was true that the most formidable opposition to the new Constitution came from that class of men whose obvious interest it was to resist any diminution in the power and influence they wielded under the present state governments, and also from those who hoped "to aggrandize themselves by the confusions of their country," Hamilton refused to dwell on "observations of this nature." With a fairness that struck a new note in American pamphleteering he agreed that much of the opposition was honest, if wrong-headed, in intent, and it was to this honest opposition that he intended to address himself. He even went further: "We are not always sure," he admitted with startling candor, "that those who advocate the truth are influenced by purer principles than their antagonists."

He foresaw, however, that a torrent of angry passions and accusations would be loosed in the controversy and warned his fellow-citizens to be on their guard against attempts to influence their judgment "by any impressions other than those which may result from the evidence of truth." He frankly avowed that he was in favor of the new Constitution; "my motives must remain in the depository of my own breast. My arguments will be open to all, and may be judged of by all. They shall at least be offered in a spirit which will not disgrace the cause of truth."

Having thus cleared the ground and set the tone in which the discussion would be held, he concluded with a survey of the points which he, Publius, intended to discuss in the following papers.

John Jay now took up the pen and wrote the next four papers. The same thread of argument runs through all of them—the indispensable necessity of a firmly united nation in order to avoid foreign aggression and a division into rival confederacies. With these four papers Jay's contribution to *The Federalist* ended, except for Number 64, well toward the end of the series.

From this point on Hamilton and Madison shared the herculean labors between them, with Hamilton taking the lion's share, though Madison's papers were equally weighty in substance and import. The numbers flowed from their pens in a constant stream to appear several times a week for a period of months in various New York newspapers. Hamilton in particular wrote furiously and in haste, snatching odd moments for the composition between the interviewing of clients and the trial of law suits. Many a time the printer, with the deadline of his newspaper staring him in the face, waited impatiently in Hamilton's office to snatch the sheets unsanded from the racing pen and rush them out to be set in type.

In four vigorous numbers Hamilton pointed out the perils and horrors of disunion which must ensue if the Constitution were not ratified. Already the signs and portents were visible. "Let the point of extreme depression to which our national dignity and credit have sunk, let the inconveniences felt everywhere from a lax and ill administration of government, let the revolt of a part of the State of North Carolina, the late menacing disturbances in Pennsylvania, and the actual insurrections and rebellions in Massachusetts, declare—!" [4] These disturbances, and especially Shays' Rebellion, were fresh in men's minds, and Hamilton employed them with telling effect to argue for a strong authority that could deal with them promptly and forcefully.

The tenth paper was written by Madison and came by messenger from Virginia. This paper is without doubt the most famous of the entire series. In it Madison took his stand solidly by the side of Hamilton and anticipated the major thesis of Karl Marx. He indulged in plain speaking and a realism unhampered by any moral judgments. "A well-constructed Union," he argued, is necessary "to break and control the violence of faction." There will always be factions,

but the most common and durable source of factions has been the various and unequal distribution of property. Those who hold and those who are without property have ever formed distinct interests in society. Those who are creditors, and those who are debtors, fall under a like discrimination. A landed interest, a manufacturing interest, a mercantile interest, a moneyed interest, with many lesser interests, grow up of necessity in civilized nations, and divide them into different classes, actuated by different sentiments and views. The regulation of these various and interfering interests forms the principal task of modern legislation, and involves the spirit of party and faction in the necessary and ordinary operations of the government.

It is ridiculous to believe, he asserted, that these opposing interests will vote or judge other than in their own favor, and "neither moral nor religious motives can be relied on as an adequate control." Accordingly, a majority in a small area, governing directly under a "pure democracy," could and necessarily would ride roughshod over the interests and liberties of a minority. Hence a republic, such as the Constitution envisaged, was the best form to protect minority rights. In the larger area no single interest could obtain a majority, and the delegation of authority to a small group of citizens chosen for wisdom, patriotism and love of justice might avoid such madnesses as "a rage for paper money, for an abolition of debts, for an equal division of property, or for any other improper or wicked project."

At this stage of their careers there was obviously very little to choose in opinions between Hamilton and Madison. Yet within the short space of two years Madison was to shift to an almost opposing pole, while Hamilton remained fixed in his position with the steadiness of the North Star.

The pen now shifted again to Hamilton in New York. Madison had laid the ground work for an economic argument for the establishment of the Constitution. Hamilton pursued the theme to emphasize the commercial importance of such a union. It could meet the European nations on an equal footing and enforce respect for its trade and commerce by a powerful navy.[5] The prosperity of commerce was the "most useful as well as the most productive source of national wealth." Knowing that this favorite thesis of his was most violently denied by those who considered agriculture as the sole and only base for a national economy, he attempted to prove that there was no serious rivalry between the two. Better still, "it has been found in various countries that, in proportion as commerce has flourished, land has risen in value." [6]

And so the papers marched on, the major portion of them written by Hamilton, a respectable minority by Madison, a few even the joint product of their pens, taking up in turn the broad, general arguments for a national government, the questions of war and peace, commerce and agriculture, finance and taxation. Then the proposed Constitution was analyzed, almost section by section and clause by clause, meeting the objections that had already been advanced, clarifying in powerful discussions the meanings and purports of the disputed clauses in such wise that later justices of the Supreme Court harked back to these papers again and again for light on points of Constitutional interpretation.

It was readily admitted by both men that the Constitution they advocated was not a perfect instrument. Madison admitted it contained errors, but charged them to a "defect of antecedent experience," which only an actual trial would point out. He compared America to a patient with a dangerous malady. Delay in treatment was fatal, and here at least was a remedy which was an obvious improvement over the old Articles of Confederation.[7]

Hamilton summed up the case in the final paper: "I never expect to see a perfect work from imperfect man. . . . The compacts which are to embrace thirteen distinct States in a common bond of amity and union, must as necessarily be a compromise of as many dissimilar interests and inclinations. How can perfection spring from such materials?" [8]

On this note of robust pessimism Hamilton ended the famous series. He had argued valiantly for what he did not truly believe in; he had no feeling that the Constitution, even if adopted, was destined to endure. It was to him a makeshift, a compromise, with fatal defects which nevertheless he was careful to gloss over in public discussion. In some respects he was of counsel, furnished with a brief it was his business to defend. Yet he was more than merely a lawyer handling a case for a client. He was a statesman, content for the moment to advocate any advance upon what he conceived to be an intolerable situation. If the Constitution could bolster the fabric of government for a time at least, the breathing spell might mean the difference between dissolution and success. He hoped that the wiser heads of the nation— among which he included his own—would then have an opportunity to weld more firmly the loose bonds of nationality and strengthen the links of true and respectable government.

The first paper of *The Federalist* appeared on October 27, 1787; the last on August 15, 1788. During most of that fateful period the controversy over the ratification of the Constitution was waged with a passion and a fury hitherto unexampled in American experience. In each of the thirteen states, in every town, village, farm and plantation, the great debate raged back and forth, the voice of the orator rose shrill and the pen of the pamphleteer dipped in gall. On the side of federalism by far the greatest champions were the triumvirate of Hamilton, Madison and Jay; on the side of the opposition R. H. Lee gave the best and most cogent arguments in his "Letters of the Federal Farmer."

There has been a tendency among certain commentators to consider the influence of *The Federalist* on ratification as much overrated, and their arguments are based on the fact that some of the states had already met in convention and ratified before the major papers of the series appeared in print. While this is true, nevertheless the pivotal states of Massachusetts, South Carolina, Virginia, New Hampshire and New York had ample time to digest much of *The Federalist* before coming to a final decision, and the proponents of ratification found it an inexhaustible arsenal of weapons for use in debate.

That it made a considerable stir among the leaders admits of no doubt. Washington wrote to Hamilton:

As the perusal of the political papers under the signature of Publius has afforded me great satisfaction, I shall certainly consider them as claiming a most distinguished place in my library.—I have read every performance which has been printed on one side and the other of the great question lately agitated... and, without an unmeaning compliment, I will say that I have seen no other so well calculated (in my judgment) to produce conviction in an unbiassed mind, as the *Production* of your *Triumvirate*.[9]

Jefferson, then in Paris as envoy to France, declared to Madison that he had read *The Federalist* "with care, pleasure & improvement," and warmly commended it as "the best commentary on the principles of government which ever was written." So well, however, were the respective contributions of the three authors hidden in the finished product that Jefferson generously assigned the lion's share to his friend, Madison, grudgingly gave Hamilton a minor portion of the papers and denied to Jay any part at all.[10]

William Maclay, the fiercely democratical senator from Pennsylvania, certainly could not be accused of tenderness toward the authors or their doctrines. On June 12, 1789, after the battle was ended, he made an entry in his *Journal: "Mem.* Get, if I can, the *Federalist,* without buying. It is not worth it." Having thus vented his spleen, he was obliged to confess that "it truly was instrumental in procuring the adoption of the Constitution." [11]

2. BATTLE IN NEW YORK

While Hamilton, Madison and Jay were spreading the gospel of the Constitution through the pages of *The Federalist*, the more practical struggle for ratification began in the state conventions especially elected for that purpose. Delaware, Pennsylvania and New Jersey ratified in rapid succession before the end of 1787. The new year had barely turned when Georgia and Connecticut followed suit. But these adherences to the new Constitution had been generally expected; the real strength of the opposition was marshaled in the great states of Massachusetts, South Carolina, Virginia and New York.

By common consent Hamilton led the Federalist forces in New York; Madison was the party whip in Virginia; and in Massachusetts Hamilton's disciple, Rufus King, worked untiringly in the common cause. The Federalist leaders wrote constantly to each other, advising, exhorting, planning, keeping one another in immediate touch with the ebb and flow of Federalist fortunes in their respective states.

The opposition was equally well organized. Taking their cue from the tactics that had served so well during the Revolution, the Anti-Federalists spread a network of committees of correspondence from the pivotal center of New York to rally all forces against the Constitution. John Lamb was made chairman of the Republican Committee of New York and his expresses went out to R. H. Lee, Patrick Henry and George Mason of Virginia, to Aedanus Burke of South Carolina, to Massachusetts and Maryland. As in Revolutionary days, the letters were sent clandestinely and under false names and covers.

In New York Governor Clinton showed no disposition to call for an election of delegates to a ratifying convention. The year 1788 was ushered in and still he made no move. Hamilton and his adherents determined to force his hand. A resolution was introduced in the assembly on January 31, 1788, to call a convention, and a similar one in the senate on February 1st. The struggle in both bodies was severe. The resolution passed the assembly by 27 to 25, and the senate by 11 to 8.[12]

The election for delegates was held on the 3rd day of April and for five days thereafter. Astonishingly, *both* sides had agreed to the base of universal adult male suffrage for the election, thereby insuring that the New York convention would be the most democratically chosen of any in the country. It is obvious why the Anti-Federals agreed to such a procedure—they felt certain that the poor and unpropertied masses would vote overwhelmingly against the Constitution. Why the Federalists should have assented is not so evident. Perhaps they felt that the rural counties were lost to them in any event, and expected to receive the accessions in the towns of the poor artisans and laborers whose votes and wills could be controlled by the pressure of their merchant employers. Curiously enough, the extension of the suffrage made very little practical difference in the final result.

When the ballots were counted it was seen at once that the Antis had won an overwhelming victory. They gathered 46 delegates, while the Federalists mustered a bare 19. The Clintonians had swept the entire state with the exception of the four lower counties of New York, Kings, Richmond and Westchester. Even Queens had gone Anti-Federal.[13] In New York City, however, the Federal majority was immense. Of a total of 2836 ballots cast, the nine Federal candidates received a minimum of 2651 votes and a maximum of 2735. The chief Anti-Federal candidate, Governor Clinton, could do no better than 134.[14]

But the city Federalists who were elected had in their ranks some of the most important men in the state. Besides Hamilton, they comprised John Jay, Richard Morris, John S. Hobart, Robert R. Livingston, Isaac Roosevelt, James Duane, Richard Harrison and Nicholas Low. To counterbalance them on the side of the Clintonians were such stalwarts as Clinton himself, elected from another county, John Lansing, Melancton Smith and Robert Yates.

The Clintonians exulted, but their exultation was tempered with the knowledge that not all of the delegates accredited to their party were opposed to the Constitution *in extremis*. A fair number of them based their objection chiefly on the ground that no Bill of Rights (as later provided for by the first ten amendments) had been written into the document. Few of them would follow the lead of young De Witt Clinton, nephew to the governor, who declared violently that "if the Constitution is adopted, I am convinced that several people who now warmly advocate its adoption will exclaim—'From the insolence of great men—from the tyranny of the rich—from the unfeeling rapacity of the excise-men and Tax-gatherer—from the misery of despotism—from the expence of supporting standing Armies, Navies, Placemen, sinecures, federal cities, Senators, Presidents and a long train of et

ceteras, Good Lord deliver us.'" But, he added somewhat cautiously,
"there is yet no prospect of it being ratified." [15] Nor did they hold
with Abraham Yates, Jr., hot-headed brother to delegate Robert Yates,
who wrote with even greater violence that "rather than to adopt the
Constitution I would risk a government of Jew, Turk or Infidle
[sic]." [16] Whether such extremists could hold their moderate comrades in line in the event the Federalists agreed to amend the Constitution in the manner indicated remained to be seen.

On the other hand, the despair of Hamilton in the face of these
dismal returns was equally tempered with a careful optimism. All was
not lost. With shrewd insight he penetrated into the heart of the
Clintonian dilemma in New York. Governor Clinton had the power
and the votes to command a quick and decisive victory in the convention against the Constitution. But Clinton was an old and wily
strategist. He had no desire to place himself irretrievably out on a
limb. If the union *should* be accepted by nine states—the number
necessary to put it into effect—and New York had openly declared
itself, then New York might indeed be isolated and subject to reprisals. In addition, as Hamilton and Jay openly insinuated, the city
of New York would then break away from the rest of the state to
join the union, leaving the hinterland cut off from its only port and
source of revenue. Clinton preferred rather to adjourn the convention
without a vote until the following spring or summer. If not enough
other states ratified, well and good. If they did, and the union began
to operate, he could adopt a policy of watchful waiting. As Hamilton
pointed out to Madison, Clinton would "see how the government
works and . . . act according to circumstances." Should any considerable discontent arise, "they will stand ready to head the opposition.
If on the contrary the thing should go on smoothly and the sentiments
of our own people should change they can then elect to come into the
Union." [17]

Hamilton at once adjusted his own strategy to meet Clinton's unfolding tactics. Clinton's desire to delay a vote agreed with his own
policy. A quick ballot would spell defeat for the Constitution, but
Hamilton had no intention of permitting the convention to adjourn.
Rather he wished to hold it in session, marking time with debates and
speeches until the situation clarified itself elsewhere. He placed great
faith in the missionary influence of the still-appearing numbers of *The
Federalist;* he wanted time for the effect of the open threat to dissociate the city from the state to seep into the consciousness of the

moderate Antis;[18] above all, he hoped for sufficient interim ratifications by the other states to establish the union without New York. Then New York must come in, or perish.

In conformity with these tactics he sent expresses to his Federal friends elsewhere urging them, nay, imploring them, if they wished to avoid civil war and destruction of their country, to speed through ratification in their own conventions. On February 16th Massachusetts had joined the procession; on April 26th Maryland ratified; on May 23rd South Carolina finally approved. With these eight states already decided, only one more was required to put the new union on a going basis. But Rhode Island was hopeless, North Carolina seemingly as bad, while for the present New York was definitely opposed. Hence either New Hampshire and Virginia *must* come in, or all the Federalist labors would prove unavailing.

It was just in these two states that the opposing forces were most evenly balanced. In Virginia a Homeric struggle was in progress. Talents and numbers were so closely divided that Madison thought, if the Constitution were to obtain a majority at all, it would not exceed three or four.[19] In New Hampshire it was just as bad or worse. The convention had met on February 19th with a decisive majority of the delegates opposed to ratification, and it was only by the tactics of the proponents in obtaining an adjournment for four months that the Constitution was saved from immediate defeat.

It was with the knowledge of these conditions that Hamilton awaited the opening of the New York convention at Poughkeepsie on June 17th. His eyes were fixed as much on distant Virginia and New Hampshire as on his native state. What occurred at Poughkeepsie would be largely determined by events and decisions elsewhere.

He wrote to Madison in Virginia suggesting a constant correspondence while their convention was in session. "It will be of vast importance that an exact communication should be kept up between us at that period; and the moment *any decisive* question is taken, if favorable, I request you to dispatch an express to me, with pointed orders to make all possible diligence, by changing horses, etc. All expense shall be thankfully and liberally paid." [20]

To John Sullivan of New Hampshire he wrote in similar vein. "You will no doubt have understood that the Anti-Federal party has prevailed in this State by a large majority. It is therefore of the utmost importance that all external circumstances should be made use of to influence their conduct. This will suggest to you the *great advantage* of a speedy decision in your State, if you can be sure of the question, and a prompt communication of the event to us." Sullivan also was to send an express to Hamilton at Poughkeepsie, if the event should prove favorable, and he agreed to pay all expenses.[21] Rufus King in Boston called on John Langdon in New Hampshire to send *him* the news so that he could forward it to Hamilton by a relay of horses. Again, the expense was no object.[22]

While waiting for the all-important New York convention to open, Hamilton intermittently attended sessions of the somewhat moribund Continental Congress, to which he had been re-elected, though not without opposition, on January 22nd. The chief business before that body was the problem of Kentucky's application for admission as a state when and if the union became effective. Hamilton opposed the move vigorously, fearing that any action in that direction might unduly complicate the already complicated fight on the Constitution. All the eastern states followed his leadership, fearing to add an ally to the southern interest, but congress passed the resolution nevertheless.[23]

The village of Poughkeepsie—it was barely more than that—overflowed with delegates, political busybodies, camp followers and the merely curious. The Federalist group of delegates departed from their city stronghold with deliberate pomp and "Eclat," and with loud expressions of their confidence in the result; yet it appeared to a keen observer of the opposite camp that they were merely whistling to keep up their courage. "I believe," he remarked, "there has not been a Time since the Revolution in which, the *Well Born*, who are the Leaders of that Party, have felt and appeared so uninfluential, as they feel and appear at this Time and Place." [24] In fact, the same commentator further declared, "the Numbers of the Antis astonish the Federalists and they look on their Case as desperate." [25]

The Federalists admitted among themselves that this estimate of the situation was just. General Knox told King mournfully that "the majority of the antis is so great at Poughkeepsie, that I ask no questions." Nor did he feel any more hopeful about Virginia. "I fear that overwhelming torrent Patrick Henry," he cried. "I would it were well over and the parchment lodged in the Secretarys office." [26]

But Hamilton, the acknowledged leader, refused to despair. He admitted that "it is not easy to conjecture the result. Our adversaries greatly outnumber us." But he circulated easily and freely among the leaders on the other side and employed every device he could think of to persuade them of the inevitability of ratification. These leaders "gave indication of a pretty desperate disposition in private conversations previous to the meeting; but I imagine the minor partisans have their scruples, and an air of moderation is now assumed." [27]

The opposition testified to the alarm felt at Hamilton's tactics in approaching their members, ably seconded as he was by Jay and Chancellor Livingston. One of them hastened to assure a friend in New York that "all the acts of a Hamilton & c[o] will have no effect;" but, he added significantly, "the latter's manners and mode of address would probably do much mischief, were the members not as firm as they are." [28]

The convention officially opened on June 17th. The first day was devoted to organization. Governor Clinton was elected president as expected, but the Anti-Federals showed a degree of moderation in giving their opponents two out of the five appointments to the committee on rules.

The strategy of both parties immediately unfolded itself. In the main it was the same—to delay and temporize. But the reasons were wholly different, as already indicated. Clinton wished to adjourn after a skirmish or two; Hamilton, with ear cocked for the hoofbeats of expresses pounding into Poughkeepsie from New Hampshire and Virginia, wanted to hold the convention in session pending the receipt of what he hoped to be dramatically favorable news.

The first skirmish resulted in a victory for the Federalists. It came on a resolution to consider the Constitution clause by clause, instead of as a whole. Sufficient Antis joined Hamilton's group to pass it, leading Clinton to remark bitterly of Melancton Smith, who had agreed to it in the belief that he could match the Federalist orators in debate, that "his vanity had lost the State." [29]

Chancellor Livingston led off for the Federalists with a general discussion of the advantages of a well-ordered government. Smith countered for the Antis with an attack on the provisions in the Constitution relating to the method of election for members of congress. Lansing and Clinton followed him, representing the heavy guns of the opposition. Livingston rose in reply to plead for the excise as a national form of revenue.

On June 20th Hamilton, who had been busy taking notes of the various speeches, jotting down on Livingston's last effort: "Bravo! as far as it went one of the most excellent energetic Speeches that ever I heard," [30] now rose to make his first major address.

The convention sat back in their chairs to listen. It was conceded by both parties that he was pre-eminently the leader of the forces calling for ratification,[31] and Clinton, scanning his cohorts with a vigilant eye, watched closely for signs that Hamilton's points were making an impression.

"Although I am persuaded this convention will be resolved to adopt nothing that is bad," he began flatteringly, "yet I think every prudent man will consider the merits of the plan in connection with the circumstances of our country; and that a rejection of the Constitution may involve most fatal consequences." [32] Then he proceeded to consider, point for point, the objections of the opposition to the particular legislative provisions under consideration.

He spoke with great earnestness and energy, and with much vehement gesture. He held the floor at great length, running over on this particular occasion to the following day. He repeated his arguments again and again, at times using almost verbatim the phraseology of *The Federalist*, employing a running fire of classical and historical examples to prove the necessity of strong governmental controls. "Men will pursue their interests," he remarked, hammering his favorite thesis. "It is as easy to change human nature as to oppose the strong current of selfish passions. A wise legislator will gently divert the channel, and direct it, if possible, to the public good."

From then on there was hardly a day that he was not on his feet, arguing, exhorting, parrying the attacks of the Antis on particular clauses of the Constitution, holding out stoutly against any attempt to require amendments before ratification would be agreed to. If amendments should be found necessary, he argued, let them be made *after* ratification and after the Constitution has had a chance to show how it actually worked in practice.

A close examination of Hamilton's speeches, both in the published and unpublished reports of the convention, makes it difficult to avoid the conclusion that his long-windedness, his continual repetitions, his dragging out of each debate to interminable lengths, were in essence a filibuster. He was marking time, holding the convention from a definite conclusion of its business until those Virginia and New Hampshire expresses could arrive. If the news they brought was favorable, he would have a dramatic moment in which to strike. If unfavorable, he was just as much lost now as then. Governor Clinton had played into his hands with his own strategy of delay, and Melancton Smith's "vanity" had aided immeasurably. For there was no question that any time during those first days of debate Clinton could have forced through a decisive refusal to ratify.

Fortunately Hamilton did not have to wait long for the break to come. The mails between Virginia and New York, and New Hampshire and New York, had been clogged with daily accounts of progress in the various vital conventions. Now the first express came galloping in, lashing the final horse of a series of horses in the long, breakneck journey from New Hampshire to Poughkeepsie. The wearied messenger thrust the impatiently expected message from John Sullivan, president of the New Hampshire convention, into the hands of Alexander Hamilton.

Hamilton ripped open the enclosures and read them with delight. On June 21st, New Hampshire had ratified the Constitution! The United States of America, as a *nation*, and not as a mere aggregation of states, had just been born!

The news, which Hamilton immediately communicated to the convention, put renewed hope into the hearts of his cohorts and consternation into the ranks of the opposition. Down in New York City the Federalists set the church bells into a wild clamor of rejoicing to commemorate the occasion.[33]

But the first wild exultation and dismay soon passed. The letters from Virginia became increasingly gloomy as to the chances for ratification, and if Virginia refused, New York would likewise refuse. For, with these two populous and powerful states standing outside the union, that union must soon collapse and disintegrate into its former disparate parts.

Clinton claimed in a private letter that "the News from New-Hampshire has not had the least Effect on our Friends at this Place."[34] If this represented a bit of whistling, Hamilton was not disposed to treat it as much less than the truth. He sent an immediate express off to Madison in Virginia giving him the good news. But, he added, "we eagerly wait for further intelligence from you, as our chance of success depends upon you. There are some slight symptoms of relaxation in some of the leaders, which authorizes a gleam of hope, if you do well, but certainly I think not otherwise."[35]

Meanwhile Madison's reports were dark with foreboding. His opponents were concentrating on demanding amendments in the form of a Bill of Rights as a *prerequisite* to ratification, and there was talk of adjournment or even secession if they failed to pass. On the other hand, Madison was fighting valiantly for ratification *first* and a recommendation of amendments to be submitted according to Constitutional provision.[36]

Meanwhile the debate at Poughkeepsie became more exigent, more exacerbated with the knowledge that the union was already a *fait accompli*. Lansing and Hamilton, who had been courtesy itself hitherto to each other, now quarreled publicly and violently on the floor of the convention. Lansing accused Hamilton of deliberate inconsistencies in his position from day to day, and Hamilton charged Lansing with a "want of candor and indecency." [37] Matters went so far that a certain Colonel Oswald issued a formal challenge to Hamilton to meet him with pistols, but satisfactory explanations were made and the challenge was withdrawn.[38]

Then another express came thundering through the dusty streets of Poughkeepsie; this time from Madison and Virginia. Virginia, after infinite turmoil, had ratified the Constitution on June 25th! Hamilton must have cried out his joy, though Madison added some cautionary words to the effect that the ratification carried some "highly objectionable" recommendations for amendments, and that Patrick Henry had announced "he should wait with impatience for the favorable moment of regaining in a *constitutional way*, the lost liberties of his country." [39]

Hamilton rushed to the convention and read Madison's letter to the delegates. An observer noted how "a visible change took place in the disposition of the House." [40] No wonder! Aside from New York, only North Carolina and Rhode Island remained recalcitrant. They were comparatively uninfluential states, and the problem of how to keep out of the union and still retain its power and prosperity now stared New York full in the face.

Yet Clinton still saw no reason for despair. He merely changed his tactics. He would be willing to accept the Constitution, he declared, *provided* it was revamped to agree with his views. To that end a whole series of amendments was suggested. Hamilton, in some perplexity, wrote to Madison for advice in the light of what had happened in Virginia. Already the passions involved had risen so high that there had been a riot and actual bloodshed in Albany between the two parties, though, he added with obvious satisfaction, while the Anti-Federalists were the aggressors, the Federalists had emerged the victors.[41] Madison's reply was firm against any compromise, even though it took the form of a reservation of the right to withdraw from the union if the proposed amendments were not later accepted. Such a conditional ratification, he asserted, "does not make New-York a member of the new

Union, and consequently... she could not be received on that plan....
The Constitution requires an adoption *in toto* and *for ever*. It has been
so adopted by the other States." [42]

Armed with Madison's opinion, Hamilton returned to the floor to
argue that the other states would refuse to permit any provisional entry
into the union on such a basis. The Clinton forces were pressing the
point for an immediate vote, fearing a further swing of the tide against
them. Hamilton pleaded with them not to call for the question, "but
retire and consider." He was ready, he said, to go as far as he thought
safe in "recommandatory and explanatory Amendments," and pledged
his party "to endeavor for their adoption; " but he begged them not to
listen to "Jealousy" or put "Liberty to the hazard" in their present
insistence. [43]

Now Clinton was hot for immediate action. He felt he had found a
formula on which he could reasonably go to the state. The proposed
amendments, he trumpeted, were vital. He was willing to enter the
union, but he wished to reserve the right to withdraw if the amendments failed of later passage.

Again and again Hamilton was on his feet, urging delay and careful
consideration, begging that no hasty action be taken. The Federalist
delegate, Hobart, moved for an adjournment in order to give the two
factions—the one for unconditional ratification, and the other for conditional—time to consider. "The Commercial people may devise a mode
to meet their Northern brethren!" he said placatingly. But Lansing
would have no waiting; it was now or never.

On July 17th the argument still raged. Hamilton declared that "things
have changed since we came here. It is therefore only decent that we
should consult our constituents." He hinted broadly that if the northern
part of the state should persist in its stubbornness the southern part would
separate and join the rest of the union. What then would be the position
of the truncated, agricultural north? "Let us take care not to oppose the
whole country!" he ended. Look at all the distinguished men who were
in favor of the union—Adams, Livingston, Dickinson, Franklin and
Washington. Think of our "departed heroes." But, in spite of his peroration, in spite of all his oratory, the motion to adjourn was defeated by a
vote of 40 to 22. [44] The Clintonians were pressing their advantage hard.

Now thoroughly on the defensive, Hamilton consented to discuss the
matter of the amendments *per se*, and especially those which involved
a Bill of Rights. On and on went the interminable discussion and changing of words and commas in the proposed amendments, Hamilton

always in retreat, yet fighting hard and giving ground slowly. He even read Madison's letter denying such a method of entry into the union. Again he tried to postpone the final question, but was compelled to withdraw his motion for adjournment. Finally he threw up his hands. The cause seemed lost; the opposition united and adamant. "We are willing to go as far as we can and be received," he cried. "The Gentlemen will see that we have made an effort to try to come to this." The Anti-Federalist, Adgate, had asserted that the Antis had compromised by being willing to come into the union with reservations; it was time now for the Federalists to meet them at this halfway station. No! countered Hamilton. We have tried to meet you on some equal ground; but we have fully decided this offer you have made will not do.[45]

With this final despairing cry the debate practically ended. Lansing pressed his motion to a vote. It called for adoption of the Constitution, with the right to withdraw after a term of years "if the Amendments are not submitted to a convention in the mode prescribed."

On July 25th the motion was put to the delegates. It was a tense moment. Hamilton and his fellow Federalists were certain of defeat. Yet, as the call proceeded, a miracle seemed to take place before their unbelieving eyes. The first break in the hitherto solid ranks of the Clintonians was the defection of Melancton Smith, hitherto their most redoubtable champion. He made a little speech avowing his conversion by the arguments of the Federalists, and voted against. The more moderate of the Clintonians followed suit. When the smoke had cleared, Lansing's motion had gone down to defeat by 28 to 31.

Delighted beyond all their hopes, the Federalists pressed their own motion for unconditional adoption with a mere recommendation of amendments. It passed by 30 to 27—a narrow margin of three votes, but sufficient to place New York safely within the union.

The long struggle was over. The union was an accomplished fact. Though North Carolina and Rhode Island had still refused to ratify, everyone knew that they could not possibly remain out indefinitely. Actually, North Carolina ratified more than a year later, on November 21, 1789, and little Rhode Island, always pugnaciously perverse, reluctantly came in on May 29, 1790.

Everyone also knew that it was Hamilton more than anyone else who had beaten down what had seemed to be insurmountable odds and thus assured the success of the new nation. "Col. H——," wrote one who had sat through the long convention, "stands the political porcupine, armed at all points and brandishes a shaft to every opposer: a shaft powerful to repel and keen to wound." [46] Everyone had heard how Melancton Smith had publicly announced his conversion, and it was faithfully believed that Hamilton's arguments had been responsible. And soon everyone was telling his neighbor of the message Hamilton had sent down to the city at a time when the Antis had still a two to one majority: "Tell them!" said Hamilton with flashing eyes and vigorous gesture, "tell them, that the Convention shall never rise, until the Constitution is adopted!" [47]

What actually caused the sudden break in the ranks of the Clintonians has never been fully explained. But doubtless several factors weighed heavily with the more moderate. Once Virginia had ratified, New York had lost its last chance of having a powerful state to stand with it outside. The threat—and it was in fact no idle one—that lower New York would break away and leave the upper state shorn of everything that made a state rich and powerful, greatly impressed the rank and file. The final offer to ratify with reservations was in itself a break from the die-hard position. And even that tenuous place of safety was ruthlessly cut away by Madison's letter, which Hamilton read to them, that the union could not and would not accept such a makeshift plan. After that there was nothing to do but to surrender. Yet it is worth noting how close the vote was, even then.

The merchants, the solidly respectable, and the well-born in New York City went wild with joy when the news was cried from the lips of hard-riding messengers. The bells set up a furious jangling and cannon roared antiphonal response. A great procession was organized. The merchants, traders, lawyers, doctors moved in front as became their dignities. Behind marched the artisans—carpenters, sailmakers, tallow chandlers, carters. Light horse, trumpeters and artillery escorted the great parade.

The carpenters built for the occasion the replica of a thirty-two-gun frigate. Its keel was twenty-seven feet and its beam ten; it was completely equipped in hull and rigging, and thirty-two seamen perched on its deck under the authentic command of Commodore James Nicholson. In honor of the services that he had notably rendered toward ratification the ship was named *Hamilton*. The sailmakers, not to be outdone, provided a stage on which another ship, *New Constitution*, sailed proudly along. Here too rose the figure of Hamilton on a great standard, bearing the "Constitution" and the "Confederation" in either hand, while Fame held a crown of laurels to press upon his amiable brow. Other groups, more modest, placed Washington with Hamilton in equal majesty on their standards.

Thus equipped, the huge parade started from the Fields—where Hamilton had made his maiden speech—to the accompaniment of a thirteen-gun salute from the good ship *Hamilton*, and moved its stately way with cheers and songs down Broadway to "Alderman Bayard's orchard" where it dispersed. That evening the festivities culminated in a huge outdoor feast, with loud hurrahs and the drinking of innumerable toasts, among which those to Hamilton were not the least, and such a cultivated, urbane spectator as the French nobleman, Brissot de Warville, admitted that the scene was "magnificent." [48]

In Boston, however, a solid merchant, Andrew Craigie, Federalist to the core, heard of the ratification by New York with a curious feeling of despair. The letter he dispatched to a business partner upon receipt of the news—which should have filled him with unalloyed delight—is a sufficient commentary on the motives that animated some of those most vociferous in behalf of the new Constitution.

"Had it been certain that the Constitution wd be adopted by. New York," he wrote, "or even probable, I should have been more anxious to secure the Certificates at the going price but knowing that they wd not probably rise higher than 5/. should all the States come in & would fall in consequence of its rejection by that State I thought it best to take the chance [of not purchasing]." Since the certificates of public indebtedness promptly rose on the news, Craigie felt he had suffered a substantial loss. Almost irrelevantly he added: "The greater part of the public Debt is held by rich people who can afford to keep their Interest." [49]

CHAPTER XVII

Mr. Secretary of the Treasury

THE GOOD SHIP *Hamilton* was quietly dismantled, the bells stopped ringing and the cannon ceased their salvoes. A nation had been born, and New York had decided to become a part of that nation; but the machinery of government was still to be manufactured and assembled.

From the triumph of Poughkeepsie Hamilton returned to his law practice and his family in New York City. Occasionally he attended sessions of the congress, to which he was still a delegate, but that body was chiefly marking time until the new Constitution would go into effect and sweep the old confederation out of existence.

He did very well in his practice. His reputation as a lawyer and as a public man brought clients flocking to him, and he and Aaron Burr shared the top honors in New York. But he had to work long and diligent hours to make enough for his expenses; for his fees were moderate even for those days. His cash books show item after item of five or ten dollars, and he charged twenty-five dollars for a matter that took him from the city. He had a large and ever-growing family to support, and his tastes were lordly. Though his income was good, at no time during his career did he have much ready cash on hand. It was always a close race between intake and expenditure. At times the race became so close as to be embarrassing. In 1791, while Secretary of the Treasury and formulating plans involving millions of dollars, he was compelled to write to a friend: "If you can conveniently let me have twenty dollars for a few days, be so good as to send it by the bearer. I have just put myself out of cash by payment of Major L'Enfants' bill." The friend sent him fifty dollars.[1]

Nevertheless he managed to buy some houses and a parcel of land on Wall Street, then the fashionable residential section of New York, and he installed his family in a fair degree of comfort. He entertained well and was even able to afford occasionally a generous gesture. The artist, Ralph Earle, had been thrown into Debtors' Prison and would have languished there indefinitely had not Hamilton induced his wife, Elizabeth, to sit for the impecunious artist in the uninviting confines of the jail while he painted her portrait. Elizabeth was so pleased with his work that she recommended other ladies of her acquaintance to him. The jail became a rendezvous of fashion, filled with the rustle of silks and the odor of perfumes. In the end Earle had made enough to discharge his debts and walk out, a free man, to other commissions and a competence.

Hamilton's domestic life was happy. Elizabeth graced his board and entertained his visitors. Brissot de Warville, the cultivated Frenchman, admired her as "a charming woman, who joins to the graces all the candour and simplicity of an American wife." [2] Stephen Van Rensselaer added his compliments. He was happy to hear, he wrote, "that you are so good a *housewife, housekeeper* & etc. The General [Schuyler] talks of nothing but you & the Esquire & says you and he will be models for us all." [3] General Schuyler was indeed inordinately proud of his dashing son-in-law and constantly sang his praises from the housetops. Elizabeth was equally proud of her husband and tendered him a devotion that lasted long after his tragic death. By this time—the summer of 1788—she had borne him four children, of whom the oldest, Philip, was six, and the youngest, James Alexander, only a few months old. Yet, though they already had a sufficiency of their own, the Hamiltons generously adopted the small orphaned daughter of a certain Colonel Antil, a former aide to Montgomery, and reared her as one of their family. [4]

If General Schuyler and Elizabeth thought well of Hamilton, Angelica Church, across the sea, considered her brother-in-law the most romantic of fellows, the most splendid of men, the most lofty of geniuses. In her secret thoughts she compared him with her husband, John Barker Church, and Church paled before the resplendent light with which she invested the distant Alexander. If she hankered for America in the midst of the glittering society of London, to which her husband's connections and money admitted her, it was almost solely because of her *petit Fripon*, one of the many endearing nicknames which she lavished upon Hamilton. And Hamilton in turn was strongly attracted to his lively sister-in-law. He wrote her the most gallant of letters, full of wit, gossip, flirtatious remarks, which she read eagerly and promptly retorted on him.

If my path was strewed with as many roses as you have filled your letter with compliments [she replied to one of these], I should not now lament my absence from *America*, but even Hope is weary of doing anything for so assiduous a votary as myself.... Church's head is full of Politics, he is so desirous of making one in the British House of Commons, and where I should be happy to see him if he possessed your eloquence.[5]

She made no secret of her feelings for her "poor dear Hamilton." Artlessly she wrote to her sister, Elizabeth:

Colonel Beckwith tells me that our dear Hamilton writes too much and takes no exercise, and grows too fat. I hate both the word and the thing, and I desire you will take care of his health and his good looks. Why I shall find him on my return a dull, heavy fellow! He will be unable to Flirt as Robert Morris; pray, Betsey, make him walk, and ride, and be amused. You will see by some of Church's letters which have caused me to shed the most delicious tears of joy and gratitude, that it will not be long before we return to America. Embrace poor dear Hamilton for me, it is impossible to know him, and not to wish him health and pleasure, and then I am really so proud of his merit and abilities, that even you, Eliza, might *envy my* feelings.[6]

But Angelica was not to return to America as soon as she thought, and years were to pass before she could see for herself whether her *petit Fripon* had retained his slimness, looks and charming vivacity.

Besides his law, family and politics Hamilton kept an abiding interest in education and educational institutions. In recognition of his services Columbia College gave him a degree of Doctor of Laws, and Dartmouth, the College of New Jersey, Harvard and Brown followed suit. In 1792 he helped found a school for Indians at Oneida, later to bear his name as Hamilton College.

He continued the reading habits of his youth, and his library was well stocked with the classics and the best of the moderns, as well as the current works on trade, commerce and history. He became thoroughly acquainted with Adam Smith's *Wealth of Nations*, whose influence is shown in many of his great reports. Yet he rejected decidedly the leading tenet of that famous book—free trade. To the end of his life he believed in the principles of tariffs and protection and tried to make the United States as self-sufficient as possible.

2. THE FINANCIER

The semi-interlude of private affairs which Hamilton had allowed himself was soon over. The ratification of the Constitution had brought a new nation into existence, but so far it was largely a theoretical one. A government had to be formed under its terms, with a president, a senate, a house of representatives, a cabinet and a host of under-officers before the eleven ratifying states could be considered as parts of an organic whole. No one knew better than Hamilton how decidedly important these first moves were. He had fought valiantly and skilfully for the ratification of the Constitution, yet he never concealed in private conversation what he vigorously denied in public—his profound belief that it was a "frail and worthless fabric." He considered "all republican government to be radically defective," as Gouverneur Morris remarked later, "because he confounded it with democratical government, and he detested the latter because he believed it would end in despotism and be in the meantime destructive to public morality." To Hamilton the truly ideal form of government would have been one similar to the British Constitution, with a monarch balanced by a parliament where birth and the possession of property were the necessary qualifications. He had resigned himself, however, to the fact that such a system was at present impossible in the United States, and he had fought for the Constitution, imperfect as it was, because, as the same observer pointed out, "he considered it as a band which might hold us together for some time, and he knew that national sentiment is the offspring of national existence." [7] And it was "national sentiment" that Hamilton desired above all else. Let Americans once become infused with the idea that they were *Americans*, and not New Yorkers or Virginians or Pennsylvanians, then even an imperfect instrument of government might eventually be modified in the direction of a strong, coherent, proud and vigorous nation.

With such thoughts as these it was absolutely essential that the first heads of government give the proper tone and strength to the shaky Ship of State. There seemed no question as to the man for the presidency. All factions, all shades of opinion, united on George Washington. Yet Washington had no desire for office. "It is my great and sole desire," he told Hamilton sincerely, "to live and die, in peace and retirement, on my own farm." [8] But Hamilton pressed him hard in letter after letter. Without Washington in the presidency, he declared, the ship was sunk before it had even quit port. "The framers of [the Constitution] will have to encounter the disrepute of having brought about a revolution in government, without substituting anything that was worthy of the effort; they pulled down one Utopia, it will be said, to build up another." [9]

Reluctantly, in response to Hamilton's urgings and the urgings of other friends, Washington finally yielded, though avowing that he would accept only to retire as fast as possible, in order "to pass an unclouded evening after the stormy day of life, in the bosom of domestic tranquillity." [10]

The matter of choosing a suitable vice-president, however, was not as obvious. The original Anti-Federalists determined to put up a candidate in the person of Governor Clinton of New York. The Federalists chiefly concentrated on John Adams of Massachusetts. But Hamilton had reservations about Adams. He had heard that he was unfriendly to Washington, and he feared that he might prove the center of a cabal "very embarrassing to the Executive, and of course to the administration of the government." He asked Sedgwick in Massachusetts to consider the matter carefully, and suggested General Lincoln or General Knox as possible alternatives. [11]

Sedgwick replied promptly that though Adams was not his particular friend, he had the highest esteem for him as a man of experience and integrity, and that it was too late to consider Lincoln or Knox for the post. [12] He followed this with some alarming news—that the Massachusetts Federalists had split on the question of choosing presidential electors by the legislature or by popular vote. In the first instance Adams was certain of the Massachusetts' ballots; in the second John Hancock might be chosen. [13]

This last news brought Hamilton up sharply. As between Hancock and Adams he preferred Adams, whose "sound understanding" and "ardent love for the public good" will correct or, he hoped, already has "corrected those jealousies which he is represented to have once been influenced by." [14] Thus early Hamilton evinced the shadow of a distrust for John Adams, which was later to flare up in a clash that disrupted the Federalist party and tumbled Adams from the presidency.

The possibility that George Clinton might run for the vice-presidency on an Anti-Federalist ticket did not disturb Hamilton very much. At the most he could garner a few votes from some of the southern states. In fact, as he told Madison, political capital might be made from the candidacy. "I should imagine, if pains are taken, the dangers of an Anti-federal Vice-President might itself be rendered the instrument of Union." What worried him more was the presence of a manifest defect in the Constitutional provisions governing the choice of the heads of government. The framers had erred in making no distinction between the electoral ballots cast for president or vice-president, with the result that, the voting being for two, there was the probability of a tie and the consequent throwing of the decision into the House of Representatives. Exactly that situation arose with Jefferson and Burr in 1800, and it finally required the passage of the Twelfth Amendment to remedy the matter.

To avoid such a possibility in this first election as between Washington and Adams, Hamilton suggested that some of the Federalist electors withdraw their votes from Adams.[15] This procedure, as advised by Hamilton, did Adams no harm in this election, but in the second almost lost him the vice-presidency to Jefferson. Adams never forgot, nor forgave.

Meanwhile, in New York, the struggle between the Federalists led by Hamilton and Jay, and the Antis led by Clinton, continued unabated. Clinton had been outmaneuvered and defeated on the Constitution, but he held his control of the state. He was still governor and, though he lost the state senate in the 1788 elections, his majority in the assembly was heavy enough to offset the defection. He had the further satisfaction of forcing through the combined legislature the appointment of an entire slate of five Anti-Federalist candidates to the Continental Congress. Not the least element in his satisfaction was the defeat of Hamilton for one of the seats. Hamilton took his defeat philosophically; the old congress could only mark time until the new congress, elected under the Constitution, was born.

On that new congress, however, another struggle impended, as well as on the electors for president and vice-president. On the latter the Clintonians called for appointments by the joint legislature, which they controlled; the Federalists for a general election. Hamilton was just as well satisfied to see the wrangle continue past the day set for the meeting of all the electors of the states because, as he put it, "the most we could hope would be to balance accounts and do no harm."[16]

The issue raised in the appointment of United States Senators from New York was more important. Here too, the Federalist-controlled state senate, under the leadership of Schuyler, and the Clinton-controlled assembly, quarreled so bitterly over the method of choosing the pair that the time passed and the first session of the United States Senate found no Senators from the sovereign state of New York in their seats.

Clinton's term as governor expired in 1789. As a matter of course he was in the running again. He had been governor for so long that he considered himself a fixture in the gubernatorial chair. But the Federalists, flushed with their gains in the legislature, felt that the time had come to defeat the perennial office-holder. They tried to persuade John Jay to run, but he declined. Disappointed, they accepted Robert Yates, who had been up to recently an Anti-Federalist, as their candidate. It was a choice of convenience rather than of conviction; they hoped through Yates to gain the more moderate of the former Antis to their side. But Clinton won the election, though by an uncomfortably close vote; the only comfort the Federalists obtained was the control of *both* houses of the legislature for the first time since the Revolution. Through this control they were finally able to send two Senators to the United States Senate—for the long term, Rufus King, the Massachusetts lawyer whom Hamilton had helped persuade to come to New York; for the short term, Philip Schuyler, Hamilton's father-in-law and Federalist party boss in the state.

Hamilton had thrown himself into the campaign against Clinton with his usual energy. As a member of a committee of correspondence to promote Yates's candidacy he toured the state, addressed the Supervisors of the City of Albany, threw off a broadside flatteringly addressed "To the Independent and Patriotic Electors of the State of New York" and published a series of letters in the newspapers which he signed "H. G." [17]

He pleaded that all parties should forget their former animosities and unite in supporting the Constitution. Clinton, he declared, was too deeply committed in opposition, and he dangled before the electorate the tempting lure of federal favor and offices if it elected Yates, who would work harmoniously with the general government. As the Clintonians, however, counter-attacked, Hamilton lost his studied moderation and lashed out in return. He examined the biography of Governor Clinton in great detail and ridiculed everything he had ever done. Admitting that he was "fair on the score of probity," he denounced him as an "artful man," cunning and obstinate, who had "betrayed a stronger attachment to his own power, influence and advantage than to the dignity, respectability and prosperity of the people." What a man, he exclaimed, to cry out upon the "men of property" in the Federalist ranks when everyone knew that Clinton himself was rich and parsimonious! During the Revolution he had commanded but once, at Fort Montgomery, where he had "made a well-timed retreat (I mean personally, for the greatest part of the garrison were captured)." He had obstructed, in peacetime, every attempt to set the union on a firm foundation, and would continue to embarrass the new government by every means in his power if he were re-elected. Nevertheless, Clinton *was* re-elected, and he too never forgot nor forgave Hamilton's most unflattering portrait of himself.

On April 30, 1789, George Washington looked down upon the assembled multitude from a Wall Street balcony in New York City and took the oath of office as President of the United States. By his side stood the short, stocky figure of John Adams, swearing in turn to execute faithfully the duties of vice-president, which he was later to describe with considerable disgust as "the most insignificant... that ever invention of man contrived, or his imagination conceived." The new Congress of the United States had already been in session since March 4th, and with the induction into office of the chief executive officers the government slowly got under way.

The difficulties were immense. The bare skeleton of the Constitutional framework had to be clothed with living sinews and coordinated tendons. The Constitution made no provision for working departments or an advisory cabinet. These had to be supplied by Act of Congress.

On May 19th Elias Boudinot of New York introduced a resolution in the House calling for the establishment of a secretary of finance. He recognized, as did everyone else, that finances would be the first and most pressing preoccupation of the infant government, as it had been of the old confederation and of the revolutionary colonies before that. Madison, who had also been elected to the House of Representatives, promptly added a provision for departments of foreign affairs and of war, and raised the Treasury secretariat to the dignity of a department.[18]

The debate immediately centered on the question whether the treasury department should be placed under a single head, or under a board of three commissioners. It was no mere routine debate. Though the Constitution had been finally put into effect, the major controversy over centralization of governmental powers as against decentralization had not been fully resolved. Nor has it been, as a matter of fact, down to the present day. Elbridge Gerry of Massachusetts called for a board to head the treasury, arguing that by putting "all this power into the hands of one great man, who is to be the head of the department... we shall establish an office giving one person a greater influence than the President of the United States has, and more than is proper for any person to have in a republican government." [19] John Page of Virginia attacked another phase of the Bill, to wit, that clause which made it the duty of the secretary to "digest and report plans for the improvement and management of the revenue, and the support of the public credit." He declared that it was not only "a dangerous innovation upon the constitutional privilege of this House," but went so far as to assert that it might even lay "a foundation for an aristocracy or a detestable monarchy," on the high ground that "members might be led, by the deference commonly paid to men of abilities ... to support the minister's plan, even against their own judgment." But Madison and others professed themselves at a loss to see where the danger lay, and the Bill finally was passed in its original form.[20]

Under such auspices, and with such qualms, the Treasury Department came into existence.

Washington was now confronted with the problem of appointing his respective heads of departments. For Foreign Affairs he selected Thomas Jefferson, calling him back from France, where he had been minister during the dust and heat of the struggle over the drafting of the Constitution and its ratification. For War he chose General Henry Knox of Massachusetts, and for Attorney-General, Edmund Randolph, former governor of Virginia. But the chief post was the Treasury. On the state of finances of the new government would depend whether the United States would continue as a going concern or split asunder in the fashion of the old confederation.

The logical man for the position was Robert Morris, who had obtained a broad, if disheartening, view of the country's financial condition as private banker and Financier during the Revolution and confederation. Washington took the logical step and offered him the post. But Morris declined. He had had enough of the thankless job. Instead he recommended Hamilton, for whose abilities he had a vast respect and whose earlier financial proposals had impressed him deeply. It is highly probable that Morris's recommendation coincided with Washington's own wishes. He too had felt the impact of Hamilton's genius and knew that he would not hesitate to adopt bold and radical measures to untangle the dark confusion of the country's finances, whereas Morris has already shown himself to be cautious and too placating. With a secret feeling of relief, therefore, he asked Hamilton to accept the post just as soon as it was organized by the action of congress.

Thus far Hamilton had managed to continue his law practice during all his immersion in public affairs. But now he had come to a parting of the ways. If he accepted the Treasury, he must give up all private affairs. The salary attached to the post was only $3,000 a year; his income from the law had been considerably more. Yet he assured Washington that he would take over the Treasury if appointed. The very next day he told his friend, Robert Troup, of the proposal and asked him to wind up his law business for him in the event he assumed the office. Troup protested vehemently, pointing out the tremendous disparity between his present income and that which he would get as secretary. Hamilton admitted that his family might not be as well provided for, but he felt that this was one department in which he could effectually promote the welfare of the country.[21] That he was sincere in this belief admits of no dispute. His was a precise, logical mind, bold to improvise, yet rigorous in detail. From earliest youth he had disclosed a profound delight in the sheer handling of facts and figures; and his letters to Robert Morris, his pamphlets and proposals in the New York assembly and the confederate congress, had disclosed his preoccupation with taxes, duties, contributions and the whole financial structure of government. From the first he had insisted that no government could exist, much less prosper, without a sound financial basis, and he was certain that he knew exactly the methods by which such a basis could be laid.

The knowledge that Washington intended Hamilton for the Treasury soon became an open secret and doubtless had much to do with the opposition in congress to granting the secretary too much power. The opponents of strong government feared his views and his undoubted abilities, and wished to hamstring him from the start. In this they failed. The debates in the Senate were secret and we do not know what, if anything, members of that body offered against the nomination. That there was opposition seems likely from the the private letters of a Boston merchant who had a financial stake in the result and who boasted of his official connections and his ability to speculate safely and with profit on the basis of his foreknowledge. On May 23rd, Andrew Craigie took it for granted that Hamilton would be secretary.[22] On July 11th he was not as certain.[23] In the end, however, what opposition there was collapsed and Hamilton's nomination was confirmed.

Craigie's business correspondence, chiefly hitherto unpublished, discloses some fascinating sidelights on the closeness with which merchants and speculators generally were watching appointments to the Treasury and what benefits they expected to derive from Hamilton's tenure in office. The disposition of the public debt—both state and national—was what interested them most.

The public debt for a long time had been a fruitful field for speculation. The promises to pay of the Continental Congress and of the several states during and after the Revolution had depreciated immensely in value, and the original holders, unless they were independently secure, had been compelled to sell them at heavy discounts. The purchasers and speculators in the securities who, as late as June, 1788, while the final ratification of the Constitution was still doubtful, had been able to obtain large quantities of paper at discounts of over eighty per cent of the face value, naturally desired an intimate view of the minds and intentions of those in official life whose actions could affect the ultimate value of their holdings. Craigie put it very frankly in a letter he wrote in May, 1788. "The public Debt affords the best field in the world for speculation—but it is a field in which strangers may easily be lost. I know no way of making safe speculations but by being associated with people who from their Official situation know all the present & can aid future arrangements either for or against the funds." [24]

Suiting action to the words, Craigie associated himself closely with William Duer in a maze of speculative contracts. Duer had married Lady Kitty, the lively daughter of Lord Stirling, whose noble title, if somewhat cloudy, lent an air of glamour to an otherwise drab American scene. By this marriage he became related to the Schuylers and therefore to Hamilton. The relationship between Hamilton and Duer deepened with the years to a warm intimacy, an intimacy which was shortly to cause Hamilton considerable public embarrassment and private dismay.

For it was through Duer that Craigie expected to achieve that inside view of official actions which he coveted. "D[uer]," he announced exultantly, "probably will be secretary to Hamilton." [25] A little later, when even Hamilton's appointment seemed doubtful and Duer, accordingly, would fall by the wayside, he nevertheless informed a Dutch firm that, "altho' Duer will not be in that Department he will no Doubt be well provided for & have great Influence which will be of importance, if secured, to your views." [26]

But Hamilton's appointment survived the storm, and he promptly made Duer his assistant. Craigie had now a friend in court; so did everyone who thought to fatten on the public funds. From distant Paris Brissot de Warville wrote to congratulate Duer on his appointment and to introduce to him Cazenove of Amsterdam, who "is to settle himself in america, & I believe to make some speculations in your funds. I am sure, knowing your obliging temper you'll give him good informations about his speculations: & I'll be much obliged to you to do it." [27]

Duer evidently obliged, as he did with Craigie and a whole horde of avid speculators. He also obliged himself. He had bought and sold the public debt before taking office, always at large profits to himself.[28] This was permissible. But once in office, another adjective must apply. Especially is this true in a case where he used his official position to force himself into a profitable federal contract as a secret partner of the original undertaker.[29]

That Hamilton knew of all the underhanded machinations of his friend and assistant is highly improbable; that he knew, however, of his speculations and associations with other speculators who were equally friends of Hamilton is incontestable. In fact, Hamilton observed the sudden outburst of activity in the evidences of the public debt with considerable complacency. The transfer of holdings from the poor to the rich tied in with his philosophy of government. There was building up in America a powerful group of moneyed men who had a direct financial stake in the perpetuation of the nation, and he could rely on them to support his policies with a passion directly proportional to the sum total of their holdings.

Nor did it unduly annoy him that they in turn considered him as their friend and supporter. If he could have read the letter which one of them wrote to Samuel B. Webb on Hamilton's assumption of office, he would have seen nothing unethical or disturbing about it. The speculator, Joseph Barrell, inquired of Webb: "You know I have a considerable Sum in indents, and as you are intimate with Mr. Hamilton, the man to whom we look for the resurrection of the Public Credit, I wish you would find out how his Ideas [are] upon that matter, and whether he purposes to do anything about them in his plan, which no doubt he will lay before Congress at their next Session; and if anything, what. I can then judge whether I had best dispose of them at the present price, or purchase more." [30]

Yet Hamilton was quick to refuse any *direct* request for information once he was in office, and his every act became subject to a hostile scrutiny. Henry Lee of Virginia wanted to know if the value of the debt was soon to improve and if the interest would be paid in specie. These queries "may be improper," Lee admitted. He did not think so, but "of this," he added magnanimously, "you will decide, and act accordingly. Nothing can induce me to be instrumental in submitting my friend to an impropriety." [31]

Hamilton delicately availed himself of Lee's magnanimity. "I am sure you are sincere when you say that you would not subject me to an impropriety," he wrote back; "nor do I know there would be any in answering your queries. But you remember the saying with regard to Caesar's wife. I think the spirit of it applicable to every man concerned in the administration of the finance of a country. With respect to the conduct of such men, *suspicion* is ever eagle-eyed. And the most innocent things may be misinterpreted." [32]

William Duer was not as circumspect. He not only handed out choice morsels of information to his business associates, but was expansively informative in larger groups as well, so that Noah Webster was able to deduce from "the outdoor talk of Col. Duer, the Vice-Secretary," that the debt would be funded and a national bank established. Accordingly, Webster was able to advise a friend that "this will be the time for your speculations." [33]

Hamilton entered upon his duties as Secretary of the Treasury on September 11, 1789. He had wound up his private affairs and turned his law practice over to Troup, so that he could devote himself unremittingly to the task at hand.

He had no illusions about the difficulty and complexity of that task. He had to create a department *de novo*, and he had but few precedents from which to gain instruction. The example of the confederation was certainly not to be followed, and the English system, which Hamilton admired, could not be applied except in part to the peculiar situation of the United States. Yet upon the success or failure of the Treasury depended the success or failure of the federal union.

Before his official induction Hamilton was already actively advising Washington on matters of government. The President sent him a list of proposed nominations for office for his comment and requested him, in conjunction with John Jay, soon to be appointed Chief Justice of the Supreme Court, to name a good man for the Post-Office in place of Colonel Osgood, who had already declined.[34]

More puzzling by far, however, to Washington was the etiquette proper for him to observe as President of the United States. There had been no office quite like it before in the history of the world, and while Washington's own predilections were for a considerable dignity and solemn investitures, he feared the cry of *monarchy* with which the former Antis were certain to greet any excess solemnity. He took his perplexity to Hamilton, who obliged with a detailed system of etiquette for the guidance of the President. Hamilton, too, would have preferred an elaborate ceremonial; he likewise realized that "men's minds are prepared for a pretty high tone in the demeanor of the executive, but I doubt whether for so high a tone as in the abstract might be desirable. The notions of equality are yet, in my opinion, too general and too strong to admit of such a distance being placed between the President and other branches of the government as might even be consistent with a due proportion." To keep as much a distance as possible, however, he provided for levees to be held by the President, specifying the exact length of time, the character of the visitors and the topics they might be permitted to discuss; he also enumerated what formal affairs should be given by the President and a list of those who might be invited, which included Senators but *not* Representatives.[35]

If either Hamilton or Washington thought that such a plan was a compromise calculated to placate "the notions of equality" they were much mistaken. Senator William Maclay of Pennsylvania, though among the elect who were permitted to attend formal functions, found *his* "notions of equality" outraged by the trappings with which Washington, the President, and Adams, the Vice-President, invested their respective offices. When Washington first appeared before the Senate, flanked by his Secretary of War, General Knox, in connection with a proposed Indian Treaty, the dour Pennsylvanian wrote acidly in his *Journal* that same evening: "I cannot be mistaken, the President wishes to tread on the necks of the Senate. Commitment will bring the matter to discussion, at least in the committee, where he is not present. He wishes us to see with the eyes and hear with the ears of his Secretary only. The Secretary to advance the premises, the President to draw the conclusions, and to bear down our deliberations with his personal authority and presence.... This will not do with Americans." [36] As for Adams' fondness for regal trappings and phraseology, Maclay's pen literally scorched the pages of his *Journal*.

CHAPTER XVIII

The Great Reports

I. FIRST REPORT ON THE PUBLIC CREDIT

HAMILTON TOOK OFFICE as Secretary of the Treasury on September 11, 1789. Ten days later the House of Representatives passed a resolution calling on him to report to it a plan for the "adequate support of the public credit."

That such a plan was highly needful was self-evident. Nothing could be more chaotic or desperate than the then state of the public credit. In fact, had it not been for the hopeless confusion into which the finances of the confederation had fallen, it is more than doubtful that the Constitution would have been ratified.

Thrust thus into the very heart of his problem before he had even a chance to accustom himself to his new duties, Hamilton set to work. It was the most difficult task that had ever been set for him in all his active career. On its successful solution depended not only Hamilton's political fate, but the fate of the nation. Yet he had no special training in finance or practical experience. He had read widely on economic and financial problems, and had studied Adam Smith; years before, he had offered with the boldness and assurance of youth, plans for the financial structure of the confederation. It was one thing to offer plans for which one assumed no responsibility, however, and another to offer them as Secretary of the Treasury. Yet Hamilton did not hesitate. He gathered information on imports and exports, on tariffs and revenue systems, on the state of the public securities—and he did what he rarely ever did—he asked for advice. In this instance he asked Madison.

James Madison had been as staunch as he in the fight for the ratification of the Constitution; certainly he had been more active and more influential in the drafting of that document. They had been closely associated in political struggles and their ideas so far seemed pretty well in agreement. Madison was now in the House of Representatives, elected from Virginia, and his advice must necessarily have an important political as well as financial basis. "May I ask of your friendship," wrote Hamilton, "to put on paper and send me your thoughts on such subjects as may have occurred to you, for an addition to our revenue, and also as to any modifications of the public debt, which could be made consistent with good faith—the interest of the public and of the creditors." Also, "what further taxes will be least unpopular." [1]

Madison considered the questions posed to him for more than a month before he replied. On the matter of additional taxes he was definite, suggesting an excise tax on home distilleries, an increase in the duties on imported liquors and a land tax. On the matter of the public debt, however, he was more cautious.

The codification of the public debt is a subject on which I ought perhaps to be silent, having not enough revolved it to form any precise ideas. I take it to be the general expectation that the foreign part of the debt is to be put on the most satisfactory footing, and it will no doubt equally gratify the public wish, if it can by that means be turned into a debt bearing a reduced interest. The domestic part is well known to be viewed in different lights by different classes of people. It might be a soothing circumstance to those least favorably disposed, if by some operation the debt could be lessened by purchases made on public account; and particularly if any impression could be made on it by means of the Western lands.

Much more confidently he considered it "very desirable that the provision to be made should be such as will put the debt in a manifest course of extinguishment." [2] In this last sentiment he was buttressed by a letter newly arrived from his friend and mentor, Thomas Jefferson, who was preparing to leave Paris to assume his duties as Secretary of Foreign Affairs. Jefferson had furnished Madison with a long disquisition against the right of one generation to bind succeeding generations with a system of perpetual debts. [3]

The interesting point to be noted in this rather careful reply to Hamilton's request is that nowhere is there any hint that the *domestic* debt—soon to be the source and fount of acrimonious debate—ought not to be paid in full, or that there should be any differentiation between its original and present holders.

Armed with facts, figures—and Madison's reply—Hamilton drafted what is now known as his First Report on the Public Credit. He worked at breakneck speed, yet the finished document discloses a logical skeleton, a careful attention to interrelated parts and a wealth of illustrations to bolster his fundamental points. [4]

He took the broad, general position that the debt of the United States was the price it had paid for its liberty and constituted a debt of honor to be firmly established and met as all debts of honor should be. But he had more potent arguments than the merely ethical. The public credit was a sensitive and delicate thing, in exactly the same category as private credit. It could be maintained only "by good faith; by a punctual performance of contracts. States, like individuals, who observe their engagements are respected and trusted, while the reverse is the fate of those who pursue an opposite conduct."

The true question was, according to Hamilton, not whether the new government should refuse to pay any part of the debt, nor whether it could, by devious methods, pay a part instead of the whole, but how to recast it and fund it in such a fashion that *all* creditors would gain confidence in its sanctity and consider its possession as a valuable and profitable asset.

He went boldly further—and by so doing, earned the suspicion and lasting enmity of such men as Jefferson and Madison. He declared that "it is a well known fact, that, in countries in which the national debt is properly funded, and an object of established confidence, it answers most of the purposes of money. Transfers of stock or public debt are there equivalent to payments in specie; or, in other words, stock, in the principal transactions of business, passes current as specie."

Having thus set the background, Hamilton proceeded to discuss details. He divided the debt into its two categories—national and state. He took up the national debt first. Here again he divided it into two branches—foreign and domestic. The foreign debt consisted of the obligations held by foreign creditors, chiefly French and Dutch. Practically everyone was agreed that this portion of the debt must be paid in full, both as to interest and eventually as to principal. It was too obvious for argument that unless the foreign obligations were "provided for according to the precise terms of the contracts" the United States would never be able to resort to any further foreign borrowing. Yet, as he hinted to both William Short and Lafayette in Europe, if they could manage to get France voluntarily, and without *direct* solicitation, to suspend a demand for the payment of installments of the principal for five or six years, while receiving the interest, "it would be a valuable accommodation to the United States." [5]

On that portion of the national debt held by *domestic* creditors, however, there was no such unanimity. Madison had suggested as much, and others were far more openly vociferous in opposition. The

trouble was obvious and simple. The *original* evidences of debt had
been given during the Revolution and immediately thereafter to soldiers in payment of wages and to merchants in payment for supplies
because the struggling nation had no money with which to meet its
obligations. But, as has already been pointed out, only the wealthy
could afford to hold on to these governmental evidences of debt. The
poorer holders, and especially the soldiers, very soon were compelled
to sell them for cash in order to continue the business of living. The
speculators and the wealthy who were willing to buy took full advantage of the necessities of the original holders. They purchased at
discounts that ranged as low as twelve cents on the dollar. The question that now agitated the country was—who was to be paid by the
government, the present or the first holders? And even—should the
debt be paid at existing market value or in full?

To Hamilton there was but one answer to this question: pay the
present owners the par value of the holdings, regardless of what they
had purchased them for. He rejected all other solutions but this simple
one as "equally unjust and impolitic; as highly injurious, even to the
original holders of public securities; as ruinous to public credit." He
argued from the analogy of common business practice, where the
buyer stood exactly in the place of the seller, regardless of the private
transaction between them. He admitted the hard case of the needy
sellers, but declared that their complaint, if any, was against the government, and not against "the persons who relieved their necessities,
by giving them the current price of their property." His additional
argument was in truth unanswerable. How *could* the government possibly be just in discriminating between classes of holders? Pay the
present holder exactly what he paid, plus accrued interest, and pay the
balance to the first holder? But most certificates had passed through
several hands, and each passage had been at a different price. How
could a Treasury unravel the tangled skein of myriad transactions and
restore each holder in the series to his original position? Would not
such a precedent also in effect establish the rule that government securities were not assignable, and what then must happen to the national credit? How about those original holders who had hastened
to sell, not because of financial needs, but because of a lack of faith
in the permanence of the new American State? Must they be rewarded
for their lack of faith, and the purchasers penalized for their faith?

As to the state debts, Hamilton considered them in exactly the same
category as the national. In fact, "an assumption of the debts of the

particular States by the Union, and a like provision for them as for those of the Union, will be a measure of sound policy and substantial justice." One national plan should involve them all.

From these considerations Hamilton moved on to methods of funding and payment. This constituted the second prong of his plan. The total amount of outstanding securities, both state and federal, was indeed enough to stagger the imagination of erstwhile colonials, and to set in motion grave doubts whether the United States could ever possibly meet such totals out of its resources. Hamilton had no such doubts. It was true that the amount, including accrued interest, ran almost to $85,000,000. Beyond his contemporaries Hamilton had an abiding faith in the indefinite expansion of the country and its later ability easily to meet obligations far in excess of the present.

For the immediate problem he proposed a new loan for the full amount of the debt, with flexible interest rates and even annuities, so that "the debt should, with the consent of the creditors, be remoulded into such a shape as will bring the expenditures of the nation to a level with its income." Here his plan became somewhat tortuous and led with some justice to the later complaint on his various series of figures that they were "intricate and so complicated it appears to one to require some time and attention to understand." The additional complaint by Joseph Jones of Virginia was perhaps more partisan, that "at first view I think it well calculated to keep us all in the dark excepting those... who thrive on speculation." [6]

To such carpings, which kept increasing in volume with the issuance of Hamilton's further reports, his staunch defender, John Fenno, was to retort in satiric doggerel:

> The Secretary makes reports
> Whene'er the House commands him;
> But for their lives, some members say
> They cannot understand him.
> In such a puzzling case as this
> What can a mortal do?
> 'Tis hard for ONE to find REPORTS
> And understanding too.[7]

If, however, neither House nor country at large could make head or tail of his involved financial schemes, there certainly was no lack of understanding of Hamilton's main principles. And on these principles the storm broke with a violence that rocked the newly established government to its foundations.

On January 4, 1790, Hamilton submitted a letter to the House of Representatives advising that body that, pursuant to its resolution of September 21, 1789, he had prepared a plan for the support of the public credit, which he was ready to deliver personally to the House. It was suggested that January 14th be fixed as the date.

This seemingly modest and correct communication touched off a long debate. The point of dispute was Hamilton's proposal to deliver his report *in person*. Elbridge Gerry of Massachusetts was on his feet immediately with an amendment to the motion "that it [the report] should be made in writing." [8] Such an amendment, if accepted, would prevent Hamilton from appearing directly before the House to read his report and submit to questioning on policy and details.

Gerry, though personally friendly to Hamilton, had already evidenced in the previous session his fear that the Treasury, if consolidated in "the hands of one great man," would possess "a greater influence than the President of the United States has, and more than is proper for any person to have in a republican government." His amendment was designed to avoid increasing that personal power. A financial report, droned to the House by a clerk, could be debated with calm and equanimity. The same report, presented with all the eloquence of a Hamilton, might dazzle uncritical members and sway them all uncritically to his view.

Boudinot, politically and personally allied with Hamilton, protested instantly that the secretary be allowed to make his report in person. "It was a justifiable surmise," he maintained, "that gentlemen would not be able clearly to comprehend so intricate a subject without oral illustration."

But he was the only one of Hamilton's supporters who spoke in favor. Clymer was definitely opposed, and even more surprisingly, Fisher Ames of Massachusetts, ultra-aristocrat, "wished these communications to be in writing; in this shape they would obtain a degree of permanency favorable to the responsibility of the officer, while, at the same time, they would be less liable to be misunderstood." Ames, it is true, did not share Gerry's fear of a danger to republicanism; rather he was afraid to establish a precedent in which a demagogic secretary might, by sheer weight of oratory, override what he hoped might be a wholly deliberative assembly.

Thus, with friends and opponents united, Hamilton's idea was overwhelmingly voted down.[9] The consequences were far-reaching. The whole course of government in the United States was set in a definite mold. Thereafter *no* cabinet member ever appeared in congress personally to explain and defend his proposals, and that interacting influence which characterizes the British form of government never became a part of the American scene. Thereafter the cabinet became an adjunct of the presidency rather than of congress. Unwittingly congress had made possible the very thing it feared—an increase in the power of the Executive.

Disappointed at the rebuff, Hamilton submitted his report, and it was received in the House on January 14th. With it he included a series of proposals for increasing the national revenues in order to meet the interest charges and eventual installments of principal. In so doing, he delivered himself of a phrase which later commentators have been wont to tear from its qualifying context and belabor acrimoniously as an example of Hamilton's secret desire to exalt the virtues of a permanent national debt. While he considered "that the proper funding of the present debt will render it a national blessing," wrote Hamilton, yet he ardently wished "to see it incorporated as a fundamental maxim in the system of public credit of the United States, that the creation of debt should always be accompanied with the means of extinguishment." This he regarded as the "true secret for rendering public credit immortal." [10]

His scheme of taxation was conservative. It added only to current duties and taxes an increase on what he termed luxuries—wines, spirits, teas and coffees. He expected to reduce the principal of the debt by means of the postal revenues, which he would employ to purchase stock in the open market whenever the price fell below its "true value." Thereby a double purpose would be served: a reduction of the outstanding debt and a bolstering of the market price.

For future consideration he left the other fundamental section of his logical structure—the establishment of a national bank.

2. THE FIGHT ON THE REPORT

The report had barely come to the Speaker's desk when the first rumblings began. From his perch in the Senate, Maclay commented indignantly: "An extraordinary rise of certificates has been remarked for some time past. This could not be accounted for, neither in Philadelphia nor elsewhere. But the report from the Treasury explained all. He recommends indiscriminate funding, and, in the style of a British minister, has sent down his bill. 'Tis said a committee of speculators in certificates could not have formed it more for their advantage." [11]

The following day Maclay collected all the gossip and wrote it down in his *Journal*. A rumor here and a hint there. Robert Morris was speculating in the securities; so was Fitzsimmons: both members of congress from Pennsylvania. There was no doubt in the plain-spoken Senator's mind that they had been tipped off in advance by Hamilton. "The business of yesterday will, I think in all probability, damn the character of Hamilton as a minister forever," he wrote.[12]

There was no doubt in many other observers' minds that Hamilton had communicated the gist of his report to private friends and avowed speculators before it appeared publicly before the House. With the inevitability of a sharp rise in price once it was known that the secretary recommended funding at face value, those with advance knowledge were in a position to make large fortunes by purchasing secretly at the lower levels. It was said, and believed, that the Schuyler family had benefited greatly as a result.

So persistent were the statements about the Schuylers that long after the event James A. Hamilton, Hamilton's son, found it necessary to state flatly that Hamilton had requested Schuyler to keep his son, Van Rensselaer, from speculating in the public securities to avoid erroneous inferences, and that Van Rensselaer had complained at the restriction, though obedient to his father's will.[13]

The evidence, however, is directly to the contrary. Philip Schuyler himself was an active speculator. During the year 1791 the New York Loan Office registered on his account securities totaling $67,509.53.[14] Even more damning were the transactions of John Barker Church, Angelica's husband and Hamilton's brother-in-law. Church was in England at the time, and Hamilton acted as his agent in negotiations with Thomas Willing of Philadelphia for the purchase and sale of the public debt. On February 24, 1790, Willing wrote to Hamilton: "I have had this day the honor of your's inclosing yr power of substitution on behalf of Mr. Church. At present the sale of stock, & indeed every other Money transaction is nearly at a stand. . . . I observe what you say respectg the sale of what remains of Mr. Church's shares, & shall do whatever may be in my power to dispose of them whenever I receive the Certificates & your Orders to make the sale." [15] The total of Church's activities, as registered in the Loan Office, are larger even than Schuyler's. One item alone amounted to $28,187.91.[16]

Thomas Willing was Robert Morris's business partner and, according to Maclay, Willing had avowed openly that he had seen Hamilton's plan in manuscript before it had been made public.[17] Further-more, it is obvious from a letter from Angelica Church to her "dear Brother" that Hamilton had communicated some details of his pend-ing report to her—and necessarily to her husband—well before it reached congress.

Angelica had made her long-anticipated trip to America to visit with her family. Not the least of those whom she desired to see was the gay and witty, the gallantly flirtatious husband of her sister Betsy. Hamilton lived up to all the expectations and the dreams she had woven around him during her extended stay on the continent. He was everything her dull, prosaic, business-man husband was not. He made her visit delightful and a whirl of social gaiety. In spite of the pressure of official and private business he squired her around. When, early in November, 1789, wifely duties called her back to England he obtained her passage and took care of her finances. In his unpublished cash book are the following entries:

Account of Angelica Church
Nov. 2, 1789—Cash paid for passages of yourself and servant—£148.5
Nov. 4, 1789—This sum advanced to take with you
　　　　　　　200 Dollars　　　　　　　　　　　　　— 80.
Nov. 10, 1789—paid account of your last landlady for rooms
　　　　　　　　& some damage done by your servants in
　　　　　　　　removing　　　　　　　　　　　　— 23.9.3
　　　　　　　This sum paid your former music teacher　40.[18]

She had barely reached England when Hamilton wrote to her. She responded on January 7, 1790:

Many thanks to my dear Brother for having written to his friend at a moment when he had the affairs of America on his mind; I am impatient to hear in what manner your Budget has been received and extremely anxious for your success. I sometimes think you have now forgot me and that having seen me is like a dream which you can scarcely believe.—adieu I will not write this idea of being lost in the tumult of business and ambi-tion does not enliven my spirits—*adieu soyez heureux au dessus de tout le monde.*[19]

Yet it is just as equally certain that Hamilton did not own or deal in a single share of the public debt, and that when he left the Treasury he was poorer than when he entered it.

The House seemed in no hurry to take up the report that Hamilton had placed in its hands. Maclay thought some of the members were deliberately holding off action to give them a chance to buy up se-

curities in remote parts of the union before the news got to the un-
wary original holders. A man coming up from North Carolina told
him that he had "passed two expresses with very large sums of money
on their way to North Carolina for purposes of speculating in certificates." Maclay also heard that Jeremiah Wadsworth of Connecticut
had sent two small, fast vessels to the south on a similar errand. "I
really fear the members of Congress are deeper in this business than
any others," he ended mournfully. "Nobody doubts but all the commotion originated from the Treasury; but the fault is laid on Duer but
respondent superior. [*sic*]" [20]

Madison added his comments on "the avidity for stock" which
raised the price from a few shillings in the pound to eight or ten even
before the report came to congress. As late as January 24th, he declared, "emissaries are still exploring the interior & distant parts of the
Union in order to take advantage of the ignorance of holders." [21]

When the House finally took up consideration on January 28th,
the surge of speculation had reached such proportions that many of
the members who had previously favored Hamilton's plan of no discrimination between the original holders and the speculative trans-
ferees of the debt now grew doubtful of their position. Jackson of
Georgia became the chief spokesman for these members.

The long-awaited debate was begun to unusually crowded galleries.
Jackson rose to address the House. He had formerly coincided with
the secretary's opinion, he declared,

but circumstances have occurred, to make me almost a convert to the
other. Since this report has been read in this House, a spirit of havoc,
speculation, and ruin, has arisen, and been cherished by people who had
an access to the information the report contained. [In a rising fervor of
passion he continued], Three vessels, sir, have sailed within a fortnight
from this port, freighted for speculation; they are intended to purchase
up the State and other securities in the hands of the uninformed, though
honest citizens of North Carolina, South Carolina, and Georgia. My soul
rises indignant at the avaricious and immoral turpitude which so vile a
conduct displays.

Everyone knew to whom he particularly referred, and Wadsworth
must have squirmed in his seat. While the galleries listened tensely,
Jackson told the members that his "mind is almost made up in favor
of some discrimination, by reason of the speculation, which has been
carried on." On the subject of the assumption by the federal government of the state debts, he wanted to hear first from the states them-

selves before he committed himself. Therefore he proposed a long adjournment of any further consideration.[22]

Those who opposed *in toto* Hamilton's plan were equally in favor of a lengthy adjournment, certainly until the still absent North Carolina delegation arrived in New York. North Carolina was definitely in the opposition. But Hamilton's supporters were insistent on immediate action. They were afraid of the mounting tide of resentment. One of them, Boudinot of New Jersey, attempted to defend the speculators. He should be sorry, he said, "if, on this occasion, the House should decide, that speculations in the funds are violations of either the moral or political law." Yet he was compelled to admit "that the spirit of speculation had now risen to an alarming height." The only way to put a stop to it, he urged, "is to give the public funds a degree of stability as soon as possible."[23]

The opposition moved to adjourn consideration until the beginning of March, but Hamilton's supporters mustered enough strength to hold postponement down for a week.[24]

In the interim there was much scurrying and tightening of lines. Hamilton was now thoroughly alarmed for the success of his plan. He had not expected such vehement opposition, and he was concerned to see some of his earlier supporters drifting away. To him the speculative activity was something to be welcomed rather than deplored. With the public debt in the hands of the strong and wealthy instead of the weak and poor, there would be that mutual binding interest between government and men of money which to him was the prime cement of any national vigor and prosperity. With the morals of the question he had nothing to do.

On February 1st Maclay acidly observed that "Mr. Hamilton is very uneasy, as far as I can learn, about his funding system. He was here early to wait on the Speaker, and I believe spent most of his time in running from place to place among the members."[25]

Meanwhile ordinary folk were reading copies of the report and getting more and more bewildered and enmeshed in its complications. One Bostonian constituent reported to Theodore Sedgwick: "I imagine you will have a hard task to digest & adopt the Secy's Budget. People here do not understand it."[26]

Henry Van Schaack, himself a political figure and a man of wide affairs, wrote in like vein to Sedgwick: "The subject of the Report is an important one—that it is complicated and difficult to be understood, while we are in an infancy in the knowledge of Finance, is not to be wondered at. After the first reading of the Report I found myself as ignorant as Uncle Toby confided himself to be to his mother." But Van Schaack persevered. "I however gave it a second and third reading by which means I am gaining ground and I know now more about our National affairs than I ever did before—some parts of the Report must remain obscure until the subject is fur[ther] explained." [27]

When, on February 8th, the House resumed consideration of the report it was as a committee of the whole. Jackson of Georgia again took the lead in critical debate. While he agreed that the *foreign* debt must be properly provided for, he feared the effects of a permanent funded debt. He would rather, he declared, impose direct taxes immediately in order to pay off the principal as fast as possible, or use the sale of public lands for the same purpose. [28]

No one, in fact, but admitted the binding obligation of the foreign debt. It was the *domestic* debt on which the artillery of the opposition was concentrated. Livermore of New York sounded the keynote of their position. The domestic debt, he argued, was "not incurred for efficient money lent, but for depreciated paper, or services done at exorbitant rates, or for goods or provisions supplied at more than their real worth." Why not then pay the holders at the current market value, which he considered high enough in all conscience. [29]

But now, for the first time, Hamilton's supporters rushed into the breach. One after another, Bland of Virginia, Boudinot of New Jersey and Ames of Massachusetts rose to the defense. Their arguments ran along the lines of the sacredness of contract, appeals to legal principles, and passing references to "honor, justice and policy." "Shall it be said that this Government," demanded Ames, "evidently established for the purpose of securing property, that, in its first act, it divested its citizens of seventy millions of money, which is justly due to the individuals who have contracted with Government!" [30]

To this exordium on the sacredness of property Livermore slyly countered with the query whether Ames would be willing to show the same tenderness for the holders of the old Continental bills, which "were issued with as much confidence, and were received with as firm reliance on the public faith, as any species of securities whatever." [31] Ames sat silent under the embarrassing query. Logically it was unanswerable, for everyone knew, as Livermore pointed out, that it would be impossible to include redemption at par on these practically worthless bills.

On February 11th a new figure arose to participate in the debate. All eyes were instantly focused on him. James Madison of Virginia carried weight and authority. He had helped draft the Constitution and had impressed it with his stamp. His learning was universally considered profound, and his logic severe. Behind him, portentous and grim, hovered the powerful men of Virginia—and especially the tall, gangling figure of Thomas Jefferson, the new Secretary of State.

Thus far Madison had failed to declare himself. It is true he had seemed to agree with Hamilton in his reply to that worthy's requests for comments. But since then he had been silent. Now he was going to speak.

Ames watched him curiously. He had earlier characterized his appearance and manner in addressing the House: "He speaks low, his person is little and ordinary. He speaks decently, as to manner, and no more. His language is very pure, perspicuous, and to the point. Pardon me, if I add, that I think him a little too much of a book politician, and too timid in his politics." Yet Ames was compelled to add: "He is our first man." [32]

In his dry, small voice Madison began. He admitted, he said, that the domestic debt was valid. But to whom was the government indebted? He divided the domestic creditors into four classes: (1) original holders who had never alienated their holdings; (2) original holders who *had* divested themselves by assignment; (3) present holders who held merely by assignment; and (4) intermediate holders no longer in possession. As to the first class there was no dispute. They must be paid in full. As to the last class, "their pretensions, if they have any, will lead us into a labyrinth, for which it is impossible to find a clew." With these two out of the way, he concentrated on the second and third groups as presenting the main issue of the debate. The second group, he felt, had never really been paid. They had been compelled, by hard necessity, to sell at a fraction of the face value. The third group—the present holders by assignment—also had claims, it was true. He even presented the arguments in their behalf fully and fairly. But it was impossible to pay *both* what good faith in the first instance, and legality in the second, demanded. And it was equally unfair to reject wholly either group. Therefore he suggested a compromise and so formally moved: "Let it [the compromise] be a liberal one," he said, "in favor of the present holders, let them have the highest price which has prevailed in the market; and let the residue belong to the original sufferers." [33]

Madison's compromise proposal became immediately the storm center of an acrimonious debate. Like all compromises it failed to satisfy the partisans on either side. The Hamiltonians accused him of having suddenly changed his position and of inducing their leader to believe he would back the report. So vehement were their attacks and so uneasy Madison's own conscience that he wrote out a memorandum on a scrap of paper and attached it to his private notes. Referring to himself in the third person he stated: "This explains the apparent change in Mr. Madison's opinion from his previous one opposed to discriminations. At that time the debts were due to the original holders." [34]

From his vantage point in the Senate, Maclay was just as sharply critical. To him, Madison's scheme was even more dangerous than Hamilton's, for it would necessitate just as heavy taxes and might be more readily submitted to by the people because of the specious plea in favor of the original holders. What Maclay wanted was to remove completely the threat of a permanent debt. To accomplish this he insisted that the interest rate be scaled down from six to three per cent, and the principal extinguished by the sale of the western lands, "in which certificates of the domestic debt only shall be receivable." [35]

The test of strength on Madison's motion came on February 22nd, and his plan was decisively defeated by a vote of 13 to 36. With this important hurdle surmounted, Hamilton's supporters jubilantly pressed for swift action. In rapid succession Fitzsimmons' original motion to appropriate permanent funds for the payment of interest on, and the gradual reduction of, the public debt, and a motion to fund the accrued interest, were passed.[36] The first great victory had been won.

3. THE FIGHT ON ASSUMPTON

So far the struggle had been over the *national* creditors. Attention now centered on the second, and what was considered on all sides more important, aspect of the report. This was Hamilton's requirement that the debts due from the respective states be assumed by the national government and funded in one indistinguishable mass with its own national debt.

At first blush it would appear that the states ought to have been gladly and wholeheartedly in favor of a plan that would relieve them of a pressing load of debts. Actually this was not the case. On no part of Hamilton's schemes was there concentrated such a torrent of abuse, such a weight of heated argument, such a maneuvering for position. Charges of bribery and corruption were tossed freely into the air, and before the smoke of battle cleared Hamilton, Jefferson, Madison and a host of minor figures had been clothed in epithets and tarred in characterizations that remained the small change of party warfare concerning them for the balance of their lives.

Hamilton's purpose in advocating assumption was open and avowed. By taking over the war debts of the respective states, these local centers of separatism and jealousy must have a continuing interest in the success of the union which had agreed to pay them. Similarly, the numerous creditors would find it to their interest to support the central government. And the fact of assumption gave the government its most powerful argument for a uniform and general system of taxation.

The states, on the other hand, viewed the matter from equally frank and various points of self-interest. The New England states, and especially Massachusetts, with the heaviest war debts of all, eagerly embraced the theory of assumption. States like Georgia, on the other hand, whose war effort had not involved large borrowings, vehemently opposed, since they felt that they would be taxed by the national government to pay off the debts of the other states. Again, those states which had already paid portions of their debts in varying degrees, wanted to know if they would receive credits from the government for the parts so paid. And in the south generally it was matter of bitter comment that their own citizen-holders of the debt had already divested themselves of ownership at tremendous discounts and that assumption would mean merely taxation for the benefit of the new northern purchasers.

The debate in the House followed closely along these lines. The positions taken by the Representatives could be deduced in advance from the particular state of the debt at home.

The struggle commenced on February 23rd and did not end until July 26th. The heaviest guns on both sides volleyed and thundered; passions rose to an almost insupportable intensity; and the foundations of the new nation sagged alarmingly in the process. A similar debate resounded in the Senate, but the secrecy of the proceedings prevented any but casual glimpses of the intensity of the battle in that chamber.

In the House, Ames and Sedgwick of Massachusetts, with Sherman and Wadsworth of Connecticut, assumed the brunt of the Hamiltonian position. Their oratory was chiefly on general principles. Aedanus Burke of South Carolina, however, frankly confessed that his state would end in bankruptcy if the measure was lost, "for she was no more able to grapple with her enormous debt, than a boy of twelve years of age is able to grapple with a giant." [37]

The opponents of assumption were quite specific. White of Virginia moved for a disclosure by Hamilton of the exact resources of the nation which he intended to apply to the payment of the state debts if the bill should pass. Jackson of Georgia declared he was opposed to assumption, "not only in its original form, but in every possible modification it might assume." He paid ironical tribute to Hamilton's abilities and talents; but, he cried, "I trust we shall not run ourselves enormously in debt, and mortgage ourselves and our children, to give scope to the abilities of any Minister on earth." [38]

The vote on White's motion disclosed the delicate balancing of the opposing forces. It resulted in a tie—25 to 25—and the casting vote of the Speaker was required to carry it.

Madison, as always, started out cautiously and in a compromising frame of mind. He hinted his suspicion that the state debts, like the federal debt, would flow inevitably into the hands of northern wealth, and he even expressed the fear that eventually it must go out of the United States altogether and become concentrated in foreign hands. But he failed to pursue the point. Instead, he called for an amendment which would provide for a mutual settlement of accounts between the states and the nation, so that those States which had paid off the major parts of their debts would not be "burthened to pay the debts of the other." [39]

Meanwhile Maclay was recording in his *Journal* that Hamilton was employing every tool at hand to push assumption through—the clergy, government officials, the Order of the Cincinnati—a group of veteran officers of the Revolution which Hamilton had helped found and which he proposed to make hereditary—and God knows whom! He had heard that a certain Representative had been offered a thousand guineas for his vote, but Maclay cynically thought it unlikely, for the man might have been purchased for "a tenth part of the sum." [40]

With the opposed forces so evenly balanced, on March 3rd Carroll of Maryland suddenly moved to discharge the House from consideration of the Bill. Instantly Hamilton's supporters were on their feet protesting. Even though Carroll explained his move, not as a final discharge, but as a halt until Hamilton could report on the information desired from him in White's bill, his motion was defeated, 20 to 28. [41]

In fact, Hamilton's report came in the following day. It proposed a series of additional duties in order to meet the interest on the state debts, when and if assumption was carried.

On March 13th, however, it was his own supporters who decided to postpone further consideration for a while. For in the meantime the picture had rapidly worsened. The reports that came in from the south, of congressional speculators and others pushing deep into the interiors to buy up state debts from ignorant and necessitous holders, had aroused tremendous indignation and caused several votes to shift. In addition, some of their staunchest men were absent—Fitzsimmons, Clymer and Wadsworth—and Fisher Ames, the leader of the Hamiltonians, thought it well to wait for their return.[42]

As a result, as Jonathan Trumbull reported to the absent Wadsworth, "the whole of the past Week has been wasted with the Quakers & the Negroes. The So. Carolina & Georgia members have taken up the matter with as much warmth & zeal as though the very existence of their States depended on the decision ... in the meantime all discussion on the Sectys Report is at a stand—& will remain so till you & Clymer & Fitzsimmons return." [43]

It was at about this time, too, that William Duer resigned as Assistant Secretary of the Treasury. His involvement in speculations and in the tangled affairs of the Scioto Company, his direct use of his office for purposes of private gain, had become matters of public report and criticism. He became a drag upon Hamilton at a most critical stage in the congressional struggle, and it was doubtless at Hamilton's suggestion that he resigned. Tench Coxe was appointed in his place.

On March 29th, the absent members having returned, the debate was resumed. On April 1st, surveying the situation, Wadsworth confessed that "I almost begin to despair of the assumption of the State debts, and with that I shall despair of the National Government." [44]

Two days later Burke of South Carolina had shifted his earlier ground to such an extent that he made a violent personal attack upon Hamilton's integrity on the floor of the House. So bitter were the insults that New York City expected momentarily the issuance of a challenge to a duel. Maclay, who considered dueling a sign of aristocratic decadence, feared that "so many people concerned in the business may really make the fools fight." [45] But Hamilton wisely decided to ignore the provocation.

On April 8th Maclay allows us a glimpse of the situation in the secretive Senate. It is a lively description, though its manifest partisanship must be discounted. "I never observed," he wrote, "so drooping an aspect, so turbid and forlorn an appearance as overspread the partisans of the Secretary in our House this forenoon.... Elsworth and Izard in particular walked almost all the morning back and forward. Strong and Patterson seemed moved, but not so much agitated. King looked like a boy that had been whipped, and General Schuyler's hair stood on end as if the Indians had fired at him." [46]

In truth, the supporters of assumption in both branches of congress had much to be perturbed about. On April 12th the measure finally came to a vote in the House, and it went down to defeat by a vote of 29 to 31.

The vote came as a stunning blow. Under the first impact Sedgwick of Massachusetts rose to deliver what was in effect a funeral oration. Massachusetts, he warned them, would never submit tamely. "We have demanded justice; we have implored the compassion of the Representatives of the People of America, to relieve us from the pressure of intolerable burthens; burthens incurred in support of your freedom and independence. Our demands and entreaties have both been ineffectual." [47]

Maclay had quit the Senate chamber to watch these portentous proceedings in the House. According to him Sedgwick was called to order for his remarks.

Some confusion ensued; he took his hat and went out. When he returned, his visage, to me, bore the visible marks of weeping. Fitzsimons reddened like scarlet; his eyes were brimful. Clymer's color, always pale, now verged to a deadly white; his lips quivered, and his nether jaw shook with convulsive motions.... Ames's aspect was truly hippocratic—a total change of face and features; he sat torpid, as if his faculties had been benumbed. [Gerry] delivered himself of a declaration that the delegates of Massachusetts would proceed no further, but send to their State for instructions. [Wadsworth] hid his grief under the rim of a round hat. Boudinot's wrinkles rose in ridges and the angles of his mouth were depressed and assumed a curve resembling a horse's shoe. Fitzsimons first recovered recollection, and endeavored to rally the discomfited and disheartened heroes. He hoped the good sense of the House would still predominate and lead them to reconsider the vote which had been now taken; and he doubted not but what it would yet be adopted under proper modifications. The Secretary's group pricked up their ears, and Speculation wiped the tear from either eye.[48]

By April 14th, two days after the debacle, Hamilton's supporters had rallied. One after another arose with motions designed to reintroduce the discredited bill under the guise of modifications. By April

22nd Madison, because of "the uncommon perseverance with which the advocates for an assumption adhere to their object," felt compelled to make a long speech on the subject, in which for the first time he introduced the question of constitutionality.[49]

On April 26th, however, Fitzsimmons suddenly moved to discharge the House from further consideration of assumption. The Antis assented joyfully, considering their cause definitely won. But it was a mere tactical retreat on Fitzsimmons' part—to give Hamilton a chance to employ other means to gain their objective.

Hamilton himself, during all the heat and dust of congressional battle, had declared his complete confidence in the final result. It must be carried, he told friends, because the rest of his plan, already passed, could not be put into effect without it.[50]

But he had other reasons for his confidence than this. And now, for the first time, the paths of the two great antagonists during the formative days of the republic converge and mingle.

Thomas Jefferson, as tall as Hamilton was short, as gangling and loose-jointed as Hamilton was erect and compact, as trustful of the essential wisdom of the farmer-yeoman as Hamilton of the moneyed man, as distrustful of centralization as Hamilton was in favor, had returned to the United States in March after an extended stay in France as Minister. He had been absent all through the extended struggle over the Constitution and during the elections. The initial phases of Hamilton's funding schemes had passed through congress, and the battle on assumption was already under way.

Jefferson later made the claim that he was "a stranger to the ground, a stranger to the actors on it," and that he "took no concern in it." [51] In a sense this was true, though he had been in touch with the leaders of Virginia and elsewhere by letter during the entire period of his absence and had kept himself informed of every step along the road of Constitution and after.

Another matter, however, arose to trouble congress during the backings and fillings on assumption. This was the question of a permanent capital for the United States. New York was the temporary capital, and the southern states violently objected to the seat of government being placed so far to the north. They demanded, nay, insisted, that the capital rightfully belonged in the south. The New Englanders as violently demanded that it be placed at some point at least equidistant between the two sections of the country. Pennsylvania clamored for Philadelphia as the logical seat. On these conflicting claims no agreement was reached nor seemingly *could* be reached. At this point of impasse Hamilton conceived his brilliant idea.

On June 14th he sent his assistant in the Treasury, Tench Coxe, as emissary to the most determined opponent of assumption in the Senate, William Maclay of Pennsylvania. Coxe proposed a bargain. If the Pennsylvania delegation could be persuaded to vote as a body for assumption, then Hamilton would see to it that the permanent capital would go to Pennsylvania. But Maclay told his *Journal* that night: "I constrained my indignation at this proposal with much difficulty." Meanwhile Hamilton was personally in touch with Robert Morris. What was needed for the passage of assumption, he told Morris, was a single vote in the Senate and five in the House. If Pennsylvania would furnish the required number, the capital was theirs—and would even be placed temporarily in Philadelphia. Morris expressed, nor hid, no such moral indignation as Maclay; instead, he agreed to consult the Pennsylvania delegation on the matter. But before it could come to a decision, Hamilton had achieved unexpected success in a wholly different quarter and sent post-haste to Morris a note calling the deal off because "his friends would not hear of it." [52]

Hamilton was less than candid with Morris. What had happened was that he had talked with Jefferson. The latter wrote the story down after long years in an attempt to justify how "I was most ignorantly & innocently made to hold the candle." Hamilton, it seems, stopped him in the street one day as he was going to see the President. Hamilton was in despair. He walked Jefferson backwards and forwards before the President's door for half an hour. He painted a pathetic picture of the temper of congress, of the disgust of "the Creditor states," of the dangers of secession. He appealed to Jefferson "that the members of administration ought to act in concert," that since the assumption had been lost by a small majority, an appeal by Jefferson to his friends might easily change the result. Jefferson replied that he was "really a stranger to the whole subject;" but if a dissolution of the incipient union would result from rejection, then something ought to be done. Accordingly he agreed to arrange a dinner at which Hamilton could meet and discuss the matter with Jefferson's "friends."

The dinner was arranged and Hamilton exercised his persuasive powers to such effect that it was agreed that some of the members of congress present at the convivial board should shift their votes so that assumption might pass. It was remarked, however, "that this pill would be peculiarly bitter to the Southern States, and that some con-

comitant measure should be adopted to sweeten it a little to them."
Curiously enough, this "pill" was exactly the same as had been previously offered to Pennsylvania. Except that now the capital was to be
placed permanently at Georgetown in Virginia. Jefferson does not say
so, but it is logical to believe that Hamilton said something about a
"pill" for Pennsylvania also, whose votes were essential to carry the
matter of the capital. In any event it was finally agreed that the capital
be placed for an interim period of ten years in Philadelphia and after
that transferred permanently to Georgetown. "So," continues Jefferson, "two of the Potomac members (White & Lee, but White with a
revulsion of stomach almost convulsive) agreed to change their votes,
& Hamilton undertook to carry the other point." And so, concludes
Jefferson, Hamilton "effected his side of the engagement, and so the
assumption was passed, and 20. millions of stock divided among favored
states, and thrown in as pabulum to the stock-jobbing herd." [53]

If such were the true facts, then Jefferson was far more naïve and
gullible, and his friends as well, than there is any reason to believe
possible. Actually, of course, it was a straight out-and-out political
bargain, a *quid pro quo,* of which Jefferson in after years bitterly
repented and attempted to cover with a veil of reminiscence.

In his private letters immediately following the "bargain" Jefferson
expressed himself with more candor. To Monroe he wrote that the
struggle in congress had reached such proportions on both questions—
assumption and the capital—that "unless they can be reconciled by
some plan of compromise, there will be no funding bill agreed to, our
credit, (raised by late prospects to be the first on the exchange at
Amsterdam, where our paper is above par) will burst and vanish, and
the states separate to take care everyone of itself." This sounds very
much like the speech of a man who has weighed the consequences and
decided on a course of action, not like one who as "a stranger" has
been taken in by specious arguments.

It is true that on the specific question of assumption Jefferson proceeded to say: "I have been & still am of their opinion that Congress
should always prefer letting the states raise money in their own way
where it can be done. but in the present instance I see the necessity of
yielding for this time to the cries of the creditors in certain parts of the
union for the sake of union, and to save us from the greatest of all
calamities, the total extinction of our credit in Europe." [54]

In any event, the bargain made was lived up to on both sides. To the profound astonishment of the outright opponents of assumption, Hamilton's measure passed in the Senate on July 21st and in the House on July 26th by a vote of 34 to 28.[55] He had won a great victory.

Not merely were men like Senator Maclay astounded, who rightly suspected a double bargain with Robert Morris and the Virginians,[56] but even those "speculators" whom Maclay and Jefferson accused of knowing every move that Hamilton made, were taken by surprise. Andrew Craigie of Boston wrote mournfully that he had not made the profit he might have made had he but known. He had purchased a large amount of the South Carolina debt under three shillings, eightpence per pound, "but was unfortunate enough a few days before the compromise took place & when the Assumption was thought by the knowing ones to be lost to part with it at 4/. in the £.... Mr. Cazenove, a Dutch Agent, I afterwards found was the fortunate purchaser & of large Sums besides on the same day." [57]

The passage of assumption provoked immediate repercussions in Jefferson's own state of Virginia. Barely had the legislature convened when Patrick Henry introduced a fiery resolution denouncing assumption as "repugnant to the constitution of the United States, as it goes to the exercise of a power not expressly granted to the general government." [58]

Though John Marshall and other conservative men fought the resolution, it passed by a large majority, and was immediately followed by an even more fiery Protest and Remonstrance which declared flatly that all powers not expressly given in the Constitution were reserved to the states, that the Assumption Act was an effort "to erect and concentrate and perpetuate a large monied interest in opposition to the landed interests," which would prostrate "agriculture at the feet of commerce" or result in a "change in the present form of Federal Government, fatal to the existence of American liberty." [59]

To Hamilton this action on the part of a powerful state like Virginia was fraught with the most serious consequences. He sent copies of the two resolutions along to John Jay with a grim note: "This is the first symptom of a spirit which must either be killed, or it will kill the Constitution of the United States. I send the resolutions to you, that it may be considered what ought to be done." [60]

Jay in this instance was the more practical politician. He advised Hamilton that the best course was to take no notice of the resolutions.

They were mere ebullitions and would only tend to diminish the influence of the states, rather than seriously affect the status of the national government.[61]

As Jay had prophesied, the Virginia resolutions had no immediate effect; but Hamilton proved the more far-sighted in his concern over the ultimate consequences. Here were the first rumblings of Nullification and Secession. Here, for practically the first time, a measure passed by congress was held by an important state to be unconstitutional. Here was the inception of the doctrine of "strict construction," which Jefferson and Madison were to wield with such telling effect in future debates.[62]

CHAPTER XIX

The Great Reports (continued)

1. THE NEW SEAT OF GOVERNMENT

THE FIRST FRUIT of the bargain on assumption was the shift in the capital of the United States from New York to a ten-year residence in Philadelphia. Hamilton, busy with the cares of his office in New York, asked a friend to find him a decent home in Philadelphia. But first he wanted to make certain where the Treasury Department would be located. "My next wish," he wrote, "would be to have a house as near my destined office as possible. A cool situation & exposure will of course be a very material point to a New Yorker. The house must have at least six rooms. Good dining and drawing rooms are material articles. I like elbow room in a yard. As to the rent the lower the better consistently with the acquisition of a proper house." [1]

A little later he wrote his agent that he had already engaged a house for an *office* at the corner of Chestnut and Third Streets and asked him to find a residence for him as close as possible to the office. [2] He finally discovered one close enough—at the corner of Walnut and Third—and Betsy and their four growing children ensconced themselves with some misgivings in their new quarters. These proved hot enough to "New Yorkers" and Hamilton was compelled to find a cooler situation, though further away from his office, outside the city and close to Robert Morris's palatial estate. There they remained for five years.

The government soon acclimated itself to the atmosphere of Philadelphia and began to work as a functioning unit. The problems that faced Washington were many and disturbing. The financial situation at home was still chaotic, but Hamilton was working feverishly and with some degree of success to straighten it out. He sent detailed instructions to William Short in Holland on the raising of a new foreign loan of $14,000,000, with which to pay off part of the existing foreign debt as it became due and to fund the remainder. [3] He sent to the

House a further Report on the Public Credit, asserting that the most essential and immediate object was the establishment of sufficient funds to pay the interest on the assumed state debts. To provide for this, he advocated further duties on distilled spirits, both domestic and foreign, and insisted on their effective collection by vigilant public officers. But he refused to suggest increased duties on imported articles of trade other than spirits. These, so the merchants had assured him, were high enough already. He went out of his way to praise the merchants of the nation as an "enlightened class of our citizens," who had shown themselves most accommodating and favorable to the national government.[4] This section of his report must have proved bitter reading to the planters of the south and especially to the frontiersmen of western Pennsylvania, whose corn, distilled to liquor as the only viable form for easy transportation and sale, was being increasingly taxed by Hamilton's measures.

The foreign situation also demanded closer attention. The year before, the great convulsion of the French Revolution had broken all Europe from its moorings. Most Americans had hailed its beginnings with gratification. The example of the New World was being followed in the Old. Even Hamilton adopted a mildly benevolent, if somewhat reserved attitude. The excesses were still to come. But more immediate and pressing to the American scene was the matter of the impending hostilities between Great Britain and Spain.

Actually, Jefferson, as Secretary of State, should have had complete charge of foreign affairs. But Washington had not yet differentiated the separate departments of the government into tight compartments of their own. He usually called on all the members of his cabinet for their opinions on moot questions. Hamilton was quick to avail himself of this privilege and, though refusing to accept interference in the running of his own department, the Treasury, from the other members of the cabinet, inserted himself wherever possible in *their* affairs. Especially in the field of foreign affairs was he active. Jefferson resented this from the beginning, and his resentment grew with the years.

Curiously enough the British-Spanish dispute came first to the attention of Hamilton. Major Beckwith approached him unofficially on behalf of Lord Dorchester to sound out the possibility that, in the event of definite hostilities between England and Spain, the United States would grant passage to British troops from Canada through the western territory to assault the Spanish possessions. Hamilton made memoranda of his two conversations with Beckwith and submitted them to Washington. In a private note for his own file, Hamilton claimed that "Mr. Jefferson was privy to this transaction." [5] But Jefferson later intimated that he was not, and the fact that Washington, on receipt of the first memorandum, discussed Beckwith's business with Hamilton and Jay, and not at all with Jefferson, would seem to bear him out.

At this discussion, it was decided by the trio that Hamilton was "to extract as much as he could from Major Beckwith and to report to me [Washington], without committing, by any assurances whatever, the Government of the U. States, leaving it entirely free to pursue, unreproached, such a line of conduct in the dispute as her interest (and honour) shall dictate." [6]

When, pursuant to these instructions, Hamilton had his *second* interview with Beckwith, then for the first time Washington decided to bring it formally before the cabinet and the knowledge of Jefferson. He asked the members of his cabinet to express their opinions on two points in the event that the two nations went to war and Dorchester formally requested permission to march troops through American territory from Detroit to the Mississippi. First: what answer should the United States return to such a request; second: "what notice ought to be taken of the measure, if it should be undertaken without leave, which is the most probable proceeding of the two?" [7]

Jefferson gave his opinion first; Hamilton took more time for his reply. Jefferson, characteristically, preferred to "avoid giving any answer" to Dorchester, should he make the request. "They will proceed notwithstanding," he went on, "but to do this under our silence, will admit of palliation, and produce apologies, from military necessity; and will leave us free to pass it over without dishonor, or to make it a handle of quarrel hereafter, if we should have use for it as such." Jefferson always shrank from coming to irrevocable decisions on distasteful matters. "If we are obliged to give an answer," he continued reluctantly, "I think the occasion not such as should induce us to hazard that answer which might commit us to the war at so early a stage of it; and therefore that the passage should be permitted." [8]

Hamilton argued the matter on historical and legal grounds, as well as weighing and considering the consequences of refusal and nonrefusal. He agreed this far with Jefferson that the United States was in the worst possible position for a war with Great Britain and that the cultivation of neutrality was our true policy, but he disagreed sharply on the matter of an evasive answer or no answer at all. "An evasive conduct in similar cases is never dignified—seldom politic," he declared. "It would be likely to give satisfaction to neither party—to effect no good—to prevent no ill." Therefore, if the request be made, grant consent. If, however, Washington should decide to *refuse* consent, and the British marched nevertheless, then resist, even to war. If, as Washington thought probable, the British moved without asking our leave, then we should be content with mere remonstrances.[9] In the end, though by diverse paths, both men came to a common ground.

Fortunately, this first threat to American neutrality never materialized. Lord Dorchester decided not to make an official request; the British troops remained in Canada; and the United States was spared a fuller consideration of its foreign policy for a few more years.[10]

2. REPORT ON A NATIONAL BANK

As far back as 1779, when Hamilton was only a youth of twenty-two, he had written a famous letter to General Sullivan on the subject of a national bank. And, during the intervening years, he had never once permitted the subject to die. In letter after letter, in address after address, in private conversation and in public debate, in Continental Congress and in Federal Congress, he had insisted unweariedly that a bank underwritten by and partially controlled by the national government was the fundamental basis for a successful system of finance.

Now, as Secretary of the Treasury, he was in a position to bring the matter to a head. Using his earlier Report on the Public Credit as a springboard, he laid before the House of Representatives on December 14, 1790, a Supplemental Report in which he set forth his plan in full.

Essentially, his proposals were the same as those he had advocated in earlier years. After a short history of public banks and a discussion of their merits, he elaborated on his scheme. He called for a capital stock of $10,000,000, divided into 25,000 shares. Of these shares the United States might subscribe to 5,000; the balance was open to private subscription. The shares were payable one-fourth in coin, and three-fourths in the six per cent public debt. The bank would be governed by a board of twenty-five directors which, by virtue of the limitations on governmental subscriptions, must necessarily represent by a large majority the private shareholders in the bank. Hamilton plainly stated that he considered it an essential ingredient in the structure of the bank "that it shall be under a *private* not a *public* direction—under the guidance of *individual interest*, not of *public policy*." The sense of private interest and of ownership, he was convinced, "is the only security that can always be relied upon for a careful and prudent administration." The chief object of combining part of the public debt in the capital structure of the bank was "to enable the creation of a capital sufficiently large to be the basis of an extensive circulation, and an adequate security for it."

The bank was to have the power to issue notes, limited only by the provision that the total of its debts could not exceed its deposits by more than $10,000,000. These notes were to be payable on demand and would be legal tender for all obligations to the United States. Its loans were to be limited to a six per cent interest rate. The government had the right to borrow the $2,000,000 it had paid into the bank, and return the loan in ten annual installments. The sole interest of the government in the bank was to consist of its share in the profits, its borrowings, and the receipt of reports as to its condition and resources. In all other respects the bank would be a private venture. The bank charter was to run for twenty years; it was to be unique during its existence; and branch banks might be established for discount and deposit.[11]

Such was the dryly detailed and seemingly uninteresting plan—from an emotive point of view—that Hamilton tossed into the lap of congress. Yet it proved a bombshell, more explosive in its possibilities and more productive of heat, if not of light, than even assumption. From its reception sprang the great debate on the theory and capabilities of the Constitution of the United States that has continued down to the present day, and has not yet lost much of its original force. From this report stemmed as the natural flower the great decisions of John Marshall and the shaping of the tremendous doctrine of "implied powers." Hamilton was its father, and Marshall reared it to a lusty giant. Without this doctrine, it is more than doubtful if the Constitution as a practical scheme of government could have survived; through the doctrine, that aged instrument, made flexible and amenable to ever-changing needs, has held the nation together through all divisive and centrifugal struggles.

The immediate effect of the publication of the report was enormous. Fisher Ames sent a copy of it to a friend, with the comment: "The late surprising rise of public stock is supposed to be owing in part to this report, because it affords an opportunity to subscribe three fourths paper and one fourth silver into the bank stock." [12] And Sir

John Temple, in charge of British interests, advised his government that "some of the Public Securities of these States have risen 16, & 17/ the pound! and are still rising! The Dutch have been great Purchasers into these funds, and if nothing shd. happen to alter present appearances, they will have made great proffit indeed by their purchases, two & three for one!" [13]

Senator Maclay, that indefatigable diarist, read the report and considered it "an aristocratic engine." He also doubted its constitutionality, yet he was afraid that the bank would come to pass. The whole course of events led him to despair. Once an ardent admirer of Washington, he was now moved to write of that erstwhile great man: "Would to God this same General Washington were in heaven! We would not then have him brought forward as the constant cover to every unconstitutional and irrepublican act." [14]

Maclay's fears were well founded. Though the report had been made to the House, his own Senate acted first upon it and passed a bill with reasonable rapidity. Maclay tried in vain to have it amended in order to give the government the right to subscribe on equal terms with individuals, and asked Robert Morris to back him. But Morris said that Schuyler had told him of Hamilton's declaration that there must be no alteration in the bill. Which led to Maclay's retort that "Schuyler is the supple-jack of his son-in-law Hamilton." [15]

In the House the report had much harder sledding. For some curious reason the members were loath to take up its consideration. Received on December 14th, it went through three leisurely readings. On the third reading the debate actually started. Then it made up in intensity for past delays. Jackson of Georgia opened the proceedings on February 1, 1791. One of the most determined opponents of every Hamiltonian measure, he declared that this particular plan was "calculated to benefit a small part of the United States, the mercantile interest only; the farmers, the yeomanry, will derive no advantage from it." Then he went to the fundamental question—the one on which the debate thereafter turned as on a wheel. This bank, he cried, is unconstitutional! We have no power to grant a charter to any private corporation! And, with a triumphant smile, he quoted from the Federalist Papers—written by Hamilton, Madison and Jay—to prove his point. [16]

When Madison arose—small, pale, precise—drama entered the stage. For here was the one man in the House who could speak with authority upon the Federalist Papers and upon the Constitution with which he had had so much to do. He well recollected, he said, "that a power to grant charters of incorporation had been proposed in the General Convention and rejected." Then he launched on his constitutional argument. It was carefully considered, dispassionate, legalistic, yet powerful. Adhering to the strict letter of the document, it was unanswerable from that point of view and became the basis of all future arguments for a "strict construction." Jefferson, in his later cabinet opinion, took over these arguments almost verbatim.[17]

The following day Ames replied. He was the ablest of Hamilton's supporters in the House, yet he did not attempt to meet Madison on his own ground. Instead, he relied on Hamilton's own indicated ground—the invocation of the doctrine of "implied powers." "If Congress may not make laws conformably to the powers plainly implied, though not expressed in the frame of Government," he asserted, "it is rather late in the day to adopt it as a principle of conduct. A great part of our two years' labor is lost, and worse than lost to the public, for we have scarcely made a law in which we have not exercised our discretion with regard to the true intent of the Constitution." Of what use was the power to borrow, as expressly provided for in the Constitution, if its most efficient instrument, a bank, was not implied in that power?[18]

With these two powerful statements of the issue, the line of demarcation between the future parties—Federalist and Republican—was plainly indicated. Stone of Maryland pointed out another significant line—a geographical line—which cut the continent in two on opinions respecting the Constitution. Giles of Virginia was even more specific—and filled with foreboding. "I have observed with regret a radical difference of opinion between gentlemen from the Eastern and Southern States, upon great Governmental questions, and have been led to conclude, that the operation of that cause alone might cast ominous conjecture on the promised success of this much valued Government."[19]

But by February 8, 1791, the opponents of the bank had exhausted their resources and their arguments, and the Bill passed by an overwhelming vote of 39 to 20.

Yet victory, seemingly within Hamilton's grasp, suddenly began to slither away. Washington hesitated to sign the Bill. The vehement outcries against its constitutionality troubled him. He asked Randolph, the Attorney-General, for his opinion. Randolph declared the measure unconstitutional. He applied next to Jefferson, Secretary of State. On February 15th Jefferson returned a written opinion to the same effect.

He maintained that the proposed incorporation did not come within
any of the delegated powers, either enumerated or non-enumerated.
"To take a single step beyond the boundaries thus especially drawn
around the powers of Congress, is to take possession of a boundless
field of power, no longer susceptible of any definition." He dismissed
as quibbling the argument that the clause ("to make all laws necessary and proper," etc.) justified the bank. The enumerated powers,
he said, "can all be carried into execution without a bank. A bank
therefore is not *necessary*, and consequently not authorized by this
phrase." [20]

With these two adverse opinions before him Washington, in still
greater perplexity, turned to Hamilton.[21] Hamilton roused himself for
his greatest effort. If the President vetoed the Bill, there would be no
chance of passing it again over that veto. He studied the opinions
of Randolph and Jefferson carefully; then sat up all night to draft his
argument to the contrary. On this argument all later discussions of
the Constitution as a flexible instrument of government were based.
When, in 1819, Chief Justice Marshall finally affirmed the constitutionality of the bank in the case of McCullough *vs.* Maryland, he drew
upon this cabinet opinion as a source.

Heavily underscoring his points, Hamilton answered the objection
that the United States had no power to erect corporations:

This *general principle* is *inherent* in the very *definition* of government,
and *essential* to every step of the progress to be made by that of the United
States, namely: That every power vested in a government is in its nature
sovereign, and includes, by *force* of the *term*, a right to employ all the
means requisite and fairly applicable to the attainment of the *ends* of
such power, and which are not precluded by restrictions and exceptions
specified in the Constitution, or not immoral, or not contrary to the *essential ends* of political society.

In other words, to the argument of the strict constructionists that
the United States had only such powers as were specifically granted,
he opposed the doctrine that any government by its very nature is
fundamentally sovereign and can only be denuded of certain powers
by *express* prohibitions to the contrary.

But he pushed the argument further. The "necessary and proper"
clause which, to Randolph and Jefferson, did not apply, was to him
a fundamental clause. "*Necessary*," he asserted, "often means no more
than *needful, requisite, incidental, useful,* or *conducive to.*" And certainly the bank was all of these in connection with the enumerated

powers of levying and collecting taxes and creating a *"convenient species* of medium in which they are to be paid."

The true criterion was: "Does the proposed measure abridge a pre-existing right of any State or of any individual? If it does not, there is a strong presumption in favor of its constitutionality." And on this test he was content to rest his case.[22]

Washington was so impressed by the force of Hamilton's opinion that he hesitated no longer and signed the Bill. The edifice which Hamilton was building was fast nearing completion.

3. THE REPORT ON MANUFACTURES

While the controversy over the bank was still raging, Hamilton tossed off additional reports and initiated a series of measures in congress to fill in the chinks in his structure. On January 28th he submitted his Report on the Establishment of a Mint. It laid down sound, if not revolutionary, principles for the minting of coins and the establishment of monetary standards. After weighing all the arguments for either gold or silver as the monetary unit, he decided in favor of both, chiefly on the ground that "to annul the use of either of the metals as money, is to abridge the quantity of circulating medium, and is liable to all the objections which arise from a comparison of the benefits of a full, with the evils of a scanty circulation." [23]

And, in addition, Hamilton's recommendations for an extension of import duties and internal excise taxes came up before congress. On the former there was no trouble, but the latter touched off another one of those violent debates which seemed to greet every one of Hamilton's measures. Congress was loath to levy any type of internal taxes— a species of taxation which the states maintained were in their sole province and which the farmers and the artisans insisted bore with unequal hardship on themselves—but the particular tax which Hamilton recommended, a tax on whisky, aroused an extreme of opposition which later culminated in actual armed resistance. For the western frontier could market its grain in the east only in the form of this easily transportable product. From no other source could it obtain the hard cash requisite for the purchases of eastern goods and supplies.

Yet congress, through the tactics of the Hamiltonians, passed the Act of March 3, 1791, which, among other rates, laid duties on domestic spirits of 9 to 25 cents a gallon.

It is no wonder that Senator Maclay, representing the Pennsylvania frontier which was hardest hit by these measures, became discouraged and even more bitter than before. The Hamiltonian juggernaut appeared irresistible. "The resolution of the Mint was foully smuggled through," he wrote. And on the Excise Bill: "War and bloodshed are the most likely consequences of all this. Congress may go home. Mr. Hamilton is all-powerful, and fails in nothing he attempts." [24]

But the triumphant Mr. Hamilton was now riding for a fall. The structure which he was rearing with infinite pains and which he hoped would solidify the "frail fabric of the Constitution" was almost, but not quite, completed. Two of the three strong buttresses were finished—funding and the bank. He began to lay the foundations for the third.

As far back as January 15, 1790, the House had requested him to report to it a plan for the encouragement of such manufactures as would make the United States independent of other nations, particularly in the matter of military supplies.[25]

Hamilton had dealt with first things first. But he had not forgotten the question. For over a year, while head over heels immersed in a tremendous sea of other business, he had been carefully, painstakingly and incessantly gathering materials on which to base such a report. The extent of his correspondence on this and other matters is almost incredible. Each letter of inquiry was written by Hamilton himself in his own bold, angular hand; each letter received was read, digested and filed. They add up to a staggering total. His inquiries went out all over the land, and all over the world. From the remotest places the replies poured in—from Canton in distant China, from London and Liverpool, from France and Glasgow, from Connecticut and Massachusetts. Hardly a village, and certainly not a town, escaped his active scrutiny.

An anonymous "Hosier" in Glasgow sent samples of cotton woven in England with a pathetic letter expressing an eagerness to emigrate to the United States and work in similar manufactories there. The letter illuminates whole areas of the problem.

It would be an Act of Humanity to the poor Hosiers in Britain—If Congress or private Societys would grant a Bounty upon all Hosiers imported from this Country. Youll get plenty by that Means—other ways No Man in that Branch will be able to Come Over to America—As it is utterly impossible for the Poor Stocking Weavers to raise as much as pay his freight & none dare indent him—for their is a penalty of £700 & 12 Months imprisonment, for every such Act. This Country is queit overstocked with Hosiers—& of Course their Wages very low—were 1000 or 2000 to be imported into America their would be plenty left in this Country; while it would serve America, it would only raise the Wages of those left in Britain to a proper Levell, with the price of Provisions. And you will by this receive the Blessing of the Poor in Britain & of every—Hosier.[26]

A man named Barton sent him a printed pamphlet, entitled "Remarks on the State of American manufactures and commerce," with the notation, "For the Hon. A. Hamilton, Esq. from the Writer." [27]

Hamilton wrote to his friend, George Cabot, to gather pertinent data in Massachusetts. Cabot in turn asked others. And Joseph Dana told him that he was getting together merchants and manufacturers to forward the information, since, as he put it, "we have full confidence, that the ultimate object is to befriend the manufacturers of our country, and not to take advantage of them." [28]

Thomas Randall, then in China, sent to Hamilton a long and detailed report on the existing trade between the United States and Canton.[29] Hamilton sent around to all his supervisors of revenue in the several states a circular letter, dated June 22, 1791, requesting them to gather information concerning the condition of manufactures in their localities. From John Chester in Connecticut, Nathaniel Hazard in New York, John Dexter in Rhode Island, Edward Carrington in Virginia, from private friends and merchants everywhere, the responses flooded in. Taken in the mass, as they exist among Hamilton's papers in the Library of Congress, they present an unforgettable picture of the state of the country, its industries and wealth. Quaintly worded, badly misspelled, they present a tale of a new country, still industrially backward, tentatively moving forward on the path of industrialization. From all sides rose reiterated refrains: "We have no capital. We have no knowledge of the business. We have no skilled workmen. We cannot compete with English goods." As Cabot put it succinctly: "Our artists have been learning their trades at our expense." [30] But from all sides rose the equally insistent cry: "Give us bounties to protect our struggling manufactories. Place heavy, nay, prohibitory duties on competing imports." It was asserted that the Congress of the United States "alone are Competent to this Business—the separate States having neither Authority or Funds for the purpose." [31]

With this enormous wealth of material on hand, Hamilton commenced work on his final, and perhaps his greatest, report—the Report on Manufactures.

"The expediency of encouraging manufactures in the United States," he began, "which was not long since deemed very questionable, appears at this time to be pretty generally admitted." Yet there were still many opposed who argued that "agriculture is the most beneficial and productive object of human industry," that capital and labor should be employed in converting the existing wilderness into farms and thus "contribute to the population, strength, and real riches of the country." These agrarians, of whom Thomas Jefferson and John Taylor, both of Virginia, were the principal exponents, objected to any government patronage of industry which would transfer its natural current "from a more to a less beneficial channel." To leave industry to private, unaided interests, they said, is "the soundest as well as the simplest policy."

Hamilton replied that it was true that agriculture was primary and fundamental to the well-being of a nation, but that certainly it was not exclusive. Nay, agriculture's real interest was advanced, not injured, by manufactures. The latter was just as real and just as productive a source of wealth to a nation. With great skill and foresight he pleaded for a division of labor, for a diversification of the resources of the country. The greater the number of industrial hands, the greater the number of mouths to consume the surplus of the land. He pointed out that "women and children are rendered more useful, and the latter more early useful, by manufacturing establishments, than they would otherwise be." He held up for admiring example that in the cotton manufactories of England "four sevenths, nearly, are women and children, of whom the greatest proportion are children, and many of them of a tender age." The social consequences of such employment did not seem to worry Hamilton, nor did he call attention to the horrible conditions under which these same women and children worked.

He was happier in his observations on the pressing need for reciprocity. While other nations were glad to sell us *their* manufactured goods, they set up injurious barriers against the receipt of *ours*. Only by making ourselves independent and competitive, could we force them to the liberal basis of a free, unimpeded and equal exchange. European nations aided their manufactures by bounties and tariffs; in order to attract capital into home industries, it was therefore necessary to do the same.

He ridiculed the argument that protection gave "a monopoly of advantages to particular classes, at the expense of the rest of the community," or that his plan would aid the north and middle states, as against the south. Yet his own arguments to the contrary limped a bit. As to the former, "the internal competition which takes place soon does away with every thing like monopoly, and by degrees reduces the price of the article to the minimum of a reasonable profit on the capital employed." As to the later, the interests of the north and south were interrelated. The "aggregate prosperity of manufactures and the aggregate prosperity of agriculture are intimately connected."

He specified the ways in which the government could aid manufactures: protective duties, which had the added merit of producing revenue; prohibition of rival imports, or prohibitive duties thereon in special instances; prohibition of export of raw materials peculiar to this country; pecuniary bounties—upon which Hamilton was particularly insistent; exemption from import duties of those raw materials essential to our manufactures; drawbacks; encouragement of inventions and their introduction from abroad; governmental inspection of manufactured commodities to prevent frauds and inferior quality; facilitation of cash remittances from one part of the country to another; and the building of good roads and canals for a similar transportation of goods.

With these general principles in mind, Hamilton went to the specific. One after another, he took up the consideration of the particular industries that required encouragement and proposed specific measures to insure their success. Thus ended, he submitted the final report on December 5, 1791.[32]

With this report Hamilton hoped to place into position the third, and most enduring, buttress of the nation. With a sound financial structure, with a national bank to make it viable, with a prosperous hum of machinery rising from every city and town in the land, he felt that the future might be faced with a degree of confidence hitherto unknown. He had followed with the keenest interest the rising tide of the industrial revolution abroad, he had read Adam Smith and adapted his doctrines to the peculiar needs of America, and he prophesied the future.

But the majority was against him. Jefferson, in particular, observed the same omens and recoiled from them in horror. To Jefferson the sound of whirring looms, the clang of machinery stitching shoes faster than the human hand could follow, were anathema. They presupposed huge gatherings of workers in congested factories, of men and women taken forcibly from the life-giving land and transformed into bestial robots or maniacal mobs. "I consider the class of artificers as the panders of vice, and the instruments by which the liberties of a country are generally overturned," he wrote in his "Notes on Virginia." "The mobs of great cities add just so much to the support of pure government, as sores do to the strength of the human body."

Jefferson envisaged a nation of sturdy yeomen, independent farmers rooted in their soil and pure in virtue. Hamilton envisaged a nation resting on the twin foundations of agriculture and manufactories. Jefferson won for the moment. The House pigeon-holed the Report on Manufactures and did nothing about it. But in the long run Hamilton's vision—in this respect—proved truer than Jefferson's. An inexorable logic moved the nation steadily along the lines of industrialization. The south fought the process right through the Civil War, vainly, gallantly.

4. THE SOCIETY FOR ESTABLISHING USEFUL MANUFACTURES

But Hamilton did not wait for congressional action on his report. By the time the report was rendered, he was already actively engaged in an ambitious scheme to implement its proposals. The report itself calls attention to the scheme. "It may be announced that a society is forming, with a capital which is expected to be extended to at least half a million dollars, on behalf of which measures are already in train for prosecuting, on a large scale, the making and printing of cotton goods."

The idea of establishing a society to promote manufactures in the United States had already floated nebulously before the eyes of theoreticians and men of capital. Tench Coxe, Hamilton's assistant in the Treasury, had proposed a scheme along those lines to Jefferson on April 15, 1791.[33] Jefferson, as was to be expected, ignored the suggestion. Perhaps Hamilton had instigated the proposal. In any event, a group of moneyed men, chiefly Hamilton's personal friends, took up the idea. Among them were William Duer, Elias and Elisha Boudinot, Jonathan Dayton, Robert Troup, Secretary of War Henry Knox, Philip Livingston and Nicholas Low.

The promoters caused a series of announcements and articles to be placed in the newspapers announcing the scheme and calling for subscriptions. An elaborate prospectus was circulated privately, which Hamilton quite probably wrote.[34] The prospectus contained in essence the later Report on Manufactures. But it also appealed to the profit-making instinct of potential investors, painted in glowing phrases the vast profits that would eventually accrue and hinted that "the pecuniary aid even of Government, though not to be counted upon ought not wholly to be dispaired of." The new society, it was announced, expected to manufacture paper, sail cloth, stockings, blankets, carpets, shoes, cotton and linen goods, and proposed even a brewery. The prospectus called for a subscription of $500,000; but the new society would apply for a charter and commence business on receipt of $100,000.

It was a bold scheme drawn to a vast scale in a day of small manufactories with limited investments. It proposed to transplant the United States almost overnight into the ranks of the great industrial nations.

The response was encouraging. Within a fairly short time the initial $100,000 was subscribed; by the beginning of October more than $250,000 had been promised or secured.[35] The first subscribers had already met on August 9, 1791, in the town of New Brunswick, and authorized Hamilton to take the necessary legal steps to procure a charter and to seek artisans skilled in cotton manufacture.[36] They had determined to fix the site of the manufactory somewhere in New Jersey as conveniently located, plentiful with cheap labor, and under the aegis of a legislature amenable to the influence of the Boudinots, Jonathan Dayton and others of the promoters.

Accordingly, Hamilton set to work. He quite probably drafted the charter, which was detailed, astonishingly comprehensive—and somewhat peculiar. It called for an authorized capital of $1,000,000, and welcomed subscriptions from state and national governments, holding out as a lure for these the right to investigate the proceedings of the society. It proposed a board of thirteen directors and a governor. It proposed exemption from all taxation of the goods and chattels of the society forever, and of the land and buildings for ten years. It proposed for the artificers and workers in the employ of the society exemption from personal taxes and from all military duty except in case of actual invasion. It gave the society the right to build canals and roads, to operate lotteries, to charge tolls and to exercise the power of eminent domain. It demanded a municipal charter for an area of thirty-six square miles, to be called "the Corporation of the Town of Paterson," and to be governed in part by the society.[37]

Yet Hamilton, appearing in the company of others before the New Jersey legislature in order to "elucidate anything that may appear obtuse" in these remarkable provisions, had no difficulty in persuading that body of lawmakers to grant the charter *in toto*.[38] On November 22, 1791, the Society for establishing Useful Manufactures (thereafter familiarly known as the S. U. M.) was officially incorporated.

The first step thus taken, Hamilton threw himself into the scheme with the same energy that he displayed in everything he touched. He had already chosen the exact site for the initial factory to be raised by the society, after a consultation with his father-in-law, General Schuyler. From the various locations proposed, they had decided on the land fronting the Little Falls, at the head of navigation of the Passaic River.[39] The town to be built there was to be called Paterson.

He proceeded personally to interview and hire workmen and superintendents. Among these were Thomas Marshall, who had learned cotton spinning under Richard Arkwright in England, William Hall, and a Mr. Most, whom Hamilton suggested be sent to Europe to engage and bring back workmen with him.[40] Hamilton, a prominent government official, knew that he was advising what in effect was a criminal act under the laws of England—the procurement of skilled workers for export from that country—yet he gave the advice and the directors of the S. U. M. appropriated $20,000 for the purpose of luring skilled hands to America, specifying in their minutes "that the whole Business of procuring such Hands be committed to the direction and management of the Governor of this Society, subject to the advice of the Secretary of the Treasury." [41]

The scheme seemed to have commenced most auspiciously. William Duer, Hamilton's friend and former assistant in the Treasury, was chosen governor of the society. Nehemiah Hubbard of Connecticut was offered the position of superintendent-general. Major L'Enfant, the French engineer who laid out Washington, drew a series of magnificent plans for the group of factories on the Passaic and for the surrounding Township of Paterson. The land was purchased, and machinery ordered. The literature put out by the society teemed with glowingly optimistic predictions.

But the first rosy premises soon shifted to a darker tinge. William Duer, the governor, ran into malodorous financial difficulties of his own and ended ingloriously in jail. His accounts with the society were discovered to be in strange confusion. Hubbard, the superintendent-general, sniffing disaster from afar, cannily refused to keep his titled post, though Hamilton asked him to reconsider. "This institution has presented itself to my mind as of such real public importance,"

he wrote Hubbard, "that I feel myself much interested in its success."[42]
In fact, Hamilton's connection had been widely and assiduously pub-
licized both by the promoters and by himself.[43] And L'Enfant's plans
were too grandiose in conception for the prosaic work at hand and
had to be abandoned, much to his disgust.

Hamilton tried heroically to stem the tide of disaster. He wrote a
careful, considered letter to the board of directors. "Among the disastrous incidents of the present juncture," he told them, "I have not
been least affected by the temporary derangement of the affairs of
your Society." He mapped out a businesslike course for them to
pursue. Among his suggestions were "that the Society confine themselves at first to the cotton branch. The printing business to commence
as early as possible;" and that, if desired, he would arrange a loan on
favorable terms.[44] He was as good as his word. Through his connection with William Seton, cashier of the Bank of New York, which
Hamilton had helped found, a loan of $10,000 was obtained with an
interest rate of only five per cent—a rate as low as the United States
itself obtained from that bank.[45] And Peter Colt, a responsible manufacturer, was obtained as superintendent in Hubbard's place.

For a while it seemed as if Hamilton's energetic actions would retrieve the fortunes of the company. But his political enemies accused
him of corruption and ambition in connection with this project of a
non-governmental nature; the crash of Duer and other financiers
brought panic to the money markets, internal dissensions hamstrung
the venture almost from the start, and the subscribers began to default
in their installments on the stock.

Though a mill was actually constructed and limited operations commenced, the vast original plan never materialized. By 1796 everyone
involved was heartily sick of the venture. The plant was put up for
sale and a plan of dissolution proposed, though never carried. From
then until the present day, the company has continued as a mere land-
holder and lessee, possessed of invaluable charter privileges. All attempts through the years to annul its charter or to curtail its rights
and privileges were successfully resisted, and the remaining stockholders and their heirs waxed wealthy on leaseholds and rentals from
the rising values of the lands and water rights the original company
had secured. As late as 1937, the Supreme Court of New Jersey refused
to grant the petition of the city of Paterson either to revoke the 145-
year-old charter of the company or rescind its exemption from taxes.[46]

CHAPTER XX

Years of Strife

I. THE BUBBLE SPECULATION

As far back as the beginning of 1791 Robert Troup had written prophetically to his friend, Hamilton, that "we are going headlessly into the bitterest opposition to the Genl Government—I pity you most sincerely—for I know that you have not a wish but what is combined with the solid honor & interests of America." Not as prophetic, however, was the final optimism that "the time will come when your enemies will blush they are in opposition to you." [1] For the enmities aroused by Hamilton increased with the years rather than diminished. Not the least of these had to do with the Bank of the United States, the especial pride and cornerstone of Hamilton's structure.

On June 20, 1791 William Seton, cashier of the Bank of New York, reported that the quota of $60,000 for New York for subscriptions to the national bank stock had been oversubscribed by $20,000 within half an hour after the legal opening, and that if Hamilton wished to increase the limit by another $60,000, "it would be immediately filled up." [2] And from Philadelphia, from Baltimore, from Boston, the reports poured in thick and fast of a wild rush of moneyed men to get in on the ground floor of the new institution. The initial success was beyond even Hamilton's most favorable predictions.

But if Hamilton's Bank was hailed with enthusiasm and a flood of subscriptions in certain quarters, it was viewed with equal alarm in other quarters. Madison wrote indignantly to Jefferson that

the subscriptions [to the bank] are consequently a mere scramble for so much public plunder, which will be engrossed by those already loaded with the spoils of individuals. ... It pretty clearly appears, also, in what proportions the public debt lies in the Country, what sort of hands hold it, and by whom the people of the United States are to be governed. Of all the shameful circumstances of this business, it is among the greatest to see the members of the legislature who were most active in pushing this job openly grasping its emoluments. ... Nothing new is talked of here. In fact, stock-jobbing drowns every other subject. [3]

And Jefferson in turn was complaining to Monroe that

the bank filled and overflowed in the moment it was opened. Instead of 20 thousand shares, 24 thousand were offered, & a great many unpresented who had not suspected that so much haste was necessary. Thus it is that we shall be paying 13 per cent. per ann. for 8 millions of paper money instead of having that circulation of gold & silver for nothing.

The only shred of comfort that Jefferson could find was that "very few subscribers have offered from Virginia or N. Carolina, which gives uneasiness to H[amilton]." [4]

But the bank stock was not the only medium for bringing out the moneyed men. The funded debt boiled over even more sharply. A veritable mania for speculation seized upon the country. The funds rose overnight and continued to rise. Everyone was buying—not merely the usual professional speculators, but small merchants, artisans, and mechanics who had a few savings to guard them against old age. A boom of gigantic proportions was in the making. Mr. Hamilton had proclaimed the unlimited future of the country, and the average man left politics and learned disquisitions of alarm to Madison and Jefferson and other voices crying in the wilderness.

The plain people could not afford to purchase aristocratic bank stock at $400 a share, but the funded debt, the deferred securities of which were selling at thirteen shillings or so, was more within their modest means. As in all boom markets, the speculators immediately entered the arena. As it seemed to their advantage they alternately boosted prices and depressed them. They even sold their holdings of bank stock in order to buy and sell in the funds. Henry Lee, en route from Philadelphia to Virginia, painted a vivid picture of the turmoil. "My whole rout," he told Madison, "presented to me one continued scene of stock gambling; agriculture commerce & even the fair sex relinquished, to make way for unremitted exertion in this favourite pursuit." [5]

The inevitable happened. The New York *Daily Advertiser* issued a public warning on August 13th: "It has risen like a rocket. Like a rocket it will burst with a crack and down drops the rocket stick. What goes up must come down—so take care of your pate, brother Jonathan."

The most active of the speculators for the rise was William Duer, who had quit the Treasury under a cloud. Hamilton heard of his shady transactions and wrote a friendly letter of advice. There were rumors that he was lofting the values of the funds by fictitious pur-

chases—in modern parlance, by wash sales—but, added Hamilton discreetly, "I know you too well to suppose you capable of such views
as were implied in those innuendoes, or to harbor the most distant
thought that you could wander from the path either of public good
or private integrity." [6]

If, as Hamilton hinted, Duer was riding for a fall, it was unfortunate
that he chose this particular time, when the market was beginning to
show signs of hesitation and shakiness, to place the government sinking fund into the market to support the price of the funds. He caused
to be transferred to William Seton, of the Bank of New York, $150,000
of the sinking fund with which to purchase the debt in the public
market,[7] and covered the transfer with a confidential letter advising
Seton that "a principal object with me is to keep the stock from falling
too low in case the embarrassments of the dealers should lead to sacrifices. . . . If there are any gentlemen who support the *funds* and others
who *depress* them, I shall be pleased that your purchases may aid the
former—this in great confidence." [8]

It was still more unfortunate that Seton promptly used substantial
portions of this government money to purchase from this same William
Duer $52,685 of securities at the inflated prices, and thereby enabled
him temporarily to escape from the consequences of his recklessness.[9]
Afterwards, when Duer finally went into bankruptcy and the whole
top-heavy structure toppled, Hamilton's seeming intervention on behalf of his friend and other speculators of the same stripe became one
of the most damaging charges to be made against him.

In fact, it was claimed by certain disgruntled speculators who were
not Hamilton's friends that he had, immediately prior to entering
the market to support prices, stated in private conversation that the
stocks were all too high and quoted figures much below the then
market as the true value sanctioned by his authority. As a result, these
speculators had hastily rid themselves of bank stock at a loss and were
therefore much mortified by the subsequent rise due to Hamilton's
manipulations. Rufus King communicated the rumors to Hamilton,
adding cautiously that "it can scarcely be believed that these gentlemen have any foundation for their assertion, but the fact will suggest
to you the utmost caution on this subject—I know you must have
regretted the late extravagance, but at the present juncture, the most
unfair advantage may be made of your remarks." As for the small
people caught in the toils of these proceedings, King had little sympathy. "It will operate," he added, "to deter our industrious citizens

from meddling in future with the funds, & teach them contentment in their proper vocations." [10]

Yet Hamilton frankly admitted that he had spoken out, for, as he explained to King, "a bubble connected with my operations is of all the enemies I have to fear, in my judgment, the most formidable." But he denied vigorously that he had quoted any prices setting forth the true values, and even gave his own figures to King to show the discrepancy with those which report had accredited to him.[11]

Nor did he refrain from throwing further cash from the sinking fund into the market. On September 7th he sent Seton $50,000 more, with a note that "I wish I could have gone farther, but my hands are tied by the want of a majority of the Trustees being present. . . . You may, however, make it known that the treasurer is purchasing here." [12]

Before Seton could spread the glad news, or commence his purchases, the secret had leaked out. "The bearer of the letter I apprehend knew or conjectured the contents, as it flew over the town like wildfire that I had orders to purchase. Therefore, before I got to the coffee-house, at noon, every one was prepared, and no one would offer to supply at less than the former price." He reported that the scrip, which had been down to 110, was now up to 135 to 145, adding philosophically that "they are now getting into the proper hands." [13]

Hamilton's intervention kept the market not merely steady, but was largely responsible for a resumption of the rise. By October the bank stock, of a par value of $400, had soared to $500, and all other stocks were higher in the same proportion.[14] By the end of January they were still higher.[15]

But by then the end was almost in sight. The first evidence that the boom was over came with the final financial crash of William Duer. That shady speculator and good friend of Hamilton had rigged his markets, juggled his transactions and exercised his political influence for the last time. The whole slippery and shifting structure of his manipulations collapsed like a house of cards.

During his short stay in the Treasury he had involved his official accounts to such an extent that even now, in 1792, the recently appointed comptroller, Oliver Wolcott of Connecticut, had been unable to make any headway in untangling them. In one transaction at least he had been guilty of criminal misappropriation. He had taken official Treasury warrants and pledged them as security for his own private loans. On his failure to meet his engagements, the warrants had been offered for sale and purchased by one A. G. Frauncis. In all good faith the Philadelphia Loan Office had duly honored the warrants on presentation, and returned them to the Treasury for payment. It was then that Hamilton discovered the fraud and refused to meet the obligation. Yet, knowing the circumstances though he did, Hamilton stood by his friend and made no public mention of the transaction. Instead, he readily accepted Duer's assurances that he would make good. But Duer did not, and the matter dragged.[16]

Now, however, when the affairs of Duer and his partner, Flint, were becoming public property, Wolcott, to protect himself, was compelled to act. He wrote to Richard Harrison, the United States Attorney in New York, to notify Duer to settle his public accounts or give proper security. In the event of non-compliance, Harrison was to commence suit.[17]

Duer had advance notice of this move and wrote frantically to Hamilton beseeching him to stave off the threatened suit. He wrote also to Jeremiah Wadsworth, member of congress, to use his influence to the same effect.[18]

Hamilton was still willing to help Duer, but the matter was already out of his hands. Much troubled, he wrote back: "Your letter of the 11th got to hand this day. I am affected beyond measure at its contents, especially as it was too late to have any influence upon the event you were apprehensive of, Mr. Wolcott's instructions having gone off yesterday." He exhorted him to meet his difficulties with fortitude and honor, ending with a "God bless you, and take care of you and your family. I have experienced all the bitterness of soul on your account which a warm attachment can inspire." [19]

Wolcott was similarly regretful, but he was more afraid of the consequences than his chief. On March 21st he wrote again to Harrison that "no person can be less disposed than I am to increase his misfortunes, yet when I consider the nature of his engagements to the public, the repeated assurances which I have personally recd. and the embarrassments which I am expecting, in consequence of his failing to perform his promises I feel no inclination to neglect my duty & sacrifice my character on his account." [20]

But by this time Duer had gone down with a resounding crash that rocked the foundations of the country and started a panic that ruined thousands. More and more unpleasant aspects of his public and private dealings came to light. He had taken usury on loans to "Widows Orphans Butchers & Carriers" at rates ranging from two to four per cent a month.[21] He had failed to account to the Society for Useful

Manufactures for substantial sums which had been entrusted to him. A wave of indignation swept his victims. On March 23rd he was clapped in jail, and the more violent openly advocated removing him from that place of safekeeping and lynching him. The indignation turned as well on those who, it was asserted, had protected him. It beat savagely upon Hamilton. "I observe with extreme anxiety the State of many minds respecting the Government—" wrote one observer. "And particularly the bitter use which the Secretary's enemies make of his attachment to Colo Duer." [22]

From jail Duer continued to call upon Hamilton for aid. But Hamilton by this time realized that Duer was beyond all help, and that his own personal honor and political fortunes were involved. With unusual caution he wrote back that he would try to get to New York to give him the benefit of his advice, but government business had delayed him, and hinted it would be wise to make his own accommodations with his creditors. "Indeed, I can hardly flatter myself that my advice could be of any real importance to you." [23] At no time, however, did Hamilton show any real awareness of the implications of Duer's manipulations. He stood by him steadily to the end, helping him in every way he could. And even though Duer never made any complete accounting to the government, somehow or other the suits instituted against him by Wolcott subsided and died from lack of prosecution.

Hamilton stood by all his friends—a commendable trait if he had not been at the time an official charged with governmental responsibility. He sheltered William Seton and the Bank of New York as well from the consequences of their own acts.

Over Hamilton's opposition the Bank of the United States had opened branches in New York and elsewhere. The New York branch competed with the Bank of New York not only in the normal business of discounts, but was obviously the natural depository for government funds. Seton wrote on November 21, 1791, to Hamilton to complain of the situation. Hamilton replied on November 25th that the branches had been established without consulting him and against his judgment. "Ultimately it will be incumbent on me to place the public funds in the keeping of the branch," he acknowledged, "but it *may be depended upon* that I shall *precipitate nothing*, but shall so conduct the transfer as not to embarrass or distress your institution." [24]

But the Bank of New York ran into difficulties, and Seton again called on Hamilton for aid. Hamilton promptly came to the rescue. He ordered the United States to forbear from drawing out any government funds from the embarrassed institution and asked Seton to be "confidential" with him. "If you are pressed, whatever support may be in my power shall be afforded. I consider the public interest as materially involved in aiding a valuable institution like yours to withstand the attacks of a confederated host of frantic and, I fear, in too many instances, unprincipled gamblers." [25]

When the Duer crash brought panic, Hamilton threw all the resources of government to the support of the market, and, incidentally, of Seton's bank. He sent $50,000 to purchase the six-per-cents at par, if they should sink below that figure. While Seton was not to declare specifically on whose account he was buying, Hamilton felt reasonably certain the truth would be conjectured and have a beneficial effect on the market.[26]

The sum helped a little, but the failure of Alexander Macomb on April 12th added fuel to the partly extinguished fire. Macomb was another speculator with whom Hamilton had been intimately associated. The two of them, in conjunction with Philip Schuyler and Henry Knox, the Secretary of War, had purchased ten townships of land on the southeastern shore of the St. Lawrence River for speculation, and Gouverneur Morris was even then trying to dispose of them in London to English investors.[27]

In the face of this new blow, Hamilton sent additional funds to Seton, which Seton declared mournfully were being gobbled up by holders of the depreciated funds as fast as he could throw them into the market.[28] Meanwhile Hamilton was declaring indignantly that "'tis time there should be a line of Separation between honest Men & knaves, between respectable Stockholders and dealers in the funds, and mere unprincipled Gamblers. Public infamy must restrain what the laws cannot." [29] Strangely, he never seemed to consider Duer and Macomb in the ranks of these unnamed "gamblers."

As a result chiefly of Hamilton's support the panic subsided, the government stocks departed from the jittery little people and found repose in "strong hands," so that by June 10th Fisher Ames was able to write to Hamilton from Boston that "all goes well in the state. The people really prosper, and, what is more, they know it and say it, and give credit to the general government for the change they have witnessed."[30]

And Seton likewise was able finally to report that all was well between his bank and the branch of the Bank of the United States, thanks to Hamilton. "With respect to ourselves & the Branch we go in in perfect Harmony, & there does not appear any disposition on their part to do otherwise." If, however, "should any Circumstances occur that augurs hostilities, I shall address myself freely to you." [31]

Later on he thanked Hamilton for ordering the Collector of New York to deposit his receipts in the Bank of New York, for, as he put it in confidence, he felt that the branch was trying to drain him of specie. "If I find they persist in the draining us, I must implore the aid of your all powerfull hand to convince them we are not destitute of aid in the hour of need." [32] Evidently Hamilton exercised his "all powerfull hand," for there were no further complaints, and the Bank of New York not only weathered the storm, but flourished.

Yet, in spite of Hamilton's somewhat blunted perceptions of public morality when it came to his friends, he was sensitive to a peculiar degree when his own personal affairs were involved. In all the orgy of speculation, when he might have made a considerable fortune from his personal knowledge of the turn of events, he remained poor. So poor in fact that on June 15, 1791, he was compelled to borrow $200 from his friend, Robert Troup, who assured him he could take his time about repaying.[33]

And, fearing that he might be accused of making personal profit from his holdings in government funds while he was engaged in supporting the market, he ordered Seton to sell them for him, though the price was then considerably below their true value. All that he owned, in fact, was a mere $800 in the three-per-cents.[34] Seton expostulated against such "extreme delicacy" in the face of the current low prices, and held off selling, in spite of Hamilton's repeated requests, until it had risen to thirty per cent over par; and then, to his dismay, "behold it has since risen four or five p Cent more very unexpectedly." [35] In spite of this accession to his bank account, all that remained as a balance on August 30th was $175.31.[36]

In another field at about this time Hamilton was equally meticulous. He owned five shares of the Ohio Company, which dealt in land grants in the Western Territory, and he now found himself obliged in his official capacity to determine the validity of some of these grants. Accordingly he turned the entire matter over to the Attorney-General and his Accounting Department for action, so as to guide himself wholly by their decision in the matter.[37]

2. COLLISION WITH MR. BURR

The national arena was sufficient of itself to absorb all of Hamilton's attention and energies; yet he dared not, even for an instant, remove his vigilant eye from the affairs of his own state of New York. For New York—with Pennsylvania—represented the balance of power by means of which he was precariously enabled to put his national program into effect. By and large New England backed him; by an equally vehement majority the south opposed him. As long as these two middle states threw their weight to him, he was safe.

But in New York a serious situation arose. Governor Clinton, that perennial leader, had been bitterly Anti-Federal since the days of the Constitutional Convention. The breach between him and Hamilton was irreconcilable. Yet as long as General Schuyler and the Livingston family controlled the legislature, Hamilton's policies were assured of support on a national basis. Schuyler and Rufus King, the transplanted Massachusetts lawyer, were rocks of strength in the Senate. But Schuyler, to whom by lot the short term had fallen, was up for re-election early in 1791. It was, seemingly, to be a mere formality, for the Federalists were safely in control of the legislature which chose the Senators.

Yet the dry routine of nomination and election exploded into stunning surprise. The name of Schuyler was rejected. And Aaron Burr, the young colonel of the Revolution, the brilliant lawyer with whom Hamilton was on fairly friendly terms, was chosen as the next Senator from New York. What had happened?

Hamilton did not know—he attributed the disaster in fact to the secret and personal machinations of Aaron Burr, and reacted with such violence that a series of events was set in motion that ended ultimately in the tragedy of his own obliteration.

Actually, his own arrogant behavior in local New York politics had been responsible for the unexpected defeat. His most powerful allies in New York had been the Livingston clan. They had supported the Constitution and backed his policies. They had a right to expect some degree of reciprocity when Hamilton became a power on the national stage. Yet Rufus King became a Senator instead of one of them. Robert R. Livingston, who hoped to become Chief Justice of the Supreme Court, was turned down in favor of John Jay. They were disregarded in local appointments by the Hamilton-Schuyler faction. As a result, their political friendship curdled to determined enmity.

In conjunction with Clinton, they seized upon the opportunity to humble Hamilton through Schuyler. To do this, however, a moderate was required—one who was not too closely identified with Clinton and extreme Anti-Federalism. Aaron Burr was that man. Thus far he had been reasonably independent in politics and had served with dignity as attorney-general of the state. The swirl of party passion had not yet ingulfed him; and Livingstonian Federals as well as Clintonian Antis could vote for him with a clear conscience.

The blow struck Hamilton with all the more force because his major measures were passing in the Senate by uncomfortably close votes. And now his most loyal supporter was out and a man chosen by his enemies in. One of his political followers in New York assessed the somber situation accurately.

A coalition of Interests from different principles produced his [Burr's] Election—He is avowedly your Enemy, & stands pledged to his party for a reign of Vindictive declamation against your Measures. The Chancellor [R. R. Livingston] hates, & would destroy you—Nay so incautious was he at a public Masonic Dinner last St. Johns Day that he declared himself to me without any Stipulation of Secrecy, that he was not only opposed to your Funding System, but that R. Morris & several other well informed Influential Characters, viewed it as a system of public injustice.... We want a Head, to repress & keep down the machinations of our restless Demagogue [Clinton], but alas where is he to be found? [38]

Burr himself had good reason to feel that his election would "be unpleasing to several persons now in Philad[elph]ia. There was uncommon animosity & eagerness in the opposition." [39] Yet he took no partisan position toward the pending Bank Bill. He was willing to consider it on its merits. As he told a correspondent, he had not yet had a chance "to read with proper attention the proposed establishment. I am therefore wholly incompetent to give an opinion of its merit.... It certainly deserves deliberate consideration—a Charter granted cannot be revoked. This appears to me to be one of those cases in which Delay can be productive of no Evil." [40]

Hamilton was right, however, in sensing that from this time on Burr was to be a far more formidable obstacle to his fortunes in New York and elsewhere than Clinton had ever been. The second collision came between them in 1792, during the gubernatorial campaign. Clinton was a perpetual candidate to succeed himself. But the Federalists were at a loss. Judge Yates was first offered the nomination, and he refused. So did Stephen Van Rensselaer. Hamilton and Schuyler became alarmed. They became much more alarmed when, seemingly from nowhere, sentiment swelled among the rank and file of Federalism to make *Burr* their candidate.

The moderate Mr. Burr was personally on good terms with a majority of the lesser, and with some of the major, Federalist leaders. He had already welded together a smooth-running machine of faithful followers, and he was popular with the artisans and democrats of New York City. Such a coalition, thought these Federalists, had a good chance of unseating the hitherto invulnerable Mr. Clinton. Even Judge Yates was considered, and justly, as favorably predisposed to the candidacy of Aaron Burr.

But Hamilton, and Schuyler with him, would rather see Clinton re-elected than be parties to Burr's elevation. Clinton was an old man, and his influence was already past its peak. Burr was young, ambitious, far more talented—and therefore much more dangerous. Hamilton foresaw New York completely slipped from his grasp, and a powerful rival raised upon the national stage. In great alarm, he persuaded John Jay to quit his secure seat on the Supreme Court and stand for the governorship. When a mass meeting of Federalists followed his lead and nominated Jay, and Judge Yates was persuaded to appear and approve, Hamilton thought he had definitely circumvented Burr.

Burr was not so easily disposed of, however. Among the Anti-Federals, or Republicans, as they now chose to call themselves, there was much agitation to replace Clinton with Burr who, they felt, had a better chance of defeating the formidable Mr. Jay. But Burr finally announced that he was not a candidate, and Clinton forced through his own nomination.

The election was bitter and closely contested. Hamilton's policies, rather than the respective merits of the ostensible candidates, became the touchstone for votes. Tillery wrote pessimistically to Hamilton that "the Bank Mania rages violently in this City, & it is made an engine to help the Governor's re-election." [41]

Even when the votes were in, and the ballots had to be canvassed by a joint committee of the legislature, the issue was still in doubt. On the count, John Jay had seemingly been elected by a majority of four hundred votes, but the Republicans among the canvassers claimed to discover irregularities in the votes from the counties of Otsego, Clinton and Tioga. If, as a result of the alleged irregularities, the votes of these three counties were rejected, then Clinton was governor.

The entire state was thrown into a fever of partisanship over the contest, and it was finally decided to submit the issue to the two

Senators from New York, Rufus King and Aaron Burr. But these two eminent luminaries disagreed—on party lines, and the board of canvassers, on similar party lines, declared Clinton elected. The legislature upheld its committee on a like party vote. John Jay, though without doubt the victor, was forced to see Clinton remain triumphantly in the gubernatorial chair.[42]

The hotheads among the Federalists wanted to call a convention to override the decision of the legislature, and there was even loose talk about forcible resistance. But the leaders—Jay, King and Hamilton— set their faces sternly against extreme courses. As Hamilton pointed out: "I do not feel it right or expedient to attempt to reverse the decision by any means not known to the Constitution or laws. The precedent may suit us to-day; but to-morrow we may see its abuse." [43] Yet, while thus counseling moderation, his inner resentment against Burr, to whose legal opinion on the disputed ballot boxes he attributed Jay's downfall, was fast reaching the exploding point. Not long after, as a matter of fact, the explosion did occur.

3. CONTROVERSY WITH MR. JEFFERSON

When, in 1789, the government had first been formed, it was universally understood that the two most important posts in President Washington's Cabinet were the Treasury and the State Departments. It was equally well understood that the two most important and able men in the country—aside from Washington himself, and possibly Madison—had been called to fill these respective posts.

But, as they first confronted each other in the cabinet, they knew little personally of each other except by rumor and report. Jefferson, the elder by thirteen years, had made his name chiefly before Hamilton had come prominently to the fore, and during the rapid rise of his youthful rival had been across the ocean in France. Thus their natural antagonism, due to diverse philosophies of life and of government, had had no opportunity to hone to a razor edge through the grinding friction of personal contact. That opportunity had now arisen.

The first contact had been most unfortunate. Jefferson considered— at least in public utterance—that he had been tricked by Hamilton into giving his support for assumption. And, as Hamilton unfolded his financial system in measure after measure, Jefferson began to fight back. Here was a system and a philosophy whose goal was opposed to everything to which his deepest instincts were committed. Hamilton believed in a strong central government, Jefferson in that minimum of government which came under the head of police powers; Hamilton favored the banker and the merchant, Jefferson the middle-class farmer; Hamilton welcomed an industrialized America, Jefferson shuddered at the idea and held aloft the vision of a nation devoted to the arts of agriculture. No two men could have been more widely divergent in present or in future goals than these two who now confronted each other in positions of prominence. It was inevitable, therefore, that sooner or later they must clash.

The clash came sooner by Hamilton's own precipitation. As much as possible Jefferson avoided open conflicts. By nature he hated them. He preferred to work by subtlety and indirection. He fought Hamilton's measures not openly, but through that group of disciples, chiefly from Virginia with some additions from Pennsylvania and New York to whom he stood in the position of philosophic guide and father. The chief of these was Madison, whom he early weaned away from the Hamiltonian fold.

The matter, however, might have remained for a considerable period in a twilight state of non-belligerency had not Hamilton almost immediately commenced poaching on what Jefferson deemed his inviolable preserves. It is true that Jefferson, through his disciples, continually meddled in the affairs of the Treasury; but he defended this course by maintaining that his interference was done through the legal channels of congress and cabinet opinions addressed to Washington. In the case of the State Department, of which he was titular head, however, Hamilton moved directly and at cross-purposes with that head. In Hamilton's defense it may be said that the first cabinet of the United States was in its experimental stage, that the various departments were fluid and had not yet received those hard, self-containing shells that were later to form about them, and that he considered the matters in which he meddled directly concerned with the affairs of his own Treasury. Yet it is also true, as Jefferson complained, that he trod aggressively and tactlessly in those precincts, and conducted himself on many occasions as if in fact *he* were the Secretary of State and not Jefferson. It is little wonder then that such combustible elements shortly burst into flame.

The immediate occasion of the quarrel was the delicate relations existing with both Great Britain and France. During the Revolution Great Britain had been the enemy and France the ally. But the years

had wrought a change. France underwent her own Revolution which
soon engulfed the European World and threatened to swallow as well
the New. Hamilton was favorably disposed at first, but as the convulsion widened and declared itself a social and economic as well as
a political upheaval, his conservative instincts became alarmed and he
returned to his old admiration for the ordered stability of the British.
Jefferson, on the other hand, passionately admired the French and
their slogan of *Liberté, Egalité, Fraternité* and was obsessed with a
hatred for England and her advocates in America. The worst epithet
that he could find for a political adversary was that he was a monocrat, meaning thereby that he advocated a monarchy on British lines.
And more and more, Hamilton became to him the chief exemplar of
that hated tribe. His *Anas*—jotted comments usually written down
long after the event—are full of reported conversations of Hamilton
and his colleagues tending to prove this thesis.

For example, On August 13, 1791, Jefferson noted that Hamilton
had declared: " 'I own it is my own opn, tho' I do not publish it in
Dan & Bersheba, that the present govnmt is not that which will answer
the ends of society, by giving stability & protection to its rights, and
that it will probably be found expedient to go into the British form.
However, since we have undertaken the experiment, I am for giving
it a fair course, whatever my expectns. The success indeed so far, is
greater than I had expected....' " [44]

But later, Jefferson claimed he heard Hamilton say "that this constitution was a shilly shally thing of mere milk & water, which could
not last, & was only good as a step to something better." [45] And,
referring to Jay and Hamilton, he wrote that "both are dangerous.
They pant after union with England as the power which is to support
their projects, and are most determined Anti-gallicans. It is prognosti-
cated that our republic is to end with the President's life. But I believe
they will find themselves all head and no body." [46] It was inevitable,
therefore, that a Secretary of State who hated England and adored
France, and a Secretary of Treasury, who reversed both in his sentiments, should come into swift and violent conflict.

Both England and the revolutionary government of France had
hastened representatives to America to gain advantages for themselves
and to create an atmosphere of hostility against the other. England
sent George Hammond as its Minister, and France sent Ternant. Each
promptly gravitated to those American officials who favored by policy
or inclination his accrediting country. Accordingly, Hammond was

soon quite confidential with Hamilton, and Ternant enjoyed an equal status with Jefferson.

Even before Hammond arrived, Hamilton hailed the appointment as a sign that "the British Cabinet wish to be thought disposed to enter into amicable & liberal arrangements with us.... I would not warrant the issue; but if some liberal arrangement with Great Britain should ensue it will have a prodigious effect upon the Conduct of some other parts of Europe. Tis however most wise for us to depend as little as possible upon European Caprice," he warned, "& to exert ourselves to the utmost to unfold and improve every domestic resource." [47]

As for France, Hamilton was willing enough to enter into a new treaty of commerce with France on a reciprocal and permanent basis. As he informed Jefferson, "my commercial system turns very much on giving a free course to Trade and cultivating good humour with all the world." [48]

Jefferson may have agreed with the principle, yet he was probably offended by the arrogant reference to *"my commercial system;"* and certainly he considered Hamilton's private negotiations with both Hammond and Ternant in the matter of treaties and foreign relations, of which he learned only by chance or by their fruits, as an affront to his dignity as Secretary of State.

Toward the end of November, 1791, for example, Hamilton had drawn Ternant into conversation on the subject of a treaty of commerce and, discovering that the French National Assembly had given him no instructions, suggested that Ternant volunteer the matter to Jefferson. He also spoke to Washington about it, who in turn suggested the negotiation to Jefferson. Thus indirectly, and to his mortification, Jefferson discovered the initiative taken by Hamilton.[49]

If Hamilton thus interfered in the relations with France, it was merely in isolated instances; with Hammond, however, he was immediately on the most confidential and intimate footing. Hammond's reports to his superior in England, Lord Grenville, are full of detailed discussions with Hamilton on matters which Jefferson was negotiating with him in an official capacity. Nor did Hamilton hesitate to communicate to the British minister his own private thoughts on these matters, even though they contradicted the official line which Jefferson was taking and even, on occassion, intimating that the United States would be satisfied with fewer concessions than Jefferson was claiming at the moment.

The chief sources of complaint between Great Britain and the

United States stemmed from the treaty of peace. Great Britain had failed to surrender its trading posts and forts in the Northwest Territory and had consistently refused to enter into a formal treaty of commerce; nor would she yield compensation for the Negro slaves who had fled from their masters under the protection of the British army. In justification of these refusals, she pointed to violations of the treaty on the part of the United States, especially with reference to the legal disabilities still thrown in the way of the collection of pre-war debts owing to British merchants.

In the negotiations on these disputed questions, Jefferson demanded full and complete adherence to the treaty on the part of Great Britain. In private conversations with Hammond, however, Hamilton indicated that the only point on which the United States would insist was in the matter of the yielding of the posts, and even there we might, if pressed, grant to British subjects privileges in those posts with respect to the fur trade. In the matter of compensation for the "kidnapped" Negroes, Hamilton partially agreed with Hammond's position, adding, perhaps gratuitously, that it "did not strike him as an object of such importance as it had appeared to other members of this government." [50]

But Hamilton was not Hammond's only source of information as to what was happening behind the scenes in American officialdom. A good many Senators were eager to bring him tidbits of confidential information. Barely had the Senators quit a secret session in which ministerial appointments to Great Britain and France had been ratified, than Hammond was sending off the results to Grenville. "In the whole course of this discussion," he reported complacently, "I have been regularly informed of the proceedings of the Senate, and have received every mark of personal and unreserved confidence." [51]

It is not a matter of wonder then that Jefferson was bitter about this backstairs diplomacy in which even Washington, through Hamilton's suggestions, seemed also to take a part. Jefferson had protested against negotiating with Ternant in unorthodox fashion, but had yielded on Washington's insistence. Now, however, when Washington came to him again with Hamilton's proposition that he negotiate with equal informality with Hammond, he rebelled; and declined to treat with either minister.[52] He went further. He told Washington openly during the course of a quarrel over the question as to whether the State or the Treasury Department had jurisdiction over the Post-Office that "the department of treasury possessed already such an influence as to swallow up the whole Executive powers, and that even the future Presidents (not supported by the weight of character which himself possessed) would not be able to make head against this department." [53]

This outburst took place on February 28, 1792. On the following day Jefferson went further. He spoke of resigning. Washington urged him not to, on the ground that it would only add to the discontents against the government. Jefferson retorted that "there was only a single source of these discontents," and that was the Treasury. He called Hamilton's system pernicious, exclaimed that it was poisoning the government and the country, and that members of congress had feathered their own nests by supporting it. He also accused Hamilton of communicating all their views to Hammond behind their backs. [54] To this unexpected explosion Washington could only interpose soothing words which, however, finally had their effect and Jefferson consented to remain in office.

Whether Washington communicated the matter to Hamilton or not is unknown, but Hamilton continued his intimacy with Hammond. Jefferson had sent a stiff reply to Hammond's note of March 5th which had set forth England's position, and Hammond hastened with it to Hamilton, complaining of its irrelevant matter "and the general acrimonious stile and manner of this letter." Hamilton deplored Jefferson's note as much as Hammond. "After lamenting the intemperate violence of his colleague," reported the British Minister to his own government, "Mr. Hamilton assured me that this letter was very far from meeting his approbation, or from containing a faithful exposition of the sentiments of this Government." That Washington in fact had not read the note, having just returned from Virginia, and "had relied upon Mr. Jefferson's assurance, that it was conformable to the opinions of the other members of the executive government." [55] This was intervention with a vengeance!

4. MR. HAMILTON AND MR. JEFFERSON HIRE PRESS AGENTS

As though the controversy between the two secretaries was not sufficiently exacerbated, they both rushed into the public prints. At first it was done secretly, through the medium of subsidized journalists; later, as the respective backings of their champions came to light, accompanied with angry outcries and mutual denunciations of corruption, they entered the lists themselves, transparently veiled in the patent anonymity of Latin pseudonyms.

Jefferson's journalistic champion was Philip Freneau, a poet of vigor and some distinction in the early American scene, as well as a thorough-going radical. Hamilton's champion in the lists was John Fenno, of a more conservative bent and possessed of a duller, if fairly competent, pen. In view of the later acrimonious charges and countercharges as to who first employed such outside aid, it might be well to examine the chronological data with some care.

In 1789 John Fenno had started the *United States Gazette* in New York. It presumed to be a semi-official newspaper, devoted almost entirely to governmental affairs. When the seat of government was removed from New York to Philadelphia in 1790, Fenno and his news-paper followed suit. The first evidence of a connection between Fenno and Hamilton appears in hitherto unpublished items in the pages of Hamilton's cash books, now reposing in the Library of Congress. On October 19, 1790, Hamilton noted a loan of $100 to Fenno; on January 8, 1791, he entered the fact of another loan of $100.[56]

Whatever further financial connection there may have been—and Freneau later pointed to the fact that Fenno's newspaper received from the Treasury $2500 of exclusive government printing within the course of a single year[57]—it soon became obvious that Fenno was whole-heartedly supporting Hamilton in all his works, and by the same token, damning his opponents, with special attention to Jefferson and Madison. By 1792 the *United States Gazette* was generally known as a Hamil-tonian organ.

In 1789 Philip Freneau had written fugitive pieces for the New York *Daily Advertiser*, of which Childs was the owner. From all the avail-able facts it is plain that for some time prior to May, 1791, both Jeffer-son and Madison were negotiating with Freneau to come to Philadelphia and set up a newspaper in opposition to Fenno's *United States Gazette*. On May 9th Jefferson wrote to Madison that "your favor of the 1st came to hand on the 3rd. Mr. Freneau has not followed it: I suppose therefore he has changed his mind back again, for which I am really sorry." [58] On May 15th Jefferson enclosed a copy of Fenno's paper to Thomas Mann Randolph, exclaiming against it as a "paper of pure Toryism, disseminating the doctrines of monarchy, aristocracy, & the exclusion of the influence of the people." Significantly he added that "we have been trying to get another *weekly* or *half weekly* paper set up excluding advertisements, so that it might go through the states, & furnish a whig vehicle of intelligence. We hoped at one time to have persuaded Freneau to set up here, but failed." [59]

Shortly afterward, however, the hesitant Mr. Freneau changed his mind once more, this time permanently. He appeared in Philadelphia and commenced a newspaper called the *National Gazette,* which promptly began a series of attacks on Hamilton and his policies which soon thrust it into the forefront as the recognized organ of Jefferson and Madison. If this were all, Jefferson was just as much within the bounds of the permissible as was Hamilton in helping Fenno to *his* start. But it wasn't all.

Freneau came to Philadelphia, not only to start his newspaper but to accept a post in the offices of the State Department as a clerk for foreign languages and translator, at a salary of $250 a year. And his appointment to this post was substantially simultaneous with the appearance of his newspaper.[60]

When Hamilton later furiously charged that Jefferson had employed his government patronage to subsidize a newspaper which continuously attacked the government and its policies, Jefferson was ingenuous, if not ingenious, in his denials. He asserted that Freneau had long before, in New York, applied to him for a clerkship, but that there had been no vacancy then. When he applied again, after the government had been removed to Philadelphia, a vacancy had arisen and his request had been granted. "I cannot recollect," he continued his defense rather confusedly to Washington,

whether it was at the same time, or afterwards, that I was told he had thought of setting up a newspaper there. But whether then, or afterwards, I considered it as a circumstance of some value, as it might enable me to do, what I had long wished to have done, that is, to have the material parts of the Leyden gazette brought under your eye & that of the public, in order to possess yourself and them of a juster view of the affairs of Europe. . . . But as to any other direction or indication of my wish how his press should be conducted, what sort of intelligence he should give, what essays encourage, I can protest in the presence of heaven, that I never did by myself or any other, directly or indirectly, say a syllable, nor attempt any kind of influence.[61]

In view of Jefferson's letter to Randolph, previously cited, it is difficult to know just how to characterize this statement.

The rival newspapers went at it hammer and tongs. Whatever one asserted was promptly attacked in the other. Whatever Hamilton did was upheld by Fenno and simultaneously excoriated by Freneau. Hamilton was described as Sir Galahad and as Sir Devil. Since Freneau was the more trenchant writer, and the more adept at scathing diatribes, Hamilton himself was stung into coming to the aid of his plodding supporter. His first entry into print was in the form of a satirical inquiry concerning Freneau, anonymously initialed "T. L."

The editor of the *National Gazette* receives a salary from government. *Quere.*—Whether this salary is paid him for *translations*, or for publications, the design of which is to vilify those to whom the voice of the people has committed the administration of our public affairs....In common life it is thought ungrateful for a man to bite the hand that puts bread in his mouth; but if the man is hired to do it, the case is altered.[62]

He followed this squib with a series of three public letters, signed "An American," which savagely attacked not only Freneau and the circumstances of his employment, but Jefferson as well, the employer. Hamilton minced no words: Jefferson had opposed the Constitution itself in the beginning and had since opposed every important act of that government of which he pretended to be a part. Jefferson had received his political education amid the intrigues of a European court. "If he disapproves of the government itself, and thinks it deserving of his opposition, can he reconcile it to his own personal dignity, and the principles of probity, to hold an office under it, and employ the means of official influence in that opposition?"[63]

The arraignment was so bitter, and so obviously Hamilton's, that James Madison was hurried into the columns of the *National Gazette*, under the disguise of "Aristides," to answer Hamilton and attack him in turn. The battle of the big guns was on.

For several months the heavy artillery on both sides volleyed and thundered: Freneau and Madison on one side, and Hamilton and Fenno on the other. Hamilton imitated the chameleon; in turn he was "Catullus," "Amicus," "Metellus," "Civis" and "A Plain Honest Man." Against this pseudo-galaxy of a single multi-masked star, Madison opposed his "Aristides" and Freneau, "Mercator." Only Jefferson remained on the sidelines, shrinking, as always, from public polemics. But the barbs of Hamilton's attacks tore at his sensitive flesh, and the festering venom was soon to find an outlet.

It was all a strange and unholy spectacle—two responsible cabinet members, together with the leading member of congress, engaged in a furious and name-calling struggle in the public prints. No one was fooled by the classical signatures of the contestants; no one doubted their identity. The whole country followed the weekly diatribes with varying emotions. Sensible and judicious men grieved, but the rank and file egged their champions on with wild glee. The sharp divisions of Hamiltonians and Jeffersonians were clearly distinct.

John Beckley, Representative from Pennsylvania, wrote to inform Madison that Hamilton considered him "his *personal* & political enemy." In another letter he paid unwilling tribute to their common foe. "It would be wise to be watchful," he warned Madison; "there is no inferior degree of sagacity in the combinations of this *extraordinary* man. With a comprehensive eye, a subtle and contriving mind, and a soul devoted to his object, all his measures are promptly and aptly designed, and like the links of a chain, dependent on each other, acquired additional strength by their union & concert." [64]

Washington was aghast at this sudden public eruption of cabinet differences of which he had long been aware and which he had hoped to keep on a dignified level and perhaps eventually reconcile. With all the massive weight of his character and office he tried to bring about at least a truce. Both men, he felt, were essential to the proper working of the government. He sent cautiously phrased appeals to the two antagonists. To Hamilton he wrote:

Differences in political opinions are as unavoidable, as, to a certain point, they may perhaps be necessary; but it is exceedingly to be regretted, that subjects cannot be discussed with temper on the one hand, or decisions submitted to without having the motives, which led to them, improperly implicated on the other; and this regret borders on chagrin, when we find that men of abilities, zealous patriots, having the same *general* objects in view, and the same upright intentions to prosecute them, will not exercise more charity in deciding on the opinions and actions of one another.[65]

Hamilton replied with all proper respect and with a frank avowal of his instrumentality in the retaliations on Jefferson, but he firmly declared that he could not recede "*for the present*." He went into the history of the quarrel and hinted at a willingness for both of the contestants to resign for the good of the administration. "Nevertheless," he added, "I pledge my honor to you, sir, that if you shall hereafter form a plan to reunite the members of your administration upon some steady principle of cooperation, I will faithfully concur in executing it during my continuance in office; and I will not directly or indirectly say or do a thing that shall endanger [engender?] a feud." [66]

Jefferson likewise answered with a defense of his acts. He started, however, with the complaint that he had been duped into a support of assumption "by the Secretary of Treasury and made a tool for forwarding his schemes, not then sufficiently understood by me." From that high ground he proceeded to an attack on all of Hamilton's measures, singling out especially the Report on Manufactures as a scheme for corrupting members of congress so as to have a "corps under the command of the Secretary of Tresury for the purpose of subverting step by step the principles of the constitution. . . ." He complained also of Hamilton's high-handed interference in his department, his attacks on him in Fenno's *Gazette,* and attempted to defend his own connection with Freneau in the manner already quoted. He ended on a venomous note: "I will not suffer my retirement to be clouded by the slanders of a man whose history, from the moment at which history can stoop to notice him, is a tissue of machinations against the liberty of the country which has not only received and given him bread, but heaped its honors on his head." [87]

Both men had offered to resign. But Washington refused to accede and finally, after much effort, induced them both to remain. There was, however, from this period on a continuous private, if not public, warfare. The lines were sharply drawn. The Federalist party of Hamilton, and the Republican party of Jefferson, were to enter the national election of 1792 openly as such.

CHAPTER XXI

Rum and Politics

---

1. STRUGGLE OVER WHISKY

THE IMMEDIATE RESULT of the assumption of state debts by the national government was the necessity for new sources of revenue whereby the increased cost could be met. The income under the Tariff Act of 1789 was clearly insufficient for the purpose. Hamilton had promptly recommended an increase in import duties and, in addition, the levying of an excise tax upon the domestic manufacture of whisky. There was little trouble in gaining assent to the first proposition, but the second brought up the whole troublous question of internal taxation by the federal government.

This was a field which the states had always claimed belonged solely to themselves. The fear of federal intrusion had been one of the most effective arguments raised against ratification of the Constitution. And, as though Hamilton had deliberately determined to force the issue to extremes, a tax on whisky was the most unpopular of all taxes that could possibly have been levied.

To the farmers and frontiersmen on the western fringes of the nation—western Pennsylvania, Virginia and North Carolina—where the line of the Alleghenies made a formidable barrier to easy traffic with the seaboard, whisky was at once the most common article of consumption and the simplest medium of exchange. It did not pay to transport grain over the Alleghenies—but grain distilled into easily portable whisky found a ready market to the east and brought the distillers their only cash with which to purchase the manufactured articles of the east. A tax on whisky therefore—payable in cash—seemed an insupportable and intolerable burden to these farmer-distillers of the backwoods.

But Hamilton's pressure, and the stark reality of a national deficit, compelled congress, albeit reluctantly, to place a sliding scale of taxes on domestic spirits ranging from nine to twenty-five cents a gallon. This Act of March 3, 1791, stirred up such a hornet's nest of wrath that the amounts were hurriedly reduced. But the frontier regions and their advocates elsewhere refused to be appeased. Mass meetings were held, petitions and memorials flooded congress. Tax collectors were compelled to flee for their lives, and the sums collected proved the merest trickle. Congress turned in despair to Hamilton: would he furnish it with information and an opinion in connection with these difficulties?

Hamilton obliged with a Report on Spirits, Foreign and Domestic, which he submitted to the House on March 6, 1792.[1] As always, he made the particular issue the basis for a discussion of broad principles. The right to levy internal taxes was just as essential to a government, he argued, as the generally conceded right to levy taxes on foreign imports. There was nothing in the one that restricted the liberty of a country more than in the other. The national government must have an adequate income, he asserted vigorously, and there was no reason why the consumer of domestic products should not pay his share just as well as the consumer of foreign articles; the small farmer and frontiersman as well as the merchant and eastern landowner.

But the western counties would have none of such general arguments. The agitation increased. The tax collectors dared not venture into the disaffected regions. Liberty poles—portentous reminders—made their appearance. The public meetings grew more turbulent.

Hamilton viewed the proceedings, if not exactly with delight, at least with a certain sense of anticipation. Here was presented an opportunity he had long coveted. The government of the United States had not yet proved itself. It had not yet shown that it was strong enough to survive. What would happen when, as seemed quite probable, a group of states or even a single state, should decide to set itself against the nation?

This was the time, he reflected, to test the strength of the government. The issue was clear-cut, and the opposition scattered and unable to mobilize as a unit. He took full advantage of the opportunity. In a series of private talks and letters he urged Washington to act with decision—and at once. Washington agreed with him on the necessity of enforcing compliance in the disaffected areas, though he was reluctant to employ military means unless they became absolutely essential. Hamilton, on the other hand, would have preferred an immediate show of force.

On August 10th he wrote Washington that "it affords me much satisfaction to observe that your mind has anticipated the decision to enforce the Law; in case a refractory spirit should continue to render the ordinary & more desirable means ineffectual. My most deliberate reflections have led me to conclude, that the time for acting with decision is at hand..." [2]

On September 1st he repeated his conviction that it was necessary to exercise the full weight of the government, even to the use of force. "If this is not done, the spirit of disobedience will naturally extend, and the authority of the government will be prostrated. Moderation enough has been shown; it is time to assume a different tone." [3]

By this time Washington was in full agreement with his bellicose Secretary of the Treasury. "Forbearance," he wrote the latter, "under a hope that the Inhabitants of that Survey would recover from the delirium & folly into which they were plunged, seems to have had no other effect than to encrease the disorder." [4]

Encouraged by this stiffened attitude on the part of the President, Hamilton wasted no time in propelling him into action. He not only advised Washington to issue a proclamation against the offenders, but submitted a draft for that proclamation. He urged haste. "Every day's delay will render the act less impressive, and defeat part of its object." [5]

But Washington suddenly became cautious. Now that he was being forced into positive, open action, the implications troubled him. Before he went ahead he wanted a united cabinet in back of him. Hamilton saw to it that Knox and Randolph endorsed the proclamation. But they were without much weight; Washington considered it to be essential that Jefferson countersign it. Jefferson, however, at the moment was home in Monticello, and though Washington agreed that delay in issuing the proclamation was dangerous, he nevertheless insisted upon sending the document down to Jefferson for signature. [6]

Hamilton fumed at the delay and at the knowledge that Jefferson would certainly oppose. Yet he was compelled perforce to bow to the will of the President. And, while the proclamation was still en route to the south, news came from the disaffected areas that the talk of resistance to the tax had ended, that the courts were still functioning and the collectors no longer in fear of their lives. Through Washington's caution the chance had vanished, and Hamilton had to bide his time for two years before the opportunity recurred.

2. STRUGGLE OVER POLITICS

The year 1792 was a presidential year—the second national election to be held in the United States. The first had passed off smoothly and easily. Washington had been chosen by universal acclamation; if there was some difficulty over John Adams for vice-president, it did not affect the result. But in 1792 parties had reared their heads; the basically differing philosophies of two great groups of Americans had found their leaders.

Washington still stood above the party battle, though the rumblings of discontent were already beginning to be heard. It was generally conceded that if he so desired, the presidency was his for a second term. By this time, however, Washington was weary of public life and would have much preferred to retire to his estate in Mount Vernon. It took the concerted urging of cabinet members, congressmen and influential individuals everywhere to obtain his reluctant consent to stand again for office.

On the vice-presidency, however, there was far from unanimity. Here the party lines showed openly and aboveboard. There was no question that John Adams, the incumbent, would be the candidate for the Federalists. Even Hamilton, who had had mental reservations about the gentleman from Massachusetts, realized that with the formation of a vigorous opposition all energies must be employed to back the present holder of office. For the Republican forces had entered the field. Not daring as yet to contest with Washington, they concentrated on Adams.

The first publicly avowed candidate for the office was Governor George Clinton of New York, Hamilton's ancient enemy. The entry of this formidable foe galvanized Hamilton into calling personally on Adams to exert himself to the utmost in his own behalf and promising him full measure of support.[7]

But if the announcement of Clinton's candidacy was disturbing, the next report that came secretly to Hamilton filled him with the most intense alarm. This was the advent of a new, and far more formidable candidate in the field than the aging governor—Aaron Burr.

Rufus King wrote the news:

If the enemies of government are secret and united, we shall lose Mr. Adams. Burr is industrious in his canvass, and his object is well understood by our Antis. Mr. Edwards is to make interest for him in Connecticut, and Mr. Dallas...informs us that Mr. Burr will be supported as Vice-President in Pennsylvania. Should Jefferson and his friends unite in the project, the votes of Mr. A. may be so reduced, that though more numerous than those of any other person, he may decline the office.[8]

The apparition of Senator Aaron Burr of New York came upon Hamilton like a thunderbolt. Clinton was bad enough—but he was a known and self-limiting quantity; he was old, stubborn, and of talents that could be weighed and provided against. But Burr was another matter. He was young—only a year older than Hamilton—brilliant, able, vigorous and with the world before him. Hamilton remembered only too well how Mr. Burr had upset all his carefully laid plans by displacing his father-in-law, General Schuyler, in the Senate of the United States. The memory of it rankled fiercely, though Hamilton and Schuyler had agreed to act in public toward Burr as though nothing had happened.[9] He remembered, too, how Burr had substantially contributed to John Jay's defeat for the governorship. Wherever he turned, Burr loomed in the path. Decidedly, this trim, smiling figure with the keen, yet subtle, brain must be eliminated by fair means or foul.

He answered King: "Though I had had a previous intimation of the possibility of such an event; yet the intelligence contained in your letter of the 17th surprised me. Even now I am to be convinced that the movement is any thing more than a diversion in favor of Mr. Clinton. Yet on my part it will not be neglected.... A good use will be made of it in this state." [10]

Decidedly Hamilton made a good use of this communication from King. In many ways it was even an extravagant use. For in his resentment against the new candidate he sent out a series of letters broadcast over the country in which he attacked Burr not merely as a politician but as a private individual. He attacked his probity, his honor, his honesty and his personal life. He called him by names which, had they then come into public view, would have forced a duel—and possibly brought about Hamilton's death—some twelve years before the actual event.

Employing King's merely political letter as a text, Hamilton embroidered on it to his correspondents. Mr. Clinton, he told them, at least was "a man of property, and in private life, as far as I know, of probity." It was far different with Burr. "Mr. Burr's integrity as an individual is not unimpeached. As a public man, he is one of the worst sort—a friend to nothing but as it suits his interest and ambition. Determined to climb to the highest honors of the State, and as much higher as circumstances may permit; he cares for nothing about the means of effecting his purpose.... In a word, if we have an embryo-Caesar in the United States, 'tis Burr." [11] To another he wrote in the same vein: Burr, he feared, "is unprincipled, both as a public and a private man.... Embarrassed, as I understand, in his circumstances, with an extravagant family, bold, enterprising, and intriguing, I am mistaken if it be not his object to play a game of confusion, and I feel it to be a religious duty to oppose his career." Here too he asserted that Burr was determined "to make his way to be the head of the popular party, and to climb *per fas aut nefas* to the highest honors of the State, and as much higher as circumstances may permit." To all of which "I pledge my character for discernment, that it is incumbent upon every good man to resist the present design." [12]

Yet, strangely, when Hamilton wrote to Steele at a later date, he was very much more cautious: "My opinion of Mr. Burr is yet to form—but, according to the present state of it, he is a man whose only political principle is *to mount at all events*, to the highest legal honors of the State..." And again, "imputations, not favorable to his integrity as a man, rest upon him, *but I do not vouch for their authenticity* [italics mine]." [13] Perhaps the shift from former categorical assertions and pledges to hesitant vagueness can be attributed to the fact that Mr. Steele was in congress and had had an opportunity to become acquainted with Mr. Burr, whereas the other correspondents knew of him only by report.

Moreover, to Washington he made no such accusations against Burr. He merely set forth the fact of his candidacy, as gleaned from Rufus King; and gave it as his opinion that it is not "anything more than a diversion in favour of Mr. Clinton." [14]

In this last opinion Hamilton was correct. The Republicans in fact concentrated on Clinton against Adams, and Burr supported his supposed rival with vigor and efficiency. Washington received the presidency without a dissenting vote, but Adams had a fight on his hands. He received 77 electoral votes; Clinton was second with 50; Jefferson picked up 10 from Kentucky; and Burr was given a single ballot by South Carolina. Hamilton's reckless correspondence might better have never been sent.

One of the aftermaths of the election was a charge directed against Hamilton's own integrity. A report came to Washington's ears that a certain Colonel Mercer of Maryland had asserted during the campaign that Hamilton had tried to bribe him with money for his vote in support of assumption. Washington considered the charge so serious that he called upon the man who had brought it to him for definite confirmation. [15]

Hamilton, in a cold rage, determined to track down the rumor. He wrote to Maryland for information and received a first-hand account from a man named William Bagly. Bagly, it seems, had heard that at an election at Upper Marlboro

Colo. Mercer had said, that Mr. Hambleton [*sic*], the Secretary had Offered him, Money if he woud Vote for the Assumption. I asked Colo. Mercer if he had said so, he Answered Yes, by God he had. Mr. Walter Bowie who was sitting by Colo Mercer said it was in a Jocular way. I then ask'd Colo. Mercer if he thought Mr. Hambleton was Serious or Jesting, he Answered, that he had a Right to take it either way. [On Bagly's further insistence, Mercer explained.] He had been Down at Mr. Hambleton's office, in Order to settle some Accounts, or to receive some money that was due to him, from the United States, but that Mr. Hambleton's Clerks, or Understrappers, would not pay it—& on Colo. Mercers Return from the Office he met Mr. Hambleton who Observed to him, if he would Vote for the Assumption—he Mr. Hambleton would pay the money.[16]

With this definite information in hand, Hamilton called on Mercer for an exact account of his words. With the implication that a duel might result, Mercer replied hastily that he "disavows his ever having impeached the integrity of the Secretary...and explicitly acknowledged what passed between him and the Secretary, on this subject, was altogether in jest." [17]

In a like jesting vein Hamilton received the pleasing information that the new French Republic had issued honorary certificates of citizenship, dated October 10, 1792, to *Jean* Hamilton, George Washington, James Madison and others of the sister republic across the seas. Hamilton grimly endorsed on the back of his certificate: "Letter from Government of French Republic transmitting me a Diploma of Citizenship mistaking *Christian* name, Oct. 1792—curious example of French finesse." [18]

3. THE GILES RESOLUTIONS

On February 27, 1793, William B. Giles, Representative from Virginia and a close friend of Jefferson and Madison, moved a series of resolutions in the House that was the most direct public attack yet made on the integrity of the Secretary of the Treasury and his official acts in office. The resolutions, nine in number, minced no words. They charged Hamilton with specific violation of an Act of Congress, dated August 4, 1790, in applying portions of appropriated funds to purposes not authorized by law. They charged Hamilton with deliberately deviating from the instructions of the President of the United States in the transfer of moneys raised by loans in Europe to the United States, and in failing to provide congress with official information of his acts in connection therewith. They charged him with a wanton disregard of the public interest in negotiating a loan with the Bank of the United States at five per cent interest at a time when ample public funds were lying idle in that and other banks. They charged him with being "guilty of an indecorum to this House" in attempting to judge of its motives in requesting information from him on these and kindred matters, and with withholding essential information in complying with the request.[19]

The charges were serious, specific, and backed by a concerted opposition determined to discredit Hamilton and drag him forever from public life. It represented the culmination of a persistent sniping at Hamilton and his financial policies that had brought months before an impassioned diatribe against his defamers.

You bring every thing to the standard of your narrow and depraved ideas, and you condemn without mercy or even decency whatever does not accord with it.... Your politics originate in immorality, in a disregard of the maxims of good faith and the rights of property, and if they could prevail must end in national disgrace and confusion.... Your principles of liberty are principles of licentiousness incompatible with all government. You sacrifice every thing that is venerable and substantial in society to the vain reveries of a false and new-fangled philosophy. As to the motives by which I have been influenced, I leave my general conduct in private and public life to speak for them.[20]

On January 23, 1793, Giles had taken the preliminary step which was to lay the foundation for the public denunciation of February 27th. He had called for a general accounting by Hamilton of all foreign loans which he had made, a statement of the balances existing between the United States and the Bank of the United States, an accounting of the sinking fund operations, together with a report on unapplied revenues and where they were deposited. The strategy had been obvious. Congress was scheduled to adjourn at the beginning of March and not to reconvene until late in the fall. It was considered impossible for Hamilton to prepare within the short space of time that was left before adjournment the voluminous and incredibly complicated data which had been called for. This would leave, during long months, the suspicion generated by the resolutions rankling in the minds of the country, and Giles and his confederates gleefully anticipated the political capital they could make of Hamilton's failure to make the report in time.

But they had failed to reckon with Hamilton's almost superhuman energy when put to the test. Working day and night, assembling figures, barely eating, snatching only scattered moments of sleep, Hamilton whipped into shape and presented to an amazed congress within twelve days after the resolutions had been passed a complete and detailed report of all his financial manipulations, with the documentary evidence to support them. Two days later he filed a supplementary report, and a third and final answer on February 13th, a week after. With open sarcasm, he inquired:

Is it not truly matter of regret that so formal an explanation, on such a point, should have been made requisite? Could no personal inquiry, of either of the officers concerned, have superseded the necessity of publicly calling the attention of the House of Representatives to an appearance, in truth, so little significant? Was it seriously supposable that there could be any real difficulty in explaining that appearance, when the very disclosure of it proceeded from a voluntary act of the head of this Department? [21]

All that the disgruntled opposition could do, after the minutest study of the reports, was to seize upon certain technical points for presentment in the formal resolutions of denunciation. Even the sarcastic query of the Secretary was made a part of the complaint. If the presentment was thin, the determination of Giles and his associates to push it to extremes was not.

Who were these associates? Mr. Jefferson and Mr. Madison. That they were co-partners in the entire proceedings now admits of no further doubt. The documentary evidence is overwhelming. There is in existence a draft of the resolutions moved by Giles in Jefferson's own handwriting, which to a large extent parallels word for word those which appeared in Congress, except for one significant omission by Giles. Jefferson had proposed a tenth resolve "that the Secretary of the Treasury has been guilty of maladministration in the duties of his office, and should, in the opinion of Congress, be removed from his office by the President of the United States." [22] Even Giles felt this was going too far.

There is also in existence a manuscript memorandum in Madison's hand analyzing in great detail Hamilton's report of January 3rd with special reference to the suspicion "that the funds raised in Europe & which ought to have been applied to the paiment of our debts there, in order to stop interest, have been drawn over to this country & lodged in the bank, to extend the speculations and increase the profits of that institution." [23] It was on the basis of this memorandum prepared by Madison that Giles hammered home his major attack.

On February 28th, the day after he had brought forward his resolutions, Giles moved to have them considered by a committee of the whole. With adjournment only a few days away, this was a clever scheme for delay. But Hamilton's supporters objected. Why delay? demanded Smith of South Carolina. Let us proceed at once to a consideration of these charges. "The question was, had the Secretary violated a law? If so, let it be shown; every member was competent to decide so plain a question." [24]

Even though the Hamiltonians failed to stop the commitment, their protests were so vigorous and their attitude so determined that they forced an immediate consideration, even though congress was scheduled for adjournment that very day.

On March 1st the all-important debate commenced. Giles led off with an attack in which he called on congress to help the President get rid of the guilty secretary. But this line of attack left him open to Barnwell's barbs of ridicule. *He* had heard nothing in the nature of a complaint from the President. Why then was the House so eager to rush to his aid? The most crushing and unanswerable argument to Giles and his resolutions, however, came from Smith of South Carolina. While regretting that the charges against Hamilton had been brought at the tag end of the session, he nevertheless was happy that "the vague charges of mismanagement, with which the public had long been alarmed, were at length cast into a shape susceptible of investigation and decision." He then proceeded with his investigation. Taking up the resolutions one by one, he pulled them to pieces, showed the animus behind them, defended the acts of the secretary with chapter and verse. So splendid was his argument and so minutely familiar with every detail of the intricate financial operations, that it is more than probable that Hamilton himself prepared at least the basis for the speech. [25]

When Smith sat down it was obvious even to the most partisan that the resolutions could never be passed. Giles attempted a weak answer, but as though realizing it was all over, he quit almost abruptly. Madison delivered one of his cautious, moderate, legalistic discussions to prove that Hamilton had violated the law. Boudinot and Ames replied. The House moved into a night session. The Hamiltonians blocked all efforts to adjourn. The hour grew very late. The candles guttered and smoked. The opposition tired. Finally the resolutions were brought on for a vote. One after another, they went down to overwhelming defeat. The best that Giles could muster was 15 to 33 on the 5th Resolution. The others ranged from 12 to 40, to 7 to 34. The next day congress adjourned.[26]

Hamilton had won a tremendous victory. Jefferson sought to minimize its importance with the comment that Giles had failed only because the House was composed of bank directors, holders of bank stock, stock-jobbers, blind devotees, ignorant people and those who were either too lazy or too good-humored.[27]

Yet when Hamilton demanded of him a statement concerning the cabinet discussion back in 1790 on the question of allocating the European loans, which made up the greater part of the resolutions of censure, Jefferson replied blandly that the matter had gone "out of my mind altogether, till the late enquiries brought it forward again." Nevertheless he felt that the President's instructions had given no sanction to Hamilton's course, and ended with the astounding assertion that "I did not take it up then as a Volunteer, nor should now have taken the trouble of recurring to it, but at your request; *as it is one in which I am not particularly concerned, which I never had either the time or inclination to investigate, & on which my opinion is of no importance.*"[28] This from the man who had drafted the resolutions of Mr. Giles!

4. EUROPEAN WAR AND AMERICAN NEUTRALITY

On the first day of February, 1793, the long-exacerbated relations between England and the revolutionary government of France culminated in a declaration of war addressed by the French National Convention against the former. The news of this important break, so vital to every internal and external relation of the United States, reached these shores first by rumor and then by official packets by the end of March and the beginning of April. Long expected though it was, the war between the two great European powers created a sensation. Washington was vacationing in Mount Vernon at the time. He cut short his visit and hastened full speed to Philadelphia. He reached the capital on April 17th; on the following day he submitted a series of thirteen questions to the members of his cabinet "with a view to forming a general plan of conduct for the executive" in this grave emergency.

It was indeed a moment of grave emergency. With the two great European powers locked in a struggle for existence, the new republic of the United States had good reason to consider its course. On Washington's present decision depended the whole future course of the American people; possibly even the life or death of the American experiment. Two huge antagonists grappling with each other would notoriously not be concerned with the niceties of international law, and the United States by its instant actions might find itself ground to pieces between the vantage heavings of the powers.

The questions that Washington posed to his advisers covered the whole field of American relations with the war. Should the United States issue a proclamation of neutrality? Should a French minister be received? Should the United States consider that the old treaties with France, based upon the alliance during the American Revolution, were still in effect, or ought they to be renounced or suspended? Ought congress to be called immediately into session?[29]

When Jefferson received the questions he saw in them the hand of his own great antagonist, Hamilton. "It was palpable from the style," he confided to his *Anas*, "their ingenious tissue & suite that they were not the President's, that they were raised upon a prepared chain of argument, in short that the language was Hamilton's and the doubts his alone." And he declared that Randolph, the Attorney-General, had confirmed him in this suspicion.[30]

There seems to be no question that Jefferson was correct in his surmise. The European war had not exactly burst like a thunderbolt upon the officers of the government. It had been long expected and long prepared against. Only the date of actual hostilities had been in doubt. On April 12th Washington had written from Mount Vernon to both Hamilton and Jefferson requesting their opinions on the impending event, though expressing at the same time his determination to adhere to a strict neutrality.[31]

But Hamilton had not waited for the President's request. Already, on April 9th, he had taken it upon himself to set forth his views on the subject to John Jay in language almost identical with that of Washington's questions, and followed it up the same day with another letter asking him to draft a proclamation of Neutrality along those lines for Washington's perusal and signature.[32] Two days later Jay obliged with a hasty draft of ideas to be embodied in such a proclamation.[33]

All this was legitimate, although Jefferson did not appear to think so. Washington had requested the opinions of his cabinet. Hamilton had answered; Jefferson had not. What troubled Jefferson, however, in the questions as Washington finally submitted them, was not so much the avowed object of a policy of neutrality as the hesitations therein expressed as to the course to be pursued in connection with France and the still-existing treaties with that country. According to those treaties the United States was in effect the ally of France in any war with England in which England was the aggressor, and had given practically a guaranty of the French possessions in the West Indies. To add to the complications, word was received that the French Republic was sending a minister to the United States. Was he to be received; and if not, what was to be done in the matter?

On these thirteen questions Hamilton and Jefferson came again to a split. Not, it must be stated emphatically, on the *fact* of neutrality. Here the two antagonists were wholly in agreement. Neither one relished the idea of throwing the United States into a war from which only the most fatal consequences could ensue for the still weak and semi-formed nation on this side of the Atlantic. But on the details of neutrality, on the infinite complexity of questions that followed inevitably in its train, there was not merely no agreement but wide divergencies.

Obviously, neither of the men was neutral in his sympathies. Hamilton had early become disgusted with what he considered the brutal excesses of the French Revolution; Jefferson calmly considered that no Revolution worthy of the name could be made without some breaking of eggs. Hamilton was by nature devoted to the British ideal of government; he had based his own system as nearly as possible on that great exemplar. Jefferson was equally by nature much more attracted to the French enunciations of Liberty, Equality and Fraternity, and hated with every fiber of his being the monarchical, aristocratic and financial structure of Great Britain. Jefferson considered Hamilton more attached to England than to America, and Hamilton reciprocated by attributing a similar bias to Jefferson in favor of France. And neither one thought the deliberations of the cabinet of such secrecy that they might not be disclosed on occasion to others. Only Jefferson talked to his fellow-Republicans—Madison, Monroe, etc., while Hamilton made a confidant of the British Minister.

Hamilton in fact talked with surprising freedom to George Hammond, the British representative. Through Hamilton, Hammond was enabled to keep his home government accurately informed of the currents of opinion inside the American government. On March 7th, even before the declaration of war, Hammond wrote home that Hamilton "has assured me that *he* shall exert his influence to defeat the success of any proposition on the part of France, which, tempting as it might appear, might ultimately render it necessary for this government to depart from the observance of as strict a neutrality as is compatible with its present engagements, and which is so essential to its real interests." Hammond sagaciously attributed this stand to "the knowledge that any event which might endanger the *external* tranquillity of the United States, would be as fatal to the systems he has formed for the benefit of his country as to his present personal reputation and to his future projects of ambition." [34]

And, on April 2nd, under the heading, *"Most Secret and Confidential,"* Hammond was able, because of Hamilton, to assure his government that the United States would not permit its treaties with France to involve it "in any difficulties or disputes with other powers." He would continue to cultivate Mr. Hamilton, he added significantly.[35]

The cabinet went into session on April 19th to discuss the questions which Washington had submitted on the impending crisis. Hamilton argued for an immediate proclamation of neutrality, while Jefferson considered its issuance unwise. Let us act neutrally, he maintained. "It would be better to hold back the declaration of neutrality," he suggested, "as a thing worth something to the powers at war, that they would bid for it, & we might reasonably ask a price, the *broadest privileges* of neutral nations." [36] He also argued that the President had no power to issue such a proclamation without the consent of congress. To this Hamilton retorted that congress was not in session and that Washington had ample authority to go ahead at least until congress convened.[37]

These differences, however, were soon ironed out by yieldings on either side. As a result, the entire cabinet joined in a unanimous opinion on April 19th advising the issuance of the proclamation. On April 22nd, Washington published his famous proclamation which Edmund Randolph, the Attorney-General, had drafted for him; though even in recent times John Jay has been considered its author. In spite of the general impression it was *not* a Proclamation of *Neutrality*. Jefferson had been the victor to that extent. The very word was carefully avoided. It merely expressed a determination on the part of the United States to "adopt and pursue a conduct friendly and impartial toward the belligerent powers," and "to exhort and warn the citizens of the United States carefully to avoid all acts and proceedings whatsoever, which may in any manner tend to contravene such disposition." [38]

With this delicate question out of the way, an even more vexing question came into prominence. This was the problem of what to do about the expected envoy from France, "Citizen" Edmond C. Genêt. It was obvious that he was coming to call upon the United States to conform to the treaties of alliance into which it had rashly entered during the last war when France and America had been allies, and which had never been abrogated or denounced. Certainly, such conformity would not only contradict the terms of the proclamation being issued by Washington, but would inevitably embroil this country in the war.

Hamilton would have very much preferred to have cut the Gordian knot by not receiving Genêt at all. But this could not be done without abandoning that very point of friendly impartiality announced in the proclamation. The next best course, according to him, was to tell Genêt plainly on his arrival that the United States reserved "to future consideration and discussion the question—whether the operation of the treaties ... ought not to be deemed temporarily and provisionally suspended." While his instinct was sound and based on a realistic conception of the present position of the United States in a world of turmoil and conflict, the arguments he adduced to support this contention were more ingenous than convincing. He maintained that the treaties had been entered into with the *king* of France, that the king had been executed, and the present government was a mere usurpation. Since the Revolution was not the "*free, regular*, and *deliberate* act of the nation," and since France was in a state of flux and uncertainty, it would be wise for us to suspend the operations of the treaty until the outcome was determined; then we could decide *de novo*.[39]

Jefferson violently opposed this jesuitical reasoning. To him the treaty was in full force and effect. He held the ground that it was the *people* who make up a nation, not its form of government, whether monarchy or republic. The treaty had in effect been made with the French people, regardless of the formal terminology. In fact, France as a republic was far more entitled to its treaty rights than it had been as a despotism.[40]

With this profound conflict in the cabinet it is small wonder that all concerned waited uneasily for the arrival of the much-heralded French minister. The delay in his appearance merely added to the excitement.

Contrary winds and perhaps a desire to land at a point in friendlier territory to his professed aims than the hostile atmosphere of the capital, Philadelphia, brought Genêt to the port of Charleston for his first contact with the United States to which he had been accredited.

Citizen Genêt was the worst possible representative that France could have sent over. Bumptious, domineering, vain, flighty, filled with a sense of his own importance, he started on a career of blundering diplomacy that instead of cementing closer the ties of gratitude between the old allies, nearly brought them to the verge of war.

At Charleston Genêt's original conceit was immeasurably expanded by the enthusiastic reception he received from the Republican sympathizers with France. Instead of proceeding, therefore, to Philadelphia to submit his credentials to Washington, he remained to bask in adulation and to arrange for the recruitment and outfitting of privateers to prey on English commerce. With a reckless hand he distributed military commissions to American adventurers for service in mythical French armies against Florida and Louisiana.

When, finally, he decided to appear before the government in Philadelphia, he traveled overland by slow stages, graciously permitting the Republican sections of the populace at each stage to welcome him in vast throngs with speeches, idolatry, cheers for France and anathemas for England.

The Federalists viewed his slow, triumphal progress with the utmost alarm. Jacobinism was in the air; and they were certain they saw in the flighty person of Genêt the imminent approach of the wildest excesses of the Reign of Terror. An excited Federalist who had observed the monstrous portent in Virginia wrote to Hamilton about "the man that we are all afraid of." Only Hamilton could save them from impending disaster. "The best men in this country rely chiefly upon your talents and disposition," he cried, "to avoid the rocks which lie upon the right hand, and upon the left, ready to dash our young government to pieces upon the least unskilful pilotage." [41]

In Philadelphia, Washington and his cabinet awaited the dilatory approach of the French envoy with sharply divergent feelings. The President, holding a firm control over the contending factions, nevertheless considered his dignity insulted by these strange and unaccountable actions to the south. Hamilton, bearing Knox in his train and half-dragging a wavering, irresolute Randolph, was furious. Jefferson, on the other hand, beamed anticipatory approval on the approaching apostle of liberty. He wrote sneeringly to Monroe that "H[amilton] is panic-struck if we refuse our breach to every kick which Gr Brit. may chuse to give it. He is for proclaiming at once the most abject principles, such as would invite & merit habitual insults. And indeed every inch of ground must be fought in our councils to desperation in order to hold up the face of even a sneaking neutrality, for our votes are generally 2½ against 1½." At the same time he described with obvious delight the wild enthusiasm of the "yeomanry" of the city at the sight of a French frigate bringing to port a captured English prize.[42]

On May 17, 1793, Genêt finally presented his credentials to Washington, five and a half weeks after his landing in the United States. Puffed up with all the adulation he had received he expected no less a reception from the President. But Washington received him with chilly politeness and a frigid exterior. Taken aback, he attributed the manner of his reception to jealousy. "Old man Washington is jealous of my success, and of the enthusiasm with which the whole town flocks to my house," he wrote home petulantly.

But while Genêt was arrogantly determined to subvert Washington's Proclamation of Neutrality in favor of an open stand for France, and, if necessary, overthrow the government itself by an appeal to the people of the United States if it refused to obey his demands, the British minister, Hammond, filed a protest against that very seizure of a British ship which Jefferson had viewed with such complacency. For it seemed that the ship, the *Grange*, had been captured in American territorial waters.

Randolph wrote an opinion agreeing with Hammond's thesis, and the cabinet, including even Jefferson, saw the force of the complaint. Genêt had the grace to agree to yield the prize and flattered himself on his magnanimity in so doing.

The case of the *Grange* was merely the first, however, of a whole series of such cases. It devolved on Jefferson as Secretary of State to take up the matters officially with Genêt. He performed his unpleasant duties with a laudable fairness, and in the process the first enthusiasm between Genêt and Jefferson began to cool. Jefferson wondered, in fact, if Genêt was not more of a burden and an embarrassment than at first he had been led to believe when he had welcomed him as the great representative of a great revolutionary people. "He will sink the Republican interest, if they do not abandon him," he decided finally, albeit reluctantly.

Hamilton suffered from no such shiftings of position. From the very beginning he looked on Genêt with contempt and loathing, and considered him the natural representative of a nation given to every kind of excess. In opinion after opinion addressed to Washington he stressed the need for strict neutrality, in accordance with the terms of the proclamation, and denounced vigorously the continued infractions by the French. "What has been done on the part of the French is a violation of our rights," he insisted, "for which we have a *claim to reparation*, and a right to make war, if it be refused." [43]

But all these matters paled into insignificance in the face of the far more serious issue that arose over Genêt's open outfitting of privateers in American ports to take the sea against the English. Within a week of his landing in Charleston four privateers had sailed with his official sanction. They played havoc with English shipping; and Hammond immediately protested. Jefferson promptly assured him that our government disapproved of Genêt's course and would take steps to prevent a recurrence.

The sincerity of Jefferson's assurances were almost immediately, and disastrously, put to the test. The *Little Sarah*, an English merchant vessel, sailing out of Philadelphia, had been captured by a French frigate and brought back to port as a prize of war. This was in May. By July 6th word came to the government that she was being secretly outfitted as a French privateer. An examination disclosed not only that this was the truth, but that she was going to sail the very next day. After a demand by Governor Mifflin of Pennsylvania that Genêt hold the ship in port had been refused with "great passion," Jefferson himself hurried to Genêt's house to request him to detain it until at least Washington, then at Mount Vernon, returned to Philadelphia. Genêt refused again, but indicated that the ship would not be ready to sail "for some time," though she would drop down the river a little way in order to continue her preparations. Jefferson incautiously took this as a promise that the *Little Sarah* would not in fact sail until Washington's return.

On July 8th the cabinet met in the President's absence to consider the situation. Hamilton, Jefferson and Knox were present; Randolph was in Virginia. Hamilton, Knox concurring, insisted on a firm, decisive stand. Just below the point at which the *Little Sarah* had dropped anchor was an island called Mud Island. The pair demanded that a battery of guns be at once placed in position on the island to make certain that the ship did not sneak out to sea. Jefferson, relying on what he held to be Genêt's promise, dissented and insisted that no action be taken until Washington's return. Faced with his dissent, and in the President's absence, Hamilton could only fume and compose a written opinion setting forth his stand. [44]

When Washington arrived, he found his cabinet in an uproar. He read the conflicting opinions and decided that it was now too late to do anything about it even if he wished. The *Little Sarah* was already down the river, and the precious forty-eight hours wasted precluded the establishment of a battery in time. Meanwhile Jefferson kept on assuring him that everything would be all right. Several days later, unmolested, the *Little Sarah* hoisted sail for the open sea to assume a career of destructive privateering.

The fat was in the fire. Pale with fury, Hamilton moved in cabinet meeting to notify France that Genêt must be recalled. Knox added that in the meantime he be considered suspended from his functions. Jefferson, though taken aback at the turn of events, merely proposed that the matter, and Genêt's abusive correspondence, be communicated to France "with friendly observations." Jefferson noted that Washington remained silent while his cabinet heads debated.[45]

Hamilton returned again and again to the attack until, on August 1st, it was agreed to demand Genêt's recall, though Jefferson and Randolph did so with the greatest reluctance.[46]

By this time Hamilton was determined to do exactly what Genêt had threatened to do in his own behalf a month before—appeal to the people. He wanted to publish the entire correspondence with Genêt and thereby bare the inner wheels of the diplomatic tragi-comedy that was convulsing the nation.

Failing in this course, due to Jefferson's determined resistance, he betook himself to the public prints as he had so often done before. Under the pseudonym of Pacificus he had already begun the task of defending the Proclamation of Neutrality against the attacks of the Republicans. The first paper appeared on June 29, 1793, in Fenno's *Gazette of the United States*. The seventh and last appeared on July 20th.[47]

Pacificus was a thoroughgoing statement of the Federalist position in the great war then raging in Europe. The chief attack by the Republicans against that position centered in the existing treaties with France. By those we were in effect an ally of France and bound in good faith and gratitude to come to her aid. But Hamilton pointed out that the treaties called for a defensive alliance, and that France had *declared* war. We were not bound to go in back of that declaration, he argued, to determine who first injured whom. "Self-preservation is the first duty of a nation," he declared realistically. "Good faith does not require that the United States should put in jeopardy their essential interests, perhaps their very existence, in one of the most unequal contests in which a nation could be engaged, to secure to France—what? Her West India islands and other less important possessions in America."

Somewhat cynically he ridiculed the argument that gratitude for French aid during our Revolution required that we come to her aid now. "The rule of morality in this respect is not precisely the same between nations as between individuals," he declared flatly. Besides, France had helped us then not from motives of altruism, but to seek revenge for former defeats at the hands of England. What price gratitude, when its preachers "are not ashamed to brand Louis the XVI as a tyrant, Lafayette as a traitor?" *These* were the men who had aided us, not the present revolutionary government.

The articles, as they appeared white-hot from week to week, aroused the utmost alarm in Jefferson. Never very good in controversial debate, he called on his mainstay with the pen to rise and respond to the mighty Pacificus. "Nobody answers him," he wrote urgently to Madison, "& his doctrines will therefore be taken for confessed. For God's sake, my dear Sir, take up your pen, select the most striking heresies and cut him to pieces in the face of the public. There is nobody else who can & will enter the lists with him." [48]

Such a frantic exhortation to rise and smite was more easily made than obeyed. While Madison expressed indignation over Pacificus he manifested reluctance to enter the lists. Cautiously he replied: "I will feel my own pulse and if nothing appears, may possibly try to supply the omission." [49] Since no one else did take up the cudgels, against his better judgment Madison finally took up his pen under the mask of Helvidius. He found the task "the most grating one I have ever experienced. . . . One thing that particularly vexes me is that I foreknow from the prolixity & pertinacity of the writer [Hamilton], that the business will not be terminated by a single fire, and of course that I must return to the charge in order to prevent a triumph without a victory." [50] To such a state had Hamilton's facile controversial pen finally reduced his hitherto most redoubtable opponent!

Now, in August, immediately on finishing his Pacificus letters, Hamilton opened fire on Genêt in another series entitled "No Jacobin." [51] Appearing in the New York *Daily Advertiser*, he appealed to the people against the Frenchman's machinations. He thoroughly aired the entire controversy over the French prizes and Genêt's conduct, and did it so well that when Genêt's recall was ultimately announced even the Republicans were reduced to a grudging acquiescence.

"No Jacobin" ended abruptly. Even Hamilton's steel-strung constitution could not stand the strain of such herculean activities. The yellow fever was raging in Philadelphia. Hamilton caught the contagion. So did Betsy, his wife, though in a lesser degree. For days Hamilton's life was despaired of. He had the dreaded illness in its most virulent form, and practically no one survived who showed his symptoms.

The Hamiltons had moved to a large house some two miles out of Philadelphia. In the city itself the dead were daily being carted away, and Dr. Benjamin Rush ruled supreme with his method of treatment.

But Edward Stevens, Hamilton's boyhood friend and now a practicing physician in the town, disagreed sharply with Rush. He declared that the treatment advocated by that famous doctor was the worst possible for the disease. His own method, however, was treated with equal contumely by the Rushites.

Dr. Stevens was called in to take care of Hamilton. He ordered cold baths in constant succession and dosage with infusions of bark. A host of attendants was required to fill the baths, carry the gasping man in and out, and attend him in accordance with the doctor's specific instructions.[52]

To everyone's amazement Hamilton recovered. On all sides it was considered a miracle due only to Dr. Stevens' ministrations. The rest of Philadelphia did not escape as fortunately. Over four thousand had succumbed to the fever.[53]

Congratulations poured in on Hamilton. Only one sour note sounded in the chorus. Jefferson's hatred for his opponent caused him to stoop to malicious jeers at the stricken man.

Hamilton is ill of the fever as is said [he wrote to Madison]. he had two physicians out at his house the night before last. his family think him in danger, & he puts himself so by his excessive alarm. he had been miserable several days before from a firm persuasion he should catch it. a man as timid as he is on the water, as timid on horseback, as timid in sickness, would be a phaenomenon if the courage of which he has the reputation in military matters were genuine.[54]

Still much enfeebled, the convalescent quit the pestilent city and, with Betsy, drove by slow stages to the Schuylers' home in Albany. It was late in October before he returned to Philadelphia, though still below his normal strength.

CHAPTER XXII

More Rum and More Politics

I. ENDLESS INVESTIGATION

HAMILTON'S ILLNESS did not soften the hearts of his enemies. Barely had he returned to Philadelphia than they set the machinery in motion again to find some flaw in his armor, some chink through which they could deliver the *coup* that would rid them forever of this colossus who stood astride the path by which they hoped to bring about a revolutionary change in the government to what they considered a more democratic system. The most vulnerable point of attack, they were certain, was his financial measures and operations. Giles had led the onslaught once before—and failed. A more skilful assault might this time bring victory. Jefferson, their leader, had wearied of almost constant defeat in the cabinet at the hands of Hamilton, and offered his resignation on the last day of 1793. Retired to his beloved Monticello, he hoped for a freer hand and a broader opportunity to retire his antagonist as well to private life.

Hamilton likewise was wearied of political turmoil and the exacting demands of his office. But he refused to resign under fire and permit his adversaries to crow over him. It seemed too much like an ignominious retreat in the face of the enemy.

On June 21, 1793, he had informed Washington of his determination to resign after the next session of congress, explaining that he was postponing his withdrawal until then to give that body a chance to bring its investigation of his official conduct to a complete close.[1]

Hamilton determined to force the issue the moment he came back to Philadelphia. He wrote a formal letter to the House of Representatives requesting "that a new inquiry may without delay be instituted in some mode, the most effectual for an accurate and thorough investigation; and I will add, that the more comprehensive it is, the more agreeable will it be for me."[2]

The opposition was caught off guard by this strategy of attack where they had expected sullen defense, but they rallied their forces and professed a willingness to oblige. After some delay, a committee was appointed to inquire into the state of the Treasury Department. Of all the vast and complicated transactions that Hamilton had been engaged in they could think of nothing better to investigate than the hoary—and already much-investigated—management of the foreign loans made under their own authority of August, 1790.

But the inquiry bogged down almost at once and dragged wearily along all the year, elucidating little light but managing to engender in the process considerable heat. The committee insisted that Hamilton turn over to it every communication that he had ever made to Washington; Hamilton retorted that he would yield only those that pertained to the issue. The committee wished to know "by what authority any portion of the moneys borrowed abroad have been drawn to the United States?" He replied with a statement that he had received a general commission from the President, and that he had likewise received specific sanctions for each disposition. He also put in evidence letters which he solicited and received from Washington as to his recollection of the original transactions.[3]

The committee was puzzled. This constant calling upon the still sacrosanct (at least in an official sense) figure of the President stopped them at every turn. Yet they persisted, even though by the end of 1794 everyone, including themselves, was heartily weary of the whole affair. It made good political capital by the very length and persistence of the inquiry. In fact, when Hamilton finally and formally announced his resignation, he was still compelled by the interminable proceedings to postdate it in order to give Congress still another chance to bring them to a close.[4]

If he thought that such extreme meticulousness in the matter would stifle hostile criticism he was mistaken. For a man named Fairly, a local New York Republican, assiduously spread the rumor that Hamilton had resigned because, as Schuyler indignantly reported it to his son-in-law, "the affairs of your department were so deranged, that it was not possible for you to extricate It from the confusion In which it was Involved." To which rumor Schuyler publicly declared that "the propagator of such a calumny was a liar and a villain."[5]

2. TROUBLE WITH ENGLAND

The difficulties with France had been surmounted triumphantly by the dismissal of Genêt—a dismissal in which even Jefferson had concurred. But the difficulties with England, the other great protagonist in the war that was convulsing Europe, were of a different order.

For England, engrossed in the sole object of bringing France to her knees, had no time to bother with the alleged neutral rights of the nation across the sea. By a series of Orders in Council the British forbade all trade with the French West Indies and seized hundreds of American ships that disobeyed those Orders. Jefferson, still Secretary of State, complained with justice of these manifest infringements on American rights. Hamilton, however, firm enough against French invasions of our neutrality, adopted a different attitude with England. He had been from the very beginning on the best possible terms with the succession of British representatives in this country; first with Beckwith, then with Hammond. At times his confidential talks with these foreign emissaries assumed a curious tone. For example, while Jefferson was officially complaining against England's Orders and the seizures of American ships and goods under them, Hamilton was privately informing Hammond that he agreed with the justice of the British measures and her view of international law, but could not be responsible for his colleagues' opinions in the matter.[6] So close and intimate were these relations, in fact, that Hammond always first consulted Hamilton—whom he designated as "No. 7" in his code—on receipt of instructions from England, and took up the business with Jefferson only when he could not help himself.[7] It was an amazing situation, for at about the same time Jefferson was himself privately tutoring Genêt in his relations with the American government.

Thus backed by Hamilton, Hammond paid little attention to Jefferson's protests against the long series of discriminations by England against American commerce. Finally, on December 16, 1793, two weeks before he resigned from office, Jefferson submitted to congress a report on the nature and extent of foreign interferences with American trade. The emphasis was all on the British. On January 3, 1794, Madison reintroduced in the House his famous Resolutions of 1791 calling for retaliation on England. The resolutions would levy additional duties on all imports and shipping coming from countries with whom the United States had no commercial treaties. This was aimed specifically against England. And they called for extraordinary tonnage duties on British vessels trading between the West Indies and the United States, from which trade the ships of the United States were excluded by the British Navigation Acts. Even as the resolutions were being laid before the House, as if to give them added weight, news came of unprecedented seizures by the British in the Caribbean under a new and harsher Order in Council, dated November 6, 1793.

The country exploded with wrath. Even the Federalists joined in the clamor. Hamilton for once turned a cold shoulder on his friend, Hammond, called the Order "atrocious" in a letter to Washington and advised the raising of an army of 30,000 men and the fortification of the ports.[8] For once the British seemed to have gone too far.

Actually, however, angry as they were, the Federalists desired above all to avoid war with England. To Hamilton such a war meant the ruin of everything he had laboriously built. Under the stress of hostilities with the powerful British fleet all his financial structure must go toppling, and with it, the prosperity and future of the country. His friends agreed with him.

To Madison's resolutions, which must, he considered, inevitably lead to war, he opposed his most determined strategy. While the Republicans pressed eagerly for immediate action his followers maneuvered for delay while they sought for other means with which to allay the agitation. When the resolutions could no longer be held up in committee, one of his adherents, William Smith of South Carolina, rose to oppose them with a powerful speech. The speech became immediately famous, and the disgruntled Republicans knew at once who had actually written it. Jefferson, by now resigned and back in Monticello, wrote to his friend, Madison: "I am at no loss to ascribe Smith's speech to it's true father. Every tittle of it is Hamilton's except the introduction.... The very turn of the arguments is the same, and others will see as well as myself that the style is Hamilton's. The sophistry is too fine, too ingenious, even to have been comprehended by Smith, much less devised by him." [9]

In spite of the speech, in spite of Hamilton's rushing into print with two anonymous letters denouncing the resolutions as *a covert design to embark the United States in the war*" on the side of a depraved and bloody France,[10] congress passed a temporary Embargo Act to last for a period of one month, and Washington duly proclaimed it.

Meanwhile a little coterie of influential Federalists met in the rooms of Rufus King, Senator from New York, to determine what course they should pursue in order to avert fast-approaching war. Devoted followers of Hamilton, they represented some of the best brains of the party. They were, besides King, George Cabot and Caleb Strong of Massachusetts, and Oliver Ellsworth of Connecticut. The first meeting was held on March 10th. It resulted in a decision that Ellsworth go to the President and propose that the country be put speedily in a state of defense and, more important, that a special envoy be sent to England to adjust all matters of dispute between the two nations and obtain satisfaction for damages already sustained. Nothing less than this, they realized, would satisfy the people in their present temper. Ellsworth was also to insinuate that "unless a person possessing Talents of the first order, enjoying the Confidence of the friends of Peace, and of the Government, and whose character was unexceptionable in England was selected, it would be fruitless to make an appointment." Who was such a man? No less a one than Colonel Hamilton.[11] Though Hamilton himself was not present at the meeting, it is safe to assume that he was aware of the fact and of the proposals that issued from it.

Ellsworth executed his mission and reported back on March 12th that the President had been "at first reserved," but finally more communicative and much impressed. However, he was doubtful that Hamilton would be a proper envoy, because he "did not possess the general confidence of the Country." In some chagrin—for the whole purpose of the proposals was to get Hamilton appointed—the little band approached Robert Morris, who promised to do what he could do in furtherance of the scheme.[12]

There the matter rested for the moment, while the country drifted closer and closer to war with England, and the Republicans were doing every thing in their power to bring about such a consummation.

On April 8th Washington sent for Morris for consultation. By this time he was convinced of the necessity of sending an envoy; the question was, who? Washington said he had thought of John Adams, Hamilton, Jay or Jefferson as possibilities. Morris objected to either Adams or Jefferson, and expressed a decided preference for Hamilton. Four days later, Jay arrived in Philadelphia to hold Circuit Court. He met King, who informed him of what his group had done and that they had picked either him or Hamilton for the post, though acknowledging that they would prefer Hamilton because of his cabinet experience and knowledge of commerce. Jay seemed to agree "in the propriety of Hamilton's appointment."[13]

Meanwhile the news had leaked out that an envoy was being considered and that Hamilton would very likely be given the mission. The Federalists exulted. "Who but Hamilton would perfectly satisfy all our wishes?" demanded Fisher Ames. "He is *ipse agmen*."[14]

From England, on an earlier intimation that Hamilton might come, Angelica Church wrote enraptured to her *petit Fripon:* "You and

Betsey in England. I have no ideas for such happiness, but when will you come and receive the tears of joy and affection?"[15]

But the Republicans rose in wrath and alarm. Monroe sat down in haste and wrote in protest to Washington that "I should deem such a measure not only injurious to the publick interest, but also especially so to your own." Which cryptic phrase he professed a desire to explain in private.[16] Washington replied briefly that "if you are possessed of any facts or information, which would disqualify Colonel Hamilton for the mission to which you refer, that you would be so obliging as to communicate them to me in writing."[17]

Edmund Randolph, who had taken over the State Department on Jefferson's resignation, employed every means possible to defeat Hamilton's appointment. The new French minister, Fauchette, was in constant conference with Randolph on the subject. Madison did what he could.

The storm over Hamilton was so great, and Washington himself was so unwilling, that Hamilton swallowed his mortification and wrote a long letter to Washington in which, after reviewing at length the instant crisis and the measures to be taken to prevent it from ending in war, withdrew his own name from consideration and recommended Jay as the proper man for the mission.[18]

Much relieved, Washington immediately sent for Jay and offered him the post. The following day the Federalist coterie, this time including Hamilton, went to Jay and urged him to accept as "the only man in whom we could confide." He agreed, and on April 16th his name was sent to the Senate. The appointment was bitterly opposed by the Republicans who, led by Monroe and Burr, openly accused him of being pro-British. Their own choice lay between Madison and Jefferson. But on April 18th Jay was approved by a vote of 18 to 8.[19]

On April 21st the group met again with Jay and laid down a series of instructions for Jay to follow in the course of his mission. The fact that Washington was the President and the proper person to issue instructions seems never to have entered their minds. The men present at this all-important conference were Hamilton, King, Ellsworth, Cabot and Jay.[20]

If Madison exulted that Hamilton, whom he had feared in the post more than any one else, had been finally "laid aside, & Jay named in his place," he was rejoicing without cause.[21] For Hamilton was writing the ticket for Jay, and it would have been far better had he gone in person to see to it that his instructions were being faithfully carried out.

On April 23rd, having first received Washington's consent, Hamilton drafted a memorandum of these instructions for Jay. They were strong enough. Jay was to demand (1) indemnification for depredations on our commerce; (2) arrangements for the future guarantying freedom from seizure of all articles except those which were specifically contraband of war; (3) prompt compliance by the British with the terms of the Peace Treaty of 1783 with respect to indemnity for the slaves who had been carried away and the surrender of the forts still held by them, in return for which the United States would pay damages for the state obstructions in the way of the recovery of debts specified in the treaty; (4) the United States to receive certain trading privileges with the West Indies, England and Ireland, and to offer in return a most-favored-nation clause on imports from England. While Hamilton allowed room for modifications on these demands, he laid down two inflexible rules: (1) no treaty was to be entered into which would affect unfavorably the existing treaty with France, and (2) American ships *must* be granted unrestricted entry in the West Indies.[22]

Since Randolph was the Secretary of State, it devolved on him to issue the formal instructions to Jay, but they were based almost entirely on Hamilton's recommendations. There was, in fact, little in them at which even an ardent Republican could cavil.

Hamilton was never more triumphant than at this moment of seeming defeat for his private aspirations. He had wearied of the duties of the Treasury and would have welcomed the mission to England which, as he fully realized, he was far better equipped to manage than Jay. In fact, on several occasions, he had offered his resignation to Washington and consented to remain only because the President requested it and the times were so critical.[23] Yet he was at the peak of his career. He had forced his chief antagonist, Jefferson, to resign his office. He dominated the much weaker Randolph, who was opposed to him, almost as much as Knox in the War Department, who was his follower. Washington listened with respect to his advice and generally followed it. He ranged far and wide over the whole cabinet. The British Minister treated almost wholly with him, exhibiting an insulting disregard for the nominal Secretary of State. The Federalist leaders were completely devoted to him. If he was unpopular with the people at large, what did that matter? Hamilton had only contempt for the people as such.

Jay, however, was a bad choice. Inflexible enough in his ideals of conduct and his intense, if narrow, probity of character, he was utterly unfitted to cope with the genial-seeming, shrewdly clever statesmen of

England. Lord Grenville, the Secretary of State for Foreign Affairs, read Jay's weaknesses at a glance and set about the necessary maneuvers to outwit him. The task proved absurdly simple.

Yet Jay had England in the hollow of his hand, had he but known it and been supple enough to take advantage of the situation. His country was ready to back him up on a strong stand. Even Hammond wrote with some surprise to his chief about "the extent of the prevailing popular ferment, by the operation of which the apprehensions or feelings of Mr. Hamilton, who has hitherto been uniformly the most moderate of the American Ministers, have been so much excited." [24] Hamilton had sent Jay off with exhortations to be firm and not to recede from certain basic demands. And, about the time of his arrival in England, Grenville had received the most disturbing information. Sweden and Denmark were proposing a general alliance of all neutral countries to oppose England's arrogant violations of their neutrality, and they were inviting the United States to join in the alliance. Such a joint action would have cut off completely England's sources of desperately needed naval stores, and at the same time, her just as desperately needed customers.

Unfortunately, Jay did not know of this development and made no attempt to gather information. He was dazzled and flattered by the warmth of his reception by the English. He submitted a draft of a proposed treaty to Grenville, in accordance with his instructions. But when Grenville smilingly refused, he backed down on practically every point. Basking in a round of entertainment, Jay wrote home to Hamilton that "appearances continue to be singularly favourable, but appearances merit only a certain degree of circumspect reliance. . . . I will endeavour to accommodate rather than dispute; and if this plan should fail, decent and firm representations must conclude the business of my mission." With more enthusiasm he listed the great English leaders with whom he was dining, warning Hamilton, however, to keep this phase of his mission quiet. "They make no part of my communication to Randolph or others," he added. [25] Since Randolph was his chief and entitled to know the exact minutiae of his mission, it is obvious how completely that unfortunate secretary was being by-passed.

Meanwhile Hamilton was doing his own share, albeit unwittingly, to sabotage Jay's mission. He told Hammond, anent the armed-neutrality proposals of Sweden and Denmark, "with great seriousness and with every demonstration of sincerity . . . that in the present conjuncture it was the settled policy of this government in every contingency, even in that of an open contest with Great Britain, to avoid entangling itself with European connexions, which, could only tend to involve this Country in disputes, wherein it might have no possible interest, and commit it in a common cause with allies, from whom in the moment of danger it could derive no succour." [26]

This amazing bit of gratuitous information was hustled off to England by fast packet and was read by Grenville with the profoundest satisfaction. The tables had been turned. Jay was now in his hands. Hamilton had yielded up what should have been, even if correct, the most closely guarded of secrets. If the United States was to embark on a policy of standing alone in splendid isolation and intended to refuse the joint assistance of her fellow neutrals, England ought to have been the last country on earth to hear about it. For such an alliance was the one thing England had feared, and the mere threat of it might have compelled her to moderate her policy. Now Jay might just as well go home.

The bewildered envoy sensed the change in the political climate, though at a loss as to what it might be attributed. Grenville, though still courteous, noticeably stiffened his attitude. He drove Jay back on point after point until the latter agreed to accept a treaty on November 14th which contained hardly a single item of the important conditions which had represented the essential part of his instructions. It was true that he received a promise to evacuate the line of forts still held by England, though the promise was vitiated by the indefiniteness of the date of evacuation; but there was very little more. All that England yielded on the indispensable item of unrestricted trade with the West Indies was a grudging, and strictly limited, permission for vessels of seventy tons or less to enter under almost prohibitive conditions and with the counter-proviso that American vessels were to be prohibited from trading anywhere in the world in molasses, sugar, coffee, cocoa and cotton; and further, that British vessels be allowed unlimited trade between the islands and the United States. This was the famous Article XII which later stirred up such a tempest of refusal in the Senate. As to the demand for indemnity for the slaves, which affected the south only, it was completely disregarded.

Jay wrote to Hamilton a few days later: "My task is done; whether *finis coronat opus*, the president, senate and public will decide.... If the treaty fails, I despair of another." [27]

What Hamilton's emotions were when he read the confidential text, or how far he realized his own responsibility for its making, are unknown. But he adopted the treaty as the best to be had under the circumstances, and proceeded with his accustomed vigor to rally every force to push it through an acceptance in the Senate. This, however, comes properly under a discussion of the events of the year 1795.

3. THE WHISKY REBELLION

As though the grim possibility of embroilment in the European war were not enough, the long smoldering discontent in the western part of Pennsylvania flared suddenly into the open again. The problem of the excise taxes upon the whisky distilled by the frontiersmen from home-grown grain had never been adequately solved. Back in 1792 the aggrieved settlers on the other side of the Alleghanies had threatened, and for a time actually failed, to pay the tax. But some placating legislation by congress and the counter-threat of force by the government had put a temporary halt to open manifestations of resistance, if not to the deep-seated causes of the discontent.

Now, however, the disaffection broke loose with redoubled force. The four western counties of Pennsylvania held mass meetings at which vehement orators inflamed the passions of their listeners. Liberty poles—reminiscent of the Revolution, and more alarmingly, of the great convulsion overseas—made their appearance. On these poles were inscriptions: "An equal tax, and no excise"; "United we stand, divided we fall"; and the significant device of a writhing snake cut squarely in two.

The meetings spilled over into riots. The riots spread down into western Virginia and as far south as South Carolina. The house of a hated inspector of revenue was burned to the ground, a United States marshal imprisoned, and the revenue collectors terrorized and forced to flee for their lives.

Washington viewed the spreading agitation with deep distress. He asked Hamilton for his opinion on the course of action the government should take. Hamilton responded promptly. It was an opportunity, he thought, once and for all to show the strength of the national government. Once before, the opportunity had arisen and weak-kneed councils had let it slip. He was determined this time not to let it slip again. The alleged rebels were attacking the two things dearest to his heart—the financial system he had constructed, in which the excise taxes played an integral role; and the majesty and solidity of the central government. In addition, the rioters were members of what he called the Jacobin Party—lovers of France, followers of Jefferson, setters-up of liberty poles, and despised democrats.

On August 2nd he sent his opinion to Washington. After a review of the long period of trouble he called for immediate and vigorous measures. The states in which the disturbances were centered had failed by local means to quell the insurrection. Let the national government act. Issue a call for 12,000 militia, he urged, to rendezvous in Pennsylvania and Virginia on September 10th.[28]

Three days later he followed it up with another and even more urgent report, and drafted a proclamation for the President to issue, calling on the insurgents to disperse.[29]

While Washington followed Hamilton's suggestions in the main, he nevertheless shrank from the ultimate use of force which his belligerent secretary was urging upon him until he had explored the possibilities of a more peaceful settlement. He requested an interview with Governor Mifflin of Pennsylvania to devise means of cooperation between the federal and state governments in handling the situation. Mifflin replied evasively. A sharp note was sent to him, signed formally by Randolph as Secretary of State, but actually written by Hamilton. The President, it informed the Pennsylvania executive, did not intend to turn over his sworn duty of enforcing the nation's laws to the shifting, indeterminate course proposed by the executive. He would call out the militia, even though he was willing to try one more experiment at conciliation by sending commissioners to the disaffected counties.[30]

When Mifflin protested at the tone of the official communication, disavowing the sentiments attributed to him, Hamilton, through the medium of Randolph, answered sharply and plainly, demanding that he suit actions to words and proceed at once to disperse and adequately punish the rebels.[31]

It may properly be said that Hamilton was not too anxious for a peaceful settlement of the alleged "rebellion." Here was the chance to test the strength of the nation, as opposed to the respective states, and he would not willingly let the chance slip. Under the pseudonym of Tully he addressed four essays "To The People of the United States" putting the question directly to them: "Shall the majority govern or be governed? shall the nation rule or be ruled? shall the general will prevail, or the will of a faction? shall there be government or no government?"[32]

Meanwhile old General Knox had resigned his position as Secretary of War, and Hamilton assumed the office temporarily in addition to his duties in the Treasury. It was dryly commented by the opposition that this was just as well; Hamilton was now performing openly what he had done before actually under the obese figurehead of Knox.

The militia assembled in accordance with Washington's call. There were 9000 foot and 3000 horse—an overwhelming force to put down what was as yet a mere scattered series of riots and mass meetings. Even as it gathered, Washington's commissioners were journeying peacefully into the western counties to treat with the alleged insurgents. And the committees of Fayette County, the center of the disturbance, drafted a set of resolutions under the guiding hand of Albert Gallatin which exhorted their followers to employ only peaceful means in agitating the repeal of the hateful tax, and not to resist in anywise the military expedition set in motion against them.[33]

With these resolutions at hand, with the commissioners already at work, with the original disturbances quieted, it seemed hardly necessary that the plans for the invasion of the reluctant counties should be put into effect. But Hamilton was determined that the militia must march to quell what was already a non-existent rebellion, and he brought Washington into agreement with his views.

Some of Hamilton's old military visions stirred to new romantic life. He had never, during all the years of domesticity and paper work, lost his secret taste for military glory. And here, unexpectedly, the golden opportunity had arisen. He would not be cheated again. He wrote to Washington his decision to accompany the troops. He placed his decision on high public grounds, but the motive is transparent.

Sir [he wrote]. Upon full reflection I entertain an opinion that it is advisable for me, on public grounds, considering the connection between the immediate ostensible cause of the insurrection in the western country and my department, to go out upon the expedition against the insurgents.

In a government like ours it cannot but have a good effect for the person who is understood to be the adviser or proposer of a measure, which involves danger to his fellow-citizens, to partake in that danger; while not to do it might have a bad effect. I therefore request your permission for the purpose.[34]

To his friend, Rufus King, he wrote almost jovially over the prospect. There are, he said, "a great number still uncomplying and violent so as to afford no appearance of submission to the laws without the application of Force. It will give you pleasure to learn that there is every prospect of our being able to apply this effectually—& of the issue being favourable to the authority of the laws. It will occasion a large bill of Costs, but what is that compared with the object?" [35]

On September 25th the militia were set in motion. On September 30th Washington, accompanied by his private secretary, Bartholomew Dandridge, and Hamilton left Philadelphia to join the expedition.[36]

Washington, after reviewing the troops, returned to the capital, but Hamilton was determined to see it through. Under the command of Major-General Lee, with Hamilton officially present as Secretary of War, the great force commenced its march. By October 25th they had reached Berlin, arriving in a heavy downpour of rain. The militia (chiefly young men of the Federalist persuasion) found the going "arduous and distressing," though there was not a single "enemy" in sight. On October 29th they were at Jones' Mill, and depressing news came to Hamilton. The "enemy" not only was resolved not to fight, but had actually appointed commissioners to deprecate the advance of the army and to proclaim their pacific intentions. But Hamilton resolved that "there is nothing which can occasion a question about the propriety of the army's proceeding to its ultimate destination;" adding, rather lamely, that "no appearances whatever of opposition occur." [37]

Such outrageous failure on the part of the insurgents to meet force with force did not suit his purposes at all. He wrote somewhat vindictively to King that "a law regulating a peace process of outlawry is also urgent;... for the best objects of punishment will fly, and they ought to be compelled by outlawry to abandon their property, homes, and the United States. This business must not be skinned over. The political putrefaction of Pennsylvania is greater than I had any idea of. Without rigor everywhere, our tranquillity is likely to be of very short duration, and the next storm will be infinitely worse than the present one." [38]

By this time Hamilton was seeing in the opposition to his precious excise tax no mere local disturbance, but an integrated rebellion led and fomented by the Democratic Societies or Jacobin Clubs for the purpose of overturning the government and establishing a mob rule similar to that in France. He infected Washington with his point of view so that Washington, normally cautious and reserved in his letters, could write to John Jay that the rebellion was due to the Democratic Societies "which have spread themselves over this country, have been laboring incessantly to sow the seeds of distrust, jealousy, and of course discontent, thereby hoping to effect some revolution in the government;" and exulting in the great outpouring of young men "possessing the first fortunes in the country, standing in the ranks as private men." [39] Unfortunately, some of the militia—obviously not of "the first fortunes"—seized the occasion to pillage the country, burning fences and stealing from the inhabitants so that in some places "they did not leave a plate, a spoon, a glass or a knife." [40]

By this time the country was beginning to laugh at the tremendous expedition, and the opposition, headed by the Republican editor of the Philadelphia *Aurora*, was lashing out at the show of force generally and at Hamilton in particular. Nowhere did the troops find a single man with arms in his hands, and everywhere they came across peaceful committees protesting their peaceful activities and offering submission. To Hamilton's indignation, no one had even fled to justify a declaration of outlawry. He complained to Washington that there were "not many fugitives from justice yet." [41]

Balked in his plans by the unaccountable lack of resistance, Hamilton determined to strike terror into the hearts of the leaders. If not many had fled and furnished thereby *prima facie* evidence of their treasonable intentions, at least he could arrest and imprison those whose submissions had been belated. Meeting in consultation with General Lee and the Federal District Attorney, they decided to arrest the agitators summarily and turn them over to the courts for swift action. "All possible means are using [*sic*] to obtain evidence, and accomplices will be turned against the others," he informed Washington. "I hope good objects will be found notwithstanding many have gone off." Hugh Brackenridge, prominent in the agitation, he called "the worst of all scoundrels." [42]

Under Hamilton's supervision the army made hundreds of arrests. He took it upon himself personally to interrogate the prisoners, seeking evidence against the leaders. His inquiries were bullying, and he threatened condign punishment against those who refused information. He wanted, he admitted frankly, to make such examples that the spirit of rebellion would be crushed forever. He kept himself also in a perpetual state of alarm. A liberty pole had been erected some sixteen miles from where he was stationed. He sent troops in hot haste to smash this new evidence of a dangerous spirit. At Pittsburgh, the final headquarters of the army, he heard of a large assemblage of fugitives from justice. Again the troops were dispatched. The enemy army disappointingly disintegrated into "small vagrant parties in that quarter, affording no point of attack." [43]

Two days later, with even baseless alarms no longer in evidence to justify his continued presence, and with the army idle at Pittsburgh, it was decided on all hands to go home. The mythical revolt had been effectually crushed, and the civil authorities were capable of handling the situation.

4. MR. HAMILTON RESIGNS

Hamilton returned to meet a storm of criticism from the opposition press. Bache, in particular, in the *Aurora*, got under his skin, though he professed an utter indifference to such manifestations of the mob. "It is long since I have learned to hold popular opinion of no value," he told Washington. "I hope to derive from the esteem of the discerning, and an internal consciousness of zealous endeavors for the public good, the reward of those endeavors." [44]

But he was tired. The double duties of Treasury and War, the arduous marches through Pennsylvania, his old determination to quit public life once his measures had been securely established and attend to his family and private fortunes, decided him this time to resign without any strings. He had barely returned to Philadelphia when he wrote out his resignation and sent it to Washington, to take effect on January 31, 1795.

Washington accepted his resignation reluctantly and with a letter of praise for his long and devoted services to his country.

The opposition was delighted to have their most formidable and dangerous antagonist out of public life, though they could not believe he meant it. Madison was afraid that Hamilton intended to become a candidate for the governorship of New York in the impending election.[45]

Hammond, the British minister, on the other hand, was sorry to see Hamilton go. He had good reason to be, for, as he lamented, Hamilton's resignation "deprives me of the advantages I derived, from the confidential and friendly intercourse, that I have uniformly had with him, when the most influential member of this administration." [46] His alarm, however, was needless. Oliver Wolcott, the comptroller, whom Washington elevated to the vacant post on Hamilton's advice, proved to be equally friendly. Five months later Wolcott was furnishing him with confidential news of the rejection of Article XII of Jay's Treaty by the Senate, though the proceedings were supposed to be secret.[47]

Before he left public office, Hamilton submitted to the Senate a long and well-matured plan for the support of the public credit. In it he reviewed the whole course of the funding of the debt, the revenues accruing to the United States and all the Acts pertaining thereto, together with a recapitulation of the fiscal system he had evolved. Then he proposed a series of propositions to complete the structure. "Credit," he told the Senate, "is not only one of the main pillars of the public safety; it is among the principal engines of useful enterprise and internal improvement.... No well-informed man can cast a retrospective eye over the progress of the United States, from their infancy to the present period, without being convinced that they owe, in a great degree, to the fostering influence of credit, their present mature growth."

It is also worthy of note, in view of the constant allegations against Hamilton that he wished to force upon the country an eternal debt structure, that he laid down as two fundamental principles for all public loans that (1) there be established at the time of contracting a debt, funds both for the repayment of the principal and interest within a determinate period; and (2) it be made a part of the contract that the fund so established "shall be inviolably applied to the object." [48]

With this, and a Report to the House on the Improvement of the Revenue, as his swan songs, Hamilton passed out of public office, never to return.

CHAPTER XXIII

Private Statesman

1. FORENSIC ELOQUENCE

HAMILTON HAD stepped down from his high office without regrets. He had accomplished what he had set out to do—place the finances of the country on a sound, immovable basis, and lay the groundwork for a nation as against a loose confederation of states.

He had private reasons as well for relinquishing the hurly-burly and the limelight. Just before he had written out his resignation, a letter came from his old friend, General Knox. "Among other reasons for wishing your return," wrote the former Secretary of War, "is Mrs. Hamilton's earnest desire. It seems she has had, or has been in danger of a miscarriage, that has much alarmed her." [1]

It was time to consider his family. It consisted of a wife and five children, the oldest of whom, Philip, was thirteen and the youngest, John Church, two and a half. More were in contemplation; the fact of Betsy's present miscarriage merely delayed the next addition. It required a substantial income to rear them properly; the salary accruing from the post of secretary was clearly insufficient for the purpose. Had it not been for the almost surreptitious aid of his father-in-law, Hamilton would have found himself in the direst financial straits.

When he quit his post he was a poor man. It is true that there were rumors afloat that he had made a good thing of his privileged position in the Treasury. Commodore Nicholson, a New York Republican politician, talked loudly of "authentic information" that Hamilton had invested £100,000 sterling secretly in the British funds. [2] When Nicholson's loud talk finally reached Hamilton's ears, steps were taken toward a challenge to a duel. The trial at arms was averted, under obscure circumstances, by the intervention of youthful De Witt Clinton, nephew to the governor. [3]

Actually, a careful examination of the financial transactions between Hamilton and William Seton, who handled his funds, as evidenced by the correspondence in the Library of Congress, discloses the indubitable fact that Hamilton was continually involved in money difficulties, overdrew his account with disheartening regularity, and was compelled at intervals to borrow petty sums of as low as fifty dollars from his friends. It was the truth that he told Tobias Lear and Major William Jackson, both of Washington's secretarial family: "I am not worth exceeding five hundred dollars in the world; my slender fortune and the best years of my life have been devoted to the service of my adopted country; a rising family hath its claims." [4]

If there was any basis at all for the canard, other than the malicious invention of political enemies who feared Hamilton even in retirement, it might have come from a distorted knowledge of the very considerable transactions which Hamilton undertook for John Barker Church, his brother-in-law and the husband of the gay and charming Angelica. These transactions really reached astonishing proportions. Church had done very well for himself in England, though Angelica pined continually for America and for the company of her amiable and adored *Fripon*—her pet name for Hamilton.

Church had large funds to invest, and he kept a shrewd speculative eye on America. Hamilton rashly consented to be his agent in America—a position that might well lead to misunderstandings at a time when he was Secretary of the Treasury and thereby necessarily in possession of advance information that would raise or lower the prices of governmental paper.

During the heat and confusion of his greatest struggles, Hamilton nevertheless diligently attended to Church's affairs. He constituted William Seton his sub-agent in the matter, with instructions to purchase or sell the funded debt and United States bank shares as the occasion might require. In 1793 the transactions involved the very substantial sum of £10,000. The circumstances were peculiar, since Church's orders to purchase bank shares, relayed through Hamilton, were not backed by cash. Seton wrote in some perturbation to Hamilton: "I think you will not blame me for making this further observation; Mr. Church's circumstances and responsibility I am totally ignorant of, £10,000 [Sterling] is a very large sum to run the risk of even a 20 p Cent [damages?] upon, Now my dear Sir for you or under your absolute guarantee of course I would commit myself for any Sum; but I must confess to you sincerely that unless I had you to look to, I should deem myself unjustifiable to my family to enter into this negotiation." [5]

Evidently Hamilton furnished the necessary assurances, for Seton commenced purchasing the shares at attractive prices until, by the end of March, 1794, he had on Church's account investments valued at £7856.1.6 Sterling. At this time the price began to fall, and Hamilton asked him to discontinue further purchases until the market was stabilized.[6] By May the bottom had been reached, and Seton went into the market again for Church to the tune of more than £10,000 and was able to report to Hamilton that their mutual client was well satisfied with his operations.[7]

Nor did the distant Church confine himself to transactions in shares alone. He lent out money, through Hamilton, at substantial rates of interest. One of the borrowers was no less a personage than Robert Morris, who had fallen on evil times in the days since the establishment of the United States. The sum was large and Morris, twisting and turning to avoid the ultimate crash and bitterness of a debtor's prison, asked Hamilton repeatedly for extensions.[8]

Hamilton was compelled by Church to insist upon an immediate settlement, and Morris offered a mortgage on 50,000 acres of land near Pittsburgh as security.[9] Meanwhile Hamilton, now practicing law, rendered legal services to his erstwhile sponsor. By 1797 his fees had mounted, with accrued interest, to the staggering total of $12,088.33. Nor had Morris been able to pay back the debt he owed Church. Hamilton lost patience. He pressed for payment on both accounts. Morris disregarded Hamilton's personal claim, and asked his help against Church. "I would fain hope that he does not wish to take advantage of my necessities and obtain my property at less than its worth," he said plaintively.[10]

When Hamilton, driven by Church, finally issued attachment against his goods, Morris cried out: "Your agency in it astonishes me, if it is for the balance of the money *you lent me*, I shall deem myself more unfortunate than ever before." But Hamilton was able to explain to him that it was not on his own account that he was suing, but on behalf of Church. Morris accepted the explanation and promised payment as soon as possible.[11] He never did get out of his difficulties. His magnificent home outside of Philadelphia was taken from him; the debtor's prison gaped; and shortly thereafter Robert Morris, who had piloted the revolutionary states through the most trying period of their existence, died broken and unlamented, except by his creditors.

If Hamilton's relations with Church were largely on a legal and financial basis, his relations with Angelica Church were of a wholly different order. Angelica, immured in London, literally pined for the presence of her dashing and gallant brother-in-law. Her letters home were filled with the most endearing terms, the prettiest phrases. When, on one occasion, Hamilton wrote that there was a possibility he might make "a short excursion to Europe," Angelica at first was wild with delight, but as the months passed and the prospect faded, she told her sister, Eliza, despairingly: "You and my dear Hamilton will never cross the Atlantic, I shall never leave this Island and as to meeting in heaven—there will be no pleasure in that." [12]

She kept up a constant correspondence. Hardly ever did she write about her businessman husband; always it was about Hamilton, his career, his prospects, her pride in his fame and achievements, her complete despair at this lengthy severance. If Hamilton's letters were discreet, as became a brother-in-law, hers were not. Even to her sister she wrote recklessly and fulsomely of her *Amiable,* and

by my Amiable you know I mean your Husband, for I love him very much and if you were as generous as the old Romans, you would lend him to me for a little while, but do not be jealous, my dear Eliza, since I am more solicitous to promote his laudable ambition, than any person in the world, and there is no summit of true glory which I do not desire he may attain; provided always that he pleases to give me a little chit-chat, and sometimes to say, I wish our dear Angelica was here.

After which breathless sentence she ended: "Ah! Bess! you were a lucky girl to get so clever and so good a companion." [13]

Angelica, poised in England, made herself the way-station through which an endless stream of noble refugees from the French Revolution were handed on to receive the hospitality of the Hamiltons in America. Talleyrand, Beaumetz, Rochefoucauld-Liancourt, Chastellux, Moreau de Saint-Méry, and a host of others found Hamilton a charming host, thoroughly sympathetic with their misfortunes and travails, agreeing with them in their denunciations of the Terror they had fled, and sighing with them for the return of a stable monarchy and the glittering Court.

Hamilton was only sorry he could not do more for these aristocratic arrivals. "I wish I was a Croesus," he wrote Angelica; "I might then afford solid consolation to these children of adversity, and how delightful it would be to do so. *But now,* sympathy, kind words, and *occasionally* a dinner are all I can contribute." [14]

If Hamilton sympathized with the exiled Frenchmen, they were enraptured with him. He had the manners, the point of view, the charm of a European aristocrat, such as they had not expected to find

in the raw American wilderness. Rochefoucauld-Liancourt thought
him "one of the most interesting men in America. He united with
dignity and feeling, and much force and decision, delightful manners,
great sweetness, and was infinitely agreeable." [15] Saint-Méry, arriving
in Philadelphia while Hamilton was still the Secretary of the Treasury,
was amazed by the Spartan simplicity of his office, though he thought
Hamilton's French, while fluent, "very incorrect." [16]

But it was Talleyrand, that brilliant and subtle fox who epitomized
in his own slight frame all the tortuousness of the old European diplomacy, who found and hailed in Hamilton his American counterpart.
They became bosom friends during the two winters that Talleyrand
was compelled to spend in Philadelphia and New York until he was
recalled to France, there eventually to rise to astonishing heights under
Directory, Empire and Bourbon Restoration. Their mutual admiration
was fervid. Hamilton considered Talleyrand "the greatest of modern
statesmen, because he had so well known when it was necessary both
to suffer wrong to be done and to do it." [17] In return Talleyrand later
was quoted as saying: "I consider Napoleon, Pitt and Hamilton as the
three greatest men of our age, and if I had to choose between the
three, I would unhesitatingly give the first place to Hamilton. He has
divined Europe." [18]

Late one evening during his stay in New York, Talleyrand passed
Hamilton's little law office on his way to a party. Through the window
he saw the spare figure of his friend bent over the desk, writing steadily
at a legal document by the yellow light of candles. Amazed at the
sight, he burst into the gay salon of brilliant costumes, chatter and
music to exclaim: "I have just come from viewing a man who had
made the fortune of his country, but now is working all night in
order to support his family." [19] Talleyrand was not one to understand
such a scene.

After Hamilton left the Treasury, he first took his family to the
Schuyler home in Albany. Eliza needed care and rest after her recent
illness, the children required attention, and Hamilton wanted time to
consider his future course. That he would re-enter the practice of law
was unquestionable, and that the natural site for his activities was New
York was equally patent. In that thriving, mercantile city were his
closest friends and most profitable future clients. There also he could
remain in touch with political trends and measures.

In June, 1795, he moved his family down to New York. He found

and furnished a small house at 56 Pine Street, which for one year constituted his living quarters and office. From there he later shifted
through several addresses to 24 Broadway, where he remained until
1802, when he moved into the country to occupy the Grange which
he himself planned and built.

By the time he was ready to commence his practice his funds had
become so depleted that he was compelled to borrow large sums of
cash from his old friend and college classmate, Robert Troup, who
had never quit the law to seek or hold public office. Troup idolized
Hamilton and shared all his political opinions. But he thought Hamilton had waited long enough before considering his own financial
future. "I sincerely hope . . . that you may by some fortunate & unexpected event acquire the means of perfect independence in spite of
all your efforts to be poor," he told him ironically, adding, "I have
often said that your friends would be obliged to bury you at their
own expense." [20] In the event this proved a rather startling prophecy.

Others of Hamilton's friends were equally anxious for his future.
James McHenry, his old comrade-in-arms, exhorted him from his comfortable retreat near Baltimore: "I have built houses, I have cultivated
fields, I have planned gardens, I have planted trees, I have written little
essays, I have made poetry once a year to please my wife, at times got
children and at all times thought myself happy. Why cannot you do
the same, for after all if a man is only to acquire fame or distinctions
by continued privations and abuse I would incline to prefer a life of
privacy and little pleasures." [21]

Hamilton expected to do just that. Events and his own nature precluded his ever sinking into quiet domesticity and "a life of privacy."
In the meantime the first news that he intended to practice law brought
him a rush of clients and retainers. They clamored for his services in
pending matters and sought to associate him with the counsel they
had already hired. At one bound he went immediately to the top of
his profession—a solitary eminence shared in New York only by
Aaron Burr—also temporarily retired from public life by the failure
of the legislature to return him to the Senate. [22]

But while Burr was already spoken of by members of both parties
as a possible candidate for the governorship on Clinton's decision not
to run again, Hamilton sincerely thought he was through with office.
When a certain David Campbell offered his services and those of his
friends to make him governor of New York, Hamilton scribbled on
the back of the letter: "This letter was probably written with some

ill design—I keep it *without answer* as a clue to future events." [23]

The new Attorney-General of the United States, William Bradford, knew him better than he knew himself, however. Writing to invite him to join in the defense of the Carriage Tax Act before the Supreme Court, he added some pertinent remarks: "I hear that you have renounced every thing but your profession—that you will not even pick up money when it lies at your feet, unless it comes in the form of a fee!—But it is in vain to kick against the pricks—You were made for a Statesman, & politics will never be out of your head." [24]

Hamilton might have made a large fortune from the law, had it not been for the utter modesty of his fees, even in the most important of cases, and his fixed belief that disputes should be settled, wherever possible, by conciliation rather than by court action. As it was, he made an average of $10,000 a year, no mean sum in those days. Again it was Burr who surpassed him in earning capacity; but Burr notoriously charged high fees.

James Kent, one of New York's greatest lawyers and internationally known judge and commentator, always considered Hamilton as the greatest of all counsel. "He taught us all how to probe deeply into the hidden recesses of the science," he later recollected, "or to follow up principles to their far distant sources. He was not content with the modern reports, abridgements, or translations. He ransacked cases and precedents to their very foundations." [25]

Hamilton became the first favorite of the prosperous New York merchants, as well for his forensic ability as for the Federalist principles with which they so wholeheartedly agreed. The Bank of New York, which he had helped found, employed him regularly. An overwhelming share of the insurance litigation came to him. At this time insurance was chiefly handled by private underwriters, of whom John Barker Church was later to become the leader. It was Hamilton who drafted the first charter for an insurance company in the country.

2. UNOFFICIAL ADVISER TO THE GOVERNMENT

For a while Hamilton found the law and the admiration of his friends sufficient. He listened with pleasure to the toasts at the banquet given in his honor at the famous Tontine Coffee House where all the assembled dignitaries vied in complimentary references. He accepted the certificate granting him the freedom of the city as a testimonial "of your merit and distinguished services in the cause of your country." [26]

But Bradford had been well-advised in his analysis of Hamilton's character. He could no more keep from public affairs and political endeavor than a moth can keep from a burning candle in the night.

He had been barely a month out of office when he was offering advice to Washington, to the heads of departments and to members of congress. Not only was his advice not spurned by the recipients, but it was actively solicited and, in many instances, gratefully followed. Out of office, Hamilton assumed the mantle of an elder statesman and was universally acknowledged by the Federalists as their guide and leader.

On one matter in particular he was vehement. Congress had unaccountably failed to heed the propositions he had outlined for the treatment of the unsubscribed debt. He felt this as a personal insult as well as a catastrophe to the nation. He wrote Sedgwick heatedly: "I am tortured by the idea that the country should be so completely and unnecessarily dishonored. A day of reckoning must come." [27] To King he unbosomed himself with even more violence and some pathos: "Am I, then, more of an American than those who drew their first breath on American ground?" he demanded. "Or what is it that torments me at a circumstance so calmly viewed by almost everybody else? Am I a fool—a romantic Quixote—or is there a constitutional defect in the American mind?" With something almost akin to frenzy he called on his friend, Senator King, to rouse himself and fight the enemy in the Senate. "I conjure you, my friend, make a vigorous stand for the honor of your country! Rouse all the energies of your mind, and measure swords in the Senate with the great slayer of public faith—the hackneyed veteran in the violation of public engagements. Prevent him if possible from triumphing a second time over the prostrate credit and injured interests of his country. Unmask his false and horrid hypothesis." [28] His frantic exhortations were in vain. The propositions were defeated.

He had greater success with the executive arm of the government. Here his advice was respectfully requested and usually followed. At times, indeed, he assumed almost a dictatorial attitude. He instructed Oliver Wolcott, his successor in the Treasury, on the minutest details of policy and execution.[29] Wolcott accepted the instructions and humbly asked for more. When the French began to prey on American shipping, he inquired as to the course he should pursue. Should he agitate for Monroe's recall from France and should a special envoy be sent in his place? "I shall be glad to know your opinion of what is to be done. If a minister is sent, who should he be?" [30]

If it was logical that the new Secretary of Treasury should avail himself of his superior knowledge and experience, the same situation did not hold for the Attorney-General. Yet Hamilton wrote in the same vein to William Bradford, expressing himself sharply on matters that came before the Cabinet. "You see," he added, with a touch of humor, "I have not entirely lost my appetite for a little politics; you must not infer that I have not a very good one for law." [31]

But his chief activities were in connection with the controversy over the ratification of the Jay Treaty which was convulsing the nation and threatening to split it into two warring and almost revolutionary camps. The Republicans denounced the treaty from the housetops. The country had been betrayed, they shouted. Once more we had become a mere subservient appendage to Great Britain. The Federalists, they charged, were trying to subvert the Revolution. They had insulted our former ally, France, and taken up with our former enemy, England. But the Federalists, they continued, were monarchists at heart and had always regretted the break with England.

Hamilton had not thought too highly of Jay's treaty, but he rallied with all his strength to its defense. Inadequate as it was, it was a step in the right direction—the cementing of peaceful and cordial relations between the two powers. Peace and trade with England were the cornerstones of his financial policy. Hostilities and rupture spelled disaster. In addition, by this time he thoroughly despised and hated France—the seat of anarchical revolution and monstrous terror. He hated as well those Republicans in America whom he in turn accused of slavishly following the French example and desiring to exalt that great beast—the mob—in America. So obsessed was he with the belief that the American Jacobins intended to follow in the bloody footsteps of their French prototypes that he saw bloodshed just around the corner in New York. He suspected, he told Wolcott, "that our Jacobins meditate serious mischief to certian individuals;" among whom doubtless was himself. The New York militia was not to be relied on; the regular soldiers in the fort had just received marching orders. He wanted Wolcott to ask the Secretary of War to countermand those orders, so that they could be on hand in case of trouble. [32]

Hamilton sought to stem the tide of anger that was threatening to overthrow the administration because of the treaty. Washington asked his advice on what to do, and Hamilton decided, under the signature of Camillus, to come out strongly in its defense. Washington noted this step with much pleasure. He had a firm faith in the efficacy of

Hamilton's pen, as had all of the Federalist leaders. There was no one else who could clarify the issues with such cogency and logic, or smash the opposition with such overwhelming fury.

It was high time that Hamilton took to the pen. He had attempted the magic of his presence and his speech at a great meeting called in New York to discuss the treaty. The turbulent audience, assembled before the City Hall, would have none of him. When Hamilton rose to speak, they shouted him down. When he tried again, a volley of stones clattered on the platform. One of them struck him on the forehead. With the blood streaming down his countenance, he bowed ironically: "If you use such knock-down arguments I must retire." But instead of retiring, he offered a resolution, declaring the confidence of the meeting "in the wisdom and virtue of the President to whom with the Senate the discussion of the question constitutionally belonged." But the infuriated crowd raised such a clamor to this that Hamilton and his friends thought it prudent to leave.[33]

Undismayed, Hamilton commenced his Camillus letters. Thirty-eight of them appeared in rapid succession in the New York *Argus*, of which eight were written in collaboration with Rufus King.[34]

He accused the demagogues, "men of irregular ambition," of seizing upon the treaty as a pretext for discrediting the administration, and intimated that both Jefferson and George Clinton had designs upon the presidency. On a higher level he argued that imperfect as the treaty might be, it was a means of avoiding a war which could end only in our utter destruction. "If we can avoid a war for ten or twelve years more," he pointed out, "we shall then have acquired a maturity, which will make it no more than a common calamity, and will authorize us, in our national discussions, to take a higher and more imposing tone."

He took up the various clauses of the treaty and examined them in the light of the objections that had been raised against them. If there had been any breaches of the original peace treaty, he declared, they had come first and chiefly from the American side. He played down the weak points and hammered incessantly on the strong. The impressment of our seamen was a complex issue, not easily remediable; on the other hand, by England's agreement to hand over the frontier forts, we had gained an immeasurable advantage. He exalted the clause calling for compensation to British creditors as recognizing "the sacred obligation of a just debt." Only on the much-abused twelfth article did he agree that the Senate had been "upon the whole,

... well judged and advised" in withholding its assent, yet he defended Jay's course in accepting it in the first instance.

The whole series was one long, sustained legal brief on behalf of a client whose case, at best, was shaky. It was brilliant, resourceful, and adept at highlighting the favorable factors and subduing the unfavorable. It made a tremendous impression on the country and did much to allay the agitation against the treaty.

Just how effective Hamilton's active pen really was may be judged from Jefferson's immediate and violent reaction to the product. From his retreat in Monticello he wrote in great alarm to Madison, his usual and sole resource in such desperate situations.

> Hamilton [he averred] is really a colossus to the anti-republican party. Without numbers, he is an host within himself. They have got themselves into a defile, where they might be finished; but too much security on the republican part will give time to his talents, & indefatigableness to extricate them. We have had only middling performances to oppose to him. In truth, when he comes forward, there is nobody but yourself who can meet him. ... For god's sake take up your pen, and give a fundamental reply to Curtius and Camillus.[35]

It is easy to envisage Madison's dismay and perplexity at the receipt of this exhortation. Long before he had tired of incessant replies to Hamilton; replies, as he had justly remarked, only goaded Hamilton to further efforts. There never was an end to any controversy in which Hamilton was the opponent.

What with Camillus, and the resolutions that poured in from all the "respectable" Chambers of Commerce and meetings of merchants throughout the country, the Jay Treaty was finally adopted by the Senate—with the offending twelfth article stricken out—and became the law of the land.

The action of the Senate, however, did not end the controversy. The House of Representatives, largely Republican in complexion, injected itself into the proceedings with a demand upon Washington for a submission to it of all the papers relating to the treaty.

This was obviously an unconstitutional procedure, and Washington resolved "to resist the principle." Just how to refuse, however, troubled the President, and he asked Hamilton to show him the method involving "the least bad consequences." [36]

Hamilton agreed wholeheartedly with Washington. In a series of communications he advised against turning over the papers. "It will be fatal to the negotiating power of the government if it is to be a matter of course for a call of either House of Congress to bring forth all the communications, however confidential." This was a matter of principle. On a more practical level, the disclosure of the instructions to Jay "would do harm to the President and the government." Again at Washington's request, he drafted a reply to be sent to the House which should give a proper base to the refusal.[37]

When the baffled House Republicans thereupon resolved to refuse a grant of funds to carry the treaty into effect, Hamilton outlined a plan for the President's guidance in that event. He was to inform the Senate and obtain its formal backing; he was to send a solemn protest to the House; while Hamilton engaged himself to obtain a flood of resolutions from the merchants and other respectable citizens of the country denouncing the House. In New York in particular Hamilton arranged "an unexampled unanimity" among the insurance people, the traders and the merchants.[38]

To Wolcott, however, Hamilton wrote privately to disclose his exasperation with the British for their course of action which seemingly justified the intransigence of the Republicans. "The British Ministry are as great fools or as great rascals as our Jacobins," he declared roundly, "else our commerce would not continue to be distressed by their cruisers; nor would the Executive be embarrassed as it now is by the new proposition." [39] Though the British continued their arrogant courses, in spite of Hamilton's insistence that the government take "a high tone" with them, the House finally receded from its proposed position, and the Jay Treaty passed into history for what it was worth.

At every turn in the delicate relations between the United States and the warring European powers, at every change in the domestic situation, Hamilton continued to be consulted. During this period when ostensibly he was a private citizen engaged in the private practice of law, his correspondence with government officials, from Washington himself down to the most obscure local leader, was just as voluminous as in the roaring days when he headed the Treasury.

If a cabinet post was to be filled, a letter requesting a suitable appointee found its way to his New York address. Edmund Randolph had quit the State Department under a cloud as the result of an indiscreet disclosure to M. Fauchet, the French plenipotentiary, of the confidential instructions to Jay. "What am I to do for a Secretary of State?" inquired Washington. "I ask frankly, and with solicitude; and shall receive kindly any sentiments you may express on the occasion." [40] Hamilton first suggested Rufus King, but King refused the post. It was finally decided to elevate Timothy Pickering of Massachusetts, one of the most bigoted and extreme of Federalists, from the War to the State Department. Then Pickering in turn inquired of Hamilton for help to choose his successor in the War office.[41] Hamilton felt that the south should receive the place, in order "to placate public opinion" in that turbulent area. At first inclining to Henry Lee of Virginia, he finally picked his old friend and comrade-in-arms, the man who had steadily exhorted him to relinquish the discomforts of public office for the Epicurean pleasures of private life—James McHenry.

This new cabinet with which Washington was to end his stay in office and which continued on into the administration of John Adams, was second-rate. It was a distinct come-down from the first cabinet, in which Jefferson and Hamilton towered like twin colossi over the land. But, whereas the earlier cabinet moved at cross-purposes and was highlighted by the dramatic feud between Jefferson and Hamilton, the later one worked with some degree of unity and common purpose. That unity was achieved in a peculiar way—Oliver Wolcott in the Treasury, Timothy Pickering in the State, and James McHenry in the War Department, were alike dependent for their guidance and instructions, not on the President whom they ostensibly served, but on an outsider, a man who no longer held any official position in the government. That man was Alexander Hamilton.

The final important appointment that Hamilton urged on Washington and caused to be made was that of Rufus King, who was "tired of the Senate," as the American envoy to England in place of Thomas Pinckney of South Carolina, who was on his way home.

3. ADAMS BECOMES PRESIDENT AND WASHINGTON SAYS FAREWELL

Early in the spring of 1796 it was well known to the intimate circle of his advisers that Washington would definitely not be a candidate for re-election. He had reluctantly assumed the presidency a second time only at urgent solicitation; he was now fixed in his determination to retire to private life. The attacks and scurrilities to which men in public office, even the highest, were subjected, aroused his deepest resentment. He had, he wrote Hamilton, "a disinclination to be longer buffeted in the public prints by a set of infamous scribblers," and he was sorry he had not published his valedictory immediately on the adjournment of congress. "It might have prevented the remarks," he pursued, "which, more than probable, will follow a late annunciation—namely, that I delayed it long enough to see that the current was turned against me, before I declared my intention to decline." [42]

He had considered the manner and substance of that valedictory as long before as May, 1792, toward the end of his first term. He had then requested Madison to draft it for him. Madison did so; but the speech was put aside with the reassumption of office. Now, at the conclusion of his second term, he took it out again. But the times had changed. Madison's address was merely a farewell; Washington, surveying the troubled foreign situation, the vast European war and the delicate situation of the United States as a neutral balancing itself between desperate combatants, determined to add to the original simple phrases some notes of warning, some outline of future policy, by which his country might steer its course in the days to come.

When he had completed his own draft, he sent it along to Hamilton "to redress it." He had a great respect for Hamilton's ability to clothe thoughts in vigorous, striking phrases, and had employed his talents on many occasions in the past for the writing of his speeches, letters, proclamations, addresses to congress, and the like.

"If you form one anew, it will, of course, assume such a shape as you may be disposed to give it, predicated upon the Sentiments contained in the enclosed paper," he wrote. [43]

From that point on, the "paper," known to history as Washington's Farewell Address, passed many times between the two men. Hamilton first drew a digest of the points he found in Washington's original draft, which he headed "Abstract of points to form an address." Then he made a major draft which he sent to Washington. Washington studied it and interlined it with changes and amendments. Hamilton again "redressed" it in conformity with these suggestions. Back and forth traveled the document—something being changed, something being added in the each shift of station—until Hamilton was finally satisfied with his own heavily amended draft. It was tedious, difficult work. Each phrase was carefully studied, each word pondered on. And Hamilton was ill. "I seem now to have regularly a period of ill health every summer," he wrote Washington. [44]

With Hamilton's major draft before him, and Madison's original statement, Washington proceeded slowly to write the Farewell Address, refining, changing, polishing up through the very last moment of printing.

The exact authorship of the address has been the subject of acrimonious debate for more than a century. Hamilton's son, and most historians since, took it for granted that Hamilton had been responsible both for the content and the phrasing of the famous farewell. Adherents of Madison claimed priority for their idol. John Jay, in 1811, insisted that Hamilton had consulted him and gone over the paper with him "paragraph by paragraph, until the whole met with our mutual approbation." [45] Washington's admirers always resented the implications, and claimed originality for *their* *i*dol. The truth may be found in the comparison of the various drafts. The *ideas* were Washington's; the *phrasing* mainly that of Hamilton.[46]

The final product ranks as one of the great documents of American history. Washington called on his fellow-countrymen to

observe good faith and justice towards all nations; cultivate peace and harmony with all. [But, he warned,] Europe has a set of primary interests, which to us have none, or a very remote relation. . . . Hence therefore it must be unwise in us to implicate ourselves, by artificial ties in the ordinary vicissitudes of her politics, or the ordinary combinations and collisions of her friendships or enmities. Our detached and distant situation invites us to pursue a different course. . . . 'Tis our true policy to steer clear of permanent alliances, with any portion of the foreign world.

This doctrine has been seized upon by later controversialists as the source and final justification of a brand of isolationism that has remained to plague us to the present day. They fail to note, however, that it had relevance to the peculiar conditions of the times and was intended to be regarded merely in connection with those conditions. Removed from that context and shifted to a world of which Washington had never dreamed, to a world in which we no longer hold a "detached and distant situation," Washington would himself have been the first to deny the validity of his original words and probably would have written a wholly different Farewell Address.

Washington's decision to retire at the end of his term caused Hamilton considerable concern. With him out of the running, Hamilton was afraid that Jefferson might become president. This was a specter not to be endured. Aside from his personal grievances against the former Secretary of State, he sincerely believed that Jefferson's election would plunge the country into the wildest anarchy. His whole coherent plan of government would go tumbling into ruins. Rather than Jefferson, almost anyone else. It was "all-important to our country," he wrote, that Washington's "successor shall be a safe man. But it is far less important who of many men that may be named shall be the person, than that it shall not be Jefferson.... All personal and partial considerations must be discarded, and every thing must give way to the great object of excluding Jefferson." He surveyed the possible candidates among the Federalists. John Adams was generally agreed upon as the logical candidate for the presidency and Thomas Pinckney, the late minister to England, for the vice-presidency. But Hamilton feared that New England might withdraw votes from Pinckney to ensure Adams' election to the major office and thereby give Jefferson an opportunity to squeeze in.[47]

As the elections of delegates who would choose the president and vice-president came closer, Hamilton became more and more alarmed. The Republicans, as had been expected, put Jefferson up as their candidate. But they added, for a second candidate, another man whom by this time Hamilton was beginning to fear and hate at least as much as he feared and hated Jefferson. This was Aaron Burr. Back in 1792, when Burr first appeared on the national horizon, Hamilton had written extravagant letters to his followers to head him off. Now Burr was again in the running.

Whereas it was obvious that no Federalist would consider voting for Jefferson, the same could not be said in the case of Burr. He was personally on good terms with a large number of party Federalists, and his aristocratic bearing, his background, his wit and talents, made him *persona grata* to men to whom Jefferson represented the horned beast. As if to give point to Hamilton's uneasiness, Jonathan Dayton of New Jersey, already at odds with the leaders in his own state, started a secret campaign to urge Federalists generally to support Burr for the presidency.

His letter to Sedgwick, one of the most influential of the Massachusetts Federalists, hitherto unpublished, is extremely important. It represents a decisive stage in the genesis of Hamilton's almost pathological concern over Burr and points directly toward the ultimate tragic end of that concern.

Dayton considered Adams' chances of election rather dim and suggested to Sedgwick the only alternative, as he saw it, of keeping Jefferson from the presidency. Pennsylvania would vote unanimously against Adams. So would South Carolina, which would try to ensure Pinckney's election. The south generally would cast its votes for Jefferson and Burr. While Massachusetts and New Jersey would throw all its first votes to Adams, what about the second? If they gave them, as planned, to Pinckney, might not then Jefferson win the first place? What did Sedgwick think?[48]

Dayton did not wait for the answer. The next day he wrote again, this time boldly stating what he had merely hinted before. "Every moment's reflection serves only to impress me more with the importance of our fixing upon some plan of cooperation to defeat the designs of Mr. J[efferson']s friends. If Mr. A[dams] cannot succeed, is it not desirable to have at the helm a man who is personally known to, as well as esteemed & respected by us both? I assure you that I think it possible for you & me with a little aid to effect this." That man was Burr.[49]

Sedgwick did not rise to the bait. He felt fairly confident that Adams would get the votes of Pennsylvania and that South Carolina would not desert him. Pinckney must be dealt with honestly, even if it meant his election over Adams. "Respecting Mr. Burr, no man better than yourself knows the estimation in which I hold him. But in my conscience I do not believe that every vote in Massachusetts would give him the least chance of an election to either of the offices." Sedgwick proved surprisingly prophetic in his analysis of Burr's relations with Jefferson and Jefferson's party among the Republicans. "They court the aid of his character & talents," he declared, but they "have not the smallest confidence in his hearty union to their cause. Indeed it is my firm belief that their views and his are not only distinct but opposite." He called Dayton's attention to the time when Monroe was chosen over Burr for the special mission to France "by the insidious machinations of that party." They had chosen Monroe not because he was superior, or even equal, in talents and integrity, but because "they knew the one would & the other would not condescend to act as their tool. They doubtless respect Burr's talents, but they dread his independence of *them*." Therefore, he was certain the Republicans on their side would deliberately draw votes away from him to avoid his election.[50]

Sedgwick's prognosis came true in every respect. Republican votes were withheld from Burr and wasted on Clinton, with the result that a new feud was started—that between Jefferson and Burr, which, quiescent for years, finally flared up and was responsible for Burr's own final downfall and tragedy.

Thus summarily rebuffed in his initial overture, Dayton dropped his scheme to make his friend, Burr, president. Sedgwick sent copies of the correspondence to Hamilton, with the warning: "I need not say that this information must be kept secret, for however proper it may be, and I esteem it highly so, Dayton would doubtless deem it a breach of confidence." [51] Thereafter Hamilton distrusted Jonathan Dayton deeply, and became even more convinced that Aaron Burr was a most dangerous man. With powerful friends in *both* parties, Burr might, unless halted, some day wrest control of even the Federalists out of his hands and gain the "highest honors" in the state. This was a consummation Hamilton was ready to oppose with every weapon at his command.

Whereupon Hamilton exerted himself to elect both Adams and Pinckney. He wrote Higginson in Massachusetts exhorting him to hold the state electors in line. Higginson communicated the letter to some of the electors and was able to report back that " a majority of them were at first inclined to throw away their votes from M. Pinckney, lest he should rise above Adams, but your information as to Vermont, with some observations made to them, showing the dangers of so doing, decided all but three, who were determined, upon interested and personal motives, to waste theirs." [52] In fact, this "wasting" of votes by Federalist electors to make certain that Pinckney would not outrun Adams, was responsible for Jefferson's moving into second place. When the final votes were counted, Adams was President, Jefferson was Vice-President, and both Pinckney and Burr trailed behind.

Hamilton viewed at least Burr's failure with considerable satisfaction. "The event," he exclaimed to Rufus King, "will not a little mortify Burr. Virginia has given him only one vote." [53] Just as Massachusetts had doublecrossed Pinckney to exalt Adams, so had Virginia doublecrossed Burr to place Jefferson in the vice-presidency.

Yet Hamilton, in the same letter, contended that "we are laboring hard to establish in this country principles more and more *national* and free from all foreign ingredients, so that we may be neither 'Greeks nor Trojans,' but truly Americans."

Meanwhile the rumor arose that Hamilton had secretly tried to defeat Adams in favor of Pinckney. Higginson wrote from Massachusetts to say that the rumor was prevalent among the partisans of Adams in that state and that feeling ran high against Hamilton.[54] Jefferson sought to sow similar grounds of suspicion in Adams' mind. In a letter addressed to the new President, in which he asserted that he had never expected or wished a different result to the election, he proceeded: "Indeed it is possible that you may be cheated of your succession by a trick worthy the subtlety of your arch-friend of New York, who has been able to make of your real friends tools to defeat their & your just wishes. Most probably he will be disappointed as to you; & my inclinations place me out of his reach." [55]

To Madison Jefferson unbosomed himself more frankly. "If mr. Adams can be induced to administer the government on its true principles, & to relinquish his bias to an English constitution, it is to be considered whether it would not be on the whole for the public good to come to a good understanding with him as to his future elections. He is perhaps the only sure barrier against Hamilton's getting in." [56]

CHAPTER XXIV

Public Emergency and Private Scandal

---

1. TROUBLE WITH FRANCE

THE ADMINISTRATION of John Adams began under clouded aspects. Linked with him as Vice-President was Jefferson, whom no good Federalist could contemplate without a shudder. He was a Jacobin, a Francophile, a Deist, a leveler. If Adams himself did not share the universal abhorrence of party men for his team mate, this was in part due to his suspicion that the more extreme of his partisans—including Hamilton—would have preferred to see Pinckney elevated to the presidency in his stead and had worked secretly to that end.

But more important than internecine machinations was the increasingly ominous state of our relations with France which he inherited from the waning days of Washington's tenure in office. The balance of power had shifted in Europe from British supremacy to the whelming tide of revolutionary France. And with this shift France, instead of England, became the tender spot in our foreign relations. French arrogance and disregard of American rights superseded the former similar arrogance of the British. Whereas, at an earlier date, the Republicans accused the administration of kowtowing to English depredations, now it was the Federalists who in turn complained of a supine submission to the insults of the French. The New England merchants, backbone of the Federalist party, had deprecated warlike threats against British attacks on neutral trade; they breathed a wholly different ardor when it came to similar assaults by the French.

At first Hamilton joined in the Federalist hue and cry. In a series of public essays he demanded the recall of the Minister from France, the obnoxious M. Adet, and warned the people that we could not, without loss of life and honor, submit much longer to the oppressive acts of the French government. To the accusation that we had stood equally as much from England, he retorted with much heat that the French aggressions were far more iniquitous than any hitherto contemplated by the British. "The man who, after this mass of evidence," he concluded, "shall be the apologist of France, and the calumniator of his own government, is not an American. The choice for him lies between being deemed a fool, a madman, or a traitor." [1]

Fisher Ames, one of the most extreme and narrow-visioned of the Federalists, was delighted with Hamilton's stand. To Ames, this country stood on the verge of anarchy and ruin. He considered himself an aristocrat and despised the popular mind and the popular process with a depth of contempt worthy of a noble of the *ancien régime*. Congress, that aggregation of fools, required a strong leader to point the way and hold it above a loathsome subservience upon the people. Hamilton was such a leader; let him go into the House of Representatives.

The silly reliance of our coffee-house and Congress prattlers on the responsibility of members to the people, &c., &c., is disgraced by every page of the history of popular bodies [he told Hamilton]. We expect, confidently, that the House of Representatives will *act* out of its proper character—for if it should act according to it, we are lost. Our government will be, in fact, a mere democracy, which has never been tolerable nor long tolerated. [2]

Hamilton did not adopt Ames' suggestion, but he shared to some extent the uneasiness of his political friends that the Jacobins in America were ready for instant revolution. Had there not been a series of suspicious fires bursting forth in various sections of the city of New York? Were not these the deliberate incendiary attempts of the Jacobins to burn down the town and thereby initiate the first stage of the revolution? His friends thought so. They armed themselves and nightly patrolled the town, dividing themselves into bands of twenty each, one to a ward. Hamilton tramped with the rest, and in one of his nightly watches turned his ankle and wrenched a tendon. Lamed and hobbling, he was compelled to keep to his house for some weeks and leave the safety of New York to other and more vigorous limbs. [3]

But Hamilton soon diverged from the extremist views of his fellow Federalists. They were breathing immediate and outright war against the monster, France. Hamilton was more cautious. The reasons which had made him decide for peaceful means to settle foreign disputes in the former emergency with England still held good in the present conflict with France. Above all else, the United States required an uninterrupted decade of peace and prosperity if it was to survive and flourish. Just as he had urged a special mission to England to settle, if possible, all points at issue, now he advocated a similar mission to France. Just before Washington gave up his office, he outlined his ideas to him. "We seem to be where we were with Great Britain when Mr. Jay was sent there, and I cannot discern but that the spirit of the policy, then pursued with regard to England, will be the proper one now in respect to France—*viz.:* a solemn and final appeal to the justice and interest of France, and if this will not do, measures of self-defence. Any thing is better than absolute humiliation. France has already gone much further than Great Britain ever did." [4]

Before Washington could act on Hamilton's suggestions, however, he had retired to private life and Adams took over the presidential office. Adams' first official act was to submit a series of questions to his heads of departments pertaining to our relations with France and requesting their considered opinions as to the course he should pursue. The members of his cabinet, inherited from the closing days of Washington, promptly turned the questions over to Hamilton for *his* opinion.

Hamilton replied to each one in great detail and along similar lines. To McHenry, Secretary of War, he suggested that a commission be appointed to go to France, consisting of either Madison or Jefferson (to placate the opposition), Pinckney and a "third very safe man, say, Cabot (or Jay)." In addition, an embargo was to be laid on trade with France when congress met, the navy was to be increased, and a provisional army raised.[5] Wolcott, of the Treasury, and Pickering, in the State Department, received like letters.

McHenry adopted Hamilton's suggestions and submitted his answer to Adams in language that followed, almost word for word, Hamilton's several points. Pickering and Wolcott, however, were reluctant to send a commission. Pickering thought it would certainly fail, and declared roundly it would give aid and comfort to the opposition at home. "This new mission is what the enemies of our government sigh for; however circumstances may oppose it." But, he added hastily, "I beg you to continue to communicate to me your ideas on public affairs especially at the present interesting period." [6] Wolcott was also intransigent, and Hamilton was compelled to bring pressure to bear upon them before they yielded, albeit reluctantly, to his point of view. "As to the mission, in some shape or other," he insisted to Pickering, "the more I have reflected upon it, the more has it appeared to me indispensable." [7]

The trouble was that the extreme Federalists, like William Smith, Uriah Tracy and others, were hot for war with France. They disliked what they conceived to be Hamilton's placating course. But the rebellion was soon crushed. As Wolcott confessed to him: "You know that I am accustomed to respect your opinions; and I am not so ignorant of the extent of your influence upon the friends of government, as not to be sensible, that if you are known to favor the sending of a commission, so the thing must and will be." [8]

And so, actually, it turned out to be, even though Uriah Tracy, in a violent and hitherto unpublished letter to Hamilton, had actually advocated a separation of the north and the south should the latter, through its representatives, "add to this their opinion by a public Vote, that the Government has injured France." He feared that the south, "increasing by frequent importations of foreign scoundrels as well as by those of home manufacture," would swallow up the north, "& the name & real character of an American soon be known only as a thing of tradition." Rather than let this happen, he, Uriah Tracy, would demand a separation of the two sections; in fact, if it should ever come to a choice, he would prefer to be a colony of Great Britain again than of France.[9] Thus, at this early date, some of the Federalists were considering the possibility of a secession.

To Hamilton, such a possibility was as abhorrent as he was disturbed by differences already existing between himself and his political friends. He wrote a sharp note to one of them, William Smith. "It is unpleasant to me to know that I have for some time differed materially from many of my friends on public subjects.... We seem now to feel and reason as the *Jacobins* did when Great Britain insulted and injured us, though certainly we have at least as much need of a temperate conduct now as we had then. I only say, God grant that the public interest may not be sacrificed at the shrine of irritation and mistaken pride." [10]

The rebellion, however, was abortive. Hamilton gained his point. Thereafter, the cabinet of John Adams meekly sought and followed Hamilton's advice on almost every issue that reared its head during their ensuing years of office. Adams was wholly unaware of this backstairs diplomacy. Not until the very end did he realize that Hamilton, out of office and ostensibly a busy lawyer immersed in private affairs, was in fact the guiding spirit of his administration, the oracle to whom his official family turned on every possible occasion for aid and comfort. He himself never called on Hamilton for suggestions or advice of any kind, nor did Hamilton attempt to proffer any to him by word of mouth or letter. When Adams *did* discover the truth, the inevitable explosion followed. By that time, however, it was too late, and the irascible controversy engendered was directly responsible for Adams' defeat and downfall in his bid for re-election.

In the meantime, without his knowledge, Hamilton was actually upholding his hands in the Federalist quarrel over the proper course to be pursued with France. Adams, as well as Hamilton, had no desire for war and was willing to do whatever he could to avoid such a catastrophe. Hamilton generously told Wolcott: "I like very well the course of Executive conduct in regard to the controversy with France." [11] This course followed, along broad general lines, Hamilton's ideas. Adams appointed a commission of three, composed of Elbridge Gerry, a Republican, and C. C. Pinckney and John Marshall to uphold the Federalist point of view. The commission sailed for France, to meet with a strange reception and to bring back an even stranger report of their negotiations.

2. THE AFFAIR OF MRS. REYNOLDS

While these public turmoils were impending, Hamilton was suddenly attacked from an unexpected quarter in such a fashion as to bring momentarily crashing the whole structure of his private and domestic life. The savage assault almost succeeded in driving him forever, discredited and ruined, from the arena of public affairs.

The roots of the attack go back all the way to 1792 and 1793, when Hamilton was still Secretary of the Treasury and driving home nail after nail into the solid financial structure of his plans. Unable to defeat him in the government or in the halls of congress, the opposition sought every rumor to discredit him. The most vicious of these, and the most widely believed, was that Hamilton was profiting financially from his schemes. This was easy to believe at the time, for that was the heyday of Duer's shady speculations in government stocks and government contracts, and Duer had been Hamilton's assistant in the Treasury and closely connected with him by ties of marriage and of personal friendship.

John Beckley, a minor Republican politician, thought he had found direct evidence of Hamilton's illicit, even criminal, speculations, and hastened to apprise James Monroe of his findings. They related to the alleged intermediate role played by one Andrew G. Fraunces, a clerk in the Treasury Department, as told to Beckley by a man named Jacob Clingman. Fraunces, according to Clingman's story, had boasted to him that "he could, if he pleased, hang Hamilton." He asserted that he had been the confidential go-between in a series of speculations which Hamilton had made conjointly with Duer. As a result of these private speculations, based on foreknowledge of what he, Hamilton, intended to do in his public capacity, Hamilton had cleared the tidy sum of $30,000. Hamilton had given him power of attorney to purchase a Revolutionary veteran's pay at a substantial discount just before the passage of Hamilton's bill for payment at par, and had given him, Fraunces, $50 for his services. Hamilton likewise had given Fraunces checks with which to pay his agents in Philadelphia who were engaged in buying up stock for him and reselling almost immediately to the United States at a considerably higher price. What turned Fraunces finally against his chief, according to himself, was the fact that Hamilton double-crossed him. Fraunces had tried a little speculation of his own on the side, on which he expected to clear $1500. When he presented his warrants to the Treasury for payment, however, they were turned down. He wrote Hamilton about it and Hamilton promised they would be met, if presented again. But a second presentation met with a second refusal.

Beckley turned all this information over to Monroe with the sage advice to take Clingman into his confidence, to play on Fraunces' well-known love of drink and money "as to obtain decisive proof" and "unravel this scene of iniquity." [12]

This was not all, however. Clingman claimed that another friend of his, James Reynolds, of New York, had been another and even more confidential agent of Hamilton in criminal speculations. Mrs. Reynolds had actually shown him letters signed by Hamilton accompanying payments of certain sums of money to her husband for services rendered. The sum total so received amounted to $1100.

All this was grist for Monroe's mill. Here was a chance to discredit irrevocably the mighty Hamilton, whom he considered the implacable foe of everything for which he and his mentor, Jefferson, stood. With Beckley's information before him, and as the result of other inquiries which he had already instituted, he called in two of his fellow congressmen—Muhlenberg and Venable—to consider what they should do. Part of the story had already come to Muhlenberg through Clingman himself, who was a clerk in his employ. Clingman and Reynolds, it seems, had fallen into the toils of the law for suborning a witness to commit perjury in an attempt to mulct the Treasury of a petty sum of money. Under arrest and faced with prosecution, Clingman besought the aid of his employer to get him out of trouble. Muhlenberg agreed to help Clingman, but not Reynolds, who continued to languish in jail. Accompanied by Aaron Burr, he interceded with Hamilton in his employee's behalf. Hamilton "signified a wish to do all that was consistent," but Wolcott, the comptroller, made difficulties. Thereupon Clingman hinted "that Reynolds had it in his power very materially to injure the Secretary of Treasury."

Faced with bigger game than he had expected, Muhlenberg consulted with Monroe and Venable. The trio of congressmen secretly visited Reynolds in jail and were fed with dark hints that this untimely persecution was intended to crush him because he knew too much, but that Hamilton must soon instigate his release. They next visited Mrs. Reynolds, a bold, florid, handsome woman, who added fuel to the smoldering fire. She showed her visitors notes addressed to her, undeniably in Hamilton's handwriting, spoke of many more she had destroyed, and insisted that her husband had dealt clandestinely with Hamilton, as a result of which Hamilton had finally threatened vengeance on Reynolds if he did not disappear from view.[13]

With all this seemingly damning data in their hands, the trio of Republican congressmen determined to confront Hamilton with their evidence. On December 15, 1792, they walked into his Treasury office, grim and accusing, to demand an explanation. Hamilton was thunderstruck. After a moment's hesitation he begged them to meet him at his home that evening, and he would lay before them certain documents that would satisfactorily explain his innocence.

When the sceptical congressmen retired, Hamilton called Oliver Wolcott and begged him to be present at the ensuing meeting as a witness. He knew it would be a fateful one. The sudden accusation had confronted him with a terrible dilemma. If he decided to remain silent, he stood convicted of public peculation and public dishonor, and he knew that his enemies would show no mercy in driving him headlong into disgrace. If he explained, however—and he had the means of explanation in his locked desk—then he stood convicted of low intrigue, of adultery. His private shame would lie exposed to the jeers and taunts of these same enemies, while Eliza, the wife who adored him and thought him the very soul of honor, must suffer an irremediable blow.

It was a difficult decision to make, yet Hamilton had made it in the single instant of hesitation after Monroe finished his speaking. Much rather his private honor should suffer than his public. Much rather his

domestic happiness should fall in ruins than the fruits of his statesmanship should wither at the moment of ripeness.

That evening the three congressmen heard an astonishing tale. Eliza
fortunately had gone on a visit to Albany with the children. Oliver
Wolcott was the only other spectator to the abasement of his friend
and chief.

The story went back to the summer of 1791. The scene was Philadelphia. One day Mrs. Maria Reynolds, then wholly unknown to him,
came to his house in great agitation. Her husband, she sobbed, had
deserted her and left her destitute. If only she had some money she
could return to New York, her native home. Would Mr. Hamilton,
who was also a New Yorker and known for his generosity, help an
afflicted woman?

Hamilton would and could. He was touched both by the story of
affliction and by the coarsely handsome features of the woman. Eliza
and the children were then in Albany and he was alone. He had no
money with him, so he took her address and promised to send her
some forthwith. Instead of sending it by messenger, however, he went
himself. A short and increasingly intimate colloquy in the lady's bedroom soon convinced him, in his own words, "that other than pecuniary consolation would be acceptable. After this I had frequent
meetings with her, most of them at my own house."

Later on Maria Reynolds pretended that she had become reconciled
with her husband, who appeared suddenly to Hamilton and demanded
employment as a clerk in the Treasury. Still telling the ignoble story,
Hamilton confessed that he had parried the request, though making
certain vague promises so as not to offend the cuckolded husband.
Reynolds became insistent, and the suspicion grew in Hamilton's mind
that husband and wife were in league. "Yet," he admitted, "her conduct made it extremely difficult to disentangle myself. All the appearances of violent attachment, and of agonizing distress at the idea of a
relinquishment, were played with a most imposing art. This, though it
did not make me entirely the dupe of the plot, yet kept me in a state
of resolution."

On December 15, 1791, the plot came to a head. Two letters came
to Hamilton, one on the heels of the other. The first was from Maria.
Misspelled, illiterate, it breathed agitation and seeming terror. "I have
not tim to tell you the cause of my present troubles only that Mr. has
rote you this morning . . . and he has swore that If you do not answer

It or If he dose not se or hear from you to day he will write Mrs. Hamilton he has just Gone oute and I am a Lone I think you had better come here one moment that you May know the Cause then you will the better know how to act. . . ."

Barely had Hamilton finished this terrifying epistle when James Reynold's letter came, breathing all the wild passion of a justly aggrieved husband. "I am very sorry to find out that I have been so Cruelly treated by a person that I took to be my best friend instead of that my greatest Enimy. You have deprived me of every thing thats near and dear to me . . . Sir you took the advantage [of] a poor Broken harted woman. instead of being a Friend you have acted the part of the most Cruelist man in existence. you have made a whole family miserable. . . . now I am determined to have satisfaction. it shant be onely one family thats miserable." [14]

Hamilton, aware now of his danger, did not go to see Maria. Instead, he sent a note to Reynolds to call at his office. Reynolds did so, uttering vague threats. Hamilton demanded that he put into writing what he wanted. Reynolds sent two letters, long, rambling, incoherent; in one place threatening to obtain satisfaction; in another changing his tune and imploring Hamilton to put himself in his place "and tell me what you would do in such a Case." Finally he came to the point: "I have this preposial to make to you. give me the Sum Of thousand dollars and I will leve the town and take my daughter with me and go where my Friend Shant here from me and leve her to Yourself to do to her as you thing proper."

Faced with this unblushing demand, Hamilton could do no other but comply. He paid over $600 on December 22nd and $400 on January 3rd, obtaining receipts marked "in full of all demands."

He might have known he was not finished with the Reynolds— blackmail feeds on blackmail—but he was not prepared for the next act in the sordid drama. It came in the form of letters from both husband and wife. Maria called on him in anguish for comfort in her loneliness, and James backed up his wife with an outright request that he do so, adding significantly that "I Rely on your befriending me if there should anything Offer that would be to my advantage." [15]

Rashly, Hamilton yielded to the solicitations of his inamorata and her complaisant husband. The next step was inevitable. It took the form of further demands for money—modest, to be sure. In small sums Hamilton paid over $165. On May 2, 1792, Reynolds suddenly changed his tune. "I must now forever forbid you of visiting Mrs. R any more," he wrote. "I was in hopes that it would in time ware off, but I find there is no hopes. So I am determed to put a finell end to it."

By this time Hamilton fully realized the extent of his danger, and was glad to obey the interdict. But this was not in the calculations of the precious pair. They had simply wished to whet his appetite, to force him to a more public series of visits so that their friend, Clingman, might later prove a witness to their intimacy. Accordingly, Maria again begged him tearfully to come, while Reynolds demanded more and more money from their victim. Hamilton sent $50, and again $200. It was to this last sum that Clingman was able to testify in his affidavit.

The astounded congressmen listened to the strange tale of degradation and blackmail as Hamilton unfolded it with chapter and verse, and the production of the weird letters from the Reynoldses. Venable and Muhlenberg stirred uneasily at the endless disclosures and protested several times that they had heard enough; that Hamilton need not go any further. Only Monroe said nothing. But Hamilton insisted on laying bare the complete story of his shame. When it was over, the trio stared at each other. They had not expected to hear anything like this. Were they satisfied now? asked Hamilton. They were, completely. They would do nothing further, they assured him. They would, as gentlemen, keep secret all the documents placed in their hands by Clingman. They would treat the whole affair as strictest confidence.[16]

There the matter rested until, in 1797, James T. Callender, a Republican scribbler, published in installments what purported to be a *History of the United States for the Year 1796*. In the fifth installment of this veracious history Callender uncovered to the public eye the long-buried tale of 1792. All Clingman's charges against Hamilton, together with the story of Reynolds as first unveiled to Monroe, appeared in all their damning dress.

Hamilton was stunned. Here were the original documents which his congressional visitors had promised on their honor to keep forever hid from public view. On July 5, 1797, he wrote to all three concerned, expressing his astonishment at the breach of faith. Muhlenberg answered promptly, lamenting the publication and disavowing all complicity in it. The papers, he averred, had never been in his hands. Venable answered to the same effect. Monroe, however, held his peace.

This seemed to put the blame squarely on Monroe. On July 11th Hamilton called on him. He took the precaution to take along with him his brother-in-law, John Barker Church, who had recently come over from England with Angelica to settle permanently in New York. Monroe was equally careful to have his friend, David Gelston, present at the interview. Gelston immediately after wrote down the minutes of what had taken place, and these manuscript notes give a lively account of the proceedings.[17]

According to Gelston, Hamilton came into Monroe's lodgings "very much agitated," and proceeded to detail at considerable length the circumstances of their earlier meeting in Philadelphia in 1792. Monroe interrupted to ask him to come to the point. Hamilton did so with some warmth, and Monroe answered with equal warmth. He declared he had sealed up the incriminating papers after that meeting and sent them "to his Friend in Virginia—he had no intention of publishing them & declared upon his honor that he knew nothing of their publication until he arrived at Philada from Europe." As for his silence in the face of Hamilton's letter he had wished first to confer with the other two involved before he replied.

Hamilton retorted that Monroe's statement was totally false. Monroe rose immediately. "If you say I represented falsely," he cried, "you are a scoundrel." Hamilton sprang to his feet. "I will meet you like a gentleman," he countered. Monroe answered: "I am ready. Get your pistols."

Gelston and Church thrust themselves between the excited antagonists, Church crying: "Gentlemen! Gentlemen! Be moderate!" Finally they persuaded them to sit down again, and Gelston suggested that the matter rest until Monroe went to Philadelphia and met Venable and Muhlenberg, so that they might issue a joint statement. Hamilton indicated that this was acceptable, and Church agreed. Whereupon the men parted, after first agreeing to forget "any warmth or unguarded expressions" that might have passed in the heat of encounter.

On July 17th Hamilton heard from Monroe. The letter was extremely evasive. It hinted even that Monroe had not considered himself bound at the time not to disclose the affair, that he had entered the proceedings with the right "to form an opinion upon it at such future time as I found convenient." [18]

Hamilton wrote back sharply that he considered Monroe's communication unsatisfactory and demanded a plainer response. When Monroe again evaded, Hamilton pressed hard. "I proposed a simple and direct question, to which I had hoped an answer equally simple and direct." Back and forth flew the communications, each edging closer to what seemed an inevitable encounter with pistols. The letters have a curious air of anticipation about them—in reply and counter-reply they resemble that later series between Hamilton and Burr. And, adding the last ironic touch, Burr soon became involved in this earlier affair.

Finally, Hamilton expressed the opinion that Monroe was deliberately driving him to publish a formal defense to avoid the imputations on his public character as a result of Callender's exposure, adding in significant phrases that "you have been and are actuated by motives towards me malignant and dishonorable."

Monroe inquired whether it was Hamilton's intention "to render this affair a personal one between us?" Hamilton disavowed any such intention, stating that he was now cutting short the correspondence and leaving the issue to the court of public opinion.[19]

This appeal to "public opinion" took the shape of a pamphlet entitled "Observations on Certain Documents contained in Nos. V and VI of *The History of the United States for the Year 1796*, in which the Charge of Speculation against Alexander Hamilton, late Secretary of the Treasury, is fully refuted. Written by himself." In this pamphlet Hamilton laid bare his shame for his stunned wife and all the world to see.

It took tremendous courage thus to avert the charge of speculation by an open confession of his private disgrace. His friends shook their heads and wondered whether he had not been precipitately rash. His enemies were gleeful. How had the mighty Hamilton fallen! Monroe himself, who had cynically endorsed the packet of documents back in 1793 with the caption: "Hamilton's Love and Speculation," [20] professed that he "was sorry for it, and think he has acted, by drawing the publick attention to it, & making it an affr. of more consequence that it was in itself, very indiscreet." [21]

But there is no question that Monroe could have avoided these consequences had he desired. At the least he had failed in his pledge of honor by letting the incriminating packet out of his hands. Who the "friend in Virginia" is to whom he entrusted the papers is not known, though there is a suspicion it was Jefferson. It is further suspected that John Beckley, the politician who goaded Monroe in the first instance, was responsible for placing them in the hands of Callender. In any event, now that the scandal broke, Monroe could have mitigated the consequences for Hamilton by a timely and frank avowal that he was satisfied of Hamilton's innocence in the matter of public speculation, and thereby avoided the necessity of publishing the sordid background of the Reynolds affair. Years later, when Hamilton had long been dead, and both Eliza Hamilton and Monroe were aged folk, Eliza refused implacably to accept Monroe's hand or apologies for the part he had played. She never forgave him, as she had immediately forgiven her erring husband and rushed to his defense.

The scandal did not end with the publication of Hamilton's "Observations." Rather, it gained in strength as in currency. For Callender retorted that the letters purporting to be from Reynolds and his wife were in fact forgeries concocted by Hamilton to avoid the more serious charge.

Hamilton, in a fury, turned on Monroe. Monroe considered certain expressions in the letter as a challenge, and replied on August 6th that if they were intended as such, "I have then to request that you will say so, and in which case, have to inform you that my friend, Col. Burr, who will present you this ... is authorized to give my answer to it, and to make such other arrangements as may be suitable in such an event."

The affair, which had rapidly assumed a deadly aspect, ended in a mutual comedy of errors. For Hamilton declared he had had no intention of challenging but had assumed that Monroe had done so. Monroe equally disavowed the intention, and Burr was able to draw up a statement which brought the exchange to a peaceful, if not amicable, conclusion.[22]

3. HOLLAND LAND COMPANY

While Hamilton was thus coming into contact with Burr in connection with the unsavory Reynolds affair, he was similarly meeting him in the field of legal matters.

Back in 1792 a frenzy of speculation in American lands had begun. Not only native operators, speculating for a boom in values, entered the arena, but a horde of English and Dutch capitalists sought quick fortunes from the virgin American soil. A group of Dutch men of wealth combined to form the Holland Land Company and appointed one Theophile Cazenove as their American agent. He purchased on their account vast tracts of land in western Pennsylvania and in New York. Burr became financially involved in these speculations.

But the New York purchases ran into difficulties. According to state law, aliens could not become unrestricted owners of New York real estate. The Holland Company sought to remove the limitation by direct action in the legislature, and were defeated. Whereupon Cazenove, in their behalf, retained Hamilton as counsel to further their interests when the bill came up again. Hamilton was successful insofar as he managed to obtain the passage of a law permitting aliens to hold land for a period of seven years. Not satisfied with this limited success, Cazenove urged Hamilton to try for a further law without any limitations.

This time Schuyler was directly interested. He had formed the Western Inland Lock Navigation Company to build a series of canals, and through Hamilton agreed to use *his* influence in the legislature in favor of the Holland Company bill if they would in turn aid him financially in his own venture. Adding point to this proposal, he pushed through an Act raising the term of alien holdings to twenty years, provided the Holland Company lent his Canal Company the sum of $250,000.[22] Cazenove, however, suddenly balked; resenting, no doubt, the hard bargain Schuyler and Hamilton were attempting to drive, he went to Burr for assistance. He had first complained to Hamilton over the onerous terms, and received in return a cautiously worded letter painting a dark picture of the company's prospects if it refused to accept the conditional Act, and sidestepping completely Cazenove's hint that he ought to see Schuyler and obtain some mitigation.[24]

Burr, with his own axe to grind, and with a *douceur* of bribes for susceptible legislators, managed to clear away the obstructive and venal Act, and put through a superseding law granting a wholly unrestricted tenure. The Schuyler family was righteously indignant at Burr's tactics, forgetting, in the process, their own attempt to cash in on the Holland Company's necessity. Church passed disparaging comments about Burr. Burr challenged. There was an interchange of shots which ended without harm to either duellist, except that Burr's coat showed a bullet hole. Thereafter the relations between Hamilton and Burr, already sufficiently exacerbated for personal and political reasons, became even more strained.

CHAPTER XXV

The War Clouds Gather

---

1. THE MONSTER, FRANCE!

ADAMS HAD SENT off his three envoys to France in a last, almost despairing attempt to keep the rapidly worsening relations between the two countries from ending abruptly in a state of war. But their mission could hardly be termed successful. Talleyrand, the old-time friend of Hamilton and now the subtle fox of the Directory, cynically demanded an enormous bribe from the Americans in return for a vague promise to keep the peace. The demand was met with an indignant "No! No! Not a sixpence!" and Marshall and Pinckney returned forthwith to report on their discomfiture.

Even before the so-called XYZ affair broke upon an astounded nation, Adams sought cabinet advice as to the course he ought to pursue if the mission failed. McHenry, as always, passed the inquiry on to "my dear Hamilton." What ought I to reply to these questions, was in effect his plaint. "I am sure I cannot do such justice to the subject as you can. Let me, therefore, intreat you to favour me, as soon as possible, with your ideas." [1]

Hamilton, as always, was willing to oblige. He thought it better not to come to a formal rupture with France, because of the "very general aversion to War in the minds of the people of this Country." He would prefer rather a state of "mitigated hostility" which, while leaving the door open to further negotiations, would put us in a strong defensive position. Suspend all treaties with France, he advised, arm our merchant vessels, create a strong navy and raise a standing army. [2]

Pickering, in the State Department, also passed on the questions to Hamilton and received a similar reply. Whereupon both McHenry and Pickering practically copied Hamilton's suggestions and sent them on to the unsuspecting President as their own ideas.

Then Marshall and Pinckney came back with their incredible tale. Pickering promptly told Hamilton about it "in perfect confidence."

The nation at large knew nothing as yet. Again, what should he do?[3]

Thus, without any official position or standing, Hamilton in effect molded the policies of government. All the official secrets of Adams' administration were laid bare for his inspection; not a single measure was taken that was not immediately conveyed to him. The three most important members of the cabinet—Pickering, McHenry and Wolcott—followed him with blind, unquestioning confidence. It was a cabinet supposedly of Adams; actually, it was Hamilton's tool and weapon. An intolerable situation for any President—and particularly so for a man of Adams' touchiness and pride. It is no wonder then that when he finally discovered the fact, a tremendous explosion was inevitable.

Besides working through the medium of these followers, Hamilton resorted to the press to arouse a nation which, in his estimation, required a good deal of arousing on the iniquities of France. Too many of the people still had a soft spot for their old ally; too many still hailed the French Revolution as the hope of the world; too many harkened to the Jacobins in their own country. From March 10th to April 21st there appeared a series of articles in the New York *Commercial Advertiser* called "The Stand" and signed by Titus Manlius. In these articles Hamilton let himself go. He was no longer the diplomat, the statesman of his letters to McHenry and Pickering; he was the reckless exhorter to hate and passion. France, he cried, was "the most flagitious, despotic, and vindictive government that ever disgraced the annals of mankind." How could Americans regard with indulgence "so frightful a volcano of atheism, depravity, and absurdity ... so hateful an instrument of cruelty and bloodshed?" Arm yourself! Prefer death rather than dishonor! Observe, he insisted, "the disgusting spectacle of the French Revolution!" Note the moral turpitude involved in the infamous XYZ affair! (By the end of the series the news had been made public to the country, and the Republicans were insisting it was a Federal canard for political ends.) Yet there were those in America, he continued, who sought excuses for the French. Without mentioning him by name, Hamilton denounced Jefferson as "the high-priest of this sect," who was "of so seditious, so prostitute a character" as to expect "to be the proconsul of a despotic Directory over the United States, degraded to the condition of a province."[4]

The United States was in fact torn into two disparate pieces. France became a touchstone that was at once simple and direct. If you admired France you were a Jacobin, an atheist, a bloodthirsty monster who wished nothing better than to murder all respectable citizens in their beds. If you denounced France you were a monarchist, a monocrat, a man who bitterly regretted having left the British fold, a hater of equalitarian principles and tainted with financial corruption.

Among all these conflicting passions Adams continued to pick a wary way. He wanted no war, though the extreme Federalists shouted loudly for instant conflict. In this path he had Hamilton, surprisingly enough, as an ally. Hamilton likewise wished for no war, though he shouted in public as loudly as the rest. There was nothing to be gained from open hostilities, he thought. But there was much to be gained from preparations for war. A standing army might be necessary some day to overawe the Jacobins in our midst and to crush the revolution that seemed impending in America itself.

With this in mind, Hamilton pressed unweariedly for the formation of a powerful regular army. He had dreams, too, in case of war, of returning to the military life he loved. Naturally, Washington would be chosen commander-in-chief; he hoped to be next in command. Accordingly, when Jay, now governor of New York, offered him an appointment as United States Senator in place of Judge Hobart, who had recently resigned, he turned it down.[5] He wished to have no commitments when the call came.

2. GENERAL IN THE ARMY

By July the call had come. Or rather, Hamilton and his closest friends had maneuvered to such good effect that Adams was forced to make the call.

Relations with France had steadily deteriorated. The Federalists increased their clamor for a standing army, a powerful navy, and eventual war. Congress passed the necessary bills of implementation. Adams, against his will, was pushed steadily along.

As everyone had expected, Washington was asked to head the new army. Living in retirement at Mount Vernon, he consented, with two reservations: that he be consulted in choosing the general staff, and that he should not be required to take active command until a real necessity arose.[6] This meant that the second in command would in effect be the active commander.

Hamilton realized the situation and insisted that he would accept no other post but that of inspector-general, which would give him that second rating.[7] To this insistence his friends, Pickering and McHenry, added their voices.

Washington accordingly made up his list for the general staff with Hamilton heading it as inspector-general, and Charles C. Pinckney and Henry Knox next in line as major-generals. But Washington had some hesitations about this arrangement. Would not Pinckney resent being placed below Hamilton? [8] He made no mention of what Knox's feelings might be.

Hamilton found plenty of arguments in behalf of himself as senior to both Pinckney and Knox. So did Pickering and McHenry, who had originally taken it upon themselves to urge the second position for Hamilton on Washington. McHenry had even made a special trip to Mount Vernon to argue his friend's case. Curiously enough, at the very time that McHenry was so vehement in behalf of Hamilton, Hamilton was complaining bitterly to everyone of McHenry's ineptitude in the War Office, and encouraging demands for his resignation.[9]

While all these intrigues and counter-intrigues were agitating a certain section of the Federalist party, President Adams continued naïvely to think that *he* had the final voice in the necessary dispositions of commands and offices. The first intimation of his error came when he consulted with Pickering, as Secretary of State, on the appointments.

"Whom shall we appoint Commander-in-Chief?" he asked Pickering.

"Colonel Hamilton," answered Pickering flatly.

"Oh no! It is not his turn by a great deal. I would sooner appoint Gates, or Lincoln, or Morgan."

"General Morgan is now here in Congress, a very sick man, with one foot in the grave," Pickering replied. "As for Gates, he is now an old woman—and Lincoln is always asleep." [10]

Finding Adams unaccountably stubborn in his refusal to give the command to Hamilton, and after he had offered it to Washington, Pickering hastily wrote the latter to insist that Hamilton at least be second only to *him* during his presence, and first in his absence.

The second intimation that Adams received of his error was the receipt of the list of officers that Washington had compiled, and which McHenry triumphantly brought back with him from Mount Vernon. Adams scanned the proposed list with surprise. Hamilton rank over Knox and Pinckney, both of whom had far outranked him in the Revolution? It was not to be borne.

He wrote sharply to McHenry that "General Knox is legally entitled to rank next to General Washington; and no other arrangement will give satisfaction." Furthermore, Pinckney also must rank over Hamilton. "Any other plan will occasion long delay and confusion. You may depend upon it," he ended significantly, "the five New England States will not patiently submit to the humiliation that has been meditated for them." [11]

Adams considered the matter settled. He was mistaken. The stubbornness of the President caused a flurry of excitement among Hamilton's friends. They redoubled their efforts and managed to convince Washington that Adams was disregarding his specific recommendations. Under the influence of their proddings, he wrote Adams a stiff note: "I have addressed you, Sir, with openness and candor, and I hope with respect, requesting to be informed, whether your determination to reverse the order of the three Major-Generals is final ..." [12] The intimation was clear; in that event Washington intended to resign his commission.

The President's eyes were now open; he saw for the first time the full implications of what had been taking place behind his back. His entire cabinet was wholly subservient to the outsider, Hamilton; congress was subservient to the same man; so, it now seemed, was Washington. Was he then to yield ingloriously, or fight back? Knox had already expressed his resentment in no uncertain terms at being placed under Hamilton. The old general wrote bitterly: "Our friend Hamilton's abilities by some have been considered so transcendent, as to be a sufficient cause in their opinion to degrade all his seniors in rank and years of the late American Army. I subscribe to his talents but I cannot serve under him." [13]

But the more Adams thought of it the more he realized that he would be compelled to yield. He could not stand out against Washington and the "Triumvirate"—as he called Hamilton and his two loyal friends. To salve his conscience, however, he dated all three commissions the same day, explaining ingenuously to Washington that he had done so "in hopes, similar to yours, that an amicable adjustment, or acquiescence, might take place among the gentlemen themselves. But, if these hopes should be disappointed and controversies should arise, they will, of course, be submitted to you as Commander-in-chief, and if, after all, any one should be so obstinate as to appeal to me from the judgment of the Commander-in-chief, I was determined to confirm that judgment." [14]

No one was deceived by this attempt at face-saving. It meant that

Adams had yielded all along the line. Hamilton was second in titular command, and first in actual command. Certainly McHenry and Hamilton understood it as such. McHenry crowed to Hamilton: "The sun begins to shine;"[15] and Hamilton responded: "I cannot but observe with satisfaction the conclusion of your letter as to the relative rank of the three major-generals."[16] Nor was Knox deceived, who peremptorily refused his own commission under the circumstances and remained in retirement, nursing his wrath.

The cup of humiliation was not yet full for Adams. He had proposed for Aaron Burr, for whose talents he had the highest regard, the comparatively minor post of brigadier-general; and Washington, instigated by the Triumvirate, had coldly turned it down. "How shall I describe to you my sensations and reflections at the moment?" Adams reminisced plaintively many years later.[17] The President knew now that he was not master in his own house.

3. PREPARATIONS FOR GLORY

As inspector-general Hamilton had complete control over all the preparations for raising, equipping and drilling an army. As second in command—since Washington persisted in his determinaton to remain inactive pending actual war—he had active command of all the forces in the field. His earlier dreams were now realized. Nothing stood between him and the full meed of glory but the improbable event that France would back down, or Adams would persist in his determination to avoid war at any cost.

Without the slightest regret Hamilton resigned his "extensive & lucrative" practice of law. He had just won an important law suit for a client, the Frenchman, Le Guen, involving a property valued at more than a hundred thousand dollars and "a new and delicate question" of law.[18] Aside from a few matters still in progress, he devoted himself wholly to his new military duties. These were arduous enough. A brand new army had to be raised from scratch. It had to be outfitted, officered and trained. Almost insuperable obstacles stood in the way. The Republican faction, with few exceptions, stood sullenly apart. Adams was bitterly hostile. The temper of the people did not favor a standing army, and it was difficult to recruit privates in what was still a time of peace. To cap the climax, Hamilton had nothing but contempt for the abilities of poor McHenry as Secretary of War. He made no secret of it to Washington and to others, though

McHenry continued to know nothing of his friend's attempts to replace him in office.

Washington agreed with Hamilton as to "the unfitness of a certain Gentleman for the office he holds," and expressed his willingness to insist to McHenry that he permit Hamilton to take full charge of matters that ordinarily belonged to the department, and not to a general.[19] Others thought the same. General Gunn wrote him:

"I am persuaded it can be no part of your plan merely to execute the feeble arrangements of other men. The President has no Talent for War, and McHenry is an infant in *detail*, and, if I am correct, Genl. Washington is not to take the field, but in the event of the provisional army being called into Service—you are of course not only charged with the command of the army, but, in a great degree, the direction of the War Department...."[20]

All this may have been flattering to Hamilton, but it entailed a tremendous amount of work. Even McHenry was only too happy to shoulder off on the inspector-general the direction of his own department, requesting him, among many other things, to draft all the bills for the provisional army which were to be submitted to congress for approval. "Permit me ... to request," began a typical communication, "that laying aside other business you will occupy yourself on the two military bills only.... If possible let me have the bills by Mondays mail or at furthest tuesdays." [21]

Yet Hamilton's position was anomalous. By a freak of congressional enactment he was technically not on active service and therefore not entitled to any salary. As he was forced finally to complain to McHenry, this put him in a embarrassing position. He had discontinued his practice as an attorney, was devoting his full time to his army duties and received no money. "Were I rich," he ended, "I should be proud to be silent on such a subject." But since he was not, he wished a definition of his situation.[22] For once McHenry responded with efficiency and dispatch. By return mail an official letter fixed Hamilton's "pay and emoluments," which, small enough for a man with a wife and six children to support, nevertheless permitted him to continue his duties.[23]

Since Washington still refused to take any but titular command, Hamilton assumed full charge of all troops north of Maryland, including those in the western territories, and allocated to Pinckney the command of the south. He found that resilient character, James Wilkinson, a brigadier-general in the west, and expressed to him his satisfaction at the new relationship between them.[24]

This was strange, considering that Wilkinson had been one of the cogs in the conspiracy directed during the Revolution against Washington and, indirectly, against Hamilton. What was still stranger was the fact that within a few months Hamilton was advocating to Washington Wilkinson's promotion to major-general. His accompanying reasons were most curious. "I am aware," he wrote Washington, "that some doubts have been entertained of him, and that his character on certain sides, gives room for doubt. Yet he ... is a man of more than ordinary talent, of courage and enterprise ... and will naturally find his interest, as an ambitious man, in deserving the favor of the government; while he will be apt to become disgusted, if neglected; and through disgust may be rendered really what he is now only suspected to be." [25]

Washington, who had righteously refused a commission to Burr because, as he put it, of his "talents for intrigue," now agreed to promote Wilkinson to a command which would give him control of the vast western territories that faced the Spanish possessions. "It would feed his ambition, soothe his vanity, and, by arresting discontent, produce the good effect you contemplate." [26]

McHenry, in the face of such august sponsors, dared not refuse. Nevertheless he was uneasy about Wilkinson. While protesting that he would not stand in the way, he wrote what was, for him, a strong letter to Hamilton. "Of this, however, be assured, that until the commercial pursuits of this gentleman with and expectations from Spain are annihilated, he will not deserve the confidence of government. Further, I recommend it to you, most earnestly, to avoid saying anything to him which would induce him to imagine government had in view any hostile project, however remote, or dependent on events, against any of the possessions of Spain. I require this caution on good grounds." [27]

This surprising letter about a man who held a high position in the American army discloses two interesting points: first, that McHenry knew, or suspected, that Wilkinson was in fact a spy and pensioner in the employ of Spain; second, that certain highly placed officials in the American government—unknown to President Adams—were contemplating the use of the newly raised army not merely as a defense in case of war with France, but as an aggressive weapon against the Spanish possessions in America.

Hamilton's letter to McHenry, crossing the above in the mail, confirms the second point. "It is a pity, my dear sir, and a reproach," he wrote, "that our administration has no general plan. Certainly there ought to be one formed without delay. If the chief is too desultory, his ministry ought to be more united and steady, and well-settled in some reasonable system of measures.... Besides eventual security against invasion, we ought certainly to look to the possession of the Floridas and Louisiana, and we ought to squint at South America." [28]

Here Hamilton let the cat out of the bag. By this time he was pretty certain that Adams had no intention of going to war with France. In fact, the President had thrown consternation into the ranks of the warlike Federalists by his nomination of a plenipotentiary to resume negotiations with the Directory. But now that Hamilton had the making of a large and well-equipped army in his own hands, he had no idea of letting it go to waste. A war of mere defense would have been routine, and Washington would doubtless have in that event taken over the command. A war of conquest and expansion, however, would be infinitely more glorious, and Washington was too old and tired to lead such a glamorous expedition. Hamilton must necessarily become the commander-in-chief. He envisioned himself as the Man on Horseback—the gallant general wresting from the nerveless hands of Spain all her vast dominions in the Americas. The Floridas, Louisiana, South America! What larger visions would ever beckon to a man thirsting for military fame and glory? The prospects were illimitable.

To assist him in this grandiose scheme, Hamilton relied on two men. One was Wilkinson. Whatever he may have known, or suspected, of his relations with Spain, Hamilton obviously felt that Wilkinson would not hesitate to disavow them or use them in furtherance of such a project, if it was made worth his while. The first step to make it worth his while was to advance his rank. Edward Everett Hale, writing many years later, asserted that he had personally examined in 1876 an old chest that had once belonged to Wilkinson, in which he found an immense correspondence between that worthy and Hamilton. It proposed a plan to rendezvous at Cincinnati with the newly raised army and proceed down the river to capture New Orleans. Once that exploit was accomplished, Hamilton and Wilkinson were then to co-operate with Miranda in his proposed overthrow of Spanish rule in the Caribbean and in South America. The flatboats to convey the expedition had already been built at Cincinnati. The plan was only abandoned because Miranda did not get the aid from England which he thought had been promised him. [29]

This brings us to the second man on whom Hamilton relied. This was "General" Sebastian Francisco de Miranda, a Venezuelan adventurer with an amazing career. He had fought the Moors in the Spanish army, had been imprisoned for insubordination and again for smuggling; he had served in Cuba and helped capture Pensacola; and finally, a refugee from the Spanish overlords, he came to the United States in 1784. By this time he had conceived the idea of liberating his native land from Spanish rule and, meeting Hamilton and Knox, broached to them his plans. Hamilton gave him a list of American officers who might be interested in helping him, and Knox even drafted a proposal for the employment of five thousand adventurous New Englanders in the army of liberation.[30]

To raise such a force required funds, and Miranda sailed to England to obtain financial aid. But the English government gave only vague words of encouragement, and no money. Discouraged, he went to the continent, took part in the French Revolution, became a general, was arrested for treason, was acquitted, re-arrested, and finally in 1798 came back to England. He had never forsaken his scheme for revolutionizing South America, and this time importuned not only the English, but Rufus King, the American minister in London. What he hoped for now was a joint Anglo-American expedition to support him. Even before this, when he was in Paris in 1797, he had written to Hamilton and attempted a negotiation with Monroe. On February 7, 1798, he wrote again—this time from London—explaining his mission. He had seen Rufus King, who seemed to him an excellent man, and had taken him into his confidence. Would Hamilton be so good as to write King on the subject? On the back of this letter Hamilton penned an acid comment:

Several Years ago this man was in America much heated with the project of liberating S America from the Spanish Domination. I had frequent conversation with him on the subject, & I presume expressed ideas favourable to the object and perhaps gave an opinion that it was one to which the U States would look with interest—He went then to England upon it— Hence his present letter. I shall not answer because I consider him as an intriguing adventurer.[31]

If Hamilton wrote this endorsement immediately upon receipt of the letter, and not several years later when it was the part of wisdom to dissociate himself from Miranda's schemes, then what followed is most surprising.

For on August 22nd, in direct contradiction, Hamilton was informing King that

I have received several letters from General Miranda. I have written an answer to some of them, which I send you to deliver or not, according to your estimate of what is passing in the scene where you are.... With regard to the enterprise in question, I wish it much to be undertaken, but I should be glad that the principal agency be in the United States,—they to furnish the whole land force if necessary. The command in this case would very naturally fall upon me, and I hope I shall disappoint no favorable expectation.[82]

This was sent out even before Hamilton had received another communication from Miranda, enthusiastic in tone. "It is the most grand and glorious project in all the world.... M. King will tell you all the rest." [33]

King, in fact, had fallen in wholeheartedly with Miranda's ideas. He helped him in his negotiations with the English; he assisted him in forwarding letters addressed to Adams and Pickering, and himself wrote personally to Hamilton, Pickering and McHenry. According to King, everything was in readiness for the great expedition.

He had delivered Hamilton's letters to Miranda, he told the former. "On that subject, things are here, as we could desire: there will be precisely such a co-operation as we wish the moment *we are* ready— The Secretary of State will shew you my communications on this subject ... your outline corresponds with what has been suggested by me, and approved by this Government." [34]

To Pickering he was even more specific. "As England is ready she will furnish a fleet and military stores and we should furnish the army; a map of the country that some time since I procured is in the hands of the engraver; the copies will be delivered in January." [35]

Miranda thankfully acknowledged the receipt of Hamilton's communication addressed to him under cover of King. He had already sent a messenger to America "carrying dispatches of the utmost importance to the President of the United States" and had begged Hamilton to tell the messenger "confidentially what you have learnt on that subject." [36] Now, with Hamilton's note in hand, he bubbled over: "All is approved, and we await only the *fiat* of your illustrious President to depart like lightning.... In effect, the moment appears most favorable, and the latest events seem to leave us a vast and tranquil field in which we can act to our entire satisfaction." [37]

But the moment, alas, never arrived. Miranda's messenger never got to Adams; or, if he did, Adams paid no attention to the magnificent scheme. England likewise unaccountably delayed until, as late as 1800, Miranda quit its shores in disgust. Several years later he suddenly reappeared on the scene, this time with a filibuster outfitted in American ports. Burr became involved, and Jefferson. When he finally did descend on Venezuela, after many vicissitudes, it was to meet with inglorious defeat and captivity. By that time, however, Hamilton was out of the picture.

4. NO WAR WITH FRANCE

All through the year 1799 Hamilton worked with almost superhuman energy at his heartbreaking job of raising an army. It seemed to him at times as though he alone was carrying the entire responsibility in a nation where the President was indifferent and uncooperative, the Secretary of War stupid and inefficient, and the people split hopelessly into feuding factions and sniping Francophiles whose opposing activities he considered long since to have passed the borderline of treason.

Yet he continued to throw himself into his multifarious and chiefly self-imposed duties with a devotion and a driving force that was almost miraculous. He barely ate or slept, he found little time for his family, he abandoned his law practice almost completely. His paper work was enormous. Every phase of organization came under his vigilant eye, and letters, orders, exhortations and plans flowed in a never-ceasing stream from his facile pen. More and more he grew disgusted with his loyal if inept, friend, McHenry. Again and again he rapped him sharply over the knuckles as though he were a mere schoolboy instead of his technical superior in the army. He even embodied his reproofs in public orders, specifically calling him to account in one for presuming to communicate directly with a subordinate officer instead of through him, the commanding general. McHenry ventured a discreet, if apologetic, protest at the ignominy of the reproof. "I think the head of the Department of war," he wrote plaintively, "ought not to be held up in a general order as having been ignorant of, or having been inattentive to, his duties; and because I perceive you entertain an opinion, that I have wantonly or ignorantly given orders to inferior officers within the command of their superior. This is not the case whatever may have been insinuated to you to the contrary." [38]

Hamilton's one comfort lay in congress and especially in the Senate. There a devoted group of Federalist lawmakers followed his every wish, obeyed his every command, and sought his private advice on every important measure before initiating, or voting on, the bills before them. John Adams might have been the President and titular head of the party; in fact, however, it was Hamilton who was the "king of the Feds," as a Republican pamphleteer jeeringly called him. Theodore Sedgwick, Harrison Gray Otis, General James Gunn and other leaders took their orders from him without a qualm.

The Republican party viewed his increasing activities with considerable alarm. Jefferson wondered: "Can such an army under Hamilton be disbanded? Even if a H. of Repr. can be got willing & wishing to disband them? I doubt it, & therefore rest my principal hope on their inability to raise anything but officers." [39]

There was some truth in this pious hope. The Federalist youth flocked enthusiastically to the colors—and commissions. But the plain folk—chiefly Republican—were disappointingly reluctant to enter the ranks; or, if they momentarily succumbed to the blandishments of the recruiting officer, deserted or obtained habeas corpus writs from friendly state judges. The total exclusion of Republicans from commissions reached such a point as to elicit a letter of warning from Hamilton himself.

> I regret... [he wrote McHenry] that the objection against Antifederalism has been carried so far as to exclude several of the characters proposed by us. We are very attentive to the importance of appointing friends of the Governt. to Military Stations—but we thought it well to relax the rule in favour of particular merit, in a few instances and especially in reference to the inferior grades—It does not seem adviseable to exclude all hope & to give the appointments too absolute a party feature. Military situations, on young minds particularly, are of all others calculated to insure a zeal for the service and the cause in which the Incumbents are employed. [40]

In other words, a few selected youthful Republicans might, if graciously permitted to join an essentially Federalist army, eventually be converted to the true faith.

Meanwhile the Federalists in congress had taken advantage of the general hysteria to jam through the Alien and Sedition Acts which aimed at deporting all aliens who spoke or wrote against the government and enacted drastic penalties against similar declarations by citizens "with intent to defame" or bring "into contempt or disrepute" the President and Congress of the United States. The Sedition Act in particular soon became an engine of prosecution and penalties against Republican editors and orators. Virginia and Kentucky promptly took a violent stand against the Acts. Under the guidance of Madison and Jefferson they drafted a series of resolves boldly declaring the abhorred Acts unconstitutional and setting themselves up individually as the sole judges of such unconstitutionality. There was even more than a hint that Virginia would resist any attempts to enforce the laws on her citizens or within the confines of her borders.

Hamilton took a serious view of the resolves. He advised Sedgwick to refer the matter to a special committee of the Senate and even, in advance, specified exactly what that committee should report to the Senate at large. The defiance of Virginia, he proceeded, emphasized the importance of a standing army. He reminded Sedgwick that in the Whisky Rebellion he had "trembled every moment lest a great part of the Militia should take it into their heads to return home rather than go forward." With a professional army, he would have no hesitation in proceding "to subdue a *refractory and powerful State*." In the instant case, let a force "be drawn towards Virginia for which there is an obvious pretext—& then let measures be taken to act upon the laws, & put Virginia to the Test of resistance." [41]

Before such a drastic "test" could be made, however, the whole picture suddenly changed. The long-suffering President woke up to the fact that the reins of power were not in his hands; that he was a President without a party, and almost without a government. Wherever he turned—in his cabinet, in congress—he came face to face with the invisible, yet potent, rule of the one man he resented more than any other—Alexander Hamilton. Against his will he was being pushed headlong into an unwanted war with France.

Once thus awakened, he acted with sudden and surprising speed. He nominated Murray as plenipotentiary to France, and charged him with making a final attempt to settle the outstanding differences between the two countries. Such action, from a President whom the extreme Federalists had come to despise and contemptuously disregard, exploded in the councils of the elect with the force of a bomb.

Hamilton and his friends saw at once that this move of "a vain, jealous, and half frantic mind," as Sedgwick sneeringly alluded to Adams, would put an end to all their plans for forging a strong and Federalist-controlled army. If the mission succeeded, then certainly there would be no excuse for it; even if it failed, the long interim must dampen enthusiasm and prevent recruitment and the provision of adequate supplies. Yet they could not go openly before the country with the announcement that they opposed a possible chance for securing peace. Hamilton suggested—and Sedgwick agreed to—Senatorial insistence on a commission of three instead of a single envoy. [42] Thereby they might either provoke Adams into stubborn refusal and give them the pretext to vote down the appointment, or at least enable them to have trustworthy men of their own stamp placed upon the commission. Adams yielded. A commission of three was appointed. But Pickering held them up with one pretext or another so that they did not reach France until the following year, to negotiate a mere commercial convention with a triumphant Napoleon. But by that time the war fever had died down completely.

Adams' bold stroke had deprived Hamilton of his last chance for glory. He was left with a skeleton army and no one against whom to employ it. Even defiant Virginia and Kentucky gave him no opportunity for displaying its mettle. Louisiana, Mexico and South America had slipped out of his grasp by a failure of circumstances.

A worse blow, even, was in the offing. On December 14, 1799, George Washington died at Mount Vernon. The news came to Hamilton as the last bludgeon of fate. Whatever his private thoughts might have been at various stages of his career about the character and human elements of the great commander-in-chief, their association had been too long and too intertwined for him not to mourn the passing with a sincere sense of loss. Other thoughts intruded as well. He had always been able to count on Washington to support him in moments of crisis, to be his shield and protector against his enemies. Now that shield was withdrawn. Could he find another? Would he be able to stand unsupported against a rising tide of disfavor?

These private concerns intrude themselves in his short note to Tobias Lear, Washington's private secretary and intimate. "Perhaps no man in this community has equal cause with myself to deplore the loss," he wrote truthfully. "I have been much indebted to the kindness of the General, and he was an *Aegis very essential to me.*" [43] To King, still overseas, he wondered: "Who is to be Commander-in-chief? Not the next in command [Hamilton]. The appointment will probably be deferred." [44] In this he was correct. Certainly Adams had no intention of promoting him, and the end of hostilities soon put an end to the army and Hamilton's military position alike.

CHAPTER XXVI

Twilight of the Federalists

I. PRIVATE AFFAIRS

THE CHARMING Angelica Church returned to the United States with her husband in May, 1797, after many years of London and Paris society. Her delight was inexpressible; London and Paris were all right in their way, but they did not have Alexander Hamilton. Throughout what she termed her exile she had waited for his letters, read them over and over, followed his career with eager attention. Now she was back, able to see him in the flesh, harken to his gallant speech, bathe in the refulgence that emanated from him.

What her husband, John Barker Church, thought of her obvious adoration is not specified. He was a practical man who indulged his wife in her social and aesthetic attitudes and who had returned to America because it was a good place for profitable investments. Hamilton had managed them during his long absence, and he was not quite sure they had been properly handled. He had barely returned when he was writing to Jeremiah Wadsworth about a mortgage held jointly by the two of them: "I will thank you as soon as you can to send me our Account Current, for our Friend Hamilton not being very accurate in his Accounts is not clear that he has not made some Mistakes respecting the Monies you have Paid him on my Account." [1]

He had also returned just in time to fortify Hamilton in his interview with Monroe over the malodorous Mrs. Reynolds' scandal. Strangely enough, the airing of this bit of ancient business did not affect Hamilton's relations with his wife, Eliza, or with the Churches. No temporary aberrations of conduct could change their unshakable loyalty, their love, their unbounded admiration. Church, practical business man though he was, later fought a duel with Burr over what was primarily Hamilton's affair—the Holland Company. Angelica hung on his every accent without the slightest trace of disillusionment. Eliza was—as always—Eliza, to whom her husband could do no wrong. Hamilton was deeply grateful for her steadfast loyalty in the face of the snickers of the world. His letters to her—during several absences at the home of her father—breathed affection as well as gratitude. And he included Angelica in the orbit of his love.

"I need not tell her," he wrote Eliza in the third person, "how very happy I shall be to return to her embrace and to the company of our beloved Angelica. I am very anxious about you both, you for an obvious reason, and her because Mr. Church mentioned in a letter to me, that she complained of a *sore throat*—Let me charge you and her to be well and happy, for you comprize all my felicity." [2]

Or, again: "I always feel how necessary you are to me—But when you are absent I become still more sensible of it, and look around in vain for that satisfaction which you alone can bestow. I dined with Angelica today—Margaret was with her." [3]

He even burst into rhapsodic compliment: "You are my good genius; of that kind which the ancient philosophers called a *familiar*..." and into verse, ending: "Adieu best of wives and best of mothers / Heaven ever bless you & me in you." [4]

But Hamilton's real affection for Eliza did not prevent him from seeking flirtatious pleasures wherever he could. His sister-in-law, Angelica, was the chief of these. So much so that it led to scandal that was whispered up and down the streets of New York and Philadelphia, and caused his most faithful friends considerable annoyance and anxiety.

Angelica was no soon arrived than she assumed the leadership of New York society. Her balls were the most lavish and the most brilliant ever seen. [5] Though Hamilton was deeply engrossed with his military matters he yet found time to dance attendance on Angelica to such an extent that Robert Troup commented sourly: "Though not yet in the field of Mars he maintains an unequalled reputation for *gallantry*— such at least is the opinion entertained of him by the ladies. When I have more leisure," he told Rufus King in England, "I will give you the history of the Ghost of Baron [Ciominie?] & Mrs. Church as published by our Gallant General." [6]

Troup watched the course of events with increasing acerbity. Whether the rumors were true or not, they certainly became damaging to Hamilton's reputation, and it seems that Troup himself believed in some of them. He disliked Angelica heartily, and he had nothing but contempt for her husband.

John Barker Church had gone into the business of insurance underwriting, and soon played "first fiddle" in the business. He was also a director of the Bank of New York, into which Hamilton had placed

him. Now he took an equally active interest in the Bank of the Manhattan Company, initiated by Hamilton's bitterest rival, Aaron Burr,
and an institution which Hamilton had fought with every political and
financial weapon at his command.[7]

In a very short time Troup was writing with extreme violence:
"Poor Church is fast declining in respectability. He talks too much—
is too fond of premiums—and too unwilling to pay losses." Worse still,
"Church is said to be much pushed for money—and indeed family
affairs are in a train which in my opinion will by & by cause an explosion which will spread general ruin around it—I mean the ruin of
almost the whole connexion. I consider it unfortunate that he ever
removed with his family to this country." [8] The "connexion" to which
he refers obviously is Hamilton.

By 1801 the scandal involving the Churches and Hamilton had
reached such a stage that Troup was wishing heartily the former would
go to the devil:

> Mr. Church is working hard at cards—underwriting—and examining
> bankrupts. How his constitution stands it is a matter of amazement to us
> all! He has at least four regular card clubs to attend every week & some-
> times they do not break up till the morning.... He is famous for litigation
> on his policies; and yet he is said to do a great deal of business.... There is
> as little respectability attached to him as to any man amongst us; and un-
> fortunately the whole family are enveloped in such a cloud that they enjoy
> nothing of esteem. The oldest daughter of Mr. Church is a most amiable girl
> and she is supposed to have a very cultivated mind & yet her family labor
> under such disadvantages that she has little prospect of marrying in a
> suitable manner!

This would not have mattered too much to Troup if his best friend,
Hamilton, were not involved.

> I believe I wrote you some time ago [he continued significantly] that
> I had ventured, at every risk, to communicate with a certain friend of
> ours on a certain subject. I fear notwithstanding that things continue in
> the same course. You can hardly [word illegible] how ruinous are the con-
> sequences of the general belief.[9]

Others of Hamilton's friends appeared to share the same general
belief. Harrison Gray Otis wrote cynically to his wife concerning a
certain dinner party he attended in Philadelphia:

> Tuesday Dined at Breck's, with Mrs. Church, Miss Schuyler, Genl. Ham-
> ilton, Champlin &c. &c. Mrs. C[hurch] the mirror of affectation, but as
> she affects to be extremely affable and free from ceremony, this foible is

rather amusing than offensive. Miss Schuyler [Angelica's and Eliza's younger sister] a young wild flirt from Albany, full of glee & apparently desirous of matrimony. After Dinner Mrs. C[hurch] dropped her shoe bow, Miss S— picked it up and put it in Hamilton's buttonhole saying 'there brother I have made you a Knight.' 'But of what order' (says Madam C) 'he can't be a Knight of the garter in this country.' 'True sister' replied Miss S— 'but *he would be if you would let him.*'

Otis also reported to his wife a conversation he had had with Christopher G. Champlin at the same party. Champlin was a member of congress from Rhode Island. He had misliked Hamilton's casting "some liquorish looks at his cara sposa" and complained to Otis that Hamilton "appears to him very trifling in his conversation with ladies." Fortunately Champlin's wife assured him she did not like the caster of the "liquorish looks" at all and, as Otis sardonically notes, "he was evidently *satisfied* with this intimation." [10]

2. HAMILTON WRITES A PAMPHLET

By the beginning of 1800 all eyes were turning expectantly to the presidential campaign scheduled for the end of the year. That it would be conducted with unprecedented bitterness and ferocity no one had any doubt. That it would be uncomfortably close was likewise not a matter of doubt. Washington had been elected for two terms without any trouble. Adams had had much harder sledding in 1796, and the Federalists had witnessed the advent of a Republican vice-president. Now, in 1800, they were mortally afraid. The Republicans were on the rampage and, unless Federalist efforts were herculean, they would win both high offices.

The Alien and Sedition Acts, the example of France overseas, the squabbles among the Federalists themselves, the growing concern over democratic procedures, the arrogance of incumbent office-holders, all contributed to an impending change in government.

To staunch Federalists, such a consummation was viewed with horror, as the end of the world in a welter of anarchy and bloodshed. To prevent it, they were prepared to proceed to almost any lengths.

The pivotal state was New York. Whoever won New York was most likely to win the nation. But the Republicans, under the skilful leadership of Aaron Burr, were strong in the state and had even invaded, through the agency of the Society of Tammany, the hitherto sacred bailiwicks of New York City itself. It was true that in the local election of 1799 Burr and his Tammany cohorts had been routed by the exertions of Hamilton and his merchant allies. This only came about, however, because the Federalists had been able to make a campaign issue of the Manhattan Company which, they charged, had ostensibly been incorporated to yield a pure water supply and instead had turned into a Republican financial institution. That the charge was false—inasmuch as the company *did* supply water—did not matter.[10] The cry of fraud and of double-dealing was sufficient to rout Burr, the company's sponsor.

Hamilton determined to keep the advantage gained in New York in 1799 by a repetition in the all-important elections to the legislature scheduled for the spring of 1800. It was the legislature who chose the presidential electors. To make doubly certain that these electors would not merely be Federalist in complexion, but directly accountable to him in their voting, he set up a ticket of candidates for the assembly who, if not of the first rank, would be pliable.

For such a strange procedure Hamilton had a definite reason. At no time had he really desired John Adams in the presidential seat. Even in 1796 it had been charged that he had secretly sought to displace him with Pinckney. Since then he had quarreled publicly with Adams, and the quarrel had opened a wide breach in the party. There were pro-Adams Federalists and pro-Hamilton Federalists. It sometimes seemed as though they hated each other worse than they hated the Republicans. If Hamilton certainly did not wish to see the Republicans triumphant, he was equally averse to seeing Adams continue as president. He thought that with an obedient set of electors from New York, he could at once keep the Federalists in power and substitute Charles Cotesworth Pinckney of South Carolina in place of Adams.

He reckoned, however, without Burr. That worthy outdid himself in putting into the field a list of the most prominent and influential Republicans he could find against the weak and colorless list set up by Hamilton. Tammany—composed chiefly of old Sons of Liberty, artisans, draymen and mechanics—was thoroughly organized and given sufficient property to qualify as voters.

Faced with such a powerful slate and with such tactics, Hamilton belatedly bestirred himself. The New York City polls were open from April 29th through May 1st. Hamilton rode on a white horse from polling booth to booth to harangue the voters; Burr did not harangue, but busied himself with seeing that the Tammany stalwarts came out *en masse*. When the votes were counted, the Republicans had a clean sweep in the city and enough to control the joint sessions of the legislature.

Faced with doom, Hamilton lost his head. He called on John Jay, the governor, to subvert the established procedure whereby the *legislature* selected the electors. Let the electors be chosen by a direct popular vote of the people in their several districts, he urged. The fact that such a procedure had been advocated by the Republicans *prior* to the May elections and had been successfully defeated by the Federalists, did not strike Hamilton as incongruous. To keep that "atheist in religion, and a fanatic in politics [Jefferson], from getting possession of the helm of state," overrode all scruples. "In times like these in which we live, it will not do to be over-scrupulous," he averred. *"It is easy to sacrifice the substantial interests of society by a strict adherence to ordinary rules."* With a new election by districts, it would be possible to gain sufficient electors to ensure the national victory.[11]

Jay read this extraordinary proposal and endorsed on it: "Proposing a measure for party purposes, which I think it would not become me to adopt." [12] He did not even answer Hamilton.

Hamilton quickly rallied from the blow. The more he thought of it, the more he was determined to keep Adams from the presidency, even if the result of his efforts was to put Jefferson in the seat. For Adams had suddenly come to life. After three years of a cabinet whose members secretly took orders from Hamilton and worked at cross-purposes with himself, his eyes were opened. He demanded that Pickering and McHenry resign. Wolcott was unaccountably allowed to remain.

But Hamilton had already written to Sedgwick:

For my individual part my mind is made up. I will never more be responsible for him [Adams] by my direct support, even though the consequence should be the election of *Jefferson.* If we must have an *enemy* at the head of the government, let it be one whom we can oppose, and for whom we are not responsible, who will not involve our party in the disgrace of his foolish and bad measures. Under *Adams,* as under *Jefferson,* the government will sink. The party in the hands of whose chief it shall sink will sink with it, and the advantage will be all on the side of his adversaries. [Yet] if I can be perfectly satisfied that Adams and Pinckney will be upheld in the East with entire good faith, on the ground of conformity, I will, wherever my influence may extend, pursue the same plan. If not, I will pursue Mr. Pinckney as my single object.[13]

The strategy was transparent. If the New England states, where Adams was strong, could be induced to cast their votes equally for

Adams and Pinckney, it might still be possible to elect Pinckney to the presidency. For he confidently expected that some of the southern states, like North and South Carolina, would cast their ballots for Pinckney and Jefferson, and as a result Pinckney would run ahead of Adams and Jefferson both.

And now that Adams had come out openly against him by dismissing Hamilton's men in the cabinet, he threw all qualms overboard. He determined to blast Adams in the eyes of all good Federalists so thoroughly that there would be no further question in their minds about the necessity of supporting Pinckney. To do this Hamilton would write a pamphlet. He turned to the deposed and disgruntled Pickering for ammunition. Before quitting the administration, he wrote, "allow me to suggest that you ought to take with you copies and extracts of all such documents as will enable you to explain both *Jefferson* and *Adams*. You are aware of a very curious journal of the latter when he was in Europe—a tissue of weakness and vanity." [14] To which Pickering replied mournfully: "I intended to have done precisely what you suggest, respecting Mr. Adams journal &c (very little of which I had ever read) but there was not time." [15]

While thus engaged in gathering damning materials for his pamphlet, Hamilton corresponded voluminously with "the 1st class leaders" of Federalism throughout the country. They were Sedgwick, Cabot, Pickering and Wolcott in New England; James A. Bayard, Charles Carroll, Robert Harper and McHenry of the south-middle states; and John Rutledge of the deep south. To all of them he spoke frankly. It was essential that Jefferson be defeated, but it was just as essential that Adams be replaced by Pinckney. Unfortunately, the leaders of "the 2nd class," especially in New England, were attached to Adams and might take alarm so as to throw away their votes from Pinckney. This must be avoided at all costs. Accordingly, the strategy was to agitate in New England that *both* Adams and Pinckney must be supported equally, and rely upon certain states like Delaware, North and South Carolina to drop Adams completely and thereby assure Pinckney's election. [16]

The replies ranged from whole-hearted agreement to cautious reservations. Bayard of Delaware promised that "if events should justify it, there will be no difficulty in leaving him [Adams] out of the tickets of this State." [17] Harper of Maryland reported, however, that there was a conviction "that no direct attempt can safely be made to drop or supersede Mr. Adams. It would create uncertainty division & defeat.

Let both men be held up till the Electors come to vote; & then let those who think Mr. Adams unfit to be President drop him silently." [18]

By August 3rd Hamilton was ready to go ahead with his pamphlet. Armed with facts and documents supposedly derogatory to the President's character and administration—supplied to him by the resigned cabinet members, Pickering and McHenry (as well as by Wolcott, who still remained), and taken surreptitiously from confidential government files—he set to work.

Writing at top speed and in a white heat of passion, he blazoned forth "The Public Conduct and Character of John Adams, Esq., President of the United States." It was an amazing document. Written in an election year, at a time when the opposition was united and stronger than ever before, it presented the chief officer of the nation— and the candidate of the Federalists for re-election—in a most unlovely light. There were "great and intrinsic defects in his character, which unfit him for the office of chief magistrate." The history of Mr. Adams proved conclusively that, from the very beginning, he had been guilty of "disgusting egotism, distempered jealousy, and ungovernable indiscretion." He had raged publicly and privately against Mr. Hamilton and overwhelmed him with "a torrent of gross personal abuse." He had harried his Secretary of State and his Secretary of War, and dismissed them contemptuously from office. He had taken contradictory and equally bad stands on the question of relations with France, veering from abrupt indignation to abrupt complaisance. He had sunk the tone of the public mind, sowed the seeds of discord at home and lowered the reputation of the government abroad. He had tried to prevent the appointment of Mr. Hamilton as inspector-general and "stigmatized" him "as the leader of a British faction." How different was Mr. Pinckney, whose character was unblemished and whose principles were of the highest. With all this, Hamilton ended on an inconsequent note. "Yet with this opinion of Mr. Adams, I have finally resolved not to advise the withholding from him a single vote. The body of Federalists, for want of sufficient knowledge of facts, are not convinced of the expediency of relinquishing him. It is even apparent, that a large proportion still retain the attachment which was once a common sentiment." [19]

Hamilton signed his name to the pamphlet—though men like Cabot had advised against it[20]—and rushed it to the printer. Though seemingly he had thrown all caution to the winds, he nevertheless so far heeded the cooler heads among his party friends as to cause the printing to be done with the utmost secrecy, and the pamphlet to be sent only to those whom he called "the leaders of the 1st class." What he intended to accomplish besides venting his private spleen is difficult to say, unless the lame ending be taken with tongue in cheek. If Adams, in spite of everything, *was* to be supported, then the pamphlet had better never been written. Doubtless Hamilton meant the final statement to be used only as a means of placating "the leaders of the 2nd class" to whom it might conceivably be shown, meanwhile planting in them by means of the rest of the pamphlet sufficient seeds of doubt concerning Adams that would eventually render them more pliable to the wishes of those who desired Pinckney as first choice.

In any event, Aaron Burr solved all difficulties and contradictions. Through means known only to himself, he managed to obtain a copy of the incriminating pamphlet while it was still fresh on the press. Recognizing it for the political bombshell that it was, Burr had it reprinted in the Republican newspapers even before the originals had reached the hands of the Federalist coterie for whom they were intended. The results were all that the most ardent Republican could have desired. A wave of laughter and glee spread through their ranks, while the rank and file of the Federalists read with dismay the whole public tale of recrimination and quarrel among the ruling hierarchy of their own party.

Many of the Federalist publicists rushed to reply to Hamilton's animadversions on the party candidate. Hamilton was violently attacked and for a while thought of issuing a second pamphlet.[21] From this course he was fortunately dissuaded. But he had wrecked his party and given the Republicans the great opportunity of winning.

If the Republicans had similar bickerings in their own ranks they managed to conceal them from the general eye. Jefferson was unanimously the choice for standard-bearer. For the vice-presidency there was a considerable amount of backstairs maneuvering, but eventually it was decided to put up Aaron Burr instead of the elderly George Clinton.

The candidacy of Burr alarmed and enraged Hamilton almost as much as that of Adams. Already, on August 6th, he had written to Bayard that "there seems to be too much probability that Jefferson or Burr will be President." If, by some chance, it should be Burr, he "will certainly attempt to reform the government *à la Bonaparte*. He is as unprincipled and dangerous a man as any country can boast—as true a Cataline as ever met in midnight conclave."[22]

But for the moment he was too busy concentrating all his big guns on Adams to waste any more ammunition on Burr. Hamilton had been taken aback by the storm of abuse his pamphlet on Adams had caused. Troup wrote that "General Hamilton is much disgusted with the reception his letter concerning the public character & conduct of Mr. Adams had met with—and he intimates often to me a very strong opinion that he will, in case of Jefferson's or Adams's election to the Presidency, retire from all public concerns." [23]

In fact, by now he had reached the point of openly preferring Jefferson to Adams. "General Hamilton makes no secret of his opinion that Jefferson should be preferred to Adams," wrote the voluminous Mr. Troup.[24] It was a case of *anyone* but Adams—anyone, that is, except Burr. He still hoped for Pinckney. The "leaders of the 1st class" were now heartily with him on that point. Even the hitherto cautious Cabot now conceded that he was all for Pinckney; and if Pinckney could not be elected president, "we should do as well with Jefferson for President, and Mr. Pinckney Vice-President, as with any thing that we can now expect." [25] The disgruntled ex-cabinet members, Pickering and McHenry, were naturally against Adams. But Wolcott, who had managed to remain in office, sniped at his titular chief with even greater effectiveness. "I understand," he wrote McHenry, "... that it is said by the 'Adamites,' that the President will have all the votes of New England, except in the State of Connecticut; the loss of which they are pleased to attribute to me. I feel much honoured by the supposition that my influence is sufficient to produce so great an effect.... If you will but do your part, we shall probably secure General Pinckney's election." [26]

But McHenry put his finger on the fatal flaw in all this orgy of letter-writing between the "leaders of the 1st class." With some asperity he wrote back: "Have our party shown that they possess the necessary skill and courage to deserve to be continued to govern? What have they done?... They write private letters. To whom? To each other. But they do nothing to give a proper direction to the public mind." [27] This was patently true. While Hamilton and the others were busy sending each other exhortations, the Republicans were out on the hustings getting votes. Even Pinckney, their solitary hope for continuance in power, refused to cooperate in their schemes to displace Adams with himself. When the Hamiltonian faction in the legislature of South Carolina, his own state, sent a delegation to him to obtain his consent to cast the vote of South Carolina equally for Pinckney and Jefferson, and thereby eliminate Adams, he firmly and decisively refused. It would be *Adams* and Pinckney, he declared, or none at all.[28]

With the Federalists at daggers' points and the Republicans triumphantly united, there could be only one issue to the election. Burr's tactics in New York had already insured the vote of that pivotal state for the Republicans. And now South Carolina, which had been willing to vote for Jefferson and Pinckney, in the face of the latter's refusal cast its electoral votes unanimously for Jefferson and Burr. When the smoke had cleared, it was discovered that the Republicans had won. Jefferson and Burr each received 73 electoral votes; Adams had 65 and Pinckney 64; a solitary independent voted for Jay. The reign of the Federalists was over; the second American Revolution had begun.

3. WHICH SHALL IT BE—JEFFERSON OR BURR?

For the first time since the beginning of the republic the Federalist Party was out of office, swept away by the internecine warfare which Hamilton had done so much to initiate. They were stunned, almost incredulous. They had been in power so long that they had assumed its continuance to be a law of nature. Surely the nation must crash without their wise and thoughtful guidance; certainly anarchy and worse lay ahead now that a group of wild-eyed radicals had seized the reins of government.

Once the stunning force of the blow had spent itself, however, they saw the glimmering of a ray of hope. They studied the election returns. Jefferson and Burr were tied in the number of votes. That meant that neither one was by right president. According to the Constitutional provision, if no one had a majority of all the votes, the final election was thrown into the House of Representatives. But the House—pre-election and lame-duck in character—was strongly Federalist. That meant that the Federalists, though defeated, might still decide whom they would elevate to the presidency—Jefferson or Burr. The fact that it was merely the inept provisions of the election laws that caused the tie—that the electors who had voted equally for Jefferson and Burr had certainly expected Jefferson to be president and Burr to be vice-president—did not disturb them in the slightest. Not once during all the passionate maneuvering and balloting that followed was this simple point raised. Not even Hamilton, the most passionate of all, ever thought of invoking in favor of his own stand the argument based on the manifest will of the electorate.

The rank and file of the Federalists hated Jefferson who, to them, was the embodiment of everything that was abhorrent. With Burr, on the other hand, they were to a large extent personally on good terms. He was a moderate, an aristocrat by temperament and socially acceptable, even though his political ideas were a trifle queer. After the first tumult of wild suggestions had subsided—and they included even the simple seizing of the government in the emergency—the Federalist leaders in congress decided to vote for Burr.

When Hamilton heard of the decision, he cast aside all initial plans of retirement. Rather Jefferson than Burr; rather the devil himself than Burr! Had he dragged down Adams only to elevate Burr? All the alarm that he had felt over the growing political career of Burr now came to a head. It was no longer reasonable or subject to logical argument. It was rooted in obscure emotions and a glowing hatred. There was more to it than mere rivalry in law and politics. It is difficult to explain just what drove Hamilton to such reckless vehemence when Burr was involved. He had been much more fundamentally at odds with Jefferson, yet now he was willing to accept Jefferson over Burr. The answer might possibly lie in another direction. Jefferson could never threaten Hamilton's hold over his own party; Burr definitely was a menace. There were many Federalists who wished Burr well. Jonathan Dayton had, in a previous national election, suggested that they ought to support him for the presidency. The New York Federalists, time and again, had toyed with the idea of supporting him for governor. There was the ever-present possibility that Burr might decide to cast his lot with the Federalists. In that event, with his obvious talents, he would constitute a serious threat to Hamilton's hitherto unchallenged leadership over the party leaders. Already the signs were visible. The Congressional caucus that had decided to support Burr over Jefferson had not taken the trouble to consult with Hamilton. The Adamsites were bitterly resentful. The rank and file openly blamed Hamilton for the loss of the election. His letter on Adams had stirred up a hornets' nest. "The influence . . . of this letter upon Hamilton's character is extremely unfortunate," reported Troup. "An opinion has grown out of it, which at present obtains almost universally, that his character *is radically deficient in discretion*, and therefore the federalists ask, what avail the most pre-eminent talents—the most distinguished patriotism— without the all important quality of discretion? Hence he is considered an unfit head of the party—and we are in fact without a rallying point." [29] Once Burr was president—with Federalist votes—what might not happen? Was there not a strong possibility that Burr would shift and obtain control of the party which was now "without a rallying point?"

To avoid such a dreadful possibility Hamilton bestirred himself. He wrote letters far and wide. To Wolcott he wrote: Burr's "private character is not defended by his most partial friends. He is bankrupt beyond redemption, except by the plunder of his country.... He is truly the Catiline of America." To this scorching characterization, however, he added a curious footnote: "Yet it may be well enough to throw out a lure for him, in order to tempt him to start for the plate, and then lay the foundation of dissension between the two chiefs." [30]

And, still more inconsistently, he sent another letter to Wolcott on the following day. If the present plan of the Federalists succeeds, he warned, "it will have done nothing more or less, than place in that station a man who will possess the boldness and daring necessary to give success to the Jacobin system, instead of one, who for want of that quality, will be less fitted to promote it. Let it not be imagined that Mr. Burr can be won to the federal views. It is a vain hope," he added significantly. The proper plan, rather, was to obtain definite assurances from Jefferson in exchange for their votes. Demand from him the preservation of the present fiscal system, adherence to neutrality in Europe, the preservation and gradual increase of the navy, and the continuance of our friends in office, with the single exception of the heads of departments.[31]

As the time approached for the convening of congress and the balloting, Hamilton's letters increased in volume and urgency. He told Sedgwick: "The appointment of Burr as President would disgrace our country abroad. No agreement with him could be relied upon. His private circumstances render disorder a necessary resource. His public principles offer no obstacle. His ambition aims at nothing short of permanent power and wealth in his own person. For heaven's sake, let not the federal party be responsible for the elevation of this man!" [32]

He would rather have Jefferson, he explained to Bayard, even though "his politics are tinctured with fanaticism...he is crafty and persevering in his objects;...he is not scrupulous about the means of success, nor very mindful of truth, and...he is a contemptible hypocrite." [33]

But hardly a single Federalist listened to Hamilton's jeremiads. He was a voice crying in the wilderness. Troup wrote mournfully to King: "Hamilton is profoundly chagrined with the prospect! He has taken infinite pains to defeat Burr's election, but he believes in vain...."

Hamilton at our club on Saturday last declared that his influence with the federal party was wholly gone—and that he could be no longer useful." [34]

But the strange situation was resolved without Hamilton's aid, and because of an unexpected turn of events in another quarter. The Federalists had all along expected that Burr would be willing to take the presidency at their hands, and commit himself to certain proposals which they offered him. They even sent an emissary to see him in New York, where he was busy with his duties in the New York Constitutional Convention and with the marriage of his famous daughter, Theodosia. The emissary returned with the astonishing news that Burr would not lend himself to their schemes and would make no commitments of any kind.

Congress went into session in the newly established capital of Washington on February 11, 1801, to cut the Gordian tie. The Federalists were still determined to elect Burr. The Republicans breathed revolution in that event and filled the nation with their cries of treachery. According to the Constitution, the ballots of the Representatives were cast by states, with a majority of the states—nine in number—necessary to elect. On the first ballot Jefferson had eight states and Burr six; two states had tied within their delegations and their votes were marked as blanks. On the *individual* votes of the Representatives Burr had received 55 to Jefferson's 51. The Republicans had voted solidly for Jefferson, while some Federalists had split away from the party caucus. Had the Federalists been unanimous, Burr would have been elected.

For six dreary days the House balloted and the deadlock continued. Finally Bayard, though asserting that "the means existed of electing Burr" if Burr had only cooperated, determined to break a deadlock that was threatening the very foundations of the country. He sought from Jefferson those assurances which Hamilton had declared requisite. According to him Jefferson gave the requisite assurances. Accordingly, on February 17th, certain Federalists by agreement refrained from voting, and Jefferson was elected president by ten states to four, two not voting. Aaron Burr became vice-president, and the long, bitter fight was over. [35]

CHAPTER XXVII

Achilles Retires to His Tents

---

1. REARGUARD ACTION

THE REVOLUTION had taken place and the Federalists waited for the earth to rumble, the skies to blaze with portents, and the fabric of society to dissolve and pass away. Nothing of the kind happened. Jefferson made a placating Inaugural Address. "We are all Republicans; we are all Federalists!" he announced surprisingly. In fact, as George Cabot wondered: "We are all tranquil as they say at Paris after a revolution. Mr. Jefferson's conciliatory speech is better liked by our party than his own." [1]

It was Jefferson's idea to draw the mass of the defeated Federalists away from their leaders.

The greatest good we can do our country is to heal its party divisions & make them one people [he wrote]. I do not speak of their leaders who are incurable, but of the honest and well-intentioned body of the people. ...both sects are republican, entitled to the confidence of their fellow-citizens. Not so their quondam leaders, covering under the mask of federalism hearts devoted to monarchy. The Hamiltonians, the Essex-men, the revolutionary tories &c. They have a right to tolerance, but neither to confidence nor power. [2]

Hamilton was in truth irreconcilable. He had done as much as any man to elect Jefferson, yet he was not happy with his handiwork. He was disgusted and sick at heart. He meditated on the thanklessness of the mob who went about its petty affairs with blithe unconcern and refused to see the handwriting staring on the wall. He viewed with alarm Jefferson's blandishments that stole away the hearts of the Federalists, including even those of some of his "2nd class leaders." He decided to retire from public affairs, cultivate his garden, and await the inevitable catastrophe.

Hamilton [the faithful Troup informed King] is supremely disgusted with the state of our political affairs. He has all along said and still maintains the opinion that Jefferson and his party had not talents or virtue sufficient to administer the government well; and he entertains no doubt that they will finally ruin our affairs and plunge us into serious commotions. Although he does not think this result will immediately take place, yet he predicts it is not so remote as many might imagine. He assures me that nothing short of a general convulsion will again call him into public life.[3]

But before he finally retired into the obscurity of private practice and domestic manners he made one or two attempts to save at least a modicum from the wreck. If only New York could be held to the Federalist line, he might be in a position, when the "general convulsion" actually came, to lead a bewildered nation once more out of the slough of Jacobinism into the bright air of sound Federalist doctrine.

Immediately following Jefferson's inauguration New York balloted for Governor. The aged George Clinton, perennial office-holder, was again a candidate. The disorganized Federalists nominated Van Rensselaer. Hamilton made a supreme effort to elect Van Rensselaer. As in the old days he addressed the electorate in a speech that rang with eloquence and brilliance. Everyone admitted—that is, the Federalists—that it was in his best vein. Troup thought "it was one of the chef d'ouvres of this great man. For strength of reasoning & at the same time for impressive & sublime eloquence it surpassed what in all probably [sic] has ever been delivered in this city." [4] On the other hand, the opposition press declared it was delivered "in his usual style of imprecation and abuse against the character of the venerable Mr. Clinton." [5]

It was all in vain. The magic had departed. When Hamilton went from poll to poll to argue the cause, the unfeeling populace jeered the erstwhile great man. They shouted epithets at him—thief, rascal, villain, scoundrel! Worse still, the so-called respectable citizens, the freeholders, who had always been the bulwark of the Federalist party, actually gave a majority to Clinton. "An event that had never happened before at any of our elections!" cried Troup in shocked amazement.[6] In truth, the old order was passing.

Hamilton made but one more effort to stem the tide after this. He attributed the downfall to the lack of a Federalist newspaper in New York. The triumphant Republicans had blanketed the field. Freneau's National Gazette, Cheetham's American Citizen, Duane's Aurora, the papers of Bache and Callender, spread Republican doctrine across the land. The few Federalist papers were weak and without influence. Hamilton determined to remedy the lack.

He called together a group of the faithful for consultation. Troup and Wolcott were the chief. After due consideration they picked William Coleman to edit a newspaper to present the Federalist position vigorously and forthrightly. Coleman was a lawyer of thirty-five who had come to New York from Massachusetts to practice his profession. Strangely enough, at one time he had been the law partner of Aaron Burr. He was a kindly, easy-going man with some pretensions to literature, but hardly the type of hard-hitting editor that was essential in that time of violent pamphleteering. Nevertheless, on Sedgwick's recommendation, Hamilton chose him to run the New York *Evening Post*.

Some time in May or June, 1801, the plan was formulated and funds raised from the faithful. Hamilton contributed about a thousand dollars to the venture. The first issue appeared on November 16, 1801. From then on it ran uninterruptedly to the present day, the oldest extant newspaper in the United States.

"We have set him [Coleman] up...as a printer," wrote Troup. "His first paper will make its appearance in October next....All our friends have Mr. Coleman's paper much at heart. We have not a paper in the City on the federal side that is worth reading." [7]

Whatever power or influence the *Evening Post* exercised was due not so much to Coleman's editing as to Hamilton's support and occasional intervention. Jeremiah Mason, in after years, told the story of the relations between Coleman and Hamilton. Coleman's friends, he remembered,

were often surprised by the ability of some of his editorial articles, which were supposed to be beyond his depth. Having a convenient opportunity, I asked him who wrote, or aided in writing, those articles. He frankly answered that he made no secret of it; that his paper was set up under the auspices of General Hamilton, and that he assisted him. I then asked, 'Does he write in your paper?'—'Never a word.'—'How, then does he assist?'—His answer was, 'Whenever anything occurs on which I feel the want of information I state matters to him, sometimes a note; he appoints a time when I may see him, usually a late hour in the evening. He always keeps himself minutely informed on all political matters. As soon as I see him, he begins in a deliberate manner to dictate and I to note down in shorthand; when he stops, my article is completed.' [8]

2. HAMILTON BUILDS A HOME AND LOSES A SON

For some time Hamilton had been seriously considering building a home for himself and his large family that would be more spacious and manorial than the cramped quarters of his city establishments. On

August 2, 1800, he purchased from Jacob Schieffelin an old farm of some fifteen acres in the northwestern area of Manhattan Island. The tract of land ran steeply up a hill from what is now St. Nicholas Avenue to Amsterdam Avenue, and extended northward from 141st to 145th Streets.

From the brow of the hill a noble view extended westward over the Hudson River and the Palisades of the Jersey shore. It was here that Hamilton determined to place his new home. He took a great deal of delight in planning and supervising the construction down to the last detail. Every weekend, for a year, he took the stagecoach or rode along the old Post Road that ran from lower New York to Albany to see how his manor was getting along. He named it the Grange as a final link with the respectability of his Scottish forbears on his father's side.

The building was completed some time in 1802 after financial difficulties that necessitated borrowing. Hamilton was making more money than ever in his law practice, but he lived and entertained lavishly, and there never was a time that he was not pinched for funds. The Grange was 46 by 50, square and solidly built. Its two stories were without gimcracks and the lines were simple. Verandas flanked it north and south. Hamilton planted a circle of thirteen gum-trees near the house to symbolize the original thirteen states, but there the symbolism ended. For the gum-trees withered and faded. He planted gardens, sought rare seeds and curious growths from the gardens of his friends. It was here that he expected to spend the remainder of his life, a paterfamilias, a radiater of good cheer, a solidly landed citizen of New York. Daily he rode the ten miles each way to his office in downtown New York and attended to his business.[9] He hoped to be as happy as a man could be who was convinced that the country was going to the dogs.

But Hamilton was not to find happiness—not even within the sheltering walls and hospitality of the Grange. For private tragedy struck in the midst of all the bustle and confusion of completion.

Of all his numerous offspring, he had placed his fondest hopes on his eldest son, Philip. Born on January 22, 1782, the boy was now nineteen. He had been graduated the year before from Columbia College, which his father had attended, and Hamilton expected him to enter law.

The young man was talented and possessed of much native ability, and his father was certain of "his future greatness," Troup wrote after the event. But, the old friend of the family pursued wryly, Philip "was however a sad rake & I have serious doubts whether he ever would have been an honor to his family or his country!"[10]

It may have been because of these wild tendencies in the young man that Hamilton wrote out for him a rigid set of rules immediately after his graduation from Columbia. They are Spartan in character.

RULES FOR MR. PHILIP HAMILTON

From the first of April to the first of October he is to rise not later than six o'clock; the rest of the year not later than seven. If earlier, he will deserve commendation. Ten will be his hour of going to bed throughout the year.

From the time he is dressed in the morning till nine o'clock (the time for breakfast excepted), he is to read law. At nine he goes to the office, and continues there till dinner-time. He will be occupied partly in writing and partly in reading law.

After dinner he reads law at home till five o'clock. From this time till seven he disposes of his time as he pleases. From seven to ten he reads and studies whatever he pleases.

From twelve on Saturday he is at liberty to amuse himself.

On Sunday he will attend the morning church. The rest of the day may be applied to innocent recreations.

He must not depart from any of these rules without my permission.[11]

From the beginning of time fathers have set down strict rules and children have flouted them. One Friday evening in November, 1801, Philip Hamilton and another young man named Price occupied a box at the theater. In the box next to theirs sat George I. Eacker, a lawyer and violently Republican. The young men, who probably had had a few convivial drinks before coming to the theater, began to comment audibly and satirically on a certain speech which Eacker had delivered the preceding Fourth of July, in which he had attacked the political views of Philip's father.

Eacker overheard—as it was intended he should. He promptly invited them out into the lobby to explain their animadversions. The explanations grew heated, and Eacker shouted something about a "damned rascal." Whereupon all three adjourned to a neighboring tavern for additional explanations. It was demanded of Eacker by the two young men to which one the epithet had been applied. He retorted that it had been applied to both of them. Whereupon they both challenged him.

Price seems to have challenged first. Eacker and he met Sunday morning at Powles Hook. Either three or four shots were exchanged. Not one took effect. Then the seconds intervened and stopped the duel.

The next meeting—between Eacker and Philip—took place on November 23rd. This time there was no futile exchange of shots. On the very first fire Eacker's bullet penetrated Philip's side just above the hip, ripped through and found final lodgement in his left arm. Philip fell, mortally wounded, and was carried away to die.[12]

"Never did I see a man so completely overwhelmed with grief as Hamilton has been," recounted Troup. "The scene I was present at when Mrs. Hamilton came to see her son on his deathbed (he died about a mile out of the city) and when she met her husband & son in one room beggars all description!"[13]

The blow was a terrible one for the stricken parents. Neither one ever completely got over it. Within a few weeks Hamilton was able to compose himself and attend once more to business, "but his countenance is strongly stamped with grief," Troup reported. To add to their misfortunes, the shock of Philip's death shook his eldest sister, Angelica, to such an extent that she became insane and remained so until her death at the age of seventy-three.

3. THE WAR-HORSE QUIVERS

With tragedy piled on tragedy, Hamilton nevertheless continued to peek at politics and the state of the nation. What he saw depressed him almost as much as his private misfortunes. Jefferson had been one year in office and, though the heavens unaccountably refused to fall, Hamilton momentarily anticipated some such cataclysm of nature. Under the pseudonym of Lucius Crassus he unbosomed his wrath over practically every one of Jefferson's measures and speeches. The President's fiscal policies, judiciary policies, foreign policies, naturalization policies, all came in for equal castigation.

But what aroused him more than anything else was Jefferson's open attempt to bring the more moderate of the Federalist rank and file over to his side. This was not to be borne. He tried to rouse the faithful to a sense of their high responsibilities. The faithful were strangely lackadaisical. Money was needed for political purposes. The New York Federalists evaded demands for contributions. Troup complained bitterly that besides himself and Hamilton, only a few others were willing to dig into their pockets. Hamilton took the refusals as a personal affront. At the club which the Federalists attended, the conversation grew more and more strained. Hamilton refused to talk with the recalcitrants and finally quit the club. "Hamilton & I have determined to trouble ourselves no more about the public weal; but to let things take their course," Troup wrote gloomily.[14]

Jefferson's placating course had been only too successful. The Federalist party was badly disorganized. The ordinary voters were deserting in droves and going over to the new false gods. A world without a Federalist party was unthinkable to Hamilton. Had he spent the prime years of life in futile exertions? Was this land to which he had come as an ambitious youth doomed to decay? Was the system which he had helped rear with such infinite effort already crumbling and leaving behind only shattered desolation? So it seemed to him in his forty-fifth year.

Mine is an odd destiny [he wrote despairingly to Gouverneur Morris]. Perhaps no man in the United States has sacrificed or done more for the present Constitution than myself; and contrary to all my anticipations of its fate, as you know from the very beginning, I am still laboring to prop the frail and worthless fabric. Yet I have the murmurs of its friends no less than the curses of its foes for my reward. What can I do better than withdraw from the scene? Every day proves to me more and more, that this American world was not made for me.[15]

It was not made for him because he willed it so. He was too inflexible in his demands and did not know how to change with a changing world. Stability, order, hierarchies, the rule of the rich and intelligent, power abroad and a firm hand at home, were his minimum requirements for a nation. He hated revolutions and the participation of the many in government. He did not realize that it was impossible for America with its youth, vitality, sprawlingness and lack of a traditional caste system to remain static. It had to experiment, to shift, to explore—or die. Nor did he realize that in England—the locus of his admiration—he, Hamilton, would never have had a chance to prove his powers or participate in its destinies.

But he could no more remain out of politics—in spite of repeated declarations to that effect—than a war horse can refrain from pawing the ground when it hears the sound of battle. Already he had attempted to obtain copies of certain letters among Washington's papers to be used as ammunition in his attacks on Jefferson, and had received a decided, if politely phrased, rebuke from Washington's executor and nephew, Bushrod Washington.

The opinions delivered to the President by the heads of departments were those I presume of a private council and intended for his information [the latter replied to his request]. From hence I conclude that they were not put upon the files of any of the public offices and are to be found only amongst the papers of the General. They could therefore be obtained from no other person but myself. Other measures of that administration may be again censured, discussed & condemned by one party, and vindicated by the other, whilst both must or at least may resort to the same quiver for arms to fight with. Acting with the fairness which shall always mark my conduct, I could not upon such a subject refuse to one what I have granted to the other party.[16]

But the measure pending before congress to repeal the Judiciary Act, rushed through by the Federalists in anticipation of a Republican victory, gave Hamilton his pretext to return to the arena. The Judiciary Act had provided for new federal courts and new justices, and the retiring President, John Adams, had sat up most of the night signing appointments to the newly created offices. Since these were for life, the Republicans, confronted with the specter of a solidly Federalist bench to thwart their every move, determined to abolish the new courts and thereby rid themselves of the appointees who filled them.

To Hamilton this was "a vital blow to the Constitution," and he called forthwith for a meeting of the leading Federalists to determine on a plan of opposition.[17]

The meeting never materialized, but another meeting occurred which Hamilton, as well as his party friends, seized upon gleefully as a means of stirring discord in the hitherto seemingly solid Republican ranks. This meeting took place on the anniversary of Washington's birthday at a gathering of Federalists to celebrate the occasion. Aaron Burr, Vice-President of the United States, suddenly appeared at the banquet and proposed a toast to the startled Federalists: *"The union of all honest men!"*

Ever since the preceding election, Jefferson and Burr had drifted apart. The suspicions then implanted had burgeoned; more and more the Jeffersonian Republicans were led to believe that Burr had intrigued to replace their idol. Jefferson deliberately overlooked Burr in the distribution of patronage and omitted him from his councils. The course of Burr as presiding officer of the Senate during the heated debates and votes on the Judiciary Bill added fuel to the flames of discord. The casting of his vote in favor of a Federalist move to commit the bill for further study, in order to break a Senate tie, convinced his opponents that he was throwing in his lot with the Federalists. His appearance at the birthday celebration and his public toast seemed like an open bid for Federalist support.

To Hamilton this strange move on the part of Burr was as alarming as any in all his complex career. "What meant the *apparition* and the *toast* which made part of the *after-piece* of the *birthday festival?*" he demanded of Morris. "Is it possible that some new intrigue is about to link the Federalists with a man who can never be anything else than the bane of a good cause? I dread more from this than from all the contrivances of the bloated and senseless junto of Virginia." However, he added, if Burr's situation could be rendered "absolutely hopeless with his old friends," so that he would break from them to form a third party, "then, if we think it worth the while, we can purchase him with his flying squadron." [18] In other words, Hamilton was willing enough to purchase Burr's aid provided only that he remained in a subservient position and could not dispute with him the titular leadership of the *Federalists.*

Bayard, to a somewhat similar letter, assured Hamilton that his apprehensions were groundless. In fact, Bayard himself had invited Burr to attend, knowing in advance the effect such an appearance would have on Jefferson, and he thought that Burr's toast was "extremely well calculated to answer our views." [19]

Hamilton expressed his gratification that the Federalists were using Burr merely as "a tool," and not as a partner. But it was essential, he pointed out, that the Federalists adopt a general plan of conduct. He had been busy preparing exactly such a plan, and he now offered it to Bayard for his consideration. It was an amazing plan and throws a revealing light on Hamilton's concepts of political morality.

"Nothing is more fallacious than to expect to produce any valuable or permanent results in political projects by relying merely on the reason of men," he wrote. "Men are rather reasoning than reasonable animals, for the most part governed by the impulse of passion." Heretofore it was the Republicans who had acted on the basis of this general truth, while the Federalists had "erred in relying so much on the rectitude and utility of their measures as to have neglected the cultivation of popular favor, by fair and justifiable expedients." Unless the Federalists "can contrive to take hold of, and carry along with us some strong feelings of the mind, we shall in vain calculate upon any substantial or durable results;" even though, he added significantly, there be "some deviations from what, on other occasions, we have maintained to be right."

What, then, were the most likely appeals that the Federalists could make to popular emotions? Why, first, the Christian religion (since all Republicans were obviously atheists); and second, the Constitution of the United States (since all Republicans obviously regarded that sacred document with distaste). If the Federalists would only wrap themselves in the holy garments of Christianity and the Constitution and denounce their opponents as the desecrators of these two invaluable institutions, there was a good chance to sway the general passion away from the Republicans and rally the "reasoning rather than reasonable animals" once again to the banners of Federalism.

To achieve this laudable end Hamilton proposed the formation of "The Christian Constitutional Society." Its objects would be twofold: first, to support the Christian religion; second, to support the Constitution. It would be governed by a president and council of twelve, with sub-councils in each state, and the membership would pay dues. The society would disseminate information and employ "all lawful means in *concert* to promote the election of *fit* men." [20] The implications of such a politico-religious organization are only too obvious to a present-day generation who have witnessed the rise of exactly such societies and the uses to which they have been put.

Bayard did not think much of Hamilton's pretentious scheme and said so: "An attempt at association, organized into clubs, on the part of the federalists, would revive a thousand jealousies and suspicions which now begin to slumber." [21] Thus rebuffed, Hamilton allowed his grand plan to wither, and nothing more was heard of it.

Disappointed in all his attempts to resuscitate a dying party, Hamilton devoted himself with redoubled energies to the law. Troup was happy; it was time, he thought, that his oldest friend consider his financial future. "Hamilton is closely pursuing the law," he announced, "and I have at length succeeded in making him somewhat mercenary. I have known him latterly to dun his clients for money, and in settling an account with me the other day, he reminded me that I had received a fee for him in settling a question referred to him and me jointly. These indications of regard to property give me hopes that we shall not be obliged to raise a subscription to pay his funeral." [22] Troup was to prove only half a prophet. His earlier prediction was more accurate than his later.

It seemed indeed that Hamilton was through with politics. Though certain Federalists at their sparsely attended dinners continued to toast their erstwhile peerless leader in effusive accents, he knew they were voices crying in the wilderness. The glasses clinked: "*Alexander Hamilton—As like in virtue as in suffer'd wrongs, so may he prove the Camillus of America, to drive from power by fraud obtain'd, the* modern Gauls and Vandals." [23] But Hamilton was writing at the time to King that "I as yet discover no satisfactory symptoms of a revolution of opinion in the mass." The one cloud he could discern on the Republican horizon was the schism between Jefferson and Burr. Unfortunately, the schism posed as great a threat to Federalist solidarity as to the Republicans, for too many Federalists were willing to attach themselves to the Burrite kite and "becoming a personal faction allied to him." This was not to be endured. [24]

Retired from the larger world of affairs—as he thought—Hamilton tended his own garden. He realized the rather wry humor of his situation. "A garden, you know," he told C. C. Pinckney, "is a very useful refuge of a disappointed politician." Would the southern squire send him some melon seeds for planting, and some brightly plumaged "paroquets" for his daughter? But the bucolic gentleman could not resist another question: "Amidst the triumphant reign of democracy, do you retain sufficient interest in public affairs to feel any curiosity about what is going on?" By implication, Hamilton did. For he proceeded to announce his fixed belief that "the *unity of our empire* and the best interests of our nation require that we shall annex to the United States all the territory east of the Mississippi, New Orleans included." [25]

In fact, shortly after, he urged on Jefferson such a course of action, even at the risk of war. "He might yet retrieve his character," he ended wistfully, "induce the best part of the community to look favorably upon his political career, exalt himself in the eyes of Europe, save the country, and secure a permanent fame. But for this, alas! Jefferson is not destined." [26]

When Jefferson, contrary to his pessimistic prediction, went far beyond Hamilton's proposal and purchased the vast territory of Louisiana, without a war, Hamilton was almost the only one of the Federalists who did not raise a terrific outcry.

4. THE GREATER THE TRUTH, THE GREATER THE LIBEL

On September 9, 1802, Harry Croswell, the obscure editor of an obscure newspaper called the *Wasp* and printed at Hudson, New York, republished with comments of his own an article by John Holt which had formerly appeared in the New York *Evening Post*. Croswell was immediately arrested and indicted for having uttered a libel. The libel, according to the indictment, consisted of the following comment: "Holt says the burden of the Federal Song is that Jefferson paid Cal-

lender for calling Washington a traitor, a robber, a perjurer; for calling
Adams a hoary-headed incendiary and for most grossly slandering the
private characters of men he well knew were virtuous. These charges
not a democratic Editor has yet dared or ever will dare to meet in an
open and manly discussion." Callender was the stormy petrel of the
Republican press, a foul-mouthed slanderer who himself had been under
prosecution.

Why the Republicans decided to arrest this obscure Federalist editor
for a mere reprint of this libel on Jefferson while the originator in the
far more influential *Post* was left unmolested, is something of a mystery.
Perhaps they felt that they might stir up a hornets' nest by bringing
Hamilton's own newspaper to trial, while their arrest of an unimportant
upstate editor would pass unnoticed. They were mistaken. For the
prosecution of Croswell took the center of the stage almost at once
and became the rallying point of all the party passions that had lain
dormant for more than a year of Jefferson's placid administration.

There are all the elements of ironic comedy and satiric volte-face
in the assault on Croswell's liberty. For it had been the Federalists who
had passed the notorious Sedition Act toward the end of their tenure
in office, and it had been the Republicans who had cried up the liberty
of the press and the right of editors to print what they would. Now
it was the Republicans who arrested editors for saying things about
their own leaders which they, in former days, had shouted vociferously
about Washington and Adams, and it was now the Federalists who
cried out upon such a tyrannical attack upon the freedom of the press.

The Federalists flocked to the support of the indicted editor. There
was only one lawyer in the country who could properly defend him,
they unanimously agreed. That lawyer was Hamilton. Schuyler wrote
to his daughter, Eliza, requesting her aid to induce Hamilton to take
the case. "I have had about a dozen Federalists with me," he wrote his
daughter from Albany, "Intreating me to write to Your General if
possible to attend on the 7th of next month at Claverack as Counsel to
the Federal printer there who is to be tried on an Indictment for a
libel against that Jefferson, who disgraces not only the place he fills
but produces Immorality by his pernicious example." [27] Neither time
nor the recent death of his wife had softened Schuyler's horror of
democratic principles.

But Hamilton was overwhelmed with business and could not find
the time to go to Claverack. On July 11, 1803, the great trial opened
before Chief Justice Morgan Lewis, sitting as a trial justice. Lewis

was an active Republican—or Democrat, as they were beginning to be called—and was later to become governor of New York. Croswell had to be content with less luminous counsel than Hamilton.

The prosecution set forth the contents of the newspaper with the alleged libel and proved that Croswell was the editor and printer. Then they rested. Croswell's counsel rose to request an adjournment so that they might subpoena Callender as a witness in order to prove the truth of the allegations contained in the article. Justice Lewis refused the request with the remark that even if the proposed witness, Callender, could prove the truth of the libel, he would not permit him so to testify. The old law of libel, he maintained, still was valid: the truth of an assault upon a man's character which brought him into ridicule or contempt was no defense. In this view of the law of libel—as it then stood—Lewis was on unassailable ground. But he went further. He informed the jury, in accordance with Lord Mansfield's ancient decision, that they "were judges only of the fact, and not of the truth or intent of the publication." This charge left the jury with nothing to decide except whether Croswell had printed the newspaper or not, and that fact had been conceded. Hence a verdict of conviction was the only one possible. Here Lewis was on less certain ground. For, at the famous trial of Peter Zenger in colonial days, a different precedent had been fixed. It was then declared that libel was a mixture of law and fact so intertwined that the jury had the right to decide on both.

Croswell was found guilty.

But the case was by no means ended. An impressive array of counsel appealed the conviction to the Court of Errors at Albany. This time Hamilton appeared for Croswell to argue the motion for a new trial. Associated with him were William W. Van Ness and Richard Harrison; for the prosecution appeared Caines and the Attorney-General, Ambrose Spencer.

The historic argument opened on February 13, 1804, before a bench of four justices—Chief Justice Morgan Lewis, who had tried the case in the lower court, Livingston, Thompson and Kent. Of these Lewis and Livingston were Republican in politics; Thompson and Kent, Federalist. The outcome might readily be deduced.

James Kent was a comparatively young man at this period whose principles had gradually shifted from Republicanism to Federalism. In large part his conversion was due to the example and precepts of Hamilton, whom he was to consider all through life as the greatest lawyer and greatest man he had ever known. Now, seated on the bench, attending to the motion, he took notes of the argument, interlarded with personal comments on the demeanor and effectiveness of the several pleaders. These hitherto unpublished notes present the most detailed analysis of the famous argument extant.

Van Ness opened the assault on the conviction. Caines and Spencer followed for the People. Then Harrison rose, again for Croswell; and the heavy artillery of the defense fired its final salvo with the powerful plea presented by Hamilton.[28]

Hamilton declared that "the liberty of the Press consists in publishing free Remarks with Truth & with good Motive on Men & Measures." How else, he inquired, would it be possible to preserve liberty and "bring down a tyrannical Faction"? He did not mean by this, he was quick to add, "an *unchecked Press*." He remembered only too well the calumnies heaped on the head of George Washington. The distinction between a "free" and an "unchecked" press lay in the truth of the publication and the good motives that lay behind the exposure. To decide on these essential elements of truth and good motive was the province, not of a permanent court, but of "an occasional and fluctuating" jury. Judges, he argued with much vehemence and some dislocation of his own established philosophy, were incompetent to judge in a libel action either the law or the facts, because they "might enter into the Views & Spirit of Government, or they may extend the construction & law of Libels."

He admitted readily enough that truth in itself was not sufficient; the publication must not be malicious. But all that was for a jury to decide. Kent noted with admiration the pleader's "most masterly & eloquent digression" on the indispensable necessity for permitting the truth at all times into evidence and the historical role of the jury as the bulwark of British liberties. In fact, the exigencies of the instant argument pushed Hamilton into an extreme position that would not have represented his considered judgment in a neutral discussion. In a criminal case, he insisted, while the jury "ought to pay very respectful regard to the opinions of the Court," if, in their own judgment, "the law is different from what the Court advances, they are *bound* by their oaths & their duty to their Creator & themselves, to pronounce according to their own Convictions."

The court adjourned at this point and resumed its session the following day. Hamilton still had the floor. The courtroom was crowded with eager spectators, Kent noted, and Hamilton "was sublimely eloquent." The advocate maintained that the right of a jury to decide mixed questions of law and fact in criminal cases was still a moot point, and that he would examine the whole matter afresh. He examined it, however, not from former decisions particularly, but from the point of view of public welfare. Our worst danger, he cried, came not from "a few provisional armies" (a manifest dig at the opposition for their recent stand), "but from *dependent* Judges—from *selected* Juries, from *stifling* the Press & the voice of leaders & Patriots. We ought to *resist— resist—resist* til we hurl the demagogues & Tyrants from their imagined Thrones."

From the defense Hamilton had shifted to the attack—an attack on Jefferson himself. "It ought to be distinctly known," he thundered, "whether Mr. Jefferson be guilty or not of so foul an act as the one charged." This permitted him to indulge in an impassioned eulogy of the dead Washington that, Kent thought, was "never surpassed—never equalled." In fact, Kent was so bemused by the eloquence of Mr. Hamilton (agreeing as it did with his own political convictions) that he added a note: "This argument & speech of General H. was a master Piece of pathetic, impassioned & sublime eloquence. It was probably *never surpassed* & made the deepest Impression. I never heard him so great."

All of Hamilton's eloquence, however, did not prevent the court from dividing on rigid political lines. Lewis and Livingston voted against the motion for a new trial; Thompson and Kent for. With an equal division the motion failed, and the conviction was upheld.

Kent claims that Livingston had actually at first declared in favor of a new trial, but that, before the decision came to be rendered, he changed his position and agreed with the written opinion of the Chief Justice. Kent hints that pressure was brought to bear on the Republican justice. In fact, he failed to appear at the final day, writing in that he was ill. Kent wanted to read his own opinion, but was persuaded not to do so by Lewis. Livingston never even read Kent's opinion, though it was offered to him. In a huff, Kent set down in full in his own manuscript notes the opinion that he had not made a public part of the record.[29]

So ended the great trial. Hamilton had been defeated, but he had established himself, if he had not already done so, as one of the great lawyers of his generation. Kent never forgot the effort. Much later, in an address before the Law Association of New York, he was to say: "I have always regarded Mr. Hamilton's argument, near the close of his life, in the celebrated Croswell case, as the greatest forensic effort he ever made."

The effect was immediate. A Bill was introduced into the legislature to permit the truth of an alleged libel to constitute a good defense, but it was not until the new Constitution of 1821 went into effect that the principle became a part of the law of the state.

CHAPTER XXVIII

Death and Transfiguration

I. HAMILTON DENOUNCES BURR

HAMILTON HAD BUT little time left him to enjoy the acclaim that greeted his unavailing efforts in behalf of Croswell. The tragedy that had been dogging his unwitting footsteps for many years now accelerated its pursuit. Within a short period it caught up with him. Fate appeared in the small, erect person of Aaron Burr. Their paths, so long crossing and crisscrossing, now rapidly converged to the final desperate junction.

Jefferson had never forgiven his running mate and Vice-President for the scare he had had during those days when the House had balloted interminably over the presidency. During the years of tenure in office the distrust had deepened. Burr was an ever-present threat to Jefferson's plans for the succession when it came time for him to retire. By assiduous politics the President undermined the position of his Vice-President to such an extent that, in the coming election, Burr knew he had no chance to gain the Democratic nomination again. If he wished to remain in public life, he must look elsewhere. He looked toward New York.

In the spring of 1804 New York was going to vote for a new governor. But the Clintons and the Livingstons controlled securely the Democratic party machinery in the state, and they were Burr's implacable enemies. They nominated Chancellor Lansing, who promptly declined when he found out that the rank and file, especially in New York City, where Tammany held the reins, were all for Burr. In alarm, the party chiefs hastily nominated Morgan Lewis, who had convicted Croswell, and he accepted.

Baffled on the regular nomination, Burr looked toward a possible joinder of independent Democrats and Federalists. The latter were hopelessly disorganized, without a candidate of their own who could be induced to accept certain defeat, and almost without leaders. Advances were made on either side. The majority of Federalists were definitely interested. Many of them liked Burr personally, and the fact that Jefferson and the Clintons hated him only added to their willingness to adopt him as their candidate.

But Hamilton roused himself from the slough of political despond to do battle with the mortal enemy. Time and again he had had to fight the sentiment for Burr within the Federalist ranks. The time had come again. He saw clearly that the party members had become restive under his own leadership, which had brought them nothing but continued defeat. Should Burr obtain the governorship with Federalist assistance and in return grant political plums to the avid "leaders of the second class," then nothing could prevent him from taking over the leadership of the revived party on a national scale. Whatever hopes Hamilton might have for some day leading the Federalists to victory again—on his own principles—must forever be doomed to disappointment.

As though to point up sharply the dilemma, Hamilton heard of the secret schemes of a group of extreme New England Federalists—Pickering, Plumer, Tracy, Hillhouse and Griswold—who were plotting to withdraw New England from the union. To achieve any measure of success, however, New York must join the conspiracy and the secession. They sounded out Burr. Burr evaded them with polite phrases, but they thought they saw in his evasions a possible later acquiescence. Accordingly they determined to support him in his fight for the governorship of New York.

When Hamilton received word of what was going on behind his back he was both enraged and alarmed. Were the leaders on whom he had formerly depended deserting him for Burr? Were they indeed hatching this insane scheme of disunion, of which he disapproved with every fiber of his being? [1]

Hamilton bestirred himself to an immense activity. At all costs Burr must be kept from the governorship. Just after Lansing had been nominated by the Democrats and before he had declined, the Federalists held a meeting in Albany to decide upon their own course of action. Hamilton attended.

Many of those present wished to support Burr. Hamilton employed all his eloquence against any such position. He would much rather, he asserted, permit Lansing to become governor unopposed. Burr, he insisted, was fundamentally a Democrat and would never espouse Federalist views just because they had helped him into office. The effect of his elevation would be "to reunite under a more adroit, able, and daring chief, the now scattered fragments of the Democratic party, and to reinforce it by a strong detachment from the Federalists." In concluding, Hamilton repeated all his old personal attacks on Burr as "a man of irregular and unsatiable ambition." [2]

The conference, held at Lewis's City Tavern, was supposed to be secret. But Burr's unexampled espionage system worked as usual. Two of his agents secreted themselves in a bedroom adjoining the dining chamber, and the *Morning Chronicle* flaunted a complete report of the proceedings within a few days.

In spite of Hamilton's vehemence, the great body of Federalists determined to vote for Burr, and Gaylord Griswold, Federalist congressman from Herkimer County, wrote to his constituents urging them to support Burr and charging Hamilton's opposition to a "personal resentment." [3]

Hamilton was despondent. He had outlived his usefulness. The men who had once obediently followed his slightest wish now paid no attention to his exhortations and prophecies of doom. There seemed little chance of avoiding Burr's election even though, as he told R. G. Harper, "it is an axiom with me that he will be the most dangerous chief that Jacobinism can have; and, in relation to the present question, a full persuasion, that he will reunite under him the popular party and give it new force for personal purposes—that a dismemberment of the Union is likely to be one of the first fruits of his elevation, and the overthrow of good principles, in our only sound quarter, the North, a result not very remote. I had rather see Lansing Governor and the party broken to pieces," he ended vehemently. [4]

When Lansing declined the nomination, Hamilton wondered whether the Federalists ought not to run their own candidate in a three-cornered race as a means of defeating Burr and electing Lewis, or even to elect their own man. He asked King if he would not accept the thankless task. [5]

King refused to offer himself up as a party sacrifice, while other Federalists, the "lower Classes of Life particularly," had made up their minds "to give [Burr] active support." In fact, one leading Federalist declared that "from what I can learn of the sentiments of the People here I do really believe that tho' the Leaders of our Party determine upon Neutrality yet that at least two thirds of the Federalists in this City will vote for Burr." [6]

The final blow for Hamilton was the defection of his own newspaper, the New York *Evening Post*. Though its editor, Coleman, declared editorially on March 23rd that Hamilton "will *take no part* in support of either of the present candidates [Lewis and Burr]," he himself showed decided leanings toward Burr and, toward the end of the campaign, practically advocated his election.

Faced with defection and what he considered betrayal in every quarter, Hamilton resorted to his ancient violent language to check the rising tide. Wherever he went, wherever he met with groups of Federalists, he denounced Burr without restraint. Everything that he had written in private letters during preceding elections about Burr's personal character and criminal ambitions he now said again, with embellishments, in private conversation.

At a cozy little dinner at Judge John Tayler's home in Albany, Hamilton, believing himself among friends, let himself go. He held forth on his favorite, and detested, subject of Aaron Burr. Exactly what he said in his remarks has never been told. But Dr. Charles D. Cooper, son-in-law to the host, unfortunately considered that a dissemination of Hamilton's opinion might make good political capital. He wrote two letters. One, dated April 12, 1804, was addressed to Andrew Brown, of Berne: "Gen. Hamilton . . . has come out decidedly against Burr; indeed when he was here he spoke of him as a dangerous man and ought not to be trusted." [7]

This was not so bad, but Cooper also wrote to Schuyler on April 23rd more specifically: "General Hamilton and Judge Kent have declared, in substance, that they looked upon Mr. Burr as a dangerous man, and one who ought not to be trusted with the reins of government. . . . I could detail to you a still more despicable opinion which General Hamilton had expressed of Mr. Burr." [8]

Somehow these two letters found their way into the public columns of the Albany *Register*, from where they went the rounds of other newspapers and pamphlets. The fat was in the fire.

Without question Burr had known for many years of Hamilton's "despicable opinion" of himself. His methods for gathering news were too efficient for him to have been in the dark. But always the accusations and epithets had been privately expressed and therefore not available for action. This was the first time that Hamilton's opinions had reached the public domain, where all might read—and wait expectantly for the outcome. If Burr accepted this public description of himself as "despicable," then, in the eyes of all who held themselves men of honor—and this included the veteran officers of the Revolution— he would be branded as a coward, too supine to act in his own behalf.

The tendency has been ever since to brand Burr's next steps and their eventual outcome as the result of a mere thirst for vengeance, the appeal to a barbarous code as a mere pretext for private hate. This represents the fallacy of viewing other times through our eyes. In those days duels were frequent and were to remain a part of a code for many years thereafter. Hamilton should have known that his widespread allegations concerning Burr must some day lead exactly where they did. He himself, on several occasions, had offered challenge for equal or lesser provocation.

2. EXCHANGE OF LETTERS

Burr waited until after the election. This was a crushing defeat for him. Lewis, aided by the regular Democrats and a minority of Federalists, received 30,829 votes; Burr received 22,139. Burr was finished politically.

On June 18th he sat in his private study and wrote a letter. It was short, concise, laconic.

SIR,

I send for your perusal a letter signed Charles D. Cooper, which, though apparently published some time ago, has but very recently come to my knowledge. Mr. Van Ness, who does me the favour to deliver this, will point out to you that clause of the letter to which I particularly request your attention. You must perceive, sir, the necessity of a prompt and unqualified acknowledgment or denial of the use of any expressions which would warrant the assertions of Mr. Cooper. I have the honour to be

Your obedient servant,

A. BURR [9]

Hamilton stared at the letter and the newspaper clippings whose contents he already knew by heart. For a moment he was silent, while Van Ness, Burr's political lieutenant, waited with formal politeness. Then Hamilton spoke. The matter required careful consideration, he said, and a reply would be sent shortly. Van Ness bowed and departed, leaving Hamilton to his reflections.

These were not pleasant. Cooper's unfortunate letters and Burr's cold remarks left him with few alternatives. If he acknowledged the use of expressions which Cooper had called "despicable," Burr would promptly challenge. If he denied them, then Cooper was a liar (which everyone knew he was not), and Hamilton would be accused of disavowing his follower through personal cowardice. This was not to be borne. Such a course would once and for all destroy whatever influence Hamilton might still possess and those hopes which he entertained for eventually leading a rejuvenated party back to power. There was a third alternative. He might evade a categoric affirmation or denial and trust to Burr to press no further.

Two days later he sent his reply. It was long-winded, rambling—and evasive. "I have maturely reflected on the subject of your letter of the 18th inst.," he began, "and the more I have reflected the more I have become convinced that I could not, without manifest impropriety, make the avowal or disavowal which you seem to think necessary." He argued over the offending phrase and tried to make it appear that it was not what it was. He spoke of the "animadversions of political opponents upon each other." He sought refuge in the fact that no specific offending phrase of his own had been mentioned. "I stand ready," he said, "to avow or disavow promptly and explicitly any precise or definite opinion which I may be charged with having declared of any gentleman...I trust, on more reflection, you will see the matter in the same light with me. If not, I can only regret the circumstance, and must abide the consequence."

This reply was the worst that could possibly have been made. Hamilton might have avoided a duel merely by denying he had used any expression that was "despicable." By so doing he would have replied exactly to Burr's proffered alternatives and forced the immediate closure of the controversy. The term "despicable" is a vague one and susceptible of many interpretations. By refusing to do so and ending with a demand for a specific offending phrase which Burr had it not in his power to deliver, he only enraged his antagonist. By using the closing sentence: "if not, I can only regret the circumstance, and must abide the consequence," he cut off all future avenues of retreat. It expressed, explicitly, a willingness to accept a challenge.

Burr's answer tore Hamilton's arguments to shreds. "Political opposition," he pointed out, "can never absolve gentlemen from the necessity of a rigid adherence to the laws of honour and the rules of decorum. I neither claim such privilege nor indulge it in others." As for Hamilton's labored attempts to parse and construe the word "despicable," Burr retorted that "the common sense of mankind affixed to the epithet adopted by Doctor Cooper the idea of dishonour." He brushed aside the syntax and grammar. "Your letter has furnished me with new reasons for requiring a definite reply," he concluded.

The controversy had now shifted to another level. What might have satisfied before would no longer help. Hamilton must now disavow "uttering expressions or opinions derogatory to my honour." This Hamilton obviously could not do without stultifying himself. He knew as well as Burr that he had used only too often exactly such "expressions or opinions."

Accordingly, he informed the waiting Van Ness that the note he had just delivered "contained several offensive expressions, and seemed to close the door to all further reply." Van Ness went away to report and, as Hamilton was well aware, to come next time with a formal challenge.

Having himself closed the door, so to speak, in Burr's face, Hamilton bethought himself for the first time of obtaining advice and a possible second in the impending duel. He called on his friend, Nathaniel Pendleton. He would have done well to have taken this step earlier, before he had given his first reply. It was now too late. Nor was Pendleton the right man for such a delicate mission.

Whether with his advice or not, Hamilton wrote another letter, dated June 22nd, which he turned over to Pendleton for delivery to Van Ness in the event he came with a challenge. Pendleton held the letter until the 25th, in the meantime conducting with Van Ness a series of personal conversations which were absorbed with the subtleties and niceties of the situation, instead of a forthright attempt to come to an understanding that would avoid the last step.

These failed. On June 25th, when Van Ness came to deliver his principal's challenge, Pendleton, acting for Hamilton, forestalled him by first handing him the letter dated the 22nd. It still persisted in dealing with subtleties. "If by a 'definite reply' you mean the direct avowal or disavowal required in your first letter, I have no other answer to give than that which had already been given. If you mean any thing different, admitting of greater latitude, it is requisite that you should explain."

But Burr was no longer in any mood for quibbles. He insisted on a general disavowal as against his first demand for a particular denial.

Thus confronted, Hamilton did what he should have done in the first instance—he permitted Pendleton to read a prepared statement that

in answer to a letter properly adapted...he would be able to answer consistently with his honour and the truth, in substance, that the conversation to which Doctor Cooper alluded turned wholly on political topics, and did not attribute to Colonel Burr any instance of dishonourable conduct, nor relate to his private character; and in relation to any other language or conversation of General Hamilton, which Burr will specify, a prompt and frank avowal or denial will be given.

It was too little and too late. Coming earlier it would have saved the situation; now it gave Burr the chance to retort that he could not be expected to give chapter and verse concerning derogatory remarks of which Hamilton had far better knowledge than he. Pendleton refused in Hamilton's name to go any further and on June 27th, with all due formality, accepted the formal challenge which Van Ness tendered him.

3. PREPARATIONS

Burr desired an immediate meeting, but Hamilton requested a delay until after the close of the Circuit Court where he had several cases pending, and for a decent interval in which to arrange his private affairs properly. After some negotiation the date of the duel was set for July 11th on the little height of Weehawken across the Hudson River.

Not a word leaked out about the proposed meeting with pistols of two of the leading figures of the country. Burr, it seems, told no one; Hamilton may have told his close friend, Rufus King, who tried his best to get him to refuse to go through with it, and failed.

On the 4th of July the Society of the Cincinnati held its annual celebration. Hamilton, who was its president, did not fail to attend. Neither did Burr. It was a strange meeting, and the assembled officers of the Revolution did not fail to observe that there was a singularity about the manner of their two famous members. Hamilton was gleeful even beyond his wont. He drank and sang with gusto, and sprang upon the festive board to troll out the stanzas of an old military song. There was something almost feverish about his behavior. Burr, on the other hand, who was ordinarily urbane, smiling and politely witty, surveyed the festive proceedings in impenetrable silence and with a gloomy, determined face. But only a few had the slightest suspicion of the cause.[10]

On July 10th, the day before the duel, a client met Hamilton on the street and stopped him to remind him of a case on which he had requested an opinion from him some time ago. Hamilton apologized for his neglect and promised that if the client would come to his office the following day at 10 A. M., he would discuss the entire matter with him. When the client appeared, as per appointment, he heard the tragic news that Hamilton had, that morning, received his mortal wound.[11]

During the intervening period Hamilton prepared himself against all eventualities. He tried to make order of his tangled financial affairs and leave his legal business in as tidy a shape as possible. That he was troubled about the duel was but natural. He had a wife and children; his life-work, he felt, was not ended. There was so much yet to do for this nation which he had helped bring into being and which had, temporarily, he hoped, cast him ungratefully aside. In his own party there were hotheads who wished to divide what he had pulled together. The night before the duel he wrote to Sedgwick: "I will here express but one sentiment, which is, that dismemberment of our empire will be a clear sacrifice of great positive advantages without any counter-balancing good, administering no relief to our real disease, which is *democracy*, the poison of which, by a subdivision, will only be the more concentrated in each part, and consequently the more virulent." [12]

He also wrote other letters in a more personal vein. Two of these he sealed and left for his wife, in case....

The first read:

This letter, my dear Eliza, will not be delivered to you, unless I shall first have terminated my earthly career, to begin, as I humbly hope, from redeeming grace and divine mercy, a happy immortality. If it had been possible for me to have avoided the interview, my love for you and my precious children would have been alone a decisive motive. But it was not possible, without sacrifices which would have rendered me unworthy of your esteem. I need not tell you of the pangs I feel from the idea of quitting you, and exposing you to the anguish I know you would feel. Nor could I dwell on the topic, lest it should unman me. The consolations of religion, my beloved, can alone support you; and these you have a right to enjoy. Fly to the bosom of your God, and be comforted. With my last idea I shall cherish the sweet hope of meeting you in a better world. Adieu, best of wives—best of women. Embrace all my darling children for me.[12a]

The second was an afterthought. He requested Eliza to aid his aged aunt, Mrs. Mitchell, and added that he had come to a definite conclusion "The scruples of a Christian have determined me to expose my own life to any extent, rather than subject myself to the guilt of taking the life of another." [13]

He had come to this final determination only after much wrestlings with his soul during the strange, sad days before the duel. He had informed his two sole confidants, Pendleton and King, of his resolve not to return Burr's first shot. They had tried to argue him out of his resolution, and failed.[14]

Hamilton had decided on this particular course of action not, perhaps, because of Christian principles—inasmuch as, at various stages of his career, he had evidenced no such scruples over dueling—but because, in the recesses of his conscience, he was troubled over the possibility that he might have been in the wrong. Only a short time before the duel he had discussed the general topic of political disputation with Judge Peters of Pennsylvania and had remarked that in New York, unlike Pennsylvania, "they never carried party matters so far as to let it interfere with their social parties, and mentioned himself and Colonel Burr, who always behaved with courtesy to each other." [15]

With all this in retrospect, Hamilton sat down to write his final apologia—his attempt to justify himself to the world and to himself. He was opposed to dueling on religious and moral grounds, he wrote. He was conscious of no personal, as opposed to political, ill will to Burr. He admitted, however, that

it is not to be denied that my animadversions on the political principles, character, and views of Colonel Burr have been extremely severe; and, on different occasions, I, in common with many others, have made very unfavorable criticisms on particular instances of the private conduct of this gentleman. [Because of this, and] because it is possible that I may have injured Colonel Burr, however convinced myself that my opinions and declarations have been well founded, as from my general principles and temper in relation to similar affairs, I have resolved . . . to reserve and throw away my first fire, and I have thoughts even of reserving my second fire, and thus giving a double opportunity to Colonel Burr to pause and reflect.

Why then, thinking as he did, had not Hamilton declined the challenge? He anticipated the query. There was a "peculiar necessity not to decline the call," he added. "The ability to be in future useful, whether in resisting mischief or effecting good, in those crises of our public affairs which seem likely to happen, would probably be inseparable from a conformity to the prejudice in this particular." [16]

In his anxiety not to lose caste with his fellows, Hamilton was to sacrifice his life in a duel for which he had not the slightest predilection.

4. DUEL

Hamilton, Pendleton and Dr. David Hosack as attending physician arrived on the little plateau close to seven in the morning. They found Burr and Van Ness already on the ground with their coats off and engaged in clearing away obstructing bushes and overhanging branches that might interfere with the deadly business in hand. The two parties exchanged the formal greetings required by such occasions. Then the seconds conferred, while the principals remained indifferently apart. Pistols were loaded, inspected and approved; the rules of the ghastly game were once more rehearsed. The two men were to take their respective positions and await the word. Then they were to fire as they wished.

The moment came. Hamilton and Burr went to the marked positions, turned and faced each other. The sun burned through the morning mist. There was a silence; then: "Fire!" called Pendleton in a loud voice. Both men raised their pistols. Two shots rang out. Burr remained erect; Hamilton convulsively raised on his toes, turned a little to the left and pitched forward on his face.

Pendleton ran to his chief, shouting for Dr. Hosack to help. By the time Hosack arived, Pendleton had lifted the wounded man to a half-sitting position in his arms. Hamilton was still conscious. "This is a mortal wound, Doctor!" he said feebly. Then he slumped in a faint. A hasty examination disclosed that the ball had entered his right side and fractured a rib. Later on it was discovered that the bullet had passed through the liver and diaphragm and lodged in the lumbar vertebra.

It was no wound for field surgery, and Dr. Hosack commanded that the unconscious man be conveyed with all speed back to New York. Meanwhile Burr had impulsively moved toward Hamilton with a gesture of regret, but Van Ness urged him to depart at once before the others arrived, in accordance with the conventions surrounding duels.

Hosack, Pendleton and the boatman picked the lifeless, pulseless body up and placed it tenderly in the boat. Then the boatman took the oars and rowed hard across the river. Halfway across Hamilton revived. His first faint words were: "My vision is indistinct." Then: "Pendleton knows...that I did not intend to fire at him."

This phrasing, and the fact that his pistol *had* gone off, stirred up a violent controversy that has not yet subsided. Pendleton claimed that Hamilton had not fired—that it was only after he had been hit that the involuntary flexure of the finger exploded the pistol. As evidence he pointed later to the clipped leaves of the tree above through which the ball had gone in erratic flight. On the other hand, Van Ness was equally positive that Hamilton had taken aim and actually fired first and missed before Burr returned the fire.[17]

Waiting on the New York shore, intensely agitated, was William

Bayard, whom King had notified. They took the dying man to Bayard's
house on Jane Street and sent a messenger forthwith to Eliza at the
Grange with the tragic news.

Poor Eliza, who had not suspected a thing, arrived frantic with grief.
So did the children. Angelica Church came post-haste to sit by the bed
of her dearly beloved, adored *petit Fripon*. The tidings spread through
the town, and friends hastened to see their dying leader. Gouverneur
Morris came to find Hamilton speechless, Eliza hysterical, the children
sobbing, friends deeply affected, and the city in a state of agitation.[18]

Dr. Hosack gave sedatives. Dr. Post was called in, as well as surgeons
from a French frigate then in harbor. Nothing helped. The ball could
not be removed, and Hamilton's sufferings were intolerable in spite of
the sedatives. For thirty-one hours he lingered in extreme agony. At
two o'clock the next afternoon, he died.

5. TRANSFIGURATION

A few days before the fatal duel, Alexander Hamilton was merely a
well-known lawyer, the leader of a moribund party whose members
by a large majority considered him a useless encumbrance rather than
an asset. The day following, he was translated into herohood and
apotheosized. There was some partisan purpose in the exalting, but
there was also a sudden knowledge that a great man had passed away.

The city went into mourning, and the nation. The newspapers out-
rivaled each other in expressions of sorrow. The clergy preached long
sermons, with the duel as their text. Mass meetings were held, in New
York, in Philadelphia, in Boston, in Albany. Church bells tolled. Aaron
Burr, indicted for murder both in New Jersey and New York, was
compelled to flee southward for his life. Execrations followed him, and
long persecution. Political advantage was sought by his enemies. Only
here and there—except in the south and west, where he was welcomed—
was a voice raised to defend him. Judge Peters, though a friend of
Hamilton, insisted that "as an old military man Colonel Burr could not
have acted otherwise than he did. I never knew Colonel Burr speak
ill of any man, and he had a right to expect a different treatment from
what he experienced."[19]

In New York City the merchants and citizens gathered at the Tontine Coffee House to mourn their loss. On the date of the funeral they
closed all stores and marched in vast procession to the muffled beat of

drums. The ships in the harbor half-masted their flags. The City Council attended in a body, and the members of the bar, party lines forgotten, decreed mourning for a period of six weeks. The mayor, members of congress, foreign ministers, the students of Columbia, the Cincinnati, Tammany and all the citizenry marched in line.

> The funeral took place on July 14, 1804, and the long procession moved slowly down to Trinity Church where Bishop Moore read the services. Ships' guns in the harbor saluted. Gouverneur Morris gave the funeral oration.

Morris had not welcomed the task. He admired Hamilton—with reservations. He discussed his proposed oration with Harrison the day before. What ought he to put in, what avoid? His illegitimate birth? His indiscretions and vanity? His opposition to republican in favor of monarchical government? His system of finances which was "in one respect radically wrong?" Further, "I cannot thoroughly excuse him without criminating Colonel Burr, which would be wrong, and might lead to events which every good citizen must deprecate.... Colonel Burr ought to be considered in the same light with any other man who had killed another in a duel." His conjugal fidelity? Well.... At least, Morris finally brightened, something could be said "to excite public pity for his family, which he has left in indigent circumstances." [20]

It can be seen that Gouverneur Morris was hardly the proper man to be chosen to deliver the funeral oration. However, he managed to go through with it, though his voice did not carry well in the open air, and barely a tenth part of the vast concourse heard what he said. "How easy would it have been," he meditated after the event, "to make them, for a moment, absolutely mad!" But it had been his duty, he told himself virtuously, to allay mob passions, not to arouse them.

For days the family was too stunned to think of anything but their grief. Eliza lived to a ripe age, but she never forgot and never ceased mourning the husband she had lost. Hamilton's friends, however, soon rallied to consider the state of affairs in which his untimely death had left his wife and children. The more they considered, the more they delved into his finances, the more they realized they had a problem that must be solved. Hamilton himself, when he wrote his will, had realized what might happen. After all debts were paid, the remainder of his estate was to go to Eliza. But he doubted that a forced sale of his possessions would bring sufficient even to pay his debts. "Though conscious that I have too far sacrificed the interests of my family to public avocations," he wrote, and therefore "have the less claim to burthen my children," yet, if nothing remained, he consigned their mother's care to them.[21]

Hamilton died heavily in debt. The building and maintenance of the Grange had proved costly; he had lost considerable sums in speculation on wilderness lands, and he had mortgaged himself and his future earnings to the hilt. Gouverneur Morris, looking into his affairs, found that he owed fifty to sixty thousand dollars. Against this there was a property which might, in time, bring in seventy to eighty thousand dollars. If brought to the hammer immediately, however, it would not fetch more than forty, less than enough to meet the debts. And there was a widow and seven young children to provide for.[22]

Accordingly, Hamilton's friends held a meeting. It was determined to raise a subscription to provide for the orphaned family, and, if possible, to save the Grange from going on the auction block by purchasing it from the estate. Morris, Wolcott, King, Egbert Benson and Charles Wilkes associated themselves as trustees. The scheme was not wholly eleemosynary; the donations were to be reimbursed from the eventual sale of a huge tract of land belonging to Hamilton, called the Scriba's Patent, in Oswego County.

By August 14th the sum of $16,100 had been subscribed, though Wolcott wrote mournfully to King that "this is certain, that it require considerable management to render Genl Hamilton's Estate solvent." [23] Eventually, $39,700 was raised. The New York Federalists rallied strongly to the cause of their departed leader. The Boston Federalists, however, proved a sad disappointment. This may be attributed to two causes: first, the lingering resentment over the feud with John Adams; second, the feeling on the part of Messrs. Pickering *et al.* that Hamilton had obstructed their dearest schemes of disunion.

The Grange was finally purchased and presented to the family. By 1808 the transaction was completed, and King estimated that about $20,000 would be left over for the benefit of the family.

Eliza's deep religious piety saved her from going entirely to pieces. She roused herself to face the world and its problems. The foremost was the question of finances and the careers of her children. She asked Hamilton's old friends to find her young son and his namesake, Alexander, a position in some "counting house." Two months after the funeral, she wrote from Albany to General Clarkson:

He is young and ... your goodness I trust will Excuse the request I make that you will have an Eye upon him, and could you permit him some times to accompany you, in your walks, that he might hear from you those just sentiments of Religion as well as those on Other subjects that have always marked your Character, for to the Grevious Affliction I am under will be aded the trembling Mothers Anxiety for her fatherless Child lest he should fall in to Error.[25]

General Clarkson replied that he would be happy to serve them. He suggested that young Alexander accept a position with Higginson in Boston, who had an opening for him.[26] Eliza declined the tempting offer. Boston, she feared, knew only the morals of the counting house. What would happen to her son's moral and religious character there? "The present day has Evils of every sort assailing a young mind, that has just steped from the studys of a college class. the advantages of having a home, ware, he will Meet, with tenderness, to make him domestick, books that will be suited to him and see a tender virtuous fathers Bust that will press on his mind, that Goodness, and Religion must be his chief support." [27]

Poor Eliza! She needed all the support of "Goodness and Religion" herself in the long years to come. Alexander Hamilton was dead, and a nation mourned his passing. In after years, it was able to assess more truly the incalculable services he had rendered it in its inception. It was also able to note the imperfections, the human frailties, of the departed hero. Not so Elizabeth Hamilton. In her heart he remained forever enshrined as the perfect knight, the shining soldier who had swept her off her feet in the camp at Morristown and who had miraculously chosen her to be his companion in the all too brief years that remained to him of mortal life.

NOTES

For convenience the titles of works most frequently referred to in the Notes will be abbreviated as follows:

Works, Lodge	*The Works of Alexander Hamilton*, Henry Cabot Lodge, ed.
Works, J. C. H.	*The Works of Alexander Hamilton*, John C. Hamilton, ed.
J. C. H., *History*	John C. Hamilton, *History of the Republic of the United States, etc.*
J. C. H., *Life*	John C. Hamilton, *The Life of Alexander Hamilton*
Intimate Life	Allan McLane Hamilton, *The Intimate Life of Alexander Hamilton*

Grateful acknowledgment is hereby given to the following institutions for permission to quote from their manuscript materials: American Antiquarian Society, Columbia University, Connecticut Historical Society, Hamilton College, Henry E. Huntington Library, Massachusetts Historical Society, New York Historical Society, New York Society Library, Pennsylvania Historical Society and the William L. Clemens Library.

CHAPTER I

1. J. T. Callender, *The Prospect before Us* (1800), I, p. 82.
2. Adams to Jefferson, 1813; *Historical Magazine*, July, 1870.
3. See in particular J. C. H., *Life*, I, p. 2, and J. C. H., *History*, I. pp. 41-2.
4. Gertrude Atherton published her discoveries in "The Hunt for Hamilton's Mother," *North American Review*, Vol. 175 (1902), pp. 229*ff*. Further material may be found in her *Adventures of a Novelist*, and the Notes to her novel, *The Conqueror*.

5. There is in existence a deed of conveyance to Dr. Fawcett and his wife, dated 1714; Atherton, "The Hunt for Hamilton's Mother," *loc. cit.*
6. Common Records of Nevis, Feb. 5, 1740 (1725-1746), p. 429; cited in Atherton, *The Conqueror*, p. 527.
7. See citations in Note 3 *supra.*
8. Atherton, *Adventures of a Novelist*, p. 352; and Johan Smertenko, *Alexander Hamilton*, p. 4.
9. John Anderson, *The Historical and Genealogical Memoirs of the House of Hamilton* (1825), Edinburgh.
10. Records of St. Christopher, cited in Atherton, "The Hunt for Hamilton's Mother," *loc. cit.*
11. Hamilton to —— Hamilton, May 2, 1797; *Works*, Lodge, X, pp. 257-8.
12. George Bancroft, *History of the United States*, VII, p. 79 (1860).
13. Memorandum dated Feb. 15, 1822; Pickering MSS., Mass. Hist. Soc.
14. James A. Hamilton, *Reminiscences*, p. 2.
15. Hamilton to Elizabeth Schuyler; *Intimate Life*, p. 7.
16. June 12, 1793; *Works*, J. C. H., V, p. 567.
17. Hamilton's "Expense Books"; *Intimate Life*, p. 3.
18. Atherton, *The Conqueror*, Notes, p. 534.
19. See Note 11 *supra.*
20. Protocol of the Dealing Court in Christianstadt, Aug. 3, 1768, quoted in Atherton, *A Few of Hamilton's Letters*, p. xv.
21. *Ibid.*, p. xvi.
22. Registers of St. John's Church, St. Croix; Atherton, "The Hunt for Hamilton's Mother," *loc. cit.*

Chapter II

1. *Intimate Life*, p. 3.
2. July 10, 1804; *Works*, Lodge, X, pp. 475-6.
3. Memorandum dated Feb. 15, 1822; Pickering MSS., Mass. Hist. Soc. Pickering's informant told him that Mrs. Mitchell was Hamilton's aunt, the sister of Rachel Fawcett.
4. J. C. H., *History*, I, p. 42.
5. Undated; *Intimate Life*, p. 4.
6. Oct. 12, 1782; Hamilton MSS., Lib. Cong. The history of this postscript is interesting. J. C. Hamilton, the son, printed it in the *Life* as follows: "I take the liberty to enclose you a letter to Mr. Kane, executor to the estate of Mr. Lavine, a half-brother of mine who died some time since in South Carolina. Captain Roberts, if you should not be acquainted with him, can inform you where he is. I shall be much obliged to you to have my letter carefully forwarded." Here are some very serious discrepancies, though Hamilton's manuscript copy is quite legible. *Cape* Roberts, the place of death, becomes Captain Roberts, and is shifted to the next sentence. Punctuation is changed, and no deletion is shown in the printed sentence, though a word, probably a name, has been erased in the manuscript. This change makes it appear that one Captain Rob-

erts, a fictitious character, knew of Levine's affairs. Actually it was someone else, whose name was so painstakingly scratched out of the manuscript before it was turned over to the Library of Congress that it is now impossible to decipher. When J. C. Hamilton later published his father's *Works*, he omitted the entire postscript (see *Works*, I, p. 318). Curiously enough, Senator Lodge followed suit in *his* edition of the *Works*, IX, p. 301, though the manuscript letter was available to him in the Library of Congress. Gertrude Atherton first noticed the missing postscript in the *Life*, and raised quite an outcry about it. No one, however, until now, ever checked the text against the original. J. C. Hamilton's belated decision to omit all references to Peter Levine is understandable, if futile. What intrigues the imagination, though, is the reason for his strange distortion of the manuscript when he *did* print it; and why the name of the man to whom Hamilton referred Greene for information as to the estate was so carefully erased. Who was this man? What was his relation to Levine and Hamilton? One senses a mystery that may now never be revealed.

7. Hamilton to Messrs. Semphill & Co., May 20, 1786; *Works*, Lodge, IX, pp. 415-6.
8. Oct. 27, 1786 (?), misdated 1783 in J. C. H., *History*, II, p. 318. This letter is here wrongly related to Hamilton's inquiry to Greene about the Levine estate, instead of to the Hallwood estate some three years later. Thereby it is insinuated that Hamilton was interested solely in an inheritance through his mother, rather than from Levine.
9. Hugh Knox to Hamilton, July 28, 1784, Hamilton MSS., Lib. Cong.
10. Nov. 11, 1769; *Works*, Lodge, IX, pp. 37-8.
11. Oct., 1771; Hamilton MSS., Lib. Cong.
12. Nov. 4, 1771; *ibid.*
13. Nov. 12, 1771; *ibid.*
14. Nov. 16, 1771; *ibid.* (See also *Works*, Lodge, IX, pp. 38-9.)
15. Nov. 16, 1771; *ibid.* (See also *Works*, J. C. H., I, p. 3.)
16. Nov., 1771; *ibid.*
17. Jan. 10 (1772); *ibid.*
18. Feb. 1, 1772 (misdated 1771); *ibid.*
19. Feb. 24, 1772; *Intimate Life*, pp. 19-20. The name of Burling, omitted in the published text, is taken from the original in the Hamilton MSS., Lib. Cong.
20. Feb. 21, 1772; Hamilton MSS., Lib. Cong.
21. Nicholas Cruger to John Harris Cruger, Mar. 19, 1772; *ibid.*
22. Quoted in full in Gertrude Atherton, *A Few of Hamilton's Letters*, pp. 261-7.
23. Agnes M. Whitson, "The Outlook of the Continental American Colonies on the British West Indies, 1760-1775," *Political Science Quarterly*, Vol. 45 (1930), p. 64.
24. J. Witherspoon, *Works* (1802), IV, pp. 185-201.
25. Hugh Knox to Hamilton, July 28, 1784; Hamilton MSS., Lib. Cong. "I have always had a just & secret pride in having advised you to go to

America, & in having recommended you to some of my old friends there."
26. J. C. H., *History*, I, p. 45.

CHAPTER III

1. "Mulligan's Narrative," Hamilton MSS., Lib. Cong. Mulligan's story, though it is the basis of all accounts of Hamilton's early days in America, must be scrutinized with great caution. He was an old man when he composed his reminiscences for the benefit of Hamilton's son; and the patina of time as well as the source and nature of the request mellowed his recollection. For example, he alleges that Hamilton tried to enter Princeton rather than King's College "because it was more republican." Aside from the obvious facts that the boy had just landed and was certainly not engrossed in politics, it is more plausible to assume that Dr. Knox, an enthusiastic Princeton graduate, had much more to do with this particular choice. And the predilections of Boudinot and Livingston were also in favor of Princeton.
2. For a fairly good, if over-laudatory, life of Hercules Mulligan, see Michael J. O'Brien, *Hercules Mulligan*.
3. Nathan Schachner, *Aaron Burr*, pp. 26-7.
4. J. C. H., *History*, I, p. 46.
5. "Mulligan's Narrative," *loc. cit.*
6. "Troup's Narrative," Hamilton MSS., Lib. Cong. The same strictures apply to this manuscript account of Hamilton's early life as to Mulligan's story. This brief sketch was written in 1810, thirty-seven years after the event, and was addressed to the Reverend John Mason, who had some idea of doing a biography of Hamilton. Aside from Troup's own passionate partisanship for his deceased friend, there was the cloth of the minister to be considered. Accordingly, it is not surprising to find that Troup makes Hamilton into a most devout and religious young man. If Troup is to be believed, Hamilton attended public worship with exacting regularity, and prayed on his knees each morning and night in the privacy of his own room. Even when he commanded a company of artillery, during the war, Troup would find him in attitude of prayer. Troup mentions a hymn he wrote at about this time, entitled "Soul Entering into Bliss."
7. *Ibid.*
8. *Maryland Gazette*, Apr. 17, 1766; cited in Agnes M. Whitson, "The Outlook of the Continental American Colonies on the British West Indies, 1760-1775," *loc. cit.*, p. 77.
9. Dec. 23, 1777; Hamilton MSS., Lib. Cong.
10. J. C. H., *Life*, I, p. 26. (See also "Troup's Narrative," *loc. cit.*)
11. Dec. 5, 1775; *ibid.*
12. J. C. H., *History*, I. pp. 54-6.
13. MS. "Ledger," Dr. Robert Harpur; N. Y. State Library.
14. *Ibid.*
15. MS. "School Exercises," 1773-1775 (?); Hamilton MSS., Lib. Cong.

16. MS. "Pay Book of the State Company of Artillery Commanded by Alexr. Hamilton, New York, Aug. 31, 1776," *ibid.* For a few excerpts from this "Pay Book," see *Works,* J. C. H., I, pp. 4-7.

17. *Ibid.*

CHAPTER IV

1. "A Full Vindication" is given complete in *Works,* Lodge, I, pp. 4*ff.*
2. *Ibid.,* p. 19.
3. "The Farmer Refuted"; *Works,* Lodge, I, pp. 54*ff.*
4. *Ibid.,* p. 113.
5. *Ibid.,* pp. 176-7.
6. Troup's Letter, Mar. 17, 1828; quoted in J. C. H., *History,* I, p. 74.
7. *Ibid.,* pp. 74-5.
8. "Remarks on the Quebec Bill"; *Works,* Lodge, I, pp. 181*ff.*
9. Biographers generally have followed John C. Hamilton in placing Hamilton in the company called "Hearts of Oak," instead of the "Corsicans"; (J. C. H., *History,* I, p. 99). Both J. C. H. and his successors were led astray by the reminiscences of Troup and Mulligan, in which such a statement is made, with the further assertion that the slogan on their leather caps was "Freedom or Death." But the Official Register of Militia as given in *Documents Relative to the Colonial History of the State of New-York* (E. B. O'Callaghan, ed.), VIII, pp. 601-2, does not mention the Hearts of Oak as in existence before 1776, by which time Hamilton had gone on to other fields. The Register, however, describes the Corsicans in 1775 with the inscription "Liberty or Death" and the green uniforms of Troup's description. Furthermore, Fleming was its captain, whom Troup mentions as the organizer of the Hearts of Oak. It is probable that the Corsicans changed its name in the following year to the Hearts of Oak, which would account for Troup's later confusion of the two; but by that time Hamilton was out, and so was Fleming.
10. This sketch of the attack on Dr. Cooper and Hamilton's part in rescuing him is a composite taken from "Troup's Narrative," Hamilton MSS., Lib. Cong.; O'Callaghan, *op. cit.,* VIII, p. 297; and Dr. Cooper's own poetic account which appeared in the *Gentleman's Magazine,* July, 1776. A sufficient sample of Dr. Cooper's muse follows:

> *Meanwhile, along the sounding shore,*
> *Where Hudson's waves incessant roar,*
> *I take my weary way;*
> *And skirt the windings of the tide,*
> *My faithful pupil by my side*
> *Nor wish the approach of day.*

11. "Troup's Narrative," *loc. cit.;* "Mulligan's Narrative," Hamilton MSS., Lib. Cong.; *Gaine's New York Gazette and Weekly Mercury,* Aug. 28, 1775. Troup asserts that a man was killed at Hamilton's side, but this is an error, for there were no fatal casualties on shore.

12. Nov. 26, 1775; Hamilton Misc. MSS., N. Y. Public Library. The letter is quoted in *Intimate Life*, pp. 24-7.
13. Dec. 31, 1775; *The Correspondence and Public Papers of John Jay*, Henry P. Johnston, ed., I, p. 41.

CHAPTER V

1. *Records of the New York Provincial Congress*. "Mulligan's Narrative," Hamilton MSS., Lib. Cong., is wholly inaccurate. He alleges that the date of the appointment was either July 10 or 12. He also alleges that the appointment was conditional upon Hamilton's ability to raise a company of thirty men, and that by nightfall Hamilton and Mulligan had already recruited twenty-five. On their report to that effect the next day the commission was unanimously granted. The official Records disprove any such conditional appointment.
2. "Mulligan's Narrative," *loc. cit.* See also J. C. H., *Life*, I. p. 52.
3. Mar. 10, 1776; W. A. Duer, *Life of Alexander, Earl of Stirling*, p. 136.
4. *American Archives* (Peter Force, ed.), Fourth Series, V, p. 1424.
5. Hamilton to N. Y. Congress, Aug. 12, 1776; *ibid.*, Fifth Series, I, p. 1509.
6. Hamilton to N. Y. Congress, May 26, 1776; *ibid.*, Fourth Series, VI, pp. 577-8.
7. *Ibid.* p. 1336.
8. MS., "Col. Webb's Orderly Book, 1776"; Conn. State Library.
9. *Ibid.*
10. *American Archives*, Fourth Series, *op. cit.*, VI, p. 1439.
11. "Mulligan's Narrative," *loc. cit.*
12. *American Archives*, Fifth Series, *op. cit.*, I., p. 1491.
13. "Mulligan's Narrative," *loc. cit.* While Mulligan's accounts must always be treated with great caution, this particular episode is confirmed by G. W. P. Custis, Washington's stepson, in his *Recollections and Private Memoirs of Washington*, pp. 343-4.
14. For a personal description of Hamilton within a year of this encounter see William Sullivan, *The Public Men of the Revolution*, p. 260.
15. Mulligan, *op. cit.*, says that Hamilton was present at Bunker's Hill and tells the story of the loss of baggage and cannon. For an account of Burr's rescue of the brigade, see Nathan Schachner, *Aaron Burr*, pp. 49-50, and citations there.
16. J. C. H., *History*, I, pp. 133-4, gives an account of Hamilton's part in the battle.
17. Custis, *op. cit.*, p. 344. Custis also narrates (p. 342) that General Greene had become impressed with Hamilton's abilities while watching him drill his company in the Fields months before; that he had invited the young captain to his quarters and eventually introduced him to Washington with recommendations. John C. Hamilton (J. C. H., *History*, I, p. 125) claims that his father first met Washington at Harlem Heights while the beaten army was hurriedly throwing up earthworks against the expected attack. Washington, on a tour of inspection, came upon Hamilton's company while so engaged, and invited the youthful officer

to his tent for an extended conversation, in the course of which Washington "received an impression of his military talent" which later led to an invitation to join his official staff. Troup ("Troup's Narrative," Hamilton MSS., Lib. Cong.) has still another version. According to him it was General Knox who first noted Hamilton's talents and recommended him to the commanding general. Of these conflicting stories the one given in the text seems the more probable. It certainly was not likely that Washington would have the leisure or the inclination to spend time in his tent discussing this and that under the urgencies of an impending attack. Nor does it ring true that Knox, who seems to have met Hamilton only during the inglorious episode of Bunker's Hill, would have developed an understanding of his special abilities or a desire to further his fortunes, under the circumstances of his own humiliation.

18. Eyewitness account; Washington Irving, *Life of Washington*, III, p. 88.
19. George Otto Trevelyan, *History of the American Revolution*, Part II, Vol. II, pp. 114, 148-9.

Chapter VI

1. W. B. Reed, *Life of Joseph Reed*, I, p. 146.
2. *Works*, J. C. H., I, pp. 24-5.
3. *Ibid.*, p. 19.
4. *Works*, Lodge, IX, p. 45.
5. Oswald Tilghman, *Memoir of Lieut. Col. Tench Tilghman*, p. 128.
6. *Works*, J. C. H., I, pp. 12-13.
7. *Ibid.*, pp. 23-4.
8. *Works*, Lodge, IX, pp. 56-7.
9. *Ibid.*, pp. 65-6.
10. *Ibid.*, pp. 71-2.
11. *Ibid.*, p. 81.
12. J. C. H., *Life*, I, p. 69.
13. G. W. P. Custis, *Recollections and Private Memoirs of Washington*, p. 346.
14. Alexander Graydon, *Memoirs of His Own Time*, p. 275.
15. *Works*, Lodge, IX, p. 85.
16. Henry Lee, *Memoirs of the War in the Southern Department of the United States*, pp. 91-2. Lee mentions three men wounded in Hamilton's boat, and none killed; but Hamilton's letter to Hancock, written the same day (see Note 19 below), is decisive.
17. *Works*, Lodge, IX, p. 101.
18. John Adams, *Works*, II, p. 438.
19. Hamilton to Hancock; *Works*, Lodge, IX, p. 102.
20. John Marshall, *The Life of George Washington*, I, p. 168.
21. Henry Lee, *op. cit.*, p. 96.
22. *The Writings of George Washington*, W. C. Ford, ed., VI, pp. 154-5.
23. *Works*, Lodge, IX, p. 105.
24. *Ibid.*, pp. 106-8.

25. *Ibid.*, pp. 109-10.
26. Gates to Washington; James Wilkinson, *Memoirs of My Own Times*, I, p. 372. (See also Hamilton to Washington; *Works*, Lodge, IX, pp. 111-14.)
27. *Works*, Lodge, IX, pp. 120-2. The date of this letter is Nov. 9, 1777; Lodge misdates it Dec. 9.
28. *Ibid.*, p. 114.
29. J. C. H., *History*, I, pp. 358-9.
30. Washington, *op. cit.*, VI, pp. 211-12.
31. Hamilton to Washington; *Works*, Lodge, IX., p. 112.
32. MS. letter, Nov. 5, 1777; Gates Papers, N. Y. Hist. Soc. That Washington's need for troops was desperate is plainly evidenced by a hitherto unpublished letter from Brigadier Jedediah Huntington to Governor Trumbull of Connecticut, dated Nov. 10, 1777, at Whitemarsh. (Jonathan Trumbull Papers, Conn. State. Lib.) The enemy, he wrote, was too strongly intrenched to hazard an attack upon them with the forces at hand. But "whenever we are in Force sufficient to risque the Consequences we shall cut off their Communication with their Ships at Chester which will immediately lay them under the necessity of fighting. We thought to be able for this when we could be joined by a Part of General Gates Army, and General Washington has sent his Aid-de-Camp Colonel Hamilton to the Northward for that Purpose, but it seems Congress in their Wisdom, have made a Disposition of those troops and subjected Genl. Washington to the Inconvenience of a Consultation with General Gates and Governor Clinton before any Alteration can be made....I do most heartily pity General Washington. It is impossible for him to operate with Vigour."
33. *Works*, Lodge, IX, pp. 112, 114.
34. Hamilton to Washington; *ibid.*, pp. 119-20.
35. Dr. Jones to Governor Clinton; *Public Papers of George Clinton*, II, pp. 541-2.
36. I. Gibbs to Governor Clinton; *ibid.*, p. 556.
37. Washington, *op. cit.*, VI, p. 198.
38. *Memoirs, Correspondence and Manuscripts of General Lafayette*, I, p. 37.
39. Wilkinson, *op. cit.*, I, pp. 372-3.
40. *Ibid.*, pp. 386-7.
41. *Ibid.*, p. 400.

Chapter VII

1. *Works*, Lodge, IX, pp. 122-7.
2. *Public Papers of George Clinton*, II, p. 865.
3. *Works*, Lodge, IX, pp. 127-31.
4. Washington to Howe; *The Writings of George Washington*, W. C. Ford, ed., VI, p. 442.
5. Elias Boudinot, *Journal of Elias Boudinot*, pp. 43-4.
6. *Ibid.*, pp. 44-5.
7. *Ibid.*, p. 45.

8. Colonels Robert H. Harrison and Alexander Hamilton to Colonels O'Hara and Hyde, Amboy, Dec. 12, 1778; MS. copy in William M. Clemens Lib.

9. Boudinot, *op. cit.*, p. 49.

10. *Works*, Lodge, IX, pp. 138-9. See also *Memoirs, Correspondence and Manuscripts of General Lafayette*, I, p. 179.

11. Hamilton to Boudinot; *Works*, Lodge, IX., pp. 140-2. The original of this letter is in the Pa. Hist. Soc. See also Washington to Lee, June 26, 1778; *Lee Papers*, N. Y. Hist. Soc. Coll., II, pp. 421-2; and Washington to Lafayette, same date; *ibid.*, pp. 422-3.

12. Hamilton's testimony; *Lee Papers*, op. cit., III, pp. 57-8.

13. G. W. P. Custis, *Recollections and Private Memoirs of Washington*, p. 219.

14. Lee's testimony; *Lee Papers*, *op. cit.*, III, p. 201; Mercer's testimony, *ibid.*, p. 114; Harrison's testimony, *ibid.*, p. 75.

15. Hamilton's testimony; *ibid.*, pp. 59-61.

16. MS. letter, dated July 2, 1778; Emmett Collection, N. Y. Pub. Lib.

17. *Works*, Lodge, IX, pp. 140-2.

18. MS. letter, dated July 8, 1778; Society Collection, Pa. Hist. Soc.

19. Hamilton's testimony; *Lee Papers*, *op. cit.*, III, pp. 60, 64.

20. *Works*, Lodge, IX, p. 156.

21. "Narrative of an Affair of Honor between General Lee and Col. Laurens," Dec. 24, 1778; *ibid.*, IX, p. 157.

22. *Lee Papers*, *op. cit.*, III, p. 363.

23. *Ibid.*, pp. 393-4.

24. Washington, *Writings*, *op. cit.*, VI, p. 103.

25. *Ibid.*, footnote, p. 238.

26. Bernard C. Steiner, *The Life and Correspondence of James McHenry*, pp. 17-8.

27. *Holt's Journal*, Oct. 19, 1778; *Works*, Lodge, I, p. 201.

28. *Holt's Journal*, Oct. 26, 1778; *ibid.*, p. 201.

29. *Holt's Journal*, Nov. 16, 1778; *ibid.*, pp. 208-9.

30. MS. letter, McHenry to Giles, Jan. 19, 1782; Hamilton MSS., Lib. Cong.

31. MS. draft, Feb. 26, 1782; *ibid.* Hamilton made several mistakes in this letter. He refers to *Wm.* Chase, and thinks he was tried before the Virginia House of Delegates. For the record of Samuel Chase's acquittal by the Maryland Legislature, see the *Maryland Journal*, Aug. 23, 30, 1781; Sept. 24, 1782.

32. J. C. H., *History*, I, p. 528.

33. *Works*, Lodge, IX, pp. 160-1.

34. *Mass. Hist. Soc. Proc.* (1924-5), Vol. 58, pp. 219-36.

35. *Smythe's Journal*, p. 98; quoted in Frank Moore, *Diary of the American Revolution*, II, p. 250.

36. *Smythe's Journal*, p. 91; *ibid.*, p. 203.

37. *Public Papers of George Clinton*, V, pp. 203-4.

38. MS. copy, Hamilton Misc. MSS., N. Y. Pub. Lib. A bowdlerized version, omitting the words, "whore or," is in *Works*, Lodge, IX, p. 201.

39. MS. letter, July 25, 1779; Hamilton MSS., Lib. Cong.
40. *Works*, Lodge, IX, p. 175.
41. *Ibid.*, p. 189.
42. Washington, *Writings, op. cit.*, VIII, pp. 259-61.
43. *Works*, J. C. H., I, pp. 81-2.
44. Washington, *Writings, op. cit.*, VIII, pp. 83-4.
45. MS. letter, John Mitchell to Hamilton, Nov. 10, 1779; Hamilton MSS., Lib. Cong.
46. Hamilton to a member of congress, Nov., 1779 (?); *ibid.* Lodge, in his edition of the *Works*, III, pp. 319-41, gives the year as 1780 and assumes that the letter was addressed to Robert Morris. But the manuscript copy in the Library of Congress bears neither date nor address. Whichever date is correct, the superscription to a member of congress must rule out Morris as the addressee, since he quit Congress on Nov. 1, 1778. Internal evidence points to Nov., 1779, as the correct date, and General John Sullivan as the probable recipient. Among other things, Sullivan was then active in congress in financial measures, and not long after, expressed himself to Washington as deeply impressed with Hamilton's knowledge of finance and practical statesmanship at a time when Washington himself was ignorant of Hamilton's abilities along those lines.

Chapter VIII

1. *Works*, Lodge, IX, pp. 187-8.
2. Quoted in Mary Gay Humphreys, *Catherine Schuyler*, p. 191.
3. Oswald Tilghman, *Memoir of Lt. Col. Tench Tilghman*, p. 90.
4. Hamilton MSS., Lib. Cong., Jan. 25, 1781. This passage is omitted from the published letter in *Works*, J. C. H., I, p. 210.
5. See Chap. I, p. 17, *supra*.
6. *Intimate Life*, pp. 97-9.
7. *Ibid.*, pp. 129-30.
8. Hamilton MSS., Lib. Cong. These passages are omitted from the published letter in *Works*, J. C. H., I, p. 135.
9. MS. letter, Laurens to Hamilton, July 30, 1780; Hamilton MSS., Lib. Cong.
10. Tilghman, *op. cit.*, p. 173.
11. MS. letter, Oct. 20, 1780; Hamilton MSS., Lib. Cong.
12. *Intimate Life*, pp. 127-8.
13. *Works*, Lodge, I, pp. 213-38.
14. *Ibid.*, IX, p. 203.
15. MS. letter, Sept. 12, 1780; Emmett Collection, N. Y. Pub. Lib.
16. The details of this narrative are taken chiefly from Jared Sparks, *Life of Arnold*, p. 246; Richard Rush, *Occasional Productions* (1860), p. 82; *Memoirs, Correspondence and Manuscripts of General Lafayette*, I, pp. 254-5.
17. *Works*, Lodge, IX, pp. 205-6. Hamilton's order to Greene is in *ibid.*, p. 206.

18. *Ibid.*, pp. 206-8.
19. Nathan Schachner, *Aaron Burr*, p. 72.
20. The Clinton Papers are located at the William L. Clements Library, Ann Arbor, Mich. Among many other notations by Clinton relating to Arnold is this one: "His wife [Arnold's] obtained for her services, which was very meritorious, 350 pounds." The whole matter has been recently examined, in the light of this collection, by Carl Van Doren, *Secret History of the Revolution, passim.*
21. *Works*, Lodge, IX, pp. 208-9.
22. *Ibid.*, pp. 209-23.

CHAPTER IX

1. MS. copy in Duane Papers, July 22, 1780, N. Y. Hist. Soc. The original is in the possession of Miss Frances R. Duane.
2. *Works*, J. C. H., I, p. 135.
3. *Pennsylvania Gazette*, Mar. 18, 1781.
4. *Secret Journals of the Continental Congress*, W. C. Ford and G. Hunt, eds., II, pp. 357.
5. Laurens to Hamilton, Dec. 18, 1780 (misdated 1779 in text); *Works*, J. C. H., I, pp. 113-4.
6. Lovell to Laurens, Dec. 17, 1780 (misdated 1779 in text); *Letters of Members of the Continental Congress*, Edmund C. Burnett, ed., II, p. 539.
7. *The Writings of George Washington*, W. C. Ford, ed., IX, p. 80.
8. *Works*, Lodge, IX, pp. 226-8.
9. *Memoirs, Correspondence and Manuscripts of General Lafayette*, I, pp. 385-6.
10. *Ibid.*, p. 366.
11. Washington, *Writings, op. cit.*, IX, p. 53.
12. *Ibid.*, pp. 53-4.
13. Hamilton MSS., Dec. 9, 1780, Lib. Cong. The paragraph here quoted is omitted from the text published in *Works*, J. C. H., I, pp. 199-200.
14. A photostat of the marriage record in the First Reformed Church is in the N. Y. Hist. Soc.
15. The *Epithalamium* is given in full in Bernard C. Steiner, *The Life and Correspondence of James McHenry*, pp. 29-30.
16. *Ibid.*, pp. 30-1.
17. *Works*, J. C. H., I, p. 201; misdated Dec. 9th in the published text. The true date is given in Washington's acknowledgment; *ibid.*, I, p. 202.
18. *Ibid.*, I, p. 189.
19. *Letters of Members of the Continental Congress, op. cit.*, V, p. 548.
20. Washington, *Writings, op. cit.*, IX, p. 131.
21. *Letters of Members of the Continental Congress, op. cit.*, VI, p. 11.
22. Hamilton to Schuyler; *Works*, Lodge, IX, pp. 232-7.
23. *Ibid.*, J. C. Hamilton, in *Works*, J. C. H., I, pp. 211-4, omits all disparaging references to Washington, and thereby gives a wholly distorted picture of Hamilton's relations with him.

24. Steiner, *op. cit.*, p. 35.
25. *Works*, Lodge, IX, p. 238.
26. J. C. H., *History*, II, pp. 176-7.
27. Washington, *Writings, op. cit.*, IX, p. 227, footnote.
28. *Ibid.*, pp. 226-7.
29. *Works*, Lodge, IX, pp. 238-9.
30. Washington, *Writings, op. cit.*, IX, pp. 229-31.
31. *Works*, Lodge, IX, pp. 240-2.

Chapter X

1. *Works*, Lodge, III, pp. 356*ff*.
2. *Works*, J. C. H., I, pp. 264-5.
3. *Diplomatic Correspondence of the American Revolution*, Jared Sparks, ed., XI, p. 364.
4. *Works*, J. C. H., I, p. 266.
5. *Ibid.*, p. 214.
6. *Ibid.*, p. 264.
7. *Works*, Lodge, IX, p. 243.
8. *The Writings of George Washington*, W. C. Ford, ed., IX, p. 321.
9. *Works*, Lodge, IX, p. 245.
10. *Ibid.*, p. 246.
11. The accounts of this incident vary somewhat. J. C. Hamilton, in J. C. H., *History*, II, p. 268, gives the name of the superseded officer as Barber. I have followed him in this, because his informant was Major Fish, second in command under Hamilton. Henry Lee, in his *Memoirs of the War in the Southern Department of the United States*, p. 501, claims that Hamilton told him afterward that it was Colonel Gimat. H. A. Muhlenberg, in his *Life of Major-General Peter Muhlenberg*, pp. 271-7, makes out a case for his ancestor as the victim.
12. Isaac Q. Leake, *Memoir of the Life and Times of John Lamb*, p. 279
13. Henry Lee, *op. cit.*, pp. 501-2; *Memoirs, Correspondence and Manuscripts of General Lafayette*, I, pp. 270-1; J. C. H., *History*, II, pp. 268-9.
14. James Thacher, *Military Journal*, I, p. 341.
15. William Gordon, *History*, etc., III, p. 258.
16. *Works*, Lodge, IX, pp. 247-50.
17. Lafayette, *Memoirs, op. cit.*, I, p. 443.
18. Elias Boudinot, *Journal of Elias Boudinot*, pp. 37-8.

Chapter XI

1. *Works*, Lodge, IX, pp. 251-3.
2. *Works*, J. C. H., I, p. 270.
3. *Works*, Lodge, IX, pp. 253-4.
4. "Troup's Narrative," Hamilton MSS., Lib. Cong.

5. *Works*, J. C. H., I, pp. 278-9.
6. *Works*, Lodge, IX, pp. 255-6.
7. *Ibid.*, pp. 259-60; also *Works*, J. C. H., I, p. 280.
8. *Works*, J. C. H., I, pp. 284-5.
9. For extended discussions of the situation in New York see D. S. Alexander, *A Political History of the State of New York*, I, *passim*; J. D. Hammond, *The History of the Political Parties in the State of New York*, I, *passim*; E. W. Spaulding, *New York in the Critical Period, 1783-89*; E. P. Oberholtzer, *Robert Morris*; and W. G. Sumner, *The Financier and the Finances of the American Revolution*.
10. MS. letter, Nov. 24, 1781; Abraham Yates Papers, N. Y. Pub. Lib.
11. *Works*, Lodge, IX, p. 262.
12. *Works*, J. C. H., I, p. 287.
13. *Works*, Lodge, IX, pp. 264-6.
14. *Ibid.*
15. MS. "Plan of Specific Taxation to be Substituted to the Present mode by assessment: Together with the supposed product and the appropriation of each tax"; Hamilton MSS., Lib. Cong.
16. *Works*, Lodge, IX, pp. 294-5.
17. *Works*, J. C. H., I, p. 304.
18. MS. report; Jonathan Trumbull Papers, Conn. State Lib.
19. *Works*, J. C. H., I, pp. 299-302.
20. MS. letter, Yates to Duane and L'Hommedieu, Oct. 19, 1782; Abraham Yates Papers, N. Y. Pub. Lib.

Chapter XII

1. "The Continentalist," *Works*, Lodge, I, pp. 243*ff.*
2. The original manuscript of this letter is in the Morgan Library; it is printed in *Works*, Lodge, IX, pp. 280-1.
3. Bernard C. Steiner, *The Life and Correspondence of James McHenry*, pp. 43-4.
4. *Works*, J. C. H., I, p. 320.
5. *Letters of the Members of the Continental Congress*, Edmund C. Burnett, ed., VI, p. 502.
6. "Madison's Notes of Debates in the Congress of the Confederation"; *The Writings of James Madison*, Gaillard Hunt, ed., I, p. 270.
7. *Journals of the Continental Congress*, W. C. Ford and G. Hunt, eds., XXIII, pp. 770-1.
8. *Ibid.*, pp. 783-4. For the complete text of the report see *Works*, Lodge, II, pp. 179-92.
9. *Works*, Lodge, I, p. 274.
10. J. C. H., *History*, II, p. 336.
11. *Works*, Lodge, IX, p. 308.
12. *Journals of the Continental Congress, op. cit.*, XXIII, p. 869.
13. *Works*, Lodge, IX, p. 309.
14. Madison, *Writings, op. cit.*, I, p. 332.

15. *Ibid.*, p. 336.
16. *Ibid.*, p. 334.
17. *Ibid.*, p. 351.
18. *Ibid.*, p. 366.
19. *Ibid.*, pp. 372-3.
20. *Ibid.*, p. 402.
21. *Ibid.*, p. 453n.
22. MS. draft, Feb. 13, 1783, N. Y. Pub. Lib. The letter appears in *Works*, Lodge, IX, pp. 310-13, misdated Feb. 7th, and with certain textual variations. See also Madison, *Writings, op. cit.*, I, p. 379.
23. *The Writings of George Washington*, W. C. Ford, ed., X, pp. 163-6.
24. *Works*, J. C. H., I, pp. 343-5.
25. *Works*, Lodge, IX, p. 326.
26. Washington, *Writings, op. cit.*, X, pp. 214-6.
27. *Works*, Lodge, IX, p. 337.
28. *Ibid.*, I, p. 304.
29. *Journals of the Continental Congress, op. cit.*, XXIV, pp. 412-3.
30. This was a second report, made on July 1st. The first report to congress on the situation was made on June 24th; *ibid.*, pp. 413-15.
31. *Works*, Lodge, IX, pp. 350-77.
32. Hamilton to Madison; *ibid.*, pp. 377-8.
33. Madison to Hamilton, *Works*, J. C. H., I, pp. 409-10.

CHAPTER XIII

1. *The Writings of James Madison*, Gaillard Hunt, ed., I, pp. 414-5.
2. *Works*, Lodge, IX, p. 337.
3. *Ibid.*, VI, pp. 463-83.
4. Capt. William Armstrong to Sir Guy Carleton, Apr. 1, 1783; Hist. Manuscripts Commission: *Report of American MSS. in the Royal Institution of Great Britain*, 1907; IV.
5. *Journals of the Continental Congress*, W. C. Ford and G. Hunt, eds., XXIV, pp. 371-2.
6. *Ibid.*, pp. 372-3.
7. *Works*, Lodge, I, pp. 305-14.
8. *Ibid.*, IX, p. 342.
9. *Ibid.*, pp. 348-9.
10. *Public Papers of George Clinton*, VIII, pp. 202-3.
11. *Ibid.*, pp. 219-20.
12. *Works*, J. C. H., I, pp. 411-12.
13. De Alva S. Alexander, *A Political History of the State of New York*, I, p. 23.
14. MS. Letter to James Duane, Aug. 5, 1783; Duane Papers, N. Y. Hist. Soc.
15. MS. Letter to R. R. Livingston, Aug. 13, 1783; Livingston Papers, Bancroft Transcripts, N. Y. Pub. Lib.
16. *Laws of New York, Sixth Session*, chap. 31.

17. MS. plea and demurrer; N. Y. Hist. Soc. Hamilton drafted several variant briefs in connection with Rutgers *vs.* Waddington. One is in the Hamilton College Library; another is among the Hamilton MSS. in the Library of Congress. Shorter versions may be found printed in *Works*, Lodge, and *The Intimate Life*, Appendix H. Henry B. Dawson, in *The Case of Elizabeth Rutgers versus Joshua Waddington*, gives a circumstantial account of the case which is inaccurate in certain particulars. By a series of misprints he places the date of the trial in 1786 instead of 1784.

18. MS. brief, Hamilton MSS., Lib. Cong.

19. Dawson, *op. cit.*, pp. 35-8.

20. New York *Packet*, Sept. 6, 1784.

21. *N. Y. Assembly Journal*, Nov. 2, 1784.

22. *Works*, Lodge, IV, pp. 230-90.

23. Mentor's *Reply to Phocion*, 1784.

24. J. C. H., *Life*, II, pp. 276-7.

25. Feb. 21, 1784; Hamilton MSS., Lib. Cong.; misdated Mar. 21, 1784, in *Works*, Lodge, IX, p. 399.

26. A vast array of letters, accounts and briefs pertaining to Hamilton's legal affairs may be found in the Hamilton MSS., Lib. Cong. Other briefs and documents are scattered in the archives of the N. Y. Hist. Soc., the Huntington Lib., the N. Y. State Lib., and elsewhere. See his letter to Egbert Benson, Dec. 10, 1784, Huntington Lib., for his willingness to compromise "to avoid hazarding additional expense to men who can ill afford it and to make an end of the controversy."

27. J. C. H., *History*, III, p. 46.

28. MS. letter, Feb. 7, 1784; Hamilton MSS., Lib. Cong.

29. *Works*, Lodge, IX, pp. 396-8.

30. MS. letter, May 2, 1784; Hamilton MSS., Lib. Cong.

31. Hamilton's "Expense Books" contain several references to purchases of slaves. Some of these are among the Hamilton MSS., Lib. Cong. *Intimate Life* (p. 235) lists an item dated May 29, 1797, showing a purchase for Hamilton's account of a negro woman and child for $225.

32. MS. letter, Feb. 7, 1785; Schuyler Papers, N. Y. Pub. Lib.

N. B.—In connection with this chapter on Hamilton's legal matters an interesting textual point arises concerning a series of letters exchanged between one John Wilkes, a New York lawyer, and Hamilton. These letters are not particularly important in themselves; but their handling by Lodge in his standard edition of Hamilton's *Works* casts a curious light upon his general editorial research. John C. Hamilton, in *his* edition of his father's *Works* (I, p. 424), printed a letter from Hamilton, dated Nov. 8, 1785, and purportedly addressed to one *John* Wilkes, sharply resenting a letter from Wilkes received that same day, in which Wilkes, a lawyer, berated Hamilton for professional discourtesy in connection with a legal matter pending between them. Wilkes' letter, so resented by Hamilton, was not printed by J. C. Hamilton; but he did print the hasty, abject apology which Wilkes returned on Nov. 9th, after receiving Hamilton's sharp note, and again cites his name as *John*

Wilkes. In his own edition of the *Works* (IX, pp. 406-12), Lodge reprinted Hamilton's letter of Nov. 8th and in a footnote quotes Wilkes' reply of Nov. 9th, but arbitrarily changes Wilkes' Christian name from *John* to *Israel*. In so doing he enters upon a long explanation purporting to show that J. C. Hamilton was mistaken in his attribution. For, remarks Mr. Lodge, John Wilkes, the famous English agitator, was in England at the time and hence could not possibly have been the Mr. Wilkes of the letters. Therefore *this* Mr. Wilkes must have been Israel Wilkes, his eldest brother, who was then resident in New York. Having thus solved the problem to his own satisfaction, Mr. Lodge proceeds to wonder: "Why Mr. J. C. Hamilton should have printed the letter as from John Wilkes cannot be determined. That the original should have been signed 'John Wilkes' seems most unlikely." We can only wonder at Mr. Lodge's wonderment, for the original *is* in fact signed 'John Wilkes,' as Mr. Lodge could readily have verified from the Hamilton MSS. in the Library of Congress with which he worked in preparing his edition. The signed letter may be found in Volume VI of the bound manuscripts, page 723. Furthermore, he obviously did not read (nor did he nor J. C. Hamilton print) the first letter of accusation from Wilkes to Hamilton, dated Nov. 8th, and likewise signed "John," which may be found on page 721 of the same bound volume. Actually, of course, this John Wilkes was a local New York lawyer of no particular prominence, and the similarity of names with the English agitator was without doubt purely coincidental.

CHAPTER XIV

1. MS. letter to Theodore Sedgwick, May 21, 1786; Sedgwick Papers, Mass. Hist. Soc.
2. MS. letter to Sedgwick, Feb. 11, 1786; *ibid.*
3. MS. letter, June 13, 1785; Hamilton MSS., Lib. Cong.
4. *Journal of the Assembly of the State of New York*, May 5, 1786; see also Troup's *Reminiscences* in J. C. H., *History*, III, p. 162.
5. There is a MS. draft of the petition in the Hamilton MSS., Lib. Cong.
6. *N. Y. Assembly Journal*, *op. cit.*, Act of May 4, 1786.
7. N. Y. *Packet*, Oct. 2, 1786.
8. MS. letter, Apr. 20, 1786; Van Rensselaer Papers, N. Y. State Lib.
9. N. Y. *Packet*, May 1, 1786. Hamilton ran fourth among the nine selected to the Assembly.
10. *American Historical Association Report*, 1896, I, p. 734.
11. *Documentary History of the Constitution of the United States of America*, IV, p. 25.
12. "Many gentlemen, both within and without Congress, wish to make this meeting subservient to a plenipotentiary Convention for amending the Confederation. Tho' my wishes are in favor of such an event, yet I despair so much of its accomplishment at the present crisis that I do not extend my views beyond a commercial Reform." Madison to Jef-

ferson, Aug. 12, 1786; *The Writings of James Madison*, Gaillard Hunt, ed., II, pp. 257*ff*.

13. *N. Y. Assembly Journal, op. cit.*, Jan. 13, 1787.
14. *Ibid.*, Jan. 19, 1787. The vote was 39 to 9.
15. *Ibid.*, Feb. 14, Feb. 24, Mar. 28, 1787.
16. *Ibid.*, Feb. 16, 1787.
17. J. C. H., *Life*, II, p. 431.
18. *N. Y. Assembly Journal, op. cit.*, Feb. 15, 1787.
19. *Works*, Lodge, II, pp. 492*ff*.
20. Schuyler to H. Van Schaack, Mar. 13, 1787; H. C. Van Schaack, *Memoirs of the Life of H. Van Schaack*, pp. 149-55.
21. *Ibid.*
22. *Journals of the Continental Congress*, W. C. Ford and G. Hunt, eds., Feb. 21, 1787.
23. For the various votes and maneuvers see the letter of Schuyler to Van Schaack, *supra;* and the *N. Y. Assembly Journal, op. cit.*, and *New York State Senate Journals* from Jan. 23, 1787, to Apr. 18, 1787.
24. Nevertheless Governor Clinton was certain he had been decisively defeated. The N. Y. *Advertiser* for July 21, 1787, said that "it is currently reported and believed that his excellency Governor Clinton has, in public company, without reserve, reprobated the appointment of the Convention, and predicted a mischievous issue of that measure. His observations are said to be to this effect:—that the present confederation is, in itself, equal to the purposes of the Union:—That the appointment of a Convention is calculated to impress the people with an idea of evils which do not exist:—therefore, that in all probability the result of their deliberations, whatever it might be, would only serve to throw the community into confusion."
25. *N. Y. Assembly Journal, op. cit.*, Apr. 14, 1787; *Works*, Lodge, IV, pp. 291-4.

CHAPTER XV

1. J. C. H., *History*, III, p. 239.
2. *The Journal of the Constitutional Convention*, in *The Writings of James Madison*, Gaillard Hunt, ed., III, p. 5.
3. "Yates' Minutes," *The Debates in Several State Conventions on the Adoption of the Federal Constitution*, Jonathan Elliot, ed., I, p. 411.
4. "Madison's Journal," in *Writings, op. cit.*, III, p. 88; "Rufus King's Notes," in *The Records of the Federal Convention of 1787*, Max Farrand, ed., I, pp. 107-8.
5. "Notes of Major William Pierce on the Federal Convention of 1787," *American Historical Review*, Vol. III, p. 327.
6. The account of Hamilton's speech before the convention and of his proposed constitution is taken from "Madison's Journal," in *Writings, op. cit.*, III, pp. 182-97; "Propositions for a Constitution," in *Works*, Lodge, I, pp. 347-50; "First Draft of a Constitution," *ibid.*, I, pp. 350-69; "Brief of Speech," *ibid.*, I, p. 374; "Yates' Minutes," in Elliot, *Debates*,

op. cit., I, pp. 417-23; "Papers of William Paterson on the Federal Convention, 1787," *American Historical Review*, Vol. IX, p. 335; "Alexander Hamilton's Notes in the Federal Convention of 1787," in *ibid.*, Vol. X, pp. 97-109. I have also compared the printed Hamilton texts against the appropriate manuscripts in Hamilton MSS., Lib. Cong.

7. *King's Notes*, in Farrand, *op. cit.*, I, p. 366.
8. Madison, *Writings, op. cit.*, III, p. 221; also "Yates' Minutes," in Elliot, *Debates, op. cit.*, I, p. 426.
9. Madison, *Writings, op. cit.*, III, p. 244.
10. *Ibid.*, p. 288.
11. Jefferson, *Writings* (Ford, ed.), I, p. 343.
12. Jonathan Dayton to Wm. Steele, Sept., 1825, printed in *National Intelligencer*, Aug. 26, 1826. Madison, in his "Journal," does not report the quip about "foreign aid."
13. *Works*, Lodge, IX, pp. 417-8.
14. *Works*, J. C. H., I, p. 437.
15. MS. letter, King to Henry Knox, July 11, 1787; Knox Papers, Mass. Hist. Soc.
16. E. Wilder Spaulding, *New York in the Critical Period*, 1783-89, p. 189.
17. *Works*, J. C. H., I, pp. 444-5, 447.
18. *Ibid.*, pp. 439-40.
19. MS. letter, Abraham G. Lansing to Abraham Yates, Jr., Aug. 26, 1787; Yates Papers, N. Y. Hist. Soc.
20. MS. letter, Aug. 28, 1787; King Papers, N. Y. Hist. Soc.
21. Madison, *Writings, op. cit.*, IV, pp. 383-4, 411, 418; "Papers of Dr. James McHenry on the Federal Convention of 1787," *American Historical Review*, Vol. XI, p. 615.
22. Madison, *Writings, op. cit.*, Vol. IV, p. 478.

CHAPTER XVI

1. The "Cato" letters commenced publication on Sept. 27, 1787; the "Caesar" letters on Oct. 11th. The latter are reprinted in *Essays on the Constitution of the United States*, Paul L. Ford, ed.; the cited quotation is on p. 287.
2. There have been innumerable editions of *The Federalist*. The ones edited by Lodge (1923) and by P. L. Ford (1898) are the most satisfactory. The exact authorship of certain of the papers in *The Federalist* has been the subject of vigorous dispute. Jay's contribution is certain— Nos. 2-5, 64. Hamilton is conceded to have written 1, 6-9, 11-13, 15, 16, 22-36, 59-61, 65-85; and Madison, 10, 14, 37-48. Both collaborated in 18-20. Nos. 17 and 21 are fairly confidently assigned to Hamilton. This leaves twelve papers—Nos. 49-58, 62, 63—as the objects of controversy. Lodge gives them all to Hamilton, though conceding that there are grounds for doubt on 49-58. E. G. Bourne is certain, however, that all the twelve were written by Madison. His arguments may be found in *American Historical Review*, Vol. II, pp. 443-60. P. L. Ford attacks his thesis in the same volume, pp. 675-82, and holds with Lodge. The

trouble is that it was only at the end of his career that either Hamilton or Madison indicated in private memoranda what they then believed to have been their respective papers. Some of their attributions overlapped, and both made some obvious errors in assigning credit.

3. "Troup's Reminiscences," Hamilton MSS., Lib. Cong.
4. *The Federalist*, No. 6.
5. *Ibid.*, No. 11.
6. *Ibid.*, No. 12.
7. *Ibid.*, No. 38.
8. *Ibid.*, No. 85.
9. MS. letter, Aug. 28, 1788; Columbia Univ. Lib.
10. *The Works of Thomas Jefferson*, Paul L. Ford, ed., V, pp. 433-7.
11. *The Journal of William Maclay*, p. 75.
12. New York *Daily Advertiser*, Feb. 8, 12, 1788.
13. The election results are conveniently tabulated by E. W. Spaulding in his *New York in the Critical Period, 1783-89*, p. 203.
14. From a N. Y. newspaper clipping, dated May 30, 1788, attached to a MS. letter from Nathaniel Hazard to Theodore Sedgwick, June 5, 1788; Sedgwick Papers, Mass. Hist. Soc.
15. MS. letter, De Witt Clinton to Gen. [James Clinton], Apr. 25, 1788; N. Y. State Lib.
16. MS. letter, Abraham Yates, Jr., to Abraham G. Lansing, June 25, 1788; Yates Papers, N. Y. Pub. Lib.
17. June 8, 1788; *Works*, Lodge, IX, pp. 432-4.
18. Jay to Washington, May 29, 1788; *The Correspondence and Public Papers of John Jay*, Henry P. Johnston, ed., II, 344*ff*: "An idea has taken root that the southern part of the State will at all events, adhere to the Union; and, if necessary to that end, seek a separation from the northern. This idea has influence on the fears of the northern."
19. Madison to Hamilton, June 16, 1788; *Documentary History of the Constitution of the United States of America*, IV, p. 705.
20. May 19, 1788; *Works*, Lodge, IX, p. 431.
21. June 6, 1788; *ibid.*, p. 432.
22. MS. letter, June 4, 1788; King Papers, N. Y. Hist. Soc.
23. John Brown to Madison, June 7, 1788; *Letters of Members of the Continental Congress*, Edmund C. Burnett, ed., VIII, p. 750.
24. MS. letter, James M. Hughes to John Lamb, June 18, 1788; Lamb Papers, N. Y. Hist. Soc.
25. MS. letter, James M. Hughes to John Lamb, June 17, 1788; *ibid.*
26. MS. letter, June 19, 1788; King Papers, N. Y. Hist. Soc.
27. Hamilton to Madison, June 21, 1788; *Works*, Lodge, IX, p. 435.
28. MS. letter, Chas. Tillinghast to Lamb, June 21, 1788; Lamb Papers, N. Y. Hist. Soc.
29. J. C. H., *History*, III, p. 484n.
30. MS. "Notes on Poughkeepsie Convention"; Hamilton MSS., Lib. Cong.
31. Wm. Kent, *Memoirs and Letters of James Kent*, p. 31.
32. *The Debates in Several State Conventions on the Adoption of the Federal Constitution*, Jonathan Elliot, ed., I, pp. 230*ff*.

33. MS. letter, Yates to Lansing, June 25, 1788; Yates Papers, N. Y. Pub. Lib.
34. MS. letter, Clinton to Lamb, June 28, 1788; Lamb Papers, N. Y. Hist. Soc.
35. June 27, 1788; *Works*, Lodge, IX, p. 436.
36. Madison to Hamilton, June 20, June 22, 1788; *Works*, J. C. H., I, pp. 458-9, 461-2.
37. MS. letter, Christopher Yates to Abraham Yates, June 30, 1788; Yates Papers, N. Y. Pub. Lib.
38. Isaac Q. Leake, *Memoir of the Life and Times of General John Lamb*, p. 330.
39. June 27, 1788; *Works*, J. C. H., I, pp. 462-3.
40. Kent, *op. cit.*, p. 310.
41. July 8, 1788, also July [?], 1788; *Works*, Lodge, IX, pp. 436-7, 437-8.
42. Madison to Hamilton, Sunday evening [July], 1788; *Works*, J. C. H., I, p. 465. Edward Channing, in his *A History of the United States*, III, p. 552n, doubts the genuineness of this famous letter on two grounds: (1) that the original was not found after diligent search by Mr. Gaillard Hunt (editor of *The Writings of James Madison*), in either Madison's or Hamilton's papers in the Library of Congress; (2) that the reports of the debates in the convention "do not bear out J. C. Hamilton's assertion that Madison's letter was read in the Convention and that a short time thereafter the Constitution was unconditionally ratified." Though it is true that J. C. Hamilton's statements are not always to be accepted without caution, in this instance he was wholly accurate. The original letter, for which Mr. Hunt searched in vain, may be found in the Library of Congress in the bound volumes of the Hamilton MSS., First Series, VII, p. 891. And, though the printed debates do not mention the reading, the unpublished notes taken by Gilbert Livingston on the floor of the convention (the manuscript is in the New York Public Library) specifically mention the reading as having occurred on July 24th. Hamilton asserted he "has taken advice with men of character—they think it will not do [conditional ratification] proposed to read a letter—reads it . . . the terms of the constitution import a perpetual compact between the different states."
43. MS. "Reports of the Poughkeepsie Convention," taken by Gilbert Livingston, N. Y. Pub. Lib.
44. *Ibid.*
45. *Ibid.* Other accounts of the Convention proceedings may be found in Elliot, *Debates*, *op. cit.*, II, pp. 230ff; and in J. C. H., *History*, III, pp. 483ff.
46. New York *Journal*, July 4, 1788.
47. Letter of Daniel Chipman; cited in J. C. H., *History*, III, pp. 522-3.
49. J. P. Brissot de Warville, *New Travels in the United States of America*, p. 166; William A. Duer, *Reminiscences of an Old New Yorker*, pp. 51ff; J. C. H., *History*, III, p. 528.
50. MS. letter, Craigie to D. Parker, July 27, 1788; Craigie Papers, Amer. Antiquarian Soc.

CHAPTER XVII

1. J. A. Hamilton, *Reminiscences*, p. 7.
2. J. P. Brissot de Warville, *New Travels in the United States of America*, p. 166.
3. MS. letter, Nov. 6, 1787; Van Rensselaer Papers, N. Y. State Lib.
4. J. C. H., *History*, III, p. 362.
5. Oct. 2, 1787; *Intimate Life*, pp. 56-7.
6. Apr. 25, 1788; *ibid*, p. 73.
7. *The Diary and Letters of Gouverneur Morris*, Anne C. Morris, ed., II, pp. 523-4, 526.
8. MS. letter, Aug. 28, 1788; Columbia Univ.
9. Sept., 1788; *Works*, Lodge, IX, pp. 444*ff*.
10. Washington to Hamilton, Oct. 3, 1788; *The Writings of George Washington*, W. C. Ford, ed., XI, pp. 328-32.
11. Hamilton to Sedgwick, Oct. 9, 1788; *Works*, Lodge, IX, pp. 446-7.
12. Oct. 16, 1788; *Works*, J. C. H., I, pp. 482-3.
13. Nov. 2, 1788; *ibid.*, I, pp. 483-4.
14. Hamilton to Sedgwick, Nov. 9, 1788; *Works*, Lodge, IX, pp. 451-2.
15. Hamilton to Madison, Nov. 23, 1788; *ibid.*, IX, pp. 453-6. See also John Trumbull to Adams, 1789; *The Works of John Adams*, C. F. Adams, ed., VIII, pp. 484-5, in which Trumbull voices his indignation over Hamilton's arrangement to throw three votes in New Jersey and two in Connecticut away from Adams.
16. Hamilton to Sedgwick, Jan. 29, 1789; *Works*, Lodge, IX, pp. 456-7.
17. The "*H. G.*" letters, broadsides, etc., are in *ibid.*, II, pp. 105-75.
18. *Annals of the Congress of the United States*, I, pp. 383, 385.
19. *Ibid.*, p. 403.
20. *Ibid.*, pp. 616, 628, 631.
21. J. C. H., *History*, IV, pp. 29-30; G. W. P. Custis, *Recollections and Private Memoirs of Washington*, pp. 349-50.
22. MS. letter, Craigie to D. Parker; Craigie Papers, Amer. Antiq. Soc.
23. MS. letter, Craigie to Messrs. N. & I. Van Statehorst & Hubbard; *ibid*.
24. MS. letter, Craigie to D. Parker; *ibid*.
25. MS. letter, Craigie to D. Parker, May 23, 1789; *ibid*.
26. MS. letter, *supra*, note 23.
27. MS. letter, Nov. 27, 1789; Duer Papers, N. Y. Hist. Soc.
28. MS. letter, Duer to John Holker, Dec. 10, 1788; *ibid*. In this letter Duer itemizes an impressive list of public securities he had bought and sold. In each case he made a tidy profit. One item will suffice: on June 24, 1788, he purchased securities of the par value of $10,000 for $1851. Within two months he resold the lot for $2500.
29. MS. letter, Jarvis to Melancton Smith & Andrew Craigie, Nov. 1, 1790; Craigie Papers, Amer. Antiq. Soc.
30. MS. letter, Oct. 8, 1789; Webb Correspondence, *ibid*.
31. Henry Lee to Hamilton, Nov. 16, 1789; *Works*, J. C. H., V, p. 445.
32. Hamilton to Lee, Dec. 1, 1789; *ibid.*, pp. 446-7.

33. Webster to James Greenleaf, Sept. 20, 1789; *Notes on the Life of Noah Webster*, E. E. F. Skeel, ed., I, p. 207.
34. MS. letter, Sept. 25, 1789; Hamilton MSS., Lib. Cong.
35. Hamilton to Washington, May 5, 1789; *Works*, J. C. H., IV, pp. 1-3.
36. *The Journal of William Maclay*, Aug. 23, 1789; p. 131.

CHAPTER XVIII

1. Hamilton to Madison, Oct. 12, 1789; *Works*, Lodge, IX, pp. 462-3.
2. Madison to Hamilton, Nov. 19, 1789; J. C. H., *History*, IV, pp. 60-4.
3. Sept. 6, 1789; *The Works of Thomas Jefferson*, Paul L. Ford, ed., VI, pp. 3-11.
4. *Works*, Lodge, II, pp. 227-91.
5. Hamilton to Lafayette, Oct. 6, 1789; *ibid.*, IX, pp. 459-62; Hamilton to Short, Oct. 7, 1789; *ibid.*, IV, pp. 294-6.
6. *Mass Hist. Soc. Proc.*, Second Series, XV, p. 122n., p. 140.
7. *Gazette of the United States*, Feb. 23, 1793.
8. *Annals of the Congress of the United States*, I, p. 1080.
9. *Ibid.*, p. 1081.
10. *Works*, Lodge, II, p. 283.
11. *The Journal of William Maclay*, p. 177.
12. *Ibid.*, pp. 177-8.
13. James A. Hamilton, *Reminiscences*, p. 18.
14. Charles A. Beard, *An Economic Interpretation of the Constitution of the United States*, p. 109; citing Treasury Dept. MSS., Lib. Cong.
15. Hamilton MSS., Lib. Cong.
16. Beard, *op. cit.*, p. 109.
17. Maclay, *Journal, op. cit.*, p. 188.
18. Hamilton MSS., Lib. Cong.
19. *Intimate Life*, p. 57.
20. Maclay, *Journal, op. cit.*, p. 179.
21. Madison to Jefferson, Jan. 24, 1790; *The Writings of James Madison*, Gaillard Hunt, ed., V, p. 435.
22. *Annals of Cong., op. cit.*, I, pp. 1132, -5, -8.
23. *Ibid.*, p. 1139.
24. *Ibid.*, p. 1141.
25. Maclay, *Journal, op. cit.*, p. 189.
26. MS. letter, Sam Henshaw to Sedgwick, Jan. 30, 1790; Sedgwick Papers, Mass. Hist. Soc.
27. MS. letter, Feb. 7, 1790; *ibid.*
28. *Annals of Cong., op. cit.*, I, pp. 1180-2.
29. *Ibid.*, pp. 1185-6.
30. *Ibid.*, pp. 1187, 1190, 1194.
31. *Ibid.*, p. 1195.
32. Ames to Minot, May 3, 1789; *Works of Fisher Ames*, Seth Ames, ed., I, pp. 35-6.
33. *Annals of Cong., op. cit.*, I, pp. 1234-8.

34. MS. memo; Madison Papers, Lib. Cong.
35. Maclay, *Journal, op. cit.*, pp. 199, 200.
36. *Annals of Cong., op. cit.*, II, pp. 1345, 1354.
37. *Ibid.*, p. 1411.
38. *Ibid.*, pp. 1446, 1428, -9, -32.
39. *Ibid.*, pp. 1387-9.
40. Maclay, *Journal, op. cit.*, p. 209.
41. *Annals of Congress, op. cit.*, II, pp. 1459-63.
42. Ames to Minot, Mar. 23, 1790; Ames, *Works, op. cit.*, I, p. 75.
43. MS. letter, Trumbull to Wadsworth, Mar. 21, 1790; Wadsworth Papers, Conn. Hist. Soc.
44. *Annals of Cong., op. cit.*, II, p. 1565.
45. Maclay, *Journal, op. cit.*, pp. 227, 230.
46. *Ibid.*, p. 234.
47. *Annals of Cong., op. cit.*, II, pp. 1577-8.
48. Maclay, *Journal, op. cit.*, p. 237.
49. *Annals of Cong., op. cit.*, II, pp. 1587-92.
50. MS. letter, Craigie to Samuel Rogers, Apr. 10, 1790; Craigie Papers, Amer. Antiq. Soc.; also Craigie to Rogers, Mar. 8, 1790; *ibid.*
51. "Anas," *The Writings of Thomas Jefferson*, A. A. Lipscomb, ed., I, p. 174.
52. Maclay, *Journal, op. cit.*, pp. 291-3.
53. "Anas," Jefferson, *Writings*, I, pp. 174-7.
54. MS. letter, Jefferson to Monroe, June 20, 1790; Monroe Papers, N. Y. Pub. Lib.; to same effect, Jefferson to T. M. Randolph, June 20, 1790; Jefferson, *Works, op. cit.*, VI, pp. 76-7.
55. *Annals of Cong., op. cit.*, I, p. 1055; II, p. 1755.
56. Maclay, *Journal, op. cit.*; see his vigorous and acid entries for the period from June 18 to July 17, 1790.
57. MS. letter, Craigie to Rogers, Aug. 18, 1790; Craigie Papers, Amer. Antiq. Soc.
58. *Journal, Virginia House of Delegates* (1790), p. 35.
59. *Ibid.*, pp. 80-1.
60. Hamilton to Jay, Nov. 13, 1790; Wm. Jay, *The Life of John Jay*, II, p. 202.
61. Jay to Hamilton, Nov. 28, 1790; *The Correspondence and Public Papers of John Jay*, Henry P. Johnston, ed., III, pp. 409-10.
62. Madison, when an old man, gave as the reason for the breach between Jefferson and himself, on the one side, and Hamilton and Washington, on the other, that Hamilton had made plain "his purpose and endeavour to administration the Government into a thing totally different from that which he and I both knew perfectly well had been understood and intended by the Convention who framed it, and by the People adopting it." Nicholas P. Trist to Martin Van Buren, May 31, 1857; Van Buren MSS., Lib. Cong.

CHAPTER XIX

1. MS. letter, Hamilton to Gen. Stewart, July 5, 1790; Stewart Papers, N. Y. Hist. Soc.
2. MS. letter, Hamilton to Gen. Stewart, Aug. 27, 1790; *ibid*.
3. Hamilton to Short, Sept. 1, 1790; *Works*, J. C. H., IV., pp. 38-46.
4. *Works*, Lodge, II, pp. 337-51.
5. *Ibid.*, IV, p. 302.
6. *The Diaries of George Washington*, John C. Fitzpatrick, ed., III, p. 143.
7. Washington to Hamilton, Aug. 27, 1790; *Works*, J. C. H., IV, p. 35.
8. "Cabinet Opinion," Aug. 28, 1790; Jefferson, *Works*, VI, pp. 141-3.
9. "Cabinet Opinion," Sept. 15, 1790; *Works*, Lodge, IV, pp. 313-42.
10. MS. letter, Washington to Hamilton, Oct. 3, 1790; Washington MSS., Lib. Cong.
11. *Works*, Lodge, III, pp. 388-443. In this connection, a letter from Tench Coxe to Hamilton, dated Mar. 5, 1790, is of interest. In a section to be found among the Hamilton MSS., Lib. Cong., and omitted from the the published version (*Works*, J. C. H., V, p. 455) we find that Coxe sent him a pamphlet he had written some time before outlining a plan for a bank.
12. Ames to Thomas Dwight, Dec. 23, 1790; *Works of Fisher Ames*, Seth Ames, ed., I, p. 90.
13. Temple to Duke of Leeds, Jan. 5, 1791; Hammond Transcripts of Brit. State Papers, N. Y. Pub. Lib.
14. *The Journal of William Maclay*, pp. 355, 351.
15. *Ibid.*, pp. 370, 401.
16. *Annals of the Congress of the United States*, II, p. 1941.
17. *Ibid.*, pp. 1945ff.
18. *Ibid.*, pp. 1954-9.
19. *Ibid.*, p. 1789.
20. *The Works of Thomas Jefferson*, Paul L. Ford, ed., VI, pp. 197-204.
21. Washington to Hamilton, Feb. 16, 1791; *Works*, J. C. H., IV, p. 103.
22. Feb. 23, 1791; *Works*, Lodge, III, pp. 445-93.
23. *Ibid.*, IV, pp. 3-58.
24. Maclay, *Journal*, *op. cit.*, pp. 409, 387.
25. *Annals of Cong.*, *op. cit.*, I, p. 1095.
26. MS. letter, July 6, 1790; Hamilton MSS., Lib. Cong.
27. Hamilton MSS., Lib. Cong. The article had originally appeared in the "American Museum," 1790.
28. MS. letter, Dana to Cabot, July 26, 1790; *ibid*.
29. MS. letter, Aug. 14, 1791; *ibid*.
30. Cabot to Hamilton, Sept. 6, 1791; Henry Cabot Lodge, *Life and Letters of George Cabot*, pp. 43-6.
31. MS. letter, Elisha Colt to Chester, Aug. 20, 1791; Hamilton MSS., Lib. Cong.
32. *Works*, Lodge, IV, pp. 70-198.
33. Jefferson MSS., Lib. Cong.

34. *Gazette of the United States,* Sept. 10, 1791; also MS. prospectus, Hamilton MSS., Lib. Cong.
35. *General Advertiser,* Oct. 6, 1791.
36. Hamilton MSS., Lib. Cong.
37. *Session Laws of New Jersey* (1791), pp. 730-46.
38. *National Gazette,* Nov. 14, 1791.
39. MS. letter, Hamilton to S. U. M., 1791; Hamilton MSS., Lib. Cong.
40. MS. letters, Marshall to Hamilton, July 19, 1791; Hall to Hamilton, Aug. 29, 1791; *ibid.* Also Hamilton to S. U. M., Dec. 7, 1791; cited in Joseph S. Davis, *Essays in the Earlier History of American Corporations,* I, p. 399.
41. Davis, *op. cit.,* I, p. 406.
42. Hamilton to Hubbard, May 3, 1792; MS. letter in Huntington Lib.
43. *Independent Gazetteer,* May 22, 1792.
44. MS. letter, Apr. 14, 1792; Dreer Coll., Pa. Hist. Soc.
45. Seton to Hamilton, June 11, 1792; Hamilton MSS., Lib. Cong. The section referring to the loan is omitted from the published letter in *Works,* J. C. H., V, pp. 511-12.
46. N. Y. *Times,* Feb. 16, 1937.

CHAPTER XX

1. MS. letter, Troup to Hamilton, Jan. 19, 1791; Hamilton MSS., Lib. Cong.
2. MS. letter, Seton to Hamilton; *ibid.*
3. July, 1791; *The Writings of James Madison,* Gaillard Hunt, ed., VI, p. 55.
4. July 10, 1791; *The Works of Thomas Jefferson,* Paul L. Ford, ed., VI, pp. 281-2.
5. MS. letter, Aug. 14, 1791; Madison Papers, Lib. Cong.
6. Aug. 17, 1791; *Works,* Lodge, IX, pp. 493-4.
7. Hamilton to Seton, Aug. 15, 1791; *ibid.,* p. 490.
8. Hamilton to Seton, Aug. 16, 1791; *ibid.,* pp. 491-2.
9. *American State Papers: Finance,* I, p. 117.
10. MS. letter, Aug. 15, 1791; Hamilton MSS., Lib. Cong.
11. MS. letter, Aug. 17, 1791; King Papers, N. Y. Hist. Soc.
12. Hamilton to Seton; *Works,* Lodge, IX, p. 496.
13. Seton to Hamilton, Sept. 12, 1791; *Works,* J. C. H., V, p. 480.
14. J. B. Cutting to P. Colquhoun, Oct. 12, 1791; *The Manuscripts of J. B. Fortescue, Esq.,* Historical Manuscripts Commission, II, p. 228.
15. *American State Papers: Finance,* I, p. 231.
16. MS. letter, Seth Johnson to Craigie, Dec. 24, 1793; Craigie Papers, Amer. Antiq. Soc.
17. Mar. 12, 1792; MS. copy in Wolcott Papers, Conn. Hist. Soc.
18. MS. letter, Mar. 12, 179[2]; Wadsworth Papers, Conn. Hist. Soc.
19. Mar. 14, 1792; *Works,* Lodge, IX, pp. 502-3.
20. MS. letter; Wolcott Papers, Conn. Hist. Soc.

21. MS. letter, James Watson to Jeremiah Wadsworth, Mar. 14, 1792; Wadsworth Papers, Conn. Hist. Soc.
22. MS. letter, James Watson to Jeremiah Wadsworth, Apr. 3, 1792; *ibid.*
23. Apr. 22, 1792; *Works*, J. C. H., V, pp. 506-7.
24. *Works*, Lodge, IX, pp. 498-9.
25. *Ibid.*, pp. 501-2.
26. Hamilton to Seton, Mar. 25, 1792; *ibid.*, pp. 503-5.
27. Knox Papers, Mass. Hist. Soc.
28. Seton to Hamilton, Apr. 16, 1792; *Works*, J. C. H., V, p. 505.
29. MS. letter, Hamilton to Philip Livingston, Apr. 2, 1792; Livingston Papers, N. Y. Pub. Lib.
30. *Works*, J. C. H., V, p. 511.
31. MS. letter, Seton to Hamilton, July 23, 1792; Hamilton MSS., Lib. Cong.
32. MS. letter, Seton to Hamilton, Aug. 6, 1792; *ibid.*
33. MS. letter, Troup to Hamilton; *ibid.*
34. Hamilton to Seton, June 26, 1792; *Works*, Lodge, IX, p. 540.
35. Seton to Hamilton, May 28, 1792; *Works*, J. C. H., V, pp. 509-10; Seton to Hamilton, June 11, 1792; *ibid.*, pp. 511-12; Seton to Hamilton, Aug. 6, 1792; Hamilton MSS., Lib. Cong.
36. MS. letter, Seton to Hamilton; *ibid.*
37. MS. letter, Hamilton to Washington, May 9, 1792; Washington MSS., Lib. Cong.
38. MS. letter, I. Tillery to Hamilton, 1791; Hamilton MSS., Lib. Cong. To same effect, Seton to Hamilton, Feb. 3, 1791; *Works*, J. C. H., V, pp. 463-4.
39. MS. letter, Burr to Sedgwick, Feb. 3, 1791; Sedgwick Papers, Mass. Hist. Soc.
40. MS. letter, Burr to Sedgwick, Feb. 17, 1791; *ibid.*
41. MS. letter, Mar. 1, 1792; Hamilton MSS., Lib. Cong.
42. For a full discussion see Nathan Schachner, *Aaron Burr*, pp. 110-14.
43. Hamilton to King, July 25, 1792; *Works*, Lodge, IX, pp. 3-4. See also King to Hamilton, July 10, 1792; Hamilton MSS., Lib. Cong.; and Peter Van Schaack to Sedgwick, Nov. 20, 1792; Sedgwick Papers, Mass. Hist. Soc.
44. Jefferson, *Writings*, I, pp. 184-5.
45. *Ibid.*, p. 236.
46. Jefferson to Wm. Short, July 28, 1791; Jefferson, *Works, op. cit.*, VI, pp. 290-1.
47. MS. letter, Hamilton to Goodhue, June 30, 1791; N. Y. Soc. Lib. MSS.
48. MS. letter, Hamilton to Jefferson, Jan. 13, 1791; Jefferson MSS., Lib Cong.
49. Jefferson, *Writings*, I, pp. 207-8.
50. Hammond to Grenville, Jan. 9, 1792; Hammond Transcripts, N. Y. Pub. Lib.
51. Hammond to Grenville, Jan. 9, 1792 (second letter); *ibid.*
52. Jefferson, *Writings*, I, p. 208.
53. *Ibid.*, p. 192.

54. *Ibid.*, p. 196.
55. Hammond to Grenville, June 8, 1792; Hammond Transcripts, N. Y. Pub. Lib.
56. "Cash Books"; Hamilton MSS., Lib. Cong.
57. *National Gazette*, Sept., 1793.
58. Jefferson, *Works, op. cit.*, VI, p. 257.
59. *Ibid.*, pp. 263-4.
60. "An American" in *Gazette of the United States*, Aug. 4, 1792.
61. Jefferson to Washington, Sept. 9, 1792; Jefferson, *Works, op. cit.*, VII, p. 149.
62. *Gazette of the United States*, July 25, 1792.
63. *Ibid.*, Aug. 4-18, 1792.
64. MS. letters, Beckley to Madison, Sept. 2, Oct. 17, 1792; Madison Papers, N. Y. Pub. Lib. In a long letter addressed to Col. Edward Carrington of Va., Hamilton reviews the history of his relations with Madison, and documents the reasons why he now considers Madison his personal and political enemy; May 26, 1792; *Works*, Lodge, IX, pp. 513-35.
65. Aug. 26, 1792; *The Writings of George Washington*, W. C. Ford, ed., XII, p. 177.
66. Sept. 9, 1792; *Works*, Lodge, VII, pp. 303-6.
67. Sept. 9, 1792; Jefferson, *Works, op. cit.*, VII, pp. 136-49.

Chapter XXI

1. *Works*, Lodge, II, pp. 368-408.
2. *Ibid.*, X, p. 11.
3. *Ibid.*, VI, pp. 339-41.
4. Sept. 7, 1792; *The Writings of George Washington*, W. C. Ford, ed., XII, pp. 181-3.
5. Hamilton to Washington, Sept. 9, 11, 1792; *Works*, Lodge, VI, pp. 342-7.
6. Washington to Hamilton, Sept. 16, 1792; Washington, *Writings, op. cit.*, XII, pp. 186-7. Washington to Jefferson, Sept. 15, 1792; *ibid.*, p. 187.
7. Sept. 9, 1792; *The Works of John Adams*, C. F. Adams, ed., VIII, pp. 514-5.
8. Sept. 17, 1792; *Works*, J. C. H., V, p. 526.
9. Schuyler to Hamilton; *ibid.*, pp. 492-4.
10. Sept. 23, 1792; *Works*, Lodge, X, p. 21.
11. Hamilton to ——, Sept. 26, 1792; *ibid.*, p. 22.
12. Hamilton to ——, Sept. 21, 1792; *ibid.*, pp. 19-20.
13. Oct. 15, 1792; *Works*, J. C. H., V, p. 535.
14. MS. letter, Sept. 23, 1792; Gratz Coll., Pa. Hist. Soc.
15. Washington to David Stuart, Oct. 21, 1792; Washington, *Writings, op. cit.*, XII, pp. 204-5.
16. MS. letter, Bagly to Hamilton, Nov. 4, 1792; Hamilton MSS., Lib. Cong.
17. N. Y. *Daily Advertiser*, Mar. 11, 1793.

18. Hamilton MSS., Lib. Cong.
19. *Annals of the Congress of the United States*, III, p. 900.
20. These passages appear in the course of a long and important communication addressed by Hamilton to Washington, defending his financial measures against the objections raised by Col. George Mason of Va.; Aug. 18, 1792; *Works*, Lodge, II, pp. 426-72.
21. *Report on Loans*, Feb. 4, 6, 13, 1793; *ibid.*, III, pp. 61-126.
22. Jefferson, *Writings*, VII, pp. 220-3. See also P. L. Ford, "The Authorship of Giles's Resolutions," in *The Nation*, Sept. 5, 1895.
23. MS. memorandum, undated; Madison MSS., Lib. Cong. Jefferson used this memo verbatim in a cabinet paper which he addressed to Washington; *Works*, J. C. H., IV, p. 334.
24. *Annals of Cong.*, op. cit., III, p. 901.
25. *Ibid.*, pp. 911-14.
26. *Ibid.*, pp. 955-63.
27. "Anas," Mar. 2, 1793; Jefferson, *Writings*, I, p. 262.
28. Jefferson to Hamilton, Mar. 27, 1793; *ibid.*, VII, pp. 270-2. Italics mine.
29. Washington, *Writings, op. cit.*, XII, pp. 280-1.
30. Jefferson, *Writings*, I, pp. 267-8.
31. Washington to Hamilton; *Works*, J. C. H., IV, p. 357; Washington to Jefferson; Washington, *Writings, op. cit.*, XII, pp. 278-9.
32. Hamilton to Jay (2); *Works*, Lodge, X, pp. 38-9.
33. Jay to Hamilton, Apr. 11, 1793; *Works*, J. C. H., V, pp. 552-3.
34. Hammond to Grenville; Hammond Corresp., N. Y. Pub. Lib.
35. Hammond to Grenville; *ibid.*
36. Jefferson to Madison, June 23, 1793; Jefferson, *Writings*, I, p. 266.
37. Hamilton's arguments were later amplified in his controversial pamphlets, signed "Pacificus." See especially No. I in *Works*, Lodge, IV, p. 442.
38. *American State Papers: Foreign Relations*, I, p. 140.
39. Hamilton to Washington, Apr., 1793 (cabinet paper); *Works*, Lodge, IV, pp. 369-96.
40. Jefferson to Washington, Apr. 28, 1793 (cabinet paper); Jefferson, *Writings*, VII, pp. 283-301.
41. John Steele to Hamilton, Apr. 30, 1793; *Works*, J. C. H., V, pp. 561-2.
42. May 5, 1793; Jefferson, *Writings*, VII, p. 309.
43. May 15, 1793; *Works*, Lodge, IV, p. 415.
44. Cabinet paper, July 8, 1793; *ibid.*, V, pp. 3-12.
45. "Anas," July 14, 1793; Jefferson, *Writings*, I, p. 291.
46. *Ibid.*, p. 305.
47. *Works*, Lodge, IV, pp. 432-89.
48. July 7, 1793; *The Works of Thomas Jefferson*, Paul L. Ford, ed., VII, p. 436.
49. July 18, 1793; *The Writings of James Madison*, Gaillard Hunt, ed., VI, p. 125.
50. MS. letter, Madison to Jefferson, July 30, 1793; Madison MSS., Lib. Cong.
51. *Works*, Lodge, V, pp. 17-49.

52. Fisher Ames to Minot, Dec. 6, 1793; *Works of Fisher Ames*, Seth Ames, ed., I, p. 132.
53. Wolcott to Washington, Oct. 20, 1793; George Gibbs, *Memoirs of the Administrations of Washington and John Adams*, I, p. 112.
54. MS. letter, Sept. 8, 1793; Madison MSS., Lib. Cong.

CHAPTER XXII

1. *Works*, Lodge, X, pp. 48-9.
2. Dec. 16, 1793; *ibid.*, III, pp. 178-9.
3. Hamilton to Washington, Mar. 24, 1794; *ibid.*, pp. 183-4; Hamilton to Committee of Congress, Apr. 1, 1794; *ibid*, p. 185; Washington to Hamilton, Apr. 8, 1794; *ibid.*, p. 190.
4. Hamilton to Speaker of House of Representatives, Dec. 1, 1794; *ibid.*, p. 199.
5. Schuyler to Hamilton, Jan. 5 (1795); *Intimate Life*, p. 164.
6. Hammond to Grenville, July 7, 1793; Hammond Transcripts, N. Y. Pub. Lib.
7. Hammond to Grenville, Nov. 7, 1793; *ibid.*
8. *Works*, J. C. II., IV, p. 506.
9. Apr. 3, 1794; Jefferson, *Writings*, VIII, p. 141.
10. "Americanus," in the *Daily Advertiser*, Feb. 1, 8, 1794; *Works*, Lodge, V, pp. 74-96.
11. *The Life and Correspondence of Rufus King*, Charles R. King, ed., I, pp. 517-8.
12. *Ibid.*, p. 518.
13. *Ibid.*, p. 519.
14. Ames to Gore, Mar. 26, 1794; *Works of Fisher Ames*, Seth Ames, ed., I, p. 140.
15. Aug. 15, 1793; *Intimate Life*, p. 58.
16. Apr. 8, 1794; *The Writings of James Monroe*, S. M. Hamilton, ed., I, pp. 291-2.
17. Apr. 9, 1794; *The Writings of George Washington*, W. C. Ford, ed., XII, p. 415.
18. Apr. 14, 1794; *Works*, Lodge, V, pp. 97-119.
19. King, *op. cit.*, I, pp. 520ff.
20. *Ibid.*
21. MS. letters (2), Madison to Jefferson, Apr. 14, 28, 1794; Madison MSS., Lib. Cong.
22. Hamilton to Washington; *Works*, Lodge, V, pp. 115-9.
23. Hamilton to Washington, May 27, 1794; *ibid*, X, pp. 65-6; Washington to Hamilton, May 29, 1794; Washington, *Writings, op. cit.*, XII, p. 433.
24. Apr. 17, 1794; Hammond Transcripts, N. Y. Pub. Lib.
25. July 11, 1794; *The Correspondence and Public Papers of John Jay*, Henry P. Johnston, ed., IV, pp. 29-30.
26. Aug. 3, 1794; Hammond Transcripts, N. Y. Pub. Lib.
27. Nov. 19, 1794; *Jay Correspondence, op. cit.*, IV, p. 135.

28. *Works*, Lodge, VI, pp. 353-8.
29. Aug. 5, 1794; *ibid.*, pp. 358-88; Aug. 7, 1794; *ibid.*, pp. 389-94.
30. Secretary of State to Mifflin, Aug. 7, 1794; *ibid.*, pp. 394*ff.*
31. Secretary of State to Mifflin, Aug. 30, 1794; *ibid.*, pp. 427*ff.*
32. Aug. 23-Sept. 2, 1794; *ibid.*, pp. 410-26.
33. *The Writings of Albert Gallatin*, Henry Adams, ed., I, pp. 4-9.
34. Sept. 19, 1794; *Works*, Lodge, VI, pp. 441-2.
35. Sept. 22, 1794; King Papers, N. Y. Hist. Soc.
36. George Washington, *Diaries*, John C. Fitzpatrick, ed., III, p. 209.
37. Hamilton to Washington; *Works*, Lodge, VI, pp. 452-3.
38. Oct. 30, 1794; *ibid.*, p. 77.
39. Nov. 1, 1794; Washington, *Writings, op. cit.*, XII, pp. 484-9. Also Hamilton to Fitzsimmons, Nov. 27, 1794; *Works*, Lodge, X, pp. 78-9.
40. Washington to Hamilton, Oct. 26, 1794; Washington, *Writings, op. cit.*, XII, pp. 480-2.
41. Nov. 3, 1794; *Works*, Lodge, VI, p. 455.
42. Nov. 8, 1794; *ibid.*, pp. 455-6.
43. Hamilton to Washington, Nov. 17, 1794; *ibid.*, pp. 459-60.
44. Hamilton to Washington, Nov. 11, 1794; *ibid.*, pp. 457-8.
45. Madison to Monroe, Dec. 4, 1794; *The Writings of James Madison*, Gaillard Hunt, ed., VI, p. 227.
46. Jan. 5, 1795; Hammond Transcripts, N. Y. Pub. Lib.
47. June 25, 1795; *ibid.*
48. Jan. 20, 1795; *Works*, Lodge, III, pp. 199-301.

Chapter XXIII

1. MS. letter, Nov. 24, 1794; Knox Papers, Mass. Hist. Soc.
2. MS. letter, Beckley to Madison, May 25, 1795; Madison Papers, N. Y. Pub. Lib.
3. Isaac Q. Leake, *Memoir of the Life and Times of General John Lamb*, p. 347. Here, however, the impending duel was blamed on differences over the Jay Treaty. In view of the immediately preceding accusations by Nicholson against Hamilton's personal honor, it is much more plausible to assume that these accusations were the motivating force.
4. G. W. P. Custis, *Recollections and Private Memoirs of Washington*, p. 352.
5. MS. letter, Nov. 26, 1793; Hamilton MSS., Lib. Cong.
6. MS. letter, Seton to Hamilton, Mar. 29, 1794; *ibid.*
7. MS. letter, May 28, 1794; *ibid.*
8. MS. letter, June 23, 1795; *ibid.*
9. MS. letter, July 20, 1795; *ibid.*
10. MS. letters, Oct. 2, Nov. 1, 1797; *ibid.*
11. MS. letters, Morris to Hamilton, Dec. 21, 1797, Jan. 17, 1798; *ibid.*
12. Hamilton to Angelica Church, 1794; Angelica to Eliza, 1794; *Intimate Life*, pp. 17, 227.
13. July 30, 1794; *ibid.*, pp. 259-60.

14. Dec. 8, 1794; *ibid.*, p. 37.
15. La Rochefoucauld-Liancourt, *Voyage dans les Etats-Unis d'Amérique*, VII, p. 149.
16. M. L. E. Moreau de Saint-Méry, *Voyage aux Etats-Unis d'Amérique*, pp. 145-9.
17. *Life, Letters, and Journals of George Ticknor*, G. S. Hillard, ed., II, p. 113.
18. Charles A. Talleyrand-Périgord, *Etude sur la République des Etats-Unis D'Amérique*, p. 192.
19. *Ibid.*
20. MS. letter, May 11, 1795; Hamilton MSS., Lib. Cong.
21. MS. letter, Feb. 17, 1795; *ibid.* This passage is omitted from the letter as published in *Works*, J. C. H., V, p. 623.
22. Nathan Schachner, *Aaron Burr*, p. 145. This was in 1797.
23. MS. letter and memo, June 27, 1795; Hamilton MSS., Lib. Cong.
24. Photostat, July 2, 1795; *ibid.*
25. William Kent, *Memoirs and Letters of James Kent*, p. 318.
26. Varick to Hamilton, Apr. 30, 1795; *Works*, J. C. H., V, p. 633.
27. Feb. 18, 1795; *Works*, Lodge, X, p. 89.
28. Feb. 21, 1795; *ibid.*, p. 90.
29. See letter of Apr. 10, 1795; *ibid.*, pp. 92-7. Also letters dated June 22, 1795; *ibid.*, pp. 104-6; and June 26, 1795; *ibid.*, p. 106.
30. June 14, 1796; *Works*, J. C. H., VI, p. 129.
31. May (10), 1795; *Works*, Lodge, X, pp. 98-101.
32. July 28, 1795; *ibid.*, p. 112.
33. J. C. H., *History*, VI, p. 225.
34. *Works*, Lodge, V, pp. 189-491.
35. Sept. 21, 1795; Jefferson, *Writings*, VIII, pp. 192-3.
36. Washington to Hamilton, Mar. 31, 1796; *The Writings of George Washington*, W. C. Ford, ed., XIII, pp. 180-2.
37. Hamilton to Washington, Mar. 7, 26, 29, 1796; *Works*, Lodge, X, pp. 145-7, 152; VII, p. 161ff.
38. Hamilton to King, Apr. 15, 18, 20, 1796; *ibid.*, X, pp. 157-61.
39. Apr. 20, 1796; *ibid.*, p. 161.
40. Washington to Hamilton, Oct. 29, 1795; Washington, *Writings, op. cit.*, XIII, pp. 127-36.
41. Nov. 17, 1795; *Works*, J. C. H., VI, pp. 67-9.
42. June 26, 1796; Washington, *Writings, op. cit.*, XIII, pp. 217-21.
43. May 15, 1796; Hamilton MSS., Lib. Cong.
44. Sept. 4, 1796; *Works*, Lodge, X, p. 190.
45. Jay to Richard Peters, Mar. 29, 1811; *Memoirs of Historical Society of Pennsylvania*, I, pp. 239-51.
46. A definitive analysis of the genesis of the Farewell Address may be found in Victor Hugo Paltsits, *Washington's Farewell Address*, N. Y. Pub. Lib., 1935.
47. Hamilton to ———, 1796; *Works*, Lodge, X, pp. 195-6.
48. MS. copy, Nov. 12, 1796; Hamilton MSS., Lib. Cong.
49. MS. copy, Nov. 13, 1796; *ibid.*

50. MS. copy, Nov. 19, 1796; *ibid.*
51. MS. letter, Nov. 19, 1796; *ibid.*
52. Dec. 9, 1796; *Works*, J. C. H., VI, pp. 185-7.
53. Dec. 16, 1796; *Works*, Lodge, X, pp. 215-7.
54. Jan. 12, 1797; *Works*, J. C. H., VI, pp. 191-2.
55. Dec. 28, 1796; Jefferson, *Writings*, VIII, pp. 259-61. The original is in the N. Y. Pub. Lib. It is quite probable, however, that this letter never reached Adams. For Madison, to whom it was sent by Jefferson for forwarding, wrote back in a hitherto unpublished letter that he was holding it up. Madison dryly remarked that Adams already was aware of Jefferson's warm feelings toward him and "it deserves to be considered whether the idea of bettering it is not outweighed by the possibility of changing it for the worse.... There is perhaps a general air on the letter which betrays the difficulty of your situation in writing it." Adams, he was certain, already knew of Hamilton's machinations, "and there may be danger of his suspecting in mementos on that subject, a wish to make his resentment an instrument for avenging that of others." Jan. 15, 1797; Madison MSS., Lib. Cong.
56. Jan. 1, 1797; Jefferson, *Writings*, VIII, p. 263.

CHAPTER XXIV

1. "The Answer"; *Works*, Lodge, VI, pp. 215-29; "The Warning"; *ibid.*, pp. 229-59.
2. Jan. 26, 1797; *Works*, J. C. H., VI, pp. 198-203.
3. Troup to King, Jan. 28, 1797; *The Life and Correspondence of Rufus King*, Charles R. King, ed., I, pp. 135-7.
4. Jan. 19, 1797; *Works*, Lodge, X, pp. 229-30.
5. Mar. 22, 1797; *ibid.*, pp. 241-3.
6. MS. letter, Mar. 26, 1797; Pickering Papers, Mass. Hist. Soc.
7. May 11, 1797; *Works*, J. C. H., VI, p. 246.
8. Mar. 31, 1797; *ibid.*, p. 224.
9. MS. letter, Apr. 6, 1797; Hamilton MSS., Lib. Cong.
10. Apr. 10, 1797; *Works*, Lodge, X, p. 256.
11. June 6, 1797; *ibid.*, p. 268.
12. MS. photostat, June 22, 27, 1793; N. Y. Pub. Lib.
13. "Observations on Certain Documents, etc.," *Works*, Lodge, VII, pp. 379-83, 412-7.
14. *Ibid.*, pp. 388-425.
15. *Ibid.*, pp. 425-9.
16. "Statements of Muhlenberg and Monroe"; *ibid.*, pp. 451-2.
17. MS. minutes of David Gelston; Gratz Papers, Pa. Hist. Soc.
18. *Works*, Lodge, VII, pp. 461-2.
19. *Ibid.*, pp. 461-76.
20. Photostat; Hamilton Misc. MSS., N. Y. Pub. Lib.
21. Photostat, Monroe to Burr, Aug. 6, 1797; *ibid.*
22. The pertinent letters are in *Works*, Lodge, VII, pp. 476-9; and in *American Book Prices Current*, 1926-7.

23. For a complete history of The Holland Company, see Paul D. Evans, *The Holland Land Company, passim.* For the quoted Act, see *Laws of New York,* Chap. 36, 20th Sess., Mar. 17, 1797. For Burr's connection with the affair, see Nathan Schachner, *Aaron Burr,* pp. 154-9.

24. MS. letters, Cazenove to Benson and Hamilton, May 29, 1797; Hamilton MSS., Lib. Cong.; Hamilton to Cazenove [Aug., 1797]; *ibid.*

CHAPTER XXV

1. Jan. 26, 1798; Bernard C. Steiner, *The Life and Correspondence of James McHenry,* p. 291.

2. Hamilton to McHenry, no date; *ibid,* pp. 291-5.

3. Mar. 25, 1798; *Works,* J. C. H., VI, pp. 274-5.

4. "The Stand"; *Works,* Lodge, VI, pp. 259-318.

5. Jay to Hamilton, Apr. 19, 1798; *Works,* J. C. H., VI, p. 281; Hamilton to Jay, Apr. 24, 1798; *Works,* Lodge, X, p. 281.

6. Washington to Hamilton, July 14, 1798; *The Writings of George Washington,* W. C. Ford, ed., XIV, pp. 40-3.

7. Hamilton to Washington, June 2, 1798; *Works,* Lodge, X, pp. 286-7.

8. *Supra,* Note 6.

9. MS. letter, Schuyler to Hamilton, Aug. 6, 1798; Hamilton MSS., Lib. Cong.

10. Pickering to J. A. Hamilton, June 14, 1821; *Intimate Life,* pp. 323-4.

11. Aug. 14, 1798; *The Works of John Adams,* C. F. Adams, ed., VIII, p. 580.

12. Sept. 25, 1798; Washington, *Writings, op. cit.,* XIV, pp. 92-104.

13. Photostat, Knox to Col. Wadsworth, Aug. 19, 1798; Gov. Joseph Trumbull Coll., Conn. State. Lib.

14. Adams to Washington, Oct. 3, 1798; Adams, *Works, op. cit.,* VIII, pp. 600-1.

15. MS. letter, Oct. 5, 1798; Hamilton MSS., Lib. Cong.

16. Oct. 19, 1798; *Works,* Lodge, VI, pp. 485-6.

17. Adams to S. B. Malcom, Aug. 6, 1812; Adams, *Works, op. cit.,* X, pp. 123ff.

18. MS. letter, Troup to King, June 3, 1798; King Papers, N. Y. Hist. Soc.

19. Washington to Hamilton, Aug. 9, 1798; Washington, *Writings, op. cit.,* XIV, pp. 65-7.

20. MS. letter, Gen. James Gunn to Hamilton, Dec. 19, 1798; Hamilton MSS., Lib. Cong.

21. MS. letter, McHenry to Hamilton, Jan. 11, 1799; *ibid.*

22. Hamilton to McHenry, Jan. 7, 1799; *Works,* Lodge, VII, pp. 50-3.

23. McHenry to Hamilton, Jan. 9, 1799; *Works,* J. C. H., V, p. 188.

24. Hamilton to Wilkinson, Feb. 12, 1799; *Works,* Lodge, VII, pp. 64-7.

25. Hamilton to Washington, June 15, 1799; *ibid.,* X, pp. 352-3.

26. Washington to Hamilton, June 25, 1799; *Works,* J. C. H., V, p. 277.

27. McHenry to Hamilton, June 27, 1799; *ibid.,* pp. 282-3.

28. June 27, 1799; *Works,* Lodge, VII, pp. 97-8.

29. E. E. Hale, *Memories of a Hundred Years,* I, pp. 65-7. Hale states that

the owner of the chest had offered it for sale to the War Dept. When they refused to pay the price he demanded, he burnt all the letters in a fit of anger.

30. William S. Robertson, *The Life of Miranda*, pp. 43, 54-5, citing Miranda MSS.

31. MS. letter and endorsement, Miranda to Hamilton; Hamilton MSS., Lib. Cong. Miranda's letters are written in French.

32. *Works*, Lodge, X, pp. 314-5.

33. MS. letter, Aug. 17, 1798; Hamilton MSS., Lib. Cong.

34. Oct. 20, 1798; *The Life and Correspondence of Rufus King*, Charles R. King, ed., II, p. 454.

35. Same date; *ibid.*, p. 453.

36. Miranda to Hamilton, Apr. 6, 1798; *Edinburgh Rev.*, XIII, p. 291.

37. MS. letter, Miranda to Hamilton, Oct. 19, 1798; Hamilton MSS., Lib. Cong.

39. Jefferson to Edmund Pendleton, Apr. 22, 1799; Jefferson, *Writings*, VIII, p. 65.

40. MS. letter, Feb. 6, 1799; Dreer Coll., Pa. Hist. Soc.

41. MS. letter, Feb. 2, 1799; Sedgwick Papers, Mass. Hist. Soc.

42. MS. letter, Hamilton to Sedgwick, Feb. 21, 1799 [misdated 1798]; *ibid.*

43. Jan. 2, 1800; *Works*, Lodge, X, pp. 356-7.

44. Jan. 5, 1800; *ibid.*, p. 360.

Chapter XXVI

1. MS. letter, May 29, 1797; Wadsworth Papers, Conn. Hist. Soc.

2. MS. letter, July 19, 1797; Hamilton MSS., Lib. Cong.

3. MS. letter, June 3, 1798; *ibid.*

4. Nov., 1798; *Intimate Life*, p. 43.

5. MS. letter, Troup to King, Jan. 23, 1799; King Papers, N. Y. Hist. Soc.

6. MS. letter, Troup to King, May 6, 1799; *ibid.*

7. MS. letter, Troup to King, June 5, 1799; *ibid.*

8. MS. letter, Troup to King, Sept. 2, 1799; *ibid.*

9. MS. letter, Troup to King, May 27, 1801; *ibid.*

10. MS, letter, Troup to King, Dec. 12, 1799; *ibid.:* "The water works of the Manhattan company go on with great rapidity. I have now a plentiful & constant supply of better water." For a detailed account of the Manhattan Company, see Nathan Schachner, *Aaron Burr*, pp. 159-66.

11. Hamilton to Jay, May 7, 1800; *Works*, Lodge, X, pp. 371-4.

12. William Jay, *The Life of John Jay*, I, p. 414.

13. May 10, 1800; *Works*, Lodge, X, pp. 375-6.

14. May 14, 1800; *ibid.*, p. 376.

15. MS. letter, May 15, 1800; Hamilton MSS., Lib. Cong. The passage here quoted is deleted from the letter as printed in *Works*, J. C. H., VI, p. 443.

16. The correspondence is voluminous, and may be found in *Works*, Lodge, X. See particularly Hamilton to Wolcott, July 1, 1800; *ibid.*, p. 377.

17. MS. letter, Bayard to Hamilton, June 8, 1800; Hamilton MSS., Lib. Cong.
18. MS. letter, Harper to Hamilton, June 5, 1800; *ibid.*
19. *Works*, Lodge, VII, pp. 309-64.
20. Cabot to Hamilton, Aug. 21, 1800; *Works*, J. C. H., VI, pp. 458-9; also Ames to Hamilton, Aug. 26, 1800; *ibid.*, pp. 463-5.
21. Hamilton to Pickering, Nov. 13, 1800; *Works*, Lodge, X, pp. 391-2.
22. Hamilton to Bayard; *ibid.*, p. 387.
23. MS. letter, Troup to King, Dec. 15, 1800; King Papers, N. Y. Hist. Soc.
24. Troup to King, Dec. 4, 1800; *The Life and Correspondence of Rufus King*, Charles R. King, ed., III, p. 340.
25. Cabot to Wolcott, Oct. 5, 1800; Henry Cabot Lodge, *Life and Letters of George Cabot*, p. 295.
26. July 18, 1800; George Gibbs, *Memoirs of the Administrations of Washington and John Adams*, II, p. 381.
27. McHenry to Wolcott, July 22, 1800; *ibid.*, pp. 384-5.
28. Dwight Foster to Caleb Strong, Dec. 12, 1800; *American Historical Review*, IV, pp. 330-1. See also C. C. Pinckney, *Life of General Thomas Pinckney*, p. 156.
29. Troup to King, Dec. 31, 1800; *King Correspondence, op. cit.*, III, p. 359.
30. Dec. 16, 1800; *Works*, Lodge, X, pp. 392-3.
31. Dec. 17, 1800; *ibid.*, p. 393ff.
32. Dec. 22, 1800; *ibid.*, pp. 397-8.
33. Jan. 16, 1801; *ibid.*, pp. 412-19.
34. Feb. 12, 1801; *King Correspondence, op. cit.*, III, p. 391.

CHAPTER XXVII

1. Cabot to King, Mar. 20, 1801; *The Life and Correspondence of Rufus King*, Charles R. King, ed., III, p. 408.
2. Jefferson to Dickinson, July 23, 1801; Jefferson, *Writings*, VIII, p. 281.
3. Aug. 8, 1801; *King Correspondence, op. cit.*, III, p. 496.
4. MS. letter, Troup to King, May 27, 1801; King Papers, N. Y. Hist. Soc.
5. Newark *Centinel of Freedom*, Apr. 28, 1801.
6. *Supra*, Note 4.
7. MS. letter, Troup to King, Sept. 14, 1801; King Papers, N. Y. Hist. Soc.
8. G. S. Hillard, *Memoi and Correspondence of Jeremiah Mason*, pp. 32-3.
9. Amer. Scenic & Hist. Preserv. Soc., *Thirteenth Annual Report* (1925), pp. 20-32; *Intimate Life*, pp. 347-8; Troup to King, Dec. 31, 1800; King Papers, N. Y. Hist. Soc.
10. MS. letter, Troup to King, Dec. 5, 1801; King Papers, N. Y. Hist. Soc. Troup's unflattering estimate of Philip Hamilton is omitted from the published version in *King Correspondence, op. cit.*, III, p. 28. The editor might have been justified in the deletion had not the context which he *did* print given rise to a complete distortion of Troup's remarks. On the basis of the text as published, all later biographers have conjured up a picture of young Philip which has little relation to the facts.

11. *Intimate Life*, p. 215.
12. N. Y. *Evening Post*, Nov. 24, 1801; N. Y. *Gazette & General Advertiser*, Nov. 24, 1801.
13. Troup to King, *supra*, Note 10.
14. MS. letters, Troup to King, Oct. 14, 1801, Dec. 5, 1801; King Papers, N. Y. Hist. Soc.
15. Feb. 27, 1802; *Works*, Lodge, X, pp. 425-6.
16. MS. letter, Nov. 21, 1801; Hamilton MSS., Lib. Cong. This paragraph is omitted from the letter as published in *Works*, J. C. H., VI, p. 526.
17. Hamilton to C. C. Pinckney, Mar. 15, 1802; *Works*, Lodge, X, pp. 428-9.
18. Apr. 6, 1802; *ibid.*, pp. 429-32.
19. Apr. 12, 1802; *Works*, J. C. H., VI, pp. 539-40.
20. Hamilton to Bayard, Apr., 1802; *Works*, Lodge, X, pp. 443-7.
21. Bayard to Hamilton, Apr. 25, 1802; *Works*, J. C. H., VI, pp. 543-5.
22. Troup to King, Apr. 9, 1802; *King Correspondence, op. cit.*, IV, p. 104.
23. N. Y. *Evening Post*, July 15, 1802.
24. June 3, 1802; *Works*, Lodge, X, p. 439.
25. Dec. 29, 1802; *ibid*, pp. 444-6.
26. "Pericles," in N. Y. *Evening Post;* reprinted *ibid.*, VI, pp. 333-6.
27. MS. letter, June 23, 1803; Hamilton MSS., Lib. Cong.
28. MS. record of the case of Harry Croswell ads. The People, written by Judge James Kent; N. Y. Pub. Lib.
29. *Ibid.* See also William Kent, *Memoirs and Letters of James Kent*, pp. 321-6; and *Works*, Lodge, VIII, pp. 387-425.

Chapter XXVIII

1. *Documents Relating to New England Federalism*, Henry Adams, ed., p. 148.
2. *Works*, Lodge, VIII, pp. 373-6.
3. Feb. 27, 1804; cited in Jabez D. Hammond, *The History of the Political Parties in the State of New York*, I, p. 208.
4. MS. copy, Feb. 19, 1804; Columbia Univ.
5. Hamilton to King, Feb. 24, 1804; *Works*, Lodge, X, pp. 448-50.
6. MS. letter, Thomas Cooper to Stephen Van Rensselaer, Feb. 29, 1804; N. Y. State Lib.
7. *Albany Register*, Apr. 24, 1804.
8. *Ibid.*
9. For the entire correspondence see William Coleman, *Collection of Facts and Documents Relative to the Death of Hamilton, passim;* Davis, *Burr*, II, pp. 294ff. For Burr's side see Nathan Schachner, *Aaron Burr*, chap. 17.
10. *Autobiography, Reminiscences and Letters of John Trumbull*, p. 244.
11. Dirck Ten Broeck to Abr. Ten Broeck, July 12, 1804; Columbia Univ.
12. *Works*, Lodge, X, p. 458.
12a. *Works*, Lodge, X, p. 475.
13. *Ibid.*, pp. 475-6.

14. Pendleton to King, July, 1804; *The Life and Correspondence of Rufus King*, Charles R. King, ed., IV, pp. 398-9.
15. *Autobiography of Charles Biddle*, p. 302.
16. Davis, *Burr, op. cit.*, II, pp. 318-21.
17. The N. Y. *Evening Post* and the *Morning Chronicle* for weeks thereafter were filled with statements from both sides, charges and counter-charges. At times it seemed as though the two seconds would themselves fight out the merits of their respective positions.
18. *The Diary and Letters of Gouverneur Morris*, Anne C. Morris, ed., II, p. 456.
19. Biddle, *op. cit.*, p. 303.
20. Morris, *op. cit.*, II, pp. 457-8.
21. Coleman, *op. cit.*, pp. 27-8.
22. G. Morris to Rob. Morris, undated; Morris, *op. cit.*, II, p. 459.
23. MS. letter; King Papers, N. Y. Hist. Soc.
24. King to Gore, Jan. 10, 1808; *King Correspondence, op. cit.*, IV, pp. 410-11.
25. MS. letter, Sept. 17, 1804; N. Y. Soc. Lib.
26. MS. letter, Sept. 24, 1804; *ibid.*
27. MS. letter, Sept. 29, 1804; *ibid.*

BIBLIOGRAPHY

The bibliography on Alexander Hamilton is enormous, involving thousands of items. It would serve no useful purpose to include herein every merely secondary volume, though I have examined practically all. But I have attempted to furnish as complete a listing of manuscript and printed source materials as possible for the use of the reader and student. Much of the included manuscript material is used here for the first time, while the great mass of the Hamilton Manuscripts in the Library of Congress, though already known in bulk, has never, I believe, been thoroughly exploited before in connection with a biography of Hamilton. The present standard editions of Hamilton's *Works*, edited by John C. Hamilton and Henry Cabot Lodge respectively, have been compared to the original manuscripts. Both editions disclose a considerable number of errors in transcription, in attributed dates, and in elisions of pertinent sections. Wherever such errors distorted the facts of Hamilton's career, or led to misinterpretation, I have indicated them either in the text or in the notes.

Manuscript Sources

American Antiquarian Society
    Craigie, Andrew, Papers
Columbia University
    Hamilton, Alexander, Misc. MSS.
Connecticut Historical Society
    Wadsworth, Jeremiah, Papers
    Wolcott, Oliver, Papers
Connecticut State Library
    Trumbull, Jonathan, MSS.
    Trumbull, Gov. Joseph, Photostats
    Webb, Col., Orderly Book, 1776

Hamilton College Library
  Hamilton, Alexander, MS. Brief and Letters
Henry E. Huntington Library
  Hamilton, Alexander, Misc. MSS.
Library of Congress
  Hamilton, Alexander, MSS., 1st Series of 84 bound vols., 2nd Series of 25
    bound vols., Cash Books, Memorandum Book, and Misc. Folders
  Jefferson, Thomas, MSS.
  King, Rufus, MSS.
  Madison, James, MSS.
  Monroe, James, MSS.
  Van Buren, Martin, MSS.
  Washington, George, MSS.
Massachusetts Historical Society
  Knox, Henry, MSS.
  Pickering, Timothy, MSS.
  Sedgwick, Theodore, MSS.
Morgan, J. Pierpont, Library
  Hamilton, Alexander, Misc. MSS.
New York Historical Society
  Bauman, Sebastian, MSS.
  Burr, Aaron, MSS.
  Duane, James, MSS.
  Gates, Horatio, MSS.
  Hamilton, Alexander, MSS.
  Jay, John, MSS.
  King, Rufus, MSS.
  Lamb, John, MSS.
  O'Reilly Transcripts
  Schuyler, Philip, MSS.
  Steuben, Baron von, MSS.
  Stevens, Ebenezer, MSS.
  Stewart Papers
New York Public Library
  British State Papers, Transcripts of Hammond Correspondence, 1789-95,
    by G. L. Ford
  Hamilton, Alexander, MSS. in Emmett Collection
  Hamilton, Alexander, Misc. MSS.
  Kent, James, MS. Record, Harry Croswell ads. The People
  Livingston Papers
  Livingston, Gilbert, MS. Report of the Poughkeepsie Convention
  Madison, James, MSS.
  McDougall, Col., Orderly Book
  Schuyler, Philip, Papers
  Washington's Farewell Address, MSS.
  Yates, Abraham, Jr., MSS.
New York Society Library
  Hamilton, Alexander, Misc. MSS.

New York State Library
  Burr, Aaron, MSS.
  Hamilton, Alexander, MSS.
  Harpur, Dr. Robert, Ledger
  Van Rensselaer MSS.
Pennsylvania Historical Society
  Dreer Collections
  Etting Papers: Bank of the United States
  Gratz Papers
  Society Collection
  Wallace Papers
William L. Clemens Library
  Hamilton, Alexander, Misc. MSS.

Printed Sources

Adams, Henry, ed.—Documents relating to New England Federalism, 1905.
Adams, John, The Works of.—C. F. Adams, ed., 10 v., 1856.
Adams, John Quincy, Memoirs of.—C. F. Adams, ed., 12 v., 1874-7.
Adams, John Quincy, Writings of.—W. C. Ford, ed., 7 v., 1913-17.
American Historical Review
  "Notes of Major William Pierce on the Federal Convention of 1787,"
    III, 310ff.
  "Papers of William Paterson on the Federal Convention, 1787," IX, 310ff.
  "Alexander Hamilton's Notes in the Federal Convention," X, 97ff.
  "Papers of Dr. James McHenry on the Federal Convention of 1787,"
    XI, 595ff.
American State Papers, Documents Legislative and Executive, Class III,
  Finance, v. I, 1822.
Ames, Fisher, Works of.—Seth Ames, ed., 2 v., 1854.
Annals of the Congress of the United States.—Gales and Seaton, eds., 1834.
Atherton, Gertrude.—*A Few of Hamilton's Letters*, 1903.
———. "The Hunt for Hamilton's Mother," *North American Review*
  (1902), Vol. 175, p. 229ff.

Biddle, Charles, Autobiography of, 1883.
Boudinot, Elias, Journal of, 1894.
Brackenridge, Henry M.—*History of the Western Insurrection in Western
  Pennsylvania*, 1859.
Brissot de Warville, J. P.—*New Travels in the United States of America*,
  1792.
Burnett, Edmund C., ed.—*Letters of Members of the Continental Congress*,
  8. v., 1921- —.

Callender, James T.—*The History of the United States for 1796*, 1797.
Callender, Tom (pseud.).—*Letters to Alexander Hamilton, King of the
  Feds*, 1802.

Chastellux, Marquis de.—*Voyages ... Dans L'Amérique Septentrionale ...*, 1788.
Cheetham, James.—*An Answer to Alexander Hamilton's Letter*, 1800.
———. *A Narrative of the Suppression by Col. Burr of the History of the Administration of John Adams*, 1802.
Clinton, George, Public Papers of.—10 v., 1899-1914.
Cole, Arthur H., ed.—*Industrial and Commercial Correspondence of Alexander Hamilton*, 1928.
Coleman, William.—*Collection of Facts and Documents Relative to the Death of ... Hamilton, etc.*, 1804.
Continental Congress, Journals of the.—W. C. Ford and G. Hunt, eds., 33 v., 1904-36.
Custis, G. W. P.—*Recollections and Private Memoirs of Washington*, 1860.

Dawson, Henry B., ed.—*The Case of Elizabeth Rutgers versus Joshua Waddington*, 1866.
Day, Edward W., ed.—*One Thousand Years of Hubbard History*, 1895.
Documentary History of the Constitution of the United States of America, 5 v., 1894-1905.
Duer, William A.—*The Life of William Alexander, Earl of Stirling*, 1847.
———. *Reminiscences of an Old New Yorker*, 1867

Edinburgh Review, "Emancipation of Spanish America," XIII (1808-9), 277ff.
Elliot, Jonathan, ed.—*The Debates in Several State Conventions on the Adoption of the Federal Constitution*, 5 v., 1859.

Farrand, Max, ed.—*The Records of the Federal Convention of 1787*, 3 v., 1911.
Federalist, The.—Edited by Henry Cabot Lodge, 1923.
Force, Peter, ed.—*American Archives*, Fourth Series, 1837.
Ford, Paul L.—*Bibliotheca Hamiltoniana*, 1886.
Ford, Paul L., ed.—*Essays on the Constitution of the United States*, 1892.

Gallatin, Albert, The Writings of.—Henry Adams, ed., 3 v., 1879.
Gibbs, George.—*Memoirs of the Administrations of Washington and John Adams*, 2 v., 1846.
Graydon, Alexander.—*Memoirs of His Own Time*, 1846.
Griswold, Rufus W.—*The Republican Court*, 1867.

Hamilton, Alexander, The Works of.—John C. Hamilton, ed., 7 v., 1851.
Hamilton, Alexander, The Works of.—Henry Cabot Lodge, ed., 12 v., 1903.
Hamilton, Allan McLane.—*The Intimate Life of Alexander Hamilton*, 1911.
Hamilton, James A.—*Reminiscences*, 1869.
Hamilton, John C.—*History of the Republic of the United States, etc.*, 7 v., 1857-64.
———. *The Life of Alexander Hamilton*, 2 v., 1834, 1840.

Harper, Robert G.—*The Case of the Georgia Sales on the Mississippi Considered*, 1799.

Higginson, Stephen, Letters of.—(Annual Report of the American Historical Association for ... 1896, v. I), 1897.

Historical Manuscripts Commission.—*Report of American Manuscripts in the Royal Institution of Great Britain*, 1907, IV.

Historical Manuscripts Commission.—*The Manuscripts of J. B. Fortescue, Esq., preserved at Dropmore*, 10 v., 1892-9.

Historical Society of Pennsylvania, Memoirs of, v. I (1826), pp. 232-58. "Papers relative to the Valedictory Address of President Washington."

Jay, John, *The Correspondence and Public Papers of*.—Henry P. Johnston, ed., 4 v., 1893.

Jay, William.—*The Life of John Jay*, 2 v., 1833.

Jefferson, Thomas, *The Works of*.—Paul L. Ford, ed., 12 v., 1904.

Jefferson, Thomas, *The Writings of*.—A. A. Lipscomb, ed., 20 v., 1904.

Kent, James.—"Address before the Law Association of N. Y.," 1836.

Kent, William.—*Memoirs and Letters of James Kent*, 1898.

King, Rufus, *The Life and Correspondence of*.—Charles R. King, ed., 6 v., 1894.

Lafayette, General, Memoirs, Correspondence and Manuscripts of, 3 v., 1837.

La Rochefoucauld-Liancourt.—*Voyage dans les Etats—Unis d' Amérique, etc.*, 1799, 8 v. in 4.

Leake, Isaac Q.—*Memoir of the Life and Times of General John Lamb*, 1850.

Ledyard, Isaac.—*Mentor's Reply to Phocion*, 1784.

Lee, The (Charles) Papers.—Collections of the New York Historical Society, 4 v., 1872-5.

Lee, Henry.—*Memoirs of the War in the Southern Department of the United States*, 1870.

Lodge, Henry Cabot.—*Life and Letters of George Cabot*, 1877.

Maclay, William, The Journal of, 1890.

Madison, James.—*Letters of Helvedius*, 1796.

Madison, James, *The Writings of*.—Gaillard Hunt, ed., 9 v., 1902.

Massachusetts Historical Society Proceedings (1924-5), v. 58, pp. 219-36.— "A Letter of Hamilton," by W. C. Ford.

Monroe, James, *The Writings of*.—S. M. Hamilton, ed., 7 v., 1898-1903.

Moore, Frank.—*Diary of the American Revolution*, 2 v., 1860.

Moreau de Saint-Méry, M. L. E.—*Voyage aux Etats-Unis de L'Amérique*, 1913.

Morison, Samuel Eliot.—*The Life and Letters of Harrison Gray Otis*, 2 v., 1913.

Morris, Gouverneur, *The Diary and Letters of*.—Anne C. Morris, ed., 2 v., 1888.

New York, Journal of the Assembly of the State of, 1787.
New York State Senate Journals, 1787.

O'Callaghan, E. B., ed.—*Documents Relative to the Colonial History of the State of New-York*, VIII, 1857.

Paltsits, Victor Hugo.—*Washington's Farewell Address*, 1935.
Parsons, Theophilus.—*Memoir of Theophilus Parsons*, 1859.
Pennsylvania Magazine of History and Biography (1905), v. 29, No. 4.— "Washington's Household Account Book."
Pickering, O., and Upham, C. W.—*The Life of Timothy Pickering*, 4 v., 1867-73.
Pinkney, William.—*A few Remarks on Mr. Hamilton's late Letter*, 1800.
Pontgibaud, Ch.valier de.—*A French Volunteer of the War of Independence*, 1897.

Seabury, Samuel.—*A View of the Controversy between Great-Britain and her Colonies, etc.*, 1774.
———. "Letters of a Westchester Farmer," *Publications of the Westchester County Historical Society*, VIII, 1930.
Southern History Association Publications, X (1906).—"Letters to James McHenry, Secretary of War."
Sparks, Jared, ed.—*The Diplomatic Correspondence of the American Revolution*, 1829.
Sullivan, William.—*Familiar Letters on Public Characters and Public Events*, 1834.
———. *The Public Men of the Revolution*, 1847.

Talleyrand, Prince de.—*Memoirs*, 5 v., 1891.
Taylor, John (?).—*An Examination of the Late Proceedings in Congress, respecting the Official Conduct of the Secretary of the Treasury*, 1793.
Ticknor, George, Life, Letters, and Journals of.—G. S. Hillard, ed., 2 v., 1876.
Tilghman, Oswald.—*Memoir of Lieut. Col. Tench Tilghman*, 1876.
Trumbull, John, Autobiography, Reminiscences and Letters of, 1841.

Van Buren, Autobiography of.—John C. Fitzpatrick, ed. (Annual Report of the American Historical Association for... 1918, II), 1920.

Washington, George.—*Diaries*, John C. Fitzpatrick, ed., 4 v., 1925.
Washington, George, The Writings of.—W. C. Ford, ed., 14 v., 1890.
Webster, Noah.—*A Letter to Hamilton*, 1800.
Wilkinson, James.—*Memoirs of my own Times*, 3 v., 1816.
Windham Papers, The, 2 v., 1913.

Secondary Sources

Adams, Henry.—*History of the United States during the Administration of Thomas Jefferson*, 4 v. in 2, 1930.
Alexander, De Alva Stanwood.—*A Political History of the State of New York*, I, 1906.
Alexander, Edward P.—*A Revolutionary Conservative, James Duane of New York*, 1938.
American Historical Review (1897), II, pp. 443-60; 675-82.—Two articles, "The Authorship of the Federalist," by E. G. Bourne and by P. L. Ford.
Anderson, Dice R.—*William Branch Giles*, 1914.
Atherton, Gertrude.—*Adventures of a Novelist*, 1932.
———. *The Conqueror*, 1902.

Bailey, Ralph E.—*An American Colossus*, 1933.
Bassett, John Spencer.—*The Federalist System*, 1906.
Beard, Charles A.—*An Economic Interpretation of the Constitution of the United States*, 1913.
———. *Economic Origins of Jeffersonian Democracy*, 1915.
Bemis, Samuel Flagg.—*Jay's Treaty*, 1923.
Beveridge, Albert J.—*The Life of John Marshall*, 4 v., 1916.
Bowers, Claude G.—*Jefferson and Hamilton*, 1925.
Brown, William G.—*The Life of Oliver Ellsworth*, 1905.
Bryce, James.—"The Predictions of Hamilton and De Tocqueville," *Johns Hopkins University Studies*, Fifth Series, IX, 1887.
Bullock, Charles J.—*Finances of U. S. from 1775 to 1789*, Bulletin of Wisconsin University Press, 1895.

Chinard, Gilbert.—*Honest John Adams*, 1933.
———. *Thomas Jefferson*, 1929.
Conant, Charles A.—*Alexander Hamilton*, 1901.
Conway, Moncure D.—*Edmund Randolph*, 1889.
Culberston, William S.—*Alexander Hamilton*, 1916.

Davis, Joseph S.—*Essays in the Earlier History of American Corporations*, 2 v., 1917.
Domett, Henry W.—*A History of the Bank of New York*, 1884.

Evans, Paul D.—"The Holland Land Company," *Buffalo Historical Society Publications*, v. 28, 1924.

Ford, Henry Jones.—*Alexander Hamilton*, 1929.
Fox, Dixon Ryan.—*The Decline of Aristocracy in the Politics of New York*, 1919.

Hammond, Jabez D.—*The History of the Political Parties in the State of New York*, I, 1852.

Hughes, Rupert.—*George Washington, 1777-1781*, 1930.
Humphreys, Mary Gay.—*Catherine Schuyler*, 1897.

Journal of Political Economy, The, v. 3 (1894-5), pp. 289-310.—"Hamilton as a Political Economist," by Edward C. Lunt.

Kapp, Friedrich.—*The Life of Frederick William von Steuben*, 1859.

Livingston, Edwin B.—*The Livingstons of Livingston Manor*, 1910.
Lodge, Henry Cabot.—*Alexander Hamilton*, 1886.
Loth, David.—*Alexander Hamilton, Portrait of a Prodigy*, 1939.

Marshall, John.—*The Life of George Washington*, 5 v., 1807.
Mason, Jeremiah, Memoir and Correspondence of.—G. S. Hillard, ed., 1873.
Massachusetts Historical Society Proceedings.—(1912-13), v. 46, pp. 412-26. —"The Indebtedness of John Marshall to Alexander Hamilton," by Prof. McDonald.
Miner, Clarence E.—*The Ratification of the Federal Constitution by the State of New York*, 1921.
Monaghan, Frank.—*John Jay*, 1935.
Morse, John T., Jr.—*The Life of Alexander Hamilton*, 2 v., 1876.

Nation, The (Sept. 5, 1895), v. 61, pp. 164-5.—"The Authorship of Giles's Resolutions," by Paul L. Ford.
Nevins, Allan.—*The Evening Post*, 1922.
New York History (Oct., 1937), XVIII, No. 4, pp. 378-85.—"The Settlement of Alexander Hamilton's Debts," by Mayer and East.

Oberholtzer, E. P.—*Robert Morris*, 1903.
Oliver, Frederick Scott.—*Alexander Hamilton*, 1928.

Palmer, John McAuley.—*General Von Steuben*, 1937.
Pinckney, C. C.—*Life of General Thomas Pinckney*, 1895.

Quarterly Journal of Economics (1888-9), v. 3, pp. 32-59.—"Some Precedents followed by Alexander Hamilton," by Chas. F. Dunbar.
Quarterly Journal of Economics (1893-4), v. 8, pp. 328-44.—"Alexander Hamilton and Adam Smith," by Edward G. Bourne.

Randall, H. S.—*Life of Jefferson*, 3 v., 1858.
Rives, W. C.—*Life of Madison*, 3 v., 1859.
Robertson William S.—*The Life of Miranda*, 2 v., 1929.
Rowland, Kate M.—*The Life of Charles Carroll of Carrolton*, 2 v., 1898.

Schachner, Nathan—*Aaron Burr*, 1937.
Schmucker, Samuel M.—*The Life and Times of Alexander Hamilton*, 1856.
Skeel, E. E. F., ed.—*Notes on the Life of Noah Webster*, 2 v., 1912.
Smertenko, Johan J.—*Alexander Hamilton*, 1932.

Sparks, Jared.—*Life of Gouverneur Morris*, 3 v., 1832.
————. *Life of Pulaski*, 1847.
Spaulding, E. Wilder.—*His Excellency George Clinton*, 1938.
————. *New York in the Critical Period*, 1783-89; 1932.
Steiner, Bernard C.—*The Life and Correspondence of James McHenry*, 1907.
Sumner, Wiliam Graham.—*Alexander Hamilton*, 1890.
————. *The Financier and the Finances of the American Revolution*, 2 v., 1891.

Talleyrand-Périgord, Charles A.—*Etude sur la République des Etats-Unis D'Amérique*. 1876.
Thomas, Charles Marion.—*American Neutrality in 1793*, 1931.
Trumbull, Levi R.—*A History of Industrial Paterson*, 1882.
Tuckerman, Bayard.—*Life of General Philip Schuyler*, 1903.

Van Schaack, Henry C.—*Memoirs of the Life of Henry Van Schaack*, 1892.

Warren, Charles.—*The Making of the Constitution*, 1928.
Warshow, Irving.—*Alexander Hamilton*, 1931.

INDEX

Adet, M., 360-1

Adams, John, 1, 66, 188, 235, 241, 309, 329, 353, 410, 414; elected Vice-President, 232-3; re-elected, 307; elected President, 356-9; administratoin of, 360ff.; and trouble with France, 374ff.; election of 1800, 392ff.

Ames, Fisher, 247, 253, 254, 256, 258, 269, 271, 288, 313, 329, 361

André, John, 115-9

Annapolis Convention, 188-90

Armstrong, John, 164

Arnold, Benedict, 114-9

Arnold, Peggy Shippen, 114, 116-8

Atherton, Gertrude, 1, 24

Bank of New York, 181-3, 281, 287, 289, 347, 390

Bank of North America, 136, 180

Bank of the United States, 287, 289; Bill signed, 273; stock subscribed, 282-3

Barber, Colonel, 140-1

Bayard, James A., 395, 397, 401-2, 411-2

Beckley, John, 302, 364-5, 371

Beckwith, Major, 266-7

Benson, Egbert, 176-7, 187, 432

Boudinot, Elias, 28, 29, 46, 78-80, 83-4, 235, 252, 253, 278, 313

Boudinot, Elisha, 26, 278

Brackenridge, Hugh, 338

Bradford, William, 347, 349

Burgoyne, John, 64, 68

Burke, Aedanus, 215, 256, 258

Burr, Aaron, 28, 118, 228, 330, 346, 366, 371-2, 379, 381, 385, 389; meets Hamilton, 49-52; Senator, 290-3; and election of 1792, 307-9; campaign of 1796, 356-8; and Holland Land Co., 372-3; election of 1800, 392ff.; tied for president, 399; becomes Vice-President, 400-2; breaks with Jefferson, 410-1; defeated for governor, 419-23; duel with Hamilton, 422-30; flight, 430

Cabot, George, 275, 328, 330, 362, 395-6, 398

Callender, James T., 369, 371, 404, 414-5

Carroll, Charles, 395

Cazenove, Theophile, 239, 372-3

Chase, Samuel, 88-90

Chase, Angelica (née Schuyler), 104, 106-7, 109, 229-30, 249-50, 329, 342-4, 370; and Hamilton, 389-92, 430

Church, John Barker (John Carter), 104, 181-2, 229, 249, 342-3, 347, 369-70, 389-91

Clingman, Jacob, 364-6, 369

Clinton, George, 71, 72, 73, 77-8, 93, 147-9, 151, 158, 159, 160-1, 171, 191, 193, 203-4, 350, 357, 397; prosecutes Tories, 173-4; forms party, 185ff.; opposes ratification, 215ff.;

Clinton, George (Cont'd)
elected governor, 232-4; re-elected,
290-3; candidate for Vice-President, 307-9; again governor, 404
Clinton, Sir Henry, 80, 81, 90, 114-5,
117, 137, 139
Coleman, William, 405, 421
Congress, Continental, 35, 36, 41, 48,
64, 66, 77-9, 88, 97, 110-2, 156ff.,
184ff., 208.
Congress, New York, 43, 44, 45, 47,
48, 57ff.
Congress, United States, 242, 325-6,
327-8, 386; first session, 235ff.; de-
bate on Report on Credit, 247-55;
on assumption, 256-63; on bank,
270-1; Whisky Tax, 304-5; Giles
Resolutions, 310-4; Jay Treaty
ratified, 351-2; decides election of
1800, 402
Constitutional Convention, and rati-
fication, 195-227
Conway, General, 68; "Cabal," 74-6
Cooper, Charles D., 422-3
Cooper, Myles, 29, 38-9, 41-2
Cornwallis, Lord, 53, 113, 138-40, 142
Corsicans, The, 40, 42
Coxe, Tench, 258, 261, 278
Craigie, Andrew, 227, 237-9, 263
Croswell, Harry, 413-8
Cruger, Nicholas, 18, 20-3, 27

Dana, William, 94
Dayton, Jonathan, 278, 279, 356-8
D'Estaing, Admiral, 86, 87, 96
Dickinson, John, 167, 189, 195
Dorchester, Lord, 266-8
Duane, James, 109-10, 113, 120, 126,
157, 171, 176-8, 185, 187, 188, 216
Duer, William, 58, 59, 186, 238-40,
258, 278, 280-1, 364; bankruptcy,
283-7
Du Portail, Colonel, 96

Eacker, George I., 407-8
Earle, Ralph, 228-9

Ellsworth, Oliver, 328-9, 330
Eustace, John S., 85-6

Farewell Address, 354-5
Fawcett (Faucette), John, 3-5
Fawcett, Mary, 3-6, 8
Federalist, The, 207-15, 221
Fenno, John, 246, 299-301, 303
Fish, Nicholas, 138, 141
Fitzsimmons, James, 158, 249, 255,
260
Fleury, Colonel, 95-6, 109
Floyd, William, 157, 163, 171
Franklin, Benjamin, 168, 195, 202
Fraunces, Andrew G., 364-5
Freneau, Philip, 299-301, 404

Gallatin, Albert, 336
Gates, Horatio, 68ff., 113; and "Con-
way's Cabal," 74-6
Gelston, David, 370
Genêt, Citizen Edmond C., 318-23
Gerry, Elbridge, 235, 247, 364
Giles, William B., 310-14
Gordon, William, 94-5, 142
Grayson, Colonel, 79
Greene, Nathanael, 18, 56, 75, 85,
123-4, 130
Grenville, Lord, 332-3
Griswold, Gaylord, 420-1
Gunn, James, 386

Hale, Edward Everett, 382
Hamilton, Alexander, birth, 1-15;
controversy over, 8-10; correspondence with father and brother,
11-13; correspondence with Scottish relatives, 13-4; youth 16ff.; becomes clerk, 18ff.; Hurricane
Letter, 23-5; in New York, 27ff.;
at school, 28-9; at King's College,
29ff.; first polemic, 31-2; first
speech, 32-3; pamphlets against
Seabury, 35-9; on Quebec Bill,
39-40; saves Dr. Cooper, 40-2; at-

tacks the *Asia*, 42-3; and Rivington affair, 43-4; captain of artillery,
45-55; meets Burr, 49-52; aide to
Washington, 56*ff.*; campaign at
Philadelphia, 64-7; mission to
Gates, 68*ff.*; and "Conway's Cabal," 74-6; at Valley Forge, 77-80;
Battle of Monmouth, 81-5; and
D'Estaing, 86-7; attacks Chase,
87-90; and Negro soldiers, 91-2;
diversions in camp, 92-3; and Dr.
Gordon, 94-5, 96; letter to Sullivan, 97-101; engagement to Eliza,
102-9; letter to Duane, 110-13; and
Benedict Arnold, 114-9; discontent
with Washington, 120*ff.*; marriage,
124-5; resignation as aide, 126-32;
letter to Morris, 133-6; assault at
Yorktown, 137-43; studies law,
144-6; tax receiver, 146-52; writes
"The Continentalist," 153-5; in
Congress, 155*ff.*; and mutiny,
163-7; and peace treaty, 168-70;
opposes ill treatment of Tories,
172*ff.*; counsel in Rutgers vs. Waddington, 175-9; law practice, 180-3;
returns to politics, 184*ff.*; in Annapolis Convention, 188-90; in New
York Assembly, 190-4; and Constitutional Convention, 195*ff.*;
writes *The Federalist*, 207-14; and
ratification, 215-27; interlude in
law, 228-30; and election of 1789,
231-5; Secretary of Treasury,
236*ff.*; Report on Public Credit,
244-55; and Assumption, 255-63;
and foreign affairs, 265-8; Report
on National Bank, 268-73; Report
on Manufactures, 273-8; and Society for Useful Manufactures,
278-81; and stock speculation,
282-9; break with Burr, 290-3; and
Jefferson, 293-303; and Whisky
Tax, 304-6; and election of 1792,
307-9; and Giles Resolutions,
310-4; and Neutrality, 314-23; ill
with yellow fever, 324; and congress, 325-6; and Jay Mission,
327-33; and "Whisky Rebellion,"
334-8; resigns, 339-40; returns to
law practice, 341-47; advocates
Jay's Treaty, 348-53; part in Farewell Address, 354-5; campaign of
1796, 355-9; and relations with
France, 360-4; and Reynolds affair,
364-72; and Holland Land Co.,
372-3; military command against
France, 374*ff.*; and Miranda, 383-5;
military duties, 385-8; and Angelica Church, 389-92; election
of 1800, 394*ff.*; attacks Adams,
396-8; attacks Burr, 397-402;
founds New York *Evening Post*,
403-5; builds home, 405-6; son
killed, 406-8; political spectator,
409-13; defense of Croswell, 413-8;
duel with Burr, 419-30; death, 430;
funeral, 430-1; estate, 431-3

Hamilton, Elizabeth (née Schuyler),
12, 104-9, 138, 139, 144, 159, 183,
229, 265, 324, 344-5, 408, 414, 427;
marriage, 124-5; miscarriage, 341;
and "Reynolds Affair," 367; loyalty to husband, 389-90; death of
Hamilton, 430; grief, 431-3

Hamilton, James, 6; emigrates to
West Indies, 7; lives with Rachel
Levine, 8*ff.*; deserts family, 11;
correspondence with son, 11-13;
death, 13

Hamilton, James (the younger), 10,
11-12, 15

Hamilton, John C., 1, 6

Hamilton, Philip, 145, 159; killed in
duel, 406-8

Hamilton, Will, 7, 8

Hamm, Archibald, 6, 8

Hammond, George, 295-8, 316-7,
320-1, 327-8, 339

Hancock, John, 66, 232

Harper, Robert, 395

Harpur, Robert, 33

Harrison, Robert R., 58, 59, 62, 78-
80, 83

Henry, Patrick, 263

Higginson, Stephen, 188, 358

Hobart, John S., 216, 224
Holland Land Company, 372-3, 389
Hosack, David, 428-30
Howe, General William, 48-50, 53, 64, 86

Jay, John, 32, 38, 43, 44, 91, 183, 209, 211, 214, 216, 217, 220, 233-4, 240, 263, 315, 317, 355, 362, 394, 399; defeated for governor, 292-3; on mission to England, 329-33; treaty ratified, 349-52; governor, 376
Jefferson, Thomas, 1, 163, 214, 236, 243, 244, 254, 271-2, 276-8, 283, 327, 328-30, 350-1, 353, 385-6, 417, 419-20; and assumption, 260-4; Secretary of State, 266-7; quarrel with Hamilton, 293-303, 305; drafts Giles Resolutions, 312, 314-5; and neutrality, 315-23, 324; resigns, 325; campaign of 1796, 356-9; Vice-President, 360ff.; election of 1800, 394ff.; tied for President, 399ff.; becomes President, 400-2; in office, 403-4, 408ff.; libeled by Croswell, 413-4.
Johnson, William S., 195, 201

Kent, James, 180, 347, 415-7, 422
King, Rufus, 184, 196, 197, 203, 204, 215, 219, 259, 284-5, 290, 293, 307-8, 328-30, 348, 350, 383-4, 401, 413, 426-7, 432; Senator, 234; Minister to England, 353
King's College (Columbia), 29-30, 33, 40, 43, 192, 230
Knox, Henry, 50-1, 67, 75, 116, 164, 219, 232, 236, 241, 278, 288, 305, 319, 321-2, 335, 341, 377-8, 383
Knox, Hugh, 7, 17, 18, 25, 28, 31, 57, 64, 93

Lafayette, Marquis de, 80-4, 87, 116, 123, 124, 131, 137, 140, 156
Lamb, John, 42, 215

Lansing, John, 194, 195, 202-4, 206, 216, 220, 225, 419-21
Laurens, Henry, 87, 141
Laurens, John, 62, 84, 85, 88, 91-2, 94, 102, 108, 114, 119, 121-2, 137, 155
Ledyard, Isaac, 179
Lee, Charles, 68; at Monmouth, 81-5
Lee, Henry, 64-6, 239, 283, 353
Lee, Richard Henry, 214, 215
Levine, John Michael, 7, 10; marries Rachel Fawcett, 5-6; deserted, 6; divorce, 14-5
Levine, Peter, 6, 15, 17, 18
Levine, Rachel (née Fawcett), 4ff.; marriage to John Levine, 5-6; and James Hamilton, 7, 8, 10; Alexander Hamilton born to, 8; deserted by Hamilton, 11; divorced by Levine, 14-5; death, 15
Lewis, Morgan, 176, 414-5, 417, 419, 423
Livingston, Brockholst, 176
Livingston, Robert R., 58, 59, 186, 187, 216, 220, 290
Livingston, William, 28, 60
Lytton, Peter, 3, 6, 10

Maclay, William, 214, 241, 249-52, 255, 257-9, 261, 263, 270, 273
Macomb, Alexander, 288
Madison, James, 158, 160-3, 167, 185, 188-9, 195, 196, 215, 218, 235-6, 242-4, 251, 257, 260, 264, 299, 301-2, 312-3, 327-8, 330, 339, 351, 354, 359, 362, 386; reports Constitutional Convention, 201ff.; and The Federalist, 209-14; and ratification, 222-5; on Report on Credit, 254-5; on bank, 270; answers Pacificus, 323
Malcolm, Colonel, 186
Manhattan Company, 303
Marshall, John, 263, 272, 364, 374
Mason, George, 206, 215
McDougall, Alexander, 32, 45, 53, 111

McHenry, James, 62, 83-4, 87, 88, 89, 116, 120, 125, 130, 156, 172, 346, 377, 379-81, 384-6, 398; Secretary of War, 353, 362, 374-5; dismissed from office, 394-6
Meade, Richard K., 62, 145
Mercer, Colonel, 309-10
Mifflin, Governor, 321, 335
Miranda, Sebastian Francisco de, 383-5
Mitchell, Ann, 16, 427
Mitchell, Thomas, 4, 6
Monroe, James, 92, 188, 262, 330, 348, 357; and Hamilton, 365-6, 369-72
Morris, Gouverneur, 58, 59-61, 195, 201, 231, 288, 431, 432
Morris, Robert, 111, 126, 133, 136, 146-51, 188, 195, 236, 249, 261, 263, 270, 329, 343
Muhlenberg, John P. G., 365-6, 369-70
Mulligan, Hercules, 27-9, 42, 49

New York *Evening Post*, 405, 413-4, 421
Nicholson, James, 226, 431

O'Hara, Colonel, 80
Otis, Harrison Gray, 386, 391-2

Page, John, 235-6
Paterson, William, 197
Pendleton, Nathaniel, 425-9
Peters, Richard, 170, 428, 430
Pickering, Timothy, 10, 362, 374-5, 377, 384, 398, 420, 432; Secretary of State, 353; dismissed from office, 394-6
Pinckney, Charles C., 364, 374, 377-8, 380, 413; election of 1800, 393ff.
Pinckney, Thomas, 353, 356-8, 362
Putnam, Israel, 49, 69, 71-3

Quebec Act. 39-40

Randolph, Edmund, 189, 190, 195, 197, 236, 271, 306, 317, 319, 321-2; Secretary of State, 330, 331-2, 335, 352
Reed, Joseph, 56
Reynolds, James, 365-8
Reynolds, Maria, 366-9
Rivington, James, 36, 43
Rochambeau, Count, 138
Rochefoucauld-Liancourt, 344-5
Rutgers vs. Waddington, 175-7

Scammel, Colonel, 123, 138, 141
Schuyler, Catherine, 104, 108
Schuyler, Peggy, 107
Schuyler, Philip, 59, 103-6, 108, 111, 121-2, 124, 129-31, 136-7, 144, 159, 183, 185, 186, 187, 193-4, 229, 233, 373, 414, 422; Senator, 234, 249, 259, 270, 280, 288, 290; defeated for re-election, 290-2
Seabury, Samuel, 35-7
Sears, Isaac, 126
Sedgwick, Theodore, 232, 252, 256, 259, 356-7, 386-7, 394-5, 401, 405, 427
Seton, William, 281, 282, 284-5, 287-9, 341-3
Shays' Rebellion, 190
Sherman, Roger, 256
Short, William, 265
Smith, Melancton, 216, 220-1, 225-6
Smith, William, 313, 328, 362
Society for Useful Manufactures, 278-81
Steuben, Baron von, 80, 85, 87
Stevens, Edward, 10, 16-7 19, 30, 31; cures Hamilton, 324
Stirling, Lord (William Alexander), 46
Sullivan, John, 97-8, 100, 125-6, 218, 222

Talleyrand, Charles Maurice de, 344-5
Tallmage, Major, 116

Tammany, Society of, 392-3, 419
Temple, Sir John, 269
Tilghman, Tench, 58, 62, 104, 108, 127-8, 138
Tracy, Uriah, 3, 62-3, 420
Troup, Robert, 30, 40-2, 62, 76, 145, 176, 186, 237, 278, 282, 289, 346, 390-1, 398, 400-1, 403-9, 412
Trumbull, Jonathan, 258

Van Ness, William W., 415-6, 423, 425-6, 428
Van Rensselaer, Stephen, 229, 291
Van Schaack, Henry, 252-3
Venable, Congressman, 365-6, 369-70
Viomenil, Baron de, 140, 142

Wadsworth, Jeremiah, 182, 251, 256, 286, 389
Warville, Brissot de, 229, 238
Washington, Bushrod, 409-10
Washington, George, 10, 28, 48-50, 52-3, 60-3, 86-7, 90, 94-6, 137-40, 195, 196, 203-4, 214, 265-8, 297, 298, 302-3, 325, 339, 348, 362, 392, 414, 417; Battle of Trenton, 54-5; at Morristown, 56-8; campaign at Philadelphia, 64-7; and Gates, 68-71; and Putnam, 71-4; and "Con-way's Cabal," 74-6; at Valley Forge, 77-80; battle of Monmouth, 81-5; and Arnold, 114-9; and Hamilton's discontent, 120ff.; at Yorktown, 140-2; and mutiny, 163-6; President, 231ff.; signs Bank Bill, 271-3 and Whisky Tax, 305-6; re-elected president, 307, 309; and neutrality, 314-22; and Jay mission, 328-30; and "Whisky Rebellion," 334-8; appoints cabinet, 352-3; Farewell Address, 354-5; commander-in-chief, 376ff.; death, 388
Washington, Martha, 97, 102, 125
Webb, Colonel 47, 49
Webster, Noah, 240
"Whisky Rebellion," 304-6, 334-8, 387
Wilkinson, James, 380-2; and "Con-way's Cabal," 75-6
Willing, Thomas, 249
Wilson, James, 161-3, 195, 197
Wolcott, Oliver, 285-6, 401, 405, 432; Secretary of the Treasury, 339, 348-9, 352, 362-4, 366, 375, 394-6, 398

Yates, Abraham, Jr., 151-2, 217
Yates, Robert, 194, 195, 202-4, 206, 216, 234, 292

(3)